STANDING
ROOM ONLY

▲●▲

STANDING ROOM ONLY

Strategies for Marketing the Performing Arts

Philip Kotler

Joanne Scheff

*Published in association with
Americans for the Arts*

HARVARD BUSINESS SCHOOL PRESS

BOSTON, MASSACHUSETTS

Library of Congress Cataloging-in-Publication Data

Kotler, Philip
    Standing room only : strategies for marketing the performing arts
/ Philip Kotler, Joanne Scheff.
      p.   cm.
    "Published in association with Americans for the Arts."
    Includes index.
    ISBN 0-87584-737-4
    1. Performing arts—Marketing. I. Scheff, Joanne. II. Title.
PN1590.M27K68   1997
791'.068'8—dc20   96-10225
                                               CIP

To my wonderful grandchildren—Jordan, Jamie, Ellie, and Olivia—for whom the performing arts will open a world of continuous pleasure and inspiration.

PHILIP KOTLER

To my father and mother for their inspiration and encouragement, to Orrin for his aesthetic and support, and to Jennifer and Lisa for the future.

JOANNE SCHEFF

We also dedicate this book to the many artists of generations past and present whose work inspires, challenges, and sustains us.

PHILIP KOTLER AND JOANNE SCHEFF

▲●▲

CONTENTS

PREFACE

THOSE OF US WHO LOVE THE PERFORMING ARTS—MUSIC, DANCE, OPERA, theater—want to see them flourish. In fact, the performing arts experienced two decades of unprecedented growth from the mid-1960s to the mid-1980s. Audiences increased, the number of professional symphonies, theaters, and dance and opera companies swelled, and contributions multiplied. Many organizations displayed their newfound affluence in more elaborate productions, larger performance halls, and bigger management staffs. Many midsized orchestras offered year-round contracts to their musicians for the first time, supporting a scale of operations that had been impossible in the past. These changes reflected optimism about continued growth in both audiences and contributions.

But today, pessimism is in the air. Opening the daily newspaper, one sees headlines such as "Is the Symphony Orchestra Dying?" and "Dancing Precariously on the Bottom Line." While few arts organizations have been forced to close their doors, many important organizations are eliminating programs while debts continue to rise, contributed support is declining, and audience sizes are stagnant at best.

Not only are many performing arts organizations in the United States facing grave challenges. In England, historically generous government subsidies to the performing arts are being reduced and companies are seeking to increase their ticket sales and find new sources for contributed support. And in eastern Europe and former Soviet countries, arts organizations that have always depended on state subsidies to provide for most of their budgetary needs are now struggling to adapt to the new market economy. To accomplish this, they must augment their earned income through more ticket sales and increased prices, encourage contributions in a climate where philanthropy did not exist in the past, recruit volunteers, add marketing and development managers to their staffs, and develop systems for accountability and control.

In these troubled times, arts organizations everywhere must learn new ways to attract the resources they need to sustain their mission and quality. Arts organizations must improve their skills in increasing and broadening their audience base, improving accessibility to various art forms, and learning how to better meet the needs of specific audience segments and contributors.

Standing Room Only: Strategies for Marketing the Performing Arts is a comprehensive and up-to-date sourcebook of marketing philosophies and methods. It focuses on strategies and techniques that can significantly improve the impact and practices of performing arts organizations, while integrating their public missions with their artistic missions. It is an indispensable tool for arts managers, marketers, fund-raisers, board members, arts management educators and students, and others who work closely with arts organizations such as foundation directors, corporate executives, consultants, and the artists themselves.

This book is divided into six sections: (1) Defining the Mission and Strategy, (2) Understanding the Performing Arts Audience, (3) Developing the Strategy, (4) Delivering the Message, (5) Managing the Organization, and (6) Securing the Future. Throughout the book we address a wide range of basic marketing and managerial strategies and issues in terms of the concerns common to performing arts managers and marketers. We address such questions as:

- How can an arts organization attract and develop new audience members?
- How can an arts organization increase the frequency of attendance of its current audiences?
- How can an arts organization develop a better understanding of its customers: their interests, attitudes, and motivations?
- How can an arts organization create offerings, services, and messages to which its target audience will enthusiastically respond, while at the same time, not compromise its artistic integrity?
- How should arts marketers package their offerings to their publics: as subscriptions, single-ticket offers, flex plans, memberships, and so on, in order to best meet the organization's needs while garnering the largest possible response?
- How can arts organizations make their performances and services an integral part of people's lives, woven into the fabric of the community?
- How can arts organizations collaborate with each other, with other nonprofit organizations, and with businesses to achieve their goals more effectively and efficiently than they could on their own?

- How can an arts organization increase its contributed income during a period of continuing funding cuts and changing priorities among many funding sources?

- How can performing arts organizations educate their publics and the next generation of attenders to enhance their appreciation and understanding of the arts?

- In today's complex and rapidly changing environment, how can arts organizations develop long-range strategic plans?

- How can arts organizations reorganize their structure and operations to perform better in the new environment?

- How can an arts organization determine how well it is meeting and satisfying the interests of various constituents?

- How can an arts organization learn to be fiscally responsible, to live within its means?

- How can an arts organization attract, train, and retain effective volunteers?

- Why should artistic directors, artists, managing directors, and board members take marketing seriously and make it a central part of the organization's decision-making processes?

- How does an art organization maintain its purpose and vigor while redefining its roles in the face of fiscal and artistic challenges?

The book is replete with examples of performing arts organizations that have innovated new approaches to audience building and resource development, organizations that can serve as models for those performing groups struggling to survive, let alone prosper, in a rapidly changing social, economic, and demographic climate.

We would like to thank the many arts managers and marketers, journalists, artists, board presidents, foundation directors, consultants, and other practitioners and lovers of the arts who have contributed their personal time, vision, and experience to help enrich the material content and focus of this book: Barbara Beerstein, Steven Belth, Dominique Bourgenon, Robert Bourne, Rich Braugh, Tony Brown, Eugene Carr, Butch Coyne, Janice Mancini Del Sesto, Stephen Eich, Tim Evans, Henry Fogel, Jerry Fuller, Patti Gessner, Morton Gould, Sandra Guthman, Cheryl Havlin, Peter d'Courcey Hero, Susan Mathieson, Jack McAuliffe, Danny Newman, Jean Oelrich, Rob Orchard, Lynn Osmond, Russ Reid, and John Zorn. We would also like to thank the American Council for the Arts for its support and encouragement for the writing of this book, and Nicholas Philipson and Barbara Roth at the Harvard Business School Press, and Alice Howard, of *Harvard Business Review,* for their extremely helpful suggestions. At the J. L. Kellogg Graduate School of Management at Northwestern University, we thank our colleagues whose work has had an important influence on this book: Max Bazerman, Bobby Calder, Donald Haider, Ann McGill, Stephen Shortell, Louis Stern, Brian Sternthal, Martin Stoller, and Ed Wilson. We also thank Dean Donald P. Jacobs for his continuing enthusiastic support of our research and writing efforts.

▲●▲

DEFINING
THE MISSION

CHAPTER 1

▲●▲

Art isn't easy.
STEPHEN SONDHEIM
*Sunday in the Park
with George*

*The arts are always
in trouble. It is their
nature to be in
trouble.*

*Artists don't see
the world the way
it wants to be seen
and the world
reciprocates.*
ARCHIBALD MacLEISH[1]

*For art establishes
the basic human
truths which must
serve as the
touchstones of our
judgment.*
JOHN F. KENNEDY[2]

THE PERFORMING ARTS: A GROWING CRISIS?

AFTER TWO BOOM DECADES, THE NONPROFIT PERFORMING ARTS INDUSTRY IN America, along with many performing arts organizations around the world, is facing crises on a variety of fronts. From the mid-1960s to the mid-1980s, there was an unprecedented proliferation of the number of performing arts organizations, the size of their audiences, and the level of contributions. Many arts organizations displayed their newfound affluence in more elaborate productions, larger management staffs, and new performance facilities with more seats to fill. For the first time, midsize orchestras gave their musicians full-year contracts instead of fee-for-service agreements, thereby providing them with a welcome measure of financial security formerly enjoyed only by musicians employed by large symphony orchestras in major cities. These changes reflected optimism about continued growth in both audiences and contributions.

Yet, in the past few years, growth has ground to a halt. Many important organizations have been forced to eliminate programs; others have closed altogether. Audience size is stagnant at best; in many areas it is shrinking. Lifestyles are changing among younger generations of potential attenders. The arts face growing

3

competition from other, more accessible and less expensive forms of entertainment as leisure time decreases and the costs of attending performing arts programs increase dramatically. Cutbacks in arts education in the schools are affecting younger generations of potential audiences. The arts have also been hard hit by declining contributed support. Cuts in government funding have become severe, and many sources of funding—especially government agencies and private foundations—have been earmarking grants for specific programs, leaving less money for general operating budgets. At the same time, arts organizations face a constant upward spiral of operating costs. As a result, debts are rising and arts organizations are finding it increasingly difficult to find the resources they need to sustain their mission and quality.

History: The Arts Expand over the Decades

In his famous ordering of national priorities, statesman John Adams said that he had to study politics and war, so that his sons could study mathematics and philosophy, in order to give their children a right to study painting, poetry, music, and architecture. Although he valued the fine arts highly, Adams feared that a strong focus on the arts might be linked with an excess of luxury, a trend Adams felt he had observed in France during his diplomatic service at the court of Versailles. Therefore, Adams reasoned, too great an interest in the arts might corrupt his fellow citizens, who were trying to forge a new nation in a vast wilderness and were preoccupied with more "practical" things. Whether Adams intended his generational hierarchy to be literal or figurative, it was nearly two hundred years before the United States government committed itself to a program of sustained, direct financial support for the arts.[3]

Before the Civil War, formal systems for presenting high culture did not exist in the United States. Serious art and popular works intermingled in public venues, where sponsoring organizations might present a relatively austere program of classical music one week and a popular extravaganza (such as "Mr. Mutie, his African monkey, and several Chinese Dogs") the next. After the Civil War, nonprofit enterprise in the arts as we know it today began to develop as the emerging urban upper classes attempted to define and legitimate a body of art that they could call their own and that would serve as a source of honor and prestige among their peers. Says sociologist Paul DiMaggio, "The institutionalization of high culture . . . can best be understood as an antimarket social movement, aimed at defining a corpus of sacred art beyond the reach of profane commercial concerns."[4] Cultural entrepreneurs of the late nineteenth century utilized the nonprofit form to bring performers under their direct employment, protecting art from government intervention and from the whims of the masses. Says DiMaggio,

Only the power to hire and fire performers, to demand their exclusive services, and to place them under the authority of a conductor hired by the nonprofit entrepreneur or trustees enabled the orchestras of the twentieth century to develop a musical canon and modern performance standards. In purely market terms, the nonprofit form was less efficient than the conventional combination of proprietary band and proprietary sponsor; but it attained ends that were unrealizable through market exchange alone.[5]

The nation's first permanent, independent, and disciplined orchestra, the Boston Symphony Orchestra, was founded in 1881 by philanthropist Henry Lee Higginson. Higginson once asserted, "I alone am responsible for the concerts of the Symphony Orchestra." He defined his role and his purpose as "to pay the bills, to be satisfied with nothing short of perfection, and always to remember that we were seeking high art and not money: art came first, then the good of the public, and the money must be an after consideration." It was Higginson who gave the money to build the symphony's hall, to manage operations, and to single-handedly cover a deficit that by 1914 had accumulated to $900,000. It was also Higginson who chose the conductors, who had ultimate authority to hire and fire musicians, and who insisted that the musicians devote themselves exclusively to the orchestra and avoid such vulgar activities as performing for dances. He also persisted in segregating the musical fare so that "light" music was increasingly relegated to summer performances by the Boston Pops Orchestra while the Symphony Orchestra "purified" its programs, presenting music that he and his conductors considered worthy, whether or not it was popular with the audiences.[6]

By the 1930s, courses in art and music were being taught in all major universities and radio brought music to small towns and rural areas, so by the post–World War II period, art became more popularized. Most orchestras, however, continued to be administered by their founders and supported by wealthy individuals. In the 1950s, cultural visionary W. McNeil Lowry, as director of the Ford Foundation's Office of Humanities and the Arts, began infusing millions of dollars of capital financing into the infrastructure of arts organizations—donating $80 million to orchestras alone. Other foundations quickly followed the Ford Foundation model. This cultural emphasis was given official life in 1965 when Lyndon Johnson signed the law that created the National Endowment for the Arts (NEA), declaring, "Art is a nation's most precious heritage, for it is in our works of art that we reveal to ourselves, and to others, the inner vision which guides us as a nation."[7]

In the thirty years from the mid-1950s to the mid-1980s, the arts sustained rapid and persistent growth. In 1955 the arts received $15 million in contributions from foundations and corporations; by 1990 that amount had increased to $500 million. A promotion boom made arts attendance more accessible and compelling to greater numbers of people, and expanding attendance levels stimulated the growth of new and larger performing arts organizations. Since 1965, the number of professional orchestras in the United States has increased from 58 to to more than 1,000 (including community orchestras); opera companies from 27 to more than 110; dance companies from 37 to 250, and professional resident theater companies from 12 to more than 400. In addition, there are literally thousands of nonprofit presenting organizations that engage artists and groups to perform in their halls: youth symphonies, university theaters, dance groups, and so on.

By 1987, ticket sales to nonprofit performing arts events exceeded spending for tickets to sports events. According to John Naisbett, the arts will continue to replace sports as society's primary leisure activity throughout the 1990s.[8] He foresees a growth of new arts patrons who are affluent, educated, professional, and increasingly female. As evidence that this trend is widespread and not confined to the major cities, Naisbett cites the example of the Alabama Shakespeare Festival, which witnessed growth in attendance from 3,000 in 1972 to more than 300,000 in 1989. Naisbett believes that potential audiences for the arts will continue to grow, as the 35–44 age group increases by six million and the 45–54 age group increases by 11 million between 1990 and 2000.[9]

ENTER THE CRISES

Although the arts achieved unprecedented growth in many important ways from the 1950s to the 1980s, in recent years the nation's nonprofit arts industry has been grappling with spiraling expenses, deficits of crisis proportions, shrinking contributed income, and stagnant audience sizes.

Expenses and Revenues

The orchestra industry's annual deficit grew from $2.8 million in 1971 to $23.2 million in 1991 and is expected to exceed $60 million by the year 2000. In the twenty-year period from 1971 to 1991, expenses of symphony orchestras increased dramatically, from $87.5 million in 1971 to $698.9 million in 1991 (an increase of 137.5 percent after adjusting for inflation). Most important, both the amount of increase and the pace of increase were greater for expenses than for revenues. (In the five-year period from 1986 to 1991, expenses increased 41.5 percent while revenues increased only 39.6 percent.)

Across the United States, almost half of the more than four hundred regional theaters are operating in the red, with budget deficits ranging from a few thousand dollars to more than half a million dollars annually. In San Diego, which was deeply affected by California's recent economic downturns, 60 percent of the sixty-four theaters that are members of the League of Resident Theatres (LORT) are running deficits, and twenty of these theaters are in severe trouble.

For the sixty-six sample theaters surveyed annually by the Theatre Communications Group (TCG), during the five-year period 1990–94 aggregate expenses exceeded income (earned and contributed) by 2.1 percent, despite the fact that nearly one-third of the theaters have significantly reduced their operating budgets. Ticket sales decreased or, at best, remained static during the years 1990–94. Aggregate attendance at main series productions fell by more than 3 percent in that five-year period, and in 1994, box office income covered only 46.7 percent of expenses—the smallest portion reported to TCG since 1982. In the 1994–95 season, box office income grew 6.9 percent over the previous year, mainly due to a surge in single-ticket and group sales.

In the years 1988–93, opera audiences increased by almost 30 percent, resulting in a similar increase in box office receipts. Yet, the aggregate deficit of American opera companies grew during those years, largely because of dwindling contributed income from both foundation and government sources. This drop was somewhat offset by a modest increase in private giving; individual contributions rose at a much higher rate than corporate and business giving.[10]

Many of the nation's major dance companies are also exhibiting severe symptoms of financial stress. The American Ballet Theatre staved off bankruptcy with radical cuts in programming and touring, but is still battling a huge deficit. From 1990–1994, the budget at the Pennsylvania Ballet shrank from $8.4 million to $5.7 million. In 1994, the Houston Ballet announced the cancellation of its New York season due to economic considerations. At the Atlanta Ballet and the Bay Ballet Theatre of Tampa, an increasing emphasis on the financial bottom line has brought many boards and artistic staffs into acrimonious conflict. The National Dance Heritage Initiative, a preservation project, was a victim of the NEA's 1994 budget cut and lost its $300,000 funding.[11]

The situation at Dance Saint Louis in 1992 typifies the problems facing many performing arts organizations today.

DANCE SAINT LOUIS MOVES TO TACKLE $400,000 DEFICIT

From 1985 to 1992, Dance Saint Louis's audience size grew impressively, ranging from 16,000 to 77,000 people annually. Along with this expansion came a less welcome one—the company's deficit grew to $400,000. The financial problems resulted from a combination of factors. In 1991, unanticipated costs of $30,000 were incurred when the company moved to a new theater, $80,000 in normally assured funds from private and public resources were lost, and the Arts and Education Council of Greater Saint Louis cut Dance Saint Louis's $160,000 in funds by 16 percent—mainly because it was dissatisfied with the company's persistent deficit!

To help reduce the deficit, the fifty-two members of the Dance Saint Louis board agreed to increase their donations, typically totaling $65,000, by 50 percent over the next three years. Also, the organization applied for a National Endowment for the Arts Challenge grant of $157,000, which must be triple-matched within three years in order for the company to be eligible for the money. The company also planned to cut some of its dance programs that are highly popular but that typically lose money, and to add more break-even performances that can drive subscription sales.[12]

Contributed Income Challenges

By the late 1980s, the entire nonprofit performing arts industry was faced with declining contributed support due to the economic recession, changing philanthropic priorities among foundations and corporations, severe funding cuts from government sources, and increased competition for contributions resulting from the significant growth in the sheer number of arts organizations competing for funds. In the American orchestra industry, contributed income from individuals rose at an inflation-adjusted 139 percent in the twenty years from 1970 to 1990.[13] However, because private giving to the arts in general increased more than 250 percent during those two decades, orchestras' share of the philanthropic arts dollar decreased by almost a third.

Theaters have also faced new contributed income challenges. Although individual contributions rose 20.7 percent from 1991–95 and foundation giving rose 31.6 percent, corporate philanthropy dropped 1 percent, federal support dropped 23.7 percent, and state support dropped 13.0 percent (all figures adjusted for inflation).[14]

U.S. government support of the arts has declined consistently in recent years, and by the mid-1990s the very existence of the National Endowment for the Arts and the National Endowment for the Humanities was at stake. What began with isolated cases of criticism of some NEA-funded arts projects by certain conservative members of Congress has become a major debate over government funding of the arts. State and local funding sources are also at risk, and many have been subject to deep cuts that have severely affected the size and number of their grants to arts organizations.

Increasingly, funders—especially government agencies and foundations—are designating their grants for specific purposes, and less funding is available for general operating support. Corporate support is becoming more commercial than philanthropic and is often conditioned on arts organizations becoming leaner, more business-oriented, and able to meet the corporations' own marketing objectives. These factors are having their effect on the quality and quantity of programs and services the arts organizations can undertake, and in many cases, funding cutbacks and restrictions are threatening organizational survival.

Internationally, countries like France and Austria provide substantial and sometimes lavish state support for the arts: the French government supports the arts with $2 billion per year. However, in other European countries such as England and the Netherlands, government patronage of the arts has historically been much less extensive. In England, where government support for the arts has been on the decline in recent years, arts organizations are reaching out to individuals for contributions for the first time in their history and are increasing their emphasis on corporate sponsorships, which currently account for about 10 percent of British arts organizations' revenue. Arts organizations in eastern European and former Soviet countries are seeking all new sources for contributed support, because, under the new regimes, their governments no longer sustain them financially.

Audience Size

At the same time, audience size remains stagnant at best, and in many areas is shrinking. Lifestyles are changing. Americans' leisure time declined by 37 percent between 1973 and 1987, from 26.2 hours per week to 16.6 hours: husbands and wives both working has become the norm; there are more single-parent households; and baby boomers have moved out of urban areas, have taken on greater job responsibilities, and are caring for young children. There is growing competition from less expensive and more convenient forms of entertainment, especially VCRs and television, while the cost—both in dollars and convenience factors—of attending performing arts programs has been increasing dramatically. Also, the lack of arts education in the schools is having an effect upon the younger generations of potential audiences.

Among those who do attend, there have been drastic changes in ticket-purchase behavior. From the late 1960s, when full-season subscriptions were first offered, through the mid-1980s, subscription sales increased dramatically and continually for many organizations. Since then, people have become more spontaneous in choosing their entertainment options and are less likely to commit a year in advance to specific dates or to an entire series of performances. This has put strain on arts marketers, who must work much harder to maintain ticket sales at their former levels and who now must find ways to create multiple offerings of smaller packages to attract new patrons without further eroding their subscriber base.

Furthermore, the country's demographics are changing dramatically, and arts organizations must learn how to include members of diverse minorities among their audiences, boards of directors, donors, and volunteers. In 1990, one out of six workers belonged to an ethnic minority; by 2000, the proportion will be one in three. By the year 2010, one in three children will be either African-American, Asian-American, or Hispanic. The Hispanic population in America is projected to grow from 24 million in 1992 to 81 million by 2050.[15]

A declining audience base is not unique to the United States. In a 1994 study of opera and ballet audiences in London, it was found that about one-third fewer people go to performances by the three major London ballet companies than attended during the years 1971–74. Opera attendance has also declined slightly despite an increase in the opportunities to attend.[16]

Such factors have led various observers to paint a gloomy picture for the performing arts industry. Articles abound with headlines such as "Orchestras Face Up to Trouble and the Bottom Line," "Arts Groups Fight Lean Times," and "Facing Their Own Recession, Regional Stages Tighten Belts."[17]

ECONOMIC CHALLENGES

Overgrowth of the Industry

The main problem creating stress for nonprofit performing arts organizations today is that while enjoying three decades of sustained growth they overinvested in fixed expenses.

Throughout the history of the nonprofit arts movement, growth has been the primary criterion for measuring success. Budget maximization has always been a major goal of arts managers because larger budgets enable directors to stage productions that are more challenging in terms of size and cost, and that offer greater freedom to experiment. Although this response may have been both workable and meaningful up to the mid-1980s, it is much less viable today.

During their period of rapid growth, arts organizations used their surplus income to invest in larger performance halls, higher-quality productions, larger staffs, more musicians, longer seasons, and so on. During the years 1977–87, overall ticket sales increased 50 percent in inflation-adjusted terms, but during the same period, employment was boosted by 161 percent in nonprofit theaters and by 83 percent in orchestras and opera companies.[18] As budgets grow, the need to continually draw a larger audience and donor base creates the need for a still bigger staff and budget. The result is likely to be spiraling costs that exceed revenues and lead to the inevitable distancing of financial decisions from artistic priorities.

Similarly, many orchestras, which previously had been scheduling performances based on current demand, responded to pressure from their musicians for year-round employment. "Now," says one symphony marketing director, "my main problem is that I have 30 percent too many concerts to sell." If managers had anticipated the slackening of demand and the shrinking funding that has characterized the period since the late 1980s, they could have used their surpluses—or at least part of them—to create endowments for future security instead of locking in such high fixed expenses. According to some estimates, the performing arts industry as a whole is attempting to function at a level 30 to 50 percent beyond the capacity of its available resources. Managers and boards of directors today are saddled with organizations and budgets too big to manage, and they are struggling to manage change.

Productivity in the Arts

The problem of spiraling expenses is persistent in the arts industry because performing arts organizations do not benefit from the productivity gains realized by other sectors of society. For most of the twentieth century, increasing efficiency in our technology-oriented, for-profit economy has been continuous and cumulative. Output per man-hour has doubled approximately every twenty-nine years. Suppose that, due to technological advances and other factors, an automobile worker's productivity increases 4 per cent per year. If, each year, the worker's wages increase by 4 per cent, the ratio between total labor cost and total output remain virtually unchanged. Productivity and wages are rising in tandem.

In contrast, productivity in the arts has actually decreased relative to the rest of the economy. A live performance of a forty-five-minute Schubert quartet will take the same three man-hours to produce as it did at the beginning of the century, and always will. But the musicians' wages rise over time, even if their productivity does not. If in a forty-hour week the string player provides just as many performances as he did the previous year, but his wage is 4 per cent higher, the cost per performance has risen correspondingly, and it will continue to increase in proportion to the performer's income. The other costs of managing organizations and mounting performances—managerial salaries, materials, rents, advertising, and so on—also keep increasing. And while Broadway theaters run productions for as long as they can attract an audience, nonprofit theaters mount several new productions every season, each requiring massive efforts in rehearsing, directing, development of sets, lighting, costumes, and promotion.

Nonprofit performing arts organizations, no matter how successful artistically, typically operate under constant financial strain. They suffer from what Baumol and Bowen call an inevitable "cost disease" of growing financial pressures and an ever-widening gap between income and expenses.[19] In 1971, the cost to the orchestra industry was $5.00 per audience member served, based on attendance at the 13,000 performances presented that year. In 1981, it cost $12.62 per audience member at the industry's 20,100 performances. By 1991, the costs had risen to an average of $26.17 per audience member served at the industry's 18,100 performances.[20] Not only does income not cover these costs, but the gap has widened dramatically, from $2.78 in 1971 to $15.91 in 1991. Orchestras represent the only performing arts discipline that registered increases in the proportion of budget earned between 1985 and 1990. During that same time period, dance, theater, and opera all showed declines in the percentage of budget earned. On average, audience members now pay for only 39 percent of the costs of the services provided to them. And few in the industry believe that this income gap can be substantially reduced through increased ticket prices. It is largely for this reason that performing arts organizations have needed to shift part of the financial burden back to their performers and managers—who are often very poorly paid by commercial standards. It is also why the recent wave of demands by musicians' labor unions has put many symphony orchestras at risk.

Of course, there are some opportunities for performing arts organizations to benefit from productivity increases. Computers increase efficiency in administrative offices and airplanes save travel time for performers. Larger-scale operations can increase productivity through the use of longer seasons, more performances of each production, and larger theaters that enable organizations to serve larger audiences with a near-constant expenditure of effort. Orchestras served 1,500 people per performance in 1991, up from 1,200 a decade before. However, the arts can never hope to match the remarkable productivity growth achieved by the economy as a whole.[21]

Other Financial Issues

Although a constant upward spiral of operating costs is likely to remain characteristic of the industry, other economic factors are affecting the financial health of arts organizations. Arts organizations are revenue intensive, meaning that they rely heavily on current income and advance ticket sales to support current expenses. They often carry sizable debt in accounts payable, which tends to accumulate slowly over a period of years. Differing lengths of seasons due to erratic bookings lead to earned-income swings. They have little or no endowment, no significant cash reserves, and limited or no lines of credit. Many organizations are beginning to use what endowment funds they do have to meet their rising operating expenses. The desire to fulfill the organization's artistic mission often leads directors to spend all available money on short-term artistic pursuits.

As arts organizations attempt to increase earned revenue with restaurants, shops, and other profitable ventures, small businesses are lobbying against not-for-profit business competition. As a result, the government is examining ways of increasing the nonprofit enterprises' exposure to income taxes—an effort that is likely to result in tax payment on some earned income.

SOCIAL AND POLITICAL QUESTIONS

Art versus Entertainment

In 1960, the state of American culture raised the concerns of August Heckscher, cultural advisor to President Kennedy. In his contribution to the president's Goals Commission Report, Heckscher examined both the popular and fine art traditions in America and found the former too often lacking sufficient substance, threatening to become "irredeemably trivial," and the latter, through no fault of its own, too often lacking a sufficient audience. Cautioned Heckscher, "An industrial civilization, brought to the highest point of development, has still to prove that it can nourish and sustain a rich cultural life. In the case of the United States, it is evident that cultural attainments have not kept pace with improvements in other fields." The same argument persists today, as was anticipated a century and a half ago by Alexis de Tocqueville when he prophesied the difficulty, if not the impossibility, of supporting a serious culture in a democratic society.[22]

Although much art deals with universal topics such as life, death, fear, joy, love, war, and peace, there is a perception that the fine arts reflect the taste of a very small cultural elite. Some sociologists recognize a cultural hierarchy that tends to polarize into a conflict between traditional high culture (fine art) and popular culture (mass culture). To high culture devotees, the product of popular culture is "kitsch":

sentimental, manipulative, predictable, vulgar, unsophisticated, and superficial. Critics of popular culture see it as a threat to Western culture itself. They maintain that popular culture is undesirable because it is mass-produced by entrepreneurs for profit, because it debases high culture, produces spurious gratification, is emotionally harmful to its audience, and they even claim that it encourages totalitarianism by creating a passive audience.

To popular culture fans, the product of high culture is overly intellectual, effeminate, snobbish, and superficial. Those who enjoy the paintings of Norman Rockwell, popular Broadway musicals, rock, pop, and country music, and so on believe they have just as much right to their taste as those who enjoy Beethoven, theater of the absurd, and opera. Supporters of popular culture argue that high culture today is an attempt to restore an outdated, elitist order at the expense of an existing cultural democracy.[23]

The sharp distinction between the "nobility" of art and the "vulgarity" of mere entertainment is due in part to the systems under which they operate. The performing arts are predominantly distributed by nonprofit organizations, managed by artistic professionals, governed by prosperous and influential trustees, and supported in a large part by funders. Popular entertainment, on the other hand, is sponsored by profit-seeking entrepreneurs and distributed via the market.[24] However, the differences between high art and popular culture are often greatest in the minds of their enthusiasts, especially in terms of the social status conferred by participation or non-participation, rather than in the intrinsic nature of the art itself.[25] Consider the fact that Mozart's *Magic Flute,* which today is performed in the world's finest opera houses, was originally commissioned by a music hall to entertain its populist audience. And, in response to criticism from the classical avant garde for writing music they considered too accessible, Pulitzer prize–winning composer Morton Gould quipped, "I'm sorry I wrote something a lot of people like. I'll try never to do it again."

To some high culture elitists, what is considered "popular" or "entertaining" is whatever draws a huge crowd. Says the director of an ethnic music festival, "There's an idea out there that if something is 'popular,' it's not very good, that if we're selling out the house we must be doing something wrong."[26] Similarly, concert pianist and educator David Owen Norris cautions, "We mustn't be forced into the idea that the fewer people who like something, the better it must be. We must make the experience relevant for the audience and either satisfy or surprise audience expectations."

An attitude of "art versus entertainment" on the part of arts managers and artistic decision makers can only work to the detriment of arts organizations. Says Robert Kelly, "The factors that drive institutional status (or vanity) are quite different from those that prevailed when the linkages between the arts and persons of high status were first formed."[27] And artist Leopold Segedin reminds us that "not only great artists and connoisseurs, but all persons have the potential to achieve satisfaction and fulfillment through creative and aesthetic experiences."[28]

Art for Art's Sake or Art for Social Purpose?

Since the 1960s, when government agencies, foundations, and corporations began substantially to fund the arts, art has taken on a social function, serving purposes previously confined to education, religion, and politics. Ronald Berman, a former chairman of the National Endowment for the Humanities, believes that this transformation has resulted in a major change in art's constituencies, leading to more emphasis on the funders and new types of audiences. Says Berman, "Art becomes a political commodity. There is assumed a direct connection between the appropriation of funds and the resolution of one or more social problems."[29]

As early as the 1950s, many claims were being made for the value of the arts in American society, largely by lay patrons and community leaders. The arts were said to be (1) important to the image of American society abroad, (2) a means of communication and consequently of promoting understanding between this country and others, (3) an expression of national purpose, (4) an important influence in the liberal education of the individual, (5) an important key to an American's understanding of himself, his times, and his destiny, (6) a purposeful occupation for youth, (7) vital to institutions mobilizing the social, moral, and educational resources of American communities, (8) good for business, especially in the new centers of population, (9) components for strengthening moral and spiritual bastions in a people whose national security might be threatened, and (10) an influence to offset the materialism of a generally affluent society. It is important to note that these arguments advanced for the arts in the fifties almost universally accepted the role of art as a means to some other end, rather than as an end in itself. However, say arts consultants and authors Bradley Morison and Julie Dalgleish, "Art does not exist to serve practical purposes. It is misguided to try to justify its support on the basis of community prestige, economic impact, urban development, corporate image, enlightened self-interest or even the chamber of commerce quality-of-life. We must accept art as art, as an end in itself, and strive to make it part of the lives of all because, quite simply, it *is* the essence of civilization."[30]

Robert Brustein, theater critic and artistic director of the American Repertory Theatre in Cambridge, Massachusetts, addresses this topic passionately in an article aptly titled "Culture by Coercion."[31]

Given the limited resources available for both social and cultural programs, the humanitarian agencies that disburse grant money no doubt believe that a single dollar can fulfill a double purpose. . . . This is surely true not only of Federal, state and civic cultural agencies, where the arts are vulnerable to populist political pressures, but also of most private funding organizations. In a recent issue of the newsletter Corporate Philanthropy Report, an unidentified contributions manager is bluntly quoted as saying: "We no longer 'support' the arts. We use the arts in innovative ways to support the social causes chosen by our company."

Staggering under large-scale deficits, our nonprofit cultural institutions are being asked to validate themselves not through creative contributions, but on the basis of community services. As Alexis de Tocqueville once predicted: "Democratic nations will habitually prefer the useful to the beautiful, and they will require that the beautiful be useful."

"Coercive philanthropy" is the name Brustein applies to the activities of many foundations, both large and small, that give their money not to general support, as in the past, but overwhelmingly to special programs conceived by their officers. "Today it is a rare foundation indeed that doesn't reserve the lion's share of its revenue for incremental multicultural projects. Artistic support, in short, is posited not on quality (most funders admit that excellence is an obsolete standard) but on evidence of affirmative action."[32] For example, the Lila Wallace–Reader's Digest Fund, which distributed $45 million to the arts in 1993, describes its three-year program for resident theaters this way: "To expand their marketing efforts, mount new plays, broaden the ethnic makeup of their management, experiment with color-blind casting, increase community outreach activity and sponsor a variety of other programs designed to integrate the theaters into their communities." Responds Brustein, "What the foundation fails to 'expand' or 'broaden' or 'sponsor' is an artistic goal. By forcing artistic expression to become a conduit for social justice and equal opportunity instead of achieving these goals through basic humane legislation, we are distracting our artists and absolving our politicians."[33]

Boston Globe critic Richard Dyer believes that

pieces should never be programmed simply because they are by a woman, a gay, a representative of some ethnic or racial community, or indeed simply because they are new (or simply because they are old). . . . A concert can rise above political, careerist or even aesthetic concerns to reveal the life of the community through the efforts of individuals conveying their aspirations, fears, convictions and concerns. The value of that cannot be called into question. [34]

Furthermore, the high purpose of art, as articulated by playwright John Guare, is "to present the vivacity of clarity, to tell the truth and to tell it compellingly on how we survive on this planet." Brustein elaborates:

As theatre artists our obligation is to penetrate the puzzles of the human heart: to honor complexity, appreciate mystery, expose secrets, invade dreams. The function of dramatic art is to disclose not the effects but the *causes* responsible for our condition, not the symptoms but the *sources* of errant and aberrant human behavior. From such disclosures we regain the capacity to be tragic human beings instead of social victims, complicated creatures of will rather than simplified subjects of sociological inquiry. . . . For the play's not "the thing" to arouse unproductive guilt in an ineffective spectator. It is an opportunity to expose the obscure elements, the hidden unpredictable qualities shared by *every* human soul.[35]

In response to Brustein's commentary, the *Chicago Tribune*'s chief critic, Richard Christiansen, writes:

> On the whole, [education and outreach programming] is a responsibility that arts groups have willingly and happily taken on, and the results have been impressive. . . . With artists perceived in some quarters as frivolous or irrelevant persons whose chief function is to undermine morality and mock religion, it is perhaps all the more important to hold up to attention the overwhelming amount of good deeds that they provide for their communities.
>
> In recent times, however, there has been a growing concern among many scholars, critics and artists that what was once a willing responsibility of conscience has become twisted into a dictated necessity of the marketplace. In short, instead of asking for general support to sustain and improve their art, arts organizations are asking for specific funding dedicated to social service. Instead of holding to the belief that art is everything, they are conceding that, in today's funding maze, art is not enough.

Continues Christiansen, "[Art has] a noble and important mission, but it is a mission we may be in danger of losing if we try to replace it instead with politically correct and socially worthy goals."[36]

MARKETING ISSUES

Art-Centered versus Market-Centered Product Choice

In 1991, the Chicago Symphony Orchestra (CSO) performed a newly commissioned work by Ralph Shapey, a piece that is highly challenging and difficult for even the most sophisticated music listeners. The Shapey concert drew a large audience because it was part of a heavily subscribed program. But in the midst of the performance, the audience evacuated the concert hall in record numbers. And those who left probably represented only a portion of those who were dissatisfied with the experience. Yet, Zarin Mehta, executive director of the Ravinia Festival, has no problem with even five hundred people leaving a performance, while two thousand remain and gain exposure to the music. One can also argue that the five hundred who left were somehow influenced by the music they did hear, and that the mere exposure may cause them to listen differently to other contemporary music in the future.

A market-centered approach calls for satisfying the customer. But, in the arts, is satisfaction the goal? If the purpose of art is to broaden human experience, it may be necessary for the artist to take an audience through an uncomfortable period of "unfreezing" before they come to terms with the new possibilities. However, even the highly respected CSO would erode its subscriber audience if the Ralph Shapey experience occurred on a regular basis; as much of the audience clamors for traditional and familiar music. Henry Fogel, the CSO's president, reflects that if he were to receive significant negative feedback from the audience on such a matter, it would be certain to affect the amount of contemporary music he would program for the next season. According to Fogel, "A serious artistic organization that ignores the market place is lying—pure and simple lying." In order for a performing arts organization to survive, it must both meet the current needs of its audiences and assist in the developmental process that will cause audiences to seek and respond to a product that is closer to the director's artistic vision.

One of marketing's major theorists, Theodore Levitt of Harvard, argues that any business must try to satisfy its customers:

> The view that an industry is a customer-satisfying process, not a goods-producing process, is vital for all businessmen to understand. An industry begins with the customer and his needs, not with a patent, a raw material, or a selling skill. Given the customer's needs, the industry develops backwards, first concerning itself with the physical *delivery* of customer satisfactions. Then it moves back further to *creating* the things by which these satisfactions are in part achieved.[37]

According to Levitt, the basic premise of the marketing concept is that a company should determine what consumers need and want, and try to satisfy those needs and wants, provided that doing so is consistent with the company's strategy and that the expected rate of return meets the company's objectives.

However, this purely market-centered philosophy is inconsistent with what the concept of art is all about. Is art presentation just another industry? Should high customer satisfaction even be the objective of a performing arts organization? If patrons were all satisfied, artistic directors wouldn't be living up to their responsibility to challenge and provoke. Said a Rockefeller report on the problems facing the performing arts in 1965, "Entertainment which makes no demand upon the mind or the body offers neither permanent enrichment of the spirit nor a full measure of delight."[38] Furthermore, say Morison and Dalgleish,

> When the goal is creating a love affair between people and a certain artist's vision of art, then changing the product does not help to accomplish that end; it betrays it. It is totally inappropriate for those who govern, manage or market the arts to suggest that the product be changed to make it sell better. In theory, they have accepted the vision of the artistic leadership and their responsibility is to support that vision and to communicate clearly and effectively its values, meaning and benefits to those who might find enjoyment and enrichment in participating as audience. If that is done and no one is interested, then eventually the maintenance of the organization will no longer be justified. Or, as an alternative to institutional euthanasia, a board of trustees may choose to select artistic leadership whose tastes and values are closer to those of a larger public. In that case, however, it would appear that *institutional survival* rather than artistic purpose is what is being pursued.[39]

The artist's perspective transcends predetermined input from the audience. Art is pure expression; it is visionary; and when successful, it leads an audience on a journey that for many is a previously unimagined experience.

On the other hand, the essence of the performing art experience resides in the communication between the performers onstage and the members of their audience. Unless the performers are speaking, singing, playing, or dancing in a language that audience members can appreciate, relate to, or be moved by, then there is an element of futility in the very act of performing. Richard Dyer believes that the best communication comes when

> pieces [are] programmed from across the spectrum of human experience, from the profoundly spiritual to the probingly sensual; some should be deeply serious and some should be cheeky and entertaining. And all should be there because the music director and the orchestra love this music, believe in it and use it to express their own feelings, knowledge and experience of life. This is the connection that is too often missing. When that connection is made, every concert is "relevant" and "authentic."[40]

Neither a pure adherence to a market-centered approach nor to an art-centered approach could work in the context of the performing arts, where both the artist and the audience must be considered. So it is necessary to explore and discover a harmonious balance between the two ends of the spectrum, a mix that benefits both the suppliers and the consumers of the product. When it is at its best, the artistic decision is well received, even demanded, by the public. And, at its best, the market-centered decision is highly artistic. Along the continuum of art-centered and market-centered choices, the ultimate product is the one in which the two concepts become one.

Education and the Arts

At a performance of *Macbeth* during Chicago's International Theater Festival, England's Royal Shakespeare Company took three curtain calls and returned to the stage to applaud the audience. One commonly asks what makes a great performance. But the flip side of that question is, What makes a great audience?

Art requires listeners and viewers who want to participate, not just "consume." Pianist Rudolf Firkusny reminisces about his youth, back in the days when the only way to hear music was to play some. Once, an orchestra came to his home town to play a Beethoven symphony that hadn't been heard there for years. Long in advance of the concert, townspeople bought the score and played the symphony in piano reduction and four-hand versions. By the time of the performance, people really knew the piece. Remarks musician and teacher John Steinmetz, "Imagine how exciting it must have been, after learning the symphony by playing reductions, to hear the music in all its orchestral splendor! Imagine playing for an audience like that!"[41]

For some people, especially in European countries, art continues to be one of the basic necessities of life, an integral part of their education and upbringing. But many fewer people in the United States have a basic music education, and fewer than ever before value the type of musical involvement that Firkusny described. In the United States, says Steinmetz,

> Orchestral and chamber music audiences have been full of people with foreign accents. Soon that generation of music-lovers will be gone. Who will replace them? Of course, we have home-grown music supporters, too, but it appears that we have not grown enough of them. . . .
>
> Art music requires some involvement from the listener. You have to have a relationship with the music. Your experience will be affected by how you involve yourself.
>
> In marketing art music, we mustn't mistake listeners for consumers. They are co-producers of our product! Without an excellent audience, we will have a lousy product.

A 1988 study conducted by the National Endowment for the Arts indicated that most Americans have not had any form of arts education. The study found that, in general, public school systems do not provide opportunities for most students to become culturally literate; they do not teach the arts sequentially in kindergarten through high school, nor do they generally evaluate students of the arts. The study also reported that many arts teachers are not prepared to teach art history and critical analysis. Although these conditions are not new, high school students' achievement in and knowledge of visual arts and music have declined in recent years as whatever arts programs schools have provided in the past have been severely reduced or cut out completely. The study warns that "the artistic heritage that is ours and the opportunities to contribute significantly to its evolution are being lost to our young people." Says noted arts critic Samuel Lipman, "The direct result of this neglect is a downtrodden army of cultureless children marching into a barren and depleted adulthood and taking American civilization with them. And the sheer numbers of these future citizens confront the nation with prospects of a diminishing cultural future."[42] This situation poses a serious threat to the transmission of culture in this country and will have a long-term negative impact on the number of people interested in attending the performing arts.[43] It creates special challenges for arts organizations both in attracting and satisfying audiences and in taking on the role of educating current and potential future audiences.

Inaccessibility

In Canada, data reveal that fewer than one in four people attend live theater, one in twelve attend live dance, only one in twenty-five attend live classical music performances; and only one in seventy attend opera.[44] But another in-depth survey shows that many more people are interested in attending the performing arts than currently do so. Of the individuals surveyed who either are already attending or are very interested, opera currently taps 17 percent of this potential audience, theater 45 percent, ballet 27 percent, and orchestral music 37 percent.[45]

A major reason for this disparity between interest and participation is lack of accessibility. Of course, lack of understanding and appreciation of the art is often a factor, but accessibility problems often pertain to more mundane issues such as time of the concert, price, ticket availability, and concern about where to park, what to wear, or when to applaud. Many arts organizations are finding that although many people are *attracted to* theater, dance, and music, several factors are acting as *barriers*, keeping them away. Throughout this book we will give many examples of how audiences have been successfully expanded with attention to such "details" and without in any way changing the artistic product itself.

The Complexities of Marketing the Arts

The art marketer's role is complex. In the commercial world the customer reigns. Goods and services are produced and distributed according to demand and profitability considerations. But the purpose of a nonprofit arts organization is to expose an artist and his or her message to the widest possible audience, rather than to produce the artist and the message that the largest audience demands. Businesses innovate only when there is economic justification to do so. Nonprofit arts organizations innovate and explore in the pursuit of social or aesthetic value, even when there is no assurance of economic success.

This situation creates three major marketing problems.[46] First, the organization must *find* a market for its offerings. Because it is presenting productions for which there may be little or no existing demand, the organization must create new needs in the marketplace, rather than just meeting existing needs. Consider the contrast between a Broadway commercial theater that will run a production for as long as it can attract an audience ("*Cats*—now and forever!") and a nonprofit theater that will close a successful show in order to open the next, probably unfamiliar production, which is likely to run at a financial loss. Second, the organization must *expand* its market. Any market is usually of a limited size. But since art is often ahead of its audience (consider contemporary classical music at any time in history), the organization limits itself from producing the works that would most quickly expand the audience. It takes a long time to develop and educate an audience, and it entails a great financial risk. Third, an arts organization must *keep* its audience. While continually innovating and experimenting to promote the growth and exposure of artists, organizations drop successful trends and repeatedly make new demands on their audience members. So an artistic organization that tries to fulfill its mission and to innovate regardless of economic rationale must operate under severe handicaps in its efforts to find, expand, and keep an audience. (It is for this reason that arts organizations are partially removed and protected from the vagaries of the market and receive contributions that compose a significant portion of their budgets). Given these conditions, an arts marketer must be aware of and sensitive to the different and perpetually changing interests and needs of a wide variety of audience segments.

MANAGERIAL ISSUES

*The Crisis
Mode of
Management*

As managers and board members attempt to alleviate current problems, they often take certain actions and decisions that contribute to the crisis instead. Crisis management, which is the process of dealing with emergency situations, becomes the norm, preventing strategic planning both for the short and the long term. And as their debt increases, organizations become driven by financial concerns—often at the expense of artistic considerations—further complicating their problems. Arts consultants Nello McDaniel and George Thorn point out, "Stress from accumulated deficits is debilitating. It affects the way they [arts people] are working, the way they're thinking. It controls what they're able to do—and not do. Institutions become debt-driven rather than art-driven." Cash shortages create the necessity for immediate and impassioned fund-raising, triggering emotional responses from both staff and the board members and undercutting strategic fund-raising efforts. In the process, organizations become secretive about their true state of affairs in an effort to keep up appearances and to maintain funding and community support. Systems falter and organizations lose "memory" as staff and board membership turn over rapidly due to stress and burnout. This description is especially true of smaller organizations and of those that produce more challenging work, because they rarely have as strong a foundation of community and financial support on which to rely in difficult times as older, more established organizations.[47] Yet, the large number of troubled mature institutions confirms that a confluence of factors have developed during the last ten to fifteen years that can overwhelm even the best of arts managers and boards.

In 1991, McDaniel and Thorn published a special report entitled "The Quiet Crisis in the Arts."[48] The authors note that they have observed growing patterns of stress in arts organizations, indicating that a fundamental problem exists throughout the field:

> While no arts organization deliberately courts failure, many create situations that preclude success. Expense budgets are driven by growth, and income budgets are created to balance those expenses without regard to whether the goals are achievable. These "mythical" income budgets set up the staff, the board and the volunteers for failure. Marketing and fund-raising staffs, who are often inexperienced, untrained and immature, feel defeated. Frequently, they are fired because unrealistic targets are not met. Board members and volunteers are berated for failing to achieve artificial goals that they, secretly, never believed in. Board members believe that if the artists would just learn what the audience wants and give it to them, they would sell more tickets and raise more money. Organizations continually place people in positions with the expectation that they will meet unrealistic goals. Consequently, they are given absolutely no chance of being successful.

Of at least equal concern is the attempt by organizations to close the gap by using human capital—thereby creating a human deficit. When budgets don't balance, one frequent response is to lay off staff and ask everyone left to work harder. This is what we mean by using or abusing human capital. . . . Too often people feel they are victims. They are smart and working hard. They are doing all of the right things. But the gap continues to grow, and a sense of being a victim begins to take hold. The number of arts professionals and volunteers who are experiencing anger, frustration and feelings of failure is growing at an alarming rate.[49]

McDaniel and Thorn identify three benchmarks for defining the stability of an organization. A *pre-edge* organization is overextended, but its problems are still at the stage where they are manageable. Cash flow problems are increasing, staff is being cut back, earned income predictions are based on successful productions, and there is no room for lack of success. When income is discussed, whether earned or contributed, it is always qualified by the word "hope," as in "We hope to raise $50,000."

An organization *at the edge* begins to feel a sense of crisis and is close to being unable to operate. Cash flow and debt problems become all-consuming, staff has been reduced, turnover is high, and morale is low. Marketing and fund-raising staff are fired or resign because they are unable to meet unrealistic income targets. Board members are highly frustrated, and fund-raising among insiders is eroding because some people don't want to support an organization that might not make it. Much energy is expended presenting a stable facade to the community.

Once an organization is *over the edge*, it is in crisis and all the conditions described above are greatly intensified. The organization is unable to operate unless its minimum expenses are provided for by board members or a granting institution. Any one of a number of events could trigger collapse, but it would take a combination of major factors to ease the crisis. For all practical purposes, decision making and planning have stopped. Hopefully, organizations will provide for intervention, diagnosis, and stabilization before these latter stages occur.

Professionalizing Management

There is a great need for the development of well-trained, experienced arts managers for top-level positions, as well as for specialists in audience development and fund-raising. Many arts managers and marketers have learned their skills on the job and lack the necessary education in modern management and marketing theory and techniques to effectively analyze, strategize, plan, implement, and evaluate.

The first generation of nineteenth-century arts managers exhibited an *impresarial* style, combining traditionalistic authority, charisma, and entrepreneurship. The impresario was a connoisseur and a gentleman, primarily engaged in wooing contributors and satisfying wealthy trustees while dominating performers and employees by an autocratic imposition of his will. It wasn't until the 1960s that the impresarial form of arts management, which had evolved slowly over the course of a century, rapidly gave way to the administrative form of arts management. By the 1960s, arts organizations had grown much larger, in terms of both number of employees and size of budgets, causing more bureaucratic structures to emerge. Also, the large number of funding agencies and other interest groups have increasingly held the organizations and their managers formally accountable. "This demand for formal accountability," says sociologist Richard Peterson, "in turn puts a premium on employing arts managers adept at working in the administrative rather than the impresarial mode."[50]

Managing arts organizations has become much more complex as they have taken on auxiliary activities such as operating retail stores, dining facilities, educational programs, real estate ventures, music recording contracts, and membership tours. Today's arts administrators must negotiate formal written contracts with artists' managers and with musicians' and backstage technicians' labor unions; they must understand labor laws, workers' compensation laws, retirement plans, medical insurance benefits, workplace safety codes, and record and television performance royalties. Furthermore, new economic developments have led to a greater focus on the private sector and the marketplace, producing an increased emphasis on marketing, fund-raising, profit-making ventures, and the commercialization of artistic enterprises. In the process, marketing and fund-raising functions have become more sophisticated and competitive, requiring the employment of more highly educated managers. The days of continuous growth and expansion have given way to the need for austerity, consolidation, and careful planning. It is no longer enough to know basic operational skills such as accounting, database management, grant-writing, and how to produce a play. Subtler and more sophisticated communication and negotiating skills are critical for managing and marketing an arts organization.

Dramatic change in the functions and functioning of arts organizations is inevitable. This change can be most productive when it is the result of strategic planning, effective implementation, and ongoing evaluation. The ability to analyze and strategize requires fluency and comfort with current management theory and techniques. Arts managers have often been content to evaluate themselves based on the "goodness of their cause" and to substitute good intentions for results. Winston Churchill once said that "Success is going from failure to failure with undiminished enthusiasm." But such enthusiasm becomes increasingly difficult to muster on the part of the managers, the artists, the audiences, and the funders alike. Contemporary arts managers need the tools to build and sustain an organization that supports its artistic mission while facing the challenges of an uncertain and changing environment.

Resistance to Marketing

Some arts professionals, especially artistic directors, refuse to join with administrators in marketing-oriented activities and to include them in decisions about programming. Sometimes they actively seek to frustrate efforts in which market response is given "undue consideration." Says Robert Kelly of such professionals,

"They are an 'enemy within'; not because they consciously wish to place their arts organizations in jeopardy but because their blind resistance to marketing may, in the end, have that consequence."

In some cases, says Kelly, "marketing is feared and even hated for what it might do to the arts; on the other [hand], there is an unquestioning conviction that marketing can work miracles for the arts. To compound matters, these contradictory beliefs are often held by the same persons." Kelly believes that arts professionals must become more, rather than less, heavily involved in the marketing decision-making process, since avoidance will lead to ineffectual marketing, not to an absence of marketing.[51]

THE MARKETING RESPONSE

Although audiences grew significantly during the boom years of the mid-1960s to the mid-1980s, the major growth emphasis was on the *supply* side of the equation. The huge infusion of funds by foundations, corporations, and government agencies resulted in more arts organizations, more performers, more performances, more and bigger halls—and many more seats to fill. Today, some of the very funding sources that provided for this growth are changing their priorities and reducing their support.

The outlook for the health and sustainability of arts organizations would be more positive if organizations worked to accommodate larger and more diverse audiences by making better use of marketing procedures. In the current environment we have a more than ample supply of arts organizations and artists, while there appear to be serious deficiencies in the size and character of arts audiences. This situation must change. The audience for the arts is limited and the range of leisure activities continues to expand. As long as arts organizations continue to define their mission as to serve only the publics they have traditionally served, those that survive and thrive will be the exception rather than the rule.

Booker T. Washington once told a story of a ship lost at sea for weeks, its crew dying of thirst for lack of fresh water. Finally, sighting another vessel, the thirsty captain signaled, "Water, water . . . dying of thirst!" The other ship signaled back, "Cast down your bucket where you are." Thinking he had been misunderstood, the first captain repeated his message again and again, only to get the same reply. Eventually, the captain thought to cast down his bucket, which came up full of fresh, drinkable water. Although adrift on the ocean, the ship was in the sea of fresh water forming the nearly shoreless mouth of the Amazon River. Like the thirsty captain, arts managers tend to look elsewhere for help, devoting extraordinary efforts to regain contributed support that is not likely to come their way in the near future. Rather, arts managers should look to the resources most immediately at their disposal and most likely to remain fruitful for many years to come: their current and potential audiences.[52]

It is necessary to emphasize the *demand* side: to broaden the audience base, to increase audience size, to increase the accessibility of various art forms and of more "difficult" productions, and to support projects that meet the needs of specific audience segments. Arts managers have historically centered their focus on their productions, their product—their art. But art does not exist in a vacuum. The essence of art is in its *communication* with the audience member. Therefore, arts organizations must shift their focus to that communication. They must shift from a pure product focus to one that balances the artistic decision-making process with audience needs and preferences. The role of the arts organization is to serve as liaison, as facilitator, as distribution channel between artists and audiences; therefore it must be sensitive to both. Together the artistic director, managing director, and marketing director can create an experience that is ultimately satisfying to the artists, the audiences, and the organization itself.

[1] Statement marking the fiftieth anniversary of the American Society of Composers, Authors, and Publishers, *New York Times*, Feb. 16, 1964.

[2] Address at Amherst College, Amherst, Mass., Oct. 26, 1963.

[3] Milton Cummings, Jr., "Government and the Arts: An Overview," in *Public Money and the Muse: Essays on Government Funding for the Arts,* ed. Stephen Benedict (New York: Norton, 1991), 31–32.

[4] Paul DiMaggio, "Nonprofit Organizations in the Production and Distribution of Culture," in *The Nonprofit Sector: A Research Handbook,* ed. Walter W. Powell (New Haven, Conn.: Yale University Press, 1987), 204–205.

[5] Ibid., 205.

[6] Lawrence W. Levine, *Highbrow/Lowbrow: The Emergence of Cultural Hierarchy in America* (Cambridge, Mass.: Harvard University Press), 1988, 127.

[7] "The Arts in America," report prepared by the National Endowment for the Arts, 1988.

[8] John Naisbett, *Megatrends 2000* (New York: Morrow, 1990).

[9] Bernard Holland, *New York Times*, June 15, 1992, Living Arts Section.

[10] Laura J. Young and Nancy Roberts-Lea, "State of the Art," *Opera News,* November 1993, 26–27.

[11] Jacqueline Maskey, "The Year in Dance," *Musical America Directory 1995,* 76.

[12] *St. Louis Business Journal,* June 1, 1992, sec 1, p. 7.

[13] The Wolf Organization, *The Financial Condition of Symphony Orchestras,* part 1, "The Orchestra Industry" (Cambridge, Mass.: American Symphony Orchestra League, 1992).

[14] Steven Samuels and Alisha Tonsic, "Theatre Facts 1995," *American Theatre,* April 1996.

[15] Judith E. Nichols, *Growing from Good to Great* (Chicago: Bonus Books, 1995), 14–15.

[16] "Lyric Theatre Review," a report commissioned by the Arts Council of England, January 1995.

[17] Holland, *New York Times;* Mary Maguire, *Chicago Tribune,* July 15, 1991; *New York Times,* October 8, 1990, sec. C, p. 11.

[18] Lester M. Salamon, "Arts, Culture and Recreation," in *America's Nonprofit Sector: A Primer* (New York: Foundation Center, 1992), 94.

[19] William J. Baumol and William G. Bowen, "Anatomy of the Income Gap," in *Performing Arts: The Economic Dilemma* (New York: Twentieth Century Fund, 1966).

[20] Wolf Organization, *Financial Condition of Symphony Orchestras.*

[21] Baumol and Bowen, *Performing Arts: The Economic Dilemma.*

[22] Robert Brustein, *Dumbocracy in America* (Chicago: Ivan R. Dee, 1994), 26.

[23] Ibid, 52–53.

[24] Herbert Gans, *Popular Culture and High Culture* (New York: Basic Books, 1974), 75–94.

[25] Robert F. Kelly, "Elitism in the Arts," presented at the 2nd International Conference on Arts Management, Jouy-en-Josas, France, June, 1993.

[26] Elizabeth Zimmer, "The World at Your Door," *Inside Arts,* Spring 1993, 18.

[27] Kelly, "Elitism in the Arts," 7.

[28] Leopold Segedin, "Interdisciplinary Studies: Evolution or Revolution?" paper prepared for presentation at the conference of the Association of Integrative Studies, Washington, D.C., 1980.

[29] Ronald Berman, "Art vs. the Arts," *Commentary* 68, no. 5 (Nov. 1979), 47.

[30] Bradley Morison and Julie Gordon Dalgleish, *Waiting in the Wings* (New York: American Council for the Arts, 1987), 139.

[31] Robert Brustein, "Culture by Coercion," *New York Times,* Nov. 29, 1994, Op-Ed section.

[32] Brustein, *Dumbocracy in America, 16–17.*

[33] Brustein, "Culture by Coercion."

[34] Richard Dyer, "What Role Should a Symphony Play?" *Boston Sunday Globe,* July 11, 1993, sec. B, p. 28.

[35] Brustein, *Dumbocracy in America, 16–17.*

[36] Richard Christiansen, "If Art Is Not Enough, What Is It Worth?" *Chicago Tribune,* Dec. 11, 1994, sec. 13, p. 2.

[37] Levitt, Theodore, *The Marketing Imagination* (New York: Free Press, 1986).

[38] Rockefeller Panel Report, *The Performing Arts: Problems and Prospects* (New York: McGraw-Hill, 1965), 4–5

[39] Morison and Dalgleish, *Waiting in the Wings, 66.*

[40] Dyer, "What Role Should a Symphony Play?"

[41] John Steinmetz, "Resuscitating Art Music," *NARAS Journal,* Summer, 1993; reprinted in *Symphony,* July/Aug., 1995.

[42] Samuel Lipman, *Designs for Arts in Education,* March/April 1990.

[43] Jeffrey L. Brudney, "Art, Evolution, and Arts Education," *Society,* Sept./Oct. 1990, 17–19.

[44] Robert F. Kelly, "The 'Enemy' Within . . . Marketing in the Arts," paper presented at the First International Conference on Arts Management, Montreal, Canada, Aug. 1991.

[45] *Marketing the Arts in Cleveland,* report commissioned by the Cleveland Foundation, 1985.

[46] Ichak Adizes, "The Cost of Being an Artist," *California Management Review,* Summer 1975, 80–84.

[47] *Back Stage,* 31 (June 8, 1990), 1A.

[48] Nello McDaniel and George Thorn, "The Workpapers: *A Special Report, The Quiet Crisis in the Arts*," FEDAPT's 1989/1990 Annual Report (New York, 1991).

[49] McDaniel and Thorn, "The Workpapers," 18–19.

[50] Richard A. Peterson, "From Impresario to Arts Administrator: Formal Accountability in Nonprofit Cultural Organizations," 169.

[51] Kelly, "The 'Enemy' Within."

[52] William M. Dawson, "The Arts and Marketing," in *Marketing the Arts,* ed. Michael P. Mokwa, William Dawson, and E. Arthur Prieve (New York: Praeger, 1980) 9–10.

▲●▲

CHAPTER 2

Sell solutions, not
just products.
KLAUS LEISINGER

Marketing . . . is
the whole business
seen from the point
of view of its final
result, that is, from
the customer's point
of view.
PETER F. DRUCKER

THE MARKETING MIND-SET

IN 1989, THE PEW CHARITABLE TRUSTS RELEASED THE RESULTS OF A COMPREHENSIVE marketing survey of Philadelphia-area cultural audiences. The purpose of the survey was to identify opportunities for arts organizations to collaborate in building new audiences and increasing the frequency and variety of attendance among current audiences through such efforts as joint box offices, joint subscription offers, and other shared promotional activities. Various aspects of the survey results were widely reported in the local media, but journalist Mark Randall focused his commentary on the nature of the study itself, attacking marketing as a totally inappropriate tool to use in conjunction with the arts. Said Randall,

> Theaters, museums and musical organizations have always regarded pandering as a vice, so it is unfortunate that the major arts philanthropies should now view it as a virtue. I say "pandering," which is a term now used mostly in the arts, of course. The philanthropes, which trace their lineage and their jargon to the business community, have another word for it.
> They call it marketing.

One thinks of marketing as promotion and selling and advertising, but, in fact, these things represent almost the antithesis of marketing as it is professionally understood. Modern marketing, strictly defined, is a method that segments the population, identifies the needs of the segments, and then fashions and differentiates products to fulfill the needs of those segments. . . .

If one had taken a moment to think about the nature of art and the limits of marketing, one could only have concluded that marketing can do nothing but harm the arts. Leaving aside the stereotypical incompatibilities between art and commerce, what an artist does and what a marketer does are exactly the opposite. An artist must do what he does and then *hope* people like it. A marketer finds out what people like and then does *that*, or, to put it in marketing terms, the marketer is customer oriented, the artist is product oriented. . . .

The arts organizations engaged in . . . the absurd little polls popping out of our programs . . . must take the defining principle of art, i.e. that it express an individual or personal vision, and pretend to subordinate it to marketing's first principles. Among these is the idea that the public is never so well served as when it gets what it says it wants, and the best way to judge the arts is to count the people in the audience and to have them rank how important it is when you see a play, for example, that the play be by Shakespeare as opposed to one not by Shakespeare, how important that it have "lavish sets and costumes" and on and on down a list of hypothetical absurdities, as if *Giselle* were the green toothpaste, Mozart the red, and the job of the arts administrator is simply to keep the shelves stocked, the stores full, and everybody happy.

. . . To the extent that we glorify the tenets of marketing, i.e. risk adversity and the sovereignty of the mass will, we compromise those areas in life beyond consumer products where creativity and individuality matter. We deny ourselves the benefits of qualities outside the realm of marketing such as leadership, entrepreneurship and individual inspiration . . ."[1]

In response, we argue that much of what is unattractive about marketing practice today is the result of a lack of appreciation of the proper way to go about *doing* marketing. The reader, by the end of this chapter, should be able to pinpoint and dispel the myths present in Randall's criticisms.

It is the purpose of this chapter to explain the marketing mind-set and philosophy and to define a marketing orientation, especially in the context of artistic mission and vision. One can be a successful marketer only if one has adopted the proper marketing mind-set. This means having a clear appreciation for what marketing comprises and what it can do for the organization.

Marketing, as it relates to the arts, is not about intimidation or coercion or abandoning an artistic vision. It is not "hard selling" or deceptive advertising. It is a sound, effective technology for creating exchanges and influencing behavior that, when properly applied, *must be beneficial to both parties* involved in the exchange. In the wrong hands (i.e., the hands of those without the proper mind-set), what is called "marketing" can be manipulative and intrusive, and an embarrassment to those of us who use marketing as it ought to be used.[2]

Marketing is not just something that an organization such as Procter & Gamble or Pepsi-Cola does. It is something professional service firms (architects, lawyers, accountants) and nonprofit organizations (social service agencies, museums, churches) do and something we do daily in our individual personal lives. All of the following represent instances of marketing:

- You send a press release to a local TV station urging coverage of an upcoming program for parents of adolescents.
- Colleges provide AIDS education to all incoming students.
- The National Endowment for the Arts lobbies for more funding.

What is common to all these situations is that someone (a marketer) is attempting to influence the behavior of someone else (a target market). Given that all these situations involve marketing, they can all benefit from the application of the best marketing management techniques.

We define *marketing management* as the analysis, planning, implementation, and control of programs designed to create, build, and maintain beneficial exchange relationships with target audiences for the purpose of achieving the marketer's objectives. *Marketing* is the process by which an organization relates creatively, productively, and profitably to the marketplace, with the goal of creating and satisfying customers within the parameters of the organization's objectives.

The key feature of this definition is that it *focuses on exchanges*. Marketers are in the profession of creating, building, and maintaining exchanges. Because exchanges take place only when a target audience member takes an action, the ultimate objective of marketing is to influence behavior.

This definition permits us to distinguish marketing from several things it is *not*. Marketing's objectives are not, ultimately, either to educate or to change values or attitudes. It may seek to do so as a *means* of influencing behavior. If someone has a final goal of imparting information or knowledge, that person is in the profession of education, not marketing. If someone has a final goal of changing attitudes or values, that person may be described as a propagandist, a lobbyist, or perhaps an artist, but not a marketer. Though marketing may use the tools of the educator or the propagandist, its critical distinguishing feature is that its ultimate goal is to influence behavior (either by changing it or by keeping it the same in the face of other pressures).

Unfortunately, many of those who *could* use marketing principles do not do so because they do not see the relevance of marketing to their tasks. But we argue that, in nonprofit organizations, public relations specialists, fund-raisers, volunteer recruiters, and employee supervisors are all at one time or another marketers. And, as such, they can all benefit from understanding the philosophy and approach to marketing we present in this book.

On the other hand, there are many in nonprofit organizations, as well as in the private sector, who *think* they are marketers but who go about it the wrong way. Consider the following examples:

1. A public relations manager claims, "We are very marketing-oriented. We research our target markets extensively and hire top-flight creative people with strong marketing backgrounds to prepare brochures. They tell our story with a sense of style and graphic innovation which has won us several awards."

2. The director of a symphony orchestra describes her marketing strategy as an educational task. "I assemble a season of programs and then promote them grouped by period and style," she says, "so that the concert-goer can readily see the similarities and differences between, say, Beethoven and Brahms or between Debussy and Stravinsky. Our brochures, newsletters and lecture programs are carefully coordinated with this approach to complete our marketing mix."

The first person is confusing *promotion* and *public relations* with marketing. However, these functions are only tools, and they may or may not be effective or appropriate in a given situation. The second person is product-oriented and assumes that people will want to know what she is presenting, and only that. This approach is incomplete, both in terms of what can be told about the product and—most importantly—in terms of the interests and needs of her audiences.

Each of these executives thinks he or she understands what marketing is all about. *They do not.* In a study of eighty-eight arts administrators, marketing was seen as primarily sales promotion, heavily tied to advertising and selling activities (particularly for special programs or unusual events).[3] But marketing involves answering deeper questions such as, Who is the customer? What does the customer value? and How can we create more value for the customer?

THE EVOLUTION OF MARKETING PHILOSOPHY

To understand modern marketing management, it is useful to trace the evolution of different business orientations toward marketing in the private sector over the last hundred years. Three orientations can be distinguished.

The Product Orientation

Marketing first emerged as a distinct managerial function around the turn of the century, in an era that venerated industrial innovation in the design of new products. It was a period that saw the development of the radio, the automobile, and the electric light bulb. In this early period, marketing also was decidedly product oriented. The belief was that to be an effective marketer, you had simply to "build a better mousetrap," and, in effect, customers would beat a pathway to your door. As the strippers sang in the musical *Gypsy*, "You gotta' have a gimmick."

Even today, many organizations are in love with their product and believe strongly in its value. They firmly resist modifying it even if this would increase its appeal to others, and even if modification would have little or no impact on the organization's artistic integrity. A chamber music association calls itself a "society," performs only traditional music, advertises in only a suburban weekly, and doesn't understand why it doesn't attract a younger audience. A *product orientation* toward marketing holds that consumers will favor those products that offer the most quality, performance, and features. Managers in these product-oriented organizations focus their energy on making good products and improving them over time. These managers assume that buyers admire well-made products, can appraise product quality and performance, and are willing to pay more for product "extras." Many of these managers are caught up in a love affair with their product and fail to appreciate that the market may be less "turned on" and may even be moving in a different direction.

The Sales Orientation

Primary emphasis on selling is another approach that many firms take to the market. This approach assumes that consumers typically show buying inertia or resistance and have to be coaxed into buying more, and that the company has available a whole battery of effective selling and promotion tools to stimulate more buying. This new orientation led to significant expansion of the role of advertising and personal selling in the marketing mix. As "salesmanship" became the byword of successful marketing in the middle of this century, playwright Arthur Miller created Willy Loman, who achieved a central role in American folklore. Said Willy in *Death of a Salesman*, "Oh, I'll knock 'em dead next week, I'll go to Hartford. I'm very well liked in Hartford."

The selling orientation is still pervasive today. Organizations often believe they can substantially increase the size of their market by increasing their selling effort. They increase the budget for advertising, personal selling, sales promotion, and other demand-stimulating activities. This is why the public often identifies marketing with hard selling and with advertising. For example, a theater mounts a large-scale telemarketing and direct-mail campaign to promote subscription sales, based on the popularity of one star performer. Such sales-oriented steps will undoubtedly work to produce more customers in the short run. But their use in no way implies that the theater has adopted a marketing strategy that will generate higher sales in the long run.

A *sales orientation* toward marketing holds that success will come to those organizations that best persuade customers to accept their offerings rather than competitors' or rather than no offering at all. Selling is only the tip of the marketing iceberg. Peter Drucker, one of the leading management theorists, explains:

> There will always, one can assume, be need for some selling. *But the aim of marketing is to make selling superfluous.* The aim of marketing is to know and understand the customer so well that the product or service fits him and sells itself. Ideally, marketing should result in a customer who is ready to buy. All that should be needed then is to make the product or service available.[4]

Thus, selling, to be effective, must be preceded by several marketing activities such as needs assessment, marketing research, product development, pricing, and distribution. If the marketer does a good job of identifying consumer needs, developing appropriate products, and pricing, distributing, and promoting them effectively, those products will sell more easily.

Marketing based only on hard selling carries high risks. It assumes that customers who are coaxed into buying the product will like it, and that, if they don't, they won't badmouth it to friends or complain to consumer organizations. It also assumes that they might forget or forgive their disappointment and buy the product again. These are indefensible assumptions to make about buyers, whether they be purchasers of an automobile, patrons at a restaurant, or subscribers to a performing arts organization.

The Customer Orientation

The orientations that characterized the earliest stages in marketing's historical development had one thing in common. Marketing planning always began with the organization and *what it wanted to offer.* However, as consumers became more sophisticated and discerning, they also became more selective and more responsive to custom-tailored options, and hence were less willing to settle for just anything the market tried to persuade them to buy. And marketers began to realize that it is consumers who ultimately decide if and when transactions are to be made—not the marketer. They recognized that they had had the marketing equation turned backward. They had been trying to change consumers to fit what the organization had to offer. But since what the customer chooses to buy determines the organization's success, the customer is truly sovereign. It follows, then, that *marketing planning must begin with the consumer, not with the organization. Outside-inside marketing* must replace *inside-outside marketing.* As Willy Loman's son Hap once told him, "The trouble with you in business was you never tried to please people."

A customer-centered mind-set is the essence of the modern approach to marketing and is the guiding philosophy for this book. It requires that the organization systematically study customers' needs and wants, perceptions and attitudes, preferences and satisfactions. Then the organization must act on this information to improve its offerings to better meet its customers' needs.

This does not mean that artistic directors must compromise their artistic integrity. Nor does it mean that an organization must cater to every consumer whim and fancy, as many managers fear. Those who warn of such consequences if the devil (marketing) is let in the door simply misunderstand what a customer orientation truly means. To restate: marketing planning must *start* with customer perceptions, needs, and wants. Even if an organization ought not, will not, or cannot change the selection of works it performs or presents, the highest volume of exchange will always be generated if the way the organization's offering is described, priced, packaged, enhanced, and delivered is fully responsive to the customer's needs, preferences, and interests. Furthermore, who the customer will be is largely up to the performing arts organization. Marketing will help maximize exchanges with the targeted audience.

Consider two examples. In response to its need to develop new audiences, the Atlanta Ballet created a direct-mail piece designed to persuade potential ticket buyers that its performances are not elitist events of interest only to stuffy, upper-class patrons. The company developed brochures and accompanying letters with testimonials from subscribers representing a diverse cross section of the general public. The testimonials allude to the motivations of ballet goers, including "an avid runner and Braves fan who marvels at the dancers' athleticism" and a man who says, "A lot of us are just pedestrians who can't do anything ourselves, but we love to watch those who can." A child is quoted as saying, "When my parents take me to the ballet, it makes me feel loved," and a woman observes that "with all the bad news today—the rushing and the deadlines and the crises—it's wonderful to be able to sit back and immerse yourself in a thing of beauty." These testimonials, along with photographs of the people who spoke them, brought ballet to a level that everyday folks could understand. Making the audience and their reactions accessible to potential ticket buyers proved to be highly effective: the campaign garnered an overwhelming response among the general public, who don't really know who goes to the ballet. After only five weeks, the mailing had generated $92,000 from the sale of 1,360 season tickets, compared to $51,025 earned the previous year after twenty weeks. Incidentally, the costs of the mailing were about the same as those for the previous year's effort.[5]

In the second example, in the early 1970s a modest university research project in the Buffalo area revealed that many consumers who indicated that they thought they *might* like to attend a concert did not do so because they expected the occasion to be very formal. As these potential target consumers put it, "We can't go because we don't have the proper clothes. We would feel really uncomfortable around all those fancy-dressed people." The orchestra itself was seen as distant, formal, and forbidding. Once the Buffalo Philharmonic understood the barriers preventing potential customers from attending, the organization took great pains to humanize the orchestra and the concert-going experience. Orchestra section members began playing shirt-sleeved chamber music programs at neighborhood art fairs and other local outdoor events. The orchestra itself even performed a half-time show at a Buffalo Bills football game! The conductor, Michael Tilson Thomas, began appearing on local television and giving brief, informal talks to audiences at specific concerts. Formality was no longer a barrier keeping potential patrons away from concerts, and rising attendance figures clearly reflected this new customer-centered orientation.

Organizations often practice the marketing mind-set automatically. A movie theater showing art films practices marketing when it chooses to open its doors in a neighborhood of educated and sophisticated culture patrons. An orchestra does so when it brings back a favorite star performer year after year, even if that performer is so expensive that a sold-out house doesn't cover the costs of the performance.

However, for most organizations, this mind-set has not developed into a true customer-centered philosophy that permeates the consciousness of every manager and every other member of the organization who has any contact with potential target customers.

We define a *customer-centered organization* as one that makes every effort to sense, serve, and satisfy the needs and wants of its clients and publics within the constraints of its mission and budget.

A common result of a customer-centered orientation is that the people who come in contact with such organizations report high personal satisfaction. Since word of mouth is known to be the best advertising for a performing arts organization (or for any product), satisfied consumers become the most effective advertisement for these institutions. And whereas a satisfied customer tells an average of three people about a good experience, a dissatisfied customer gripes to eleven people. Clearly, bad word of mouth travels farther and faster than good word of mouth and can easily poison public opinion about a company or product. A Japanese businessman once said, "Our aim goes beyond satisfying the customer. Our aim is to *delight* the customer." This higher standard may well be the secret of the great marketers.

An example from the business sector illustrates this point. Gordon Segal, founder and CEO of Crate and Barrel, a contemporary and highly successful housewares and home furnishings company based in the Chicago area, says that he has told his favorite Nordstrom's story to employees on at least two hundred occasions. Nordstrom's is known for customer service, and the following incident, as told by Mr. Segal, exemplifies the company's philosophy well.

A gentleman had two feet of significant difference in size, so that one foot was a size ten, the other, size eleven. The man always purchased his shoes in size ten and a half, so that one shoe was too large, and the other too small. After having his feet measured in the shoe department at Nordstrom's, the salesman brought the gentleman one size ten shoe and one size eleven shoe. Upon being asked how the shoes felt, the gentleman replied that no shoes ever felt better on his feet, but he had no intention of purchasing two pairs of shoes. "I'm not selling you two pairs of shoes," said the salesman. "I'm selling you one size ten and one size eleven." "But, what will you do with the extra shoes?" asked the gentleman. "Sir," replied the salesman, "that is Nordstrom's problem, not yours." The positive word of mouth from this delighted customer had a major impact on Nordstrom's image and sales. In fact, this story has taken on the dimensions of legend for the company. No single paid advertisement could have done nearly as much. Besides, Nordstrom's was probably able to replace the missing "pairs" from the manufacturer.

This Nordstrom's salesman had carried out the company's marketing philosophy, which was presented to him through successful *internal marketing*. Internal marketing is the task of successfully hiring, training, and motivating able employees to serve the customers well. In fact, internal marketing must precede external marketing if the organization's philosophy is to be carried through every link in the system. Jan Carlzon of Scandinavian Airlines believes that every encounter with a customer is a "moment of truth," an occasion on which a customer has a chance to form an impression of the organization.[6] An otherwise enjoyable evening at the theater can be severely marred by an unpleasant encounter with box office personnel or with a surly usher. And not only should the front-line people, those who come directly into contact with the customers, be customer-oriented, but there must be systems in place to support them. Often, well-intentioned employees are afraid to buck organization policy to satisfy customers, subjecting customers to delays and ill will while they check with management—or, worse, claiming that what the customer wants is against company policy. So front-line people must be empowered to take action to satisfy customers, and to understand that *what is best for the customer is what is best for the organization in the long run.* This approach requires that management accept some misguided, but well-meaning, staff actions. But the payoff in customer satisfaction and long-term loyalty can prove to be dramatic, as Nordstrom's well understands.

Employees of performing arts organizations often face situations of customer dissatisfaction that require immediate response. A ticket holder finds herself behind a pillar and complains. An understudy is announced and some people want their money back. What should the theater do? Are the responses for such situations planned for in advance? Are they communicated to the ushers and the box office personnel? Is the company's customer philosophy understood well enough by the employees so that they can make appropriate spontaneous decisions when necessary?

DETECTING AN ORGANIZATION-CENTERED MARKETING ORIENTATION

Most organizations are not customer-centered. Some lack sufficient financial resources to hire, train, and motivate good employees and to monitor their performance. Some managers do not make sure that their employees in direct contact with the public, such as box office salespeople, are adequately representing the organization and maintaining a high standard of customer satisfaction. Some organizations prefer to concentrate on things other than customer satisfaction to serve the interests of their own internal stakeholders, and may intentionally be unresponsive to the publics they are supposed to serve. On the other hand, many managers wish to be customer-centered, and, in fact, wrongly believe that they are. There are several clues that reveal an organization's *organization-centered* philosophy. Among them are the following.

The organization considers its offerings to be inherently desirable. Arts administrators often find it hard to believe that any right-thinking person would not wish to attend their productions. Waving the banner of the artistic "imperative," arts managers often place themselves above the marketplace, attributing lack of organizational success to customer ignorance, absence of motivation, or both. Some managers admit that they simply haven't yet found the right way to communicate the benefits of their offerings or created the right incentives to overcome inertia among target consumers. However, a significant number of nonprofit managers actually view the customer with some contempt. These are often the same managers who present esoteric works without making them accessible to a less than highly sophisticated audience, who write program notes in "artspeak," and who package their events to appeal to wealthy, status-seeking individuals. By reinforcing the elitist aspects of arts attendance, such managers engage in what Robert Kelly calls "social work among the rich."[7]

A minor role is afforded to customer research. Without access to the results of the research conducted by an independent organization, the Buffalo Symphony would never have known that it had an image of stuffiness and formality that was keeping potential patrons away. Organizations cannot second-guess the attitudes or motivations of their publics, and they must devote both human and financial resources to challenge some managers' assumptions about their customers. Not only should research be used to analyze current audiences, but it should be proactive in order to forecast and anticipate changes in customer needs.

Marketing is defined primarily as promotion. Promotion is only one aspect of the total marketing mix. To focus marketing efforts on promotional devices alone is to ignore the full range of benefits that marketing can provide. At best, it provides short-term solutions to long-term problems. A customer may be lured to attend a performance because of a two-for-one price offer, but, unless the product itself, the location, and the total experience are satisfactory it is unlikely that the customer will return for another production. Therefore, promotion must be considered as only one tool within the marketing field.

Marketing specialists are chosen for their product knowledge or their communication skills, rather than for their knowledge of marketing principles and methods and especially of consumer behavior analysis. While product and communication skills are useful, they do not represent a full range of marketing skills. The best marketing managers in the private sector are those who know their consumer markets and their competitors well. They make active use of consumer research and know how to develop and implement systematic marketing plans. In contrast, many nonprofit managers believe that marketing *their* organizations is so different that there can be little transferability of skills. Many business managers of arts organizations were once performers themselves or were formally trained in music or other artistic disciplines. Their product orientation leads them to be more comfortable working with others who have a similar perspective. Indeed, arts marketing requires special sensitivity—sensitivity to the nonprofit point of view in which quality is maximized rather than the bottom line, and sensitivity to the artist's imperative for freedom of expression. An artist would never create a painting to appeal to the public in the way a brand manager designs the box for a consumer product (except maybe Andy Warhol). However, a marketing professional knows how to "package" the artist's creation and the organization's vision in order to make it appeal to a specific or broad audience.

Some nonprofit arts organizations no longer insist on hiring performing arts *product* specialists for their marketing positions, but rather choose public relations specialists or advertising personnel. What these potential "marketers" have in common is that they are good communicators. Their communication skills, and their emphasis on persuasion, reflect a view of marketing only slightly different from that found in the product-oriented organization. This emphasis on persuasion, as may be obvious by now, is consistent with a "selling" approach to marketing.

One "best" marketing strategy is typically employed in approaching the market and is viewed as being all that is needed. An arts administrator may perceive the market as monolithic or at least as having only a few crudely defined market segments. Thus, marketing strategies are aimed at the most obvious market segments, usually determined by age or family status. This approach ignores subtle distinctions and bypasses major opportunities. A climate of managerial certainty precludes experimentation either with alternative strategies or with variations of a single strategy applied across a number of subtle market subsegments.

From another perspective, many nonprofit managers who come from nonbusiness backgrounds may fear even carefully calculated risk-taking. They often believe that simple, consistent strategies are the best choice for career safety. They fear that too much change, too much variation, too much experimentation may be perceived as uncertainty. If an organization's losses are readily made up by generous donors and funders, this low-profile strategy may be tactically sound. If not, aggressive and creative marketing strategies are a necessity.

Generic competition is ignored or misunderstood. The managing director of a theater asked a marketing consultant which other theaters were its greatest competitors. The consultant answered that none of them were—that this theater, which attracted an elderly, middle- and upper-middle-class audience, was mainly in competition with VCRs and winters in Florida and Arizona. Organizations compete at many different levels. It takes a customer-focused perspective to understand that when a couple chooses to attend a play, the choice is not made solely in the context of what other plays are available, or what other plays are available within a certain distance from home, or what other live performances are available. Rather, the selection is likely to have been made among several forms of entertainment. Thus, concerts compete with museums for cultural outings, and theaters compete with educational television for art lovers, and with movies and restaurants as places to socialize.

CUSTOMER-CENTERED MARKETING MANAGEMENT

In the preceding sections we have analyzed product-centered and selling-centered organizations and described what a true marketing orientation is *not*. Now we will identify the characteristics that are observable in an organization that has fully adopted a modern marketing orientation.

A rationale that can help even the most reticent arts administrators accept the customer-centered approach to marketing is the fact that *customers are hard to change— the organization is not.* The organization is under management control; the customer is not. The process of changing the organization to accommodate customers ensures that consumer trends will be carefully monitored. Again, this does not mean that an organization must deny its artistic vision and present more programs that appeal to a broader audience. It means that the organization's approach to marketing the entire experience must give the customer a central focus. In a sophisticated marketing organization, all marketing analysis and planning begins and ends with the customer. A customer-centered organization always asks:

- Who is our current audience? How can we define and categorize them?
- Who is our most likely potential market for future development?
- What are their current perceptions, needs, and wants?
- How satisfied are our customers with our offerings? In what ways can we make them more satisfied? In what ways can we create and market satisfaction for other potential audiences as well?

The following features characterize a customer-centered organization.

It relies heavily on research. Even when an organization's product stays the same over time, as is the case with a Shakespeare festival or a company dedicated to presenting music of the Baroque, the customers themselves may change. Because the consumer is central, the management must have a profound understanding of consumer perceptions, needs, and wants, and must constantly track changes so that the organization can respond to even subtle shifts as they occur. To take this a step further, an organization should be proactive, not just reactive, in its strategic planning, and should develop a forecasting capability that can anticipate changes from the audience perspective. For example, when subscription renewals are eroding, an organization may offer smaller packages, custom-designed packages, or memberships, or design other ways to maintain some level of audience loyalty. In order to determine how best to meet changing audience needs and take advantage of new opportunities for audience development, performing arts organizations may undertake consumer segmentation research and then use preexisting information from inside and outside the organization to answer questions involving such issues as products, locations, facilities, pricing, ad copy, and competitors.

It creatively and strategically segments the audience into target groups. Many marketing managers of arts organizations do think of segmentation when planning strategy, but in our experience, they do so only from time to time and in the most general terms. Managers of symphony orchestras, for example, are well aware that their prospects are better in high- than in low-income households, among women than among men, among the well educated rather than the less educated, and among certain age groups. This understanding certainly helps to determine where budgets are concentrated, but all too often these budgets are spent on a single "best" program, usually aimed at upscale households, who, in marketing lingo, are known to be the "heavy users."

Yet, even within this market, many possibilities for more subtle segmentation exist. A study commissioned by the National Endowment for the Arts revealed that, despite wide industry "intuition" to the contrary, the best predictors of likely symphony attendance were not the traditional demographic characteristics, such as income and education, that are commonly researched on audience surveys, but lifestyle factors, attitudes toward actual attendance, past experience, and childhood training.[8] Considering only the lifestyle measure, the study clearly showed that there were two major lifestyle groups interested in symphony attendance. One group was the "traditional" Cultural Lifestyle Group, who made cultural events the center of their leisure pursuits. They tended to patronize the theater, opera, and museums as well as the symphony. They were very much interested in the program content and the artists when selecting performances to attend, and tended to be relatively insensitive to atmospheric factors or prices. The cultural experience itself was their primary reason for attendance. This group is undoubtedly the one that many theater and symphony marketers have in mind when they design their "one best" strategy.

The research, however, identified a very different lifestyle group that also included excellent prospects for the symphony, which was named the Socially Active Group. Respondents in this group went out a lot, not only to the symphony but to all sorts of nonclassical events, and they liked to give and attend parties. Symphony attendance for these people was largely a social experience, an opportunity to meet with friends, to plan a dinner before the concert and perhaps dessert or cocktails after. *Going out* was the point, and the content of the program was of far less interest than who among their friends were going or what restaurant they should attend.

Obviously, the appropriate strategies to reach these two groups are very different, and a strategy developed to appeal to one group may be unattractive to the other. For example, to attract the Cultural Lifestyle Group, print ads, public relations releases, direct-mail pieces, and interviews could emphasize aspects of the works to be performed, such as the difficulty and obscurity of a particular piece or the conductor's mastery of the composer's works. Such an ad might cause the Socially Active Group to see the event as formal and stuffy, a program for the aficionados and not one that they would understand and enjoy. But at the same time, a marketing strategy could be developed to attract the Socially Active Group, emphasizing the informality of the audience and suggesting possibilities for making an evening of the occasion. This approach, in turn, could signal to the Cultural Lifestyle Group that the concert program may not be very challenging or that many of those unsophisticated socializers are likely to be in attendance, applauding in all the wrong places.

It may not be possible to appeal to all target segments for the same program. Commonly accepted marketing principles don't even recommend it, as we will discuss in more detail in later chapters. However, the lesson from this example is clear: ignoring sophisticated segmentation possibilities can mean not only missed opportunities for attracting new customers, but also the possibility of driving away both current and potential audiences.

It defines competition broadly. An organization-centered marketer naturally defines the competition as "other organizations like us." But, in reality, competition is whatever the customer thinks it is. If a potential patron is deciding between going to the theater or to a movie, that movie is the competition. If a family is negotiating between seeing a live Sunday matinee performance of *The Nutcracker Suite* or attending a football game, the sports event is the competition. If a potential donor is deciding whether to give money to the theater to which she subscribes or to give more to the American Cancer Society, then that organization is the competition.

It develops strategies using all elements of the "marketing mix," not just communication. The marketing mix is one of the key concepts in modern marketing theory. The marketing mix is the set of marketing tools that the firm uses to pursue its marketing objectives in the target market. McCarthy popularized a four-factor classification of these tools called the four Ps: product, price, place, and promotion.[9] More recently, a fifth "P" has been added to the list: people.

- *Product:* The choice of works to perform is primarily in the domain of the artistic director, not the marketer. But the product also consists of marketer-designed offerings such as singles nights, flex plans, preperformance lectures, and outreach programs.

- *Price:* Performing arts organizations set prices differentiated by many factors, including seat location, timing of purchase (early subscriber discounts and hour before performance discounts), audience members (student and senior discounts), and occasion (opening night premium price). Developing these pricing structures is an important part of planning the marketing mix.

- *Place:* Place refers to the channels or access points through which the product is made available to the public. Many variations are possible in performing venues and ticket distribution, and creative distribution concepts are being successfully enacted by many performing arts organizations.

- *Promotion:* Promotion consists of all efforts that communicate to the public, including advertising, public relations, direct mail, telemarketing, and personal selling. Promotion is the final step in the marketing process. It is the communication of the strategies and tactics developed through the other aspects of the marketing mix.

- *People:* This refers to the arts organization's staff, particularly those who come in contact with customers, donors, and others. Contact personnel, depending on their attitudes and people skills, can help or hurt the organization's marketing effectiveness.

Consider the following example of how an organization puts to work various elements of the marketing mix.

PUTTING IT ALL TOGETHER: THE INTERNATIONAL THEATRE FESTIVAL

In the spring of 1992, the International Theatre Festival of Chicago presented its third biannual roster of theatrical performances by companies from all over the world, including such countries as Ireland, France, Venezuela, Japan, Canada, Poland, and Great Britain. The festival even presented a company from a small village in Siberia. The productions varied from such serious drama as Shakespeare's *Macbeth* to a six-hour epic entitled *The Dragon's Trilogy* and a magical musical by Circus Oz. Many performances were presented in each company's native language, and stereo earphones provided audience members with translation. Two years of traveling and planning culminated in the four-week-long festival, during which several productions were performed simultaneously at different venues across the city.

Potential audiences for the festival as a whole and for each production individually were taken into careful consideration as multiple marketing strategies and tactics were developed and implemented. For example, a production from Mexico was presented at the Mexican Fine Arts Center to draw a large Spanish-speaking audience that rarely attends traditional local theaters. The festival collaborated with a Venezuelan bookstore, which took ticket orders in Spanish over the phone and faxed the orders in English to the box office. Notice of this ticketing facility was advertised via Spanish-language radio stations and newspapers. This strategy was highly effective in drawing a new and very enthusiastic audience.

Five-dollar tickets were made available to artists and students in order to make the performances accessible to this highly appreciative but nonaffluent audience. And full ticket exchange privileges were initiated for all patrons who purchased "subscriptions" in advance for at least three productions, so that concern about conflicting schedules did not discourage early multiple purchase.

The Customer Orientation: How Far Does It Go?

Marketing is a tool—actually a process and a set of tools wrapped in a philosophy—for helping the organization do what it wants to do. Marketing is a *means* for achieving the organization's goals, and using marketing and being customer-centered should never be thought of as a goal in itself.

Marketing is a subarea of management. It is not necessarily positioned at the top of the organization. Clearly, top management has a responsibility to decide what role it will allocate to marketing. Management must decide which goals marketing can help achieve, and how. It is management's prerogative to say that certain decisions will be made with little or no attention to marketing concerns. Thus, the management of a theater company may decide that it will choose the season's program on the basis of the interests of its directors, who in turn will consider both past programming and the availability of performing and production talent in choosing specific plays, operas, dances, or musical works. Marketing may then be assigned the task of maximizing audience revenues for that given program. This of course does not mean that marketing should fall back upon a selling philosophy. It simply means that marketing planning must start with customers in deciding whom to target and how to describe, package, price, and distribute a given program.

At the other extreme, a theater manager may decide to be very customer-driven. He or she may very carefully survey the potential audience, consider past revenues and audience reactions, and consider which artists and works are available to maximize future attendance. This organization would then establish an offering that gives only limited attention to achieving artistic objectives but that maximizes sales. *These two approaches are equally customer-oriented.* They differ only in the management goals they were designed to achieve.

Most managers operate between the two extremes. Artist-driven and customer-driven performances are often mixed over the season. (It has been estimated that presentations of the *Nutcracker* make up more than 30 percent of dance performances in the United States each year. The revenue gained from these popular, well-attended productions help support each company's more artist-driven, experimental and less familiar productions that have narrower appeal.) Or an organization may present productions that are artist-driven with respect to content but audience-driven with respect to talent, place of performance, pricing, or special events. For example, people are as likely to go hear Itzhak Perlman perform whether he is playing Beethoven or a contemporary composer. A singles night at the theater is likely to draw a crowd, whatever the performance. A concert in the park will probably draw different and larger audiences than one in the symphony hall. Arts managers, therefore, have a great deal of flexibility in choosing how audience-driven the programming will be for a particular planning period, but the way they market the offering should always be customer-centered.

Dispelling the Myths

At the beginning of this chapter we quoted an article entitled "Artist Meets Marketer," which is highly critical of the application of the marketing philosophy to the world of the arts. Having explored the marketing mind-set and philosophy, we can now answer the author's contentions in terms of what marketing is *supposed* to be.

According to Webster's Dictionary, *pander* means "to provide gratification for others' desires, especially in terms of catering to or exploiting their weaknesses." The writer Herman Wouk once commented cynically, "The audience is vulgar and stupid; you've got to pander to them." Writer Marya Mannes takes the opposite viewpoint. She says, "The artist of today says to the public: 'If you don't understand this you are dumb.' I maintain that you are not. If you have to go the whole way to meet the artist, it's his fault."[10] In other words, the artist and the organization presenting the artist's work have a responsibility to the audience. Efforts to bring the arts to the public— and the public to the arts—do not represent pandering to lowly desires, but rather provide access to man's highest achievements and, more basically, to man's humanity. The marketer has the responsibility of packaging and communicating the artist's product to appeal to the broadest possible audience by meeting their needs and preferences. The artistic experience exists in the communication between the performer(s) on stage and the patrons in the hall; it is the role of the manager, the marketers, and the artistic directors to help facilitate that communication, thereby fulfilling the mission of the organization.

Randall complains that a marketer "fashions and differentiates products to fulfill the needs of [identified market] segments." But a good marketer will use audience surveys to understand the nature of the audience, in terms of both demographics and psychographics, in order to determine which segments to build—who will actually or potentially appreciate the product. An arts marketer will not seek to fulfill needs of the whole population. The purpose of segmentation is not to appeal to the "sovereignty of the mass will," as claimed by Randall, but rather to appeal to the *right* publics, using not only the artist's product but also a bundle of benefits and methods of communication that are centered around the needs and desires of the target segments.

Contrary to Randall's warning, the function of marketing is not to deny leadership or inspiration. Marketing exists in conjunction with other functions in order to enhance them and to find the most effective means for sharing inspiration with the public. The key is how to make the product more *accessible* to the patron, not how to change the artist's vision or the organization's mission.

Although Randall sees lavish sets and costumes as "hypothetical absurdities," innovations in these areas in recent years have elevated the visual aspect of the opera-going experience to the level of the musical aspect, creating a total experience that is highly appreciated by artists and audiences alike. Similarly, even the Metropolitan Opera, which was among the last holdouts in the American opera world against translated supertitles, has "succumbed" because of the proven importance of this feature in increasing the audience's understanding and appreciation. An important by-product is that supertitles provide artistic decision makers the freedom to venture beyond the traditional, well-known repertoire and produce unfamiliar works by well-known composers as well as works in such languages as Russian and Czech. In other words, customer-centered, marketing-oriented supertitles have served to "keep the shelves better stocked, the stores [and halls] full," and have truly made "everybody happy."

The marketing mind-set is beneficial to audiences and arts organizations alike. Many professional marketers have applied their skills, creativity, and leadership, resulting in the high satisfaction of all involved.

[1] Mark Randall, "Artist Meets Marketer," *Philadelphia Inquirer,* June 16, 1990, final edition, Editorial section.

[2] Much of the information in this section is taken from Philip Kotler and Alan Andreasen, *Strategic Marketing for Nonprofit Organizations,* 5th ed. (Upper Saddle River, N.J.: Prentice-Hall, 1996).

[3] Steven E. Permut, "A Survey of Marketing Perspectives of Performing Arts Administrators," in *Marketing the Arts,* ed. Michael P. Mokwa, William M. Dawson, and E. Arthur Prieve (New York: Praeger, 1980), 47–58.

[4] Peter F. Drucker, *Management: Tasks, Responsibilities, Practices* (New York: Harper & Row, 1973), 64–65.

[5] "Testimonials Persuade Ticket Buyers That Ballet Is Not Just for the Elite," *Chronicle of Philanthropy,* July 14, 1992, 31.

[6] Jan Carlzon, *Moments of Truth* (Cambridge, Mass.: Ballinger, 1987).

[7] Robert Kelly, "Elitism in the Arts," paper presented at the 2nd International Conference on Arts Management, Jouy-en-Josas, France, June 1993.

[8] Alan R. Andreasen and Russell W. Belk, "Predictors of Attendance at the Performing Arts," *Journal of Consumer Research,* Sept. 1980, 112–120.

[9] E. Jerome McCarthy, *Basic Marketing: A Managerial Approach* (Homewood, Ill.: Richard D. Irwin, 1981). Two alternative classifications are worth noting. Frey proposed that all marketing-decision variables could be categorized into two factors: the *offering* (product, packaging, brand or organization, price, and service) and *methods and tools* (distribution channels, personal selling, advertising, sales promotion, and publicity). See Albert W. Frey, *Advertising,* 3d ed. (New York: Ronald Press, 1961), 30.

[10] *Life,* June 12, 1964, 64.

▲●▲

*There are three types
of organizations:
those that make
things happen, those
that watch things
happen; those that
wonder what
happened.*

ANONYMOUS

*Start where you are,
do what you can,
use what you have.*

ARTHUR ASHE

A PROMISING ANSWER: STRATEGIC MARKET PLANNING

CENTRAL TO EFFECTIVE MANAGEMENT AND MARKETING IS CAREFUL AND thorough planning. Yet many artists and administrators think, "Why plan at all?" The managerial environment and the marketplace are increasingly complex and changing. It is difficult to make predictions about funding levels, audience development, and even programming opportunities. Also, in some organizations there is disagreement as to what the mission is or should be, so there is no clear consensus as to which strategies will best carry out the mission. Consider the following example.

STRATEGIC PLANNING IN THE ARTS

In the autumn of 1990, the Toronto Arts Council and the Certified General Accountants of Ontario cohosted a day of strategic planning workshops for small and medium-sized art organizations in the Toronto area. The lecturer presented ideas commonly accepted in the private sector: the need to develop a mission statement and the importance of organizational goals and objectives, strategies, and action plans.

The session was well attended by administrators of small theater groups, contemporary music ensembles, regional arts service organizations, and artist-run centers. But many administrators, who intuitively accepted the wisdom of strategic planning, questioned its use in their own circumstances. They exhibited a growing impatience with the lecturer and asked repeatedly what strategic planning had to offer *them.*

The arts administrators had attended this workshop largely because many governmental and foundation funders require even small organizations to submit a strategic plan, especially when multiyear funding commitments are being considered. The Ontario Arts Council asks professional and community orchestras for three-year plans. The Canada Council's Dance Office asks its dance company clients for long-term plans. As a result, many arts managers draft plans primarily to give funders a document, and use the plans mainly as a tool to achieve greater funding.

Whereas profit-making firms can pursue a well-defined goal of profit maximization, nonprofit organizations pursue a more complex set of goals and must use different measures of success. An arts organization might measure success by a mix of such factors as subscriber growth, total audience size, media critiques, performance opportunities for the artists, and the number of inner-city children exposed to educational programming, in addition to the organization's financial health. Arts administrators have great difficulty in assigning appropriate weights to these different and sometimes incompatible goals. Furthermore, strategic planners and arts administrators find it difficult to communicate. To many arts administrators, business language is alien, if not offensive. This situation creates a gap in communication and can obscure common purpose, diluting the organization's efforts to attract corporate sponsors and business board members.

Paradoxically, such conditions warrant even stronger strategic planning, which promises several benefits. Strategic planning (1) directs the arts organization to identify long-term trends and their implications, (2) helps define the key strategic issues facing the organization, (3) opens better communication among the key players in the organization, and (4) improves management control by setting objectives and providing measures of performance. Strategic planning helps an organization to develop a shared vision of its policies, goals, objectives, and activities. It defines the organization's planned trajectory.

To be effective, the strategic planning process requires the input of all the organization's stakeholders. It requires collaboration between the board of directors, the business managers, and the artistic personnel. Once the executive director, the board of directors, the artists, and the other upper-level managers have formed a consensus, the executive director disseminates the strategic vision and plan throughout the organization. Then the marketing director develops and implements an annual marketing plan and special campaign plans to achieve the target objectives and goals.

When is strategic planning needed? Strategic planning should inform decision making when any of the following conditions is present.

The organization's survival might depend on choosing the right managing or artistic director. For example, when Kevin McKenzie and Gary Dunning became the new directors at the American Ballet Theatre, they reached out to mend the company's vital relationships with Mikhail Baryshnikov and Twyla Tharp, which had been damaged during their predecessor's short but detrimental tenure.

A decision involves committing a high proportion of resources: financial, managerial, and/or physical. The commitment may be risky, entailing severe losses if the decision turns out to be incorrect. A large midwestern theater was built before the capital funding campaign was completed, with the anticipation that adequate funds could be raised once the curtain was up. Several years later, the theater is still trying to raise funds for the building while simultaneously coping with high operating expenses.

Making a particular choice will close off other options that are also attractive. This is called the "irreversibility" problem. For example, before undergoing extensive and costly renovations at their existing performance halls, the Chicago Symphony Orchestra and the Lyric Opera of Chicago considered cooperatively building a new performing center. The new center would have provided better facilities than each organization's current space limitations would allow, even with extensive renovations—and for little more cost. However, a majority of the symphony's board of directors believed strongly in maintaining the long-standing tradition of the current Orchestra Hall, and opted for renovation.

The choice takes the organization into technologies or geographical areas in which it has little experience. For example, a chamber orchestra may consider making and distributing a recording for the first time, or a dance company may wish to launch a national tour.

The choice involves "long-cycle feedback," meaning that it will not be known for some time whether or not the decision was correct. For example, although arts organizations are well aware of the advantage of providing educational programming in the schools to build future audiences, transferring much-needed resources from short-term projects to such long-term, less certain projects is a difficult choice.

The choice involves defining the organization's responsibilities in a new way. Such decisions may involve taking a strong stand on censorship or multiculturalism, or on internal actions such as pay cuts or downsizing.

The choice will give the organization a different image. In 1992, managers of the Sydney Opera House in Australia reordered their priorities. Rather than primarily considering the Opera House as a cultural center, they emphasized the mission of preserving and promoting it as a unique symbol of Australia and its number-one tourist attraction. Such a change might not please artistic directors, but the increased prestige and revenue should lead to greater artistic freedom.

Implementation of a strategy will dramatically change the organization's culture or pace of events. Opened in 1933, Prague's E. F. Burian Theatre was a typical Czechoslovak company—nationalized, burdened with an overmanned bureaucratic structure, and artistically stagnant. After the 1989 political upheavals, the city council wanted to inject some new life into the company. Ondrej Hrab was selected as the new artistic director. Hrab abandoned the repertory format and turned the theater into a multifaceted performing arts venue geared to presenting Czech and international contemporary theater, opera, dance, music and art. Hrab named his project Archa Theatre, after Noah's Ark, the biblical vessel that carried the potential for a whole new world.

The key members of the organization are themselves divided on what to do. For example, the government officials of Eisenstadt, a small town in Austria, wanted to sponsor a new music festival that would bring visitors to their city. After some debate, they decided to give the festival a clear identity and present only the works of Haydn, their most famous resident. Some officials worried that people would tire of the narrow range of programming. Yet the festival has developed a loyal following of knowledgeable and enthusiastic patrons and tourists who come to see the city by day and attend concerts in the evening.

The *strategic market planning process* consists of the following four steps:

1. *Strategic analysis:* (a) Analyze the organization-wide mission, objectives, and goals; and (b) Assess the organization's strengths, weaknesses, opportunities, and threats.

2. *Market planning:* (a) Determine the objectives and specific goals for the relevant planning period; (b) Formulate the core marketing strategy to achieve the specified goals; and (c) Establish detailed programs and tactics to carry out the core strategy.

3. *Marketing plan implementation:* Put the plan into action.

4. *Control:* Measure performance and adjust the core strategy, tactical details, or both as is needed.

These components constitute an integrated set of steps. The control process is used to reformulate current strategies and to help plan future strategies. In this sense, planning is an ongoing process without a beginning or an end.

Integral to strategic planning is organizational self-assessment. Peter Drucker recommends that managers consider these five questions:

1. *What is our business (mission)?* What results does the organization seek to achieve? What are its priorities? Its strengths and weaknesses? To what extent does the mission statement currently reflect the organization's goals and competencies?

2. *Who is our customer?* Who are our current and prospective customers? Who are the primary and supporting customers? What are their levels of awareness of and satisfaction with the organization's service?

3. *What does our customer value?* For each primary customer group, what specific needs does the organization fulfill? What satisfaction and benefits does it provide? How well is it providing value? Is the same value available from other sources?

4. *What have been our results?* What criteria do we use to measure success? To what extent has the organization achieved the desired results?

5. *What is our plan?* In what areas should we focus our efforts? What new results should be achieved? What activities should be abandoned, expanded, or outsourced?

ANALYZING THE ORGANIZATION'S MISSION, OBJECTIVES, AND GOALS

Strategic market planning starts with analyzing and defining the organization's mission, objectives, and goals.

Mission

Effective nonprofit organizations have four characteristics: (1) a clearly articulated sense of mission, (2) a strong leader and culture that motivate the organization to fulfill its mission, (3) an involved and committed volunteer board that provides a bridge to the larger community, and (4) an ongoing capacity to attract sufficient financial and human resources.[1]

The mission of an organization comprises its purpose and the results it wants to achieve.[2] Says management strategist Peter Drucker,

> The mission focuses the organization on action. It defines the specific strategies needed to attain the crucial goals. It creates a disciplined organization. It alone can prevent the most common degenerative disease of organizations, especially large ones: splintering their always limited resources on things that are "interesting" or look "profitable" rather than concentrating them on a very small number of productive efforts. . . . Good intentions are no substitute for organization and leadership, for accountability, performance, and results. Those require management and that, in turn, begins with the organization's mission.[3]

DEFINING THE MISSION

Although the question "What is our mission?" sounds simple, it is really the most challenging question an organization can ask. Different members will have different views of what the organization is about and should be about. Frequently, organizations hold numerous meetings over a period of several months to develop consensus. A theater should not define its mission by listing the plays it wants to produce. It should identify the underlying needs it wants to address and the satisfactions it wants to deliver.

In defining the mission, it is helpful to establish the organization's scope on three dimensions. The first is *consumer groups,* namely, *who* is to be served and satisfied. An organization's consumers include all the parties that it intends to serve, including the artistic director, the performers, and the various audience segments. The second dimension is *consumer needs,* namely *what* is to be satisfied. The goal may be, for example, to entertain, inspire, or educate the audience—but how to accomplish each goal depends on the tastes and levels of sophistication of the audience members. The third is *technologies,* namely, *how* consumer needs are to be met. A summer festival may be created to entertain an audience in the context of a casual ambience. Performances held in neighborhood settings may provide entertainment for members of particular ethnic groups.

An organization should strive for a mission that is *feasible, motivating,* and *distinctive.* Feasibility means that the mission should be realistic in terms of the organization's financial and human resources. The organization should avoid a "mission impossible." An institution should reach high, but not so high as to create an unachievable goal or to produce incredulity in its publics. In the mid-1980s, the Australian Opera attempted to present Wagner's entire *Ring Cycle;* but the stage, the pit, and the potential audience were too small, and the project had to be canceled halfway through its projected run. The mission should also be motivating: it should embrace goals that excite the organization's staff, board, and artists, who should feel they are worthwhile members of a worthwhile organization. And a mission works best when it is distinctive. If all theaters in a city resembled each other, there would be little loyalty to or pride in any one company. Also, certain consumer needs would be overserved while others wouldn't be met at all. By cultivating a distinctive mission and personality, an organization stands out more and attracts more loyal patrons.

THE GUTHRIE THEATER: A MISSION RECAPTURED

The highly respected Guthrie Theater in Minneapolis, Minnesota thrived for many years with a mission of presenting fine-quality performances of the classics. After fifteen years, a new director arrived. Trying to be more things to more people, he changed the programming, presenting some classics, some new and experimental plays, and some popular entertainment shows. The number of subscribers dropped from 23,000 to 13,000. The Guthrie had lost its grip on its purpose and its audience. For the next several years, the board of directors struggled with the Guthrie's identity—what kind of theater to be. It finally returned to its role as a theater offering vital productions of the classics. By the end of the second year, subscriptions were up 70 percent to 22,000, the highest since the inaugural season.

THE MISSION STATEMENT

The mission statement should succinctly describe what the organization does, whom it serves, and what it intends to accomplish. It should be broad enough not to need frequent revision and yet specific enough to provide clear objectives and to guide programming. It should be understandable to the general public and should be brief.[4]

Here are some sample mission statements:

- To perform classic, contemporary, and cutting-edge dance with virtuosity, energy, and artistic excellence to local, domestic and international audiences . . . to challenge, educate, entertain and thereby enrich our audiences (Hubbard Street Dance Chicago).

- To present in an attractive setting artistic events of excellence and diversity; to provide a unique opportunity to advance the professional capabilities of gifted, young performers; to promote actively the appreciation of the performing arts among all the people of the Chicago area; and to provide and maintain an inviting and comfortable setting for performers and patrons (Ravinia Festival Association).

- To present on a professional basis the following theatre disciplines—opera, ballet, drama, modern dance, music, symphony orchestras, and experimental theatre productions—under the following principles: a credo that demands the highest possible artistic standards; the belief that continual cultural contact with the international world is essential for further development of theatre in South Africa; a striving, through the arts, to create harmony and further unite all our people and various cultures in South Africa; a theatre free of prejudice and open to all (The Performing Arts Councils of South Africa).

Objectives

The organization's mission suggests more about where it is coming from than about where it is going. Each organization must also develop specific objectives and goals for the coming period that are consistent with its mission statement. Organizations might develop a large number of objectives, such as broadening the audience base to include more ethnic groups, improving performance quality, producing new works, improving the physical plant, and lowering the operating deficit or building a surplus for future improvements. Not all of these objectives may be mutually compatible or even affordable. Therefore, in any given year, organizations will choose to emphasize certain objectives and either ignore others or treat them as constraints. For example, if a theater has been losing subscribers, it may decide to devote more resources to retaining current subscribers and reattracting lapsed subscribers while devoting fewer resources to attracting single-ticket buyers.

Thus, an organization's major objectives can vary from year to year depending on the administration's and the board's perception of the major challenges facing the organization.

For-profit businesses normally aim to maximize their profits. Nonprofit organizations pursue other objectives, whether artistic, marketing-related, financial, or managerial. Some of those objectives are discussed here.

Surplus maximization. A performing arts group might want to accumulate as much cash surplus as possible in order to build a new theater or renovate a current one. Such an organization will concentrate on increasing revenue and/or reducing costs.

Revenue maximization. The management of a dance company might feel that a high total revenue indicates to current and potential contributors that the organization is doing a good job, and thus that increasing revenue will lead to greater confidence and more donations to the organization.

Usage maximization. Many nonprofit organizations are primarily interested in maximizing the number of users of their services. Granting institutions and certain other contributors typically look at each organization's attendance growth to determine how much to budget for the next year's contribution.

Capacity targeting. Organizations with fixed service capacities typically set their prices and marketing expenditures with the goal of drawing a capacity audience. For example, a symphony orchestra experiencing low attendance might offer special discounts to students and senior citizens to fill more seats. If the potential number of ticket seekers exceeds capacity, the orchestra might raise prices to improve its revenue.

Full cost recovery. Many performing arts organizations are primarily interested in breaking even each year. They would like to provide as much service, programming, and talent as they can as long as their sales revenue plus contributed income covers their costs. Many organizations want to spend just short of reporting a deficit. They may also want to avoid achieving a large surplus, lest it lead to lower donations.

Partial cost recovery. Other organizations operate with a chronic deficit each year. Their aim is to keep the annual deficit from exceeding a certain amount. Private foundations, corporations, and individual donors are often solicited to cover the annual deficit.

Budget maximization. Many organizations attempt to maximize the size of their staff, the number of offered programs, or the elaborateness of their programming. They seek program grants and donations without fully considering their ability to use the contributed funds effectively. They are reluctant to trim programs or staff even when such action is warranted. Trimming operations would cause the organization to look less successful in the eyes of the staff and public.

Producer satisfaction maximization. Performing arts organizations exist to express the artistic vision of their leaders while also meeting the needs and wishes of their customers. However, there is a fine distinction between a focus on an artistic perspective and the primacy of the personal preferences of the artistic leaders. If a theater presents a broad range of classics but has not produced a George Bernard Shaw play in over ten years, is that a "pure" artistic decision or does it reflect the fact that the artistic director doesn't like Shaw's work? If the director does not like Shaw, he or she probably wouldn't do justice to it anyway, and may be justified in not producing it. But, in some cases, "the product is created mainly for the satisfaction of producers themselves. . . . The organization will modify its product away from the one which gives its own members the most satisfaction only insofar as is necessary to obtain enough revenue from these customer groups to survive financially."[5] It has even been argued that most professionals are basically self-serving and oriented primarily toward promoting their own interests.[6] It is important that managers study their choices and their audiences to seek a fit that will allow the organization to survive and prosper.

Setting Goals

Before objectives can be achieved, they must be restated in operational and measurable terms, called *goals*. The objective of increasing subscriptions must be turned into a goal, such as a 15 percent increase in next season's subscriber base. A goal statement permits the institution to think about the planning, programming, and control aspects of pursuing that objective. A number of questions may arise: Is a 15 percent increase feasible? What strategy would be used? What resources would it require? What activities would have to be carried out? Who would be responsible and accountable? How will we track achievement? All of these questions must be answered as goals are adopted.

GOAL SETTING AT HUBBARD STREET DANCE CHICAGO

Hubbard Street Dance Chicago (HSDC), well known in the Midwest and gaining broader recognition as it repeatedly performs both nationwide and internationally, has the long-term goal of being one of the top five dance companies in the country. In aspiring to this goal, the management must address several issues. What does it mean to be a top-five company? Does top-five status refer to the performers, choreography, variety of repertoire, size of the company, benefits to customers, rave reviews—or all of the above? As to the goal's feasibility, where does the company now rank in the hearts and minds of its patrons? In how many areas and by what percentage in each area must it improve in order to attain this goal? What is the competition that must be challenged in order for the goal to be achieved? How is progress or success to be measured—by increases in audience size, increases relative to competitors, quality of reviews? How will the relevant information be obtained?

Finally, what benefits will HSDC gain by achieving this goal? Will it help to sustain current audiences and build new ones? Will it attract better dancers and choreographers? Will it attract more funding? The organization must carefully consider all these questions in adopting any goal.

INTERNAL AND EXTERNAL ENVIRONMENT ANALYSIS

The second strategic planning step is to analyze the organization's internal environment (i.e., strengths and weaknesses) and its external environment (i.e., opportunities and threats). This is known as a SWOT analysis.

Internal Analysis: Strengths and Weaknesses

Every organization has strengths that can be exploited in the pursuit of its goals. Prahalad and Hamel refer to an organization's real strengths as its core competencies.[8]

> The [organization], like a tree, grows from its roots. The root system that provides nourishment, sustenance, and stability is the core competence. You can miss the strength of competitors by looking only at their end products, in the same way you miss the strength of a tree if you look only at its leaves. . . . The skills that together constitute core competence must coalesce around individuals whose efforts are not so narrowly focused that they cannot recognize the opportunities for blending their functional expertise with those of others in new and interesting ways. Core competence does not diminish with use; competencies are enhanced as they are applied and shared. But competencies still need to be nurtured and protected; knowledge fades if it is not used.

STRENGTHS OF THE DEUTSCHE BALLET

At the Deutsche Ballet, director Peter Schaufuss would like to do less traditional programming. But for that he needs a second house—an experimental theater with 500–600 seats, dancers trained in a variety of styles, and financial and audience support. In the meantime, says Schaufuss, "you work with the tools you've got." Schaufuss works with such strengths as the 1,900-seat theater of the Deutsche Opera House, a traditionally trained company, a strong audience base, and government support for classical ballets. Using these strengths, Schaufuss presented a

Tchaikovsky cycle to commemorate the one-hundredth anniversary of the composer's death and, in that one season, tripled the number of subscriptions.[7]

A great opportunity is no opportunity if the organization lacks the required resources and capabilities. Performing arts organizations need the following competencies:

- *Program quality:* The higher the program quality relative to direct competitors, the greater the organization's strength.

- *Efficiency level:* The more efficient the organization is at producing a program, renewing its subscribers, and attracting new patrons, the greater its organizational strength.

- *Market knowledge:* The more the organization knows about its customers, the greater its market strength.

- *Marketing effectiveness:* The more proficient the organization is at marketing, the greater its effectiveness in audience building and fund-raising.

Each organization has certain weaknesses. Managers may be unaware of these weaknesses, may not recognize the extent to which they hurt operations, or may be unsure of how to correct the problems. Management would profit by periodically commissioning an outside audit of the organization. This audit can be performed by a professional consultant, by business volunteers, or by students in a business school or arts administration program who are eager to assist an organization. When no outside person is available or affordable, managers and board members should undertake the audit themselves.

ROYAL ALBERT HALL: MEETING THE PUBLIC'S NEEDS

Built in 1871, Royal Albert Hall had become more of a historic monument than an accessible and desirable venue. So, since 1989, extensive reconstruction has been under way, including improvements in disabled access to the building and a new thrust stage so the audience's view is no longer restricted for ballet performances. Also, the hall expanded its box office hours from eight hours per day to twelve, thereby increasing the availability of a service important to promoters and visitors.

Yet, concert promoters were still booking their concerts elsewhere. So executive director Peter Deuchar engaged a consultant to identify the hall's weaknesses in order to make the necessary improvements, and to develop an identity for Royal Albert Hall in order to enhance its position as a viable performance space.[9]

In evaluating the organization's strengths and weaknesses, managers should rate each factor as to whether it is a major strength, minor strength, neutral factor, minor weakness, or major weakness. It is also necessary to rate the importance of each factor—high, medium, or low. Not all factors are equally important for succeeding as an organization. When combining performance and importance levels, four possibilities emerge, as illustrated in Figure 3-1. In cell A fall important factors where the organization is performing poorly: managers should concentrate on strengthening these factors. In cell B fall important factors where the organization is already strong and should keep up the good work. In cell C fall unimportant factors where the organization is performing poorly: improvement in these areas should be given lower priority. In cell D fall unimportant factors where the organization is performing well: it is possible that too much effort is being expended in such areas.

This analysis tells us that even when an organization has a major strength in a certain factor (i.e., a *distinctive competence*), that strength does not necessarily create a competitive advantage. It may not be a competence of importance to the organization's customers and, even if it is, competitors may have the same or greater strength in that area. Also, an organization does not have to remedy all of its weaknesses, since some are unimportant to its operations or customers. The strategic question is whether an organization should limit itself to those opportunities where it now possesses the required strengths, as did the Deutsche Ballet, or consider better opportunities where it might have to acquire or develop new strengths, as was the case for the Royal Albert Hall.

External Analysis: Opportunities and Threats

An organization operates in a constantly changing and often turbulent external environment. The macro environment consists of large-scale fundamental forces—demographic, social, cultural, economic, and political—that shape opportunities and pose threats to the organization. These forces are largely uncontrollable but must be monitored for purposes of both short- and long-term planning. Most

---

Figure 3-1

PERFORMANCE-
IMPORTANCE
MATRIX

	Performance	
	Low	High
High	*A. Concentrate here*	*B. Keep up the good work*
Low	*C. Low priority*	*D. Possible overkill*

(Importance)

commonly, environmental forces create the need for an organization to change its approach. The Royal Albert Hall's managers found that they could no longer succeed by merely emphasizing the building's historical significance. So they capitalized on market-centered trends and improved their facilities and service. However, at the Guthrie Theatre, the board of directors found that their eroding audience support was due to the weakening of the theater's original identity. In this case, success resulted from recapturing past strengths.

The most successful organizations maximize opportunities by identifying attractive markets and developing the organizational strengths required to appeal to those markets. Four types of opportunities can be distinguished:

- *Build opportunities* are those present activities that warrant more investment because they improve audience interest and/or size, attract more funds, and so on.

- *Hold opportunities* are those that warrant maintaining the present level of investment. Although full-subscription purchases and renewals have slackened in recent years, organizations are maintaining their subscription efforts at present levels while offering new, smaller packages to encourage frequent attendance and loyalty to the organization.

- *Harvest and divest opportunities* are activities that should be reduced or dropped in order to free up resources that can be better used elsewhere. Thus, due to waning audience interest, many orchestras have harvested or divested chamber programs and recital series.

- *New product opportunities* are programs or services that might well be added to the organization's current offerings, such as Rush Hour and Saturday afternoon casual concerts, singles nights, and other events planned for special interest groups.

These opportunities should be classified according to their attractiveness and their probable success. Market attractiveness is made up of factors such as those listed here.

- *Market size:* Large markets are more attractive than small markets.

- *Market growth rate:* High-growth markets are more attractive than low-growth markets.

- *Surplus building:* Larger surplus-building programs are preferred to lower surplus-building programs. An organization may wish to present programs that are widely attractive to help subsidize its artistically driven programs that have narrower appeal.

- *Competitive intensity:* Markets with fewer or weaker competitors are more attractive than markets that include many or strong competitors. This does not mean that weak competition justifies entry; the market must also be attractive on other grounds.

- *Cyclicality:* Cyclically stable art forms and art organizations enjoy relatively consistent levels of demand over long periods of time. Unstable art forms go through periods of high and low attendance, reflecting changes in demand. The most unstable markets attract quick and broad attention but peak early and decline rapidly.

- *Seasonality:* Seasonality provides opportunities for special programming (*A Christmas Carol, The Nutcracker Suite*); on the other hand, it may lead to uneven attendance and cash flow.

- *Scale economies:* Programs for which unit costs fall with large-volume production and marketing or that build on previous efforts are more attractive than constant-cost programs.

- *Learning economies:* Programs that get better or more efficient with each performance or new startup are more attractive.

Opportunities can also be identified through the use of a product/market opportunity analysis. An organization may look at its present offerings in terms of building on what already exists, making modifications to current offerings, or developing entirely new products. Markets may be analyzed in the same way: building current markets that have potential for growth, modifying current markets, or developing new markets.

Market penetration consists of broadening the organization's infiltration of current markets with current products. This is often the easiest strategy; it requires the fewest changes. This strategy is most workable when there is significant room for growth in currently sizable markets with existing offerings. Offering better programs and increasing advertising and promotion to the target market will help the organization deepen its market penetration. For example, a chamber music group gave four free tickets to each board member and encouraged them to introduce their friends and business associates to the organization. The promotion included a postperformance reception with the artists to build involvement and enthusiasm.

Geographical expansion consists of taking the organization's current offerings into additional geographic markets by such means as performing in alternative venues in outlying areas, going on tours, and distributing recordings and videos through various media. Many symphonies and dance companies regularly tour internationally. Chicago's Steppenwolf Theater has performed some of its productions in New York and London. Many organizations offer outreach programs in local schools, neighborhood parks, and other community locations.

New markets involves finding new groups to attract with current offerings, such as new age or ethnic groups and special interest groups. It also includes attracting more distant audiences by offering special transportation, dinner-theater packages, group plans, and price incentives. The marketing director of Hubbard Street Dance Chicago reserved a car on the commuter train from downtown Chicago to the suburban Ravinia Festival where the company was performing. More than one hundred singles who lived in the downtown area responded to the targeted mailing offering a package that provided transportation, the dance program, beverages and snacks on the train, and a postconcert party and reception with some of the performers and staff.

Offer modification may involve changes that make programming more accessible to various target markets. The time or length of the program may be geared to specific audience segments, or a concert may be advertised as casual in order to encourage spontaneous attendance. The New York Philharmonic has added performances at the lunch hour and the rush hour, appealing to people who live in outlying areas and who would not return to the city for an evening program. Casual, hour-long, Saturday afternoon concerts provide an appropriate setting at a convenient time for parents to share fine music with their children.

Offer innovation involves the development of new product offerings, such as the creation of a subscription or a group sales plan when none previously existed. Other examples include the special children's series at the New York Philharmonic and the new jazz series at Lincoln Center.

Geographical innovation involves offering a new program in a new geographical area. A theater may develop a program of plays by African-American playwrights and perform them in African-American neighborhoods. Theaters may air select productions on radio stations.

Total innovation refers to creating new offerings for new markets. Dancing in the Streets creates new choreography for each location and market in which it performs.

Thus, the product/market opportunity analysis stimulates thinking about new opportunities in a systematic way. New opportunities are evaluated, and the better ones are pursued.

Along with opportunities, organizations face various threats. An environmental threat is a challenge posed by an unfavorable trend or development in the environment that, in the absence of purposeful marketing action, would harm the organization. Although such changes are largely uncontrollable, an organization should prepare for contingencies. If a recession is expected, the organization should think about how to develop other revenue sources. If the audience is aging, the organization should start attracting younger patrons. When fewer patrons are interested in full-season subscriptions, the organization should offer alternatives that appeal to its customers' needs for lower commitment levels and more spontaneity.

Threats can also come from groups and organizations that compete for the same audience. Although competitors are generally viewed as threats, many opportunities exist for arts organizations to develop mutually beneficial collaborations with one another and with leisure-oriented businesses such as restaurants, hotels, and other tourism providers. Issues of competition and collaboration are discussed in Chapter 7.

The Organization's Publics

Publics are individuals, groups, and organizations that take an interest in the organization. Publics can help or harm an organization, and their needs and interests must be served or accommodated. Figure 3-2 shows the many publics of a performing arts organization.

An organization is really a coalition of several groups, each giving different things to and seeking different things from the organization. Publics can be classified by their functional relation to the organization. An organization can be viewed as a resource-conversion machine in which certain *input publics* (playwrights, choreographers, composers, donors, suppliers) supply resources that are converted by *internal publics* (performers, staff, board of directors, volunteers) into useful goods and services (performances, subscription packages, benefits, educational programming) that are carried by *intermediary publics* (advertising agencies, reporters, critics) to *consuming publics* (audience members, local residents, activists, the media).

Not all publics are equally active or important to an organization. Some are central to its functioning, such as the artists, staff, donors, and volunteers. Certain publics may at times represent the organization's strengths and opportunities, and at other times may be the source of its weaknesses or threats. The common purpose may break down when one group pursues its own interest to the detriment of the organization. For example, orchestral musicians are a symphony's lifeblood, but they may put the organization at risk when they go on strike. The media may help bolster an organization with extensive promotional material or it may harm an organization's image by exposing internal strife. More peripheral groups, such as governmental agencies, may become particularly active when issues of general interest arise.

Figure 3-2

AN ARTS ORGANIZATION'S PUBLICS

An organization must pay special attention to its internal publics. *Internal marketing* involves motivating and educating the organization's personnel. The internal publics define, refine, and carry out the organization's strategy. Effective marketing requires that all the key internal publics—the management, the artistic staff, the board of directors, the support staff, and the volunteers—understand and internalize the marketing mind-set. Often, it is the lowest-paid employees—the box office personnel, the ushers, and the parking lot attendants—who have the most direct contact with the patrons. Each must be trained to deal competently and courteously with the patrons and must learn how to create goodwill even during difficult encounters.

Once the strategic market analysis has been prepared, the managers must translate recommendations into specific plans and budgets. Systems must be developed for implementation and overseen for timely and mid-course adjustments and proper long-range evaluation and control. These aspects of the strategic market planning process will be covered in Chapter 17.

In the next several chapters, we will explore the performing arts market; marketing principles, strategies, and tools; and communication theories and methods. This will provide the foundation on which management can build and implement practical and effective plans.

------

[1] E. B. Knauft, Renee A. Berger, and Sandra T. Gray, *Profiles of Excellence: Achieving Success in the Nonprofit Sector* (San Francisco: Jossey-Bass, 1991), 19.

[2] Peter F. Drucker, *The Five Most Important Questions You Will Ever Ask about Your Nonprofit Organization* (San Francisco: Jossey-Bass, 1993), 9.

[3] Peter F. Drucker, "What Business Can Learn from Nonprofits," *Harvard Business Review,* July/Aug. 1989, 89.

[4] Knauft, Berger, and Gray, *Profiles of Excellence,* 120.

[5] Michael Etgar and Brian T. Ratchford, "Marketing Management and Marketing Concept: Their Conflict in Non-Profit Organizations," *1974 Proceedings* (Chicago: American Marketing Association, 1974).

[6] John McKnight, "Professional Service Business," *Social Policy,* Nov./Dec. 1977, 110–116.

[7] Mary Thomas, "Freedom to Move," *International Arts Manager,* Oct. 1992, 32–33.

[8] C. K. Prahalad and Gary Hamel, "The Core Competence of the Corporation," *Harvard Business Review,* May/June 1990, 80–84.

[9] "Music in the Round," *International Arts Manager,* April 1993, 14–15.

▲●▲

PART II

UNDERSTANDING
THE
PERFORMING
ARTS MARKET

▲●▲

UNDERSTANDING THE PERFORMING ARTS AUDIENCE

Last year, more Americans went to symphonies than went to baseball games. This may be viewed as an alarming statistic, but I think that both baseball and the country will endure.

JOHN F. KENNEDY

AT THE CORE OF EFFECTIVE MARKETING STRATEGY IS AN UNDERSTANDING OF consumer behavior. Marketing planners must understand the motives, preferences, and behavior of their organizations' current and potential consumers. In recent years, researchers have been working to assist organizations in understanding the performing arts audience. They seek to answer such questions as What motivates a person to purchase a ticket? To buy or renew a subscription? What factors create satisfaction and stimulate loyalty to a performing arts organization?

A study conducted by the Australian Opera indicated that the major factor in a person's decision to attend was the reputation of the opera itself.[1] *La Boheme* was more appealing than the less familiar *Lulu.* Yet, in another study of cultural patrons, researchers found that some audience segments have an appetite for new experiences, meaning both new and unfamiliar works.[2] How is an opera company to strike a balance in its programming when some audience members look forward to hearing *Boheme* each season and others prefer not to hear it again for several years?

For many people, it is not the work being presented that informs the attendance decision, but other aspects of the total concert- or theatergoing experience. Consider

67

what marketers at the Saint Louis Symphony learned about the people they were trying to attract to their concerts.

**ATTRACTING
NEW
AUDIENCES
AT THE
SAINT LOUIS
SYMPHONY
ORCHESTRA**

Symphony administrators at the Saint Louis Symphony Orchestra
(SLSO) thought people who didn't attend their concerts were not
aware of their international tours, their awards, and their great
reviews. When they hired a market research firm to find out what
people thought about the orchestra, they got some surprises.
People did know about the SLSO's fine reputation. But they were
not attending for other reasons—largely because of factors that
created anxiety for them. People wanted to know: "What kind of
people go to the symphony concerts? Are they people like me?
Where do I park?" In fact, the symphony's prestige actually contributed to people's anxiety.

So, in response to the research report, the orchestra ran a new
sales campaign that soft-pedaled its strong reputation in favor of
an emotional appeal. Rather than advertising, "Virtuoso musician coming to orchestra hall," they used such lines as "When
Wynton Marsalis was here, killer wails were heard in the hall!"
They even offered a money-back guarantee for the opening
weekend, which stimulated a significant increase in ticket sales.
The success of the campaign was proved by the fact that no one
asked for a refund.[3]

MAJOR FACTORS INFLUENCING CONSUMER BEHAVIOR

Most factors that affect a consumer's arts attendance decisions, interests, needs, and
satisfaction levels go beyond issues specific to the artistic offering. Factors as broad
as macroenvironmental trends and as specific as an individual's own psychology
play a major role in influencing people's attitudes about what they purchase, how
much they spend, which leisure activities they pursue, and which needs they try to
fulfill. The major factors influencing consumer behavior, described in Exhibit 4-1, are
discussed in the following sections.

*Macro-
environmental
Trends*

Large social, political, economic, and technological forces influence our attitudes, our
values, our important decisions (education, career and job choices, and investment
decisions), and our day-to-day decisions (including how to spend our leisure time).
John Naisbett says that macroenvironmental trends, which he calls *megatrends*, last
for about a decade. And during the decade of the 1990s, with the millennium rapidly

| *Exhibit 4-1* | **FACTORS INFLUENCING CONSUMER BEHAVIOR** |

I. Macroenvironmental Trends
Social, political, economic, and technological forces

II. Cultural Factors
Nationality, subcultures, social class

III. Social Factors
Reference groups, opinion leaders, innovativeness

IV. Psychological Factors
Personality, beliefs and attitudes, motivation

V. Personal Factors
Occupation, economic circumstances, family, life-cycle stage

approaching, change is accelerating, our awareness is heightened, and we are compelled to reexamine ourselves, our values, and our institutions.[4]

In a study commissioned by Dance/USA, researcher David Meer observes the impact of people's changing values upon their leisure-time activities.[5] He notes a hunger for the classic family and a focus among young adults on child-centered activities, especially as people work longer hours. There is also a greater focus on productive leisure: staying healthy and in shape, other self-improvement activities, and building relationships. People often feel guilty if they do not achieve these goals. Conversely, one of the latest "crazes" is to "veg out": read, watch TV, and have large periods of unplanned time.

Trend analyst Faith Popcorn recommends thinking of trends as a kind of database about consumers' moods, a rich source that can be tapped to help solve marketing problems.[6] Popcorn believes that marketers should scan today's culture by checking the best-seller list of books and movies, identifying popular products, picking up unfamiliar magazines, and reading other industries' trade reports, to develop a sensitivity to what is going on and to watch for signs of the future. She has identified several trends that, taken together, she believes, create a portrait of the new turn-of-the-century consumers.

| **FAITH POPCORN'S CONSUMER TRENDS FOR THE 1990S** | 1. *Cocooning,* the tendency for people to look for a haven at home, has manifested itself in skyrocketing sales of VCRs, take-out food, mail-order merchandise, cellular phones and minivans (for drive-time cocooning), and in the fact that by 1991, 18.3 million Americans were working out of home offices. Says Popcorn, "Don't expect consumers to come to |

you anymore. You'll have to reach them in the cocoon itself." On the one hand, this trend may represent a form of competition for arts marketers. On the other hand, people may crave more experiences outside the home, and that desire can be capitalized upon by performing arts marketers.

2. *Fantasy adventure* refers to the desire to have exciting exploits, heartfelt experiences, exotic adventures, and broad sensory and emotional experiences—but to undertake them in the safest possible ways. This trend represents a wonderful opportunity for performing arts marketers, who offer risk-free risk taking: adventure by association, a range of emotional, aesthetic, and fantastic experiences from the comfort and security of a theater seat.

3. *Small indulgences* is a trend in response to the greed of the eighties, when people overextended themselves to buy showy luxuries. Today, people buy accessories to update last year's outfit, a massage instead of a spa trip, a long weekend trip instead of a two-week jaunt to Europe. This trend is not just about cutting back, but is about buying the best there is in one or two lifestyle categories. For arts marketers, it may translate into the opportunity to encourage current patrons to upgrade to the best seats in the house, or to encourage infrequent attenders to subscribe to a full season rather than taking a weekend away. (It's something to look forward to all year long.)

4. *Egonomics* refers to the consumer's need for personalization. As market niches grow smaller, each consumer's preferences for product features, packaging, distribution, and pricing grows in importance. The performing arts marketer who personalizes communications to various audience members will gain a competitive edge.

5. *The vigilant consumer* wants companies to become more human, more moral and responsible in product representation, more sensitive and responsive to consumer concerns and desires. Consumers want to be heard, and performing arts organizations can gain by being more receptive to their needs.

6. *Ninety-nine lives* is the trend to do it all and be it all (work, parent, volunteer, travel, stay fit, achieve self-fulfillment,

socialize, read, and on and on). What people really want is to buy back time. What this means to marketers is that whatever can be done to speed service, increase the ease of ticket purchase, and fit performing arts events into people's lifestyles and time constraints will help increase performing arts attendance.

Cultural Factors

Of the several groups of factors that affect consumer behavior, it is the cultural factors—from national identity to membership in small social groups—that exert the broadest and deepest influence. A growing child acquires a set of values, perceptions, preferences, and behaviors through the process of socialization into his or her culture(s).

NATIONALITY

It is frequently asserted that Europeans are more predisposed to arts attendance than are Americans. Europe has a longer cultural history, and Europeans are more habituated to arts attendance; for them it is not an unusual practice. In Europe, the arts receive more government support and subsidy, and performances are often more affordable, attracting working-class people as well as the upper classes.

In the United States, by contrast, the performing arts come across as more elitist. People feel they must be highly educated and capable of making sophisticated responses to appreciate opera, ballet, and chamber music. In one survey of adult Americans, more than 90 percent of the 1,059 people questioned said they felt the arts and humanities were important to freedom of expression, were life-enriching, and were a means of self-fulfillment. However, 57 percent said that the arts and humanities played only a minor role in their lives as a whole and little or no role in their daily lives.[7] To J. Carter Brown, chairman of the National Cultural Alliance, the survey indicated that Americans are "an enormously receptive population" for the arts, and that we must find ways to provide opportunities for more involvement. It has been suggested that if theaters were built in shopping malls, more Americans would attend.[8] If Americans could be as comfortable attending the theater or dance as they are with a movie, both the public and the arts organizations would benefit.

SUBCULTURES

Each culture consists of *subcultures*—religious groups, racial groups, regional groups—that provide more specific identification and socialization for their members. These subcultures influence a person's tastes, preferences, and lifestyles, as well as the nature and extent of one's interest in performing arts. Even when programming is directed to a specific subculture, various factors come into play. When a Central

American play, performed in Spanish, was presented in a city's central theater district, no native Spanish-speaking people attended. However, when the production was moved to the Mexican Cultural Center, the Latino community filled the house.

SOCIAL CLASS

A person's *social class* also affects his or her behavior and attitudes. Social classes are hierarchically ordered, relatively homogeneous, and enduring divisions in a society. Their members share similar values, interests, and behavior.[9] A person's social class is determined by the interaction of a number of variables, such as occupation, income, wealth, education, and values, rather than by any single variable. Persons within each social class tend to behave more alike than persons from two different social classes. Social classes show distinct product and brand preferences in their leisure activities as well as in their choice of such consumer goods as clothing and automobiles. They also differ in their media preferences. Upper-class consumers are more likely to be reached through magazines, whereas lower-class consumers prefer television. Even within a media category such as TV, upper-class consumers prefer news and drama while lower-class consumers prefer soap operas and quiz shows. There are also language differences among the social classes. The advertiser has the challenge of composing copy that rings true to the targeted social class and presenting it through the medium that is most likely to reach that target group.

The characteristics of each class's members give marketers clues as to how to reach them. In one case, theater tickets were being sold at the local supermarket, creating an air of accessibility for the performance itself. How intimidating and elitist could the performance be if it was promoted in such an ordinary and comfortable setting? As a result, middle-class consumers attended an area theater in unprecedented numbers. Similarly, working-class consumers may be encouraged to celebrate a birthday or anniversary with an inexpensive dinner and theater package, while members of the upper middle class may be encouraged to entertain their clients with box seats and cocktails in the "members only" room.

Social Factors

Social factors such as reference groups, family, social roles, and status affect a consumer's mind-set and behavior.

REFERENCE GROUPS

A person's *reference groups* usually have a direct influence on the person's attitudes or behavior. Since leisure-time activities have a strong social component, group affiliations are highly influential for involvement and attendance patterns. The more cohesive the group, the more effective its communication process, and therefore the greater its effect on the individual. Reference groups include informal primary groups such as family, friends, neighbors, and coworkers and more formal secondary groups, such as religious and professional groups. People are also influenced by groups to which they do not belong. Someone aspiring to be a member of the board of trustees of the local opera society may make large donations and attend special events to cultivate acceptance by the group's members.

In 1985, a study of Cleveland's cultural patrons was conducted to compare the relative importance of peer group influences and childhood arts education for later arts attendance. Interviewees were asked: "To what extent do childhood exposure to the arts, arts instruction and the behavior of adult friends affect attendance at cultural activities?"[10] The results are exhibited in Figure 4-1. As expected, it was found that instruction or education in the arts during childhood is a powerful factor in shaping future attendance patterns. Those who received such instruction are much more likely to patronize those art forms as adults. However, mere exposure of children to culture appears to have little effect on later attendance habits.

Adult reference groups play a key role in attendance patterns. Performing arts attenders are about twice as likely as nonattenders to have friends who participate in

Figure 4-1

RELATIVE IMPORTANCE OF PEER GROUP INFLUENCES AND CHILDHOOD ARTS EDUCATION

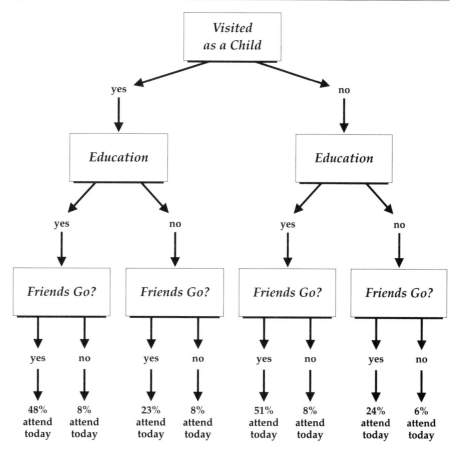

Source: "Marketing the Arts in Cleveland: An In-Depth Survey," conducted by Ziff Marketing, Inc., and Clark, Martire & Bartolomeo, Inc. Commissioned by the Cleveland Foundation, 1985. Reprinted with permission.

the same cultural activities. Adult reference groups are so important that where they are absent, the effects of childhood exposure and education tend to dissipate.

The results of this study indicate that there is a strong interaction effect between the influence of early education or instruction and the presence of adult friends who attend the arts. Individuals who have both are most likely to be arts attenders. One implication for arts marketers is that attendance can be stimulated by promoting group sales among various membership groups and businesses, by offering gift tickets with subscriptions, and by encouraging the purchase of gift certificates.

OPINION LEADERS

Consumers are also influenced by *opinion leaders*—those whose opinions they value. Opinion leaders are found in all strata of society. A specific person can be an opinion leader in certain areas and an opinion follower in others. The more highly a person esteems the opinion leader, the more influential the opinion leader will be in shaping that person's product and brand choices.

INNOVATIVENESS

People differ greatly in their readiness to try new products. An *innovative* person is quicker to adopt new ideas than other members of his or her social system. Rogers has identified five categories which are defined by how long people take to adopt innovations. Innovators, who represent 2.5 percent of the population, are venturesome and are willing to try new ideas at some risk. Early adopters, who make up 13.5 percent of the population, are guided by respect; they are opinion leaders in their community and adopt new ideas early but carefully. The early majority, comprising 34 percent of the population, are deliberate; they adopt new ideas before the average person, though they rarely are leaders. The late majority, comprising another 34 percent of the population, are skeptical and tend to adopt an innovation only after a majority of people have tried it. Finally, laggards, who make up the last 16 percent of the population, are tradition bound and adopt an innovation only when it takes on a measure of tradition itself.[11]

The adopter classification has many implications for arts marketers. It suggests that an avant-garde theater should research the demographic, psychographic, and media characteristics of cultural innovators and early adopters and direct communications specifically to them. Certain cultural innovators may subscribe to a new theater that performs in a church basement with only a hundred seats. The majority of the population will wait for the cue of opinion leaders and jump on the bandwagon only after the theater has received repeated critical and audience acclaim. A company that performs the classics with original-style sets and costumes will be appealing to the late majority and the laggards. A new chamber group that performs early music on period instruments may be positioned to appeal to both the innovators, who may never have experienced such a performance, and the laggards, who are attracted to such dedication to tradition.

Psychological Factors

A variety of personality traits, self-concept issues, and emotions also affect people's attitudes and behavior.

PERSONALITY

Personality may be described in terms of such traits as self-confidence, dominance, autonomy, deference, sociability, and adaptability. Cultural innovators and opinion leaders are likely to be more self-confident, dominant, and autonomous than the less innovative people, who may be more deferential and more interested in the social benefits of arts attendance.

Self-concept is composed of how one views oneself (actual self-concept), how one would like to view oneself (ideal self-concept), and how one thinks he or she is viewed by others (others self-concept). A message such as "You belong there!" for opening night at the symphony may reach all of these groups, including those who believe the message and those who want to believe it.

A person may undergo psychological passages or transformations during which his or her needs or tastes change. The factors that motivate someone to purchase a ticket to a play or that actually restrain them from doing so may operate at a subconscious or unconscious level. The subject of a play may stir anxiety for a person who is grappling with particular emotional issues. Or a young woman may go to the ballet to recapture the memories of similar such outings with her mother when she was a child. The title of a play, a review, or a word-of-mouth description can trigger emotions that will stimulate or inhibit response.

It is often assumed that behavior follows what Ray has called the "think-feel-do" model of consumer behavior.[12] That is, consumers presumably take in information, form some emotional response, and then act when the appropriate resources are available. However, Ray suggests that in many situations, people are influenced to take action by their feelings, following the "feel-do-think" model. This alternative model has led to growing attention in the private sector to influencing emotions. Through television or magazine advertisements that communicate few if any actual facts, advertisers attempt to create feelings or moods and provoke positive associations with an organization's offering. Coca-Cola would "like to teach the world to sing in perfect harmony," creating warm feelings and sudden thirst in its listeners. The National Basketball Association, in its ads during the playoffs and finals, shows exciting "dunks" followed by the single phrase: "I love this game." One can readily see how this approach is likely to be more emotionally appealing than the logo "Where acclaimed theater begins."

BELIEFS AND ATTITUDES

Through socialization and the learning process, people acquire beliefs and attitudes that influence their buying behavior. A belief is based on either knowledge or opinion and may or may not carry an emotional charge. People act on their beliefs. A young couple might believe that all theater performances are expensive and that tickets are scarce on the day of the performance. Yet if marketers make them aware that half-price tickets are available on the performance day, their beliefs are likely to change. The performing arts organization may want to launch a campaign to create awareness of half-price tickets and last-minute availability.

An attitude is a state of readiness to respond in a characteristic way to an object, concept, or situation. Attitudes tend to be more enduring than beliefs, and they lead people to behave fairly consistently. They allow people to economize on energy and thought, rather than having to interpret and react to every object or situation in a fresh way. In general, attitudes are difficult to change.

The traditional persuasion approach to marketing assumes that attitude change must precede behavior change. This approach seeks to modify consumers' anticipations about possible consequences. Based on the relationship between attitudes and behavior, arts organizations are trying to change people's attitudes about what kind of experience they will have attending a performance. For example, Lincoln Center has a "Serious Fun" series, and the Milwaukee Chamber Theatre asks, on the cover of its season brochure, "Wanna Play?"

However, this model has been challenged by a number of scientists who argue that we often adjust our attitudes to fit our behavior rather than vice versa. This alternative approach, known variously as *instrumental conditioning* or *behavioral modification,* is most closely associated with the work of B. F. Skinner.[13] Rather than seeking to modify consumers' anticipations about possible consequences, behavior modification attempts to modify the consequences themselves. By teaching the target individual that a particular action will lead to a desired reward, the probability of the action is increased. Thus, if a dance company offers a special singles night including a wine-and-cheese reception after the performance, people who have never been interested in attending dance performances may attend (change their behavior) in order to gain a desired reward unassociated with the performance itself (the social hour) without changing their attitudes about dance. Some of the attendees may find that the performance was far more accessible and entertaining than they had anticipated and that, as a result, their change in behavior has stimulated a change in attitude. This change may be further reinforced by the provision of additional incentives, such as a coupon for two tickets for the price of one for a return visit. Reinforcement for the behavior change may be social as well. When discussing his evening at the dance at work the next day, the new attendee may get positive feedback in the form of conversation, attention, and praise from his coworkers. So a more effective strategy for arts organization may be to seek behavior change directly rather than worrying about first changing attitudes.

MOTIVATION

A person has many needs at any given time. Some needs are *biogenic,* arising from physiological states of tension such as hunger, thirst, or discomfort. Other needs, which are less immediate, are *psychogenic,* arising from psychological states of tension such as the need for recognition, esteem, or belonging. A motive is a need that is sufficiently pressing to drive a person to act. Satisfying the need reduces the felt tension. Psychologists have developed theories of human motivation. Two of the best known—the theories of Abraham Maslow and Frederick Herzberg—offer implications for consumer analysis and marketing strategy.

According to Abraham Maslow, motivation is driven by particular needs at particular times, from the most pressing to the least pressing.[14] (See Figure 4-2.) Maslow proposed that the more basic needs require gratification before a person is able to achieve substantial gratification of higher-level needs. Gratification at each level contributes to the person's maturation.

Maslow characterized the first four needs as "deficit-driven." People must be able to satisfy the basic physiological needs for food, sleep, and sexual expression; otherwise they will not be able to move to higher need levels. Next they must satisfy safety and security needs, which include both physical security and a sense of psychological well-being. Social needs—for belonging and love—must then be met. People will also seek gratification of esteem needs. An individual's substantial success in

Figure 4-2

MASLOW'S HIERARCHY OF HUMAN NEEDS

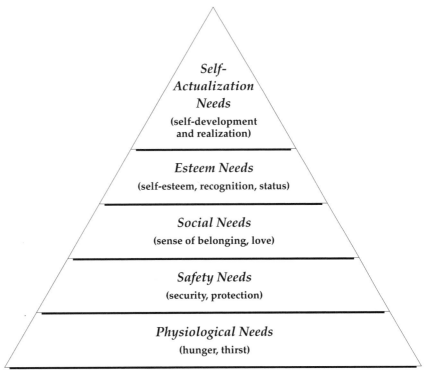

Source: "Hierarchy of Needs" from *Motivation and Personality,* 2nd ed., by Abraham H. Maslow. Copyright 1954 by Harper & Row Publishers, Inc. Copyright © 1970 by Abraham H. Maslow. Reprinted by permission of Addison-Wesley Educational Publishers Inc.

gratifying these four deficit-driven needs lessens the potency of the drives behind those needs, thus freeing up psychic energies to meet growth needs. Performing arts organizations can meet these needs in a variety of creative ways. For example, social needs are met when a theater offers a special night once a month for gays and lesbians. Esteem needs are fulfilled when arts organizations recognize donors on plaques and in program listings.

Maslow envisioned self-actualization as a level of maturity at which a person is beyond striving, beyond basic psychological fear, beyond a need to demonstrate who he or she is, beyond shaping his or her own life largely around the expectations and views of others. It is a stage of life characterized by a high level of well-being, healthy self-esteem, and a positive outlook on life, in which a person is "being all he or she can be."[15] Self-actualizing people represent an important target market for performing arts attendance. The mature adult will be discussed in more depth later in this chapter.

Another psychologist, Frederick Herzberg, developed a "two-factor theory" of motivation, which distinguishes dissatisfiers (factors that cause dissatisfaction) and satisfiers (factors that cause satisfaction).[16] For example, lack of parking adjacent to a performing arts center may be a dissatisfier, keeping away senior citizens who are concerned about safety, inclement weather, or managing long walks. If an orchestra does not offer ticket exchange privileges, this policy may be a dissatisfier that keeps frequent business travelers from making advance purchases. Arts managers must anticipate and counteract dissatisfiers. At the same time, appealing programming and other satisfiers are necessary to actually stimulate sales.

Personal Factors

A variety of other personal characteristics affect a consumer's preferences and behavior. These factors include the person's occupation, economic circumstances, lifestyle, and life cycle stage.

OCCUPATION

It is useful for marketers to identify the *occupational* groups that have above-average interest in the arts. The Los Angeles Philharmonic found that among subscribers to its classical series, 54 percent were professionals, 29 percent held executive, administrative, or managerial positions, and 9 percent held technical, sales, or clerical positions. The Los Angeles Philharmonic also found that various occupational groups have different programming preferences. For example, CEOs and senior corporate officers constituted 7 percent of all managers attending classical concerts and 16 percent of managers attending pops concerts. College-level teachers represented 7 percent of professionals at classical concerts but only 2 percent of professionals at pops concerts, while 11 percent of classical audiences and 5 percent of pops audiences were physicians and dentists.

With this kind of information, marketers can reach potential patrons through their professional publications and they can place stories and advertisements in the media read by high-interest occupation groups. Messages can also be designed to reach people directly in their workplaces. One arts organization arranged with a sponsoring corporation to announce its performances as a heading on all interoffice memos and citywide fax messages.

ECONOMIC CIRCUMSTANCES

People's *economic circumstances* consist of their spendable income (its level, stability, and availability over time), savings and assets, and borrowing power, as well as in their attitude toward spending versus saving. Marketers of income-sensitive goods and services pay constant attention to trends in personal income, interest rates, and attitudes toward the economic climate. If economic indicators point to a recession, arts marketers must take steps to redesign, reposition, and reprice their products in an effort to hold on to their audiences. Miniseries, discount coupons, and blocks of lower-priced seating are among the offers that have been developed by arts organizations in order to attract patrons with less discretionary income.

LIFESTYLE

People coming from the same subculture, social class, and occupation may nonetheless lead very different *lifestyles*. One person may choose a "belonging" lifestyle, spending a lot of time with family and voluntary organizations. Another person may choose an "achiever" lifestyle, working long hours on challenging projects and playing hard at travel and sports.

Lifestyle is a dynamic factor—each person may lead different lifestyles at different times in life. Lifestyle refers to a person's pattern of living in the world as expressed in his or her activities, interests, and opinions. Here is the lifestyle description of an achiever: He lives in a three-story brownstone house on an elegant street, across from the park and a five-minute drive from downtown, where he works as an upper-level corporate executive. He travels frequently on business and entertains some of his clients at sports events, others at cultural events. He eats at fine restaurants, but doesn't patronize expensive spots that are "all style." He runs in the park, has a regular tennis game with friends, and skis several times each winter. He drives a German car, drinks fine wines and San Pellegrino water, and likes goat cheese and understated Italian clothes. He reads several business, news, and political publications, and alternates between reading best-sellers (especially recent historical nonfiction) and the classics. He subscribes to the symphony, the opera, and the modern dance series, but often has to exchange or give away his tickets because of his frequent travels.

Such descriptions can help a performing arts organization to select performances that will appeal to achievers and to develop ad copy using the symbols that appeal to this lifestyle group.

As we observed earlier in this chapter in the discussion of macroenvironmental influences, the achievement lifestyle may be giving way to other values.

There is a growing trend toward the pursuit of emotional and physical well-being, including gaining fulfillment from work, having a less stressful life, having loving relationships, eating in a healthful manner, exercising regularly, and living in a less polluted environment. As economic success becomes more difficult to achieve, people are changing their definitions of what it means to be successful. Instead of relying on income level as a badge of success, people are prioritizing other lifestyle factors.[17]

According to Boyd and Levy, people are artists of their own lifestyles, and marketers have the opportunity to provide them with the pieces of the mosaic from which they can pick and choose to develop their own composition. "The marketer who thinks about his products in this way will seek to understand their potential settings and relationships to other parts of consumer lifestyles, and thereby to increase the number of ways they fit meaningfully into the pattern."[18] Chapter 5 discusses leisure and cultural lifestyle patterns in more detail.

FAMILY

Family members constitute the most influential of the primary reference groups that shape a buyer's behavior. For this reason, marketers have extensively researched the roles and relative influence of the husband, wife, and children in the purchase of a large variety of products and services. It has been found that decisions about certain purchases, such as life insurance, automobiles, and televisions are husband-dominated; decisions about carpeting, kitchenware, washing machines, non-living-room furniture, and groceries are wife-dominated; and for such purchases as vacations, housing, and outside entertainment, there is usually equal input by the husband and wife. The art marketer's job, then, is highly complex. Some of the factors affecting arts attendance, such as early education in the arts, occupation, and lifestyle factors may differ between the husband and wife. Since arts attendance among married people is often decided as a couple, both the husband and wife must be reached by the arts marketer.

LIFE CYCLE STAGE

A person's lifestyle and family situation are closely related to his or her *life cycle stage*. Each person passes through several life cycle stages. Belk and Andreasen have studied the effects of family life cycle on arts patronage. They defined family life cycle stages by the categories shown in Figure 4-3 and then described the mean number of theater and symphony performances attended by people in each life cycle stage.[19]

Of the respondents in the study, the most frequent performing arts attenders are unmarried people under the age of 41 with no children. Attendance then drops off dramatically as people marry and have children. There are several possible explanations for this. Children may cause budgetary constraints that preclude former luxuries like arts attendance (an economic explanation). Or the former arts attender may choose to spend more time with the family and respond to the preferences of younger family members to attend nonarts events (a sociological explanation). If a performing arts marketer understands the reasons for the decline in attendance of this group, it may be possible to devise appropriate strategies to win them back.

A major opportunity for arts marketers lies in attracting young adults: those who are educated, have disposable income, and have no family responsibilities eroding their leisure time. The characteristics of today's young adults are dramatically

Figure 4-3

MEAN NUMBER OF THEATER AND SYMPHONY PERFORMANCES ATTENDED AS A FUNCTION OF FAMILY LIFE CYCLE STAGE

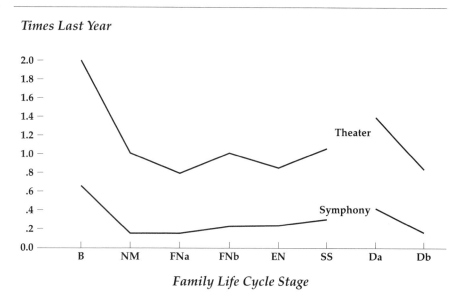

Times Last Year

Family Life Cycle Stage

FAMILY LIFE CYCLE OPERATIONAL DEFINITIONS

Stage	Operational definition
Bachelor (B)	Never married, under 41, no children
Newly Married (NM)	Married, under 41, no children
Full Nest I (FNa)	Married, youngest child under 6
Full Nest II & III (FNb)	Married, youngest child 6–19 (in-house)
Empty Nest I & II (EN)	Married, no children at home, over 40
Solitary Survivor (SS)	Widowed, no children at home, over 40
Divorced I (Da)	Divorced or separated, under 41
Divorced II (Db)	Divorced or separated, over 40

Source: Russell W. Belk and Alan Andreasen, "The Effects of Family Life Cycle on Arts Patronage," *Journal of Cultural Economics*, Dec. 1982, 25–35. Reprinted with permission.

different from those of the twenty-somethings of the 1980s (the "me" generation), who were characterized as flashy, overambitious, and status-conscious. Consider the following description of Generation X.

UNDER-STANDING GENERATION X

The behavior and interests of Generation X are characterized by genuineness, authenticity, and simplicity. They are straightforward and honest, but do not take themselves too seriously and enjoy a touch of irony. They like their clothes and their cars to exhibit utility and practicality: work shoes, flannel shirts, and jeans; Jeeps. Today's younger generation has a statistically higher propensity for self-reflection and search for truth than their parents. They are inspired by humanism and are not motivated by hype. Angst, stress, and disillusionment are often by-products of their mind-set.

Says Elaine Powell Cook, vice president of marketing at the Atlanta Symphony Orchestra (ASO), when marketing to today's 18- to 35-year-olds, "Address this market using a style and sensitivity that supports the artistic and humanistic quality of the art form. Avoid overcommercialization. 'Dumbing down' the message is not only not necessary; it could in fact be a turn-off."

To attract this younger audience, the Atlanta Symphony developed a campaign called "Join the Movement." The goal was to portray classical music composers as real human beings, struggling for identity, suggesting that creating great music is the composer's ultimate expression of his individuality and creative genius. The campaign features a coffeehouse series entitled "Coffee with a Dead Composer," where participants gather for casual evening discussions about works by classical composers. Those who attend receive an Atlanta Symphony CD of the featured composer's work. Posters depicting composers with their eccentricities (Jean Sibelius had a Mohawk haircut) help promote the series in coffeehouses, in bookstores, and on college campuses. Radio stations, MTV, and specialty coffee manufacturers have become willing partners and sponsors of the effort. As a result of this campaign, the ASO has an increasing number of 20- to 35-year-old repeat buyers of single tickets.[20]

In contrast to family life cycle stages, David Wolfe has defined three experiential stages in adult life that largely define consumer behavior, especially in terms of discretionary purchase behavior. First is the *possession experience stage*, which usually develops in young adulthood, reflecting the stage of life when the acquisition of possessions, both animate and inanimate (house, car, jewelry, spouse, child), drives consumer behavior. Possession aspirations are strongly linked to the establishment and maintenance of the image one wishes to project to others. By age 40 and the onset of the midlife crisis years, the possession aspirations normally move beyond their peak potency, although they continue to be important, and *catered experience* aspirations are ascending. These are the experiences involving the purchase of services, rather than things: season tickets to the theater, a weekend getaway, a fine meal in an elegant restaurant. The more possession and catered experiences a consumer has had, the more those *things* that once mattered so much decline in importance. This is the time when *being experiences,* essentially of nonmaterialistic origin, take center stage. A being experience may range from watching a beautiful sunset to learning something exciting to listening to music. Being experiences enhance a sense of connectedness, sharpen one's sense of reality, increase one's appreciation for life, and contribute to inner personal growth.[21] Because art often creates an environment and serves as a catalyst for self-actualization, people who seek being experiences are a naturally fruitful target group for performing arts marketers. Consider the following analysis of this segment of the population.

THE MATURE ADULT MARKET

Although performing arts managers are concerned about the aging of their audiences, they should appreciate that mature adults have always been a vital, substantial, loyal, and therefore essential audience for the arts. At the Los Angeles Philharmonic, 44 percent of subscribers to the classical series are retired persons, and many of them have been with the organization for as long as thirty years. At the Dallas Opera, the percentage of "over 65s" nearly doubled in the ten years from 1981 to 1991. Furthermore, over the next several years the 65-plus population is expected to increase at the rate of 1.7 per cent per year; as the baby-boomer generation reaches middle age, the older segment will only continue to grow.

The mature adult market is truly a lifestyle market. It is interested less in the attributes of a particular offering, and more in the experiences to which it can lead. Maslow describes the following personality attributes of the mature, self-actualizing people:

- *Superior perception of reality,* which makes them more discerning when evaluating advertising claims.

- *Increased acceptance of self and others,* resulting in a higher capacity for humor and for coping with stress.

- *Increased spontaneity.* Mature people are more likely to live day by day and respond well to the unexpected and to the spirited.

- *Increased detachment and desire for privacy.* Advertising images should acknowledge the unique individuality felt by mature adults.

- *Increased autonomy and resistance to enculturation.* Mature people know what they want, and they resist efforts by others to change their minds. Give them facts, not value-inflated, self-serving claims.

- *Greater freshness of appreciation and richness of emotional reaction.* Touch their hearts and they will allow you to enter their minds.

- *Greatly increased creativity.* First invoke the poet in the mature consumer, but be sure not to abandon the rational side of the process.[22]

Based on Maslow's theories, David Wolfe has developed a set of principles for positioning an offering to mature adults:

- *The Gateway-to-Experiences Principle.* Mature consumers tend to be motivated more by the capacity of a product or service to serve as a gateway to experiences than by the generic nature of the product or service itself.

- *The Age-Correlate Principle.* Age is a correlate, not a determinant, of consumer behavior in mature markets and hence should not be used to define and predict specific consumer behavior among older people. Stage of life, expressed in terms of *personality* maturity, has a far greater influence on consumer behavior than chronological age or social, economic, or career position.

- *The Price/Value Principle.* Consistent with the desire for quality, mature consumers tend to place a higher value on price in purchasing basics, but in their more discretionary purchases, they tend to place a higher value on the potential experience resulting from the purchase. That is, mature consumers tend to spend "tightly" on goods and services necessary to maintain lifestyles and more "loosely" on products and services that *enhance* lifestyle.

- *The Altruistic Factor.* Mature adults tend to respond more favorably to marketing messages that emphasize introspective or altruistic values and less favorably to marketing messages that emphasize selfish interests.

Performing arts marketers can use these principles to develop relevant programming and messages. The goal is to create in consumers' minds multiple perceptions of what the offering can do for them. This approach requires that marketers be creative in the art of positioning an offering in terms of what it *might be,* rather than simply in terms of what it is.

There is a complex interplay among the cultural, social, psychological, and other personal factors that shape consumer behavior. If the marketer's goal is to influence behavior, the marketer must develop a thorough understanding of the factors that affect behavior and must promise a favorable exchange. All these factors must be taken into account when a marketer segments and selects the target audience, and positions, prices, and communicates the offering.

THE BUYING DECISION PROCESS

For many performing arts attenders, the decision to purchase a ticket is stimulated by the mere receipt of an attractive announcement of an interesting performance.[23] A study conducted for the Theatre Royal Stratford East in England concluded that "respondents go to the theatre because they want to see a particular performance or a particular actor."[24] For such people, arts attendance is often routine and familiar, and the buying decision is a relatively simple, *low-involvement* one.

But in the case of *high-involvement* exchanges, the buying decision process is far more complex. High personal involvement typically occurs when the type of exchange is new to the decision maker and the consumer does not know much about the product category. The consumer is also highly involved when the purchase decision is important, expensive, or risky; when it reflects upon the consumer's self-image; or when reference-group pressures to act in a particular way are strong.

The renewal of a theater subscription for the fifth consecutive year by a satisfied patron is a low-involvement decision. The decision has become so routine that there is little or no observable decision making. This type of purchase decision is sometimes termed a *straight rebuy.* In a straight rebuy, the buyer does not need much information because she knows the organization, and the costs and benefits it confers, from previous experience. Requiring a higher level of involvement is the *modified rebuy,* such as the decision by a couple who are longtime subscribers to the symphony to add to their subscription to the orchestra's new chamber music series. The couple is familiar with the organization, and they are merely modifying a purchasing decision they have made in the past. This is a case of decision making with experience, but one that requires more information than a straight rebuy. The decision to attend the opera for the first time can be considered a high-involvement decision. This situation represents a *new task* for a couple who is faced with a new offer of an unfamiliar kind from an unfamiliar seller. In this context, it is easy to understand why organizations avidly promote subscription renewals: it is much easier for a marketer to sell a straight rebuy than a new task purchase.

Yet, theorists believe that even low-involvement decisions actually involve cognitive activity that is a simplified version of the process involved in more elaborate decision making. Furthermore, it is likely that the same factors that make a decision relatively trivial at one time may make it more deliberate at another time—such as when a longtime subscriber becomes dissatisfied with the programming and considers not renewing his or her subscription, or when a significant price change alters the patron's typical response to an offer. Therefore, it is important for arts marketers to understand the process involved in highly complex decisions.

The typical highly complex decision is one in which the consumer is considering undertaking an action or behavior for the first time. The decision process proceeds through five stages:

1. *Need recognition:* We have a baby-sitter and no plans for the evening.
2. *Information search:* What entertainment options are available to us?
3. *Evaluation of alternatives:* Should we go to a play or to a concert?
4. *Purchase decision:* The play will be here for another few weeks; maybe we should wait and go with friends.
5. *Postpurchase behavior:* I really liked that soloist and I want to get tickets for her next performance.

Breaking down the buying decision process into five stages makes it clear that the decision process starts long before the actual purchase and has consequences long afterward. This insight encourages the marketer to focus on the factors and influences that can affect each stage of decision making.

Need Recognition

The buying process starts when the consumer recognizes a problem or need, which may be triggered by either internal or external stimuli. An internal stimulus may be a desire for an enjoyable, entertaining evening or a desire to support an organization by means of a subscription and a donation. External stimuli include advertisements and word-of-mouth recommendations from friends or colleagues. By gathering information from a number of consumers, the marketer can identify the most frequent stimuli that spark interest in a performance or subscription. The marketer can then develop marketing strategies that trigger consumer interest.

Information Search

An interested consumer is inclined to search for more information. For example, someone driving home from work may be thinking about how to spend Saturday evening. That person will be likely to have heightened attention when the local theater reviewer comes on the radio. Upon arriving home, the person may begin an active information search, looking up theater schedules and prices, phoning friends, and checking for ticket availability. How much search the person undertakes depends upon the amount of information he initially has, the ease of obtaining additional information, the value he places on additional information, and the satisfaction he gets from the search itself. Some people are content to respond to one seemingly viable offering; others need to investigate all their options before making a selection. In general, the amount of search activity increases as the consumer moves from limited problem solving (Shall we go to the jazz concert or to the movies tonight?) to extensive problem solving (Which one of these three worthwhile theaters shall we subscribe to next season?).

Of key interest to the marketer are the major information sources that the consumer will turn to and the relative influence each will have on the subsequent purchase decision. Consumer information sources may be *personal* (family, friends, and colleagues), *commercial* (advertising, posters, etc.), *public* (mass media, award-granting institutions such as the "Tony"), or *experiential* (based on previous experience with similar products). Generally speaking, the consumer is exposed to the most information about a product from commercial sources, which are marketer dominated. On the other hand, the most effective exposures come from personal sources, which perform a legitimizing and/or evaluation function. One theater has a radio announcer read an ad that sounds as though he has seen the play and is recommending it to friends, combining aspects of both the personal and commercial sources.

Arts marketers often survey their audiences to determine which information sources play a part in their decisions and to assess the relative importance of each source. The responses of the patrons help organizations to prepare effective communications for the target market. Of course, it must be remembered that this approach only analyzes the responses of *current* patrons. If an organization would like to attract new target markets, the information-seeking habits and preferences of the target groups must be researched. This process is not necessarily as difficult as one might think. One arts organization arranged with a car repair shop in a target neighborhood to keep track of the radio station to which each incoming car was tuned. One could even limit such a search to certain brands of cars!

Evaluation of Alternatives

If consumers evaluated alternatives based solely on the information they collect, the marketer's job would be relatively simple. But the process is complicated by all of the cultural, social, personal, and psychological factors that influence consumer behavior. The consumer sees each product as a *bundle of attributes,* which have varying capabilities of delivering the sought benefits and satisfying certain needs.

Consumers will differ as to which product attributes are seen as relevant or salient. One person may choose to attend a certain concert because of the symphony being performed, another because she likes a featured soloist, another because she was invited to join friends with whom she wanted to spend the evening. Other factors also play a part in the evaluation process, such as ease of parking or ticket prices, and their influence will vary with different consumers. There is a significant difference between the *importance* and the *salience* of product attributes to consumers. A symphony may make its awards and great reviews salient in its ads, for example, but other attributes such as programming and ancillary social events may be more important to consumers. Marketers should emphasize those attributes that are most important to the targeted audience.

There are several tactics a marketer may employ to influence the consumer's evaluation process. Consider a modern dance company performing at an outdoor music festival in a new city. First, the marketer can attempt to change consumers' beliefs about modern dance ("You think modern dance is for highbrows? Well, you'll be dancing in the streets after this performance!"). Second, the marketer may attempt to increase the perceived weighted importance of certain factors (Listen to the "worldwide acclaim" the company has received). Third, the marketer may attempt to change beliefs about competitors ("And you thought basketball is athletic and beautiful to watch!"). Fourth, the marketer may call attention to neglected favorable consequences ("Enjoy a picnic in the park and under the stars before the show") or add new favorable consequences to the decision ("Mention this ad and get a 20 percent discount on your tickets").

Purchase Decision

The decision-making process in arts attendance is made more complex by the fact that the target consumer is often not an individual, but a group. Five different roles may be played by people involved in the decision process:

1. *Initiator:* The initiator is the person who first suggests or thinks of the idea of becoming involved in a particular exchange.
2. *Influencer:* An influencer is a person who offers or is sought out for advice on the decision.
3. *Decider:* The decider is the person(s) who ultimately determines any or all parts of the decision to participate in the exchange: whether to take action; what action to take; how, when, or where to take action.
4. *Transactor:* The transactor is the person who completes the actual transaction.
5. *Consumer:* The consumer may or may not participate in the actual purchase decision roles.

For example, Betty reads in her local paper that *A Christmas Carol* will be performed during the holiday season. She thinks that this would be a wonderful outing for the whole family. As the initiator, Betty calls Mary, whose family has seen the production previously, to ask whether they enjoyed it. She also reads an article in the newspaper written by the local theater critic about the production. Both Mary and the critic act as influencers. Betty then calls her husband Bob and they jointly decide to buy tickets. Bob offers to buy the tickets at the box office on his way home, thus becoming the transactor. Betty, Bob, and their children will be the consumers.

A performing arts organization wishing to attract an audience would do well to know the role allocation strategies of the target groups in its market. These buying decision roles apply not only to audience members but to families solicited for donations and to corporations solicited for sponsorship.

Postpurchase Behavior

After purchasing and experiencing a performance, a consumer will register some level of satisfaction or dissatisfaction. There are two major theories that explain whether consumers will be satisfied with a performance.

EXPECTATIONS-PERFORMANCE THEORY

This theory holds that a consumer's satisfaction is a function of the consumer's expectations and the perceived outcome.[25] If the outcome matches expectations, the consumer is satisfied; if it exceeds them, he or she is highly satisfied; if it falls short, he or she is dissatisfied. This theory suggests that the marketer should not overbuild expectations. If anything, the organization should *under*promise and *over*deliver so that consumers will experience higher-than-expected satisfaction. Consumers form their expectations on the basis of messages and claims by the organization, other communication sources, word of mouth, and past experience. If the consumer is satisfied, he or she will exhibit a higher probability of purchasing the product again. The satisfied customer will also tend to say good things about the experience to others, and marketers know that their best advertisement is a satisfied customer. If the seller makes exaggerated claims, consumers will experience disconfirmed expectations, which lead to dissatisfaction. The larger the gap between expectations and performance, the greater the consumer's dissatisfaction. When a play is touted as being "hilarious," and most patrons find it mildly funny, there will be much dissatisfaction and people will be less likely to believe future claims by the organization.

COGNITIVE DISSONANCE THEORY

This theory holds that making any choice always involves giving up other things, and therefore some postdecision regret, or cognitive dissonance, might be felt.[26] The consumer has to deal with the dissonance or discomfort. Dissonant consumers will resort to one of two courses of action. They may try to reduce the dissonance by vowing not to repeat the choice ("I'll never go to modern dance / an experimental play / that theater again!"). Or consumers may try to reduce the dissonance by seeking information that might confirm the high value of their action ("Now that I reread the critic's review, I appreciate the play more").

Arts organizations strive to satisfy audience members over many productions and seasons. An important part of this effort is to take positive steps to reduce postpurchase dissonance and help patrons feel good about their choices. Warm letters of welcome should be sent to new subscribers. The organization can provide interesting information about the performances and human interest stories about the performers and staff. They can also solicit suggestions and complaints from the patrons by providing them with easy means to voice their interests and concerns.

Since the objective of marketing is to create satisfaction among target consumers, it is essential that all strategic planning start with understanding consumer behavior. This understanding allows the marketer to develop a marketing program that meets the needs of its publics.

[1] Jeremy Eccles, "Focusing on the Audience," *International Arts Manager,* Jan. 1993, 21–23.

[2] Philadelphia Arts Market Study, commissioned by the Pew Charitable Trusts, prepared by Ziff Marketing, 1989.

[3] Heidi Waleson, "Marketing: What Can We Do for You?" *International Arts Manager,* Jan. 1993, 17–18.

[4] John Naisbett and Patricia Aburdene, *Megatrends 2000: Ten New Directions for the 1990's* (New York: Avon Books, 1990), xvii.

[5] David Meer, "Marketing Trends in the '90s for the Performing Arts," *Dance/USA Journal,* Summer 1991, 16–23.

[6] Faith Popcorn, *The Popcorn Report* (New York: Harper Business, 1992), 22.

[7] "Americans Back Arts, but Don't Feel Touched," *New York Times,* March 1, 1993, sec. B, p. 2. Article based on an opinion poll conducted in October 1992 by Research and Forecasts Inc. for the National Cultural Alliance.

[8] Elisa Monte, "The Artist's Voice," *Inside Arts Magazine* 5, no. 1 (Spring 1993), 12–13.

[9] Philip Kotler, *Marketing Management,* 7th ed. (Englewood Cliffs, N.J.: Prentice-Hall, 1991), 166.

[10] "Marketing the Arts in Cleveland: An In-Depth Survey," conducted by Ziff Marketing, Inc., and Clark, Martire & Bartolomeo, Inc., commissioned by the Cleveland Foundation, 1985.

[11] Everett M. Rogers, *Diffusion of Innovations* (New York: Free Press, 1962).

[12] Michael L. Ray, "Psychological Theories and Interpretations of Learning," in *Consumer Behavior: Theoretical Sources,* ed. S. Ward and T. S. Robertson (Englewood Cliffs, N.J.: Prentice-Hall, 1973), 45–117.

[13] Michael Rothschild and William C. Gaidis, "Behavioral Learning Theory: Its Relevance to Marketing and Promotions," *Journal of Marketing,* Spring 1981, 70–78.

[14] Abraham Maslow, *Motivation and Personality* (New York: Harper & Row, 1954), 80–106.

[15] David B. Wolfe, *Marketing to Boomers and Beyond* (New York: McGraw-Hill, 1993), 135–140.

[16] Frederick Herzberg, *Work and the Nature of Man* (Cleveland: William Collins, 1966).

[17] Meer, "Marketing Trends," 21.

[18] Harper W. Boyd, Jr., and Sidney J. Levy, *Promotion: A Behavioral View* (Englewood Cliffs, N.J.: Prentice-Hall, 1967), 38.

[19] Russell W. Belk and Alan Andreasen, "The Effects of Family Life Cycle on Arts Patronage," *Journal of Cultural Economics* 6, no. 2 (Dec. 1982), 25–35.

[20] Elaine Powell Cook, "Hip Not Hype: Reaching Younger Audiences," *Arts Reach,* June/July 1995, 6–7.

[21] Wolfe, *Marketing to Boomers and Beyond,* 117.

[22] Ibid., 164–165.

[23] Chris Blamires, "What Price Entertainment?" *Journal of the Market Research Society,* 34, no. 4 (Oct. 1992): 377.

[24] Artlink, 1987, Theatre Royal Stratford East Audience qualitative research.

[25] John E. Swan and Linda Jones Combs, "Product Performance and Consumer Satisfaction: A New Concept," *Journal of Marketing Research* (April 1976), 25–33.

[26] Leon Festinger, *A Theory of Cognitive Dissonance* (Stanford, Calif.: Stanford University Press, 1957), 260.

▲●▲

IDENTIFYING MARKET SEGMENTS, SELECTING TARGET MARKETS, AND POSITIONING THE OFFER

MARKETING PLANNING MUST START WITH STRATEGIC MARKETING—NAMELY, *segmenting, targeting,* and *positioning*. The marketer first identifies a variety of dimensions along which to segment the market and develops profiles of the resulting market segments. Then the marketer selects those segments that represent the best targets for its efforts. Finally, the marketer designs marketing strategies and positions the organization and its products to have the greatest appeal to the target markets. Consider the following illustrations.

REACHING NEW AUDIENCES

All of the characters in Clare Booth Luce's *The Women,* a 1936 stage classic, are women. But in a recent production, all of the players were men, as were many of the audience members. The audience consisted largely of gay men, who were lured to the play with the camp casting approach. Some theaters are choosing not only actors, but programming, with gay audiences in mind. At the Goodman Theatre in Chicago, the AIDS-themed *Marvin's Room* and gay performance artist David Cale have been featured in recent seasons. A wide variety of marketing approaches are being used as well to attract gay audiences. Following the lead of New York's Roundabout Theater, Chicago's Steppenwolf Theatre has instituted a gay and lesbian subscription night, which includes a preperformance lobby reception for subscribers.[2]

At the inaugural concert of the Raymond F. Kravis Center for the Performing Arts in Florida, the choirs of several predominantly black churches, more accustomed to gospel music, joined with the Florida Philharmonic Orchestra to perform Beethoven's Ninth Symphony.[3] Similarly, the Dance Theater of Harlem has set up an audience development task force of African Americans and Hispanics. The goal of the task force is to "increase awareness, make people feel comfortable about attending performances, and sell blocks of tickets so that people can attend in groups."[4]

The Kravis Center also has instituted an Adults at Leisure series, consisting of afternoon concerts with reduced pricing, aimed at retired people. The center has also developed a Snowbird series, which involves joint presentations with the Brooklyn Center in New York and is intended to hook wintertime residents who live in northern states the rest of the year.[5]

These programs have been developed to reach people who have not typically attended arts performances. Their planners recognize that customers vary greatly in their needs, attitudes, interests, and buying requirements. Since no organization can satisfy all consumers, each organization should identify the most attractive market segments that it can serve effectively.

Strategic marketing enables organizations to spot market opportunities and to develop or adjust their offerings to meet the needs of the potential markets. The steps in the strategic marketing process are described in Figure 5-1.

SEGMENTATION

The first responsibility of a marketer is to segment its consumer base, by aggregating consumers into similar groupings. These groupings may be geographic (distance from the theater, neighborhoods of most-likely attenders), demographic (age,

Figure 5-1

STEPS IN
MARKET
SEGMENTATION,
TARGETING,
AND
POSITIONING

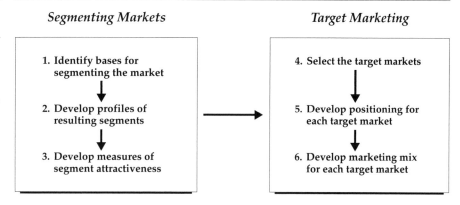

Segmenting Markets   *Target Marketing*

education, income, gender, family status), or psychographic (lifestyle measures such as activities, interests, and opinions; social class; family life cycle). The aim of segmentation is to identify groups within a heterogeneous market who share distinctive needs, preferences, and/or behaviors. Although, ultimately, each member of a market is unique, segmentation aims to identify broad groups for whom specific offers can be developed. The role of the marketer is to develop an offer whose perceived ratio of benefits to costs is higher than those of alternative offers and actions the consumer is considering. Of course, various market groupings, or segments, exhibit different responses to offerings; what appeals to one group may be unattractive to another.

Alternative Bases of Segmentation

There are usually several ways to segment a given market, and forming meaningful segments is as much an art of insight as it is a science. The segmentation variables most commonly used by arts organizations are demographic: age, gender, income, education, occupation, religion, race, family size, position in family life cycle, and geographical factors. Even when the target market is described in terms of nondemographic factors, such as personality type, the link back to demographic characteristics is often necessary in order to determine the size of the target market and how to reach it efficiently. Demographic characteristics play a significant role in identifying current and potential performing arts attenders. People who frequent the performing arts often have a college education, are affluent, are white, live in or near a metropolitan area, and do not have young children to care for.

Changes in demographics can have a significant long-range effect on an arts organization's audience base. Consider the fact that more women than men attend the performing arts. Today, 70 percent of women are in the work force. By the year 2000, that number will grow to 80 percent. Will increasing demands on women's time mean that there will be less time available for leisure pursuits such as attending the theater or ballet? Also, new census projections predict that by the year 2050, Hispanics will overtake African Americans as the largest minority (21 percent of the population in 2050), Asians will be the fastest-growing population (12 percent of the population in 2050), and minority segments will grow to 47 percent of the total population. Clearly, these projections indicate the need for arts organizations to determine how best to reach out to, engage, and meet the needs of a wide variety of ethnic groups. Yet, due to recent increased fertility (more women are having babies later) and longevity trends, the population as a whole is expected to increase by more than 1 percent a year, presenting opportunities for healthy long-term growth of performing arts organizations.[6]

Often an organization segments a market by combining two or more demographic variables. For example, education and income are two prime indicators for performing arts attendance. High levels of education and income together form a stronger predictor of attendance than either variable alone. Among the highly educated, professionals and educators tend to be the most frequent arts patrons. Among those with significant discretionary income, empty nesters have the most time for leisure events. So, adding more variables such as occupation and life cycle stage can only serve to enrich the analysis. Here we illustrate how certain variables have been applied creatively to segment markets.

GEOCLUSTERING

Geoclustering yields richer descriptions of neighborhoods than traditional demographics can supply because it takes into account the socioeconomic status and lifestyle of the inhabitants. Claritas, Inc., has developed a geoclustering approach called PRIZM, which classifies all American residential neighborhoods into sixty-two distinct lifestyle groupings called PRIZM Clusters. The groupings take into consideration thirty-nine factors in five broad categories: (1) education and affluence, (2) family life cycle, (3) urbanization, (4) race and ethnicity, and (5) mobility. The neighborhoods are broken down by five-digit zip code, nine-digit zip code, or census track and block group. The clusters are given descriptive titles that convey their essence, such as "Blue Blood Estates," "Young Influentials," "Urban Gold Coast," "Gray Power," "Mid-City Mix," "Pools and Patios," "Shotguns and Pickups," and "Towns and Gowns."

PRIZM is based on the maxim that birds of a feather flock together. The inhabitants in a cluster tend to lead similar lives, drive similar cars, have similar jobs, read similar magazines, and share other things in common. Marketers can use PRIZM to answer such questions as Which clusters (neighborhoods or zip codes) produce our most valuable customers? Which other clusters have inhabitants with similar characteristics? How deeply have we already penetrated these segments? Has our mix of customers changed over time? Is it changing in the direction we desire? Which markets, performance sites, and promotional media provide us with the best opportunities for growth?

An arts organization can use PRIZM information to locate appropriate markets and to learn what would appeal to each market. When the National Symphony Orchestra (NSO) in Washington, D.C., profiled its ten thousand subscribers in 1985, it discovered that four times more residents in "Money and Brains" neighborhoods attended concerts than those in "Winner's Circle." The major difference between the two clusters is that the former is composed of cosmopolitan singles and couples while the latter consists of affluent suburban families with young children. As a result, the NSO's 1986 telemarketing campaign focused on cultivating previously ignored neighborhoods like Capitol Hill, where the childless "Bohemian Mix" reside. In some of the targeted areas, subscription sales jumped 25 percent.[7]

The "Young Literati" cluster is described by Claritas as likely to attend live theater. The following description of the Young Literati's characteristics can help arts managers learn where best to reach them with publicity and promotions; which product features and benefits are likely to interest them; how to make appropriate positioning, pricing, and place decisions; and which corporations may be interested in sponsoring a particular arts organization in order to reach the same target market.

THE YOUNG LITERATI CLUSTER

The "Young Literati" cluster consists primarily of upscale urban singles and couples without children, most of whom are college graduates, and have professional, managerial, or other white-collar occupations. They earn a median household income of $52,100 and own (48.6 percent) or rent (51.4 percent) multi-unit housing in urban uptown areas. The median home value is $245,200; 24.5 percent have moved within the past year; 14.3 percent last moved 20 or more years ago. Their predominant age ranges are 25–34 and 35–54, with a median age of 43.4. Among the Young Literati, 23.5 percent are married, 14.7 percent are married couples with children, 5.1 percent are single parents, and 56.8 percent are single. Other characteristics are as follows:

ETHNIC ORIGIN:	U.S.	CLUSTER
White	83.2%	84.1%
Black	12.4	7.4
Asian	5.4	14.9
Hispanic	9.9	9.4
All other races	4.4	8.5

LIFESTYLE: MORE LIKELY TO

- Rent foreign videos
- Travel to Japan, Asia
- Go jogging
- Spend $60+ per month for dry cleaning
- Go scuba diving/snorkeling
- Attend live theater
- Use home pregnancy tests
- Play racquetball
- Buy hardcover books
- Go to the movies

PRODUCTS & SERVICES: MORE LIKELY TO

- Have travel insurance
- Own state/local government bonds
- Own tax-exempt funds
- Have a gold/premium credit card
- Use an ATM card
- Own stock valued $10,000+
- Own an Audi
- Buy a Montblanc/Waterman pen
- Own a Volkswagen
- Buy gourmet coffee beans
- Buy a $100+ sweater
- Drink imported beer often
- Own pagers/beepers
- Buy designer jeans
- Use olive oil
- Drink gin, low/no-alcohol beer
- Eat Wheaties
- Buy Quaker Puffed Rice
- Own a CD player
- Buy Adidas shoes

RADIO & TV: MORE LIKELY TO

- Listen to progressive rock radio
- Watch the Travel Channel
- Listen to soft contemp radio
- Watch BET
- Listen to urban contemp radio
- Watch MacNeil/Lehrer NewsHour
- Watch Masterpiece Theater
- Watch Cinemax
- Watch *The Simpsons*
- Watch *Entertainment Tonight*

PRINT: MORE LIKELY TO

- Read newspaper business section
- Read *Self*
- Read *Metropolitan Home*
- Read Newspaper style/fashion section
- Read *Rolling Stone*

- Read *GQ*
- Read *Penthouse*
- Read *Elle*
- Read *Time*
- Read *Road & Track*

Claritas also provides a map showing where Young Literati clusters can be found. They are most densely concentrated in Northern and Southern California, Minnesota, Texas, and the greater Metropolitan areas surrounding Boston, New York, Philadelphia, and Chicago.

Source: PRIZM, Claritas Inc., 1995. Reprinted with permission.

Geoclustering, which gained popularity in the 1980s, is growing in importance as a segmentation tool due to three major trends. First, census reports release more detailed data for smaller geographic divisions. Second, the U.S. population is growing in diversity because of faster population growth among certain ethnic groups, more women in the work force, changing household structures, and the changing size of age groups, largely due to the baby boomers. Further, marketing to microsegments has become possible even for small organizations as database costs decline, computers proliferate, software becomes easier to use, and data integration increases.

GENDER SEGMENTATION

Audience surveys and other research projects indicate that women dominate attendance at performing arts events. Furthermore, in many cases the men who are in attendance are there to accompany a female partner, and it was she who actually made the decision to attend. There is no logical reason to expect biology to account for this difference between the sexes. The explanation may be in socialization differences. Women may be more involved with the performing arts because as girls they were more commonly provided with early arts training than were boys—dance and music lessons and the like—as well as attendance experiences. This may be the result of cultural assumptions about the relative importance of the arts in the rearing and education of girls and boys.

An alternative explanation may lie in personality dispositions. Feminine gender identity is characterized by traits such as expressiveness and emotionalism and a largely communal (other) orientation, while masculine gender identity is characterized by independence and activity and an agentic (self) orientation. It is possible that the intrinsic characteristics of the live performing arts hold more appeal for individuals of either sex who exhibit the cluster of traits measured by feminine gender identity scales. It means that rather than targeting women, organizations should target the personality characteristics that stimulate involvement in the arts, namely expressive and communal dispositions. It also means that persons with a strong masculine gender identity can be targeted by emphasizing the individuality that can be expressed through the arts, the athleticism of the dancers, or the fact that audience members can become involved with a theatrical production as they are with a sporting event.[8]

LIFESTYLE SEGMENTATION

Lifestyle measures are sometimes called *psychographics* to denote their combining of psychological with demographic measurements. Lifestyle has been identified as a better explanatory variable for arts attendance than any traditional socioeconomic characteristic, such as income or education. Lifestyle segmentation is also more dynamic than segmentation by personality. Whereas personality is seen to be an enduring, perhaps lifelong characteristic, lifestyle is more transient and is likely to change many times throughout one's lifetime. Lifestyle segmentation is based on the notion that we do what we do because it fits into the kind of life we are living or want to live.

There are several different approaches to identifying lifestyle groups, most of which are based on measures of consumers' activities, interests, and opinions (AIOs). Andreasen and Belk used information on the leisure-time activities of respondents in four southern cities to group potential attenders at symphonies and theater according to six broad categories. The six groups were labeled Passive Homebodies, Active Sports Enthusiasts, Inner-Directed Self-Sufficients, Active Homebodies, Culture Patrons, and Social Actives. The profiles of four of these groups are reported in Exhibit 5-1. The researchers found that membership in the Culture Patron lifestyle group was a very good predictor of attendance at theater and symphony, presumably because the aesthetic benefits of symphony performances fit their lifestyles. Membership in the Socially Active group predicted symphony attendance only, suggesting that it is the symphony performance *event* that meets the lifestyle needs of this group.

Another lifestyle scheme was developed in a study of the cultural market in Philadelphia. Five segments were identified (see Exhibit 5-2), each representing about one-fifth of cultural participants.[9] The most active cultural participants tended to be people who see themselves as sociable, who like to seek self-improvement and challenge, and who like to relax in their leisure-time activities. They place more importance on quality than on cost, they like to plan ahead, and they are confident by nature.

Exhibit 5-1	**ACTIVITIES AND INTERESTS OF LEISURE LIFESTYLE GROUPS**

Passive Homebodies

They agree with or do the following:

- Television is my primary source of entertainment (interest).
- I am a homebody (interest).
- I watch TV in order to relax quietly (interest).
- I would rather spend a quiet evening at home than go to a party (interest).

They disagree with or do not do the following:

- See a movie in a movie theater (activity).
- Go bowling (activity).
- Attend a sports event (activity).
- Work on an arts or crafts project (activity).
- Go out to dinner at a restaurant (activity).
- Play tennis (activity).

Active Sports Enthusiasts

They agree with or do the following:

- Go bowling (activity).
- Go to a sports event (activity).
- Play tennis (activity).
- See a movie in a movie theater (activity).
- I like to attend sporting events (interest).
- I can't see myself going to an opera (interest).

They disagree with or do not do the following:

- I would rather spend a quiet evening at home than go to a party (interest).
- Many of my friends are interested in theater and/or symphony concerts (interest).
- I usually know which symphony concerts and plays are being performed around here (interest).

Culture Patrons

They agree with or do the following:

- Went to a play, symphony orchestra concert, and visited an art gallery or museum in the last 12 months (activity).
- The arts are more important to me than to most other people (interest).

They disagree with or do not do the following:

- My major hobby is my family (interest).
- Television is my primary source of entertainment (interest).
- I watch TV to relax quietly (activity).
- If cultural organizations cannot pay their own way, they should go out of business (opinion).

Socially Actives

They agree with or do the following:

- Go to a meeting of a social or service club (activity).
- Give or attend a party (activity).
- Go on a picnic (activity).
- I usually know which plays are being performed around here (interest).

They disagree with or do not do the following:

- I'd rather read a good book than a newspaper (interest).
- I would rather spend a quiet evening at home than go to a party (interest).
- I can't see myself going to an opera (interest).
- I like to read nonfiction books (interest).
- I have less leisure time compared to other people I know (interest).

Source: Alan R. Andreasen and Russell W. Belk, "Consumer Response to Arts Offerings: A Study of Theater and Symphony in Four Southern Cities," in Edward McCracken, ed., *Research in the Arts* (Baltimore: Walters Art Gallery, 1979), 13–19.

Exhibit 5-2	**PHILADELPHIA'S CULTURAL MARKET**

Young Traditionalists

- Value traditional tastes and habits.
- Unlikely to be among the first to try something new.
- Usually in their 30s and 40s.
- Virtually all are married with minor children living at home.
- Likely to live in the suburbs well outside the city limits.
- Least likely of all cultural participants to be nonwhite.
- Many are homemakers; few are retirees.
- Report highest annual household earnings (63% earn $50,000 or more).
- Attend art museums, classical music, theater.
- Light cultural attendance in general.
- Make charitable contributions, but not to support the arts in particular.

Solid Supporters

- Likely to be subscribers or members of cultural institutions.
- Prefer a quiet, secure life and unlikely to follow styles and trends.
- Likely to be in 50s and 60s or older.
- Moderately high incomes (39% report annual household incomes of $50,000 or more).
- Higher proportion of men than most segments (although majority of individuals in all segments are women).
- Very frequent attendance at art museums, classical music, and theater; moderate attendance at several other disciplines.
- More likely than most segments to contribute to the performing arts.

Young Trendies

- Least likely of the segments to be subscribers or members.
- Most likely to take risks—to be first among their friends to see something new, to be willing to try anything once or to take chances, and to feel comfortable in unfamiliar situations.
- Tend to be in their 20s or 30s; 71% are single.
- Income is comparatively low, with only 21% reporting annual household income of $50,000 or more.
- Majority are women, but fairly high proportion of men.
- Most frequent attendees of art museums and new music.
- Moderately frequent attendance at many other disciplines, showing varied interests.
- Least likely among the segments to report a charitable contribution.

Exhibit 5-2	**PHILADELPHIA'S CULTURAL MARKET** *continued*

Homebodies

- Traditional; prefer quiet, secure life.
- Less willing to take chances or to try something new, and least likely to say they are comfortable in unfamiliar situations.
- Likely to be in 60s or older.
- Segment with highest proportions of retirees and persons of nonwhite ethnic origins.
- Report comparatively low income: 20% report household earnings of $50,000 or more.
- Report lowest overall attendance, but do attend theater with some frequency.
- Least likely segment to report visiting any kind of museum.
- Least likely segment to report giving to the visual arts, although their other giving is about average.

Confident Benefactors

- More likely than most to take chances, to feel at ease in most situations, and to be comfortable with the unfamiliar.
- Less likely to say they check prices of small items, to say they prefer a quiet, secure life, or to seek relaxing activities.
- Tend to be in their 50s and 60s.
- Mostly professional; some retirees.
- Report comparatively high incomes (56% report annual earnings of $50,000 or more).
- Report the most varied and the most frequent cultural attendance.
- Report the most charitable contributions and the most frequent incidence of gifts in excess of $100.

Source: Philadelphia Arts Market Study, prepared by Ziff Marketing, Inc. Commissioned by the Pew Charitable Trusts, 1989. Reprinted with permission.

From these descriptions, we can see how consumer lifestyles capture many influences—cultural, demographic, social, and family—that present opportunities for arts managers to create complementary situational influences.

USAGE SEGMENTATION

Very often, the best predictor of future behavior is past behavior. Consider the so-called 80–20 rule: that 80 percent of the purchases in a category are made by 20 percent of the potential consumer base. This group is usually referred to as *frequent* or *heavy users.* The remaining 80 percent are the *light users* and *nonusers.* Marketers know that it is much easier to stimulate increased attendance by current patrons than to attract those who never attend. Most marketing resources have been devoted to efforts to increase the frequency and variety of attendance among the culturally active segments of the population. In recent years, however, the culturally active group has become saturated, their participation has stagnated or slightly declined, and marketers are now enlarging their targets in efforts to increase audience size.

Frequent users, light users, and nonusers share common characteristics with other members of their category. To develop a profile of these three segments, the Cleveland Foundation and the Pew Charitable Trust in Philadelphia commissioned studies of their area populations. *Frequent users* were found to place a high value on leisure-time activities that spark the imagination or are new and different. They accept the arts as an important part of their lives, are predisposed toward active participation, and generally attend a variety of cultural events. For this group, satisfaction improves with more diversified use; the highest satisfaction levels are reported by those who attend six or more cultural organizations. They attach little importance to activities associated with performing arts events that allow them to see and meet other people. The only problems indicated by these frequent patrons are cost and convenience.

Light users are defined as those who attend one performing arts organization only, or who sporadically attend a few organizations. Cost, comfort, and convenience are central to their decision-making process. Meeting and seeing a variety of other people is also very important, as is self-improvement. *Nonusers* report that it is essential that their leisure-time activities be fun and entertaining, feel relaxed and informal, involve family and friends, and be convenient and inexpensive. They believe that cultural participation could involve family and friends, but few expect that a visit would be relaxed and informal, fun and entertaining, or inexpensive. (Interestingly, frequent users do tend to find performing arts attendance comfortable, relaxing, and enjoyable to share with friends. Performing arts managers can work to emphasize this perspective when reaching out to nonusers.)[10]

Nonparticipants surprisingly report fewer demands on their time than participants and do not feel that time constraints limit their participation in cultural activities. It was actually found that in almost every case, cultural participants engage in competing activities involving sports, television, or VCRs as much, if not more, than nonparticipants.

In these studies, nonparticipants are slightly older than participants and include more individuals in their 60s and 70s and fewer in their 30s. They report significantly lower annual earnings and are more likely than cultural participants to be married and have family responsibilities. Nonparticipants are also more likely to live in areas outside the city limits. However, distance does not appear to be a deterrent to attendance: nonparticipants are willing to travel about as long as participants are to reach activities of interest to them.

Most nonparticipants have consciously or unconsciously eliminated the arts as being of any possible interest or value in their lives. They have drawn a "cultural curtain" and have turned off to anything that is written or said about arts activities. Thus, converting nonparticipants will be difficult and will succeed gradually at best, because it often involves changing basic attitudes.[11]

However, Morison and Dalgleish believe that arts marketers have overfocused on regular attenders and should now explore innovative ways to communicate with more elements of society. They suggest that marketers turn their attention to attracting a group they call the "Maybes," who represent the greatest potential for future audience growth and development. The Maybes tend to be uncertain about whether or not the arts are important to them. Some Maybes are intimidated by what they perceive as the formality of performance halls and the crowds who gather there. They are also insecure as to whether they know enough to be able to appreciate the arts. They will try an arts event that appears accessible and unintimidating, and will continue to attend on occasion as long as their experiences are positive. According to Sidney Levy, marketers must address nonusers' inhibitions and stereotypes:

> Nonparticipants harbor many inhibiting images of the arts as relatively austere and effete, effeminate, esoteric, inaccessible, too demanding of study and concentration, arrogant, et cetera. Coping with these attitudes is not easy, but progress is made when experience shows the contrary or reorients the negative value. To bring about the experience, marketing usually recommends incentives, free samples, easy trial, and starting with examples that most contradict the opposed imagery. Personalities help in this endeavor—men ballet dancers who are masculine, such as Edward Vilella, and opera singers who are not foreign divas, such as Leontyne Price. English translations help, as in the television broadcast of Verdi's *Otello.*

The arts marketer should begin the process of attracting Maybes at a *point of entry,* a place that is familiar and accessible aesthetically and/or geographically to prospective patrons. Intermediate stages of commitment are developed through internal communications such as continuous direct mail, learning programs, promotions, and advertising. Development of commitment to the organization is arranged in progressive stages, providing people with the opportunity to learn about the art form and increase their commitment to the organization at a gradual pace. Rather than encouraging subscriptions from Maybes from the start, audience development should be a long-term process of encouraging and assisting an audience member to become increasingly more involved in the life of an arts institution. [12]

SEGMENTATION BY AESTHETICS

Aesthetic interest is a key factor in arts attendance. Some people perceive the arts to be hopelessly beyond them; they feel unequipped to participate, even to the point of hostility toward the arts. Others who feel alienated from the arts usually express flat disinterest, a lack of experience, or ignorance, or they may emphasize the esoteric nature of the arts.

Sidney Levy has observed, however, that many of these people have significant aesthetic interest that has found expression through other means. He identified specific aesthetic attributes and clustered them into six sets that he called factors.

Respondents were asked to complete the idea "The objects in my life should be . . ." by choosing words from the factor sets. The opposites to the words in each factor are in parentheses. Levy's findings, described below, are open to creative interpretation by arts marketers.

Factor I: *bold, exciting, thrilling, crowded, active (retiring, peaceful, soothing, alone, leisurely)*. Factor I suggests that people in general want stimulation, a feeling of liveliness, activity, movement, and excitement. Most respondents selected all five stimulation words, and almost three-fourths of the sample chose "bold" and "active." Men chose "thrilling" and "crowded" more often than women. Factor I was especially pronounced among younger people and was more important to middle-class people than to lower-class people.

Factor II: *familiar, real, symmetrical, matching (strange, fanciful, asymmetrical, contrasting)*. Factor II is the realism factor. The term "real" was selected by 86 percent of respondents and "familiar" by 79 percent, reflecting the fundamentally conservative or conventional orientation among this population. The realism factor is most strongly preferred among the lower class; the concepts of "strange" and "fanciful" are most acceptable to the young.

Factor III: *hard, sturdy, practical, technical, powerful, profitable (soft, delicate, decorative, emotional, graceful, social)*. Factor III suggests a conventional sex identity dimension, with traditional masculine characteristics opposed to traditional feminine characteristics. Responses were predictable by the gender of the participants, although there was a general tendency toward preferring the "sturdy" and "practical." There was a greater interest in "feminine" attributes among the upper middle class compared to the lower class.

Factor IV: *stage plays, curved, paintings (movies, angular, photographs)*. Factor IV may relate to the performing arts in general, and their open, life-like, human quality, compared with the stiffer, impersonal, canned character of photography. There is a strong preference for the "curved" rather than the "angular," which may relate to the three-dimensional rounded character of theater or the flowing character of painting. Movies were more frequently chosen by men, lower-class people, and young people. Legitimate theater had greater acceptance by higher-status people, women, and mature people.

Factor V: *sophisticated, outstanding, luxurious (sentimental, customary, comfortable)*. Factor V is oriented toward social status. Eighty-two percent of the respondents prefer "comfortable" to "luxurious" (at least *claiming* to be sensible in this regard), and would like things to be outstanding. The lower social classes were more oriented toward the "sentimental" and "customary."

Factor VI: *dramas, serious, dramatic, alone (musicals, funny, pretty, crowded)*. Factor VI deals with seriousness and frivolity. Women and young people are more inclined to prefer the "funny," the "pretty," the "crowded," the "soft," and "musicals." Men, older people, and upper-status people incline in the opposite direction.

This analysis indicates that attitudes and behavior toward the arts are derived from fundamental factors such as excitement, realism, sex identity, performance type preferences, social status, and seriousness. These factors offer clues to marketers as to what underlies the differences among individuals and groups regarding their aesthetic dispositions.[13]

BENEFIT SEGMENTATION

People often base their performing arts attendance decisions on anticipated benefits. *Quality buyers* seek out the best reputed offerings: critically acclaimed plays, performances by superstars, or works by renowned composers, playwrights, and choreographers. For them, cost is generally not a concern. *Service buyers* are sensitive to the services provided by the organization, such as ticket exchange privileges, a convenient location, adequate parking, or educational and social events to complement the performances. *Economy buyers* favor the least expensive offers such as the low-priced community orchestra, free concerts and plays in the park, and half-price tickets on the day of the performance. Benefit segmentation works best when people's benefit preferences are correlated with their demographic and media characteristics, making it easier to reach them efficiently.

OCCASIONS

Buyers can be distinguished according to the occasions when they develop a need, purchase a product, or use a product. For example, the "need" for attending a production of the *Nutcracker* may be triggered by the desire for holiday entertainment. The purchase decision may be triggered when out-of-town guests arrive or the children are on vacation from school. New occasions for use have been created by the New York Philharmonic and the Cleveland Ballet, which present hour-long rush hour performances to attract commuters. People may attend the arts to celebrate birthdays and anniversaries or to entertain clients and friends. Marketers should consider the many possible occasions when people might attend performances and create messages and incentives to promote attendance on those occasions.

LOYALTY STATUS

A market can be segmented by consumer loyalty status. Sometimes people are loyal to a specific type of offering and will attend musicals, Shakespeare plays, Beethoven symphonies, certain ethnic productions, or appearances by their favorite performers. Organizations that present specific repertoires, such as Shakespeare, classical ballet, or Baroque music, are likely to develop customer loyalty based on their offerings, as long as they maintain a satisfying level of quality and service. Some people may be loyal to an orchestra or theater to which they have subscribed for years, and will attend no matter what the production. Such organizations must develop customer loyalty to the organization itself by creating trust, interest, and even enthusiasm for productions that people would not be likely to see if they were not subscribers. Development and maintenance of customer loyalty will be discussed in Chapter 11.

BUYER READINESS STAGE

At any given time, people are in different stages of readiness to buy a product. Some people are unaware of the product; some are aware; some are informed; some are interested; some are desirous of buying; and some intend to buy. Their relative numbers make a big difference in how the marketing program should be designed. Suppose a dance company is performing in a city for the first time. The entire community will have to be made aware of the performances, and many people will have to be introduced to the company and its offerings. The thrust of the marketing effort should be awareness-building advertising using a simple message. If the community is already familiar with the company and has developed interest based on rave reviews, extensive publicity, and good word of mouth, advertising may focus on encouraging those who missed the company in previous years to attend. A popular company that tends to sell out quickly may publicize convenient locations for ticket purchase and encourage people to buy early. In general, the marketing program must be adjusted to the changing number of people in each stage of buyer readiness.

Criteria for Segmentation

From among the many segmentation possibilities, each organization must decide which approaches to segmentation would be the most useful for its own needs. Yet, any optimal segmentation scheme should possess the following characteristics:

- *Mutual exclusivity:* Each market segment should be conceptually separable from all other segments. Separating donors into present givers and past givers, for example, would be confusing for a respondent who is both a past and present giver.

- *Exhaustiveness:* Every potential target member should be placeable in some segment. If segmentation is done according to household status, there should be categories to cover relationships such as unmarried couples, single parents, empty nesters, communal-style livers, and so on.

- *Measurability:* In order for marketers to make appropriate targeting decisions and to track the effectiveness of their strategy, the size, purchasing power, and profile of the segments should be readily measurable. Certain segments, such as the gay and lesbian populations, are difficult to measure because some of their members do not wish to identify themselves publicly as such.

- *Substantiality:* Each segment should be substantial in that it has a large enough potential membership to be worth pursuing. For example, although single parents are a growing segment of the population, they are unlikely to be frequent performing arts attenders while they have children to care for. On the other hand, a divorced parent who has weekend custody of the children is an ideal target for family-oriented programs presented on Saturday and Sunday afternoons.

- *Actionability:* Actionability refers to the degree to which the segments can be effectively reached and served. For example, even if widows over 70 years of age were frequent theater attenders, there may be no efficient advertising medium for reaching them specifically. And even if an advertising medium were available, its cost may exceed the available budget.

By analyzing the attractiveness of each segment, managers can prepare to make the following strategic decisions:

- *Quantity decisions:* How much of the organization's financial and human resources (if any) are to be devoted to each segment?

- *Quality decisions:* How should each segment be approached in terms of specific product offerings, communications, place of offering, prices, and the like?

- *Timing decisions:* When should specific marketing efforts be directed at particular segments?

Assume that a dance company wants to attract men and women, using different ads and appeals. The marketer knows that women primarily enjoy the grace, beauty, and creativity of the dancers, and that men respond most strongly to their athleticism. A single ad that tried to combine the two approaches could result in a confusing message, so the more "graceful" ad could be placed in the lifestyles section of the newspaper, and the more "athletic" ad could be placed in the sports section. The dance marketer might find that the added cost of placing two such ads is more than covered by the additional audience members the performances attract.

TARGETING

Having evaluated a variety of market segments, an organization hopes to find one or more segments worth entering. The decision of which and how many segments to serve is the problem of *target market selection.* A target market consists of a set of buyers, having common needs or characteristics, that the organization decides to serve. Before selecting target segments, an organization should learn as much as possible about each segment under consideration to determine whether and how it can meet that segment's needs, interests, and desires. For example, consider the following discussion of baby boomers as potential performing arts attenders.

TARGETING BABY BOOMERS

Baby boomers grew up during the years when their parents' generation was fueling the arts boom of the 1970s. Totaling 76 million, they make up nearly half of all adult Americans. One would assume that due to their sheer numbers and to the arts socialization they received as children (music lessons, trips to museums and theater), baby boomers would be major participants in the arts as adults. However, the decline in total arts audiences since 1984 has been attributed largely to the fact that the participation rates of boomers is lower than that of the older generations. Compared to their elders, baby boomers attend art museums and jazz concerts more often, and listen more often to classical radio. However, they participate less in symphony, opera, musicals, serious theater, and even modern dance. For young adults with little leisure time and disposable income, and often with a child or two, museums are like shopping malls in terms of ease, cost, and timing of access. Museum visits need not be planned or paid for in advance. The context of jazz also permits casual and spontaneous attendance, fitting in with baby boomers' lifestyle demands.

Although baby boomers are unlikely to become subscribers to any one performing arts organization, they may find a united arts membership appealing. Several arts organizations may collaborate to create joint subscriptions in which one modest fee generates discounts and other benefits at each participating organization. A central box office can provide extensive information about each member organization's offering, deep discounts the day of performance, and coordinated educational efforts. Short-term arts festivals and weekend afternoon concerts with concurrent chaperoned programming for children may also appeal to this segment.

Of course, baby boomers represent a broad spectrum of demographic and psychographic characteristics, and marketers can discover additional opportunities by segmenting this group further according to benefits sought, occasions for use, and other variables.[14]

Patterns of Target Market Selection

Various patterns of target market selection may be considered by an organization: single-segment concentration, product specialization, and selective specialization.

SINGLE-SEGMENT CONCENTRATION

An organization such as a children's theater, a Yiddish theater, or a theater that produces plays for, by, and about gays, African Americans, or any other specific group, is basically a single-segment provider. Through concentrated marketing, the organization is likely to achieve a strong market profile owing to its greater knowledge of the segment's needs and the special reputation it builds. However, concentrated marketing carries high risks. The particular segment may withdraw its support for a variety of reasons, or a competitor may decide to pursue the same market segment. When an organization is a single-segment specialist, it should focus its efforts on penetrating that segment as deeply as possible.

AN UNINTENTIONAL SINGLE- SEGMENT ORGANIZATION	The board of directors of a small chamber music society in a wealthy, quiet, suburban neighborhood became increasingly concerned about the fact that their audience consisted almost exclusively of gray- and white-haired people and that, over the years, few new or younger people had attended. They engaged the services of a marketing consultant to determine ways to attract younger patrons. The consultant recommended that the society (1) change the timing of its programs from Sunday afternoons, which is normally a family time, to an evening when baby-sitters are readily available; (2) change the name of the organization to eliminate the elitist term "society"; (3) add some adventuresome music to the currently traditional programming; and (4) present some performances in areas where younger people work and reside.
	The board members were unwilling to adopt any of these suggestions, since they felt such changes would drastically contrast with their own vision of the organization. So, understanding and accepting their now more clearly defined direction, they developed strategies for enlarging their current market. Within three years, the audience—which remained quite homogeneous —doubled in size.

PRODUCT SPECIALIZATION

A Shakespeare festival, an early music group, and a Brazilian dance company each concentrate on a specific product that appeals to certain market segments. This strategy creates a strong identity and a potentially loyal following among those who have a particular interest in the offering. The downside is that if demand for the product slackens, the organization may be poorly equipped to alter its offerings. Some organizations enhance their specialized product with complementary offerings that add interest and variety to the experience. Music of the Baroque performs in several Chicago-area churches, allowing patrons to experience Baroque music in varied theme-appropriate and charming settings throughout the season. Consider how a small town in Austria capitalized on having been Haydn's home.

101 INTERESTING THINGS TO DO WITH HAYDN

Every year, Eisenstadt, a small Austrian town on the Hungarian border that has the distinction of having been home to Haydn during some of his most creative years, is host to the Haydntage, a two-week festival of Haydn's music. The Haydntage has an interested and loyal audience, many of whom return annually for an average stay of seven days. Tickets for the festival sold out for the four consecutive years from 1989 through 1992. The festival has gained a reputation as a dynamic organization promoting not only the full scope of Haydn's music, but the town as well. Daytime concerts are offered as part of tours around Eisenstadt that go from one "Haydn-venue" to the next. A "magical mystery tour" includes a trip to a castle in Hungary where a concert is given. Under the theme "hunting and wine," visitors are taken to the hunting park outside Eisenstadt, where Haydn performed, and to the Fischerkirche in Rust, famous for its wine. Concerts of music with hunting and wine themes are performed in both locations.

To reach out to new, international audiences, managers have been inviting journalists from abroad to visit the festival. This strategy has been very successful. For example, one article about the festival in the Italian newspaper *La Republica* stimulated six hundred individual responses.[15]

SELECTIVE SPECIALIZATION

Most commonly, arts organizations select a number of segments, each of which is attractive and matches the organization's objectives and resources. The strategy of multisegment coverage has the advantage of attracting a broader base of the art-going public and of diversifying the organization's risk. For example, if a large proportion of a theater's yuppie audience members begin to have children and focus on more home-centered activities, the theater can continue to attract an older (or younger) audience that has more discretionary time. Arts organizations should study trends and environmental factors that signal opportunities for targeting new segments or for concentrating their efforts on building certain current segments.

The following examples of audience-building efforts represent some creative and effective targeting strategies being undertaken by arts organizations.

TARGETING PEOPLE WITH DISABILITIES

In 1990, President Bush signed the Americans with Disabilities Act (ADA), which established accessibility requirements for the private and nonprofit sectors. Although these requirements create some financial, structural, and spatial stress for organizations, some arts professionals insist that the ADA can be turned to an organization's advantage. Instead of viewing the disabled community as adversaries, some organizations are recognizing the opportunities inherent in targeting people with disabilities as potentially viable customers.

When a fire severely damaged the Mill Playhouse in Mulburn, New Jersey, in 1980, rebuilding was done with accessibility in mind. Elevators go to every level of the theater, and the box office has a special Dutch door that opens at wheelchair height so a customer in a wheelchair doesn't need a periscope to buy tickets. Two performances of each production are sign interpreted and three feature audio description—a live play-by-play account of what's happening onstage for visually impaired theatergoers. Corporations have been happy to underwrite the cost of the audio descriptions and the sign interpretation programs. Pretheater workshops are offered that allow blind people to touch the props and costumes. All staff members undergo sensitivity training to help them serve the needs of people with disabilities.

The result is a new audience that is growing every year. The theater has found that disabled people often attend with companions who themselves have never been patrons in the past. Another benefit is that older theatergoers are pleased to be offered ramps instead of stairs, large-print programs, and audio enhancement systems.[16]

Other theaters are developing similar programs. The Apple Tree Theatre in Highland Park, Illinois, has raised the height of its first row of seats so that wheelchairs may be conveniently set along the front. There are also plans to install removable seats so that patrons using wheelchairs can sit next to their companions.

TARGETING THE GAY AND LESBIAN COMMUNITY

In an article headlined "Anyone Not Advertising to an Audience This Big, This Affluent, This Influential, Just Isn't Thinking Straight," *Advertising Age* magazine reported that gays and lesbians are estimated to represent 10 percent of the U.S. population and to have a combined annual income of $514 billion.[17] Furthermore, compared to the average American consumer, gay men and lesbians are 5.6 times more likely to have traveled to Europe in the past three years, 6.5 times more likely to buy at least ten hardcover books per year, and 10 times more likely to buy 13 or more compact discs per year.

Based on these statistics, and in accord with its mission to "reach out into the many-faceted populations of Texas," the Austin Lyric Opera decided to target the estimated 50,000 gays and lesbians in its community. The statewide weekly gay publication, the *Texas Triangle,* which had demonstrated a strong dedication to journalistic integrity and provided effective editorial coverage of politics, business, arts and leisure, sports and community events, was a logical and willing sponsor for the opera's upcoming gay and lesbian event. The *Triangle*'s publishers and, through their contacts, other prominent gay men and women joined a steering committee to develop the event, which was named "Triangle on Stage." The committee identified gay-owned businesses as potential sponsors for graphic design, printing, flowers, food, and entertainment. The event itself was simple: the gay community was invited to purchase tickets for the final performance of *The Abduction from the Seraglio,* followed by a backstage tour and champagne reception. The event was promoted through four weeks of free ads and editorial promotions in the *Triangle,* invitations were mailed to the Octopus Club, a mailing list used for AIDS-related fund-raising in the gay and lesbian community, and press releases were sent to a national gay media list from the *Triangle.*

The "Triangle on Stage" event attracted about a hundred guests, including a state legislator, journalists from the mainstream press, and several cast members. The steering committee planned to offer similar free promotions targeted to gays and lesbians as a subscriber benefit for the following season. Guests and even current Austin Lyric Opera subscribers expressed their sense of unity and pride in the company's recognition of the gay and lesbian community, showing that not only box office success but more intangible assets contribute to a company's worth and image.[18]

Choosing among Market Selection Strategies

The actual choice of target markets depends on specific factors facing the organization. The more limited the organization's resources, the more likely it is to concentrate on a few segments. The more homogeneous the market, the less the organization needs to differentiate its offerings. If competitors have already captured certain segments, the organization will need to identify other segments to enter.

Each organization has to evaluate the best segment(s) to serve in terms of its relative attractiveness, the requirements for success within the segment, and the organization's strengths and weaknesses in competing effectively. The organization should focus on market segments that it has a differential advantage in serving.

POSITIONING

Once an organization has segmented the population and selected viable target market segments, it will want to promote the aspects of the organization's offerings that appeal most strongly to its target market. This is the process of developing a focused positioning strategy. We define *positioning* as the act of designing the organization's image and offer so that it occupies a distinct and valued place in the target customers' minds. Positioning involves (1) creating a real differentiation and (2) making it known to others.

The specific positioning the organization undertakes will depend largely on its analysis of its targeted market segments, its own strengths and weaknesses, and its competition. Many organizations will develop a "niche" or specialty. An organization can specialize according to customer, product, or marketing-mix (product, price, place, promotion) variables. A children's theater is a customer specialist, creating offerings for children. A Shakespeare company is a product specialist. A free community orchestra is a price specialist, while its high-priced competitor, the city's symphony orchestra, is a quality specialist. The Stratford Festival in Ontario, Canada, is a place or geographic specialist, in that an entire community of hotels, restaurants, and shops has been developed to serve tourists who vacation in Stratford to attend the performances.

The advantage of defining a position in a target market is that it almost dictates the appropriate mix of marketing strategies. If an arts organization adopts a "high-quality" positioning, then its programs should be of uniformly high quality, its prices should be above average, it should have high-quality facilities, and it should advertise in the best media. If any element is lacking, the desired marketing outcome may be sabotaged. A high-quality position can be undermined by seemingly minor factors such as low-quality stationery, hand-lettered signage, or inarticulate contact personnel. Conversely, an organization seeking contributions to correct a budget deficit should indicate frugality by using inexpensive mailers and conveying a no-frills attitude.

Some organizations prefer to leave their position less well defined in the hope of attracting more disparate market segments. Although such an approach might succeed on occasion, especially when there is little competition, it is our view that the organization that establishes a distinct identity increases its chances to survive and prosper in the long run. Other common positioning errors that managers should avoid are (1) entering a crowded marketplace, that is, taking a position that is already held by other organizations, thereby gaining no distinctiveness; (2) focusing on an unimportant attribute, that is, a factor that is of relatively little importance to the target audience; and (3) myopic positioning, that is, focusing more on the seller's offer than on what the consumer wants. Positioning, then, is a matter of both substance and perception. The organization must truly have a set of offerings that differentiates it from the competition and that gives it a clear identity in the mind of the consumer.

According to advertising executives Al Ries and Jack Trout, positioning *starts* with a product. But positioning is not what you do to a product, it is what you do to the mind of the prospect.[19] Thus a children's theater may choose to position itself as an educational experience or an entertainment experience in trying to attract an audience. Or consider what the Atlanta Ballet did to reposition its place in the minds of its potential audiences.

POSITIONING THE ATLANTA BALLET

The Atlanta Ballet Company, which had always attracted a traditional ballet-going audience, was seeking to attract a broader audience. The ad agency of Ogilvy and Mather donated time to the company to help shed light on how people viewed the ballet and to help the company reposition its message. At the time, the ballet's principal direct-mail subscription solicitation depicted a cutesy *Nutcracker* toy drum major assuring the reader, "I never met a subscriber I didn't like." This message clearly had nothing to do with artistic director Robert Barnett's approach to dance, or with the needs of prospective season-ticket buyers.

After conducting research, Ogilvy and Mather recommended the following: "The Atlanta Ballet should focus on its entertainment appeal. We want to make Atlanta Ballet fans of people who may never have seen a dance performance—people who have the money and the interest to discover new kinds of entertainment. Our positioning should be: The Atlanta Ballet is entertainment everyone can enjoy."

By the following season, the company's theme had become "What makes the Atlanta Ballet the most exciting show in town? It's athletic! funny! sensuous! chilling! The Atlanta Ballet is different." In response to this campaign, the subscription audience quickly doubled. The new language worked because it changed Atlanta's *perception* of what was already on stage. This was not an attempt to turn the company into the Rockettes, to alter or misrepresent the product. Rather, it addressed the company's eclectic repertoire and artistic director Bobby Barnett's perspective on dance, while positioning the company in the marketplace aggressively and distinctively.[20]

Positioning Strategies

Clearly, every product and/or organization needs a focused positioning strategy so that its intended place in the total market—and in the consumer's mind—is clearly reflected in its communications. The strategy requires coordinating all the attributes of the marketing mix to support the chosen position. Some alternative bases for constructing a positioning strategy are listed and illustrated here.[21]

POSITIONING ON SPECIFIC PRODUCT FEATURES

A theater may position itself as presenting the classics. The fact that a play has endured for decades or even centuries indirectly implies a benefit, namely a highly satisfying, high-quality theatergoing experience.

POSITIONING ON BENEFITS, PROBLEM SOLUTION, OR NEEDS

The Atlanta Ballet's new position focuses on the benefits the consumer will receive by attending, namely having an "exciting, fun, sensuous, chilling" experience. It is extremely useful for marketers to understand in detail the needs of each of their target markets and the benefits sought by each.

POSITIONING FOR SPECIFIC USAGE OCCASIONS

The New York Philharmonic's Rush Hour Concerts are positioned for commuters who can attend a concert after work, avoid traffic, and still have an evening at home. Similarly, the orchestra's casual Saturday afternoon hour-long concerts are positioned to appeal to families, shoppers, and anyone who would like to enjoy a concert as just one part of their afternoon in Manhattan.

POSITIONING FOR USER CATEGORY

The Arena Stage in Washington, D.C., promotes its Gay and Lesbian Series as its most successful event series. The series, which is offered on select Friday evenings, is positioned as "an alternative to the bar scene, a great way to meet others who share your love of the theater." After the show, a special reception is offered with food, drink, and conversation and is attended by members of the cast and guest speakers.

POSITIONING AGAINST OR ASSOCIATING WITH ANOTHER PRODUCT

By claiming it is "different, athletic, and funny," the Atlanta Ballet is differentiating itself from other ballet companies, or as different from what people *expect* ballet companies to be like. It is also associating itself with other leisure pursuits that people tend to consider more entertaining. Such association can strengthen the product's position in the mind of consumers. Say Ries and Trout, "The basic approach of positioning is not to create something new and different, but to manipulate what's already up there in the mind, to retie the connections that already exist."[22] For example, "You won't find an 'uncola' idea inside a 7-Up can. You find it inside the cola drinker's head." Based on this concept, "beautiful-music" radio station WLKW in Providence, Rhode Island, transformed itself from an also-ran station to number one with the theme "WLKW, the unrock station."[23]

POSITIONING AS NUMBER ONE

People tend to remember *number one* and to value it much more highly than any other offering or person that may be a close runner-up. For example, when asked, "Who was the first person to successfully fly alone across the Atlantic Ocean?" we will answer "Charles Lindbergh." When asked, "Who was the second person to do it?" we draw a blank. This is why managers fight for their organizations, productions, and performers to have the number-one position, either as the "largest" or "oldest" or "most famous." Such a position can be held by only one organization, production, or person. What counts is to achieve it with respect to *some* valued attribute. Thus the Ravinia Festival positions itself as the most delightful spot for a concert.

THE EXCLUSIVE CLUB STRATEGY

Sometimes a number-one position in terms of a meaningful attribute cannot be achieved, or it may otherwise benefit an organization to associate with other organizations of its kind. For example, the Lyric Opera Company of Chicago emphasizes the level of its quality by quoting, on the cover of its season brochure, a critic's comment that it is "one of the world's greatest opera companies."

In general, positioning must be done with a particular target group in mind. The more the performing arts organization knows about its target audience, the more effective it can be in positioning itself.

Repositioning

When an organization wishes to change the way it is perceived in the marketplace, it can reposition its offerings in a variety of ways—from altering its basic, core product; to changing the way the product is packaged, priced, or promoted; to simply changing the way the product is *presented* to the public.

An extreme example of presenting the product in a new "package" occurred when the Denver Symphony Orchestra, which had declared bankruptcy and closed its doors, was brought back by rock promoter Barry Fey under the new name of the Colorado Symphony with rock-and-roll-style glitz and promotions. On one occasion, the orchestra played to 12,000 screaming fans at Denver's McNichols basketball arena; on another occasion they performed with strobe lights flashing. One advertising campaign featured the entire orchestra glowing in the dark with the theme "Turning up the power." The next season, ticket sales rose by 34 percent, the orchestra's financial statements went into the black, and the average age of the patrons dropped from 58 to 42. The Atlanta Ballet's new promotional campaigns, described earlier, illustrate repositioning based purely on changing customer perceptions about the organization.

As another illustration, consider the positioning changes undertaken by Chamber Music Chicago.

32-YEAR-OLD ARTS PRESENTER ANNOUNCES CHANGE OF NAME AND INSTITUTIONAL FOCUS

During the decade from 1982 to 1992, Chamber Music Chicago underwent a major transformation. As a result of market segment research undertaken to learn how to attract a wider range of ethnic groups, the organization broadened its concept of chamber music by including a wide variety of ethnocentric forms of music, extending far beyond the traditional Eurocentric chamber performances. This approach brought new audiences into the organization's performing spaces, brought its performances into ethnic neighborhoods, and stimulated the formation of collaborative efforts with such organizations as the Mexican Fine Arts Center.

To reflect this change in philosophy, as well as the diversification that has occurred in its own programming and audience base, Chamber Music Chicago changed its name in 1992 to Performing Arts Chicago (PAC). This positioning change has opened up many new opportunities for the organization. While chamber music remains an integral part of the programming, other programming is now receiving equal recognition and importance. New programs include performance art, dance theater, modern opera, and a series called *dejAvant*. The name combines *deja vu*—a haunting sense of the past—with *avant-garde*—that which is new and challenging. These new programs and their quality, innovativeness, and variety have greatly increased PAC's prestige and profile in the community and have further enlarged the size and diversity of the audience base.[24]

The starting point for any repositioning strategy is developing an understanding of how the organization is perceived by its current or potential audience. This process involves measuring the organization's image, which is the sum of beliefs, ideas, and impressions people have of its offerings.

An image differs from a stereotype. A stereotype suggests a widely held image that is highly distorted and simplistic and that is associated with a favorable or unfavorable attitude toward the object. An image, on the other hand, is a more personal perception of an object that can vary from person to person. Many methods have been proposed for measuring images. We will describe a two-step approach: first, measuring how familiar and favorable the organization's image is, and second, measuring the organization's image along major relevant dimensions.

The first step in obtaining the familiarity-favorability measurement is to establish, for each public being studied, how familiar its members are with the organization and how favorable they feel toward it. To establish familiarity, respondents are asked to describe their familiarity with the organization by circling one of the following:

| Never heard of | Heard of | Know a little bit | Know a fair amount | Know very well |

If most of the respondents place the organization in the first two or three categories, then the organization has an awareness problem.

Those respondents who have some familiarity with the organization are then asked to describe how favorable they feel toward it by circling one of the following:

| Very unfavorable | Somewhat unfavorable | Indifferent | Somewhat favorable | Very favorable |

If most of the respondents check the first two or three categories, then the organization needs to repair its image.

Knowing levels of familiarity and favorability is not enough. The organization must go further and research the *content* of its image. One of the most popular tools for this assessment is the *semantic differential.*[25] It involves identifying a set of relevant dimensions for the organization. People are asked, "What do you think of when you consider a theater?" If someone suggests "quality of the performances," this dimension is turned into a bipolar adjective scale—perhaps with "high-quality performance" at one end of the scale and "low-quality performance" at the other end. This can be rendered as a five- or seven-point scale. The total number of scales should be kept small to avoid respondent fatigue. Three types of scales may be used: (1) evaluation scales (good-bad qualities), (2) potency scales (strong-weak qualities), and (3) activity scales (active-passive qualities). An example of a semantic differential scale for a theater is shown in Figure 5-2.

Figure 5-2

IMAGES OF A THEATER COMPANY (SEMANTIC DIFFERENTIAL)

superior-quality performances •——•——•——•——•——• inferior-quality performances

specialized offerings •——•——•——•——•——• broad-spectrum offerings

high ticket prices •——•——•——•——•——• low ticket prices

accessible programming •——•——•——•——•——• limited-appeal programming

customer-oriented service •——•——•——•——•——• inadequate service

highly entertaining experience •——•——•——•——•——• boring experience

popular, well-known company •——•——•——•——•——• unpopular, not well known

Image analysis may be used by an organization for several purposes, as described in the following paragraphs.

To compare before and after. For example, an organization discovers that the audience views it as providing inadequate customer service. Resources are dedicated to improving service and, the following year, another image survey is administered to track progress in this area.

To compare the perceptions of different segments. An organization may discover that highly educated audience members like the programming, but less educated audience members find it boring. Arts managers can use this information to prioritize target markets for future growth or to make changes that will broaden the program's appeal.

To compare the image of two or more competitors. Arts managers can ask respondents to rate the strengths and weaknesses of the organization along with those of its close competitors. This will help the organization decide where to direct its resources.

In order for an arts organization to do a good job of segmenting, targeting, and positioning, it must have knowledge of the methods and tools available for conducting research among current and potential audience members. That is the subject of the next chapter.

[1] Donald Michaelis, *Divergent Views on Promoting the Performing Arts* (New York: ACUAA, 1976).

[2] Sid Smith, "Courting Gays," *Chicago Tribune,* July 4, 1993, sec. 13, p. 10.

[3] Mike Farish, "A Place in the Sun," *International Arts Manager,* Jan. 1993, 41.

[4] *Public Relations Journal,* Feb. 1992.

[5] Farish, "A Place in the Sun," 42.

[6] "PRIZM: The Next Generation," Claritas, Inc., Seminar Series 1994 (duplicated).

[7] Michael J. Weiss, *The Clustering of America* (New York: Harper & Row, 1988), 2, 15.

[8] Brenda Gainer, "The Impact of Gender on Marketing the Arts," *Proceedings,* Second International Conference on Arts Management, Groupe HEC, Jouy en Josas, France, June 23–25, 1993.

[9] Philadelphia Arts Market Study, prepared by Ziff Marketing, Inc., commissioned by the Pew Charitable Trusts, 1989.

[10] "Marketing the Arts in Cleveland: An In-Depth Survey," conducted by Ziff Marketing, Inc., and Clark, Martire & Bartolomeo, Inc., commissioned by the Cleveland Foundation, 1985.

[11] Bradley Morison and Julie Dalgleish, *Waiting in the Wings* (New York: American Council for the Arts, New York, 1987).

[12] Morison and Dalgleish, *Waiting in the Wings.*

[13] Sidney J. Levy, "Arts Consumers and Aesthetic Attributes," in *Marketing the Arts,* ed. Michael P. Mokwa, William M. Dawson, E. Arthur Prieve (New York: Praeger, 1980).

[14] Judith Huggins Balfe, "The Baby-Boom Generation: Lost Patrons, Lost Audience?" in *The Cost of Culture,* ed. Margaret Jane Wyszomirski and Pat Clubb (New York: American Council for the Arts, 1989), 9–21.

[15] "Haydn, Hunting, and Wine," *International Arts Manager,* Oct. 1992, 19–22.

[16] Heidi Waleson, "Audiences with Disabilities Act," *International Arts Manager,* June 1993, 21–22.

[17] *Advertising Age,* Jan. 1993.

[18] Revah Anzaldua, "Testing the Waters of the Gay Market," *Arts Reach,* April/May 1993, 2–13.

[19] Al Ries and Jack Trout, *Positioning: The Battle for Your Mind* (New York: McGraw-Hill, 1986), 34.

[20] William Rudman, *Market The Arts!* (New York: Foundation for the Extension and Development of the American Professional Theatre, 1983), 165.

[21] Yoram J. Wind, *Product Policy: Concepts, Methods, and Strategy* (Reading, Mass: Addison-Wesley, 1982), 79–81; Ries and Trout, *Positioning.*

[22] Ries and Trout, *Positioning,* 5.

[23] Ibid., 34.

[24] Performing Arts Chicago, press release, March 2, 1992.

[25] C. E. Osgood, G. J. Suci, and P. H. Tannenbaum, *The Measurement of Meaning* (Urbana: University of Illinois Press, 1957).

▲●▲

DETERMINING MARKET SIZE AND DESIRES: MARKETING RESEARCH

Historically, managers have devoted most of their attention to managing their products, their money, and their people, while paying less attention to another of the organization's critical resources: information. In recent years, the emergence of sophisticated information technologies, such as computer databases and fax machines, has revolutionized information handling and has made it accessible to the smallest organizations.

In the 1990s, the need for marketing research information is greater than any time in the past. First, as marketing segmentation strategies become more sophisticated and segments become smaller and smaller, organizations need to learn more about the needs and wants of their various target markets. Second, as consumers have become more selective and demanding in their buying behavior, sellers find it harder to predict buyers' responses to different features, benefits, packaging options, and other attributes unless they turn to marketing research. Third, as price becomes a less important variable to many consumers, sellers require more information on the effective use of such marketing tools as advertising, public relations, product differentiation and positioning, and other product features.

Marketing research plays a critical role in understanding customer attitudes and behavior and in planning marketing strategy. What distinguishes marketing research from simple observation is that it is planned and is tied to specific decision-making situations. We define *marketing research* as the systematic design, collection, analysis, and reporting of data and findings relevant to a specific marketing situation facing the organization.

Although marketing research can benefit performing arts organizations, its use is not widespread. Performing arts organizations have limited budgets and assign higher priority to other expenditures. Marketers' knowledge of the correct use of marketing research and its technical aspects is limited. And artistic directors often resist the use of marketing research findings to influence their decision making. In the following paragraphs we refute these reasons for resistance to marketing research.

Costs of marketing research. Marketing research need not be expensive. There are low-cost forms of marketing research, such as systematic observation and use of focus groups. Much can be learned from just listening to audience comments during intermission or inviting audiences to stay after performances to discuss their reactions. And focus group discussions with eight to twelve participants can yield rich data, often for only the cost of offering complimentary tickets. Another low-cost method is the analysis of currently available information, such as ticket sales, by production, performer, time of year, day of week, time of day, or by audience segment. Even when higher levels of sophistication are needed, such as when careful field study projects are being planned, arts organizations can get low-cost assistance from marketing students and professors. Also, arts organizations can invite marketing research professionals to sit on their boards of directors.

Once managers begin to realize the benefits gained by regularly administered, well-planned and -executed marketing research, they will not only value but come to depend on the process, and they will provide for it in their budget allocations. And when a specific decision is important enough, significant expenditure for research is well justified.

Technical knowledge. Arts marketers planning to undertake research programs should acquaint themselves with the various approaches to marketing research, the marketing research process, and the rudimentary principles of probability sampling, questionnaire design, and interpretation of results. But arts marketers need not be focus group leaders, survey designers, statisticians, or computer experts. They should be familiar enough with market research methods and processes to facilitate communication with the researcher and to guarantee that the organization's research needs are fulfilled.

Resistance by artistic decision makers. There is concern among some managers and artistic directors that applying marketing research results will compromise the artistic mission and integrity of the organization. A music director might fear that the audience will favor eliminating slow movements from symphonies (too boring) and abandoning twentieth-century music (too dissonant).

These artistic directors are missing an opportunity to use market research information to their advantage.[2] For example, managers could identify opportunities to repackage the programs they are already providing. Based on consumer feedback, the Vancouver Symphony developed a "Great Composers" series and placed its more adventuresome programming in other concerts. This allowed for a more focused choice on the part of the patrons, and therefore, greater satisfaction among both the more traditional music lovers and those who prefer the new and different.

THE SCOPE AND USES OF MARKETING RESEARCH

Marketing research aims to help managers make better decisions, including such decisions as whether to move a theater to a new location, to add a new subscription series, or to develop a marketing plan for a new target group; where to place advertising; how to adjust pricing structures; or which customer service components should be improved. Consider the following examples.

- The Ballet Foundation of Milwaukee surveyed ballet patrons to determine their media usage patterns.
- The Atlanta Ballet added a highly successful Sunday-afternoon series based on audience surveys.
- The Actors' Theatre of St. Paul polled both patrons and nonpatrons to assess their attitudes toward a physical relocation.
- The Network surveyed the executive directors of Minneapolis performing arts organizations to determine their perception of its services.
- Telemarketers at the Chicago Symphony Orchestra gathered data on the preferences of buyers of multiple single tickets in order to offer custom-designed three-concert subscriptions.

In the following example, marketing research helped the American Conservatory Theatre (ACT) in San Francisco to make a pricing decision.

25¢ BROCHURES AT THE AMERICAN CONSERVATORY THEATRE?

The American Conservatory Theatre (ACT) used to distribute a glossy, lavish program produced by a commercial publisher for the use of all theaters in the San Francisco area. It included a few pages about ACT and its current production, but also described other cultural events in and around San Francisco. The costs of this brochure were increasing, and ACT found that the only way it could afford to continue distributing it would be to charge 25¢ a copy.

So ACT surveyed its subscribers and asked them whether they wanted to pay 25¢ a copy or whether they preferred a free, but much less elaborate, brochure created at ACT. Despite the $50-plus cost of a subscription, 80 percent of the respondents said "no" to the 25¢ charge. Maybe they just didn't want to be bothered searching for a quarter when they got to the theater. Maybe they were voting their support for the theater's frugality and attention to buying quality where it counts. Consequently, ACT canceled its contract with the printer and began to produce less elaborate programs—with the added benefit of being able to include more organization-specific information.

Uses of Marketing Research

By using the various tools available to market researchers, arts organizations can carry on a range of studies, which generally have one of three purposes: description, explanation, or prediction.

DESCRIPTION

Marketing research can be designed to tell management what the marketing environment is like: how many people from which demographic and psychographic profiles attend each performance, where they heard about the production, how frequently single-ticket buyers attend, what product features they prefer, and so on. Descriptive data usually serve management decisions in three ways: (1) by monitoring sales performance to indicate whether strategy changes are needed, (2) by describing consumers to inform segmentation decisions, and (3) by serving as the basis for more sophisticated analysis.

EXPLANATION

Usually a manager wants to understand the forces that lie behind the descriptive findings. The simplest level of explanation is to discover what seems to be *associated* with what. A manager may use research to help identify some common socioeconomic, demographic, or lifestyle characteristics of the people who allowed their subscriptions to lapse in the past year. The findings would help management develop stronger appeals to the lapsing audience. The next level of explanation is *causation.* For example, management may think that lapsed subscribers were dissatisfied with the programming, but research may reveal that lapsing subscribers were primarily unhappy with their seat locations. The ultimate level of explanation is to know not only that A caused B, but *why* A caused B. Suppose many of the nonrenewing subscribers asked for better seats, but their requests were ignored. Management can then attempt to reattract them with even better seats than those they had previously requested. In the future, a personal contact explaining why a particular request cannot be met may serve to appease subscribers who might otherwise become displeased with the organization. Management must often dig for deeper explanations if research is to lead to the right decisions and actions.

PREDICTION

Descriptions or explanations can prove more useful if they lead to predictions. Suppose management is willing to lower the price of subscriptions by x dollars for seats that have poor visibility. It would be useful to predict how many more subscriptions will be purchased and/or retained and how this will affect revenue and costs. Consider the situation at Centre East Theatre that created a critical need for extensive and in-depth market research.

CENTRE EAST'S STRATEGIC DILEMMA	While many other area theaters have been struggling for their very survival, Centre East in Skokie, Illinois, just north of Chicago, has been able to keep its head above water financially while earning a remarkable 90 percent of its revenues from ticket sales and rental income. (On average, nonprofit performing arts organizations earn 50 percent of their income; the remaining 50 percent comes from grants and donations.)

The keys to Centre East's success have been its entertaining and diverse offerings of performances for adults, families, and children, and its ability to garner $250,000 annually in rental income for its 1,310-seat theater.

Now Centre East faces a loss of much of its earned income. Having lost its current space to the expansion and renovation of the college where the hall is situated, Centre East will occupy Skokie's soon-to-be-built North Shore Center for the Performing Arts. This new center features an 800-seat theater, meaning that Centre East faces a 40 percent drop in seating capacity, which will have a severe impact on ticket revenue. And the North Shore Center management will control all rentals, so Centre East faces the loss of rental income as well. In order to survive, Centre East must adjust its programming, pricing, and operating policies.

With these issues in mind and with a grant from the Illinois Arts Council, Centre East commissioned a marketing consultant to oversee a comprehensive market research study.[3] The goal was to determine what direction future Centre East programming should take in order to remain as successful in the new North Shore Center as it has been since its inception fifteen years ago.

APPROACHES TO MARKETING RESEARCH

Data Sources

Central to the marketing research process is data collection. Two broad categories of data may be gathered: *secondary data* and *primary data*. An organization may choose to collect one or the other, but most often it will use both to enrich the quality of the information.

SECONDARY DATA

Secondary data consist of information that already exists somewhere, having been collected for another purpose. Researchers usually start their investigation by examining secondary data to see whether their problem can be partly or wholly solved without costly collection of primary data. A rich variety of secondary data sources are available, including external sources (government publications, trade magazines, other periodicals and books, foundation reports, and competitors' publications such as annual reports and season brochures) and internal sources (organizational financial statements, sales figures, information on subscribers and single-ticket buyers, and reports of prior research).

On occasion, a foundation, a government agency, or a trade organization will undertake basic research on behalf of a number of arts organizations. For example, in June 1992, the American Symphony Orchestra League disseminated its report "The Financial Conditions of Symphony Orchestras" to its member organizations, and the following year, it published "Americanizing the American Orchestra," a report on the research conducted by its national task force to analyze how orchestras may become more relevant and more broadly accepted in an increasingly complex environment.[4] Similarly, the Cleveland Foundation, the Pew Charitable Trust in Philadelphia, and the John D. and Catherine T. MacArthur Foundation in Chicago each hired a marketing research firm to survey attitudes toward the arts among people in their metropolitan areas, with the goal of helping local arts organizations find ways to build their audiences. Basic research might not have immediate application to specific management decisions, but can lay the groundwork for better decisions in the future.

Researchers can use internal documents to track the popularity of various programs according to such variables as market segment, scheduling factors, prices, and the nature and extent of advertising used. They can also analyze how audience response has changed over time to an organization's various offerings. Secondary data provide a starting point for research and offer the advantages of lower cost and quicker findings. On the other hand, the data needed by the researcher might not exist, or the existing data might be dated, inaccurate, incomplete, or unreliable. In this case, the researcher will have to collect primary data—at greater cost and with longer delay, but probably with more relevance and accuracy.

PRIMARY DATA

Primary data consist of original information gathered for the specific purpose at hand. Most marketing research projects involve some primary data collection. When the arts marketing researcher thinks of carrying out primary research, the first technique that comes to mind is a field survey using questionnaires, conducted by mail, telephone, or at performances. However, other techniques are available that may be more effective and efficient for the situation at hand. The next section presents the approaches available to market researchers for primary data collection.

Approaches to Primary Data Collection

When planning a research project, the research manager needs to know the full array of methodologies that might be used to solve the particular problem in order to select the process that will best meet the management's decision-making needs. Primary data can actually be collected in three broad ways: through exploratory research, which includes observation, individual in-depth interviews, and focus groups; through descriptive research, which includes surveys, conjoint research, and panel studies; and through experimental research.

OBSERVATIONAL RESEARCH

Useful data can be gathered simply by observing the relevant actors and settings. Researchers might listen in on calls to the box office as people make their programming and pricing choices or circulate in the lobby during intermission to hear how patrons talk about the different performances they have attended. Organizations can also utilize "mystery shoppers"—persons who pose as customers and rate the performance of personnel such as ticket sellers or ushers. The researchers can attend competitors' performances to observe their offerings firsthand and listen to consumer reactions. These are simple and inexpensive techniques for learning more about audiences and their reactions to offerings.

INDIVIDUAL IN-DEPTH INTERVIEWS AND FOCUS GROUP RESEARCH

Individual in-depth interviews involve lengthy questioning of a small number of respondents (rather than brief questioning of large samples) one at a time, often using disguised questions and minimal interviewer prompting so that the interviewees will not be influenced by biased questions. Focus groups involve bringing together groups of six to twelve consumers, usually (but not always) relatively homogeneous, to discuss a specific set of issues under the guidance of a leader trained to stimulate and focus the discussion. Exhibit 6-1 indicates a range of conditions under which each technique might be used.

The objective of both individual in-depth interviews and focus groups is to get beneath the surface of some issue and beyond the parameters by which market researchers and the organization's marketing manager define the problem.

Exhibit 6-1

WHICH TO USE: FOCUS GROUPS OR INDIVIDUAL IN-DEPTH INTERVIEWS?

Issue to consider	Use focus groups when . . .	Use individual in-depth interviews when . . .
Group interaction	interaction of respondents may stimulate a richer response or new and valuable thoughts.	group interaction is likely to be limited or nonproductive.
Group/peer pressure	group/peer pressure will be valuable in challenging the thinking of respondents and illuminating conflicting opinions.	group/peer pressure would inhibit responses and cloud the meaning of results.
Sensitivity of subject matter	subject matter is not so sensitive that respondents will temper responses or withhold information.	subject matter is so sensitive that respondents would be unwilling to talk openly in a group.
Depth of individual responses	the topic is such that most respondents can say all that is relevant or all that they know in less than ten minutes.	the topic is such that a greater depth of response per individual is desirable, as with complex subject matter and very knowledgeable respondents.
Interviewer fatigue	it is desirable to have one interviewer conduct the research; several groups will not create interviewer fatigue or boredom.	it is desirable to have numerous interviewers on the project. One interviewer would become fatigued or bored conducting the interviews.
Stimulus materials	the volume of stimulus material is not extensive.	a large amount of stimulus material must be evaluated.
Continuity of information	a single subject area is being examined in depth and strings of behaviors are less relevant.	it is necessary to understand how attitudes and behaviors link together on an individual pattern basis.
Experimentation with interview guide	enough is known to establish a meaningful topic guide.	it may be necessary to develop the interview guide by altering it after each of the initial interviews.
Observation	it is possible and desirable for key decision makers to observe firsthand consumer information.	firsthand consumer information is not critical or observation is not logistically possible.

Exhibit 6-1	WHICH TO USE *continued*		
	Issue to consider	Use focus groups when . . .	Use individual in-depth interviews when . . .
	Logistics	an acceptable number of target respondents can be assembled in one location.	respondents are geographically dispersed or not easily assembled for other reasons.
	Cost and timing	quick turnaround is critical, and funds are limited.	quick turnaround is not critical, and budget will permit higher cost.

Source: Mary Debus, *Handbook for Excellence in Focus Group Research* (Washington, D.C.: Academy for Educational Development, 1993), 10. Reprinted with permission.

Therefore, it is often helpful to utilize one or both of these methods in advance of designing a survey questionnaire. When talking at length with a sympathetic and resourceful interviewer or when stimulated by the camaraderie and comments of others, participants can be encouraged to define the issues in their own terms and to propose possible solutions. Exhibit 6-2 shows several techniques that skilled interviewers and group moderators use to achieve this kind of interaction.

SURVEYS

The survey is the most popular and widely used device for investigating, describing, and measuring people's knowledge, beliefs, product and media preferences, satisfaction levels, demographics, competitive choices, and decision-making processes. An arts organization can survey the views of subscribers, single-ticket buyers, donors, and others about its programs and services. Questionnaires can be stuffed into programs or can be mailed to random samples of current, past, or potential patrons. Surveys can also be administered by telephone, providing a forum for a more personal and more thorough response. We will examine survey research in depth in the next section.

Related approaches include *conjoint research techniques,* which are nontraditional methods for analyzing consumer choice processes that may be applied within the context of a survey, and *panel studies,* another descriptive research method that serves to analyze changes in consumer behavior over time.

CONJOINT RESEARCH TECHNIQUES

Traditional survey approaches that ask about choices one at a time ignore the reality that most consumer choices involve trade-offs among desired benefits. Conjoint research techniques are specifically designed to capture this process. They permit analysts to estimate the importance to an individual or group of each quality or

Exhibit 6-2	**SUGGESTIONS FOR SOLICITING RESPONSES IN FOCUS GROUPS**

1. *Top-of-mind associations:*

   What's the first thing that comes to mind when I say modern dance (opera, classical music, etc.)? What else comes to mind? Or, What comes to mind when I say Stratford Festival? Shaw Festival? etc.

2. *Constructing images:*

   Who are the people who attend opera? What are their lives like? How do you feel when you attend the opera? Describe what the experience is like for you.

3. *Asking the meaning of the obvious:*

   What does *avant-garde, classical, dramatic* mean to you?

4. *"Man from the moon" routine:*

   I'm from the moon; I've never heard of opera. Describe it to me. Tell me about the experience from the perspective of the audience. Why would I want to attend one? Convince me.

5. *Conditions that give permission and create barriers:*

   Tell me about two or three situations in which you would decide to attend this performance and two or three situations in which you would decide to do something else.

6. *Chain of questions:*

   Why do you subscribe to this theater? Why is that important to you? Would it ever not be important?

7. *Best-of-all-possible-world scenarios:*

   Forget about reality for a minute. If you could design your own subscription plan for a symphony, what would it be like? What other benefits would you enjoy? Use your imagination. There are no limits. Don't worry about whether it is possible or not.

8. *Sentence completions:*

   The ideal concert program is one that . . . The best thing about this theater is that . . . Attending this theater/play makes me feel . . .

9. *Pointing out contradictions:*

   Wait a minute, you just told me you would like our plays to be less heavy, and now you're telling me this play was great because it is so intense, deep, and emotional—how do you explain this?

Source: adapted from Mary Debus, *Handbook for Excellence in Focus Group Research* (Washington, D.C.: Academy for Educational Development, 1993), 32–33. Reprinted with permission.

attribute and to project the likely success of new choices not included in the original set. Currim, Weinberg, and Wittinck employed this technique for the Lively Arts Program (LAP) at Stanford University.[5] A mail survey of current LAP subscribers asked respondents to rank their preferences of attributes of a subscription series from the following set of factors:

Attribute	Levels
Driving time	$\leq$ 30 min; > 30 min.
Number of series events	5; 8
Seating priority	Yes; no

Single-ticket price	$5; $8; $12
Subscription discount	$30%; 15%; none
Performer renown	World; national; regional

The researchers reasonably assumed a preference ordering for the levels *within* several of the attributes (that is, everyone would prefer less driving to more, seating priority over no priority, a ticket for $5 over one at $8, and so forth). By looking at the trade-offs consumers made *among* these factors, the researchers concluded that driving time was most important, followed by performer renown, price, seating priority, number of events, and percentage discount. The power of the conjoint technique is its ability to detect these interactions.

PANEL STUDIES

Researchers may wish to monitor the performance of a target market over time. For example, they may want to analyze patterns of single-ticket buyers becoming subscribers or subscribers reverting back to single-ticket purchase. Researchers can study changes in consumer behavior in the following ways:

1. *Retrospectively,* by asking a single sample of consumers what they are doing now and what they did at some past point in time.

2. *Cross-sectionally,* by comparing behaviors of consumers at different stages in a process (for example, comparing theater attendance of 25–35-year-olds with that of 35–45-year-olds, or comparing theater exposure patterns of sudden subscribers [those who subscribe without previous attendance] with those of gradual subscribers [those who subscribe after building attendance frequency over a period of time]).

3. *Cross-sectionally over time,* by asking about behaviors of different samples at two points in time (such as different age groups changing their attendance patterns over time).

4. *Longitudinally over time,* by taking behavioral measures of the same panel of consumers at different points over time. Government or foundation funders may choose to do truly long term studies on people who are exposed to the arts at a young age and measure the impact of various factors on their future performing arts attendance patterns.

EXPERIMENTAL RESEARCH

The most scientifically valid research is experimental research. Experimental research calls for selecting matched groups of subjects, subjecting them to different treatments, controlling extraneous variables, and checking whether observed response differences are statistically significant. The purpose of experimental research is to capture cause-and-effect relationships by eliminating competing explanations of the observed findings. For example, a theater can send out two different season brochures to two randomly selected groups of subscribers. If the brochures differ only in that one group is charged a higher price for the same set of offerings, researchers can then analyze the impact of the price differential on the subscription rate. At the end of the research project, subscribers who paid the higher price are refunded the difference, and, if the test results are favorable, prices can be raised the following season for all subscribers. To the extent that the design and execution of such an experiment eliminates alternative hypotheses that might explain the results, the research and marketing managers can have confidence in the conclusions.

Budgeting for Market Research

Although marketing research should be an ongoing function, rarely are specific funds set aside for marketing research. Unfortunately, marketing research is usually treated as a discretionary activity rather than an essential tool for effective management.

A cost-benefit approach is the most effective method for determining an appropriate market research budget. Management specifies research needs for the planning period and then determines the costs of the research. These costs are then compared to the expected benefits. Specifically, the steps are as follows.

1. Ascertain upcoming information needs and list all possible projects that might be undertaken in the planning period.

2. Estimate the costs of meeting the various information needs.

3. Estimate the value or benefit of each study in terms of the likely improvement in organizational performance.

4. Compare costs to expected benefits, and include all projects where the latter exceed the former.

5. All ongoing research projects should be reevaluated each year, and an assessment should be made as to how to improve the effectiveness and efficiency of each project.

6. The total costs of both newly selected and ongoing projects will make up the year's research budget.

THE MARKETING RESEARCH PROCESS: THE SURVEY

Effective marketing research involves five steps: defining the problem and research objectives, developing the research plan, collecting the information, analyzing the information, and presenting the findings. In this section we investigate the marketing research process in the context of designing and applying the survey questionnaire, the most common instrument for collecting primary data.

Defining the Problem and Research Objectives

The first step in research calls for the managers and the marketing researcher to define the problem carefully and agree on the research objectives. Unless the problem is well defined, the cost of gathering information may well exceed the value of the findings. The manager should make clear to the researcher what the decision alternatives are and what additional information is required to make those decisions. Also, the manager should share with the researcher those financial, political, and other constraints under which the organization operates that may affect the way the research is approached and evaluated.

CENTRE EAST: DEFINING THE PROBLEM AND RESEARCH OBJECTIVES

Some members of Centre East's board of directors have suggested raising all ticket prices by 25 percent to help make up for decreased ticket sales in the smaller hall. The executive director is concerned that her audience would find such a substantial price increase excessive, so instead she is considering cutting costs by presenting less expensive performers. She knows that less expensive performers are also less well known and will attract a smaller crowd, which is appropriate for the new space. However, either of these changes is likely to destroy the niche the theater has maintained successfully for many years and will have a major effect on the audience segments Centre East attracts, the nature of its competition, and its fund-raising potential. Centre East's first task is to face the central issue of whether anticipated programming and/or pricing changes are compatible with the organization's mission. Centre East's mission statement reads, in part, "Centre East is dedicated to presenting quality professional performing arts and cultural events that are accessible to diverse audiences in the greater Chicagoland area of all ages and interests. Centre East is committed to showcasing emerging artists and playing a leadership role in establishing and developing arts and educational programs."

Clearly, Centre East's mission not only allows but encourages management to present programming outside the mainstream, which, in general, is also less expensive to the organization. Nothing in the mission statement prevents the management from raising prices; that factor will be strictly limited by market response. In reviewing Centre East's commitment to appeal to audiences of all ages and interests, the marketing consultant, the management, and the board agreed that they should not try to appeal to a huge range of audience segments, but should focus on certain target groups that best fit the organization's current and future circumstances.

For the management and board of Centre East to make the major decisions they are facing, there are many things they need to know. It would be helpful for them to

- Analyze sales over the past two years to identify areas of strength and weakness
- Know audience preferences and satisfaction levels with regard to programming and pricing factors
- Measure the market potential for new offerings
- Determine the current market's demographic and psycho-graphic characteristics
- Study competitive offerings
- Forecast short- and long-run demand

The marketing researcher and the decision makers must determine exactly which decisions are to be made using research results. For example, assume that they want to know whether they can raise prices enough to make up for the loss of five hundred seats in the theater. They will need to know the following: How many people will attend if they raise their prices by 10 percent? 20 percent? 30 percent? 50 percent? Which performances are the most (and least) suitable for the largest price increases? Is there potential for more price differentiation according to seat location than now exists? What about differential pricing by day of the week? group sales? subscriptions? special promotions? special events? Are there new audiences the organization can target with higher-priced programming? If so, what amenities can be added to attract those audiences?

If Centre East changes the nature of its programming, such as from folk music to jazz, or changes the level of fame of the performers it presents, how many former patrons will continue to attend? How many new patrons will be attracted to these performances and to shows by performers with lower name recognition?

Developing the Research Plan

The second stage of marketing research calls for developing the most efficient plan for gathering the needed information. The manager cannot simply say to the marketing researcher, "Find some patrons and ask them if they would come if we present chamber music instead of jazz / rhythm and blues, or if we charge $33 instead of $26."

The research questions must be defined more carefully. Designing a research plan calls for decisions about the sampling plan, research biases, contact methods, and questionnaire design.

THE SAMPLING PLAN

The marketing researcher must design a sampling plan that determines who will be contacted to respond to the questionnaire (the sampling unit), specifies how many people will be contacted (the sample size), and ensures that the organization obtains a representative sample of the target groups (sampling procedure).

First, the marketing researcher must define the target population that will be sampled. The appropriate sampling unit is not always immediately apparent.

CENTRE EAST: THE SAMPLING UNIT	Centre East wanted to sample current frequent attenders and infrequent attenders of a wide range of their offerings. They also wanted to sample people who had not attended Centre East performances but who enjoy the types of programming that the organization was considering presenting in the future. To locate potential attenders, Centre East requested and received from each of five key area arts organizations two hundred randomly selected names and addresses. In the end, nonattenders were eliminated from the sample. The survey was designed to include many questions about each respondent's reactions to the programs they had attended in the past at Centre East and about how they viewed Centre East's image and services. Designing and tabulating a separate survey for nonattenders proved to be too costly.

When a research project is not limited to current patrons, "snowball sampling" may prove useful as a technique for finding rare populations. Participants in the study can be asked to suggest the names of others "like them" who could be contacted. This adds to the sample a group that (1) does not have the familiarity biases of the first group, (2) is likely to cooperate in the study (especially if the initial respondents allow their names to be used as references), and (3) closely matches the first sample in terms of socioeconomic characteristics.

Sample size Large samples give more reliable results than small samples. However, it is not necessary to sample the entire target population, or even a substantial portion, to achieve reliable results. Samples of less than 1 percent of a population can often provide good reliability, given a credible sampling procedure. Rather than thinking in terms of surveying a specific percentage of a large population, researchers will generally seek a specific number of responses.

Sampling procedure   To obtain a representative sample, a *probability sample* of the population should be drawn. Probability sampling allows the calculation of confidence limits for sampling error, so that one could conclude, for example, that there is a 95 percent chance of being correct that single-ticket buyers at Centre East attend an average of 1.5 performances per year. There are three types of probability sampling:

1. *Simple random sample:* Every member of the population has a known and equal chance of selection.
2. *Stratified random sample:* The population is divided into mutually exclusive groups (such as age groups), and random samples are drawn from each group.
3. *Cluster (area) sample:* The population is divided into mutually exclusive groups (such as blocks), and the researcher draws a sample of the groups to interview.

When the cost or time involved in probability sampling is too high, marketing researchers often take *nonprobability samples.* Some marketing researchers feel that nonprobability samples can be very useful in many circumstances, even though the sampling error cannot be measured. For example, if the management is chiefly interested in frequency counts (say, of words used by consumers to describe the organization's offerings or of complaints voiced about its staff), sampling restrictions need not be so tight. Three examples of nonprobability samples are:

1. *Convenience sample:* The researcher selects the most accessible population members from which to obtain information.
2. *Judgment sample:* The researcher uses his or her judgment to select population members who are good prospects for accurate information.
3. *Quota sample:* The researcher finds and interviews a prescribed number of people in each of several categories.

CENTRE EAST: SAMPLING PROCEDURE

Centre East's marketing director used a combination of nonprobability sampling techniques to provide researchers with 2,000 names and addresses, including 500 people who had made a donation at any level to Centre East and 1,500 who had attended at least one feature performance in the past two years. (Adults who had attended *only* children's programming were eliminated from the sample.)

RESEARCH BIASES

Research can be effective only if it avoids the two major sources of error, *sampling error* and *systematic bias.*[6]

Sampling error   No sample is likely to produce results that are precisely the same as those for the entire population from which the sample was drawn. There is always some chance that those who are included in the sample are not perfectly representative of the whole population. It is always possible to pick, strictly by chance, a particular group who happen to be different in some important attribute from the population as a whole. If such differences between the sample data and the population data result purely by random chance, this is known as sampling error. Smaller samples are more likely to differ from the population than are larger ones, so smaller samples are subject to greater sampling error. The higher the sampling error, the lower the reliability; therefore, the smaller the sample, the lower the reliability of the data.

Since it is impractical to measure the entire population, researchers and statisticians usually think of sampling error in terms of comparisons between similar samples. Data from a sample is relatively free from sampling error and is reliable if another sample of the same size, taken from the same population with the same selection technique, is very likely to provide results that are the same or very similar.

Systematic bias   Systematic bias refers to extraneous sampling factors that affect survey results and reduce the validity of the data. It is difficult to avoid and correct for. The word *systematic* simply means that the bias is not random; its effect is to push results in a specific direction. Systematic bias in a survey usually results from one of the following sources:

- *Frame bias* is caused by drawing a probability sample from a poor representation of the universe. For example, estimating the proportion of men who attended ballet during the past year by sampling spectators at a football game would systematically underestimate the true value, because many male ballet fans are not avid sports enthusiasts.

- *Selection bias* results when the procedure for drawing actual sample members *always* excludes or underrepresents certain types of universe (frame) members. This would occur if telephone interviewers called only during the day, thereby underrepresenting people who work. It would also occur in field surveys if interviewers were allowed to pick and choose whom to interview. Suppose a survey were conducted to measure how satisfied or content people are. If the field-workers tended to only interview people who looked like they were very friendly, the data would reflect a bias in the direction of greater satisfaction.

- *Nonresponse bias* results when a particular group of those contacted declines to participate out of lack of interest, antagonism, or busyness.

- *Interviewer bias* results when an untrained interviewer deliberately or inadvertently leads the respondent to deviate from the truth. This can occur, for example, when interviewers read or "clarify" a question in a way that suggests that a particular answer is preferred.

- *Questionnaire bias* can arise due to poor or confusing wording, leading questions, identification of the research sponsor when this information is supposed to be withheld, or omission of important possible responses.

- *Respondent bias* occurs when respondents lie or unwittingly distort answers. Often this type of bias manifests itself when respondents "upgrade" their income or education level or their frequency of attendance. Such bias usually results not from malice, but from a misplaced attempt to "help out."

- *Processing bias* would occur if the interviewer (or the respondent in a written study) wrote down the wrong answers, if the office entered the answers into the computer incorrectly, or if the computer analysis was programmed incorrectly.

Catching all these glitches is not easy. It takes careful attention to the design process, to interviewer training, to checking on data processing, and to reviewing reports for errors. However, this process is so important that research funds are often better spent on catching errors than on increasing the sample size.

CONTACT METHODS

Respondents to a survey may be contacted by mail, by telephone, or in personal interviews.

The *mail questionnaire* is the most cost-effective way of reaching a large number of people. It is also the best way to reach individuals who would be unwilling to give personal interviews or whose responses might be biased or distorted by the interviewers. However, the response rate is usually low and can be very slow.

For patron surveys, arts organizations are in the enviable position of having a "captive" audience. By placing questionnaires in programs and collecting them at intermission or at the end of the performance, researchers can benefit from the advantages of mail questionnaires while avoiding the problem of sparse or slow responses.

Telephone interviewing is an effective method for gaining information quickly; the interviewer is also able to clarify questions if they are not understood. The response rate is generally higher than in the case of mailed questionnaires. However, the sample size will necessarily be much lower because calling is labor-intensive. Furthermore, these interviews have to be short and not too personal.

Personal interviewing is the most versatile contact method. The interviewer can ask more questions and can record additional observations about the respondent, such as body language or dress. Yet personal interviewing is the most expensive method and requires the most administrative planning and supervision. It is also subject to interviewer bias or distortion. Personal interviewing takes two forms, *arranged interviews* and *intercept interviews.* In arranged interviews, respondents are randomly selected and are either telephoned or approached at their homes or offices and asked to grant an interview. Intercept interviews involve stopping people at a shopping mall or busy street corner and requesting an interview. Intercept interviews have the drawback of using nonprobability samples, and the interviews must be short. Often a small payment or other incentive, such as free tickets to a performance, is presented to respondents in appreciation for their time.

Designing the Questionnaire

Questionnaires must be carefully developed, tested, and "debugged" before they are administered on a large scale. Exhibit 6-3 shows several types of errors that may be found in an unprofessionally prepared questionnaire.

The questionnaire is a very flexible tool: there are a wide variety of ways to ask questions. In preparing a questionnaire, the marketing researcher must carefully develop the questions and their form, wording, and sequence.

The questions asked A common type of error concerns the nature of the questions asked. The researcher must be careful to include all pertinent questions and to exclude questions that cannot, would not, or need not be answered. Each question should be checked to determine whether it contributes to the research objectives.

Exhibit 6-3

A "QUESTIONABLE" QUESTIONNAIRE

Suppose a theater asked respondents the following questions. Think about each question before reading the comment in italics.

1. What is your income?

   People do not generally want to reveal their exact income. Broad categories should be provided so people can indicate their income range. Furthermore, a questionnaire should never open with such a personal question.

2. Are you an occasional or a frequent theatergoer?

   How do you define occasional versus frequent attendance? What seems frequent to one person may be considered occasional by another.

3. Do you like this theater?   Yes ( ) No ( )

   "Like" is a relative term. Besides, will people answer this honestly? Is yes–no the best way to elicit a useful response to the question?

4. How many advertisements have you read or heard on the radio for this theater this season?

   Who can remember?

5. What are the most salient and determinant attributes in your evaluation of theatrical productions?

   What are "salient" and "determinant" attributes? Don't use big words like those. Ask clear questions if you want clear answers.

6. Don't you think it is outrageous for the government to cut NEA funding for the arts?

   Loaded question. Don't ask questions with built-in biases.

Questions that are merely interesting should be dropped because they increase the response time required and strain the respondents' patience.

Managers should be given the opportunity to review the questions in advance. Some managers express concern that certain seemingly innocent questions may set up unrealistic expectations on the part of their audience members, resulting in disappointment. One symphony director requested that researchers exclude from their survey a question asking patrons if they would like a baby-sitting service, because he was not interested in providing such a benefit. Management participation in the design decision has other advantages. It serves to win managers' support of marketing research and deepens their understanding of research details. Participation will also sensitize management to the study's limitations. The researcher might ask the decision maker "If I came up with these numbers, what would you do?" The researcher may discover that management would take the same course of action no matter what the results. Such a conclusion would suggest that that part of the research design should be eliminated.

The form of the question　The form of the question can influence the response. Marketing researchers distinguish between *closed-end* and *open-end* questions. Closed-end questions specify all the possible answers, and respondents make a choice among them. Closed-end questions provide answers that are relatively easy to interpret and tabulate. Open-end questions are especially useful in the exploratory stage of research, when the researcher is looking for insight into how people think rather than measuring how many people think in a certain way.

Exhibit 6-4 provides examples of some commonly employed forms of closed-end and open-end questions.

Wording of questions　Care should also be exercised in the wording of questions. The researcher should use simple, direct, unbiased wording so that the questions do not stimulate the respondent to think about the organization in a certain way. The questions should be pretested with a sample of respondents before they are formally included in the survey.

Sequencing of questions　Care should be exercised in the *sequencing* of questions. Whenever possible, the lead question should create interest. The questions should follow a logical order. Difficult or personal questions should be asked toward the end of the interview so that respondents do not become defensive. Classificatory questions about the respondent are asked last because they are more personal and less interesting to the respondent.

Collecting and Analyzing the Data

The data collection phase is generally the most expensive and the most susceptible to error. Once an adequate sample has been obtained, the next step is to extract pertinent findings from the data. The researcher tabulates the data and develops frequency distributions, averages, and measures of dispersion. Based on this

Exhibit 6-4	TYPES OF QUESTIONS	

Closed-end questions	Example
Dichotomous: a question offering two answer choices	Is this the first time you have attended this theater? Yes ( ) No ( )
Multiple choice: a question offering three or more answer choices	With whom are you attending this performance? No one ( ) Spouse ( ) Other relatives/friends ( ) Business Associates ( ) An organized group ( )
Likert scale: A statement with which the respondent shows the amount of agreement/disagreement	Good critical reviews are an important factor for me in choosing to attend a performance.

	Strongly disagree	Disagree	Undecided	Agree	Strongly agree
	1 ( )	2 ( )	3 ( )	4 ( )	5 ( )

Closed-end questions	Example
Semantic differential: A scale is inscribed between two bipolar words, and the respondent selects the point that represents his or her opinion.	High ticket prices Low ticket prices ___ • ___ • ___ • ___ • ___ Convenient location Inconvenient location ___ • ___ • ___ • ___ • ___
Importance scale: A scale that rates the importance of some attribute.	"Ticket exchange privilege to me is . . ."

	Extremely important	Very important	Somewhat important	Not very important	Not at all important
	1 __	2 __	3 __	4 __	5 __

Closed-end questions	Example
Rating scale: A scale that rates some attribute from "poor" to "excellent"	The quality of our productions is . . ."

	Excellent	Very good	Good	Fair	Poor
	1 __	2 __	3 __	4 __	5 __

Closed-end questions	Example
Intention-to-buy scale: A scale that rates the respondent's intention to buy.	"If subscriptions were offered for packages of three productions, I would . . ."

	Definitely buy	Probably buy	Not sure	Probably not buy	Definitely not buy
	1 ( )	2 ( )	3 ( )	4 ( )	5 ( )

Open-end	Example
Completely unstructured: A question that respondents can answer in an almost unlimited number of ways.	"What is your opinion of Centre East Theatre?"
Word association: Words are presented, one at a time, and respondents mention the first word that comes to mind.	"What is the first word that comes to your mind when you hear the following?" Theater _____ Chamber music _____ Centre East _____
Sentence completion: Incomplete sentences are presented, one at a time, and respondents complete the sentence.	"When I choose a performance to attend, the most important consideration in my decision is _____ _____"

information, the researcher analyzes the results in terms of the managerial decisions to be made and forms a series of recommendations.

CENTRE EAST:
COLLECTING
AND
ANALYZING
THE DATA

At Centre East, the 2,000 recipients of the mailed survey were given an incentive of $5 off a feature performance or $2 off a family performance as thanks for filling out the survey. (The surveys were anonymous, but people had to provide a name and address if they wanted the discount coupon. Many did.) There was a healthy response of nearly 25 percent. In all, 471 surveys were completed and returned by the cutoff date, about six weeks after the mailing.

Based on the pricing questions in the survey, the researchers determined that for the most part, prices that would allow Centre East to break even for most of its popular performers in the new, smaller hall were much too high. (Detailed analyses were made on the pricing sensitivity of several demographic groups for each of fourteen performers with a wide range of appeal.) Researchers assumed that prices could be raised somewhat higher than respondents indicated they would be willing to pay, especially since the new theater would have more of an upscale image than the current auditorium. But the prices that would have to be charged to make certain performers affordable in an eight-hundred-seat hall involved massive increases. (For example, prices for Tony Bennett, the Kodo Drummers of Japan, and Philip Glass would have to be raised from the recent $26 to $45, $55, and $50 respectively.) It was recommended that Centre East continue to present some of the most popular performers at a less than break-even price to maintain satisfaction and the current customer base and attempt to make up the financial loss by presenting more emerging, lower-priced performers at a price above the break-even level.

Many programming recommendations were derived from research results. For example, Jazz/Rhythm & Blues was found to be popular among the under-35 age group and the 35–44 group. There are few offerings of this genre on Chicago's North Shore, so Centre East has an opportunity to fill this programming gap. Also, this genre is often offered in a club setting, and Centre East may be able to take advantage of a room with a club atmosphere in the hotel connected to the new performance center either during, before, or after performances. This social component will be highly attractive to these under-45 age groups, especially since few places on the North Shore are open late for an after-show drink and conversation. A club atmosphere also provides an opportunity for singles events and other special group offerings. Furthermore, parents who attend family programming are most often in the 35–44 age group, meaning that these people are already familiar with Centre East and can be reached at family programs or through targeted mailings.

Preparing the Research Report

The research report is the document submitted to management that summarizes the research results and conclusions. First, the researcher will present an executive summary of the findings, which reports and analyzes the results and makes recommendations in a few succinct pages. It is all that many executives and board members will see of the research effort, and it becomes the standard by which the research is judged. In the executive summary, the researcher should not overwhelm the management with a multitude of numbers and descriptions of complex statistical techniques. Instead, the summary should present the major findings that are relevant to the marketing decisions facing management. The study will be useful only if it reduces the management's uncertainty concerning what action should be taken.

Generally, the researcher will also submit an extensive, detailed report of the findings and analyses of each part of the questionnaire. Such detailed information is useful to the marketing manager and sometimes to the executive director or a marketing professional on the board; these are usually the only people who have the patience and the necessary skills to wade through all the data.

It is imperative that the research report be clear and accurate, since no matter how well all previous steps have been completed, the project will be no more successful than the final report.

Implementation and Evaluation

The traditional research project concludes when the report is dropped on the manager's desk. This approach is shortsighted. The process began with the researcher and the manager thinking collaboratively about how the research would assist in managerial decision making. Now that the data are in hand, the researcher should continue to be involved. He or she understands the data and its nuances and has already thought hard about what the results should mean to the manager. Therefore, continued teamwork by the manager and the researcher through the application stage will increase the likelihood of good decisions by ensuring that the data are mined as thoroughly as possible and that they are not subject to inadvertent or wishful misinterpretations. The researcher may also make a presentation about the major findings at a meeting of the board of directors.

Furthermore, the research process just undertaken should be thoroughly evaluated. The researcher and manager should ask whether there are ways in which the research could have been carried out more effectively. Only by evaluating and improving the process will the organization get the maximum benefit from its resources.

MEASURING AND FORECASTING MARKET DEMAND

Many marketing decisions require an understanding of both the current and the probable future market. Whether an arts organization is getting a reasonable share of the existing market and whether it should venture into a new market are questions that can be answered only after present and future market potential have been carefully assessed. This analysis requires an understanding of who the market is (market definition), how large the current market is (current market size measurement), and an estimate of the probable future size of the market (market forecasting).

A.R.T.: ENTERING A NEW MARKET

In 1980, the American Repertory Theatre (A.R.T.), under the leadership of artistic director Robert Brustein, moved from Yale University to the Loeb Drama Center in Cambridge, Massachusetts, under the sponsorship of Harvard University. With the exception of a summer theater and occasional special attractions, the Loeb's main stage had been dark for much of the year. Although Boston had the reputation of being "the Athens of America," Bostonians had little exposure to theater and dance of the first rank. Several theaters had come and gone, and the four surviving legitimate theaters mainly presented Broadway shows on tour and revivals. No permanent, professional, resident theater had developed in the Boston area.[7]

Defining the Market

To define its market, each organization must distinguish between its customers and noncustomers, and must define its offer. We define a *market* as a set of actual or potential customers who might engage in a given exchange.

The term *customers* encompasses a number of possible subsets such as subscribers, single-ticket buyers, and donors. Customers can also be individuals, families, groups, or corporations. A *given exchange* is shorthand for all offers of programs, services, or goods to which target customers can respond. Those in the market have three characteristics in common: interest, the ability to transact, and access.

A.R.T.: DEFINING THE MARKET

A.R.T. management went to great lengths to assemble relevant market data. The information that was collected included:

- Ford Foundation survey data on exposure to the arts in different U.S. cities in 1974. These data were a little dated but still offered useful general insights into audience composition and behavior.

- Information gained through visits by a staff member to four regional theaters across the country, including practical managerial insights based upon actual experience.

- Information on the pricing policies of other Boston-area performing arts organizations.

- Results of a specially conducted mail survey in the Boston area. The goal of the research was "to find the people who wanted our kind of theatre." More specifically, A.R.T. wanted to obtain survey data that would predict how many people would come to A.R.T., how much to charge them, and how best to attract them.

THE POTENTIAL MARKET

The first step for managers of a new or changing product offering is to estimate the number of people in the community with a potential interest in attending the theater. The potential market is the set of consumers who profess some level of interest in a defined market exchange.

A.R.T.: THE POTENTIAL MARKET

Carolyn Clay, arts critic for the *Boston Phoenix*, distinguished two disparate theater audiences in the Boston community. The first was a group located primarily in the suburbs who would come downtown to large commercial theaters and preferred seeing a show that had already been a hit in New York. The other group resided mainly in Cambridge and consisted of more intellectual theatergoers. They patronized improvisational revues, college and experimental productions, and the classics. To both of these groups, however, "recognizability" was essential, and it was understood that the audience for truly avant-garde theater was "wildly limited" in Boston. The college student population, which helped to support a number of art cinemas in the area, was rarely visible at legitimate theater productions.

THE AVAILABLE MARKET

Consumer interest is not enough to define a market. Market size is further restricted by the ability to transact and access. Since a price is attached to the offer, potential consumers must have adequate income to afford the purchase. Interested consumers must also be able to attend at the time and place the offering is made. Those who fit all these criteria make up the *available market*—the set of consumers who have interest, ability to transact, and access to a particular market exchange.

A.R.T.: THE AVAILABLE MARKET

Sam Guckenheimer, A.R.T.'s marketing director, said, "Our prices should be high enough so that anyone who can and will pay a lot to attend will do so. At the same time, anyone who really wants to come should be able to." Following interpretation of the survey results and a review of the ticket prices and subscription plans offered by other Boston arts organizations, a pricing matrix was established. Prices ranged from a low of $4 (equal to the lowest-priced nonstudent nonprofit theater) to a high of $18 (just below the top figure for commercial theater). In return for a substantial contribution from Harvard University, A.R.T. planned to offer full-season student pass subscriptions to Harvard/Radcliffe undergraduates at $10 per pass.

Performances were scheduled in repertory; each play was offered over a period of three months. On-street parking was limited, and the nearest parking lot was four blocks away. However, public transportation service to the area was extensive, and downtown Boston could be reached by train in ten minutes.

THE QUALIFIED AVAILABLE MARKET

For certain offers, organizations establish restrictions regarding with whom they will transact. Orchestras generally do not allow children below a certain age to attend other than "family" performances. More subtly, a performing arts organization may "qualify" its audience by limiting its offerings to productions that appeal to a select portion of the available market. The *qualified available market* is the set of consumers who have interest, ability to transact, access, and qualification for the particular market exchange.

A.R.T.: THE QUALIFIED AVAILABLE MARKET

From the beginning, everyone involved in the survey project shared the conviction that A.R.T. should not use the results of market research to shape the company's offerings. As Guckenheimer phrased it: "We were going to do a certain kind of theatre no matter what people wanted. Our task was to find the people who wanted our kind of theatre."

THE TARGET MARKET

An arts organization has the choice of going after the whole qualified available market or concentrating its efforts on certain segments. If the latter choice is made, the organization must identify a *target market:* the part of the qualified available market that the organization attempts to attract and serve.

A.R.T.: THE TARGET MARKET	A.R.T. decided that direct mail would be the most effective medium for a subscription campaign. Since A.R.T. was new to the Boston area and had no track record there, the organization targeted the mailing lists that had yielded the highest returns in their survey.

THE PENETRATED MARKET

Those who actually choose a particular marketer's offering are called the penetrated market. We define the *penetrated market* as the set of qualified available consumers who are actually participating in the marketer's exchanges.

A.R.T.: THE PENETRATED MARKET	Once A.R.T. established a customer base of both subscribers and single-ticket buyers, they would have a ready-made list of high-potential repeat users. Yale Repertory Theatre's reputation preceded A.R.T. to Cambridge, enabling the new theater to attract 14,000 subscriptions in its opening season. Programming for this first season was relatively popular, and renewals for the second season were high (69 percent).
	In the second season, however, some of the plays were more controversial. The audience was unprepared for this, and only 31 percent of second-year subscribers renewed. The following year was a precarious one for A.R.T., but Harvard continued its support, along with a very solid core group of subscribers. Over the next few seasons, A.R.T. continued to develop its artistic reputation while cultivating a subscriber base more attuned to its goals.[8]

Measuring Current Market Demand

In order to examine the market demand for a current offer, an organization may consider two types of estimates: total market demand and organization market share.

TOTAL MARKET DEMAND

Total market demand is the total volume of exchanges with all marketers that would be made by a defined consumer group in a defined geographical area, in a defined time period, in a defined marketing environment under a set of defined marketing programs. Total market demand is not a fixed number, but is a function of the specified conditions. These conditions may be as broad as the state of the economy or as specific as the marketing programs (product features, promotional expenditure level, prices).

A.R.T.: TOTAL MARKET DEMAND

At A.R.T., Guckenheimer used results of his survey to analyze total current demand. His mailing list was drawn from two sources: 2,023 names were drawn from the seven Boston-area census tracts that showed the highest median educational level and the highest incidence of professional and managerial workers in the labor force. Another 2,235 names were obtained from the mailing lists of ten art-related organizations in Boston, each of which had been asked to supply a random sample of 300 names.

Respondents were asked to identify which types of live performances they had attended in the past year (symphony, chamber music, opera, ballet, theater, etc.). Then theater was broken down into four categories: musical on a Broadway tour, drama on a Broadway tour, production at a professional regional theater, and university theater productions. Respondents were also asked how often they had attended performances at specific places, to which arts organizations they had subscribed, to which they had purchased single tickets, and how many times they had attended as single-ticket buyers. From this information along with the secondary data he obtained, Guckenheimer was able to formulate a reasonable estimate of total market demand for the performing arts in the Boston area and for specific types of theatrical productions.

The *market potential* is the upper limit to the market demand, suggesting that marketing expenditures higher than a certain level would not stimulate much further demand. Knowing the market potential provides the organization with a basis for determining whether it is doing well or poorly in comparison to what it *could* do. The arguments for A.R.T.'s use of direct mail exemplify this concept.

A.R.T.: MARKET POTENTIAL

Survey respondents were a select group of current or likely cultural participants. Direct mail to this group would cost about $300 per thousand. On the other hand, the cost of stuffing the Boston edition of the Sunday *New York Times* with a flyer amounted to only $100 per thousand. But only 35 percent of survey respondents read the Sunday *Times* more than half the time, meaning that a far smaller portion of *Times* readers would respond. Stuffing a flyer in the newspaper would not be likely to generate much demand beyond those already identified for the survey. So direct mail to the survey lists with the highest response rate was determined to be the most effective and efficient use of the available funds.

ORGANIZATION MARKET SHARE

The organization may also wish to estimate its *market share* in comparison with that of its competitors. The organization's own volume does not tell the whole story of how well it is doing. Suppose the organization's volume is increasing at 5 percent a year and its competitors' volume is increasing at 10 percent. The first organization is actually losing its relative standing in the industry.

Estimating market share requires identifying the other organizations serving the same market, which is not a simple task because of the many definitions of a market. The organization must carefully define its real competition as the first step in developing an estimate of total sales and its share of sales. Then it has to estimate the volume for each competitor. The easiest way to do this is to contact each competitor and offer to exchange information. In this way, each organization can measure its performance against every other organization and against the total volume for the industry. However, some competitors are not willing to divulge such information.

Another solution calls for a trade association to collect the data and publish the results for each organization, the industry total, or both. In this way, each organization can evaluate its performance against specific competitors or the industry as a whole. Nationwide associations such as Opera America, the Theatre Communications Group, and the American Symphony Orchestra League regularly survey their members for such data, as do some local trade associations such as the League of Chicago Theaters.

Forecasting Future Market Demand

Very few industries lend themselves to easy forecasting. Forecasting is especially difficult for arts organizations, whose total demand and organizational demand are not stable and which generally lack good historical data upon which to base analysis of trends. However, good forecasting is particularly important for arts organizations, because they are subject to high fixed costs that must be met no matter how demand varies. Consider a theater that not only has been selling out its performances, but has been turning people away at the box office. The management is considering moving to a space with 50 percent greater seating capacity. The organization needs to know whether demand will continue to grow over the next several years so that it will, in effect, grow into the new space. It also needs to know whether demand will sustain itself over a sufficient period of time to make the move a viable one. As we noted in Chapter 1, many of the economic problems in the performing arts world today are the result of extensive growth among arts organizations while demand was increasing at a rapid pace. The eventual slackening of the market was not anticipated, and many organizations have been unable to reduce their costs accordingly.

When attempting to forecast market demand, one should list all the factors that might affect future demand and predict each factor's likely future level and its effect on demand. Consistent with the strategic market planning process (see Chapter 3), the factors affecting demand might be classified into three categories: (1) *noncontrollable macroenvironmental factors* such as the state of the economy, life-cycle characteristics of key population segments, and changing lifestyles; (2) *competitive factors* such as competitors' products, prices, and promotional expenditures; and (3) *controllable organizational factors* such as the organization's own products, prices, and promotions.

All forecasts are built on one of three information bases: what people say, what people do, or what people have done. The first basis, what people *say*, involves systematic determination of the opinions of buyers. This may be done through buyer intention surveys or through the use of expert judgments. Building a forecast on what people *do* involves market testing. Understanding what people *have done* involves using computer programs or statistical tools to analyze records of past buying behavior.

BUYER INTENTION SURVEYS

Forecasting is particularly difficult when one is dealing with new offerings or markets that have dramatically changed. One way to form an estimate of future demand is to ask a sample of target buyers, either individually or in focus groups, to state their buying intentions for the forthcoming period. In the A.R.T. survey, respondents were asked:

"If you heard about an interesting professional theater production at the Loeb, would you be likely to attend?" (Response percentages are in parentheses).
( ) Probably   (88.1)   ( ) Probably not   (11.9)

This question requires the respondent to make a fairly definite choice. Some researchers prefer the following form of the question:

"Would you (a) definitely attend, (b) probably attend, (c) probably not attend, or (d) definitely not attend?"

These researchers feel that the "definitely attends" would be fairly dependable as a minimum estimate and some fraction of the "probably attends" could be added to arrive at a forecast. Even when the *absolute* levels of demand derived from buyer intentions are unreliable, the relative levels are often reliable. Thus, if an arts organization measures buyer intentions over several years, it may know that each specific estimate is fallible but that if the buyer intention index is up 20 percent between periods, demand may be expected to rise. Even where past indexes are unavailable, forecasts of *relative* demand for different kinds of market offerings can be derived by asking target audience members a series of "what if" questions. Following are some of the "what if" questions A.R.T. researchers asked their survey respondents. (Percentages of responses are in parentheses.)

A.R.T. SURVEY EXCERPTS: FORECASTING DEMAND

Many cities now have professional resident repertory theaters where a permanent acting ensemble produces a season of several plays from the broad range of dramatic literature. The productions alternate performances in repertory, and one actor may appear in two or three plays in a given week. If such a repertory theater were established in Boston, is it likely that you would:

( ) Not attend at all   (5.8)

( ) Probably attend just one performance   (13.4)

( ) Probably subscribe to a four-play half season   (21.4)

( ) Probably subscribe to a full eight-play season   (8.4)

( ) Probably attend more than one performance,
     but not subscribe   (51.0)

What factors would *encourage* you most to subscribe to a theater season or series of performances? (Check up to three items which you consider to be most important.)

( ) Discount ticket prices   (55.0)

( ) Restaurant or parking discounts   (10.8)

( ) Guaranteed priority seating   (35.7)

( ) Guaranteed ticket availability   (17.4)

( ) Ease of ordering tickets   (28.2)

( ) Special ticket exchange privileges   (17.3)

( ) Membership newsletters   (9.7)

( ) Greater likelihood of attending regularly   (19.8)

( ) Desire to support the institution   (16.1)

( ) Ability to attend with friends more easily   (8.5)

( ) Want to attend many shows by one group   (3.4)

( ) Interest in particular performances   (52.9)

What factors would *discourage* you most from subscribing to a theater season or series of performances? (Check up to two items which you consider to be most important.)

( ) Too much money to commit at once   (34.2)

( ) Too much advance planning required   (32.4)

( ) Unfamiliarity with performance group   (31.4)

( ) Limited interest in attending so many performances of one ensemble   (16.6)

( ) Limited interest in the particular selection of performances (52.6)

( ) Too inconvenient (live too far away, difficulty leaving the house at night, etc.)   (18.5)

EXPERT FORECASTS

Assessment of buyer intentions may be helpful for near-term forecasting, especially for new offerings. When carrying out long-term forecasting, however, these groups may not have sufficient perspective, experience, or wisdom to give reliable estimates. Experts such as trade organization executives, marketing consultants, or managers of other arts organizations and of governmental agencies may be invited to share their knowledge in order to develop a consensus about long-range trends. In a technique called the *Delphi method,* experts work individually or in groups to supply estimates and assumptions that are then reviewed by an analyst, revised, and subjected to further rounds of estimating. This pattern may be repeated over additional cycles until a consensus is reached and the variance around the group's estimates is reduced considerably. The technique is costly, but the Stanford Research Institute (SRI) found it extremely useful in attempting to estimate how the American populace will budget their time and expenditures for leisure activities 15 to 30 years in the future.

MARKET TESTS

In situations when buyers do not plan their future behavior carefully or are very erratic in carrying out their intentions, and when experts are not likely to be very good guessers, a more direct market test of probable behavior is desirable. A direct market test is especially desirable in forecasting the sales of a new product or the probable sales of an established product in a new territory. Where a short-run forecast of likely buyer response is desired, a small-scale market test is usually a highly accurate and reliable method.

COMPUTER-ASSISTED DEMAND ANALYSIS

Arts organizations generally use computers in some phases of their operations, such as for mailing lists, payroll, fund drives, subscriptions, and ticketing. Rarely do arts managers take advantage of computer systems that actually help them in their decision-making process. However, one such system, called the ARTS PLAN system, consists of three major components: a forecasting system to predict attendance at an event, an interactive planning model by which the manager can test the impact of different choices of performing arts events on total attendance for the year, and a routine for assessing the impact of extensive promotion on different events.

To develop a forecasting procedure at the Lively Arts at Stanford program, researchers used data available from 93 performances over a three-year period. Examination of these data using the statistical technique of multiple linear regression revealed that 80 percent of the variation in attendance around the average attendance level could be accounted for by the type of performing arts event (for example, dance, jazz, chamber music), the quarter in which it was presented (fall, winter, spring), and certain other factors. Most important, it was found that the name of the individual performer was not needed to explain this 80 percent of the variation. This meant that a forecasting system could be built for performers who had not previously been on campus and that seasonal effects could be segregated from others. The ARTS PLAN system predicted total attendance of 20,875 for the following year; actual attendance that year was 20,882.[9]

Evaluation and Control

The arts organization's marketing research strategy should be routinely and formally evaluated. Questions should be raised about methodologies and personnel. Managers should investigate the value of the information they receive and ask for possible improvements. And from time to time, an independent outside consultant should be brought in to ascertain the quality of the research.

[1] Harold Geneen, *Managing* (Garden City, N.Y.: Doubleday, 1984).

[2] Paul DiMaggio and Michael Useem, "Decentralized Policy Research: The Case of Arts Organizations," manuscript, Center for the Study of Public Policy, Cambridge, Mass., n.d.

[3] The study was conducted by Joanne Scheff. The survey was administered and results were tabulated and reported by Creative and Response Research Services, Inc., of Chicago.

[4] "*The Financial Condition of Symphony Orchestras,*" prepared by the Wolf Organization, Inc., Cambridge, Mass. (Washington, D.C.: American Symphony Orchestra League, 1992); "*Americanizing the American Orchestra,*" report of the National Task Force for the American Orchestra: An Initiative for Change (Washington, D.C.: American Symphony Orchestra League, 1993).

[5] Imran Currim, Charles B. Weinberg, and Dick R. Wittinck, "Design of Subscription Programs for a Performing Arts Series," *Journal of Consumer Research,* June 1981, 67–75.

[6] Much of the description of sampling errors and sampling biases is taken from Pamela L. Alreck and Robert B. Settle, *The Survey Research Handbook* (Homewood, Ill.: Irwin, 1985), 67–68.

[7] C. H. Lovelock and P. P. Merliss, "American Repertory Theatre," Harvard Business School case study 9-580-133, 1980.

[8] C. W. L. Hart, J. I. Ayala, and J. K. Falstad, "American Repertory Theatre—1988," Harvard Business School case study 9-688-120, 1988.

[9] Charles B. Weinberg, "Marketing Planning for the Arts Organization," in *Marketing the Arts,* ed. Michael P. Mokwa, William M. Dawson, and E. Arthur Prieve (New York: Praeger, 1980), 108–9.

◮●◮

CHAPTER 7

*We all have our
special talents.
Willows are good
at greenness, but
flowers are better
at being red.*

SAIKAKU IHARA,
17TH CENTURY

*The toughest thing
about success is that
you've got to keep
on being a success.*

IRVING BERLIN

IDENTIFYING THE COMPETITION AND POTENTIAL COLLABORATORS

MOST PEOPLE READILY IDENTIFY COCA-COLA AND PEPSI-COLA AS MAJOR competitors. But how many people think beyond the soft drink industry when considering the competition facing these two industry giants? Consider the fact that in the last few years, soft drink consumption has exceeded that of water. And even French winemakers, who already endure intense competition within their own industry, are concerned with how much the soft drink industry is infringing on their sales. A major reason that Coke and Pepsi are so successful is that they have broadly defined the business they are in: not the soft drink business but the thirst-quenching business.

In the performing arts world, a broad conception of competition is just as crucial as in private industry, for two reasons. First, when a couple is making a decision about whether to subscribe to Theater A or Theater B, this is likely to be a relatively narrow, industry-specific choice, like a preference for Pepsi or Coke. But when the decision is about where to go on a Saturday night, the competition is likely to include many forms of entertainment, such as movies, sporting events, restaurants, and even videos at home. Second, many arts organizations are discovering creative solutions to financial, audience-building, and managerial problems by collaborating with other arts organizations, other types of nonprofit organizations, and businesses. Therefore, a broad conception of *competition* for arts organizations should include approaches to *collaboration* as well.

COMPETITION

Arts organizations face several different types of competition. In New York City or London where people can choose from thirty or more live stage plays on any given evening, there is intense *intratype* competition. A patron's choice between subscribing to the symphony or to the opera represents *intertype* competition. The symphony and opera companies face *substitute* competition if patrons choose to listen to recorded music or watch an opera performance on video instead of attending a live performance. Finally, there is *indirect* competition when patrons decide to attend a sports event, go to a movie, or entertain at home instead of attending a performing arts event.

Although people generally consider competition as a negative force that must be overcome, competition actually is beneficial for two important reasons. First, the existence of two or more competitors in the marketplace, clamoring for attention, spending money on advertising and public relations, can stimulate increases in the size of the total market. Second, competition can sharpen the competitive skills of the marketers. It is when business is booming and marketers become complacent that they are in danger of becoming insensitive to changing consumer needs. To compete, marketers have to continually rethink how their product is positioned. They have to look more carefully at their audience to see if there are better ways to meet their needs and wants. They have to consider the possibility of changing prices, features, benefits, and advertising. This reevaluation and continuing close attention to marketing details can only help the art organization's overall performance.

Primary and Selective Demand

In efforts to build their audiences, there are two types of demand that may be stimulated by marketers: *primary* and *selective.* When marketers stimulate primary demand, they attempt to enlarge the whole "pie" of their category's consumer base by increasing the total number of people who attend the symphony, opera, dance, or theater—or, in a broader sense, all of the performing arts. When marketers stimulate selective demand, they seek a larger piece of the current "pie" for their specific organization, usually by attracting people who are attending competitive events.

Arts marketers can attempt to expand demand in three ways:

1. Current attenders can be encouraged to attend the same type of event more frequently. This strategy is the basis for subscription series and is the driving force behind "second stage" or other additional performances that current patrons are encouraged to attend.

2. Other events and art forms can be suggested to current attenders. This strategy aims to introduce current arts attenders to other art forms or other organizations. Thus, a patron of classical theater may be encouraged to attend a modern dance or experimental theater performance. This strategy can be carried out by individual organizations, collaborating organizations, or umbrella organizations such as theater guilds that promote all their members' offerings.

3. Nonattenders can be converted to attenders. The goal is to increase the overall number of persons who attend performing arts events. This may be accomplished, for example, by exposing new people to classical music by way of free concerts in the park or by providing special events for target groups.

Of these strategies, the first is the easiest to accomplish. The second is more difficult and requires not only a change in consumer behavior but also cooperation between organizations. The third strategy is the most difficult, as it necessitates changing basic attitudes and influencing tastes among the nonattending public.

Primary demand stimulation is of great interest to arts marketers because, in recent years, overall attendance has been shrinking somewhat and is static at best. Primary demand stimulation, when undertaken by individual organizations, is best accomplished by the industry leaders with huge market share. Consider that in the business sector, Sunkist need only say "buy oranges," and Kodak can say "take pictures." Likewise, the Metropolitan Opera can encourage operagoing and the major symphonies in many cities can promote live classical music attendance. Smaller organizations are not in a position to stimulate primary demand on their own. They cannot afford the advertising and promotional budget necessary to build overall demand. Furthermore, if they did so, small organizations with small market share would mainly be building demand for their competitors. Rather, for the many small arts organizations in any given area, the most effective means for stimulating primary demand is through organizations with a broader scope such as foundations, community-wide associations, and schools, and through collaborative efforts between arts organizations.

Even under situations of the toughest competition, worthwhile efforts can be made by arts marketers. During the National Basketball Association playoffs and finals, all other generic forms of entertainment—movie houses, theaters, and restaurants—sit nearly empty. Imagine the performing arts banding together with an appeal to arts aficionados. Their advertisement could show actors, dancers, and musicians bouncing a basketball forlornly on stage and looking out at a sea of empty seats. This may serve as a humorous reminder that the rest of the entertainment world doesn't stop when Michael Jordan is center court.

Types of Competition

Selective demand stimulation is the responsibility of individual arts organizations. They encourage artsgoers to "subscribe now" or to attend their "highly acclaimed" performances. In doing so, they face several types of competition.

It is useful for arts organizations to consider from another perspective the different levels of competition they face when developing strategies for a particular target market. The competition can be categorized as follows.

1. *Desire competitors:* other immediate desires that the consumer might want to satisfy.
2. *Generic competitors:* other basic ways in which the consumer can satisfy a particular desire.
3. *Form competitors:* other forms that can satisfy the consumer's particular desire.
4. *Enterprise competitors:* other enterprises offering the same form that can satisfy the consumer's particular desire.

Consider a young professional woman in New York City trying to decide what to do on a particular evening. She realizes that she has several desires—finishing a project at work, getting some exercise, meeting household responsibilities, or being entertained. Once she determines that the *desire* she will satisfy is to be entertained, she has to consider various *generic* competitors, such as TV or a video at home, a movie, or a live performance. Choosing to be entertained by a live performance, she has to consider various *forms* of live entertainment—a symphony, a dance, a jazz club, or a legitimate play. Finally, after settling on a legitimate play, she has to choose from among the offerings of various theatrical *enterprises* that are of interest to her.

Of course, the decision-making process is not always as straightforward as this model may suggest. In fact, the consumer may eliminate alternatives across types of competition, rather than just within them, before moving on to the next level. Consider the example of parents who are planning a day with their children during the winter holiday. They are considering four options: sledding, a visit to Santa and viewing window decorations, a performance of *The Nutcracker Suite,* or a performance of *A Christmas Carol.* The parents eliminate sledding because of foul weather conditions, and the *Nutcracker* because tickets are unavailable. So their final decision, between Santa Claus and *A Christmas Carol,* will be at the generic level, a full two steps above where it should be according to the previous model.

When a performing arts organization is experiencing poor sales, the cause may be inadequate marketing strategy at any or all of the four levels of competition.

DESIRE COMPETITORS
People have so many demands competing for their limited time that they might not have the luxury of satisfying their desire for an evening of entertainment. At this

level of competition, about the best that the entertainment industry can do is to collaborate in promoting the idea that "in this stressful, work-conscious world, you need more entertainment to relax, to replenish, to grow."

GENERIC COMPETITORS

At the next level of competition, if too many promising customers are not choosing live entertainment as the preferred generic form of entertainment, two directions can be taken. First, managers of all the performing arts may combine their resources to get people out to "the world of live entertainment," emphasizing the benefits in their offerings absent from other forms of entertainment. Second, managers may explore the roadblocks that prevent people from choosing their performance offerings over other forms of entertainment. Some issues, such as cost and concern over last-minute ticket availability, are within the control of management, and the marketer can position the product to compete at this generic level. A theater might promote $10 tickets on the day of the performance for certain low-attendance days, then advertise that its live event is just as available as and little more costly than a movie.

FORM COMPETITORS

Sometimes the main competition exists within the form of performing arts. For example, dance has always had a smaller audience base than theater or symphony orchestras, although it combines elements from both of these competitors. Dance marketers may want to advertise their beautiful classical music, their dramatic story line, and their vivid sets to attract patrons of their form competitors.

ENTERPRISE COMPETITORS

The most intensive competition is usually at the enterprise level. The fine-quality, highly professional New York City Opera faces tough competition from the larger-scale, higher-budget, more famous Metropolitan Opera. The dozens of small theater companies in Chicago are in competition with one another for name recognition, for access to good plays to produce, and, of course, for patrons.

Some performing arts organizations may find it useful to compare themselves to others. First, managers should know the trends in the industry as a whole. Are subscription rates declining? miniplan purchases increasing? total audience numbers increasing or declining? Such information can help managers understand the responses of their own publics and plan for the future. Managers may also want to study the financial activities of other organizations similar in scope and objectives, or of a group that the organization wishes to emulate. The purpose of comparisons is not to replicate what others have achieved, but to identify alternative directions and goals that might be considered.

Arts organizations must understand who their competitors are and what a competitive advantage can offer. Managers need to understand their own strengths and weaknesses, and they should gather as much competitive information as possible in the process of determining their best strategies.

Formulating Competitive Strategy: A Structural Analysis of the Industry

The essence of formulating a competitive strategy is relating an organization to its environment; and the key aspect of an organization's environment is the structure of the industry in which it competes. The state of competition in an industry depends on the five basic competitive forces shown in Figure 7-1. All five competitive forces jointly determine the intensity of industry competition. Not all forces apply equally in each industry or at any point in time. But analysis of the strongest forces is central to strategy formulation.[1]

Threat of New Entrants

When new organizations enter an industry, they have an impact on the audience and donor base of existing organizations—especially on small and unstable groups. We refer to the factors that prevent new entrants from joining an industry as *barriers to entry*. If the barriers are high, the threat of entry is low. Some of the barriers facing nonprofit arts organizations are described in the following paragraphs.

LACK OF CONTRIBUTED SUPPORT
Unless a start-up organization has a founder who is willing and able to provide substantial support, or enters a niche that is highly attractive to funding sources, it will have difficulty gaining financial support. Most funders' resources are scarce and are

Figure 7-1

STRUCTURAL ANALYSIS OF INDUSTRIES

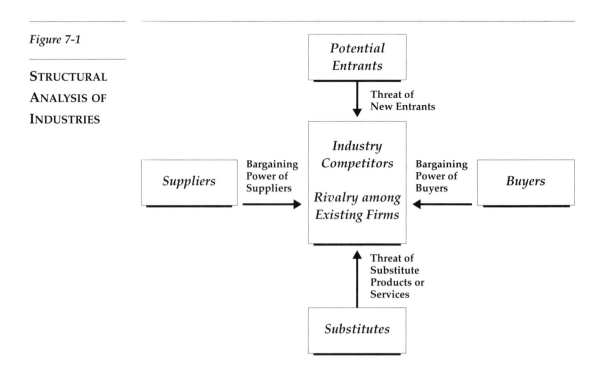

already committed. Start-ups are especially reliant on donated income, because they have no audience base on which to rely for ticket sales.

CAPITAL REQUIREMENTS

The level of capital required by an organization will affect its ability to enter the industry. A small theater company can rent a hall by the month and hire actors and production staff for one production at a time. A dance company must train and sustain an ongoing troupe of dancers. Operas, by nature, require large amounts of capital to mount their huge productions. Thus, small theaters sprout up more commonly than do more capital-intensive organizations.

PRODUCT DIFFERENTIATION

Established organizations have developed an identity and earned customer loyalty based on such factors as reputation, tradition, product characteristics, customer benefits, advertising, and customer service. New entrants are forced to differentiate their products, either finding ways to overcome existing customer loyalties or carving out a viable niche that is not currently being filled by other organizations. For example, throughout the New York City Opera's fifty-year history, one-third of the operas presented have been by twentieth-century American composers, unlike the far more traditional repertoire presented at the Metropolitan Opera.[2]

COST AND REVENUE DISADVANTAGE

Established organizations may have both cost-containing and revenue-generating advantages that cannot be duplicated by potential entrants. Such advantages may result from commitments for individual, corporate, and government support; a major head start on endowments; real estate ownership; and access to special products and supplies, such as warehouses of sets and costumes or ownership of concert grand pianos.

EXPERIENCE CURVES

The experience of existing organizations can be an entry barrier to new hopefuls, especially when that experience is proprietary and not available to competitors and potential entrants by way of copying, hiring a competitor's employees, or engaging consultants. The relevant experience may take the form of a resident choreographer, conductor, or manager, or the network of contacts that have been built over the years through extensive touring engagements or the work of a talented public relations specialist.

GOVERNMENT POLICY

Strict requirements must be met in order for a new enterprise to gain 501(c)(3) status as a tax-exempt nonprofit organization. Other government regulations may also deter entry of new competitors to the market.

Intensity of Rivalry among Existing Competitors

Rivalry may lead to the use of such tactics as price competition, advertising battles, product innovations, and improved customer service. These behaviors typically increase costs for all competitors. The factors discussed in the next few paragraphs interact to determine the intensity of the rivalry.

SLOW INDUSTRY GROWTH

Slow industry growth intensifies rivalry because any gains in sales by one organization must come at the expense of its competition, rather than through overall market growth. During the period of rapid growth in arts attendance in the 1970s and early 1980s, new entrants to the scene caused little concern among the existing organizations. In more recent years, audience growth has stagnated, and the size of the market is insufficient to support the existing arts organizations, much less to fuel industry growth.

HIGH FIXED COSTS

High fixed costs create strong pressures for all organizations to operate at capacity. When the booming audiences of the 1970s and 1980s provided arts organizations with surplus revenue, many organizations increased the size of their staffs and made other commitments that increased their fixed costs of operation. Now, in the more dreary economic climate, organizations are finding it difficult to meet those costs, and many face the necessity of serious cutbacks. For example, seating capacity tends to be augmented in large increments. When a number of organizations outgrow their space and acquire greater capacity at nearly the same time, the supply-demand balance is disrupted and the entire industry faces a period of overcapacity.

Many midsized orchestras like the Buffalo Philharmonic, the Sacramento Symphony, and the Louisville Symphony have contracted to pay their musicians for a full rather than partial calendar year, dramatically increasing their fixed costs. The driving force behind the increased number of concerts these orchestras began to offer annually was not demand for tickets, but guarantees to musicians. So demand was not adequate to meet the new cost structure. In contrast, a small orchestra such as the Cedar Rapids Symphony pays its musicians per concert, so it does not have the same concern over fixed costs.

FEE COMPETITION

At the New York City Opera Company, the top fee for singers and conductors is $1,750 a night, compared with a $12,000 limit at the Metropolitan Opera and even higher fees in Europe. This fee structure makes for a transient roster at the City Opera, because performers do not return once they are able to command higher fees elsewhere. This situation creates artistic and commercial frustration for City Opera managers.[3]

HIGH EXIT BARRIERS

Exit barriers are economic, strategic, and emotional factors that keep organizations in business even though they experience ongoing financial distress. In nonprofit arts organizations, emotional and sociocultural factors predominate in keeping managers and boards of directors from closing their doors. People involved in the arts believe in their products; many artists and arts managers will take severe pay cuts, and devoted contributors will donate large sums of money, in order to attempt to keep their organizations alive.

Pressures from Substitute Products

Substitute products, like Coca-Cola instead of water or French wine, or like home videos instead of live entertainment, have a negative impact on the size of the specific industry they replace. The fact that people have increasingly more options available for entertainment is probably the strongest competitive force facing nonprofit arts organizations. The challenge for arts organizations is to identify the benefits they provide that cannot be obtained elsewhere and to disseminate this information widely through advertisements, public relations activities, and education.

Bargaining Power of Buyers

The buyer, or audience member, "competes" with the industry by forcing down prices, by demanding higher quality or more services, and by playing competitors against each other. Frequent users, light users, and low-income arts enthusiasts all possess "power" with arts organizations.

FREQUENT USERS

Frequent users make up a concentrated buyer group that purchases large volumes relative to total sales, thereby increasing the seller's dependence on them. This principle accounts for the routine discounts given to subscribers and for group sales. The most frequent users are also the most sensitive to and demanding of quality and service options, requiring organizations to devote more and more resources to satisfying their regular patrons.

LIGHT USERS

These buyers are casual, infrequent users for whom the product is relatively unimportant and for whom alternatives may be highly attractive. Their power derives from their high sensitivity to such factors as price and other special offers, such as singles nights. This group is the most susceptible to expensive mass advertising channels. Also, they tend to be less sensitive to and appreciative of the high-quality products and services to which the organization is already devoting extensive resources to appeal to frequent users.

LOW-INCOME USERS

This group of buyers, which includes students, retirees, and blue-collar employees, have less earning power. Buyers without much discretionary income are likely to be the most price sensitive with regard to leisure-time alternatives in general.

Bargaining Power of Suppliers

Suppliers can exert bargaining power over participants in an industry by threatening to raise prices or to reduce the quality of their goods and services. In the performing arts industry, the most important suppliers are the artists and production staff. The Metropolitan Opera Company must negotiate with more than thirty unions, including singers, musicians, set designers, lighting designers, stagehands, ushers, and so forth. The Sacramento Symphony declared bankruptcy because the musicians' contractual power made it impossible for the orchestra to extricate itself from its dire financial situation. Other supply costs may also vary, such as printing and mailing costs, rental and upkeep of concert halls, and materials for sets and costumes. A supplier group is powerful if the buyer is more dependent on the supplier than the supplier is on the buyer, which is likely to be the case in the following circumstances.

CONCENTRATED SUPPLIER GROUP

A concentrated supplier group is dominated by a few companies or individuals and is more concentrated than the industry it sells to. Suppliers selling to more fragmented buyers will usually be able to exert considerable influence over prices, quality, and terms. A compelling example of this effect is that superstars can command very high fees for their performances. Such names as Itzhak Perlman, Luciano Pavarotti, and Yo Yo Ma are a magic draw for audiences, and demand for their appearances far exceeds the supply. Their fees are so high that even a large hall with a full house sometimes sustains a loss in order to present them. However, the goodwill generated and the season subscribers gained by presenting a superstar at just one concert per year can justify the expenditure, so even smaller-budget organizations seek them out.

LACK OF SUBSTITUTES

If substitutes are lacking, the supplier group's power will be greater. Orchestral musicians, for example, are highly trained professionals who gain access to their positions through a rigorously selective and competitive process. Therefore, they are not readily substitutable, and both their presence and their mental well-being are crucial to the orchestra's success. The musicians are in a strong position to press for their interests, and many labor contracts with orchestral musicians are detailed and lengthy. On the other hand, some orchestras in smaller cities and towns are made up of community members who may or may not be professional musicians and who usually are not paid for their services. These musicians are more readily substitutable than those in world-class symphonies. Similarly, nonunion actors who perform in small, local theaters are available in great oversupply and command salaries for their performances that do little more than cover their commuting costs.

IMPORTANCE OF THE INDUSTRY

Suppliers are prone to exert more bargaining power on their smaller buyers than their larger ones. For example, the performing arts industry is not crucial to the success of most printers, advertising agencies, and office equipment suppliers.

SWITCHING COSTS

When the supplier's products are unique or when switching costs are high, the buyer's ability to play one supplier against another is reduced. Consider a theater that is deciding between two different computerized ticketing software systems. The management may choose the less preferred system because the preferred alternative is not compatible with hardware currently owned by the organization and switching hardware would be prohibitively expensive.

Strategic Groups and Mobility Barriers

Arts organizations can be classified into strategic groups. Strategic groupings may be delineated by product type, size of budget, quality and prestige level of the organizations, audience segments they attract, location of venues, ticket prices, and even by the types of promotional activities undertaken by the organizations. A product type grouping may indicate that a theater performing classic plays competes for audience members more closely with classical music presenters than with theaters presenting contemporary plays. Likewise, since there is very little crossover in patronage between the Boston Pops and the Boston Symphony, each may be strategically grouped by product type with other similar forms of entertainment, either popular or classical, rather than with orchestras in general.

Other strategic groupings may relate to the organizations' prices and/or geographical locations. A metropolitan area may boast a world-class professional orchestra with a budget of $40 million a year and smaller community orchestras that perform only several times a year, have volunteer musicians, and have small budgets to support their minimal operating expenses and soloist fees. These small orchestras can never compete with the major institution on quality, variety, prestige, or fame of the guest artists. Instead, community orchestras offer their patrons convenience of location and a much lower cost. The major orchestra is likely to be in most direct competition with the opera, while the community orchestras compete with other activities in their own geographic area, from the community theater to an orchid exhibit at the botanical gardens.

Arts organizations sometimes move from one strategic group to another. The Steppenwolf Theater of Chicago outgrew its original location in a suburban church basement and then two more centrally located venues before it launched a successful capital fund drive and built a larger, state-of-the-art theater to its own specifications.

In the process, the company changed its strategic groupings related to location, budget, quality, and prestige, developing from a local to a regional company to an internationally known performing group.

Organizations often devote resources to improving their quality by means such as buying the rights to produce award-winning plays or hiring higher-priced performers. Sometimes these efforts work well for organizations, but often there are *mobility barriers* that deter an organization from moving from one strategic position to another. In a metropolitan area that already boasts a large, famous orchestra, a community orchestra cannot achieve the budget or status of its more prestigious competitor because the community cannot engender the contributions or audience base necessary to sustain two major symphonies. For other organizations, a substantial increase in budget and audience size would be possible only by instituting a programming change that would run counter to the organization's artistic mission. In such a case, the maintenance of artistic values acts as a mobility barrier to enlarging the audience base.

New barriers can arise when there are changes within the industry or new social forces at work. For example, *customer service* has come to define a strategic grouping in recent years. The organizations best positioned to provide full ticket-exchange privileges, free adjacent parking, social events, pre- and postperformance discussions, informative newsletters, and so on, create mobility barriers for other organizations that cannot readily put such systems into place.

An assessment of where an organization stands in relation to the various competitive forces will reveal the areas where the organization should confront competition and where to avoid it. It will also help an organization to identify its strengths and weaknesses and to formulate a competitive strategy. The analysis may help suggest which audiences an organization should target, what products it should offer, and how most effectively to position and present them.

COLLABORATION

As the nation's nonprofit arts industry has been grappling in recent years with spiraling expenses and deficits of crisis proportions, it has become clear that fundamental changes in the way arts organizations conduct business must be considered.[4] In response to this need, many nonprofit arts organizations, which have historically viewed other organizations as competitors, are now discovering creative solutions to their growing economic difficulties by building mutually beneficial collaborations with one another, with businesses, and with public-sector organizations.

Strategic Collaborations

The term *collaboration* is commonly used by nonprofit arts organizations to represent a variety of joint activities, such as citywide arts festivals or corporate sponsorship of single events. However, these efforts are typically *tactical* in nature, characterized by informal relationships that exist without any commonly defined mission, structure, or planning effort. Information is shared as needed, and authority is retained by each organization so there is virtually no risk. Resources are kept separate, as are the rewards achieved.

In contrast, we consider a collaboration to be a *strategic* alliance, connoting a more durable commitment and a more pervasive relationship. Authority is determined according to a new collaborative structure that is created to carry out the common mission. The parties engage in comprehensive planning and create well-defined communication channels. They pool resources and share the resulting benefits. Since each member of the collaboration contributes its own resources (including its reputation), the risk each accepts is much greater than in more informal and short-term relationships.

Well designed and well executed strategic collaborations help arts organizations expand their customer base, develop new funding sources, and cut costs—without compromising the organization's mission or quality. They can also help organizations achieve goals that they cannot achieve on their own, such as funding the construction of a new performance space. Strategic collaboration can represent a major opportunity for both nonprofit arts organizations and their partners, provided they understand clearly what it is, when it can be useful, and how and with whom it can be achieved.

Partnering with Other Arts Organizations: Collaboration versus Competition

Operating on the assumption that their relationships are largely competitive, arts organizations rarely turn to one another to find ways to achieve their mutual goals. Yet, many collaborative opportunities exist, both for building audiences and for cutting costs.

BUILDING AUDIENCES

In 1989, a comprehensive marketing survey of Philadelphia cultural audiences demonstrated that cultural institutions are not necessarily in competition with one another. For example, the study found substantial crossover between jazz, theater, and dance audiences. Capitalizing on that finding, a special subscription series combining the three art forms was put together, resulting in an increased audience size for each. In another example, the study found that Philadelphia's African-American Historical and Cultural Museum plays the role in the black community of a "cultural gateway" by promoting other cultural events. For many blacks, the museum represents their first membership in a cultural institution, but many in the museum's audience eventually become active in the larger cultural community.

The researchers in the Philadelphia study analyzed the preferences of single-ticket buyers as opposed to subscription buyers and the reasons people gave for not renewing their subscriptions. Two conclusions attest to the value of collaboration between arts organizations. First, attendees' appetites for experiencing new and unfamiliar works often exceed the ability of a single organization to mount new exhibitions or produce new works. Second, some audience segments clearly shop the cultural market for particular artists and/or particular works of interest to them, and are unlikely to develop loyalty to a particular organization.

These findings are not unique to Philadelphia. In another study, nearly 3,500 persons in the greater Cleveland area were surveyed to explore the possibilities of creating synergies among local organizations. The survey's results strongly support cross-institutional cooperation: 70 percent of area users attended more than one organization in the previous year and 47 percent attended three or more organizations. Satisfaction levels actually increase with more diversified use: the highest levels of satisfaction are reported by those who attend six or more organizations annually.

One might assume that the high degree of satisfaction is attributable to the preexisting interest and commitment of the individual attendee. But Danny Newman, father and promoter of subscription series, believes strongly that "by attending all of our productions, season after season, [the patron] develops discernment and perspective. . . . His repertoire-acceptance threshold constantly rises. His awareness of everything connected with the art form heightens. . . . He is involved—hooked."[5] Although these observations describe patrons who repeatedly attend single organizations, they apply cross-institutionally as well.

The studies in Philadelphia and Cleveland concluded that arts organizations should think beyond their own boundaries and that their participation in cooperative ventures will enliven audiences rather than exhaust them. Although arts organizations are concerned about losing patrons to one another through joint subscriptions, collaborative box offices, and other cross-promotional efforts, the economies of acquiring new patrons through these techniques are likely to more than offset the occasional loss of a patron to another organization.

A vivid example of this concept in action is the New Jersey Theatre Group's (NJTG) Theatre Sampler Series, a three-play theater package that permits patrons to buy, for $55, a ticket for one play at each of three different theaters with priority seating and flexibility. During its first eighteen months, the program sold more than 5,000 tickets, effectively increasing attendance at every NJTG member theater from the small, urban Ensemble Theatre Company in Newark to the lavish, suburban Paper Mill Playhouse in Milburn. Significantly, most people who ordered the tickets had never attended even one NJTG member theater.

INTERDISCIPLINARY CROSSOVERS

According to the Philadelphia study, efforts to cross-cultivate audiences that share a natural link (as indicated by a relatively high degree of crossover attendance) are most likely to meet with success. Partnerships in the disciplinary combinations shown in Exhibit 7-1 are likely to appeal to larger market segments than other combinations. Interdisciplinary attendance among those surveyed ranged from a high of 90 percent (opera attendees who also visited an art museum) to a low of 12 percent (classical music attendees who also visited an African-American cultural institution). Organizations with larger bases of attenders are likely to attract participants from virtually every discipline.

Most significantly, individuals who reported frequent attendance at any one organization tended to report frequent arts participation overall. Therefore, efforts by one organization to attract people are likely to have a ripple effect, causing more frequent overall cultural arts attendance. Since many cultural participants are interested in broadening their cultural activity, they would most likely be receptive to efforts to cross-cultivate audiences.

Since the demise of the Model T (available in any color, as long as it's black), automobile manufacturers have recognized the value of providing a variety of options to their publics, from small sports cars to family-size sedans, vans, and trucks. It is possible for a family to meet all its vehicular needs with only Toyotas or Chevrolets in the driveway. However, no performing arts organization is in a position to provide theater *and* dance *and* music *and* visual arts, fulfilling all of their patrons'

Exhibit 7-1 | **INTERDISCIPLINARY AUDIENCE CROSSOVERS**

Discipline	Crossovers
Ballet	Art museums, opera, classical music, theater
Modern dance	Art museums, theater
Opera	Art museums, dance, classical music, theater
Art museums	All other disciplines
Science organizations	Classical music
Arboreta	Opera, classical music, theater
Classical music	Art, dance, opera, theater
New Music	Art, dance, theater
Theater	Art, history, and culture museums, opera, classical music
Jazz	Art museums, theater
African-American organizations	All other African-American cultural organizations, especially art museums, modern dance, theater.
Children's museums	Dance

Philadelphia Arts Market Study, commissioned by The Pew Charitable Trusts, prepared by Ziff Marketing, Inc., Sept. 7, 1989, pp. xiii–xv. Reprinted with permission.

arts interests. This fact alone implies that cooperative efforts between cultural institutions can be valuable in building frequency of attendance and satisfaction among the patrons.

CROSS-FERTILIZATION OF AUDIENCES

In February 1993, the Brooklyn Philharmonic Orchestra performed the works of an unlikely combination of composers, Philip Glass and David Bowie, to an equally unusual audience, which consisted of at least as many people under 35 years old as over 60. The audience was composed of the orchestra's regular subscribers, who were accustomed to relatively traditional symphonic programs, and the younger, more adventurous fans of the Brooklyn Academy of Music's Next Wave Festival, one of America's leading venues of new performance. Bringing the two audiences together had been one of the chief goals of conductor Dennis Russell Davies, who wants to help bridge the gap between the organizations and their audiences. Davies argues that people are hungry for new sounds in the concert hall, but classical music managers and musicians too often fail to update their programs. Says Davies, "The audiences are generally more open to new music than the professionals." By bringing these two audiences together for the Glass-Bowie concert, the orchestra exposed each audience group to new and different music to which it could relate.[6]

COST-CUTTING COLLABORATIONS

By combining various administrative functions and overhead expenses, arts organizations can realize economies of scale. Producing concerts, marketing, dealing with boards, and raising money are similar processes from one organization to the next. Consolidating those functions across two or more organizations can lead to better quality as well as lower costs.

The American Symphony Orchestra (ASO) in New York City has developed an innovative managerial collaboration with the Concordia Orchestra. The ASO presents six concerts a year, taking a thematic approach to presenting less familiar symphonic repertoire. Concordia presents four concerts a year, focusing largely on jazz influences in concert music. Their audiences are as different as their music, so they do not consider each other direct competitors. Concordia has contracted with the ASO and its highly professional management team to perform its administrative functions. The two orchestras share the same executive director, the same marketing director, the same address, and most of the same staff. Each has its own stationery, mailings, and logo. Concordia retains its own board of trustees and financial books, and pursues its own artistic vision.

The collaboration has allowed Concordia to reduce its administrative costs by 40 percent and the ASO to earn additional income by providing management services. The ASO designates some of these earnings to strengthen its administrative infrastructure for the benefit of both organizations. When there are two marketing staff positions rather than one, people can be hired for their specific skills, and quality and effectiveness are improved. "What we're trying to do," explained Eugene Carr, executive director of the two orchestras, "is to create a new way to manage the arts by combining resources. It seems ridiculous that if you have a dozen organizations, each producing a small number of events every year, you also have a dozen executive directors, a dozen office leases, a dozen marketing departments. None of the organizations can really afford to engage as much staff as it needs."[7] As an added benefit, both organizations are able to show foundations that more of their contributed grant money actually goes toward artistic programs, rather than toward light bulbs and rent.

COMMON GROUND

In what may well have been the first collaborative effort of its kind, the Chicago Music Alliance, the Chicago Dance Coalition, and the League of Chicago Theaters held a joint day-long conference in July of 1993, entitled "Common Ground." Knowing that many of their problems are common to the industry as a whole, representatives of nearly one hundred organizations came together with the following goals:

- To identify the environmental influences having an effect on their work and to develop strategies to deal with them.
- To develop a better understanding of their common issues, no matter what their mission, size, or organizational culture.
- To develop new insights and approaches for dealing with their problems.
- To identify processes with which they can build a sense of community.
- To take responsibility for themselves and their community to create change for the cultural life in Chicago.

In the course of their dialogue, the group identified several ways in which they can work individually and together to increase their effectiveness. On an individual basis, it was suggested that arts managers and board members join their local chamber of commerce, school boards, and other community organizations in order to develop a voice and a strong presence in the community. As a group, they agreed they could join forces to increase their bargaining power with suppliers. Some opportunities identified were the pooling of resources for sharing full-time bookkeepers, rather than separately hiring part-time bookkeepers; joint contracting and negotiating with printers to empower the arts organizations to force printing prices down; and joint advertising in the print media—to encourage price reductions, but also to gain a stronger voice in encouraging editors to provide more arts coverage. The participants formed a steering committee, which is charged with furthering the goals of the Common Ground conference.

Collaborating with Other Nonprofits

Arts organizations can also benefit from collaborating with other types of nonprofit organizations. The Saint Louis Symphony Orchestra (SLSO), for example, developed a community partnership program called In Unison with its neighborhood African-American churches. Powell Symphony Hall, the performing center for the SLSO, is located in an African-American neighborhood, but area residents have criticized the orchestra for being aloof from its community. The partnership has created not just better community feelings but also an enthusiastic new audience segment for the orchestra.

The SLSO staff focused its outreach efforts on African-American religious institutions for several reasons. Churches are a central component in family and community life; members share an interest in music; and African-American churches have played a significant role in nurturing talent for the classical concert stage and other arenas of music. Interestingly, the SLSO has found that it can attract more African-American professionals through their church affiliations than through their professional associations, an avenue it had pursued before the In Unison collaboration.

In Unison membership is free to the churches and their congregants. The only membership obligation for participating churches is that the congregation agree to purchase twenty or more tickets, at a 50 percent discount, to six of the nine concerts included in the In Unison concert package. (Discounted ticket prices start as low as $6.) The concerts in the In Unison series are specially selected to appeal to members and feature some of the most popular programs of the season, including violinist Itzhak Perlman, pianist Andre Watts, the Boys Choir of Harlem, and the world premiere of a new jazz piano concerto.

In addition to high-quality programming and low cost, several other features of the program contribute to its success. Orchestra members offer one free ensemble performance in each participating church. The church can use this concert as a fundraiser or as cost-free entertainment for the congregation and their guests. The orchestra provides access to music education materials, including information on African-American composers and artists, details about training and auditioning for the SLSO chorus and Youth Orchestra, and other topics of interest to the congregation. Backstage tours are provided for congregation members and their guests, as are invitations to postconcert receptions and free Saint Louis Symphony Youth Orchestra tickets for children. The orchestra donates tuition for three children from each church's Sunday School to attend the annual week-long Symphony Camp. This program introduces young children to classical music under the guidance of music professionals. Pastors of In Unison member churches receive a one-year honorary membership in the Symphony Society Green Room Association, entitling them to a range of special services and establishing a social forum where they can relate to other symphony regulars.

Each congregation is represented by an In Unison project coordinator, selected by the church leadership, who works with symphony personnel and church leadership (Sunday School teachers, choir directors, and pastors) to schedule In Unison services.

At the churches, symphony representatives work to dismantle preconceptions about the concert-going experience: "Be comfortable, be yourself. Don't worry if you clap in the wrong place—you'll catch on real soon." When In Unison members arrive for a concert at Powell Hall, they are greeted by African-American staff and ushers.

By the second season, In Unison had built relationships with nearly 13,000 members of twelve area churches, and it was recouping program expenses through ticket sales, even with the substantial discount. The free ensemble performances in the churches commonly draw an audience of 250 people—more than many of the chamber performances at Powell Hall.

Art and Business Collaborations

Corporations are discovering that they can serve their own strategic goals by teaming up with arts organizations. Involvement in and support of the community in which it does business improves a firm's operations and its profitability. A thriving cultural community can help attract and retain highly educated and talented personnel and promote goodwill among customers, clients, and employees. By supporting the arts, businesses add a human element to their corporate image. By linking up with the arts organizations' image, appeal, and customer base, they gain visibility and an enhanced profile. In fact, 33 percent of businesses surveyed in 1994 indicated that a portion of their support to the arts came from their public relations budget, compared to 17 percent in 1991.[8] Businesses are increasingly able to justify attributing the cash expenses of their collaborative ventures with arts organizations to marketing budgets. This trend is of significant value to arts organizations, because corporate philanthropic budgets fluctuate according to economic circumstances and philanthropic priorities. And by providing noncash contributions in the form of management expertise, technology, volunteers, and products, corporations can increase their contributions to the arts even when budgets are tight.[9]

SPONSORSHIPS

According to Lesa Ukman, cofounder of the International Events Group, the growth of sponsorship has outpaced that of advertising and sales promotion every year since 1985, and sponsorship will be the single fastest-growing area of marketing into the next millennium. There are several reasons for this. First, people are not as reachable through mass media advertising anymore. Ads have lost some of their effectiveness as people increasingly change TV channels and radio stations and fast-forward through ads on videotapes. Herbert Schmertz, former public relations chief of the Mobil Corporation, believes that a growing number of consumers consider much product advertising infantile, shallow, and misleading. Sponsorship promotions reach people in an environment that matches their lifestyle, rather than intruding on it.

Second, sponsorship responds to the consumer demand that companies give something back to their communities. It implies a degree of altruism absent from more commercial types of marketing. In a Cone/Roper Benchmark Survey,

78 percent of adults said they would be more likely to buy a product if it is associated with a cause. Sponsorships provide the potential for creating an emotional bond with the consumer by tying the product or company to something bigger and more meaningful.

Third, people will increasingly crave live contact. With more people than ever working from their homes, many are turning to arts events and festivals for shared social experiences. Sponsorships give companies the opportunity to open up more direct and more involving lines of access to customer groups and to tie in product purchase with events that customers consider meaningful and enjoyable. Says Schmertz of Mobil Oil, "After fifteen years of artistic and cultural activity, we now find that when we give certain publics a reason to identify with the projects and causes that we have chosen to support, they will translate that identification into a preference for doing business with us." In a public opinion survey of upscale college graduates in the Boston area, respondents identified Mobil with quality programming, and 31 percent bought Mobil gas most often, compared to far lower percentages for Exxon, Gulf, and Texaco.[10]

Although $4.7 billion was spent on sponsorship in 1995, only 6 percent, or $277 million, went to the arts. Sports receive the largest share—65 percent—of sponsorship dollars, followed by pop music/entertainment at 10 percent, festivals/fairs/annual events at 10 percent, and causes at 9 percent. A niche sport like windsurfing gets more than $25 million in sponsorship, while sponsorship of every symphony orchestra in the United States totals less than $7.5 million. Says Ukman, "The spending gap does not reflect any inherent lack of value in the arts. The ability of the arts to increase their share of sponsorship dollars is totally in the hands of the people selling sponsorship. It is up to them to make their property more valuable to potential sponsors."[11]

Sponsorship, says Ukman, "is a cash or in-kind fee paid to a property in return for access to the exploitable commercial potential associated with that property."[12] Jackie van Aubel, a Brussels-based sponsorship consultant, says that "the whole idea of sponsorship is promotion. A company should assess a sponsorship proposal in the light of the business benefits received."[13] So the thrust of arts proposals must change from an entitlement perspective ("We do good work so we deserve your support") to become more market-driven. When seeking a sponsor for a special project, an arts organization should attempt to match the project's expected audience with a business that has a similar customer profile. For example, one regional theater in Canada learned through a member of its board of directors that a local bank was developing special services for people over 55 years of age. The theater approached the bank for support, using audience survey results to show bank managers that a large proportion of their audience members were upscale people over age 55. Arts organizations should also offer businesses ways to extend the impact of their support. At one theater, a wine company sponsored just one play of the season, but also was designated as the "house wine," samples of which were served during the intermission of each play all season.

Arts marketers can develop attractive sponsorship opportunities by borrowing ideas from successful sports and entertainment properties and by creating benefits that go beyond signage and the use of marks and logo. Arts organizations provide benefits that other media do not: live audiences, loyal members, opportunities for client entertainment and for on-site sampling and displays, category exclusivity (an opportunity for a company to differentiate itself from its competitors), access to data-bases, access to cosponsors for cross-promotions, and access to a network of volun-teers who can help sell the promotion.

Every sponsor must be provided with special attention that goes well beyond individual donor recognition. Key benefits should be reserved for top-level sponsors, but each sponsor's employees should be offered special discounts or other perks. The program should be turnkey, so that the budget includes all expenses, including details like signage and printing. The sponsor's managers will want to be directly involved in the many publicity and marketing decisions associated with the project so that they will be sure to meet their image- and awareness-building goals. Arts managers should keep in mind that although their organization benefits right away from the dollars provided by a corporate sponsorship, the results of the corporation's image marketing are more difficult to assess and are not likely to appear immedi-ately. Therefore, arts organizations must continue to be sensitive to the corporation's needs over time and help them continue to generate the maximum residual benefit from a special project sponsorship.

CAPITALIZING ON CORE COMPETENCIES

The EDS Corporation and the Detroit Symphony Orchestra (DSO) have created what they call a "virtual partnership," a strategic collaboration that focuses on what each does best to the advantage of both. In the early 1990s, EDS was seeking to develop community involvement as a strategic marketing tool to build its image and estab-lish its identity as an information technology expert. The DSO, whose expertise is in making and marketing music, was struggling to upgrade its information systems without much success. In the collaboration, EDS agreed to serve as the orchestra's information technology department. EDS provides the DSO with a full range of tech-nological support: standardized personal computer hardware, software, and usage training for all employees; network links; and project management for developing and implementing a new marketing and fund-raising database system. The inte-grated computer systems are also improving collaborations within the organization, as DSO financial, marketing, and development directors share the same database, develop strategies together, and learn techniques from one another.

In return, EDS receives market exposure of its products and services in all the orchestra's mailings, at the concert hall, through visibility with the orchestra's board of directors, and through touring opportunities. When the DSO toured Europe in the spring of 1995, EDS sent representatives to host receptions for European corporate sponsors. The conductor and staff members carried their portable computer notebooks, emblazoned with the EDS logo.

Building a long-term relationship with a prestigious organization such as the DSO provides EDS with the kind of exposure that will help the corporation gain further visibility and business opportunities for years to come. Both partners believe their ten-year contract will be renewed indefinitely.

TEAM SPIRIT

Collaborations between arts organizations and businesses can extend well beyond traditional businesses. For example, the Oakland Ballet Company and the Oakland Athletics baseball team collaborated to form what one journalist dubbed "BaseBallet." The team sought to increase its community service and visibility off-season, and the ballet company was looking to expand its audience and contributed support. Tapping into the huge market segment made up of sports fans makes sense as a way to attract new people to dance. And the collaboration is natural because of the athleticism required by both dancers and ball players.

Every year between 1986 and 1994 (with one exception), several members of the baseball team danced in one performance of the *Nutcracker* alongside the regular company dancers. In 1994, pitcher Dave Stewart even performed a solo choreographed especially for him. The Oakland A's flew its players home for the off-season week of rehearsals and performance, paid for costume rentals (which are necessary because the ballplayers are so much larger than the dancers), and supplied public relations staff to manage media coverage of the event. The players took their rehearsals and performance very seriously and were astonished by the athleticism required for ballet dancing.

The results of this collaboration are that the event sells out the house and the intensive media exposure helps boost ticket sales for other *Nutcracker* performances as well. When A's manager Tony LaRussa, a member of the Oakland Ballet's board of directors, makes a fund-raising pitch during the dance intermission, he generates significant donations for the ballet company. The team also helps to leverage new corporate donors for the ballet; the partnership enhances the ballet's image and its attractiveness to other local corporations. The extensive publicity that this event generates each year burnishes the team's image and magnifies its off-season visibility.

In 1995, A's Night became All-Star Night, as a variety of professional athletes from the Bay Area participated in the event.

Collaborating with Multiple Organizations

Multiple collaborators can be necessary in some circumstances. This is especially true when small and midsized organizations contemplate the construction of a new performance facility, a project usually beyond their financial capacity. Also, when tie-in promotions are developed to include a city's cultural, entertainment, and tourism providers, the resulting synergies benefit all the participating organizations as well as the consumers they serve.

BUILDING PROJECTS: "CONSTRUCTIVE" COLLABORATIONS

Chicago has long needed a midsized performing hall. In the mid-1980s, organizations such as Hubbard Street Dance Chicago and Performing Arts Chicago attempted to combine their resources to renovate or build a hall, a project they could not afford to undertake individually. Nor could any one Chicago-area foundation support such a building project on its own.

In response to this unmet need, leaders from six foundations banded together to begin the project, which eventually became the Music and Dance Theater (MAD), a nonprofit organization that represents the collaboration of six foundations and a dozen performing arts groups. The foundations have contributed approximately half the project's $33 million cost: $28 million for the land and building; $5 million for an endowment. A full-scale fund-raising campaign is under way to raise the rest of the money. If goals are met, the building will be ready for occupancy in the fall of 1998. Working cooperatively, the twelve participating organizations have agreed to a master annual schedule without stalemating over who gets the season's opening night or the New Year's Eve performance.

The Music and Dance Theater has attracted other collaborators. Corporate partners include local hotels, parking facilities, and restaurants, all of which are providing financial support and gifts-in-kind in exchange for the additional name recognition and business the new facility will bring them.

SHARING CONTRIBUTIONS TO INCREASE THE PIE

Several years ago, David Packard, then chairman of the Hewlett-Packard Company, had tired of the many fund-raising pleas from scores of local arts groups. Envisioning a one-stop giving program that would distribute money more fairly and give the groups more long-term financial stability, late in 1992 he helped organize the Silicon Valley Arts Fund, based in San Jose, California. The fund is a collaboration of eleven cultural groups: ten large arts organizations and one consortium of several small-budget organizations. The fund is managed by the area's Santa Clara County Community Foundation. Historically, arts groups, particularly the larger and better-established ones, have been protective of their "own" contributors. However, because the California economy was suffering one of the worst recessions in decades and performing arts organizations were not meeting their fund-raising goals, they responded eagerly to this collaborative project.

Whereas most fund-raising efforts address a single need, this fund addresses all the financial needs of the arts organizations. Fifteen percent of the money is designated to help participating groups pay off existing deficits. Seventy-three percent is earmarked for endowments, which provide a predictable source of capital for the groups and signal to the community that these institutions are truly established—a crucial factor in their independent fund-raising. The final 12 percent is for a venture fund to allow the groups to support new activities through interest-free twelve-month loans.

When the fund-raising was discontinued on March 31, 1995, $12 million of the $20 million goal had been raised, all but one of the groups had eliminated their deficits, and all had created endowments; only three of the eleven groups had had endowments before the project began. Even after the fund's drive officially ended, additional bequests and deferred gifts were promised.

By collaborating, each organization has raised more money than it would have raised alone. The project has built a spirit of philanthropy in what has been a notoriously tight-fisted community, and many Silicon Valley corporations are contributing to nonprofits for the first time. The project's strategy of meeting all the financial needs of the organizations and of supporting the arts community as a whole, has created a focus on investing in the stability and future of the arts community rather than on giving to individual groups for short-term needs. This novel strategy and the early success of the Silicon Valley Arts Fund have attracted the attention of other communities around the nation, especially in fast-growing cities that have been in the shadow of more established neighbors, as San Jose is to San Francisco.

TIE-IN PROMOTIONS

Economic impact studies have shown that for every dollar spent on a performing arts ticket, another $5 to $10 is spent on related enterprises such as restaurants, parking facilities, and even dry cleaners.[14] So it is only natural that such businesses would collaborate with the arts organizations. Consider the San Jose "Arts Card," which jointly benefits a number of organizations and businesses as well as the consumers they serve. The Arts Card collaboration is an alliance between three partners: the San Jose Arts Roundtable, which represents prominent performing arts groups and museums; the San Jose Downtown Association, a business group; and Alive After Five, a consortium of restaurant and entertainment business owners.

The San Jose Arts Card is offered free to subscribers and members of the Roundtable groups. Cardholders are guaranteed VIP treatment at any of fifteen recommended restaurants and receive dining discounts (15 percent off, free appetizers or a bottle of wine, etc.) and other special offers at clubs or cinemas in downtown San Jose. Used often enough, the card easily recoups the cost of a performance series or membership, while encouraging patrons to dine locally before or after a show. Subscribers can use the card at any time, not just the evening of a performance, and may extend the discount to as many as three guests per use. The discounts apply to the arts organizations as well. Cardholders may purchase discounted tickets to performances at any participating organization; they may also save on purchases at museum gift shops. Interestingly, the 18 percent of Arts Card holders who cross over to the other arts organizations rarely take advantage of this discount offer—rather, they choose to support the nonprofits by paying full price. Cardholders also receive a complete arts calendar, which shows the dates of all events at the participating arts organizations and helps subscribers to multiple organizations anticipate conflicts in advance.

For the businesses involved, the Arts Card program is cost-effective sales promotion and advertising. The arts groups give them constant exposure in brochures, newsletters, programs, and lobby displays. More than 200,000 Arts Card guides are distributed annually in hotels, in convention centers, and at the airport. And the restaurants benefit from the glamour and cultural image of the arts groups. In fact, the proportion of arts patrons eating downtown before or after a performance has grown from 15 percent to 85 percent in the nine years of the program's existence. In addition to successfully bringing more people to downtown San Jose, the Arts Card allows the arts organizations to give something back to the businesses they often solicit for support. Contributing to a spirit of community enhances the influence of the arts groups.[15]

Not every town has an Alive After Five organization to tap into. Jim Clark, executive director of the Lutcher Theater in Orange, Texas, a town of about 20,000, says that his town is definitely not alive after five, making it difficult for his theater patrons to enjoy the total experience of an evening on the town, combining theater with dinner. So Clark collaborated with two nearby restaurants, which now remain open on performance evenings. The theater provides the restaurants with its mailing list; the restaurants do a booming business on performance evenings, which, in turn, stimulates business for them on other evenings. The patrons, meanwhile, have a higher level of satisfaction with their experience. And the theater's staff gets an extra benefit: the restaurant owners often deliver special dessert trays for them, simultaneously picking up new names for their mailing lists (meaning that the staff has to go on a diet after a good collaborative season).

Forging Viable Partnerships

Each of the preceding examples demonstrates the advantages of collaboration. But success depends on a number of critical factors in the collaboration's design and implementation that maximize the benefits and minimize the risks involved.

SETTING GOALS

First, the organization initiating the collaboration should decide on its key objectives: targeting new audiences, reducing overhead, garnering expertise in a key function, providing scale for a capital drive. Then, it should identify what kinds of collaborations and which potential partners would help meet those needs, and determine what opportunities the arts organization can offer to potential collaborators. A strategic collaboration must be designed to be mutually beneficial rather than just to fill in the gaps in one organization's existing program. Each organization should integrate the project into its own long-range plan to secure the commitment of the organization and its staff, volunteers, and other constituents.

It is important that goals be set not just for each participating organization but for the collaboration as a whole. This requires a shared vision on the part of all participants. The Silicon Valley Arts Fund had particular potential for conflict of interest because its areawide capital campaign could have a negative impact on each organization's annual fund-raising ability. Says Rich Braugh, president of the board of directors of the Silicon Valley Arts Fund, "Each group had to buy in conceptually to the idea of the fund, to its mission. Details were avoided so we could be flexible, but our trust document had checks and balances built in to make all participants secure."

BUILDING CONSENSUS

Once two or more organizations have agreed to work together, the collaborative effort has just begun. The participants must build consensus for each decision throughout the project's life. At Chicago's Music and Dance Theater, the collaborators had a clear common goal of building a new performing space, but they had to develop consensus as to how each organization could meet its own individual requirements in such areas as space design and scheduling, and serve the common good as well. During the lengthy site-selection process, the foundations not only studied their options but also learned to work together. Says Sandra Guthman, president of the theater's board of directors, "Different priorities had different weights to different people. We were trying to project the future, and everyone's opinion was equally valid. So we would debate, research, and invest more time until we reached a consensus on what and where this performing hall should be. The time was more about institution-building than site selection." Consensus for the building design was developed step by step. First, each organization was polled as to its preferences for stage width, wing size, rehearsal space, number of dressing rooms, and so on. The responses were merged and the organizations were brought together to discuss their differences. Finally, their leaders presented a new set of priorities to the whole group with the goal of creating a workable space that would meet each organization's basic requirements.

Organizations involved in consensus building must decide whether "consensus" means a majority or a unanimous vote. Different standards may be set for different issues. Whatever the decision, each participant must agree to the rules being set. Consensus building continues beyond the planning stages throughout program implementation. And in multiorganizational and multifaceted projects such as the Music and Dance Theater and the Silicon Valley Arts Fund, consensus partners are likely to shift during the course of the projects. This means that consensus has to be built and rebuilt so that each group continually feels a sense of ownership and equal involvement in the project.

BUILDING TRUST

Among collaborators, trust is considered the most important factor for success. Trust is the key to consensus building and to effective communication. Participating organizations must learn to understand each other's culture and way of doing business.

This is true whether the collaboration is between nonprofits and business organizations or between arts organizations.

According to Sandra Guthman, trust cannot be built in the abstract by thinking, planning, and talking about it. The best way to build trust is to get to work. If possible, organizations should start out on a small scale. In Chicago, several Music and Dance Theater dance companies collaborated on the city's annual Spring Festival of Dance in 1995. Their joint efforts on scheduling, subscription sales, and advertising resulted in more tickets sold and a better bottom line than most of the organizations would have achieved on their own. Most important, they learned how to work together and trust one another in a discrete, short-term situation with lower commitment levels than their joint venue collaboration would allow. Guthman emphasizes the general significance of trust in such matters as scheduling: "In working out a master performance schedule that a dozen organizations agree to, it is not the schedule that is important, but the process for working it out that matters." As circumstances change, each group must feel confident that the concessions it makes for a partner's welfare will be returned in kind at another time.

COMMUNICATING

An essential ingredient for building and sustaining trust is frequent communication. Regular meetings keep collaboration partners informed and able to respond quickly to problems. All meetings should be well recorded, and minutes of the meetings should be distributed within a few days for the benefit of those unable to attend a session. To facilitate communication, EDS went so far as to assign a staff member to be in residence at the Detroit Symphony Orchestra for the first year of the collaboration.

Good communication is also necessary for the organizations to be able to respond effectively to unanticipated situations. The American Symphony Orchestra and Concordia signed a letter of agreement that covered the critical issues of their collaboration, not a twenty-page legal document addressing a multitude of details. The agreement allows them to be flexible in responding to situations as they arise. Their executive director, Eugene Carr, says that "collaborators must be willing to be flexible and take the risks, not react stodgily like big corporations. Much of our success in forming an agreement (and doing it in only two and a half months) came from the fact that our board members were willing to treat our collaboration entrepreneurially, and not scrutinize every detail as they would in the multimillion-dollar corporations many of them run."

Good communication with constituents outside the collaboration is also a must. For example, a broad-scoped program such as the Silicon Valley Arts Fund is likely to raise questions and concerns from the community at large. Barbara Beerstein, managing consultant to the Arts Fund, urges collaborators to "plan your response to critical issues or community concerns that relate to your collaboration. It is important that all those involved—including board, staff, and volunteers—respond to critical questions with the same answers.[16]

DESIGNING LEADERSHIP AND INVOLVEMENT STRUCTURES

Structure is critical to effective collaboration. Leadership must be clearly defined. The multiorganizational collaborations such as the San Jose Arts Card and the Music and Dance Theater benefit from having the leadership of an umbrella organization established specifically for that purpose. Participants in smaller collaborations must allocate leadership roles according to their relative core competencies and that are in the collaboration's best interests.

Each collaborative alliance should be a partnership of equal and supportive members working to create a win-win situation for all involved. Participation parameters may be hard to draw. For the San Jose Arts Card, distribution of many of the tasks is straightforward; for example, the participating restaurants pay for printing the brochures, while the arts organizations are responsible for distributing them. However, participation in the Silicon Valley Arts Fund was far more complex. The Fund established three different task forces—one made up of executive directors, one of trustees, and one of corporate CEOs and civic leaders—so that issues could be dealt with from different perspectives. Some organizations participate more actively than others, which placed a particular burden on the active members to keep abreast of the less active participants' interests and needs and to make those groups equal beneficiaries of the process. This structure was cumbersome and its operation time-consuming. But without all the task force meetings and resultant consensus-building efforts, the project would not have happened at all, according to the Santa Clara County Community Trust, which provided oversight for the project.

The strongest indicator of the success of the Silicon Valley Arts Fund collaboration may not be the money it raised, but the fact that the collaborators are seeking new ways to work together.

COMMITTING ADEQUATE RESOURCES

Collaborations require an enormous amount of time and commitment from all parties. It is especially important to dedicate enough funds to administrative costs. No single person can handle the entire process alone. In one situation, collaborators hired one person to manage all aspects of the project: fund-raising, public relations, and working with all participating arts organizations. Even though the manager did an excellent job and managed her time well, the burden of responsibilities caused aspects of the project to fall short of the highest standards. Collaborators who designate adequate resources up front find the long-term results of their projects to be well worth the investment.

Strategic collaborations, which have become common within the business sector in recent years, are equally valuable in nonprofit arts organizations. If arts organizations are careful to select appropriate collaborators, if collaborators have similar or complementary goals, and if the relationship is managed successfully, strategic collaborations can help all participants achieve their organizational goals and better manage their financial, human, and physical resources. In this way, arts organizations will more fully realize their own mission and will better serve their customers, their collaborative partners, and their community as a whole. This is no small accomplishment for arts organizations struggling to survive as vital institutions in a drastically changing environment.

[1] Case packet, Marketing D30, J. L. Kellogg Graduate School of Management.

[2] "City Opera Turns 50, but Who's Counting?," *New York Times,* "Arts and Leisure," Sunday, July 25, 1993, pp. 1, 25.

[3] "City Opera Turns 50."

[4] *"The Financial Condition of Symphony Orchestras,"* prepared by the Wolf Organization, Inc., Cambridge, Mass. (Washington, D.C.: American Symphony Orchestra League, 1992).

[5] Danny Newman, *Subscribe Now!* Theater Communications Group, New York, 1983, 17.

[6] "High and Low," *International Arts Manager,* Feb. 1993, 29.

[7] Allan Kozinn, "Orchestras Merge Business Resources," *New York Times,* Sept. 7, 1994.

[8] "The BCA Report: 1995 National Survey of Business Support to the Arts" (New York: Business Committee for the Arts, 1995).

[9] Craig Smith, "The Emerging Paradigm," *Corporate Philanthropy Report,* Feb. 1995.

[10] Thomas Harris, *The Marketer's Guide to Public Relations* (New York: Wiley, 1991), 219–220.

[11] Lesa Ukman, "Mutual Attraction," *International Arts Manager,* Dec. 1995/Jan. 1996, 24–26.

[12] Lesa Ukman, "Presentation Outline: The Future of Arts Sponsorship" (Chicago: IEG, Inc., 1995).

[13] Jackie van Aubel, "The Medium and the Message: Communicating Effectively through Sponsorship," *European Leaders,* Spring 1995, 77.

[14] Reported by Schuyler G. Chapin, Commissioner of Cultural Affairs, New York City, at a meeting of the Arts and Business Council of Chicago, Sept. 13, 1994.

[15] Elisabeth Geismar, "Dining Out on the House: San Jose's Arts Card Means Business," *Arts Reach,* Premiere Issue, 1992.

[16] Barbara Beerstein, "How Collaborating with Other Organizations Can Work for You," Barbara Beerstein and Associates, Santa Cruz, Calif. (photocopy).

▲●▲

PART III

DEVELOPING
THE STRATEGY

▲●▲

CHAPTER 8

*The "product" is
what the product
does; it is the total
package of benefits
the customer
receives when he
buys. . . .*

E. RAYMOND COREY[1]

DEFINING AND POSITIONING THE PRODUCT OFFERING

Tʜᴇ sɪɴɢʟᴇ ᴍᴏsᴛ ɪᴍᴘᴏʀᴛᴀɴᴛ ᴇʟᴇᴍᴇɴᴛ ᴏғ ᴛʜᴇ ᴏʀɢᴀɴɪᴢᴀᴛɪᴏɴ's ᴍᴀʀᴋᴇᴛɪɴɢ ᴍɪx is its *offering*. Marketing's ultimate objective is to develop an offering that will satisfy the needs of one or more target audiences. Even the most creative and dramatic advertising cannot sell an audience on a fundamentally weak offering. Furthermore, a performing arts event is more than music or a performer; it is an experience. Customers acquire products or services, or seek experiences, *for what these products or experiences can do for them.* All aspects of the customer's experience must be taken into account by arts managers.

To complicate matters, what people consider attractive changes over time. People's interests, needs, and tastes change with repeated exposure and experience. Audiences change generation by generation. Therefore, organizations must periodically redefine what is attractive to any given segment of the population. In this chapter we will define the product of a performing arts organization and discuss perspectives in programming and approaches to positioning the product. We will also explain the product life cycle concept and discuss how arts organizations can manage their products through different life cycle stages.

DEFINING THE PRODUCT

Why do people purchase certain products? According to marketing strategist Theodore Levitt,

> People buy products . . . in order to solve problems. Products are problem-solving tools. A product is, to the potential buyer, a complex cluster of value satisfactions. The generic "thing" or "essence" is not itself the product. . . . Customers attach value to products in proportion to the perceived ability of those products to help solve their problems. Hence a product has meaning only from the viewpoint of the buyer or the ultimate user. All else is derivative. Only the buyer or user can assign value, because value can reside only in the benefits he wants or perceives.[2]

Consider a person shopping for a drill bit. That person is not interested in the bit itself, but rather in what it can provide: a hole in the wall. Similarly, Shakespeare may have said "The play's the thing," but what is truly the "thing" for the audience is the entertainment or the aesthetic, intellectual, emotional, and/or social experience.

The Product as an Experience

To determine what kind of experience people seek and what they find satisfying, Dominique Bourgeon surveyed nearly fifteen hundred people in the regions of Caen, Dijon, and Nancy, France. Frequent and occasional performing arts attenders were asked:

- In general, what does the theater represent to you?
- What positive feelings do you associate with a theatrical performance?
- What negative feelings do you associate with a theatrical performance?
- After seeing a play, what factors make you say, "I had a good time?"
- After seeing a play, what factors make you say, "I had a bad time?"

Responses were categorized as follows:

Experience	Frequent Attenders	Occasional Attenders
Associations with the theater	Experimentation	Entertainment
	Dream, thought, relaxation	Comedy
	Escapism	Realism
	Enrichment	

Experience	Frequent Attenders	Occasional Attenders
Positive emotions	Aesthetic pleasure Curiosity Admiration Surprise	Relaxation Laughter
Negative emotions	Irritation Boredom	Boredom Abstruseness Sadness
Reasons for having a good time	Enjoyment of text Quality and humor of production	The play Good atmosphere (ambience) Beautiful scenery Comedy, laughter, cheerfulness, amusement Message
Reasons for having a bad time	Text Quality of acting Quality of production	The play Ambience Mediocrity Difficult to understand

Bourgeon found that, in general, the play itself is the main determinant of a frequent attender's feelings about the performance. But for occasional attenders, other intangible and atmospheric factors are more important. What this suggests for building frequency among occasional attenders, and for building new audiences, is that the total experience should appeal to the imagination, to emotions, and especially to pleasurable, joyful feelings. This does not mean that theaters must always present lighthearted plays; it means that the organization will attract a broader audience if it makes the total theater-going experience a source of emotional satisfaction.

The Total Product Concept

The definition of the arts organization's product extends beyond the work presented on stage to include all the organization's offerings. Visually, one can describe a product as comprising the three levels shown in Figure 8-1:

Figure 8-1

**THE TOTAL
PRODUCT
CONCEPT**

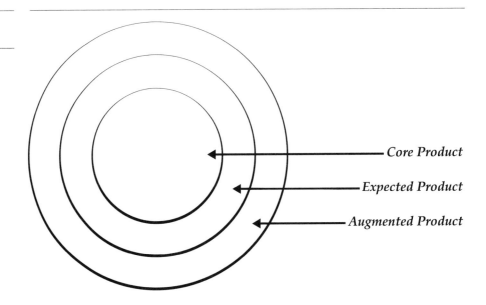

Core Product

Expected Product

Augmented Product

THE CORE PRODUCT

The *core product* is that which is visibly and essentially being offered to the target market for purchase or consumption. The core offering of a symphony orchestra may be a single piece of music to be performed (Tchaikovsky's *1812 Overture*), the program for an entire concert (a Tchaikovsky Spectacular), the collection of programs for an entire subscription series (a Great Composer Series), or the programs and series for an entire season. It may also be considered in terms of the specific orchestra, the conductor, and the guest soloist(s).

Consider a performance of the Tchaikovsky Violin Concerto, by Itzhak Perlman with the Chicago Symphony Orchestra, conducted by James Levine at the Ravinia Festival. There are six components to this product, each of which are valued differently by different members of the audience. Perlman's name is the magic draw for most, and many patrons will pay premium prices to attend his performance. Some patrons will base their attendance on the musical selections being performed; others on the orchestra's high quality. The ambience of picnicking at Ravinia on a warm summer evening is also a draw.

THE EXPECTED PRODUCT

The *expected product* includes the customer's normal expectations regarding the purchase and consumption of the product. Customers may expect to be able to purchase tickets for a performance by phone or fax with a credit card number. Subscribers expect ticket exchange privileges. They may expect a well-lit parking lot, especially if the theater is in an unsafe neighborhood. Customers may expect the air-conditioning to be functioning on a hot summer evening. They expect to be treated well by box office personnel and ushers. When a performer becomes ill, patrons expect a skillful backup to step in.

The expectations of different audience members, of course, will vary. Some patrons may expect that the acoustical quality of the hall will be high; for others, adequate leg room may be more important. Elderly and disabled patrons may not attend unless there is ease of access, no matter how attractive the evening's performance may be.

THE AUGMENTED PRODUCT

The *augmented product* consists of features and benefits beyond what the target audience normally expects. In some cases, product augmentations serve to enhance the experience of current patrons, thereby building satisfaction and commitment. For example, the Lyric Opera of Chicago sells box meals during the intermissions of long operas. Some organizations mail newsletters and program notes to their subscribers in advance of performances. Other product augmentations for current patrons may include discounts at nearby restaurants and pre- or postperformance lectures.

A variety of augmented product features can also be designed to attract new audiences. The START program in Cincinnati provides young people with citywide cultural membership and incentives to attend varied arts performances. Offering ticket exchange privileges to single-ticket buyers might stimulate advance purchase by frequent business travelers and others who have changing time constraints.

The Product as a Service

Performing arts organizations are basically in the service business. A *service* can be defined as any act or performance that one party can offer to another that is essentially intangible and does not result in the ownership of anything. Certain characteristics that are unique to services have special implications for marketers.

INTANGIBILITY

Services are intangible; they cannot be seen, heard, felt, tasted, or otherwise experienced before they are bought. A patient having plastic surgery cannot see the result before the purchase; a theatergoer cannot see the play before the performance. To reduce the uncertainty inherent in the purchase decision, the service buyer seeks signs or evidence of quality—thus, the importance of a big name, reputation, and good reviews. The service provider seeks to "manage the evidence," to "tangibilize the intangible."[3] Whereas tangible product marketers are challenged to add abstract ideas (McDonald's "Happy Meal" links entertainment with eating), service marketers are challenged to associate physical evidence and imagery with their abstract offers (Prudential Insurance says, "Get a piece of the rock").

Performing arts marketers can tangibilize their offerings in a number of ways. When promoting relatively unknown performers, marketers refer to concrete symbols of their quality such as awards or past performances at Carnegie Hall. Such symbols function the way brand names do for physical products. Special attention must be paid to "atmospherics."[4] The visual quality of the brochures and the character of the facilities can affect the customers' expectations. A no-frills auditorium sets the stage for the young, adventuresome theater company as well as a marble lobby does for the opera company.

People are also important conveyors of the positioning of a performing arts organization. Publicity photos of formally dressed chamber musicians create different expectations than do photos of musicians in brightly colored silk shirts. Even the audience provides a tangible signal about the appeal of the performance. By showing which people go, how they dress, and the serious or animated expressions on their faces, marketers can convey an image of the nature of the concertgoing experience.

Price can serve as an important clue about the service product's quality. Price can build up the customer's confidence in the product, or lessen it. It can raise customer expectations ("This is expensive, it had better be good") or lower them ("You get what you pay for").[5] One suburban, university-affiliated concert hall advertises that they have the same quality performers as the symphony hall downtown, but at one-third the price. The university hall's managers do not recognize the discrepancy in their message and wonder why concertgoers are not lured by this price "break."

PERISHABILITY

Among an arts marketer's greatest challenges is the fact that services are perishable. Services cannot be stored or preserved. A car or radio can be kept in inventory until it is sold, but the revenue potential of an unoccupied theater seat is lost each time the curtain rises. As interest in a theatrical production builds over time, the empty seats from earlier performances cannot be filled. And an organization presenting a once-only concert has no opportunity to benefit from the interest generated afterward. Perishability is less of an issue when demand is steady, as is the case for heavily subscribed organizations. But when demand fluctuates widely, perishability is a serious problem. This is why arts organizations seek advance publicity for their performances, offer discount pricing for previews, and promote subscriptions.

INSEPARABILITY

Unlike physical goods that are manufactured and put into inventory, services are typically produced and consumed at the same time. A service is inseparable from the source that provides it. Consider the emotional impact on an audience expecting to hear Pavarotti perform if an announcer tells them that Pavarotti is indisposed and that John Smith will substitute.

This concept applies to the organization's customer service as well. An enjoyable evening can be sabotaged by unresponsive or unhelpful personnel. Unfortunately, some factors that affect a patron's satisfaction with the experience are beyond the organization's control, such as a flat tire on the way to the performance or an emergency at home in the middle of the evening. But there are external factors to which the organization can respond. When a bad snowstorm or a major traffic jam affects many patrons, the curtain can be delayed a few minutes or patrons can be seated late, against custom. Such efforts go beyond a customer's expectations and may actually serve to add to satisfaction and enjoyment the patron would have experienced had the inconvenience not occurred at all. The effect may be somewhat offset, of course, by the dissatisfaction felt by those who arrived on time.

VARIABILITY

Since a service is so closely linked to its source, its quality can vary depending on who is providing it and when it is being provided. A performance by Isaac Stern is likely to be of higher quality than the same concerto played by a young prodigy. And the quality of Stern's performance can vary depending on his mental state, energy, and various external factors such as the temperature in the hall or the quality of the orchestra and conductor with whom he is performing. Purchasers of services are aware of this high variability, and the more unknowns there are about a service provider (performer, playwright, composer, director, presenting organization), the more those purchasers will engage in risk-reducing behavior to learn whether the offering is worthwhile.

Service providers also can manage variability within the organization. Consistency can be attained with good personnel selection and training and by routinizing as many parts of the service as possible. Also, organizations should develop adequate customer satisfaction monitoring systems, using suggestion and complaint systems, customer surveys, and comparison shopping with other arts organizations.

CUSTOMER INVOLVEMENT AND EXPECTATIONS

The nature of the customer's involvement is an integral aspect of the service exchange. A first-time operagoer will respond far differently to a production of *La Boheme* than will someone who has seen it five times. A great performance of the Brahms Violin Concerto will be "consumed" differently by the various audience members according to their knowledge, preferences, backgrounds, and mental states at the time of the performance. To help minimize consumer disappointment, art marketers can try to teach consumers to be better art consumers. Symphonies can offer preconcert lectures; theaters can offer postperformance discussions and informative newsletters.

Performing arts organizations should make their purpose and positioning clear to their target audience. When patrons are repeatedly unmoved by performances, then they either think that they are missing something or that they just do not enjoy the art form. The resulting disappointment and bad word of mouth that result can be avoided if the organization targets and informs its audience carefully. Organizations should try to make service users' expectations more realistic. A major source of dissatisfaction on the part of many service customers is not inferior service, but exaggerated expectations. A theatergoer should know in advance if a play will be depressing. A bittersweet play with a few comic moments should not be billed as "hilarious."

Disappointment is often engendered by too much hype. Bernard Holland, music critic at the *New York Times,* says that reading brochures about the upcoming music season is "like stepping off the curb and getting hit by a truckload of hyperbole." Instead of presenting a "Great Performers Series" or a "Season of Musical Giants," Holland ironically suggests a keyboard series called "A Couple of Terrific Pianists, a Few Average Ones and a European We've Never Heard but His Agent Says He's Good."[6] Such brutal honesty might be counterproductive, but it is true that consumer satisfaction will increase as people's expectations are geared more closely to their actual experiences.

The essence of services marketing is fine service. When the product is a performance, whether that of the pianist, the advertisers, or the box office personnel, nothing is more important than the quality of that performance.[7]

DETERMINING THE PRODUCT OFFERING

The artistic product is not tailored for its audience in the way an automobile manufacturer tests seat designs with a wide variety of people to determine the best fit. Yet programming is only partially driven by the artists' and the artistic decision makers' vision. Selecting programming is a complex activity. It requires that the artistic director and the managing directors work together to solve their perennial riddle: how to create a series of programs that have artistic merit, are congruent with the organization's mission, competencies, and constraints, and serve the needs and interests of the community. There is a distinction and delicate balance that must be maintained between art for art, art for society, and art for the survival of the organization.

Although the artistic product derives from a unique vision, even creativity does not occur in a social vacuum. All artists are sensitive and responsive to the worlds in which they live. Shakespeare created Nick Bottom and other colorful characters after the "common folk" he observed at the Globe Theater. Haydn composed a *forte* portion in his "Surprise Symphony" at the point where he knew his patrons were likely to fall asleep.

A performance is essentially a communication between the artist/performer and the audience. This communication cannot take place if the audience does not relate to what is happening on the stage. But audiences vary widely in their backgrounds and interests and, therefore, in their receptiveness to artistic offerings. Furthermore, in keeping with their mission, many performing arts organizations program works that are highly challenging to even their most sophisticated audiences. Therefore, arts organizations should capitalize on their many opportunities to help facilitate communication with their audiences. Such opportunities include thematic programming, programming for the community, scheduling accessibility, new approaches to presenting the performance ritual and environment, use of multimedia technologies, and presenting events. In determining its product offerings, the organization must always keep in mind its own mission, strengths, and cost considerations.

Thematic Programming

Thematic programming has become popular in recent years. It is most applicable for concerts, since a variety of music is played at each performance, but the concept may also be used by a theater in programming its entire season.

One common orchestral approach is the musical theme: Romantic Music, The First and Last Works of Beethoven and Bartók, Sounds from Norway, From Classical to Jazz, and so on. Often these programs are unique and include rarely heard musical selections. However, they are timid, product-centered efforts to attract new listeners into the concert hall that do little to enhance the audiences' experience or to create new levels of understanding or appreciation.

Consider instead how the American Symphony Orchestra (ASO) in New York City takes a customer-centered approach to thematic programming to offer an accessible, meaningful, and enriching experience for its audience. According to Music Director Leon Botstein, the ASO has a mission of taking bold steps "to reimagine the tradition of orchestral music and concerts within the larger culture—to link music to the visual arts, literary life, and politics as well as popular culture."

MISSION STATEMENT OF THE AMERICAN SYMPHONY ORCHESTRA

The American Symphony Orchestra strives to define the cutting edge of programming, audience development and cultural education in the New York, national and international cultural community. The ASO seeks to become a role model for how a symphony orchestra can more centrally integrate itself into American culture at the turn of the 21st century. . . .

The ASO will attempt to revive the orchestral concert-going experience for a new public, through an innovative approach to programming and audience development. The Orchestra's mission is to provide offerings which allow the public to appreciate the music of the orchestral tradition from a new perspective.

The ASO will accomplish this by presenting programs which are both intellectually stimulating and musically gratifying, organized in surprising concert formats which do not subscribe to the traditional mold. . . .

To do this, we program theme-based concerts, linking our performances to current New York art exhibitions and cultural events. We provide written guides to concert goers, and deliver pre-concert and mid-concert talks to open every possible avenue for education within the performance.

Leon Botstein and the ASO have developed thematic programming into an experience that is emotionally satisfying, instructive, and entertaining for an audience that enjoys multiple cultural and social pursuits. Botstein provides access to the music and enriches its meaning by integrating it with literature, visual arts, and politics and by deepening his audience's understanding of the music's idiom and history.

One ASO program was designed to demonstrate Shakespeare's impact on music in Europe and America during the nineteenth century. It featured four rarely heard Shakespeare tone poems: Tchaikovsky's *Hamlet Overture,* John Knowles Paine's symphonic poem *The Tempest,* Dvorak's concert overture *Othello,* and Richard Strauss's symphonic poem *Macbeth.* Before each composition was played, actress Claire Bloom presented literary images in readings from Shakespeare's own works. The words of Lady Macbeth and Hamlet foreshadowed the ominous and fateful themes in the music that followed. Botstein gave preconcert and midconcert lectures to enhance the audience's understanding of what was to come. Extensive program notes presented historical, musical, and personal perspectives from several literary contributors. To promote the concert, the ASO collaborated with local bookstores to provide special events and discounts on Shakespeare books.

In another program entitled "Berlin 1894," the ASO recreated an 1894 orchestral program to illustrate how radically concert programming has changed in the last century. In another program, Botstein scrutinized how some Russian composers prefigured the breakup of the Soviet Union; in still another, how Reaganomics and junk bonds may have found counterparts in new American music of the eighties. Other programs and special events have been organized in conjunction with the Swiss Consul General, the Metropolitan Museum of Art, the Harriman Institute of International Studies at Columbia University, the Berlin Film Archive, and the Martha Graham School, among other partners.

According to *New York Times* critic Ed Rothstein, Leon Botstein has become "the dominant figure in the most important contemporary trend in concert programming during the last 50 years."[8] As proof of the importance of this trend, after two seasons of thematic concerts, the thirty-two-year-old orchestra, which had been moribund in 1991, reported vastly improved ticket sales and a measurably younger audience. In the 1992–93 season alone, ticket sales increased by 86 percent. In addition, foundation grants increased by 730 percent, corporate grants increased by 164 percent, and private giving was up 80 percent.[9] Several critics have written that they eagerly anticipate future ASO events, validating the artistic integrity of this approach and expressing their hunger for meaningful new approaches to concert presentation.

Programming for the Community

Some organizations find they can be most effective when programming specifically for the community of which they are a part. For example, as a civic, volunteer orchestra, the Washington Civic Symphony (WCS) looks to its community to inspire its themes and events. This process, according to board president Milton Kotler, relies upon an understanding of the community's cultural dynamics. For example, the WCS presented an event to celebrate the history of America's labor unions and to honor the Labor Heritage Foundation. The concert was sponsored by several labor unions, which filled the house with many of their members—people who may never have attended a symphony concert. Pete Seeger performed his own works, which were arranged for full orchestra, and Studs Terkel, who canonized the working man, narrated Virgil Thomson's "Plough That Broke the Plains." In another concert, geared toward Washington's business community, the orchestra featured choral music composed by Dr. W. Edwards Deming, the leading guru of the Total Quality Management movement.

The San Antonio Symphony nearly folded in the 1980s, largely because of the rapidly changing demographics in its community. Now the symphony has developed an impressive long-term plan for involving the city's Hispanic population, which makes up 60 percent of its residents. Music director Christopher Wilkins programs orchestral music written by Latin American composers, has staged works by Falla and Mendelssohn using Hispanic actors, and has recently begun commissioning orchestral works from Hispanic composers. Two Hispanic composers-in-residence are writing symphonic music influenced by conjunto and tejano, varieties of Tex-Mex folk and pop styles. Mr. Wilkins said the program has led to "massive increases in support from the city and business communities." Over time, it may also lead to unusual musical hybrids, and perhaps to new audiences for more traditional programming as well.[10]

Specific recognition of the arts organization's interest in the community can develop not only a larger audience but one that is proud to have an orchestra or theater that cares. If the area has a dominant ethnic background (as Minnesota has a large Scandinavian population), the orchestra can plan an appropriate concert or festival. If an important historical event has shaped local history, the orchestra can schedule a concert of music from the period, perhaps including a neglected American work of the time. If the city is celebrating a special anniversary, the orchestra can use it to advantage. A tricentennial, for example, could involve music from three hundred, two hundred, and one hundred years ago as well as a commission for the occasion. If a corporation, hotel, or other business is promoting a major anniversary, it can show its appreciation for the community by commissioning a work for *their* orchestra.

Scheduling Accessibility

Accessibility can be enhanced by varying the standard approach to programming and scheduling. For example, rather than presenting a short, contemporary work now and then to expose the audience to various composers, Kurt Masur, music director of the New York Philharmonic, focused on contemporary composer, Alfred Schnittke, throughout the 1993–94 season. By providing sustained exposure to Schnittke's unfamiliar and difficult works over several concerts, and by explaining the music from the podium during the concerts, Masur turned this relatively unknown composer into a celebrity. Most importantly, he won people over to music that they found shocking at first exposure.

In Leipzig, Masur once conducted a joint Beethoven-Shostakovich cycle in which Beethoven works were featured in the first half of each concert and Shostakovich in the second. Some people turned up for the first half and left before the second. One night, Masur went on stage and claimed that "for technical reasons" the preannounced running order would be reversed. When forced to listen to the twentieth-century works, many audience members found that they enjoyed them. "Now," joked Masur, "there are a lot of Shostakovich lovers in Leipzig!"[11]

Approaches to Presentation

A report published by the American Symphony Orchestra League entitled "Americanizing the American Orchestra" urged orchestras to rethink not only their programming, but also their approaches to concert presentation. Harvey Lichtenstein, president and executive producer of the Brooklyn Academy of Music, has been a leader in questioning every aspect of the concert experience. Says Lichtenstein, "The orchestra, more than most cultural instruments, needs a radical approach, because it's stuck in the past, and it has more of a problem gathering a young audience. And let's face it: the orchestra, visually, is fairly dull. You've got to keep questioning all the old traditions. Some of them may be valid. But lots of them just make no sense." Arts organizations are taking up the challenge of making performances more inviting, exciting, relevant, and accessible by varying the performance rituals and environment.

THE PERFORMANCE RITUAL

Arts organizations have traditionally followed a ritualistic pattern of performance presentation. The symphony concert, in particular, is generally characterized by a short opening work, a concerto with soloist, an intermission, and then a longer symphonic piece, all performed by up to one hundred musicians identically dressed in formal attire. But there are many ways in which this ritual can be altered to enliven the experience, including concert-related activities during intermission, small ensemble and solo performances during the orchestra concert, shorter concerts and concerts with different starting times to accommodate people with different schedules, more variety in the kinds of works presented, and unscheduled encores in the middle of the program. Harvey Lichtenstein envisions concerts with dance, theatrical events, and opera. The use of color can add excitement and interest to a normally staid and formal art form. At one concert, when the women players arrived wearing brightly colored long gowns, the atmosphere immediately became more festive.

Imagine an evening dedicated to French music. The performance might begin at 7:00 P.M. with a half hour of medieval French music; at 8:00, the orchestra could begin a concert ranging from Lully to Milhaud; then at 10:30 a chamber ensemble from the orchestra could play music of Boulez and beyond. Not all events need be presented on the stage in the concert hall. Parts of the evening could take place in the lobby area. Food service might be coordinated with the French theme; refreshments could be served during longer-than-usual intermissions. The food servers could be wearing French country costumes. Audience members would be free to participate in the whole evening or just in the parts that interested them.[12]

THE PERFORMANCE ENVIRONMENT

Ambience is a critical factor in the audience's performing arts experience. Creating an ambience that enriches the programming is a unique challenge for each organization—unique because it is dependent on the nature of each organization's product offering, its physical, financial, and human resources, and its audience's preferences, interests, and needs. Consider how lingering at New York's Lincoln Center or London's Barbican Centre makes the whole concertgoing experience more pleasant. Patrons can browse among music-related books and recordings. Meals provided before a performance and/or during intermission accommodate those who do not have time to eat before the show. Postconcert wine and cheese or dessert bars in the lobby, or even on the stage, stimulate socializing and discussion about the performance. Postconcert events also answer such questions as "Where should we go after the concert?" "Where can we meet some new people?" and "How can we learn more about the performance/performers/composers?" A public "green room" allows audience members to meet the musicians, dancers, or actors after the concert and provides an opportunity for management to hear audience comments and answer questions.

Every aspect of a patron's evening out should be taken into consideration by marketers. At the end of a rave review of a "brilliant" theatrical performance, a critic stated: "Be warned that attending this production . . . involves horrible traffic, dreadful parking, uncomfortable seating and lousy sight lines. It's worth all of that."[13] Who can say how many potential patrons would decide that it's *not* "worth all of that"?

Using Multimedia

Arts organizations can capitalize on modern technology to enhance the audience's experience both within and outside the performance hall. A focus group study for the Pittsburgh Symphony revealed that audiences "liked the idea of the occasional use of multi-media—utilizing on-stage cameras to relay video images of the conductor and performers to on-stage monitors or a projection screen to the rear of the stage."[14] A visual component may also be added by using film projected on scrims or screens, most often with live musical accompaniment, as was done when composer Philip Glass created instrumental and vocal music for filmmaker Jean Cocteau's *Beauty and the Beast*. Through such innovations as "enhancing" the New World Symphony with slide projections, Harvey Lichtenstein is gambling that he can get the young, hip, Next Wave audience to do the unthinkable: go to an orchestra concert.[15] Orchestra purists worry that this approach will distract from the music, but music director Dennis Russell Davies draws an interesting parallel.

> If you hear a performance of Bach's B-minor Mass in a cathedral setting, and then in Carnegie Hall, both are acoustically justifiable. But the light coming through the stained glass, the religious objects and the large Gothic spaces create a very different ambience. If we can find a way to expand the concert-hall experience through modern

technology—to bring the ambience of the cathedral into the concert hall, if you will—this might be a way to attract a new audience.

Outside the performance hall, arts organizations can use modern technology to increase exposure, familiarity, and comfort levels with the arts. Audio tapes that play and discuss some of the major themes in the music can be distributed before the concerts to help audience members become better "tuned in" to what they are about to hear. Community access cable television and public television and radio can provide forums for orchestras and theaters to introduce new repertoire to potential audiences. As use of the Internet, interactive video, and CD-ROM becomes more widespread, arts organizations will be able to utilize such technologies to communicate with audiences and to provide opportunities for interactive exposure and learning.

The Event

As the well-known Stratford, Ontario, Shakespeare Festival and the Bayreuth Festival demonstrate, an event may provide the basis for an organization's total programming. Jazz presenters in Montreal capitalized on this principle to create their own successful festival.

THE MONTREAL JAZZ FESTIVAL

In the late 1970s, people would not come out for a jazz concert and Montreal jazz clubs were folding. When legendary bassist Charles Mingus came to town, only 600 seats were sold, and the concert's producers lost money. Yet, in 1980, the same producers presented Montreal's first jazz festival, launched as a weekend event with a budget of $250,000. It attracted 12,000 Montrealers. By the next year, 22,000 listeners appeared; by 1990 the festival had hit the 1 million attendance mark for a staggering schedule of three hundred concerts. "That's the difference a festival can make. It makes people pay attention," said Alain Simard, president and cofounder of the event. The festival offers a two-week combination of free outdoor performances, ticketed indoor concerts, special film screenings and premieres, themed concert series, cabaret performances, and more. The festival site is used ingeniously; performances are staged inside and outside the city's spectacular Place des Arts complex and in nearby auditoriums as well.

"At first, the city of Montreal and the merchants weren't very excited about the jazz festival," says Montreal jazz broadcaster Katie Malloch. "But eventually the city, the business people, everyone figured out that the jazz festival is a great thing for Montreal."[16]

Events may also be launched to build enthusiasm for the kinds of performances that audiences have come to take for granted because of year-round availability. For example, on the occasion of its sixtieth anniversary, the Orchestre Symphonique de Montréal (OSM) presented the first Canadian concert of Berlioz's *Les Troyens* and released the first digital recording of the work. A video recording of the production was also made, from rehearsals to the final performance, to be released for broadcast on network television. This mammoth event was accompanied by a huge publicity drive. The OSM arranged for 750,000 copies of a 24-by-36-inch promotional insert headlined "60 Years of Excellence" to be distributed in newspapers. An exhibition of sixty photographs—one image for each of the orchestra's seasons—toured venues around the city. Said OSM's marketing director Serge Langlois, "We were interested in bringing back memories to the community. The photo exhibition was a way of being creative and reflecting the message of the orchestra."

Although events are an effective means for building interest and enthusiasm, creating an event should not be an end in itself. Rather, says Langlois, "it is important not to be overshadowed by ourselves. The celebrations have to be the seed of something more ongoing."[17]

The Organization's Perspective on Programming

Each organization must take many concerns into account when determining its programs. Even if a particular program meets artistic and customer-related criteria, other issues add to the complexity of the programming decision. Are the rights to the projects available? Will the desired actors or singers be available when the director is ready to work? Are other theaters in the area considering the same projects? Is the production feasible within the budget? Russell Vandenbroucke, artistic director of the Chicago area's Northlight Theatre, likes to present a variety of issues, points of view, and styles that cause "heat" when rubbed together. Even so, programming the season is, for Vandenbroucke, light years from picking his five favorite plays. In the end, his work boils down to balancing personal vision, audience impact, and costs.[18]

THE ORGANIZATION'S MISSION AND OPPORTUNITIES

When evaluating current or potential product offerings, managers will want to ascertain that they are working to realize the organization's mission and are taking advantage of its best opportunities. To do so, managers may wish to use the criteria of *centrality, quality,* and *market viability.* Centrality is the degree to which a program or activity is central to the organization's mission. The quality and/or reputation of the program or activity should be evaluated relative to the organization's own standards and those of its competitors. Market viability is the degree to which the market for the program or activity is sufficient in size and growth potential.

These issues may not all carry equal weight for a performing arts organization. For example, an orchestra with a strong mission to educate its public may choose to program more contemporary and unfamiliar music despite the resistance of a large segment of its audience (high centrality, low anticipated market viability). On the other hand, consider a symphony orchestra that presents orchestral, chamber, and solo recital series of a broad range of classical music. The director is considering adding a jazz series to its programming because there is sizable demand; the move will increase revenues, may stimulate interest in the classical programming, and is not in conflict with the orchestra's mission (high quality, high market viability, neutral centrality).

COST CONSIDERATIONS

Many organizations not only manage within the financial constraints of the current season, but carry deficits from previous seasons as well. Ardis Krainik, general director of the Lyric Opera of Chicago, attributes her organization's firm foundation to rigorous financial vigilance. Ms. Krainik always determines her season within the constraints of a balanced budget, which frequently means "dusting off" an old production rather than creating a new one.

After suffering severe financial problems for many years and with little prospect for increasing contributed income, managers at the Vancouver Symphony Orchestra (VSO) concentrated on improving the returns on performances. To do so, they examined the economies of previous program offerings and estimated the costs of future programming options. A procedure called *marginal contribution analysis* was used to assist in the process. The steps in the procedure are as follows.

1. *Calculate revenue* from ticket sales, fees, sponsorship, restricted grants, etc.
2. *Less (subtract) variable costs:* (promotion, guest artists fees, production expense, materials).
3. *Equals* total contribution to overhead (musician and staff salaries, building costs, etc.).
4. *Divided by* the number of orchestra services consumed by the activity (a rehearsal or a performance is one service).
5. *Equals* per-service contribution to overhead.

The results from those calculations should be used as follows: If the result is a negative number, the activity should be discontinued (unless it has extraordinary redeeming artistic or community value); the overall financial result would be improved by *not* doing it. If the number is positive but low compared to other activities, *and a superior alternative use exists,* the services used by the activity should be reallocated to the alternative.

The VSO's managers used a marginal contribution analysis to calculate the financial contribution of each activity the orchestra presented from the 1986–87 season through the 1990–91 season. The results allowed the management to make comparisons both between series and within a particular series over a number of seasons.

The analysis was used to eliminate the "Choral Masterpieces" series in 1989–90 and the "Cafe Royal" series in the following season and to plan future seasons.[19] Techniques such as marginal contribution analysis help managers keep their organization on track financially while making programming decisions.

POSITIONING

A major responsibility of the marketer is working out how to position and present the product offering to the public. The marketer's expertise lies in augmenting, promoting, and delivering the core product creatively and sensitively to meet the needs and preferences of target markets. But for some marketers, positioning merely connotes a segmentation decision; to others it is an image question; to still others it means selecting which product features to emphasize. Few marketers consider all of these alternatives. Often, the positioning decision is based on flashes of insight rather than on a systematic approach that allows alternatives to be identified and evaluated.

In the following example, two similar organizations attracted completely different audiences for the same generic product because they adopted different positioning strategies.

ONE CORE PRODUCT— TWO POSITIONS

In the fall of 1993, both the Chicago Symphony Orchestra and the National Symphony Orchestra in Washington, D.C., opened their respective seasons with a performance of the Verdi Requiem. The core product was the same, but it was in the way that each positioned and promoted its concert that the two organizations defined their products and their target audiences.

In Chicago, the evening was an elegant, exclusive fund-raising event. Tickets were priced at a premium for both the concert and the gala benefit dinner that followed the performance in tents set up on Michigan Avenue, which was blocked off to traffic for the occasion. In contrast, the National Symphony presented Verdi's Requiem as a eulogy for the children killed by random violence in the city, contextualizing the music in such a way as to make it personally meaningful to new audiences. Seats were popularly priced to attract a broad range of Washington's diverse population.

A product or organization evokes many associations, which combine to form a total impression. The positioning decision involves selecting which associations to build upon and emphasize and which to remove or deemphasize. The positioning decision is central to influencing customers' perceptions and choice decisions. A clear positioning strategy also ensures that the elements of the marketing program are consistent and mutually supportive.[20]

An arts organization can base its positioning on various attributes. Some attributes apply to the organization itself, such as the director's charisma, the programming focus, the organization's reputation, or the fine performance hall; others apply to an individual production, such as a star performer or a famous composer. The arts organization can also base its positioning on a set of attributes. Generally speaking, however, a marketer will select the one or two attributes that appear to be the most attractive to the target audience to create a strong positioning statement, whether it be for the season brochure or to advertise an individual production. Some examples of positioning strategies follow.

Positioning by Director's Charisma

The American Repertory Theatre (A.R.T.) has built its positioning on the reputation and charisma of its artistic director, Robert Brustein. Audience comments often refer to Mr. Brustein directly. ("Theatre as presented by Mr. Brustein here is exciting and challenging.")[21] Although Brustein fills a large part of each season with experimental works, and sometimes people are dissatisfied with some productions, patrons generally remain loyal because they trust Brustein's vision. Similarly, symphonies and opera companies with prestigious music directors take full advantage of this fact in their positioning statements. Newspapers all over the country announced that Placido Domingo will become music director of the Washington Opera in 1996, creating a new positioning basis for the company.

Positioning by Programming

Organizations like the Shakespeare Repertory Company, the Music of the Baroque, the Old Town School of Folk Music, and Mostly Mozart are so clearly program-focused that their programming is positioned right in the name of the organization. Other organizations become known for certain types of programming, such as the Court Theater in Chicago, which frequently performs the classics, and the Bailiwick Repertory Company, which produces many plays on gay themes. By contrast, those organizations that produce a wide variety of works cannot develop a strong, clear position based on their diverse programming and must position on other attributes as well.

Positioning by Performers

People rarely attend a concert, play, or dance production with the express purpose of seeing one of the company's regular performers, such as an orchestra member or repertory company actor or dancer. Of course there are exceptions, such as Mikhail Baryshnikov, who is the featured attraction for the White Oak Dance Project. Star performers are such an important audience draw that arts organizations will sometimes knowingly take a financial loss in order to present them. Star performers for even a single event can serve to elevate the image of the organization and stimulate subscription sales. ("If you want to guarantee your seats to see Albert Finney, subscribe to Steppenwolf for the entire season," said a Steppenwolf Theatre ad.)

Positioning by Location and Facilities

Some performing halls have such a reputation for quality and prestige that just being there is an event in itself. The most familiar example of such a place is Carnegie Hall. Capitalizing on this, a recent brochure stated in part: "Climbers dream of Mount Everest; Divers dream of the Great Coral Reef; Music lovers dream of Carnegie Hall." Canada's Stratford Festival calls itself "One of life's great stages." The Sydney Opera House in Sydney, Australia, because of its startling architecture, has attracted millions of visitors to concerts independently of what program might be performed.

Positioning by Reputation and Image

What other field besides the performing arts presents awards and recognition to its members so publicly? These awards stimulate demand; people like to see a winner. Arts organizations usually take advantage of the recognition they receive by quoting critical praise and listing awards in their promotional material. Image positioning can also be used to establish people's expectations about the spirit of the experience they will have at a given performance. To help attract younger audiences, the Royal Philharmonic and the London Philharmonic are hoping to change their image with a new wardrobe for their musicians.[22]

Positioning by Price or Quality

A major opera company, a well-established theater, or a gala benefit opening may be positioned as higher in price and higher in quality than others. An award-winning young theater or a free performance in the park by the local symphony may position itself as high in quality but lower in price. Because arts organizations cannot achieve the productivity increases or economies of scale possible in the commercial sector, and because they do not operate with a profit motive, they do not generally compete with other similar organizations on the basis of price.

Positioning by Use or Applications

The "Serious Fun" series at Lincoln Center tells people the type of experience they can expect to have when attending a performance. Similarly, an orchestra may title a program or series "Celebrate" to encourage people to come for a special occasion. The occasion may be of general interest, such as Mozart's bicentennial; of local interest, like a theater's twenty-fifth anniversary; or a personal occasion being celebrated by the potential patron.

Positioning by Product User

Probably the most common example of positioning by product user is children's or family theater. As described earlier in this chapter, the Washington Civic Orchestra develops each program with a special constituency in mind.

Positioning by Product Class

When a program or series is called "Pops," "Jazz in June," or "Chamber Music Series," it is being positioned by product class. Sometimes these titles may create expectations in the audience that do not mesh with the changing vision of the organization. "Mostly Mozart" presents less Mozart now than in its early years. "Performing Arts Chicago" changed its name from "Chamber Music Chicago" because traditional expectations of what constitutes chamber music proved too limiting for the organization's broadening perspective.

Positioning by Competitor

In a newspaper advertisement, the New York Philharmonic called itself the "Home Team" with a byline quote from a critic saying "The home team hasn't sounded this good in years." The ad ran during the football championships, so there is no question that the orchestra was positioning itself against its major competitor of the moment.

Positioning by Multiple Attributes

When presenting an entire series that includes widely varied programming, an arts organization may position itself as having something for everyone. Consider how Vienna's Konzerthaus made a virtue out of the audience members selecting the attributes of most interest to them.

VIENNA'S KONZERTHAUS POCKET BOOK PROGRAM

The purpose of the "pocket book" program of Vienna's Konzerthaus is to present every possible aspect of a concert to every potential audience member. The book contains details of 250 concerts and 22 subscription series. A single concert at the Konzerthaus, therefore, may be presented to the public as a performance by a great international orchestra, as a chance to see a world-famous conductor or soloist at work, as a series of works by a particular composer, as a piece of music that creates a particular emotional response, as a work typical of a particular era, or simply as a concert that takes place at a particular time of day.

Care is taken to avoid making one series much more attractive than the others. Those that might be too popular can be sold as special "hidden series." When all the Beethoven symphonies appeared in one season, selling a Beethoven Symphony series would have adversely affected sales of some of the smaller series. So the Beethoven series never appeared in the program and was sold, at a premium, only to Diners Club members.[23]

The more strengths an organization has, the better it can position competitively to engage various audience interests. Furthermore, each environment presents a different set of challenges; each organization must nurture the attributes that will help it meet those challenges. To that end, managers must identify what makes their organization, series, or particular program distinctive and attractive. The more crowded the cultural scene, the more difficult it is to create an individual identity. But as the process becomes more difficult, it also becomes more necessary.

MANAGING PRODUCT LIFE CYCLE STAGES

During an organization's lifetime, managers will normally reformulate their marketing and positioning strategy several times. Not only do economic and competitive conditions change, but each organization, product offering, star performer, and even each industry (e.g., symphony orchestras, classical dance companies) passes through new stages with respect to audience preferences and requirements. Therefore, arts organizations must be able to anticipate and capitalize on change.

   In the popular performing arts, consider the rapid rise and fall of disco music, and the fact that interest in tap dancing, which waned after the heyday of Fred Astaire and Gene Kelly, is again on the increase. Such drastic and rapid changes are uncommon in the fine arts; in fact, the primary characteristic of the classics is their endurance. However, even interest in Mozart and Beethoven passes through life cycle stages. One researcher studied changes over time in audience responses to the repertoire presented by two professional Japanese orchestras. The researcher found that Beethoven's popularity in the early 1970s was superseded by Mozart in the late 1970s and early 1980s. In 1973, Mozart's Requiem Mass was the favorite piece; by 1977 it had dropped to fifth place. Mahler's Symphony #2, which was the favorite piece in 1971, was not even among the top fifteen choices in 1973.[24]

   Changes in audience preference apply not only to individual composers and pieces, but to types of presentation, such as orchestral, chamber, and solo recitals as well. Piano recitals used to be popular, heavily attended events. But in recent years, audience interest has been waning. To build enthusiasm, arts managers have tried to focus on the product factors that they think the audience will find attractive: "Winner of the Van Cliburn competition!" (tested by experts); "music by Chopin and Brahms" (highest-quality ingredients, famous brand name). They have even had to offer two-for-one tickets to try to fill the hall for "star" performers. But sometimes the cycle cannot be broken, and by the 1994–95 season, the Allied Arts Piano Series at Chicago's Orchestra Hall was reduced from twelve to ten recitals.

   Sometimes, as an organization grows, changes over time may conflict with its mission and goals, requiring it to rethink its product offerings. Consider the impact of life cycle factors on the Mostly Mozart Festival.

In 1994, after twenty-eight seasons, the Mostly Mozart Festival at Lincoln Center entered the endangered species category despite the fact that it continues to attract sizable audiences. In fact, its 1993 performances of thirty-nine New York concerts played to nearly 90 percent of capacity in Avery Fisher Hall, and a Tokyo tour earned $1.9 million in ticket sales, for the second-highest annual revenues in its history. But, the festival is an obstacle to the goals of Lincoln Center's management and board of directors.

The Center yearns for a young audience, and wants to have as great an impact on younger people as Mostly Mozart did in the 1960s and 70s. One reason for the change in audience may be the change in ticket prices. In 1966, its first summer, every seat cost $3. But prices climbed in the 1980s, and they now vary throughout the hall and from concert to concert, peaking at $40. The increase reflects administrative costs, soloists' fees, orchestra members' salaries, and the fact that the orchestra, which was formerly a pickup group, now operates under a contract.

Another reason for the change is that the cultural impact sought by Lincoln Center among the younger generation cannot be made right now with the classical repertory, despite the declaration by Mozart biographer H. C. Robbins Langdon that Mozart's legacy is "as good an excuse for mankind's existence as we shall ever encounter."[25]

Most discussions of product life cycle (PLC) portray the history of a typical product as following an S-shaped curve (see Figure 8-2). This curve is typically divided into four stages, known as *introduction, growth, maturity,* and *decline.* Each performance form, organization, or specific offering, and all levels of the product (core, expected, and augmented) may be subjected to life cycle analysis.

Audience response to full-season subscription offerings follows this typical S-shaped pattern. Season subscriptions went through a huge growth phase over a period of many years after they were first introduced in the late 1960s. Later, a maturity phase set in. Now, as fewer people are willing to commit to an entire season and as competition for subscribers has become intense, many organizations are experiencing a decline in season subscriptions. The more flexible and lower-commitment packages being offered in response are currently enjoying a growth phase.

Not all products exhibit an S-shaped product life cycle pattern. For example, the pattern for disco music can be visualized as similar to Figure 8-3a, and the classics exhibit a pattern like that shown in Figure 8-3b.

In the classic PLC pattern, the following four stages occur:

1. *Introduction:* A period of slow sales growth as the product is introduced in the market. Financial return is weak in this stage because of the heavy expenses of product introduction, especially promotional expenditures, or because of slow acceptance by the public. (Examples: a new theater company; recordings and performances by a "rising star"; modern music).

2. *Growth:* A period of rapid market acceptance, encouraging audience attendance, increasing ticket sales, and substantial financial improvement. (Examples: world [ethnic] music, thematic programming, minisubscriptions, a Tony award–winning play).

Figure 8-2

TYPICAL PRODUCT LIFE CYCLE

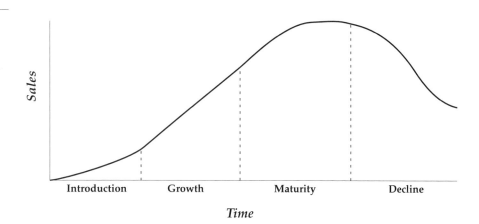

Figure 8-3

SOME ALTERNATIVE PRODUCT LIFE CYCLE PATTERNS

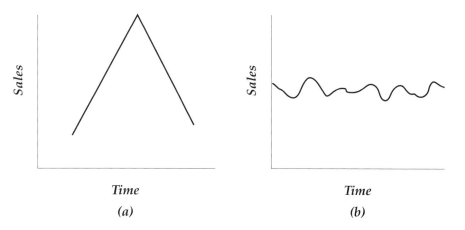

3. *Maturity:* A period of a slowdown in sales growth because the product has achieved acceptance by most potential buyers. Financial return stabilizes or declines at this stage. (Examples: *A Chorus Line* after several years on Broadway; the Steppenwolf Theatre three years after the excitement of moving into its new space.)

4. *Decline:* The period when sales show a downward drift and financial return erodes. (Examples: solo recitals; full-season subscriptions).

Corresponding to these stages are distinct marketing strategy opportunities and problems.

Introduction

In the introduction stage, the main challenge is to build organization and product awareness. Artists' managers and record companies will heavily advertise and promote new young soloists. New organizations will actively employ public relations and other low-cost promotional approaches. Music directors may "introduce" contemporary composers or compositions with special events and educational programming.

Growth

The growth phase is the period during which the arts organization capitalizes on the audience's strong response and seeks to develop patron loyalty. The organization works hard to convert single-ticket buyers into season subscribers, to sell blocks of tickets to corporations and social organizations, and to build a broad base of contributors. An organization can use several strategies to prolong the growth stage:

- Improve product quality and add new product features and benefits. Make visible improvements in the performance hall, the quality of the performers, the productions, and customer service.

- Add new products: a chamber music series, matinee concerts, staged readings, special events.

- Cultivate new market segments, perhaps by offering rush hour concerts to attract businesspeople, matinees to attract families, and special student subscriptions.

- Consider new distribution channels: perform in neighborhood churches or schools, give free concerts in the park, perform on local cable channels, collaborate with area retailers and corporations, or go on tour to broaden the customer base outside the region. Sell tickets through a new Web site.

- Shift some advertising from building product awareness to bringing about product conviction and purchase. This requires a change in advertising focus, but not necessarily an increase in advertising dollars.

Many of these market-expanding strategies may increase the organization's costs. But everyone likes to support a "winner," so by spending money on product improvement, positioning, and promotion, the organization's backers can seize the opportunity to capture a dominant position.

Maturity

At some point, the rate of sales growth slows for most products. When this occurs, the product has entered a stage of relative maturity. The slowdown in the rate of sales growth creates overcapacity in the industry, which leads to intensified competition. A shakeout period begins, and weaker competitors withdraw.

Some observers believe that many of the problems currently facing the performing arts stem from the fact that the industry as a whole is in a maturity phase. Arts organizations are competing for both earned and donated revenue in an ever-tightening market. The maturity stage normally lasts longer than the previous stages, and it poses formidable challenges to marketing management. Marketers need to systematically consider strategies of modifying the market, the product, and the marketing mix.

MARKET MODIFICATION

The organization might try to expand its market by working with the two factors that make up sales volume: the number of users and the usage rate per user.

Number of users The organization can try to expand the number of users in three ways:

- *Convert nonusers:* The organization can try to attract nonusers. Since a huge majority of the population are not arts attenders, this presents an enormous opportunity. However, building new interest in the performing arts is a daunting task. Individual organizations may develop special programming and distribution systems to reach certain target markets. Recall the program of the Washington Civic Symphony celebrating the history of the labor movement. Free tickets were distributed through labor unions to attract their members to fill the 3,700-seat auditorium. The real challenge is to build on these attendees' initial interest so that they will choose to attend other arts performances.

- *Enter new market segments:* The organization can try to enter new geographic or demographic market segments. For example, chamber music groups can perform at universities to attract music students, professors, and others for whom convenience of location is important.

- *Win competitors' customers:* The organization can attempt to attract competitors' customers. Suppose the competition is defined as cinema or home videos. The organization can try to encourage moviegoers or video watchers to experience a *live* performance. Also, small musical, theatrical, and dance groups may perform at art museums to attract museum-goers to their art form.

Usage rate The organization can also try to encourage current attenders to increase their attendance rate. Here are three strategies:

- *More frequent use:* The organization can encourage patrons to attend more frequently. For example, single-ticket holders may be converted to miniplan subscribers, and miniplan subscribers may be encouraged to take out a full-season subscription or additional minisubscriptions.

- *More usage per occasion:* The organization can encourage patrons to bring friends or family members or to arrange group events for their membership organizations. Some theaters offer half-price tickets to teenagers who accompany their parents.

- *New and more varied usage:* The organization can influence patrons to attend performances on different occasions. Some organizations celebrate events, such as the conductor's special anniversary with the orchestra, to stimulate attencance. Or the organization may encourage groups to center their social events and fund-raisers around performances.

PRODUCT MODIFICATION

The maturity stage of a product can be prolonged through product modification. For example, the organization can alter its product mix. A dance company that is equally adept in performing classical and contemporary dance can shift toward more modern dance if research indicates a growing market for contemporary choreography. By altering the season slightly, perhaps doing three contemporary and two classical ballets instead of the opposite, and by stressing the modern dimensions of the company's programming in its promotions, the company can attract modern dance enthusiasts without losing those who prefer more traditional fare.[26] Thematic programming and other creative approaches to presentation are likely to stimulate new interest among consumers.

Managers can also stimulate audience demand by modifying the product's characteristics. This can take several forms.

- *Quality improvement:* Investing more heavily in production values may help to garner awards, which helps an organization earn the label "best" in some category. Moving to a finer-quality performance hall, appearing on television, making recordings, or featuring a star performer or award-winning play may signal to the audience that the organization has "made it," thereby improving the public *perception* of the organization's quality.

- *Feature improvement:* New features contribute to an image of the organization's progressiveness and leadership and help to win the loyalty of market segments that seek those features. Generally, they can be adopted or dropped quickly and made optional to the patron. Examples are special social events for certain market segments, such as a gay and lesbian night or singles night; preconcert chamber concerts or lectures; adding multimedia technology to a program; offering box meals during intermission.

- *Style improvement:* A strategy of style improvement aims at increasing aesthetic appeal. Tactics may range from redesigning the organization's logo and brochure to giving the hall a "face-lift." A new style can indicate progressiveness and can contribute to an organization's unique market identity.

MARKETING MIX MODIFICATION

Managers should ask the following questions about the nonproduct elements of the marketing mix in trying to stimulate demand for a mature product.

- *Prices:* Would a price cut attract new triers or lapsed subscribers? Or would it be better to raise the price to signal higher quality?

- *Distribution:* Can the organization present its performances or special events in other locations? Can it introduce the product through new distribution channels, such as making tickets available through the organization's Web site?

- *Advertising:* Should advertising expenditures be increased? Should the advertising message or copy be changed? Should the media mix be changed? Should the timing, frequency, or size of ads be changed?

- *Promotion:* Should the organization increase the use of promotional tools—discounts, gifts, or special event perks?

- *Personal selling:* Should the quantity of telemarketers be increased or should their training be improved? Should the volunteer board be encouraged to host coffees to attract new patrons or to bring new people to performances? Can a new network of personal sellers be developed?

- *Services:* Can the organization increase convenience and better meet the needs of certain publics—for ticket sales, access for people with disabilities, convenient parking, and so on?

An organization must determine which tools would be most effective for meeting its needs. For example, would more be gained by increasing advertising or by offering special price breaks? Should services be improved, or should more be invested instead in new distribution channels? Each organization faces trade-offs and must weigh the relative benefits and costs of each opportunity.

Decline

If a product or organization has not sustained itself or been rejuvenated through the maturity stage, its sales will eventually decline. At some point many products and organizations outlive their value to their consumers. Once strategies to bolster inadequate audience demand have been exhausted, withdrawal from the market may be the logical course of action.

One regional dance company operated for several years with the minimum acceptable level of audience support—a "shaky" maturity stage. Two things happened: a dance company in a neighboring city grew quite strong, attracting superior dancers, and occasionally performing in the first dance company's home city. Second, national dance companies began to tour the area more frequently, siphoning off dance enthusiasts. The regional company's attendance sagged, and it appeared that most of the potential dance market had already been tapped. The company disbanded.

An astute arts director will recognize a deteriorating situation. Managing in the face of decline can benefit from a decision-making process that has been laid out in advance. For example, an organization facing an uncertain upcoming season may specify the following plan: (1) if audience levels fall below 40 percent of capacity for the season *and* the financial deficit exceeds $40,000, execute option 2. (2) Exhaust all possible sources of subsidy and seek merger with another regional company. (3) If option 2 fails to improve the situation, dissolve the company.

The decline stage of an arts organization is difficult and unpleasant to manage; managers' commitment to their artistic function delays a surrender to economic realities. However, a preplanned withdrawal is preferable to a wrenching demise brought on by shortsighted financial management.[27]

But a state of decline does not necessarily portend a death knell for an arts organization. As many orchestras are faced with financial crises and are struggling to survive, orchestra managers are reevaluating their organizations' roles in society, their programs, and their modes of presentation. Orchestral musicians are becoming more realistic about the necessity of reducing the number of weeks in their season contract in light of their current and anticipated future audiences and supporters. Those who think broadly enough to imagine how artistic integrity can be maintained within the context of sweeping changes are the most likely to avoid decline. For the rest, the future is at risk.

[1] E. Raymond Corey, *Industrial Marketing: Cases and Concepts* (Englewood Cliffs, N.J.: Prentice-Hall, 1976), 40–41.

[2] Theodore Levitt, *The Marketing Imagination* (New York: Free Press, 1986), 76–77.

[3] Theodore Levitt, "Marketing Intangible Products and Product Intangibles," *Harvard Business Review,* May/June 1981, 94–102; and Leonard Berry, "Services Marketing Is Different," *Business,* May/June 1980, 24–30.

[4] Philip Kotler, "Atmospherics as a Marketing Tool," *Journal of Retailing,* Winter 1973/74, 48–64.

[5] Leonard L. Berry and A. Parasuraman, *Marketing Services: Competing through Quality* (New York: Free Press, 1991), 101–102.

[6] Bernard Holland, "Everything is Great! Just Great!" *New York Times,* Aug. 29, 1993.

[7] Berry and Parasuraman, *Marketing Services,* 190.

[8] Ed Rothstein, "Shakespeare as Muse in Symphony Concert," *New York Times,* Sept. 28, 1993.

[9] Allan Kozinn, "The American Symphony's Programming Experiment Pays Off," *New York Times,* Apr. 28, 1994.

[10] Ed Rothstein, "Orchestra League Peers at the Future and Sees Trouble," *New York Times,* June 21, 1994, sec. B, pp. 1, 4.

[11] Kurt Masur, "The Beauty of Life," *International Arts Manager,* May 1994, 19, 23.

[12] "Americanizing the American Orchestra," Report of the National Task Force for the American Orchestra: An Initiative for Change (Washington, D.C.: American Symphony Orchestra League, June 1993).

[13] Richard Christiansen, "Imagery Propels Lepage's 'Needles,'" *Chicago Tribune,* June 3, 1994, p. 28.

[14] *Pittsburgh Symphony Marketing and Promotions Study,* Tripp, Umbach & Associates, Aug. 1991.

[15] Robert Schwartz, "The Crises of Tomorrow Are Here Today," *New York Times,* Oct. 31, 1993, 31–32.

[16] Howard Reich, "Music Lessons," *Chicago Tribune,* July 17, 1994.

[17] Serge Langlois, "Many Happy Returns," *International Arts Manager,* May 1994, 11–13.

[18] Sid Smith, "A House of Cards," *Chicago Tribune,* Aug. 16, 1992, Arts, p. 14.

[19] Andrew F. Cypiot under the direction of Robert Augsburger, "Vancouver Symphony Orchestra (B)," case study, Stanford Graduate School of Business, 1991.

[20] David A. Aaker and J. Gary Shansby, "Positioning Your Product," *Business Horizon,* May/June 1982, 56–62.

[21] C. W. L. Hart, J. I. Ayala, and J. K. Falstad, "American Repertory Theatre—1988," Harvard Business School case study 9-688-120, 1988.

[22] "London Orchestras Dress to Impress as RPO Faces Further Financial Woes," *International Arts Manager,* June 1994, 6.

[23] James Odling-Smee, "The Hidden Agenda," *International Arts Manager,* Oct. 1992.

[24] Yoshimasa Kurabayashi, "Dynamic Changes in Audience Preferences to the Orchestral Pieces in Socio-Economic Perspective: A Longitudinal and Multi-Variate Statistical Analysis of a Panel Data Set for Japanese Audience," *Proceedings,* First International Conference on Arts Management, Montreal, Canada, Aug. 1991.

[25] Edward Rothstein, " 'Mostly' is a Hard Act to Follow," *New York Times,* May 22, 1994, sec. H, p. 34.

[26] Gene R. Laczniak, "Product Management and the Performing Arts," in *Marketing the Arts,* ed. Michael Mokwa, William M. Dawson, and E. Arthur Prieve (New York: Praeger, 1980), 135.

[27] Laczniak, "Product Management and the Performing Arts," 136.

▲●▲

Everything is worth
what its purchaser
will pay for it.
PUBLILIUS SYRUS,
FIRST CENTURY B.C.

Nothing is
intrinsically
valuable; the value
of everything is
attributed to it,
assigned to it from
outside the thing
itself, by people.
JOHN BARTH,
The Floating Opera, 1956

PRICING THE PERFORMANCES FOR COST AND VALUE

FOR ARTS MARKETERS, PRICING IS AN ESPECIALLY COMPLEX ISSUE. IN MOST industries, prices are determined largely by costs so that profitability is ensured. In nonprofit organizations, monetary costs are only one of a myriad of factors that inform pricing decisions. Income generation is a means to fulfilling the organization's mission, rather than an end in itself. For example, arts organizations often want to attract as broad an audience as possible, and therefore will set ticket prices at a level many people can afford. Yet, even though contributed income plays a major role in meeting the organization's financial needs, continually rising costs translate into increased ticket prices. This is especially true for opera companies, whose substantial production costs are the highest among the performing arts.

OPERA TICKETS: NOT JUST FOR A SONG

If you want to hear Luciano Pavarotti or Placido Domingo sing at the Royal Opera House in London's Covent Garden, be prepared to spend as much as $402 per ticket. For operas that do not feature such superstars, $200 will buy a ticket in the grand tier, while $44 will get you a seat in the upper balcony. Much to

219

the chagrin of management, prices had to be increased 126 percent in the period from 1987 to 1992, making Covent Garden a
place only for the rich, even with a 32 percent government subsidy.[1] American opera companies seem cheap in comparison.
Top prices at the Metropolitan Opera are $137 on weekends;
$107 at the Lyric Opera of Chicago. Although this is still a steep
price by most standards, the $107 accounts for only about 60
percent of the production costs. American companies receive
negligible government funding, but U.S. tax laws make it easier
to raise money privately.

In formulating pricing decisions, arts managers must take several factors into consideration: (1) the costs faced by their organization; (2) the costs to the consumers relative to their perceptions of value; and (3) the organization's pricing objectives,
which are determined on the basis of its long- and short-term goals. These factors
help the manager choose the most effective pricing strategies.

THE COSTS TO THE ARTS ORGANIZATION

Among the important factors an arts organization must take into consideration when
developing pricing strategies are its costs. In addition to the tangible monetary costs
common to all businesses, arts organizations face certain intangible costs due to the
nature of their productivity, their societal and aesthetic values, and their place in the
competitive environment.

Intangible
Costs

As we discussed in Chapter 1, arts organizations are, for the most part, unable to benefit from the productivity gains realized by other sectors of the economy as a result
of improved technology or economies of scale. (A forty-five-minute quartet will take
the same three man hours to produce as it did at the beginning of the century, and
always will.) Productivity gains help to keep prices down by partially offsetting
upward-spiraling costs. Because productivity in the arts is actually decreasing in
comparison with the rest of the economy, arts organizations need to pursue potential
sources of income to help narrow the ever-widening gap between productivity and
costs. Yet, for several reasons, increases in ticket prices have consistently lagged
behind increases in the costs of performances.

First, arts organizations believe in the social value of their product, and on moral
grounds, seek to make it widely available by maintaining affordable prices. The same
organizations, however, are directed by the high professional standards of their
artists, who often value innovation and risk, meaning narrower appeal and therefore
higher cost per audience member.[2] According to Robert Brustein, artistic director of

the American Repertory Theatre, "The profit motive requires an appeal to the lowest common denominator for the widest possible audience . . . the more serious artist does not always make his or her appeal known immediately. It takes some time before the audience catches up in some cases. . . . What do we do about our James Joyces and our Stravinskys and our Picassos and our Ibsens and our Brechts until they've become absorbed into the culture and become more popular? We have to serve them, we have to subsidize them, we have to support them. And that's why some institutions exist."[3]

Because of their goal to keep prices affordable, nonprofit organizations often resist raising prices even when there is excess demand. At the Metropolitan Opera, the performances are typically sold out, but prices have not been raised to the levels the market will bear. Similarly, the Lyric Opera of Chicago avoids significant increases in ticket prices, even while selling more than 100 percent of its seats by reselling tickets turned back to the box office by subscribers.

The second factor restraining prices has to do with the relative demand for the arts. Arts managers assume that if performances become too expensive, most people will choose to get along without them. This assumption inhibits price increases, although it is difficult to validate. Consider that a ticket for a Chicago Bulls playoff game may go for $300 or more, while the top price at the Lyric Opera is just over $100. Similarly, many students and lower-income employees, two groups often cited as the rationale for low pricing strategies, may balk at spending $25 to attend a play or symphony concert but willingly spend twice that amount to go to a rock concert. One can argue that the general public isn't willing to pay as much to attend artistic performances as for spectator sports and rock concerts, but the fact remains that some costly entertainment options *are* pursued by lower-income people.

Third, ticket prices are held down by the fact that there are convenient and low-priced substitutes for live performance. Since cultural performances can be seen in the movies or on television, and music can be heard on compact discs and radio, technology limits prices through the competition of the mass media. On the other hand, it is widely believed that as people are exposed more and more to technological reproductions, they will increasingly crave and appreciate live performances.

Monetary Costs

Arts organizations incur three types of monetary costs: *fixed, variable,* and *incremental.*

FIXED COSTS

Fixed costs are those that are incurred even if no performances are held. This institutional overhead comprises such costs as building rent or mortgage and salaries of administrators and artists under annual contract. An orchestra with a large hall and staff and up to a hundred musicians under contract has high fixed costs. Conversely, a theater company that has a small staff, rents a hall, and hires artists on a per production basis has relatively low fixed costs. Many arts organizations that greatly enlarged their administrative staffs and other fixed costs during the 1980s boom are struggling in today's leaner times to manage with excessive fixed costs that are difficult to reduce.

VARIABLE COSTS

Variable costs are the expenses associated with each staged production or those that are easily increased or reduced. They include wages of part-time actors, musicians, directors, and other temporary personnel; royalties paid; transportation; sets, costumes, and other production costs. These costs vary from show to show, depending on the number of people involved, the extent of special effects, performers' fees, and so on. Although a certain level of marketing expenses for advertising and direct mail will be necessary, these costs are not fixed and may be adjusted according to the organization's needs and constraints.

The fixed nature of the production schedules of most nonprofit arts organizations exacerbates their variable costs. In any organization with a subscription series, repertory rotation, or other short-run scheduling constraints, a company cannot "milk" a successful production indefinitely, as a Broadway theater might. Nor can a flop be closed before its appointed time to make room for a more popular show.[4]

When pricing levels are at least in part determined by a production's variable costs, managers generally employ a *break-even analysis.* A break-even analysis helps to determine, for an anticipated level of demand, what price must be charged to fully cover the production's costs. This is known as the break-even price. The break-even analysis also helps determine, for any proposed price, how many tickets would have to be sold to fully cover the production's costs. This is known as the break-even volume. Assume that the cost of staging a particular show is $75,000. Dividing $75,000 by the anticipated average ticket price (or anticipated demand) will indicate how many tickets need to be sold at each price (or what price should be charged) to break even—that is, to cover the costs of staging the show.

However, just covering the costs of a particular show, or even earning a surplus, does not necessarily guarantee financial solvency for the organization. Managers must keep their *total costs* in mind, which are the sum of the organization's fixed and variable costs. For the organization to remain solvent, either the total surpluses achieved on all shows must be sufficient to cover these fixed costs, or grants and donations must be sought to bridge the gap. Often, donors and grant-makers prefer to fund specific productions or projects rather than to support the fixed operating costs of an organization. In such cases, contributed revenues are designated to the variable production costs and unrestricted gifts and earned ticket revenues are applied to the fixed operating costs.

INCREMENTAL COSTS

For an arts organization pricing its performances, incremental costs may be described as the additional costs involved in selling one more seat. Such costs tend to be extremely low. Box office personnel are already on hand, tickets and program booklets are preprinted, and most advertising is done through the mass media. The significance of low incremental costs to arts marketers is that the cost of selling an empty seat for a performance that is about to start is close to zero, so the incremental revenue of each empty seat sold is, in effect, the price of the seat. This is the economic justification for offering day-of-performance discounts, student rush tickets, and other promotions that sell otherwise unsold seats at a deep discount.

CONSUMER COSTS AND VALUE

Today's arts marketers face a growing dilemma. As costs rise and attracting contributed income becomes more of a challenge, they must raise ticket prices. But as marketers try to expand their audiences and maintain satisfaction among current attenders, they fear that price increases will act as a barrier to their success. So, arts marketers ask, How important is price? And for whom is price important?

In a study of 1,298 regular performing arts attenders in Great Britain, it was found that "price was not a significant reason for nonattendance and the motivation to attend or not to attend because of price is vastly outweighed by other considerations." Only 4% of the respondents spontaneously mentioned cost as a barrier in attendance. The researcher concluded that the potential for price increase is substantial, although he warns that such price increases can be disastrous unless accompanied by other efforts that maintain or improve the event's value to the market.[5]

In contrast, in a study of infrequent attenders at the Crucible Theatre Sheffield and Playhouse Theatre Leeds, price was found to play a role in consumers' ticket purchase decisions. Fifty-three percent of respondents reported that they had been put off by price in deciding whether to attend some event. But, choice, value, and enjoyment were reported to be as important as price in motivating ticket purchase. Seventy-six percent of arts-oriented respondents rated price in the second tier of issues, comparable with the importance of the performers, author, and company, as well as seat comfort and parking; but well below the first-tier rating of quality of performance, entertainment value, and subject matter, all of which had at least ninety percent importance ratings.[6] Another study investigated audience attitudes about the effects of a possible price rise at the Welsh National Opera (WNO). The summaries of fifty focus group discussions concluded that price increases had a significant impact on certain sectors of the audience (the medium- and lower-interest groups) who, it was felt, reacted to price increases by becoming more selective or reducing the price level of seats taken.[7] The report concluded that a specific 20 percent price increase planned by the WNO would significantly reduce the size of the audience.

For the purpose of analyzing the impact of price among nonattenders, P. Walshe drew a distinction between the *non-intenders*, those for whom pricing is not an issue since they do not intend to purchase a ticket for other reasons, and the *intender-rejectors*, those who would like to attend but become alienated as a result of pricing policy. He developed the following decision-making model for performing arts attendance:

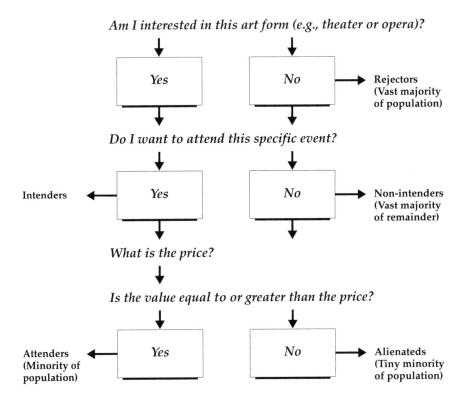

This analysis demonstrates that for the vast majority of people, rejection has set in before price becomes a consideration, since for these people there is a probably irreversible barrier: lack of interest. Therefore, one can conclude that there is little point in trying to use major price cuts to access the mass market; price cutting will not generate full houses. A second conclusion can be drawn: pricing strategies should be based only on the intenders—those who express an interest in attending a given, very specific event (and not an event type).

Arts consultant Chris Blamires holds that pricing strategy research should be conducted on future or hypothetical events, in order to assess their appeal, rather than on events already attended. His rationale is that if one asks an individual if she or he would have paid more than the ticket price of say, $15, to see each of the three plays attended in the last twelve months, the answer would be "of course" if the play was as good as the best play the person has ever seen; "of course not" if the play was as bad as the worst. Price, then, is a screening device used by those with a desire to attend a given event. It tests the value placed on the *promise* provided by the information received about the event.[8]

Actual and Perceived Costs

The price of a ticket is only one of the costs a consumer has to pay in order to attend a performance or to subscribe to a series. The consumer's actual and perceived costs of a proposed exchange can be defined as the sum of all expected negative outcomes. Consider the nonmonetary costs faced by Greensboro Symphony patrons in the following example.

THE COSTLY MOVE OF THE GREENSBORO SYMPHONY

In 1993, the Greensboro Symphony Orchestra in North Carolina moved to a new, 2,400-seat performing center, located in a special event complex that also housed another performance hall and a 25,000-seat coliseum. Some events were scheduled simultaneously in the three facilities at the complex, meaning that many thousands of cars could be entering and leaving the parking lot at the same time. Furthermore, when the season began, the complex's huge parking lot was still under construction, creating physical barriers and persistent mud. This was more than some of the Greensboro Symphony's patrons were willing to tolerate, and as a result, the symphony lost 200 of its 2,100 subscribers. Attempts were made to remedy the situation by providing shuttle buses to and from another lot, but the benefit was too little and offered too late to recover the lost customers.

Also consider the costs incurred by a couple with young children who live in the suburbs and are planning to attend a symphony concert downtown. In addition to paying for tickets, they must hire a reliable baby-sitter, travel thirty miles in heavy traffic, and locate a parking lot that will not charge a high fee and require a long exit line after the concert. There are also psychic costs involved in attending the concert that may or may not influence this couple. Many potential performing arts attenders avoid going because they do not want to feel ignorant about what is being presented or because they feel they have to "dress up" or might not "fit in" with the crowd. Some people may not attend theater in run-down areas because they fear being hurt or robbed.

Such costs may serve as greater barriers to attendance than the actual price of the ticket. Arts marketers must determine which perceived costs are influencing each target segment and develop strategies that can be used to reduce these costs. Some costs are outside the marketer's control, such as baby-sitters and traffic conditions. However, the arts organization can provide a guide to nearby parking facilities, along with discount coupons where appropriate. Posting staffers and bright lighting in front of theaters might augment the perception of personal safety.

When selecting strategies to reduce perceived customer costs, the marketer must keep two questions in mind: (1) What is the marketer's cost of reducing a perceived customer cost? (2) What response can be expected from the customer to given levels of perceived cost reduction?

Consumer responses are usually a reaction to a bundle of perceived costs and benefits. The problem in managing perceived costs is to figure out which of many costs to reduce and how much to spend to reduce them. For a given expenditure, the issue is which perceived costs should be targeted to yield the largest net gain in audience size and satisfaction.

Suppose a theater wants to reduce one or more of the following customer costs:

- Parking difficulties and the accompanying frustrations.
- Uncomfortable seats in the theater.
- Inadequate restroom facilities.
- Unattractive lobby area.

The marketer should determine the organization's monetary cost of reducing each customer cost. Suppose renting a nearby, well-lit parking lot from a retailer and making it available at no cost to patrons will cost three times as much as upgrading the lobby. Replacing the seats will cost twice as much as the parking lot rental, and increasing restroom facilities is nearly impossible because of space limitations. The marketer may then collect data from a representative patron sample on the significance and relative importance of these factors. For example, market research may indicate that patrons express far more dissatisfaction with the parking situation and inadequate restroom facilities than with the seating comfort and the ambience of the lobby. This customer information should then be matched with cost data to inform the proper investment choices. The theater may decide to invest in renting the parking lot and to extend the intermission time to compensate for the shortage of restrooms, and to deal with the less pressing customer costs at a later time.

Perceived Value

The corollary to the concept of perceived costs is the principle of perceived value. Most goods and services have a generally easy-to-determine *producer value,* which can be broadly defined as the cost of production, distribution, and marketing plus a profit factor that is within the range of industry norms. Perceived value, on the other hand, is determined by the buyer. *Perceived value* represents the margin of difference, either positive or negative, between the producer value and what a consumer feels the offering is worth regardless of its production costs. In the business sector, a good or service must be worth to the consumer at least its producer value, or it will not be produced. In most nonprofit arts organizations, the ticket price of a performance is significantly lower than its producer value, creating a gap that must be filled by other funding sources. Arts organizations explain to their prospective donors that earned income covers, for example, only 50 or 60 percent of their producer costs.

Perceived value varies by audience segment. For example, many mature audiences value experience potential, what Abraham Maslow calls the self-actualizing experiences. A couple in their fifties or older might take coupons to the grocery store to save $3 or $4, then spend $200 that evening at a fine restaurant and a concert. They may drive a car that has clocked over 100,000 miles that they hope to keep a lot longer, yet spend $12,000 on a trip to Asia or Europe. While they may spend tightly on goods and services necessary to *maintaining* lifestyles, they are likely to spend loosely on products and services that *enhance* lifestyle.[9] This market segment has a high perception of the value of performing arts experiences.

For many arts patrons, factors other than price are so central to creating value that prices can be raised significantly without eroding the organization's customer base. To research the importance of subscription series discounts among the benefits offered to subscribers, Ryans and Weinberg surveyed subscription buyers for the American Conservatory Theater (ACT) in San Francisco. Survey respondents reported that the main reason for buying a subscription series was *not* the savings, but to make sure they went to the theater more often and were assured of a good seat. Fewer than 25 percent of respondents even indicated discount as a valued benefit of subscribing. According to the report, "If a discount is a significant factor in converting occasional attenders into subscribers, then its use may be economically justified. On the other hand, if subscribers are primarily those who are the most enthusiastic theatre goers, then offering a discount may essentially be a price reduction for those who would attend in any case."[10] Validating the research results, ACT abandoned its subscriber discount the next season with no significant impact on subscription sales.[11] At the Chicago Symphony Orchestra (CSO), price reductions do not appear to be necessary to induce people to subscribe. Subscribers do not receive any discount off the single-ticket price, but they continue to make up more than 85 percent of audience capacity. In 1991, the CSO increased all its ticket prices, by amounts ranging from 5 percent for the lowest-priced seats to 25 percent for the best seats, without any identifiable decrease in sales. Although Danny Newman strongly advocates subscriber discounts as an important promotional technique, perhaps the operative factor is *promotion*, not discounts.[12] Thus, many organizations may be pricing their tickets lower than the market will bear, as a result of underestimating the perceived value of their product to many of their customers.

SETTING PRICING OBJECTIVES

There are two basic objectives an arts organization may attempt to achieve through pricing its performances: *revenue* (or *cost recovery*) *maximization* and *audience size maximization*.

When the American Repertory Theatre (A.R.T.) opened at the Loeb Theatre in

Cambridge, Massachusetts, its managers wanted to maximize box office income while simultaneously maximizing attendance. According to marketing director Sam Guckenheimer, "Our prices should be high enough so that anyone who can and will pay a lot to attend will do so. At the same time, anyone who really wants to come should be able to." There were other constraints on pricing. A.R.T. management felt it important to have a top ticket price "high enough to distinguish us from the church basement productions," as Guckenheimer put it; "but on the other hand, we do depend on outside funding, and for that reason we can't be out for blood like the commercial theatres."

Many arts organizations seek prices that will maximize revenue or at least recover a "reasonable" percentage of their costs. What is considered reasonable cost recovery for one organization may be quite different from that sought by another. In a study of thirty North American opera companies, earned income ranged from as high as 87 percent to as low as 18 percent of the annual budget. At the 215 theaters surveyed by the Theatre Communications Group, total earned income, including that from ticket sales, touring, royalties, concessions, rentals, and so on, accounts for, on average, 63.2 percent of expenses.[13]

Arts organizations also seek prices that will achieve the objective of attracting the largest possible audience. One might think this means setting a low, affordable price to stimulate demand. But in 1990, when Chicago's Remains Theatre lowered all ticket prices to $10 and made seating by general admission only, this attempt to maximize audience size actually had a negative effect. Patrons who expected to pay more became skeptical about the quality of productions offered at such low prices. Some patrons even offered to pay more if they could reserve seats in advance. Before long, a dual price structure for reserved and unreserved seating was put into place. The following season, ticket prices were raised to $20, with all seats reserved, and a half-price "rush" was offered the day of the performance. This new policy generated more income for the theater while still supporting its objective of audience maximization. But a study of this strategy concluded that it can be further improved by making rush tickets available only to students. Other people, who would have been willing to pay $20, had been waiting until the day of performance to purchase tickets to take advantage of the savings.

In one controlled experiment involving a U.S. symphony orchestra, it was found that performing arts patrons are *price inelastic,* meaning that price increases had relatively little effect on their willingness to buy a ticket (or subscription). In this study, current subscribers, occasional attenders, and high-income prospects received a booklet consisting of eight sections. Each section described a local live entertainment activity; for example, a repertory theater, an opera company, the symphony, or a professional baseball team. Each section described the offerings and listed available ticket packages by location in the auditorium, number of performances, and price. Respondents were asked which ticket package, if any, they would purchase.

The respondents were randomly assigned to one of several groups. Each group received a booklet identical in all respects except for the price structure listed for the symphony. The results showed that although ticket demand decreased as prices increased, the rate of decline was moderate. Furthermore, up to levels more than double the current prices, projected total revenue increased, verifying an organization's opportunity for revenue maximization.[14]

Therefore, although maximizing revenue is not likely to result in the largest possible audience, the cost in terms of audience size may not be significant. This finding demonstrates that it is possible for many arts organizations to approach their revenue maximization and audience maximization goals simultaneously.

This concept can be further illustrated by a demand curve, which describes how customers respond to alternative prices (see Figure 9-1).[15] Assume a situation where the price is the same for any seat in a 1,500-seat hall. Table 9-1 shows the gross revenues resulting from the number of admission tickets sold at each given price marked on the chart. From this table we can see that an objective of revenue maximization would lead to charging $7.50, thus yielding gross revenues of $7,125. But at this price the hall would only be 63 percent full (950 divided by 1,500). If we charged $3.00, we would sell out the house and turn away 500 people; but we would take in only $4,500. By studying the curve we can see that at high prices the vertical slope is fairly steep, signifying that demand is relatively *price inelastic.* In other words, a 25 percent cut in price (from $20.00 to $15.00) attracts only 17 percent more people. At a lower price level the same percentage cut, from $10.00 to $7.50, attracts 46 percent more people—so in this price range we can say that demand is relatively *price elastic.* Notice that between a $4.50 and $5.00 price, and again between a $12.00 and $20.00 price, the attendance loss is exactly compensated by the price increase. If the objective is to sell 1,500 tickets to fill the hall, the price should be $4.50, which would generate the same revenues as a $5.00 price—$6,750. This price maximizes attendance and comes reasonably close to the highest potential gross revenue of $7,125, so both objectives are approximately met.[16]

The arts organization is likely to favor this audience maximization price because it is likely to create two additional benefits. The larger audience will generate more positive word of mouth—assuming that the performance meets or exceeds expectations. The larger audience also increases the number of people who might make donations to the organization.

This analysis is based on the simplified case of a hall that charges one price to all patrons at all times. However, there may be substantial portions of the population, particularly those in middle- and lower-income groups, for whom these prices are too high. And, other segments who are willing to pay higher prices in order to gain certain benefits. Fortunately, arts organizations have the opportunity to combine various pricing strategies, allowing them to attract and accommodate widely varied segments of society while still meeting their economic and social objectives.

Figure 9-1

**DEMAND
SCHEDULE FOR
AUDITORIUM
ADMISSIONS**

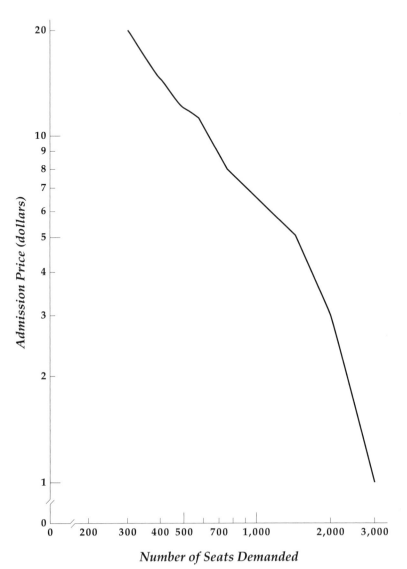

Number of Seats Demanded

Source: *Marketing the Arts,* ed. Michael P. Mokwa, William M. Dawson, and E. Arthur Prieve. Copyright © 1980 by Praeger.

Note: Ratio (logarithmic) scales have been used on both axes.

Table 9-1			

POTENTIAL GROSS REVENUES

Price (dollars)	Number Demanded	Potential Gross Revenues	Gross Revenues with 1,500-seat Constraint
20.00	300	$6,000	$6,000
15.00*	400	6,000	6,000
12.00	500	6,000	6,000
10.00	650	6,500	6,500
7.50	950	7,125	7,125
5.00	1,350	6,750	6,750
4.50	1,500	6,750	6,750
3.00	2,000*	6,000	4,500
1.00	3,000*	3,000	3,000

Source: *Marketing the Arts,* ed. Michael P. Mokwa, William M. Dawson, and E. Arthur Prieve. Copyright © 1980 by Praeger.

*Demand exceeds supply.

CHOOSING PRICING STRATEGIES

Arts managers may employ a broad variety of pricing strategies when planning their programs, arranging their seasons, and targeting specific audience segments. Here we will examine competition-oriented pricing; discriminatory pricing options; and yield management, a technique for monitoring the efficiency of the organization's pricing policies. Different strategies may be emphasized at different times, depending on the organization's goals, needs, and opportunities.

Competition-Oriented Pricing

An organization may choose to set its prices chiefly on the basis of what its competitors are charging, rather than on the basis of its own cost or demand. It may charge the same as the competition, a higher price, or a lower price. Most often, an organization will try to keep its prices at the average levels charged by its own industry group, such as repertory theaters or community orchestras. A presenting organization is likely to account for the cost of engaging the artist or performing group in its pricing of their performances, since each artist's pricing is competitively based. This is called *going-rate* or *imitative pricing,* and is popular for several reasons. Where costs are difficult to recover, it is felt that the going rate represents the collective wisdom of the industry concerning the price that would yield a fair return and elicit reasonable demand. Also, due to extensive competition from the many substitute forms of entertainment, it is felt that conforming to a going price would be least disruptive of industry harmony. Another reason imitative pricing is attractive is the unpredictability of buyers' and competitors' reactions to price differentials. The more homogeneous the product, the more likely it is that going-rate pricing will be employed. Daring to charge more than the going rate would attract virtually no customers, and deciding to charge less is unnecessary.

The more differentiation there is between the arts offerings, the more latitude organizations have in their pricing decisions. Product differences serve to desensitize the buyer to existing price differentials. An organization may position itself distinctly from other similar organizations based on such factors as quality, size, reputation, and location. Consider a large metropolitan area with a major symphony orchestra and several small community orchestras. The community orchestras will price their performances similarly to one another and much lower than the symphony downtown. But what if the community orchestra were to engage the famous piano soloist who also performs downtown? Even though the performance quality is identical, prices probably cannot be raised to the level that would be charged by the metropolitan symphony. Conversely, if ticket prices are not raised at all, it will be difficult to convince consumers that they are getting a more special, higher-quality product than usual.

Discriminatory Pricing

Discriminatory pricing occurs whenever an organization sells a product or service at two or more prices that do not reflect a proportional difference in costs. The use of various discriminatory pricing techniques can go a long way toward simultaneously maximizing audience size and revenue.

CUSTOMER SEGMENT PRICING

With customer segment pricing, different customer groups are charged different prices to acknowledge differences in their willingness or ability to pay. For example, a theater may offer half-price tickets to senior citizens for Wednesday matinees, stimulating demand for a performance time inconvenient for most other patrons. Similarly, a symphony may offer half-price tickets to students beginning two hours before the concert, filling otherwise empty seats. The Roundabout Theater Company offers reduced-price tickets for children aged ten to eighteen in connection with a parent's subscription, encouraging families to attend theater together. The New York Shakespeare Festival has started a Pay-What-You-Can Series at the Public Theater to lure young audiences by removing price as an obstacle. At one designated performance of every play, audiences can pay whatever they want. At the first such event, a specially scheduled weekend matinee, ninety-two people showed up to fill the hundred-seat theater, paying from $1 to $25, and the take was about one-fourth the receipts of a typical performance.

Group sales are another form of customer segment pricing, as discounts are given to customer groups purchasing a block of tickets for a single performance. Gift certificates and gift subscriptions may also be offered at a special price to encourage current patrons to draw in friends and family.

PRODUCT FORM PRICING

In product-form pricing, different versions of the product are priced differently. Thus, a ticket to hear Itzhak Perlman play a violin concerto will be more costly than a ticket to hear younger virtuosos such as Midori or Sarah Chang. (It can be argued, however, that a performance of the Bruch Violin Concerto by Perlman and one by Chang are two different products, not two versions of the same product.) A concert by a full orchestra and soloist is priced higher than a piano recital. A theater may charge more for a full-scale musical production than for a two-actor drama, although all productions in a subscription series are usually identically priced.

IMAGE PRICING

Organizations can capitalize on image differences in pricing their products. Patrons will pay a higher price for a particular play at an established, well-respected theater than for the same play at a new, start-up company, even if the production values are equivalent. Similarly, patrons will pay a significant premium to attend opening night because of its glamorous, exciting image. When a theater extends the run of a popular play, it may raise its prices because the production has gained the imprimateur of quality and broad acceptance.

LOCATION AND TIME PRICING

Different seat locations and days of performance are priced differently, even though the cost of offering each seat is the same. Thus patrons will generally pay a steep premium for the best seats, and higher prices are charged for the more desirable weekend performances. Because patrons who buy high-priced seats are relatively price inelastic, arts marketers often increase the price of their most costly seats by a much greater percentage than that of the lower-priced seats.

Pricing according to time factors can depend upon the time of purchase as well as the time of the performance. For example, an organization might offer an "early bird" discount on a subscription to those who subscribe before a certain date. Such a discount can have a beneficial impact on the organization's cash flow and provide valuable clues as to how many people will resubscribe. The marketing director can then get a head start on developing plans for attracting the laggards.

For single tickets, discounts are generally offered according to level of demand. In cases of weak advance demand, two-for-the-price-of-one tickets may be offered seven to ten days before a performance. This strategy is commonly used for onetime or short-run events. For ongoing productions, discounts are usually offered the day of or two hours before the performance. Some cities like London, New York, and Chicago have ticket booths where half-price tickets to a variety of theaters can be purchased on the day of the performance.

The Center Theatre Group in Los Angeles has instituted a public rush, which, minutes before performance time, makes all remaining tickets available for $10 each. Robert Schlosser, audience development director, defends this policy using the example of a couple who had $80 budgeted for theatergoing one year, which at his theater, would mean one show, at $40 apiece. With public rush, they can attend *four* shows, and more importantly, they get into the habit of attending the theater.[17]

SCALPING AND HALF-PRICE TICKET BOOTHS

It doesn't happen too often in the nonprofit arts world that demand for tickets exceeds the readily available supply, but when it does, and when convenience is highly valued, ticket scalpers are in a position to benefit. Either by telephone or standing outside performance halls and museums, scalpers sell tickets at a significant premium to people who are willing to pay dearly for the privilege of admission. The arts organizations do not benefit financially from the extra price paid for the tickets, but they do benefit indirectly from the word-of-mouth interest generated in the production ("If my friend paid that much for a ticket, it must be highly desirable"). However, undercover officers in New York and New Jersey are enforcing new restrictions on reselling tickets at marked-up prices, and the attorneys general of those two states are prosecuting well-publicized cases against more than a dozen ticket brokers.

Rather than supporting legal sanctions against scalping, economists argue that the restrictions inconvenience the public, reduce the audience size, waste the police's time, and actually drive up the cost of many tickets. Economist William Baumol believes that "it is always good politics to pose as the defender of the poor by declaring high prices illegal. . . . But when you outlaw high prices you create real problems." Dr. Baumol was one of the economists who came up with the idea of selling same-day Broadway tickets for half price at the TKTS booth in Times Square, which theater owners and managers thought dangerously radical when the booth opened in 1973. But a new clientele has been found for tickets that would have otherwise gone unsold, illustrating the free-market tenet that both buyers and sellers benefit when price is adjusted to meet demand.

The half-price ticket booth discriminates in favor of people who are willing to wait in line for two hours or more in order to save $10 to $30. Ticket scalpers discriminate in favor of people for whom the convenience is worth an extra $10 to $30. According to economist Richard H. Thahler, "Some people think it's fairer to make everyone stand in line, but that forces everyone to engage in a totally unproductive activity, and it discriminates in favor of people who have the most free time. Scalping gives other people a chance, too. I can see no reason for outlawing it."[18]

OPPORTUNITIES FOR SURPLUS MAXIMIZATION

Certain conditions create the opportunity for a performing arts organization to price tickets at a level that engenders a surplus after fully covering allocated costs. Tickets for opening night performances and special events, celebrations, or holidays are often priced high to benefit from three discriminatory pricing factors: time (the *first* performance; New Year's Eve), image (unique event, often including special benefits such as refreshments and/or a guest star), and customer segment (elitist, upscale, and/or motivated to exhibit their high interest in the production or organization).

Consider the 1994 production of *Camel Gossip III,* presented by the now defunct International Theatre Festival of Chicago at Navy Pier. Tickets for regular performances ranged from a low of $5.50 (children under twelve attending a preview performance) to a high of $26.00 (adults, Friday and Saturday evenings), with several categories in between for previews, weekdays, weekends, children under twelve, and adults. However, for the opening of the production, the Festival offered "The Picnic on the Pier—a party like you've never experienced before!" with the following price categories and benefits:

$60	Bring your own picnic
	General admission for *Camel Gossip III*
	Admission to all party exhibits and attractions
$125	Above plus picnic supper
	Admission to a seated picnic dining area
$350	Above plus reserved seating area for *Camel Gossip III*
	Reserved seating in the picnic dining area
$500	Above plus a special reception aboard the *Half Moon,* a replica
	of a seventeenth-century Dutch sailing ship

The Festival arranged with the owners of the *Half Moon* to use the ship for an evening at no cost in exchange for enclosing promotional material about the ship with the invitations. No cost was incurred to the Festival for any of the other benefits either, except the minimal cost of a picnic supper. (Such costs are often absorbed by corporate sponsors in exchange for promotion.) Interestingly, *all* of the responses the Festival received for the opening were in the $350 and $500 categories. Maybe people who would have liked to attend at the $60 or $125 level may have chosen not to do so because it would have been obvious to other patrons or their guests that they had not paid for reserved seating. Whatever the reasons, the event sold out in the higher price categories, thereby maximizing surplus to the organization.

CONDITIONS FOR PRICE DISCRIMINATION

If price discrimination is to work, certain conditions must exist. First, the market must be segmentable, and the segments must show different intensities of demand, such as greater demand by senior citizens for weekday matinees. Second, members of the lower price segment must not be able to resell the product to the higher price segment. So, for example, a deeply discounted student ticket must be clearly identifiable as such. Third, the cost of segmenting and policing the market must not exceed the extra revenue derived from price discrimination. Fourth, the practice must not breed customer resentment and ill will, meaning that customer segments not eligible for a particular price advantage should not feel discriminated against. Fifth, of course, the particular form of price discrimination must not be illegal.

Yield Management

Yield management is a method that helps marketers decide what prices to charge for different pricing options. For example, managers may want to determine the optimum price to charge for different seating locations in the hall—a process known as "scaling the house." Managers must first study how many seats have sold in each price category. If the higher-priced seats are selling out and many of the lower-priced seats are empty, management should add some seating rows to the higher-priced category, if this is feasible given the physical layout of the theater. Another alternative is to raise the price of the higher-priced seats. If the situation is reversed and many of the higher-priced seats are left empty while lower-priced seats are consistently filled, management may choose to decrease the number of higher-priced seats offered. Managers may evaluate the efficiency of a pricing system by computing the yield ratio, in which the denominator consists of the sum total of available seats at each price level multiplied by their prices. The numerator consists of the sum of the number of seats *sold* multiplied by their prices. Assume that a theater with 400 seats offers 150 seats at $30 and 250 seats at $23. If the theater sells all of its $30 seats and 200 of its $23 seats, the efficiency ratio is 89 percent. If the theater sells 100 of its $30 seats and all 250 of the $23 seats, the efficiency ratio is 85 percent. If 25 more people would have been willing to purchase $23 tickets, making those seats available would raise the efficiency ratio to 93 percent.

In the arts, as well as in many other industries, price is considered by consumers to be a strong indicator of quality. Pricing strategists must carefully match their prices with their product quality, or they may have to answer to many dissatisfied patrons. It is also important to remember that price is just one variable in the marketing mix; all the variables must be considered jointly to develop one coherent marketing strategy for each target segment. Also, the organization must recognize that it exists in a constantly changing environment. Pricing strategies must be regularly revised in light of he organization's current and potential markets, its competition, and its funding sources.

---

[1] Ray Moseley, "London's Controversial Music Scene," *Chicago Tribune*, Dec. 6, 1992, Arts, p. 22.

[2] Ichak Adizes, "The Cost of Being an Artist," *California Management Review* 17, no. 2 (Summer 1975).

[3] C. H. Lovelock and P. P. Merliss, "American Repertory Theatre," Harvard Business School case study 9-580-133, 1980.

[4] Ibid.

[5] P. Walshe, quoted in Chris Blamires, "What Price Entertainment?" *Journal of the Market Research Society* 34, no. 4 (Oct. 1992), 378–379.

[6] RSGB Study, Omnibus Arts Survey for the Arts Council of Great Britain, 1991.

[7] Blamires, "What Price Entertainment?"

[8] Ibid.

[9] David Wolfe, *Marketing to Boomers and Beyond* (New York: McGraw-Hill, 1993), 124–128.

[10] Gary Show, "American Conservatory Theatre," case study UVA-M-254, Darden Graduate Business School, rev. Dec. 1991.

[11] Adrian B. Ryans and Charles B. Weinberg, "Consumer Dynamics in Nonprofit Organizations," *Journal of Consumer Research*, Sept. 1978, 89–95.

[12] Danny Newman, *Subscribe Now!* (New York: Theatre Communications Group, 1983).

[13] Steven Samuels and Alisha Tonsic, "Theatre Facts 1995," *American Theatre*, April 1996, 3.

[14] Imran S. Currim, Charles B. Weinberg, Dick R. Wittink, "Design of Subscription Programs for a Performing Arts Series," *Journal of Consumer Research* 8 (1981), 67–68.

[15] Christopher Lovelock and Phillip Hyde, "Pricing Policies for Arts Organizations: Issues and Inputs," in *Marketing the Arts,* ed. Michael P. Mokwa, William M. Dawson, and E. Arthur Prieve (New York: Praeger, 1980), 248–249.

[16] This analysis, along with many other points in this chapter, is drawn from Lovelock and Hyde, "Pricing Policies for Arts Organizations," 240–260.

[17] Robert Schlosser, "Reinventing the Audience," *American Theatre,* May/June 1993, 38–39.

[18] John Tierney, "Tickets? Supply Meets Demand on Sidewalk," *New York Times,* Dec. 25, 1993, Living Arts.

▲●▲

MANAGING LOCATION, CAPACITY, AND TICKET DISTRIBUTION SYSTEMS

Above all else, the Metropolitan Opera House is a place. To music critic Alex Ross, it is "an extravagant point in space" with an oversized budgetary and artistic scale.[1] Much of the repertory both before and after the nineteenth century's elaborate operas is ruled out there, as small-scale sets are virtually lost on the Met's gargantuan stage and in the house's cavernous interior. The four-thousand-seat house also creates a huge public whose collective taste must be satisfied with the productions. With a big house, the stakes are higher and fewer chances can be taken. Some critics say this necessarily leads to a least-common-denominator approach to both repertory choice and set design. In 1993 Benjamin Britten's *Death in Venice*, the Met's adventuresome late-twentieth-century production, drew a mere two-thirds capacity audience. Many an opera company would be thrilled with an audience of 2,600 people. But for the Met, it was a near financial disaster, and plans to bring the work back the following season were scrapped. The musical worldview of music director James Levine dominates the Met's repertory selections, but there is no question that the place itself is a crucial factor in deciding what will be produced and how each opera will be presented.

In contrast, consider an organization called Dancing in the Streets, which performs just about anywhere. Under the direction and inspiration of founder Elise Bernhardt, Dancing in the Streets has performed in Coney Island, Grand Central Station, on the waterfront at Beard Street Pier in Brooklyn, at Orchard Beach in the Bronx, at Astoria Pools in Queens, and at many of New York City's parks. For one park performance, children from local schools and community groups were invited to make murals as set designs to hang on the fences surrounding the performance area. Ms. Bernhardt has also "planted" performances in office buildings in Chicago and Los Angeles, on several bridges in Newcastle, England, and all over Paris. The company danced on the rafters of the Wexner Center for the Visual Arts in Columbus, Ohio, while the building was still under construction. Ms. Bernhardt especially relishes events created for particular places, but not all events are site-specific. Most important, Dancing in the Streets performs for free in a wide range of neighborhoods, making the performing arts accessible to people who are not likely to go into a theater to see a performance, and providing creative and enriching new experiences for those who do.

For the marketer, *location* implies three different meanings. First, it refers to managing the benefits and constraints of the organization's own performance venue in efforts to realize audience building and customer satisfaction objectives. Second, location refers to all the places an organization can consider performing and/or providing lectures and demonstrations. Third, location may refer to all the ticket distribution sites and methods the marketer may use to make the product offering available to the public. Decisions about facility size and features, performance location, and ticket delivery systems should be consciously related to the organization's overall marketing strategy and its specific marketing objectives.

MANAGING THE ORGANIZATION'S PERFORMANCE SPACE

Determining Facility Needs

The definition of a "perfect" performing space may be different for each organization, or even for each performance. The Lookingglass Theater Company in Chicago describes itself as "nomadic" and "itinerant." Members of the company feel that owning a space forces a company to produce works that fill the space. Renting, in contrast, offers Lookingglass financial and artistic flexibility. The company views each show as a work of visual art: the play is the picture and the theater space is the frame. Thus, performance spaces are chosen to complement the productions and maximize the artistic experiences. Also, by continually staging its productions in different areas, Lookingglass can become part of each local community, whose residents hopefully will follow the company to other locations.

In contrast, Chicago's Victory Gardens Theater considers owning space and maximizing its use to be vital to an organization's success, since an owned hall cannot be closed down or have its rents raised. Also, the theater generates rental income from its building's restaurant, and earned income through the workshops, seminars, and classes it sponsors. In a worst-case scenario, the management could sell the building to pay off debts.

Determining Location

When organizations begin to consider how to serve their markets more effectively, their thinking about distribution patterns and systems is usually colored by their existing investment in facilities. They consider how to attract people to their current facilities, selected at some point in the past for reasons that may or may not be relevant today. Grand halls for orchestras and opera were built early or midcentury in the central locations most preferred by the social elite. These facilities tend to have tremendous symbolic, social, and political significance for those who have traditionally provided financial support and volunteer leadership for the organizations. But for many organizations, past decisions about location have created imbalances in recent times. As arts organizations try to broaden their audience base to include multicultural populations and younger people, they will have to reach out to those audiences in areas and venues that they find comfortable and familiar.

The organization's uniqueness and the nature of its product also affect the decision about location. People readily travel hundreds of miles to attend the Oregon Shakespeare Festival and travel thousands of miles for the Bayreuth Festival. But a local community orchestra is unlikely to draw from outside its neighborhood because it faces close competition in terms of both product and proximity.

MANAGING CAPACITY

The degree to which available seats are sold is critical to the artistic and financial success of an organization.[2] And posting Sold Out or Standing Room Only signs indicates that the organization is successfully meeting its publics' needs and interests. Capacity utilization can vary according to three factors. First is the degree of fluctuation in demand. This factor is usually managed through subscription sales. A heavily subscribed organization is far less susceptible to fluctuating demand than one that relies primarily on single ticket sales. (The complex and important subject of subscription sales is treated in Chapter 11.)

The second factor is the degree to which capacity exceeds usual minimum demand. Too many empty seats in the house can have devastating effects not only on financial return but on the quality of the experience itself for both the audience members and the performers. A full house makes the mood more fun and festive, and reactions from audience members enrich the experience. This is the rationale for distributing free tickets ("comps") before a lightly sold performance to staff, artists, and others who rate professional courtesy.

The third factor is the degree to which capacity is fixed. Fixed capacity is a function not only of the number of seats in the hall, but also of the feasibility of extra performances during and after the show's normal run. Just beyond the status of sold out is the point where patrons must be turned away. Once demand exceeds capacity, an organization is exposed to a potential permanent loss of business. This has not only negative financial implications, but impacts the organization's ability to expose its artistic product to the largest possible audience, a factor which may be central to the organization's mission.

Managing Growth and Expansion

Even more than capacity utilization, growth has always been considered a key determinant of success. In the 1970s and 1980s, when the entire performing arts industry was growing at a rapid pace, many arts organizations expanded their facilities or moved to larger ones, while new arts organizations appeared on the scene. At the then current rate of audience growth and financial support, few managers doubted whether such a dramatic increase in available seats and live performances would be sustainable over the long term. In retrospect, as demand and contribution levels have slackened in the past few years, it is apparent that excessive optimism and inadequate demand forecasting have led to a great deal of strain on an industry that has little room for error.

A thriving organization that has attained full capacity utilization and is considering expansion should ask itself such questions as: Is strong current demand largely a response to certain "hot" productions? Has demand been growing steadily? Are current demand levels sustainable for the long term? How much further growth in demand do we foresee?

If growth seems to be the right choice, an organization has many options to consider. It may modify or expand current facilities, move to a new venue, or keep the current venue and build or rent additional locations. Following are descriptions of how some arts organizations have managed the growth and expansion of their own performance spaces.

Moving to Larger Venues

Many arts organizations start out small and, as they prosper, move to larger venues. Consider how the Steppenwolf Theatre changed its venue several times to meet its growth needs.

STEPPENWOLF THEATRE MOVES TO LARGER VENUE: AGAIN AND AGAIN

The Steppenwolf Theatre of Chicago sprouted in 1976 when several college classmates formed a company to stage performances in a suburban Highland Park church basement. Their adventuresome plays and talented performers attracted a small but loyal following, including a "parental" style board of directors whose members searched their attics for costumes and furniture and contributed enough money to help keep the organization financially viable.

By 1979, the company had outgrown its 88-seat space and was anxious to become a part of Chicago's theater scene. It was ready for organizational growth as well. Along with a move to Chicago's 134-seat Hull House Theater came a formalization of the organization's structure, including a separation of management and artistic functions and the establishment of budgetary controls. The management developed a style to balance and support the impetuousness of the artists. The board also "grew up" at that time, and specialists such as accountants, marketers, and business executives, as well as people with more money to give, were recruited to lead the organization into a new growth phase.

In 1982, Steppenwolf seized the opportunity to move into a yet larger (211 seats) and more centrally located venue on Halsted Street that had been vacated by another theater company. Steppenwolf brought along 800 subscribers, growing visibility, and a reputation bolstered by great successes with *Balm in Gilead, Of Mice and Men,* and *True West.* The company had some of its worst failures in those years as well, but the momentum of its successes propelled it into the future. Steppenwolf began to aggressively market subscriptions for its five-play seasons, and by 1987 the theater had 3,500 subscribers. Steppenwolf's reputation had become so widespread that some people were calling the box office for tickets without even knowing what play was on stage, and the theater was unable to accommodate them all. To deal with the undercapacity, Steppenwolf rented space at the nearby Apollo Theater. One play per season was produced there so that the production run of the other four plays could be extended. When one of the four remaining shows was very popular, it was also moved to the Apollo and the run was extended even further. However, this rented venue had a low ceiling and severe technical limitations; it provided, at best, a temporary solution to a long-term problem.

It took several years for the Steppenwolf's financial situation to catch up to the level of its artistic recognition. At first, there were huge budgetary swings; each production seemed to have either terrific or disastrous audience response. Eventually, the subscription base grew large enough to make up for poor box office response to the less popular plays. In 1985, a deficit, which had accumulated from overspending combined with an outstanding loan from the Highland Park days, was finally cleared, and a new era of balanced budgets began. By 1987, the company had locked in its financial stability, with ticket sales generating a hefty 70–75 percent of income. It was time to expand again.

Now Steppenwolf's challenge was to build and sustain its own new, larger, custom-designed theater. In order to make this dream a reality, first the board of directors had to be overhauled. In recent years, the managers had developed expertise in marketing, financial management, and other areas, so they were no longer reliant on board members for their professional skills. What they now needed were strong donors and fund-raisers—people with a lot of their own money to give and people with strong connections to the corporate world. The board change-over was accomplished under the dedicated leadership of the board president, Bruce Sagan. After four years of planning, fund-raising, and some anxiety-ridden board meetings, $5 million was raised for the $9.5 million building project, plus $1 million for operating costs.

The theater was built with a strong emphasis on state-of-the-art production values, and the stage, according to managing director Steven Eich, is better than that of any Broadway house. The house has a rough interior that some people think is unfinished, but it mirrors the company's "edgy" vision and provides an unobtrusive, no-frills backdrop that works for a wide range of programming.

The new space also features a studio theater that flexibly accommodates a variety of configurations and anywhere from one hundred to three hundred seats. The studio was designed to present programming that would attract new, younger audiences, to develop a new audience for the mainstage, and to ensure the company's long-term survival. In its first year, the studio attracted 45,000 patrons, only 20 percent of whom were former mainstage subscribers and many of whom were significantly younger. Maintaining a balanced budget became an integral factor in the artistic decision-making process, and an important financial objective of the studio theater was to have the productions fund themselves. According to Eich, "we walk a fine line between artistic risk and financial responsibility. Sometimes the business decisions must supersede the artistic ones."

The investment in this expensive and larger hall created an intense business transition for the company. While riding the wave of excitement over the new theater space, subscriptions jumped from 13,000 to over 18,000. However, management anticipated a slump to occur sometime after the second or third year, and in fact, by 1992, subscriptions had dropped to 15,000. Then, in the 1992–94 seasons, the company produced a series of box office flops, and subscriptions continued to drop, back down to near the 13,000 level. While Steppenwolf had previously sustained minimal financial setback from poorly received productions, now more than ever they needed the audiences to like all their shows. This meant that rather than mounting productions on the whim of the artists, long-range artistic planning had to be put in place that would create dependable, consistent, and high-quality productions. The 1994–95 season was planned with several productions of guaranteed broad appeal, and systems were being put into place for strategic artistic and audience development.

Steppenwolf is engaged in further growth. The theater has purchased two lots adjoining the current location. When enough capital is raised, a new building will be constructed to increase administrative office space and build a rehearsal room. The planned parking structure will accommodate three hundred cars. Steppenwolf's history of three moves in eleven years shows that expansion and growth is much more a matter of *people* than of *place.* Over the years the artistic directors, the management, and the board have continually evolved and rebalanced to meet the organization's growing needs and the changing needs of its publics.

Modification and Expansion

Sometimes an organization prefers to modify and/or expand its existing venue rather than to move. This is especially the case when the venue has become a historic source of pride for the organization's prime constituencies, as exemplified by the major project undertaken for Chicago's Orchestra Hall in 1995–97.

THE CHICAGO SYMPHONY ORCHESTRA EXPANDS AND MODIFIES ITS VENUE

The Chicago Symphony Orchestra (CSO) is undergoing a major expansion of its facilities. The need for this project dates back to the 1950s when office space began to encroach on public space, virtually cutting the lobby space in half. Also, Orchestra Hall has the smallest number of square feet per seat of any hall in the world. Seats are small, leg space is cramped, and aisles are too narrow to evacuate the hall in reasonable time. The stage is much too shallow for the physical comfort of a large orchestra, and acoustics are restrained by both the shallow stage and the low ceiling. There is no room to allow for peripheral activities such as restaurants, a music listening room, or a smaller hall for chamber concerts, which are among the items on the CSO's wish list. Administrative space is scattered, and some offices have been moved to a nearby building.

In the 1960s and 1970s, when the orchestra was modernizing and the staff was growing, the resolution of the space problem had to be postponed. The organization was losing money each year, and the endowment was grossly inadequate to support new growth. With the arrival in 1985 of a new executive director, Henry Fogel, came an era of balanced budgets and huge growth of the endowment fund. During the same period, issues of personal comfort became more important to concert-goers, and competition for the patrons' time and dollars became more intense. It became obvious that major changes would have to be made to what Mr. Fogel called a "ridiculously outmoded facility."

In 1989, the idea of building a Lincoln Center–type performing arts center in Chicago was introduced. At the time, the Lyric Opera was exploring how to manage its own severe space problems, and several foundations had recently collaborated to find a new home for midsized music and dance organizations in the city. The Lyric was delighted at the prospect of joining forces with the CSO for a new state-of-the-art performance center, and the smaller organizations knew they would benefit from an affiliation with the two giants. A blue-ribbon committee of Chicago's corporate leaders investigated the feasibility of raising enough money to support the construction of such a center. When the committee reported back to the arts organizations that indeed there was adequate support for such a project, the CSO board of directors delved more deeply into the matter from its own perspective. Board members were concerned that many new performing halls have not turned out very well. Furthermore, the vast majority of the board was adamant that the CSO should not abandon its beloved Orchestra Hall. Once a feasibility study determined that the orchestra's needs could be met in the present location, planning for expansion and renovation began. Lyric Opera board members felt that they could not sustain a new construction project without the CSO, so they too looked to renovation as their only viable alternative.

Mr. Fogel and the board set the following objectives for the Orchestra Hall redevelopment plan: artistic improvements (including acoustics), audience safety and code compliance, audience comfort, a full-time music center environment, and facilities for outreach programs.

Plans for renovation and expansion suffered from major disappointments and difficult transactions along the way as adjacent property to the north that the CSO had counted on purchasing became unavailable. Finally, adjacent property to the west and northwest was purchased to extend the stage, to build administrative offices, to house peripheral facilities, and eventually to build a smaller, second performing hall when more money can be raised. The first stage of the project is expected to cost approximately $100 million. (An entirely new structure for the CSO, built as part of the proposed performing arts center, would have cost an estimated $125 million.)

The trade-offs and compromises within the plan are complex and costly. Consider the first balcony, which, because it has the most desirable acoustics and view, is often sold out. The first fifteen rows have forty seats per row. Each 20-inch-wide seat is being replaced with a 21-inch seat, resulting in a net loss of thirty seats. One row was lost altogether to increase leg room between rows, accounting for the loss of another forty seats. So, for the 112 subscription concerts per year, with each ticket averaging $60, the CSO loses more than $468,000 in annual ticket revenue. Furthermore, patrons who may have held the same seats for decades have to be told that their seats no longer exist and they will have to take other, possibly inferior seats. To make up for the loss in part, $2 million is being spent to extend the balcony one row forward. Mr. Fogel expects that ticket income from those seats will cover their cost within four years.

Two hundred of the 275 total seats lost throughout the house will be replaced with seats behind the stage at box level; however, these seats will be unusable during choral concerts. Although many European houses have such rear-stage seats, the desirability of their location, and therefore the appropriate level of their pricing, is in question.

Comfort, code, and ethical issues have made these costly modifications a necessity. It is hoped that the costs of these changes will turn out to be a small price to pay for the benefits gained—in particular, the preservation of a historic hall.

Adding a Facility

A third way to add capacity is to build an additional performance hall. Consider how the Orange County Performing Arts Center and one of its main tenants, the South Coast Repertory Theater, evaluated the opportunities and the difficulties inherent in such a choice.

THE ORANGE COUNTY PERFORMING ARTS CENTER: THE TIME FOR GROWTH?

The Orange County Performing Arts Center (OCPAC) opened its 3,000-seat Segerstrom Hall in 1986, and by 1991 it averaged 81 percent of capacity paid attendance at its performances. The center maintains a 50–50 balance between serving as landlord for regional groups including the South Coast Repertory Theater, the Pacific Symphony Orchestra, Opera Pacific, and the Master Chorale of Orange County and presenting touring groups such as the American Ballet Theater, the Kirov, the Royal Ballet, and Broadway shows. The regional groups are generally given first choice of performance dates at OCPAC, and touring groups fill in the rest of the calendar. Dance companies can usually fill small "holes" in the schedule, but Broadway shows generally require larger blocks of time.

In 1992, *The Will Rogers Follies* was available to the center for two weeks on an all-or-nothing basis, and had to be refused because of lack of space. Director Tom Kendrick felt that this loss of what was sure to have been a popular show was a good selling point to convince the board of the need for an additional facility. Although Kendrick feels that the arts in general should be focusing on improvement in quality rather than on expansion during the coming decade, he feels that the center must continue to grow. Says Kendrick: "With a single theater, our programming capability is severely limited. Events like opera are booked years in advance, as are international tours. We don't have the flexibility to respond."[3]

So OCPAC management and board members began to analyze the feasibility of building and sustaining a new 850-seat theater. With a balanced budget, a highly committed corps of volunteers, and their previous $73 million construction debt paid entirely by private funders, they felt that the necessary money could be raised for the project. The next step was to analyze usage patterns for the new space. Consultants for OCPAC assumed that the South Coast Repertory Theater (SCR) would account for 55 percent of its occupancy, renting the space for 27 weeks out of every year for 135 performances.

Access to the new space at the center would represent an opportunity for SCR to expand its activities and enhance earned revenue. To date, operating needs not covered by earned revenue had been met with increased contributed income. But given the recent economic recession, management and board members felt that counting on growth in contributed revenue would be risky. In recent seasons, SCR had consistently sold more than 95 percent of the seats to all its performances, and the new theater would be an opportunity to increase subscription and single-ticket revenue. A new, smaller theater would also give SCR the opportunity to respond to the recent demographic changes in Orange County and address the interests of a broad range of cultures and ethnic groups.

Yet the recession was also beginning to affect attendance levels. People had become more reluctant to commit to an entire season, and many attenders were opting instead to purchase individual tickets to a smaller number of performances. Other less committed artsgoers were spending their entertainment dollars on less costly and less risky activities, such as hit movies or blockbuster musicals. And the new, multicultural audiences who were commonly attracted to the few ethnic-oriented performances in the series typically did not return for other productions. By mounting more such productions, SCR could risk alienating its traditional audience, to whom it still had to appeal for most of its support.

Furthermore, the organization's leadership questioned the artistic staff's ability to maintain its quality standards if SCR got any larger. From an artistic perspective, management had to decide whether to "bump up" productions from the main stage and second stage to the new site, or to produce entirely new plays for the theater and bear the concomitant staffing and production costs.[4]

A powerful group of board members were also concerned about the financial resources necessary for growth and the fundraising effort that would be required. Participation in the OCPAC expansion effort would dilute SCR's own attempts to enhance its endowment and raise capital in order to build space for storage, set design, costume design, and new play development. Before committing to this new space, SCR managers also needed to forecast how much it would cost to operate there and whether its greater seating capacity would translate into increased earned revenue. Managers were also concerned that the proposed location of the new theater was not optimal, due to its lack of visibility from the street and its distance from SCR.[5]

While SCR was undergoing this decision-making process, OCPAC managers and board members put the project on hold. They felt that the necessary fund-raising could not be accomplished during the current economic recession. Furthermore, they faced new competition from the nearby Cerritos Performing Arts Center, which had just been built and was bent on attracting audiences from Orange County.

MANAGING ALTERNATIVE PERFORMANCE LOCATIONS

Increasing capacity does not have to involve huge capital campaigns and enormous financial risk for an organization. Some organizations may be able to meet their own needs best by performing in a variety of venues, in addition to or in place of a home base. Other venues may have the important added benefit of being more community based than traditional performing venues and may provide the key for building new audiences. Regional, national, and international touring opportunities can provide increased visibility and prestige for an organization, broadening its audience base geographically and building loyalty at home. Following are examples of how some arts organizations have met their space and location needs with low-cost alternative venues, touring opportunities, and out-of-town residencies.

Low-Cost Alternatives

Creative use of a variety of atypical venues can reduce an organization's overhead costs and provide accessibility to a broad range of audience segments. Germany's Schleswig-Holstein summer festival, although nominally based in the city of Hamburg, presents most of its 140 events across the countryside. Concerts take place in barns and manor houses, stables and riding schools, in medieval walled cities and tiny seaside villages. The festival features some of the world's most famous musical performers as well as some gifted amateurs. Founded by Leonard Bernstein, its relaxed, informal, magical atmosphere attracts more than 200,000 visitors annually.[6]

CHURCHES AS CONCERT HALLS

While the directors of New York City's concert halls are looking for ways to attract new listeners and worrying about raising money to pay the high costs of their venues, an alternative concert world is flourishing in the city's churches. Since the mid-1980s, as the expense of renting conventional concert halls has increased, the number of religious institutions opening their doors to performers and sponsoring their own concerts has increased significantly. When the Christ and St. Stephens Church, near Lincoln Center, allowed its sanctuary to be used as a concert hall, the Jupiter Symphony concert series was revived. It had been disbanded because the cost of presenting the concerts in Alice Tully Hall, their previous home, far exceeded the performances' ability to meet its high rental cost. The church's rental fee was a fraction of the hall's. Other churches regularly present ensembles of international stature. Small opera companies, young recitalists, shoestring chamber music groups, and some orchestras have found that they can present concerts within their limited budgets at churches and synagogues.

For the churches, the concerts are a wonderful form of outreach to the community. Church representatives enjoy the opportunity to offer musicians an artistic and spiritual home. And musicians enjoy performing in such venues as the Christ and St. Stephens Church because the sanctuary is a lovely, intimate, warm setting, both visually and acoustically. Most important, audiences are responding. Concerts performed in sanctuaries that seat from 250 to more than 1,500 people are attracting nearly full houses. Tickets are priced from $2 to $50, and parishioners account for only ten percent of audience members.[7]

Touring

Touring is a primary objective for many performing arts organizations. A tour enables the organization to share its performances with a broader audience and serves to establish a regional, national, or international reputation and raise the organization's public profile.

THE CHICAGO SYMPHONY ORCHESTRA ON TOUR

In 1971, when Sir Georg Solti took the Chicago Symphony Orchestra on its first European tour, the musicians consistently played to full houses and drew rave reviews. Upon their return home, they were greeted as victors as Mayor Daley hosted a ticker-tape parade down La Salle Street in their honor. If critics in London, Paris, Vienna, and Berlin called the CSO the best orchestra in the world, it must really be so. Ticket sales and contributed income increased as Chicagoans responded with pride, respect, and loyalty to their world-class institution.

In addition to international destinations, the Chicago Symphony tours regularly to major cultural centers in the United

States. It also has "run-outs" to other cities in the midwest such as Decatur, Illinois, and Ann Arbor, Michigan. Within its own city, orchestra members perform in small groups at schools and in cooperative ventures at the Art Institute, Northwestern and Loyola Universities, and other institutions.

Touring has a strong economic motive as well. When an organization such as a dance company or symphony orchestra has a limited audience in its home town, touring allows the organization to extend the length of the season for its artists. Because many orchestras have negotiated significantly longer contracts with their musicians in recent years, it has become especially important for them to find opportunities to use the additional time productively. However, touring requires a huge financial commitment and extensive preparation, so careful planning and budgeting must be undertaken.

The Vancouver Symphony Orchestra (VSO) felt that it was constrained from achieving world-class status only because it was financially unable to contract its musicians for an entire fifty-two-week year as do the top ten North American symphonies. Vancouver's small population forced the VSO to program creatively in order to stretch its offerings across its forty-week season. Touring appeared to be the VSO's only opportunity to further lengthen its season. Besides, touring to major cities would be a boon to the organization's popularity.[8]

A plan to tour North American cities in the spring of 1988 had to be canceled late in 1986 because of financial constraints. But in 1990, the orchestra was contracted by a Japanese presenter to tour Japan for $150,000 plus all out-of-pocket expenses. An additional $150,000 in funding was supplied by the Canadian Department of External Affairs, the Department of Communications, the Province of British Columbia, and corporate patronage. Because the tour involved no financial risk for the VSO and the concerts met with considerable critical acclaim, this touring arrangement allowed the symphony to meet both its financial and artistic objectives.

Out-of-Town Residencies

The difference between touring and out-of-town residencies is that residencies involve not only performances, but also opportunities for interacting with the community. Through residencies, a community is exposed to more and different performing arts events.

THE NATIONAL SYMPHONY ORCHESTRA IN RESIDENCE

The National Symphony Orchestra, under the leadership of Music Director Mstislav Rostropovich, has traveled to Alaska and Louisiana as part of its "American Residencies" program. Some of the 150 performances and educational events during the ten-day stay in Louisiana included six orchestral concerts, six youth concerts, and six chamber music recitals in various cities; seven days of in-school programs, with eleven groups of musicians visiting forty schools; professional coaching for members of youth orchestras in three cities, and master classes at seven universities and other institutions; preconcert lectures, workshops for teachers, and unannounced "Art Attack" miniconcerts in various public places.[9] The relationship between the orchestra and the community did not end when the residency was over. A Louisiana composer was commissioned to write a chamber work to be premiered at the Kennedy Center; six gifted young musicians were brought to Washington for three weeks of training in the Summer Music Institute; a Louisiana teacher was given a one-month fellowship for career development; and two Louisiana student soloists were invited to play with the NSO during young people's concerts.

Joint Ventures

In addition to taking their own show on the road, arts organizations have the option of sharing their productions with other organizations. An itinerant company might manage the production values of a play (selecting the play, casting, directing, set design, lighting, and costumes), then present the show in another organization's venue. Each organization then absorbs certain risks, and they share the revenue earned. When a theater must close a successful run for scheduling reasons, it can move the show to another venue whose staff will manage the operation and who will share earned revenue with the project's initiator. Opera companies that have similarly configured stages can reduce costs by sharing in the design and production of new sets. Joint ventures can also serve as a source of earned revenue, as when the Stratford Festival of Canada rents its elegant, handmade costumes to other Shakespeare presenters. Theaters may specialize in developing educational materials to use in their outreach programs and sell them to other companies producing the same play.

TICKET DISTRIBUTION

In addition to determining the location and nature of performance spaces, managers must make strategic decisions about how and where tickets to performances will be made available. For some consumers, the nature and ease of access to tickets is central to their purchase decision; for committed buyers, easy access is important to their satisfaction with the process.

Choosing a Ticket Distribution System

The first step in choosing a ticket distribution system is to examine the existing pattern of distribution to determine its strengths and weaknesses. Then objectives may be set to amend current patterns or develop new systems that respond to target market opportunities and take advantage of new technology. The distribution plan will address four questions:

1. *Who* will be responsible for delivering the service to target markets? Which outlet(s) will be used to make tickets available to the public? Which internal and/or external systems are most effective and efficient for reaching our markets?

2. *How many* outlets should be used? The concern here is with the appropriate level of distribution intensity. Intensity can be viewed in terms of both facilities and services and involves trade-offs between costs and accessibility. Intensive distribution entails having many physical facilities and/or long hours for phone orders, in addition to other commonly used methods such as mail and fax sales. Selective distribution entails having few physical distribution facilities. Exclusive distribution entails having tickets available at only one location, usually the box office.

3. *Where* should the outlets be located? A good site location must be accessible (geographic proximity) and visible (public awareness of the availability). The most common outlet that is both accessible and visible is not the local record store but the telephone, with a broadly published phone number to call.

4. *When* will the service be offered? What schedule of operating hours is most feasible and effective for each outlet? Scheduling should be governed by the audience's needs, not the administrators' convenience.

After these decisions are made, the service is delivered and its results are monitored. The results are then evaluated against the established distribution objectives, and appropriate adjustments are made.[10] Most important, the distribution system should be considered not as a facility or series of facilities, but should be planned in terms of the results it achieves for customers.

Ticket Distribution Options

Different distribution options such as the organization's own box office, centralized ticket agencies, new technology, and other outlets within the community offer distinct sets of benefits.

THE BOX OFFICE

The organization's own box office provides the key link with the customer. But this potential connection is generally not utilized to its full advantage; the encounter between ticket buyer and seller tends to be treated as a mere transaction that takes place after the customer's decision has been made. Customers could be encouraged to call the box office not just to make the purchase, but to request information that would assist in the decision-making process. The well-informed ticket seller can provide information about the performances, the composers/playwrights/choreographers, and the options for seating locations. Information about parking and restaurants and offers of advance program notes can further enhance the customer's total experience and satisfaction levels.

The ticket seller can also stimulate interest in other performances by discussing the caller's interests and preferences. If information is available in a database on a caller's past attendance patterns, the ticket seller has a readily available history of the customer's interests for use in designing and recommending minisubscriptions. Special needs and requests, such as handicapped access, special seating requirements, or transportation information may also be kept in the database so that each caller can be guaranteed personal attention. The process of anticipating and responding to customers' individual preferences and needs will help to build satisfaction, commitment, and loyalty to the organization. Of course, such time-consuming efforts may require additional staffing for the box office, but the results are likely to indicate that those marketing dollars are well spent.

CENTRALIZED TICKET AGENCIES

In the for-profit entertainment business (for example, at Broadway theaters and sports events), most tickets are sold through Ticketmaster and other intermediary agencies. By utilizing such agencies, the organization saves having to staff its own ticketing office. Also, Ticketmaster promotes its offerings through mailings and in the newspaper, supplementing the marketing efforts undertaken by the individual organizations. However, agencies like Ticketmaster charge high fees to small organizations, making their services prohibitively expensive for most nonprofit arts organizations. Furthermore, these agencies do not share customer names, addresses, and ticket purchase behavior data with the organizations they serve, meaning that organizations lose access to this valuable marketing information.

Nonprofit performing arts groups could derive the benefits of intermediary ticketing agencies without incurring their disadvantages by collaborating with other arts organizations in their area to form a nonprofit central ticket agency. Hours of operation could be extended beyond those of each organization's box office if many organizations shared the costs. Specially trained and well-informed salespeople could provide valuable information to callers about each organization's offerings. Furthermore, the organizations could share their patrons' names and addresses for marketing purposes, and, when appropriate, develop joint offers, such as a sampler series.

PERSONAL SELLING

Personal selling has distinct advantages over the box office encounter, which requires that the consumer already have a high level of conviction before initiating the call or visit.

**PERSONAL
SELLING IN
AUSTRALIA**

A highly effective personal selling approach launched in Australia is called DARTS, or District Arts Representative and Ticket Service. The DARTS program, which has pioneered a variety of direct selling approaches, was inspired by audience survey results that revealed the importance of word of mouth as a ticket purchase motivator. The program consists of a network of community sales representatives who combine direct selling with community networking—a sort of cross between doorstep salesmen and Avon ladies. The representatives work part-time for all the area venues in neighborhoods rich in potential new audiences. They work their territory selling to groups, individuals, people they meet in shops and at bus stations. One representative specializes in group bookings via formal presentations. Another targets the family market and romantic couples market through a direct approach, and another representative successfully wins support from community organizations. Each booking is classified as either a "repeat" (existing customer), a "hoppie" (someone who is trying a new venue or art form for the first time), or a "newie" (completely new customer to the arts). In a typical two-month period for one venue, 58 percent of the sales value came from people new to the arts. The DARTS representatives earn for the organizations they serve more than three times the cost of running the program, while generating great potential expanded audiences due to repeat visits.[11]

Another approach to personal selling, which is effectively utilized by the Chicago area's Ravinia Festival, is a coupon book sales program. Coupon books, which can be used as payment for tickets to any Ravinia Festival performance, are sold at a 20 percent discount by volunteers to friends and associates, and by restaurants, dry cleaners, music stores, and numerous other outlets in neighborhoods throughout the Chicago area. Merchants are usually happy to participate in this community service project, which can increase their own visibility. And people are far more likely to purchase the booklets spontaneously when asked to do so by friends or associates, or when doing neighborhood shopping, than to travel to the box office or mail order them.

Danny Newman suggests that social gatherings in the homes of board members, guild members, friends, subscribers, and other enthusiasts are an effective means of getting people to subscribe to an arts organization. The gatherings may be coffees, teas, cocktail parties, brunches, or patio parties, according to the customs of the sponsors. Hosts are asked to invite their relatives, friends, neighbors, and business associates with a goal of having about thirty people present. The intimate-sized groups permit more personal attention. An essential ingredient for the gathering is the speaker, who may be the organization's artistic director, the general manager, or any staff member, board member, or other volunteer who is capable of making a convincing talk about the organization, its offerings, and the benefits of subscribing. The event can be greatly enriched by a performance, such as two actors from a theater company performing a short scene or a few of a symphony's musicians playing chamber music. Following the speech and/or performance, brochures, order forms, seating charts, and pens and pencils should be distributed and an all-out effort should be made to pin down subscription sales while the people are there.[12] Not all guests will subscribe, but the response is usually much greater than when the same people are approached by direct mail or telemarketers.

Given the organization's objectives, the personal selling strategy should be specially designed for each target audience, for each product category (subscriptions, group sales, individual tickets, coupon books), and for each territory.

NEW TECHNOLOGY

The most important things the consumer looks for in the ticket purchase transaction are convenience and choice. Beyond the convenience of the now-common phone and mail orders, modern office technology can play a significant role in improving the ticketing process. For example, the choice of seat location, which directly correlates to the quality of the performance experience, is usually out of the customer's control. Mail and even fax orders are fairly convenient, but do not offer options such as available alternative dates or seat locations. Some box office representatives, and even New York's Tele-Charge and Ticketmaster, provide seat assignment information. However, to truly make sense of the location information, the buyer needs a seating diagram.

One solution is to provide on-line, interactive access to ticketing systems via personal computers or other automated terminals. Commercial on-line services such as Prodigy and America Online have graphic display capabilities, and Prodigy already provides its subscribers access to purchasing services for groceries and airline tickets. Computer systems can easily provide the customer with direct access to ticketing for performing arts, including diagrams of the seating plan. This method can ensure an unprecedented level of customer choice and eliminates the inefficiencies of transferring data from paper renewal forms.

The San Jose Civic Light Opera (SJCLO), which advertises its e-mail address on all of its printed material and advertisements, is receiving orders for subscriptions and single tickets with credit card numbers via e-mail. Most of the e-mail list, which has more than a thousand addresses and adds ten to twenty new ones per day, is composed of people 30–45 years old, with a sizable percentage of females and even several septuagenarians. To build its list, the SJCLO advertises a drawing for free tickets for everyone who enters by e-mail and requests to be on the list.

The San Jose Symphony features its schedules, performer bios, and even recorded excerpts of music from the season's offerings on the Internet. In one case, a person "cruising the Net" happened upon the symphony's site. Realizing he was going to be in San Jose on business when the symphony was performing Gershwin, he called the box office and purchased a ticket. The San Jose Symphony plans to feature its sponsors as well, so anyone who wants more information about a sponsoring corporation can simply select its image on the computer screen.[13] (See the section in Chapter 13 on advertising on the Internet.)

As an alternative, Automated Ticket Machines (ATMs), similar to the Automatic Teller Machines used by banks, are being put to use in selected cities. The installation cost for these computerized sales terminals may be high, but their use leads to fewer staff hours and the availability of round-the-clock spontaneous ticket purchase in convenient locations. Most important, the accessibility of tickets in key neighborhood locations can serve to build new audiences while increasing the satisfaction of current customers.[14] Consider the ATM technology launched in May of 1994 by the Wolf Trap Foundation for the Performing Arts in Vienna, Virginia.

ARTS TICKETS TERMINALS AT THE LOCAL GROCERY STORE

In the first two months after ticket kiosks were installed in twelve Safeway stores in the Washington, D.C., area in 1994, about 21,800 people purchased tickets to the Wolf Trap Foundation for the Performing Arts and another 10,000 used the machines to request information.[15] The terminals, developed by ProTix, Inc., of Madison, Wisconsin, are fast, simple, patient, and highly informative. By making selections on a touch-sensitive video screen, which is low enough to be wheelchair accessible, patrons can either request the best seats available to a particular show or pick from the seats in a specific section. Patrons can even "test-drive" their seat selections by requesting a view of the stage from that spot; actual camera shots from each seat have been programmed in.[16]

Customers can use their credit cards to buy tickets to any Wolf Trap event, order souvenirs, or pick up their previously ordered "will call" tickets. They can also print out calendar information or directions to the hall without purchasing anything. Service charges, which average $3 when ordering tickets by phone, are reduced to about $2 at the kiosks.

A major part of the kiosks' appeal is their location in Safeway stores that are frequented by much of the population. ProTix hopes to have them in all 120 area Safeway stores before long. In the meantime, ProTix executives are hoping to add more venues to the network, allowing people to buy tickets to a variety of events at each outlet.[17] They are also looking to new cities and have targeted Kansas City, where they are giving Ticketmaster some local competition, hoping to round up enough clients to justify a kiosk network there.[18]

In a similar vein, the Dutch company LVP Reserveringsystemem, which holds a 66 percent share in the computerized box office market in the Netherlands, has collaborated with the country's privatized post office to equip post office outlets with an on-line connection to a central ticketing system. Ticket purchases can be paid by credit card, by debiting the customer's bank account, or by cash at the post office. Each venue records into the system information on performances, prices, and seats, while the post office records the identity of customers and performance details. The central server keeps track of the number and price of tickets sold by each post office for each venue and performance. As for competitors in the Dutch box office market, LVP sees commercial collaboration as an inevitable step. The goal is to create a vast nationwide network that has direct and immediate access to all tickets at each concert venue. [19]

While seeking to influence participation and commitment, the arts marketer is concerned not only with the offering itself, but with where and how it is delivered. Because trade-offs and compromises are inevitable, goals and priorities must be kept firmly in mind to ensure that the organization's needs and constraints are met and the consumer's best interests are served.

[1] Alex Ross, "The Met Edges into the Future," *New York Times,* May 15, 1994, Arts and Leisure.

[2] Adapted from James L. Heskett, W. Earl Sasser, Jr., and Christopher W. L. Hart, *Service Breakthroughs* (New York: Free Press, 1990), 135–139.

[3] Robert Augsburger, "Orange County Performing Arts Center (A)," case study, Stanford Graduate School of Business, 1992.

[4] Beth Vito, "South Coast Repertory Theater," case study, Stanford Graduate School of Business, 1992.

[5] Theatre Communications Group survey, 1990, cited in ibid.

[6] Jamie James, "The Sights and Sounds of Music," *Hemispheres,* June 1994, 151–52.

[7] Allan Kozinn, "More Churches Are Doubling as Concert Halls," *New York Times,* Sept. 7, 1993, sec. B, pp. 1–2.

[8] Andrew F. Cypiot, "Vancouver Symphony Orchestra (A)," case study, Stanford University Graduate School of Business, 1991.

[9] Joseph McClellan, "NSO to Take Up Bayou 'Residency,'" *Washington Post,* Jan. 12, 1994.

[10] Charles W. Lamb, Jr. and John L. Compton, "Distributing Public Services: A Strategic Approach," in *Cases and Readings in Marketing for Nonprofit Organizations,* ed. Philip Kotler, O. C. Ferrell, and Charles Lamb (Englewood Cliffs, N.J.: Prentice-Hall, 1983).

[11] Christopher Travers, "Case Study: Cardiff Arts Marketing (CAM)," *Australian Journal of Arts Administration* 2, no. 4 (Spring 1990); 3, no. 1 (Summer 1991), 21–22.

[12] Danny Newman, *Subscribe Now!* (New York: Theatre Communications Group, 1983), 206–208.

[13] John Zorn, "Themes and Variations on Building Audiences with Technology," *Arts Reach,* April/May 1995, 25.

[14] Reed Waller, "An Essay on Productivity: An Excerpt," *Arts Management Perspectives,* American University, Spring 1994 (newsletter).

[15] Kathleen Day, "Cutting Corners at the Kiosk," *Washington Post,* July 22, 1994.

[16] Eve Zibart, "Paper, Plastic or Tickets?" *Washington Post,* May 13, 1994.

[17] Laura Outerbridge, "A Loaf of Bread, Jug of Wine and Wolf Trap," *Washington Times,* May 6, 1994.

[18] Robert Trussell, "Battle of the Box Office," *Kansas City Star,* Aug. 20, 1994.

[19] Marika Thorogood, "Just the Ticket," *International Arts Manager,* Nov. 1994.

▲●▲

BUILDING
AUDIENCE
FREQUENCY
AND LOYALTY

Many reasons have been given for the "cultural boom" that has occurred in the past thirty years, including the fact that the mere existence of a wide variety of performing arts events has stimulated attendance. However, according to public relations expert Danny Newman, a major cause of the boom is the great promotional effort undertaken by arts organizations, especially to attract subscribers. Since Newman's Dynamic Subscription Promotion campaign (DSP) was introduced in 1961, the widespread application of subscription drives has created a substantial and loyal audience base for hundreds of performing arts organizations. Yet, in recent years the public's interest in the full-season subscription has waned, and alternatives such as minisubscriptions, flex plans, and membership plans have sprung up in response. Of course, single-ticket buyers will always remain a significant part of any audience; therefore arts marketers must also consider how to most efficiently attract patrons to single performances and how to encourage them to become more frequent attenders. This chapter will address various methods by which performing arts organizations can build loyalty and frequency among their audiences.

SUBSCRIPTIONS

Very few nonprofit performing arts organizations sell enough single tickets to fill their houses on a regular basis. Most theaters, symphony orchestras, dance companies, and opera companies simply could not exist without the support of their loyal subscribers. Not only has the great success of subscription campaigns led to dramatic audience growth, but, according to Mr. Newman, it has resulted in an unprecedented proliferation of new arts-producing organizations as well. Before subscription offers were introduced in 1961, there were only four nonprofit resident professional theaters in the United States. Hundreds of stage companies opened during the 1940s and 1950s, but virtually all closed quickly because their economies were based on the hope of selling most of their capacity to the general public through single-ticket sales. Such high single-ticket sales could only happen if all the shows produced were commercial "hits"—obviously an impossibility for any theater producer. In the 1960s and 1970s, backed by the Ford Foundation and its creation, the Theatre Communications Group, Mr. Newman helped more than four hundred new theaters thrive by rooting them in the subscription concept and teaching them how to attract subscribers in significant numbers.

Also in those years, hundreds of ballet schools in cities throughout the country trained thousands of dancers who could find no professional stages upon which to appear. In 1966, despite the opposition of its administrative staff but with the support of George Balanchine and his collaborator, Lincoln Kirstein, the New York City Ballet entered its first subscription drive, and in the first season attracted 28,000 subscribers. The momentum thus gained encouraged the inception of numerous new professional dance companies, with intensive subscription drives always the prerequisite. Symphonies and opera companies soon followed suit, and before long, subscription drives became the backbone of most every performing arts audience development campaign.

*Subscriptions:
The Rationale*

In his popular book, *Subscribe Now,* Danny Newman presents several explanations for the importance of a strong subscriber base, which are summarized in the following paragraphs.[1]

THE SLOTHFUL, FICKLE SINGLE-TICKET BUYER

Single-ticket buyers tend to "pick the raisins out of the cake," attending only the biggest hits of the season. For the more esoteric shows with limited appeal, for productions without big-name performers, and on below-zero temperature nights, reliance on single-ticket buyers usually means playing to near-empty halls. Not only does this hurt the organization financially and morally, but it deprives the organization of the opportunity to inspire and educate. Through repeated exposure, people are converted into knowledgeable, experienced, regular attenders with a rising threshold of repertoire acceptance.

THE ROLE OF THE CRITIC

For an organization without a strong subscriber base, especially smaller, grass-roots companies without big-name productions or star performers, critical acclaim can be a matter of life and death. Large subscription audiences greatly reduce the power of the critics to close a play—and possibly the entire institution—with bad reviews. While critical disapproval of any individual production is grounds for concern, the real critical power belongs to the subscribers, who cast their vote at renewal time each year on the basis of their reaction to the entire season. And with a guaranteed audience, arts organizations can afford to be more adventuresome in their programming, thereby providing the critics with more interesting and novel fare.

THE ARTISTIC BENEFIT

A strong subscriber base gives artistic directors more latitude to experiment than they have when dependent upon single-ticket buyers. As stated by Newman,

> The saintly season subscriber is the art organization's ideal. . . . If we occasionally let him down, he takes his punishment in good spirit and, in most cases, doesn't hold it against us at renewal time. By attending all of our productions, season after season, he develops discernment and perspective. . . . He has become a wonderful instrument for our artists to play upon. . . . He underwrites our right to experiment. . . . He is our hero.[2]

THE ECONOMIC BENEFITS

The costs to an organization of attracting and renewing subscribers are far lower than the costs of attracting single-ticket buyers to each production. (See the discussion of the lifetime value of subscribers later in this chapter.) Subscribers also provide the organization with a guaranteed source of income, which is often paid many months in advance of the season. This helps the organization to even its income flow during the off-season and/or to earn interest through short-term investments. Furthermore, subscribers, motivated by their regular attendance and sense of belonging to the organization, become prime resources for contributions.

Subscriber Benefits

The rationale we have outlined for developing a sizable subscriber base has focused primarily on the benefits realized by arts organizations. But if a subscription drive is to be attractive, and therefore viable, it must provide benefits to patrons that are at least equal in value to the benefits those patrons provide to the organizations to which they commit and pay for a season of performances months in advance. Say Morison and Dalgleish, "For an audience, the *process* of discovering and exploring, of being challenged and puzzled and surprised, of growing their involvement with art —can in itself be a source of enjoyment and should be the objective of an arts organization's audience development philosophy, distinct from the year-to-year need to sell tickets and increase earned income."[3] This involvement with the art and the artistic process is the ultimate benefit an arts organization can provide its subscribers. But, most commonly, this intangible benefit alone does not induce subscription purchase, and other benefits must be offered that create a sense of value and urgency for the subscription offer. Organizations should survey their current and potential subscribers to determine which benefits they value and to what degree. If the benefits offered are not valued by the people they are designed for, then they are not benefits at all, and the organization would be better off investing its resources elsewhere.

The popular benefits most valued by subscribers are discounts, seating priority, and ticket exchange privileges. A myriad of other benefits may be designed by arts organizations. Some arts marketers have found that the more perks they must offer to attract subscribers, the less likely it is that those people are coming for the "right" reasons and the more likely they are to drop their subscriptions after the first season. Some benefits may not induce subscription purchase but serve to increase satisfaction and thereby build the loyalty of current subscribers.

DISCOUNTS

Many performing arts organizations offer subscribers five plays for the price of four, a 20 percent discount off the single-ticket price, one play free, or some similar offer. The amount of discount an organization should offer is directly related to its success and popularity. The American Conservatory Theatre in San Francisco dropped its subscriber discount after finding that this benefit appeared to have no effect on subscriber renewal rates or on new subscriptions. When an organization sells out many of its performances and can advertise "Were you turned away last season?" then the assurance of a guaranteed seat is enough, and discounts are not needed.

Frequent performing arts attenders tend to be in higher income categories than the general public, so their attendance is generally not dependent on getting significant discounts—except for students and other target low-income groups, for whom special price offers should be made. Each organization should carefully research what level of discount will provide the desired incentive so that it will not be overly generous. An organization can often greatly increase its ticket income by reducing the discount that it offers to subscribers.

Yet, the discount is one of the most effective promotional instruments for audience building, because so many people like to get a bargain. When designing discount offers, the organization should estimate the demand and cost implications of each offering. For example, if an organization were to offer new subscribers a 50 percent discount for the first year, either the offer would have to be repeated year after year, at great financial cost to the organization and at great risk of annoying other subscribers who were not offered the same benefit; or the organization would have to expect to lose many of these new patrons when the price goes up. On the other hand, if the organization offers all new and resubscribing subscribers a 10–20 percent discount each season, the offer can serve as a viable incentive to subscribe that helps build a loyal audience base at low cost to the organization.

SEATING PRIORITY

A popular subscriber benefit is seating priority. In heavily subscribed organizations, people wait years to work their way up to preferred seats. Some subscribers who consider dropping their subscriptions for a season or two do not do so because they are afraid of losing their seats. In organizations with a low subscribership or with an intimate hall that has uniformly good sight lines, it is harder to make a compelling case for a campaign offer to "Guarantee your seats!" Yet, the "best" seats are still a draw for many people, and long-term subscribers and generous contributors should always be granted first seating priority.

The Saint Louis Symphony offers a day-long new subscriber event in the spring, featuring the orchestra playing excerpts from the upcoming season along with a seating lottery. New subscribers draw a number and in turn select their seats from the available inventory. By allowing new patrons to participate in the selection process, to see exactly which seats are available, and to test out various choices, the organization greatly reduces customer dissatisfaction with the seat location.

TICKET EXCHANGE PRIVILEGES

Subscribers generally expect ticket exchange privileges as a benefit for committing so far in advance to attend on specific dates. Heavily subscribed theaters usually require that tickets be exchanged for the same production only. Theaters with many empty seats may benefit from allowing subscribers to exchange tickets for other productions as well. The subscribers may bring their friends to use their "extra" seats for the production, thereby bringing new patrons into the organization. Also, people who travel frequently or spend winters away may be more likely to subscribe if they can count on such flexibility. This benefit has become so important to subscribers that most U.S. orchestras, which have long held out against this policy, are now offering ticket exchange privileges to their subscribers for any season performance. Box office personnel complain of being burdened with multiple exchange requests, but they must learn to consider this a minor inconvenience compared to the great advantages of having a strong subscribership.

OTHER BENEFITS

The many other benefits organizations may provide may be less likely to induce purchase but may serve to increase consumer satisfaction. Subscribers can be given the first opportunity to purchase tickets for special productions outside the regular season, such as an annual *Christmas Carol* or *Nutcracker* event, or for special events included in the subscription season. Other subscriber benefits may include opportunities to "meet and greet" the artists, new subscriber welcoming events, parking discounts, discount coupons at local restaurants and record stores, discounts on items like T-shirts and mugs, and so on. Special lectures, discussion groups, and other educational opportunities help audience members become more knowledgeable about the organization's core product, and consequently help to increase satisfaction levels.

New Subscriber Segments

It has long been assumed that the entry pattern of subscribers can be divided into distinct stages: (1) starting as a single-ticket buyer, then (2) purchasing tickets to several performances over a few seasons, and finally, (3) becoming a season-ticket subscriber. In fact, it has been claimed that customers are unlikely to skip stages in this gradual subscriber sequence.[4] However, a significant percentage of subscribers do not follow this pattern at all. Consider a study of the entry patterns of subscribers at the American Conservatory Theatre (ACT) in San Francisco, where subscribers were found to fit into three basic patterns:[5]

- *Gradual subscribers* (31 percent of respondents): These respondents followed the pattern of no involvement to some involvement to subscriber during the previous five years.

- *Sudden subscribers* (21 percent of respondents): These respondents subscribed to ACT without any attendance at an ACT performance in the prior five-year period.

- *Continual subscribers* (32 percent of respondents): These respondents were subscribers for at least five seasons. It is unknown at what pace they committed themselves to the organization.

The presence of such a large sudden subscriber segment was particularly surprising to the management of ACT. As a cross-check, the analysis was repeated in the following season using only the most recent group of new subscribers. It was found that 40 and 33 percent of these subscribers were gradual and sudden subscribers, respectively. The sudden subscriber pattern is not limited to ACT. In a similar study undertaken by the Chicago Symphony Orchestra, it was found that 83 percent of subscribers were not frequent single-ticket purchasers before becoming subscribers.[6]

The ACT study also identified different characteristics among the gradual and sudden subscriber segments. It was found that gradual subscribers tend to choose from among many cultural (and other) activities. In contrast, sudden subscribers participate in fewer cultural activities and, in some cases, their ACT subscription was their introduction to the performing arts. It is possible that precipitating events, such as changes in income or marital status, may have been contributing factors to the decision to subscribe. It appears that ACT's major competition in the gradual subscriber segment is probably other cultural activities, whereas the major competition in the sudden subscriber segment is presumably noncultural activities or simply spending time at home. The differences between the sudden subscriber segment and the gradual subscriber group suggest that marketers should consider different strategies for reaching each group, emphasizing different benefits and advertising via different media.

ATTRACTING SUDDEN SUBSCRIBERS

Since sudden subscribers are not current patrons of the organization and may not be patrons of other area cultural organizations, cultural mailing lists, promotions stuffed in program booklets, and other means used for attracting present users will not be effective with them. Instead, organizations can use mass media and "upscale" mailing lists, such as lists of charge card holders at prestige stores, to reach the potential sudden subscriber. For example, the Manhattan Theater Club has had some success with younger, upscale types by mailing its brochures to the lists of Lands' End and Williams-Sonoma catalog users in New York, New Jersey, and Connecticut. One can assume that sudden subscribers already have an interest in attending the performing arts and that the right promotion at the right time is the incentive they need to become committed attenders.

ATTRACTING GRADUAL SUBSCRIBERS

For the largest segment of the population, the performing arts are unfamiliar; and for the initiated but undereducated, possibly unsatisfying. The organization must provide these people with the opportunity to learn about the art form and about the organization itself. This is the long-term process of audience development—encouraging and assisting audience members to increase their commitment at a gradual, natural pace with the goal of building a loyal and committed audience.

Morison and Dalgleish have developed a system for audience development, which they call the *Strategy to Encourage Lifelong Learning,* or SELL. SELL begins by introducing new people to the organization for the first time at an accessible point of entry: the place that for the consumer is the most familiar and the least intimidating.

People are generally brought into the organization for the first time through external communication channels—the media and other commercial marketing techniques. Then the marketer's key task is to capture names and addresses of the new patrons so that the process of increasing the involvement of new people can be carried out through internal communication—direct mail, phone, and personal contact. Internal communication has two important advantages. First, it is less expensive and more cost-effective than broad, less precisely targeted marketing communication. Also, the long-term process of developing loyalty and commitment is a personal one. The organization increases frequency of attendance over time by expanding and deepening the person's involvement. Commitment to the organization is developed in progressive stages, with the organization providing such options as a "discovery" series, miniseries, flex plans, memberships, coupons, and creative learning programs that are challenging but also interesting and entertaining. These offers serve as stepping stones for developing a full commitment to the organization, meaning season subscriptions and possibly volunteering and contributing. The message for the gradual subscriber should be to "Subscribe later!" not "Subscribe now!"[7]

The Full Subscription Offer

Whatever the size and scope of an organization and its offerings, all subscription offers should have certain qualities. The offer should speak to the market; it should make a compelling statement about the organization and about why the recipient should respond. The organization's positioning strategy is crucial here. An up-and-coming organization may focus primarily on the uniqueness of its programming. A heavily subscribed organization may focus on the scarcity of seats available for single-ticket purchase. The target market for each offer should be clearly identified so that the right language is used to attract the audience. This means that the organization may choose to develop more than one season brochure with differing positioning in each. The order form itself should clearly restate the offer, its conditions and benefits, and it should be easy for the respondent to fill in. Finally, the offer should be renewable year after year, so that once a subscriber has selected a series, day, time, and seat location, it will not be necessary to go through the decision process again unless changes are desired.

Designing a full subscription offering is a relatively simple task for an organization that produces no more than five or six productions a year. On the other hand, large orchestras that may offer forty or more different productions in a single season have to divide up their season into different packages of balanced offerings, creating combinations of concerts that will appeal to the various subscriber segments. This is a complex task that is best accomplished with much experience and detailed records of past sales and ticket exchanges. Furthermore, theaters, opera companies, and orchestras that used to have many eight- or nine-production subscriptions have been modifying their offers in recent years to accommodate the preference of many subscribers for shorter series.

The Subscription Campaign

A subscription campaign requires involvement at every level of the organization including staff, members of the board of directors, and volunteers. The roles and responsibilities of each will vary according to the size and structure of the organization. In larger organizations, the marketing staff will do most of the work; in small organizations, board members and other volunteers may play a more central role, with one or two employees managing administrative details. Qualities to seek in persons managing the campaign are initiative, leadership, and the ability to inspire, motivate, supervise, provide incentives, and otherwise involve the staff and volunteers. The campaign leadership should have direct contact with each volunteer at regular intervals throughout the selling period. The knowledge that there is an ongoing reporting procedure will have a positive effect on sales.

SETTING GOALS

Someone must be responsible for long-range planning and structuring. When launching a subscription campaign, arts managers should have specific goals in mind. The goals will provide guidelines and structure for both management and volunteers in their efforts to bring more subscribers into the organization. The marketer should set goals for how many current subscribers to renew, how many gradual subscribers to recruit from among the single-ticket buyers, and how many spontaneous subscribers to recruit from other sources.

A subscription campaign should be formulated in detail, considering all opportunities for potential audience growth. Danny Newman outlined the hypothetical campaign described in Exhibit 11-1 for a large resident theater company that has 8,000 current subscribers and a capacity of 15,000 seats for the run of each play.

This sample campaign allows for an intentional "overkill" of 1,495 subscriptions, permitting the organization to come in under the goal on one or more components and still meet the overall goal. There are many other possible components of a subscription campaign: radio and television promotion; inserts of brochures into newspapers and other publications; personal selling and special committees to bring in subscribers among professional groups, membership groups, corporations, and so on.

Objectives should be set realistically so that each campaign's goals are attainable. Each year, the organization may choose to set its overall goal at a certain percentage above the previous year's subscribership. This target increase may be a small increment, or there may be a major drive to substantially increase the number of subscribers, based on the appeal of an upcoming award-winning play, a new venue, or other attractions that may provide extra incentive for new subscribers. For a new organization, the goal may be a certain number of subscribers based on the size of the hall and on market opportunities.

Timing the Campaign

Renewal of past subscribers is the first step in the annual subscription campaign, but efforts to gain new subscribers must begin long before the renewal effort is over. A successful organization generally renews between 60 and 90 percent of its subscribers, meaning that it must compensate for attrition before it even begins to increase the subscriber base.

The subscription drive is usually initiated in early spring to allot the marketer enough time to follow up with patrons who have not responded before the season begins, and runs through the season's first production so that single-ticket buyers can be encouraged to apply the cost of their ticket to the price of the season subscription.

The organization should do everything possible to make sure its current subscribers renew. For every person who expresses annoyance at being contacted several times by mail or phone, there are likely to be many others who express appreciation for being reminded. Assume an organization begins its renewal campaign on March 1. A second notice should be mailed to those who have not

Exhibit 11-1	**SAMPLE CAMPAIGN OUTLINE**	

Total Subscriptions Available: 15,000

Component		Goal
Renewal	Reenrollment of 70% of current list of 8,000 subscribers	5,600
Conversion of single-ticket buyers	Sale of 2 subscriptions each to 5% of list of 2,500 single-ticket buyers	250
Restoration of dropouts	Sale of 2 subscriptions each to 10% of list of 1,250 dropouts	250
Current subscriber participation	Recruitment of 200 current subscribers to sell 2 pairs of subscriptions each	800
Parties	Sale of 4 pairs of subscriptions at each of 50 coffee parties	400
Bloc sales	Sale of 5 pairs of subscriptions each to 50 corporations	500
Sale on commission	Recruitment of outside philanthropic, civic, and religious organizations to sell subscriptions on commission	1,000
Christmas card list	Recruitment of 50 board members, guild members, and other volunteers to write 100 personal letters each to friends and associates, with anticipated return of 7% ordering 2 subscriptions each	700
Telephone campaign	Sale of 2 subscriptions each to 4% of 7,000 people contacted by phone	560
Student discounts	On-campus sale of specially priced subscriptions to students	500
Senior citizen discounts	Sale of specially priced subscriptions to senior citizens	500
Scholarships	Sale of 5 subscriptions each to 50 individuals, corporations, or service clubs, sponsoring scholarship subscriptions for students	250
Donated subscriptions	Sale of 5 subscriptions each to 50 donors, earmarked as contributions for needy individuals or groups	250
Special letter to subscribers	Letter to renewing and new subscribers asking them to identify potential subscribers among their family and friends	275
Direct mail phase I	Sale of 2 subscriptions each to 0.33% of 350,000-name brochure mailing list during the spring and early summer	2,330
Direct mail phase II	Sale of 2 subscriptions each to 0.33% of 350,000-name brochure mailing list during a second mailing in the late summer and early fall	2,330
Total Campaign Goal:		16,495

Source: Reprinted from *Subscribe Now!* by Danny Newman, copyright 1977 and 1983 by Theatre Communications Group. Reprinted by permission of the publisher.

responded on April 1, followed by a third on May 1. By May 15, a telephone campaign should begin to follow up with the recalcitrants. One professional telephoner at a major symphony orchestra says that his most effective line of approach has been "listening." He finds listening to be a greater selling tool than any "pitch" could be. By listening carefully to patrons' concerns and complaints, he is able to respond to each case on an individual basis. He provides the catharsis that often earns the patron's gratitude and leads to the sale.

A deadline can be set and enforced after which the subscriber's seats cannot be guaranteed. If the "official" campaign deadline was May 31, the organization may want to extend a grace period to those who have technically allowed their subscriptions to lapse. They may be contacted and told that they are considered members of the subscriber family, that it is hard to accept their withdrawal, and that the door is still open for them to retain their seats and other benefits for a certain period of time. At this point, it is appropriate to have someone special in the organization, rather than regular telemarketing personnel, make the contact. Even when a person does not respond to such efforts, he or she should not be considered irretrievably lost and should be approached again in early fall amid the excitement of the new season getting under way. Of course, the person's old seat locations will have already been sold, but the best seats available at that late date, on a priority basis over orders from the general public, can be offered.

The marketing director should coordinate timing with the artistic director to avoid scheduling the more "difficult" works either for the first production, when new subscribers may be getting their first impression of the organization, or during the renewal period. This will avoid giving subscribers too convenient an opportunity to express their dissatisfaction and abandon the organization. The marketing director should also coordinate schedules with the fund-raising director so that subscribers, especially those new to the organization, have a chance to attend two or three performances before being solicited for contributions.

Once a subscriber renews, the organization should not wait to respond until the late summer when tickets are sent. Rather, an acknowledgment and thanks should be sent within three to five days following the renewal with notification as to when the tickets can be expected. When the tickets are mailed, a special "helpful hints" flyer should be inserted highlighting important points on ticket exchange information, parking, special educational programs, dining information, and so on.

Budgeting for a Subscription Campaign: Lifetime Value Analysis

Business managers and board members often balk at budgeting significant amounts for building subscription audiences. But an analysis of the lifetime value of a subscriber clearly indicates that over time, the costs of attracting and maintaining a subscriber base are negligible compared to the benefits. Consider the following example.

An orchestra runs a subscription campaign and generates 100 new subscribers at a subscription rate of $150 per subscriber. The campaign cost was $5,000 for printing, mailing, telephoning, advertising, and so on, or $50 per new subscriber. There is generally a large attrition rate after the first year, but attrition drops significantly in following years. Assume the orchestra follows a typical pattern of retaining 50 percent of new subscribers after the first year, 80 percent after the second year, and 90 percent each successive year. Subscribers who stay with the organization over time continue to generate revenue each year at a minimal cost to the organization. Assume that the cost of renewing subscribers averages $5 per year per patron and that the cost of a subscription remains at $150 for the next five years.

Year	Percent Renewing	No. of Subscribers	Revenue	Cost
1		100	$15,000	$5,000
2	50%	50	7,500	250
3	80%	40	6,000	200
4	90%	36	5,400	180
5	90%	32	4,800	160
		Total	$38,700	$5,790

After five years, only 32 of the original 100 subscribers are still subscribing. But, from this one subscription campaign alone, the organization has generated revenue of $38,700 at a cost of only $5,790. The organization still comes out far ahead financially even if the campaign cost exceeds the first year's campaign revenue. Imagine that the 100 subscribers and $15,000 revenue were obtained at a cost of $20,000:

Year	Percent Renewing	No. of Subscribers	Revenue	Cost
1		100	$15,000	$20,000
2	50%	50	7,500	250
3	80%	40	6,000	200
4	90%	36	5,400	180
5	90%	32	4,800	160
		Total	$38,700	$20,790

Although at first the campaign costs exceed revenue earned, over time the revenue grows to exceed the costs by a continually greater amount. One must also consider that many subscribers will remain with the organization beyond five years; that many will bring in new subscribers; and that many will become regular contributors. In other words, the lifetime value of this one subscription campaign is much higher than the chart indicates. Furthermore, in each of the five years, the organization will conduct its annual subscription campaign, bringing progressively more subscribers into the organization.

Renewals and Retention

Once an organization has successfully captured a strong subscriber base, managers must work hard to retain their subscribers, for it is easy to lose them to competitors. The cost of getting a subscriber to renew is a fraction of the cost of recruiting a new one, and ongoing subscribers represent an important contribution source. Moreover, contributions tend to grow with duration of involvement.[8] Therefore, it is crucial to build a strong renewal program. Whether the subscriber has been with the organization for one year or ten, the marketing manager should continually monitor customer satisfaction levels and consider ways to meet subscribers' changing needs and preferences.

RENEWING FIRST-YEAR SUBSCRIBERS

Since it is not uncommon for 50 percent of first-year subscribers to fail to renew their subscriptions, every effort should be made to increase their satisfaction and involvement levels. Increasing first-year renewals by even 10 percent can amount to significant audience growth over time. Starting on the day they subscribe, new subscribers should be greeted with welcome packets containing information about the organization, the productions, the performers, educational opportunities, and other activities. Meet-the-musician or season overview receptions may be held for new subscribers, where they may also receive gift items appropriate to the experience. The organization may distribute to subscribers cassette recordings with season offerings performed and discussed and/or a course or series of lectures on the forthcoming programs. The names of all new subscribers may be listed in the program for the first production or in the first newsletter of the season, welcoming them into the "subscriber family."

During the season, the organization should regularly stay in touch with new subscribers via newsletters and special mailings that may include critical reviews and performance reminders. New subscribers should also receive at least one customer-service phone call during the season asking them to evaluate the overall experience and their special benefits, and to express any concerns or suggestions they may have. The organization should follow up on all customer requests. If seat locations cannot be improved as requested, the organization might offer two complimentary tickets to a performance to deflect disappointment. If a patron has missed one or more productions, the organization may offer extra tickets to an upcoming production.

All first-year subscribers should receive a special prerenewal letter encouraging them to stay on as members of the subscriber family. This letter should address the most common concerns expressed by new subscribers who have allowed their subscriptions to lapse in the past. A personalized renewal letter should be sent to each new subscriber. If a response is not received in a reasonable amount of time, a follow-up call should be made by the staff—or, when possible, by the artists themselves. It is hard to resist a request such as, "Hi. This is _____, the principal cellist of the symphony. I hope you have been enjoying your first season's subscription. Is there anything we can do to make next season even better? Do you have any questions about the music? Can I take your renewal order now?"

To facilitate the renewal process, the organization may offer a delayed credit charge option or complimentary upgrade offers for small package buyers. Subscription and renewal booths should be available at all performances during the drive, and a special new subscriber renewal event may be offered. In order to provide these services, the organization should allocate a budget for new subscriber retention that is two to three times the amount allocated for longer-term subscribers.

RENEWING LONG-TERM SUBSCRIBERS

If fewer than 50 percent of long-term subscribers are renewing, the organization may be in serious trouble, for this means that each year more than half of the current number of subscribers will have to be replaced. In such cases, the organization must carefully determine the reasons for customer dissatisfaction and make dramatic efforts to improve its products and/or services.

At many organizations, a renewal rate of 80–90 percent or more among longstanding subscribers is not unusual, and renewal can be *assumed* rather than solicited. Many arts organizations think they have to *ask* their subscribers to subscribe again each year, and they send current subscribers the same brochure they send to new prospects, requiring that a form be filled out in detail with personal information, preferred day, time, seating, and so on. However, just as with magazine subscriptions or membership organizations, the renewal process should be routinized. Current subscribers can be sent a statement, preprinted with the customer's name and address, and their past year's seating location, day, time, and series information. Patrons are instructed to indicate any changes they would like to make and to enclose a check or credit card information in the preaddressed envelope. One symphony marketing manager who adopted this principle received 75 percent more responses by early June than she had in previous years. When the subscription renewal is presented as a routine process, the patron no longer has to decide whether to subscribe, or when, or in which seating section at which price. Those decisions have already been made. If the marketer assumes that the customer will renew, then the customer is more likely to do so. And the simpler the renewal process, the more quickly the customer will respond.

BUILDING ENTHUSIASM AND LOYALTY

For those subscribers whose renewal involves a higher level of decision making, arts organizations seek ways to help build enthusiasm and dispel concerns. Because many patrons are unsure whether they will like the upcoming season of performances, some organizations are offering audio cassette tapes and sneak preview performances to their subscribers.

The Pacific Symphony Orchestra sends an audio cassette tape to all subscribers each year. Entitled "Nine Great New Reasons to Subscribe!" it presents musical highlights of the next season's programs. Musical director Carl St. Clair narrates the twelve-minute tape with special interest stories about the selections and the composers. He encourages patrons to subscribe and announces a phone number to call for ticket information. The phone number is also printed on the cassette itself. Free copies of the tape are left at the box office for people to pick up and are distributed at target locations throughout the city. The tape is inexpensive to produce—about one dollar for each tape, not including distribution. Musical excerpts are taken from commercial recordings. The tape is coproduced and cofinanced by a local record store, which advertises on the insert. The Pacific Symphony's marketing director, John MacElwee, notes a "bump" in renewals right after the tape is sent (it goes out a couple of weeks after renewal notices are sent). He also receives letters and calls from grateful subscribers. Moreover, the tape is described in the season brochure. If new prospects want to hear the tape, they simply call the symphony or request it by mail. Their names become hot leads for the telemarketers.[9]

Faced with an upcoming season containing significantly more unfamiliar repertoire and fewer "name" guest artists than in recent years, the Oregon Symphony held a free "Season Preview Concert" in the spring of 1994 for subscribers and their guests who wanted to learn more about the music of the upcoming season. The invitation mailed to subscribers suggested that they bring guests, up to a limit of four tickets per household. The response to the Preview Concert invitation was so great that the symphony had to add a second concert, playing to a total of 4,200 people. At each performance, instead of receiving a program, patrons were given the Symphony's 1994–95 season brochure. Music director James DePriest, who is known for his magnetism on the podium, provided commentary on each excerpt the orchestra performed. Subscribers were encouraged to renew in the lobby at intermission or after the concert, and the symphony received about $10,000 in renewal orders at each concert.[10]

The cassette tape and the preview performance serve as gestures of appreciation for past patronage. Even when significant increases in renewals cannot be attributed to such programs, they provide sufficient goodwill that organizations should repeat them annually, as long as the programs' costs are reasonable.

Other special perks and benefits should be made available to long-term subscribers. If special benefits are offered to new subscribers, many of whom do not last more than a year, why not honor those who have been loyal subscribers? The organization can plan "anniversary" events for various groups: after five years, ten years, and twenty years or more of subscribing. Since subscribers get to "know" the resident actors and musicians, why not let the performers get to know their patrons as well? Five-year subscribers can be made to feel like "family" by participating in backstage tours, on-stage parties with performers, preseason previews, or postseason celebrations. Ten-year subscribers can be invited to a cocktail reception with the artistic director; twenty-year subscribers can be invited to dine with the artistic director. Also, considering how inexpensive it is to renew subscribers compared to attracting new ones, why not give renewers an occasional souvenir like a mug or T-shirt imprinted with the organization's name? If a company has had a particularly disappointing season, a personalized letter can thank them for their continued support, remind them of past successes, and promise good things to come.

Current subscribers are the art marketer's most valuable asset. Effort commensurate with this value should be devoted to their satisfaction and retention. In most cases, because of the already high renewal rate of long-term subscribers, preferred treatment of this group is more likely to result in larger donations than in a significant increase in the renewal percentage.

MULTIYEAR SUBSCRIPTIONS

Another way to ease, routinize, and assure renewal for loyal subscribers is to offer multiyear subscriptions. Just as with a magazine subscription that people can commonly renew for one, two or three years, regular concert- or theatergoers can be offered the opportunity to make a long-term commitment to a performing arts organization of their choice. The arts organizations benefit by knowing the seats are sold well in advance and by having the money working for them. (According to general accounting standards, income is not to be realized until the service—or performance—is provided. But in practice, arts organizations use early subscription income to cover out-of-season expenses and special production costs.) The long-term subscriber receives specially designed benefits such as appropriate gifts or invitations to special events. And, of course, in special circumstances such as an out-of-town move, extended illness, or death, the payment for future years can be refunded. Long-term subscription offers are most ideally suited to well-established organizations with a clear identity and relatively strong subscriber base. Young organizations and those in transition with a new artistic director, theater location, or programming focus are less likely to command a long-term commitment.

Although multiyear subscriptions guarantee a loyal audience base into the future, some arts marketers believe that such offers are not in the organization's best interest. First, subscription prices may rise faster than the time value of money. So if the money from a three-year subscription paid at current subscription rates is invested, by the third year, the price of a new subscription may be higher than the value of the invested money. Second, multiyear subscribers are likely to be the organization's most loyal and generous contributors. But it is difficult to ask them for donations during the same season when they have paid for an expensive, long-term subscription. Third, some organizations find the bookkeeping for multiyear subscriptions to be complex and not worth the effort. Finally, there are so many unknowns: if an organization has a disappointing season or two, loses its beloved artistic director, or makes a major change in the nature of its programming, multi-year subscribers may feel "stuck" with their long-term commitment and may find it more satisfying to *act* on their long-standing loyalty to the organization and opt to renew for one more year.

Lapsed Subscribers

Some people are unfamiliar with the organization and its offerings but are willing to try it out for a season and then find it is not for them. Some people are lured by various benefits and premiums, by a special event, or by a star performer. These are among the reasons that a significant percentage of subscribers do not renew after the first year. It is helpful for the organization to understand why its patrons cancel their subscriptions. The organization should regularly survey both current and lapsed patrons to

- Identify the package bought.
- Ask why the package was chosen.
- Ask patrons to evaluate the overall experience, such as programming, guest artists, parking, and box office encounters.
- Ask patrons to evaluate the quality and importance of benefits offered, such as discounts, seat location priority, exchange privileges, priority notice of upcoming events, lectures, program notes, dining offers, etc.
- Ask lapsed patrons why they dropped their subscription.

The survey can be mailed or conducted by phone. Results should be tabulated according to the number of years subscribed, by the type of package purchased, and by demographic and psychographic audience segmentation variables.

In a survey of short-term lapsed subscribers, the Los Angeles Philharmonic found that the main reasons for dropping subscriptions were programming choices (usually too much modern music) and time and convenience factors. In a similar survey, the Saint Louis Symphony found that 20 percent of lapsed subscribers dropped their subscriptions because some tickets had gone unused due to last-minute schedule conflicts. Another 13 percent said their primary reason for lapsing was that they had been forced to buy tickets for programs they did not like. The organizations might be able to retain such patrons by being flexible in response to their concerns.

Among long-standing subscribers, there are various reasons for attrition. Some people become disappointed over time if the offerings do not consistently deliver the expected level of quality. As some people age, they find the seats less comfortable and the acoustics less vivid. Some people are faced with changing economic conditions. Consider the situation confronted by the Dallas Symphony several years ago when a significant number of its subscribers suffered severe economic constraints.

THE RECESSION HITS DALLAS SYMPHONY SUBSCRIBERS

In the mid-1980s, Texans were hit particularly hard by the recession. About four hundred people who had been loyal subscribers and generous donors to the Dallas Symphony found they had to drop their subscriptions. The symphony's marketing director knew this was a matter of necessity, not choice. So she personally telephoned each of these people, thanked them for their long-standing support, and offered them a complimentary subscription for the following season. Each of them gratefully accepted.

This marketer knew that loyalty is a two-way street. Not only could the symphony rely on its committed patrons to subscribe each year and make donations, but in times of special need, the symphony could extend loyalty and appreciation to its patrons in return.

Almost everyone who received this special treatment resubscribed the next year. The goodwill that came from this act was reflected in the donations that grew as the patrons regained financial stability.

Although the Dallas Symphony's situation is highly unusual, it signifies the importance of subscriber retention and the lengths to which an organization can go to meet its subscribers' needs. By intensively directing efforts to bring back lapsed subscribers, an organization can expect to restore 5 to 20 percent of dropouts.[11] If the organization has not been pursuing these efforts annually, there can be a potential bonanza in restoring subscriptions. Consider a performing arts group that has about 15,000 season-ticket holders and a yearly attrition of about 25 percent, which it has been replacing with new subscribers. This amounts to 11,250 dropouts over a three-year period. A successful push to bring 15 percent of them back into the organization will result in almost 1,700 subscriptions. Therefore, it is imperative to keep clear and up-to-date records that identify lapsed subscribers and to develop offers and implement plans that will bring them back.

Complaint Management

Customers are the ones who define excellent service; it is the management's responsibility to focus on *their* definitions. Researchers have found that customers are dissatisfied with their purchases about 25 percent of the time. Yet only 5 percent of customers take the trouble to complain. Most apparently believe that no good would come of it or that it would be too much trouble to complain. Yet resolving complaints satisfactorily substantially raises the likelihood that consumers will continue to patronize an organization.

Solicitation of suggestions and complaints provides the organization with opportunities to improve its effectiveness, and represents an inexpensive form of market research. Arts organizations must also conduct customer satisfaction studies, not just complaint studies, to get a true picture of the level of customer satisfaction. A study of cultural audiences in Philadelphia found an inverse relationship between frequent cultural participation and satisfaction, suggesting that regular patrons have high expectations. Complainers tend to be more upscale, more vocal, and more verbal. Therefore, the organization should maximize the opportunity for its customers to voice their positive and negative opinions. In analyzing customer complaints, it is important to remember that a customer's *perception* is what matters, not the accuracy of that perception. Reality is what consumers think it is. In handling complaints, managers must respond and make amends as soon as possible. Bad feelings fester and can lead quickly to bad word of mouth. The phone is a better medium than the mail; it is faster and more personal. The complaint manager should be empathetic and listen carefully. The manager should not excuse the organization's behavior, but rather offer a remedy that will satisfy the complainer.

There are times when complaints can be anticipated in advance. An outdoor festival raises its lawn admission significantly or begins charging for parking for the first time. A theater is being renovated and washroom facilities are at a minimum. In these cases, dissatisfied consumer reaction should not only be expected, but planned for. Each employee who comes in contact with the public should be informed as to what to say and do when the issue arises. No organization, of course, can fully satisfy all customers. Rather, it should strive to produce as high a level of satisfaction as is possible within its budgetary and personnel constraints. The organization will always face trade-offs. It may have to choose between enlarging the adjacent parking lot and improving access for the handicapped; between improving the air-conditioning system and reupholstering the seats.

ALTERNATIVE OFFERS

Despite their many benefits, subscriptions present some limitations for arts organizations. Gregory Mosher, former director of Lincoln Center Theater and the Goodman Theater in Chicago, argues that the full subscription series that has sustained so much not-for-profit theater doesn't work anymore. "The work is not nearly as good as the work that most of these artists are capable of doing, and that's because it's perforce watered down to meet the needs of subscription programming," he says. "Theater artists never get to rehearse under this system as long as they'd like or as long as they should, and you end up closing your hits early and overrunning your flops."[12]

Also, at highly popular and world-class organizations such as major operas and symphonies, tickets are both expensive and hard to get. Therefore the casual, infrequent, and less wealthy patron is left out, and growth and development of new audiences is stymied. Yet it is exactly those organizations with a first-rate product and roster of stars that are most likely to be able to draw new audiences to the performing arts. The dilemma is not easily resolved.

Furthermore, in a recent survey of American theaters, it was found that it is becoming increasingly more difficult to attract new subscribers. Among sixty-six theaters surveyed, thirty-three reported declines in subscribers for the 1995 season, selling 3.8 percent fewer subscriptions than they did in 1990. The percentage of available main-stage seats filled by subscribers declined from 51 percent in 1988 to 41.4 percent in 1995.[13] The shift away from subscriptions is attributed in part to a weak economy that has seriously affected personal discretionary income. But these trends also point to a discernible shift in the public's attitude. In fact, of the sixty-six theaters that reported a significant decline in their subscription base, 60 percent reported increases in attendance primarily because of the growth of single-ticket and group sales. In a study of single-ticket buyers undertaken by the Chicago Symphony Orchestra, the primary reasons given for not subscribing were not wanting to commit in advance (53%), wanting to choose exactly what concerts to attend (42%), inflexibility of personal schedules (36%), and deeming it too great a financial commitment (34%).

Many arts managers refuse to offer any package short of the full subscription offer, yet they often wonder why many single-ticket buyers fail to convert to full subscription packages. What some managers fail to understand is that subscribers share certain characteristics that are not common to everyone interested in attending cultural events. In the survey of Chicago Symphony Orchestra attenders, it was found that subscribers tend to be planners; when they purchase single tickets to additional performances, they often do so a month or more in advance. Nonsubscribers, on the other hand, are more spontaneous and tend to make more last-minute decisions. Also, 78 percent of subscribers go downtown for entertainment at least once per month. Of the nonsubscribers, on the other hand, 51 percent travel downtown five times per year or less. Therefore, it is not surprising that 58 percent of nonsubscribers tend to view an evening at the symphony as a "special" evening and attend the symphony only on special occasions, whereas only 34 percent of subscribers consider the activity in those terms.

These facts indicate that a significant portion of the concertgoing public are unlikely ever to become full-season subscribers. As a result, while constantly being attuned to the needs of potential, current, and lapsed subscribers, arts organizations are actively seeking alternatives to the full-season subscription to build their audience size and develop loyalty. Some options available are miniseries, flex plans, coupon books, memberships, and group sales. Although more and more organizations are adopting these alternatives, most often they are offered only after the full subscription campaign has run its course, so as not to tempt full subscribers to switch to a reduced commitment. However, full-season subscribers rarely opt for smaller packages. The reduced benefits—especially lower seating priority—make these alternative offers less attractive. Besides, season subscribers enjoy attending all the performances, and they have the time and money to do so. Whether small-package buyers are unwilling or unable to commit to a full season's offerings or are gradually building their commitment to do so, their preferences should be valued as highly as those of the season subscribers.

Consider the parallel with donors. Someone who gives $100 may be more "generous" relative to her financial situation than someone who gives $1,000. And of those who give $1,000 or more, how many started at that level in the first place? It is because they were nurtured by the organization that they increased their commitment over time. Therefore, small-package buyers should not be treated as an afterthought by the organization. From the inception of the subscription campaign, renewal programs should be instituted for all the packages offered, large and small. Of course, special efforts should be made to encourage small-package buyers to purchase multiple packages, attend special events, or in other ways increase their involvement in the organization. But small-package buyers should be granted the kind of special attention all subscribers deserve. Cheryl Havlin, marketing director of the Saint Louis Symphony, says that her orchestra has the best renewal rate of the top fifteen orchestras because she works to renew small subscription packages, whereas other orchestras only want to upgrade to full subscriptions. Says Havlin, "It is irresponsible to continue to aggressively market only full subscription offers."

Adam Glaser, marketing director of the University Musical Society at the University of Michigan in Ann Arbor, who engineered a 70 percent subscriber increase in one year (1995–96), believes that the age of the "typical subscriber" is over. Says Glaser, "We should continue to create packages designed to please our traditional subscribers who, indeed, comprise the 'bread and butter' foundation of many subscriber bases. After all, there is nothing redeeming about even the most adventurous marketing plan if it somehow alienates the 'faithful.' Unless, of course, it pays little mind to the 'curious.'" Furthermore, says Glaser, "Today's subscribers differ not only from the 'typical subscriber,' but from *each other*. They like jazz. They hate jazz. They like the Stones. They hate Mick Jagger. They're single. They're parents clocking 110 hours weekly. They're single parents. This is one incredibly diverse group of people we're courting. That simply means we, in turn, need to diversify both the points of entry we offer *and* the levels of commitment to which they can ascend in our organization."[14]

Mini-subscriptions

Minisubscriptions can provide several benefits for patrons. First, they offer a smaller package of performances for those who are unwilling or unable to attend a full subscription series. Second, minisubscriptions can be designed around specific programming such as a piano series, a great classics series, a modern music series, and so on. This serves to attract potential patrons with specific interests and eases the decision process for people who may be attempting to select from forty or more different programs. For its 1995–96 season, the University Musical Society offered fourteen packages of three, four, or five concerts in addition to the long-standing ten-concert Choral Union series and an eight-concert Chamber Arts series. Among the small, genre-specific series were the World Tour, Jazz Directions, Six Strings (guitar), Stage Presence (theater), Moving Truths (dance), and African-American Stories. While these series attracted a huge response, not only was the subscriber base for the longer series maintained, but it *increased* for the first time in years. Furthermore, a number of Choral Union subscribers purchased additional smaller series along with their regular ten-concert package.

Third, minisubscriptions can be packaged around the lifestyle characteristics of certain consumer segments. For example, the Roundabout Theater Company in New York City offers a Wine-Tasting Series, a Gallery Series, a Tea Series, a Sundae Series (free sundaes offered in a Sunday series), and an Early-to-Bed Series (five plays with a 7 P.M. curtain). In response to a tiny item in the Roundabout's regular subscription brochure announcing a singles series with complimentary refreshments after the show, all 250 available subscriptions sold out in one week. The success of the series engendered five different singles nights, including one for gay men and lesbians. The black singles series engendered the support of a corporate sponsor; the program is now officially the Johnny Walker Black Singles Series.

Minisubscriptions are most effective for organizations that provide a wide variety of programming throughout the season. For organizations with more limited offerings, a flex series or membership plan may be more appropriate.

Flex Series

There are many people for whom a preselected miniseries is unattractive, but who are willing to commit to attending multiple events. For these people, a flex series, which allows the patron to select which programs to attend, may be appealing. Flex plans allow patrons to experiment with different types of programming or to experience more variety in their season. Consider an older couple who enjoy regular concertgoing but who spend winters in the south. These "snowbirds" would be unlikely candidates for a season subscription, but could be amenable to a flex plan so they could select from concerts or plays performed in the fall and spring. Similarly, people who travel frequently on business, have small children, or are not interested in seeing every production offered in the full-season subscription are likely to respond to a flex plan offer. Among Chicago Symphony Orchestra single-ticket buyers, 39 percent expressed interest in a series of three concerts of their own choice.

Some organizations request patrons to select in advance the programs and dates of their choice. Other organizations invite people to subscribe in advance and to choose their programs and attendance dates whenever convenient, with the understanding that they will get the best available seats at the time of their call. The Saint Louis Symphony allocates three hundred seats for each performance, scattered in various locations around the hall (excluding the main floor, which is sold out to subscribers), for its "Pick-a-plan" program. Pick-a-plan subscribers receive a 10–12 percent discount, whereas regular subscribers receive 17–20 percent discounts. Pick-a-plan buyers have been found to be more entertainment-oriented than regular subscribers, so their package has been designed to include discounts and other special perks at area restaurants. At renewal time, Pick-a-plan subscribers are invited to upgrade to a higher level of commitment, but they are also offered the opportunity to renew the same package. Whereas for regular subscribers renewal means guaranteeing the same seat location, for Pick-a-plan buyers renewal guarantees attendance, priority seating over single-ticket buyers, special mailings, and other features.

The Steppenwolf Theatre understands which issues keep theatergoers from buying full-season subscriptions. Consider how Steppenwolf directly addresses those issues in its FlexPlan offer.

STEPPENWOLF'S FLEXPLAN	Too **busy** to plan ahead? **Out of town** a lot? Do things **spur** of the **moment? Prefer to wait** for reviews and articles on a play? Difficult to **plan a sitter?**
	Then FlexPlan is your Ticket to Steppenwolf!
	The FlexPlan works with any theater lover's busy schedule. The FlexPlan is a new way of seeing Steppenwolf shows when you want to see them. Purchase a FlexPlan and receive vouchers which may be used anytime throughout the season in any combination—use them all at once, from show to show, or come to only the shows that interest you.
	When you call ahead to make a reservation to redeem your vouchers Steppenwolf will guarantee you the best available seats! Save up to 16%.
	Source: Steppenwolf Theatre FlexPlan Brochure, 1993–94.

Arts managers have two concerns about offering flex series: that full subscribers will convert to purchasing a flex series instead and that flex patrons will select only the most popular shows. However, there is little threat of significantly eroding the current subscriber base with a flex series. At Steppenwolf, virtually all of the FlexPlan subscribers are new to the organization or come from the ranks of single-ticket buyers. Similarly, only 4 percent of Chicago Symphony subscribers expressed a possible interest in a flex series. Regular subscribers are reluctant to give up their hard-earned seats in order to self-select performances. Besides, as we have already seen, they like to plan in advance and to attend multiple performances. Also, some marketers admit that in effect, subscribers already have a flex plan. The Los Angeles Philharmonic, which offers a full ticket exchange plan to subscribers, has noted that a substantial number of subscribers exchange their tickets to experimental and unfamiliar programs for more popular programs. This means that the organization is already allowing its subscribers to choose which concerts to attend—to select the "best" shows—but is incurring greater transaction costs due to the issue and reissue of tickets and the logistical hassles involved in facilitating exchanges.

Organizations can also offer benefits to encourage flex series and minisubscription holders to attend additional and more adventuresome programming. For example, a steep discount can be offered for certain additional performances after a customer has purchased tickets to at least three performances at the flex plan rate. This is an effective tactic for inducing trial of less popular programs and a wider variety of styles.

Membership

A membership plan is an even more flexible and spontaneous option than a flex series. Rather than committing to a certain number of seats for the season, members pay an annual fee that makes them eligible for a discount on tickets to performances of their choice and for the opportunity to purchase tickets in advance of the general public. The Lincoln Center Theater is a highly successful practitioner of this approach. For an annual $25 fee, members can attend any play for $20. After attracting 47,000 members, the theater closed its membership and established a waiting list.[15]

The American Symphony Orchestra in New York City offers the following benefits for its "First Call" program, in exchange for a membership fee of $25.

- Before concerts are advertised to the general public, members get first chance to purchase the best available seats.

- Members of First Call can buy their first two tickets for the price of one—at as little as $10 per ticket.

- New members are entitled to two free CDs and a discount card good at local record and electronics stores and at selected Lincoln Center area restaurants.

The membership concept is similar to that practiced by museums. It gives people a sense of belonging and provides them with a range of benefits, without requiring commitment to specific programming or frequency of attendance. This option is highly attractive because the initial expenditure is quite low. In fact, the cost of the membership is often "paid back" with the purchase of the first two-for-one tickets.

Performing arts organizations may collaborate in a joint membership plan. This option can have special appeal to smaller and newer organizations as a means of inducing trial. The customer is entitled to subscriber rates and special benefits at all of the participating performing groups, and can select which performances to attend at each. This creates a low commitment, buffet-style involvement on the part of the customer, but may well generate future loyal subscribers.

Coupons

Coupon offers can be developed in different ways to appeal to the frequent ticket buyer. At the Ravinia Festival, coupon booklets are sold in advance and for three weeks into the season at a 20 percent discount. These coupons can be redeemed throughout the season for any seat purchase or lawn admission. People tend to overestimate how often they will attend, and approximately 20 percent of the coupons remain unredeemed, representing a significant income source for the organization.

Some coupon plans have been developed to appeal to the lower-budget frequent ticket buyer. At the Los Angeles Philharmonic, "Philharmoney" coupons, costing $20 each, are redeemable for the best seats available the day of performance. The most expensive seats usually sell out at the beginning of the season, but occasionally Philharmoney holders are lucky and get $50 seats for their $20 coupon. Most often, their seats are worth $18 to $30. These coupons are promoted to single-ticket buyers through telemarketing, direct mail, and some newspaper ads. Coupon sales the first year (1991) amounted to $70,000; by the second year they grew to $200,000, of which $50,000 worth were unredeemed and represented found money for the organization.

Frequent Ticket Buyer Programs

Arts organizations have the opportunity to borrow from the success of the airlines in building customer loyalty by offering free tickets. This program is especially effective for organizations such as festivals that do not offer subscriptions but attempt to generate frequent attendance. When designing frequent ticket buyer offers, it is important that the marketer provide subscribers significantly more benefit than frequent ticket buyers. If a series of five productions offers one free show to subscribers, a frequent ticket buyer program might offer a single free ticket once the fourth *pair* of single tickets was purchased. (The optimal number of tickets purchased to earn a free ticket should be determined through market analysis of ticket purchase patterns before the program is implemented.) The organization must also determine whether someone who purchases ten tickets to one performance should receive the same benefit as someone who purchases two tickets to five performances. Since the goal of the frequent ticket buyer program is to get single-ticket buyers into the habit of attending multiple performances, some minimum number of performances attended should be required. A simple method would be to divide the number of tickets purchased by the number of performances attended and round down to the nearest whole number: 10 tickets divided by 4 performances = 2.5, resulting in 2 free tickets. This method might motivate patrons to purchase enough tickets so that they avoid having to round down.

The organization must also address the issue of expiration. If some single-ticket buyers are in the habit of going to only one performance a year, it is unlikely that the frequent ticket buyer program would motivate them to go four times in one season just to get a free ticket. However, these patrons may choose to go to two performances per year for two years and take advantage of the program.

Bonus credits could also be awarded for attending more than four performances in one year, for benefit performances that are priced high, or for performances that are not selling well. Conversely, some performances with a high probability of selling out could be blacked out so that revenue is not lost by allowing frequent ticket buyers to attend free. Certain market segments such as students could be awarded bonus points for each performance attended, as an extra incentive to attend multiple performances. The Los Angeles Philharmonic offers students a special discount and one free ticket on three-ticket packages. The organization loses money on this offer, but managers feel it is worthwhile for building future subscribers. The number of student buyers has increased 20 percent each year in the four years since inception of the program. Arts organizations can also collaborate with airlines, hotels, restaurants, credit card companies, and other natural partners that can encourage people to enter the program and help them earn extra points.

While motivating single-ticket buyers to purchase enough single tickets to receive one or more free tickets, marketers can expose them to the other benefits subscribers enjoy, such as first choice of best seats available, ticket exchange privileges, guaranteed seats for sold-out performances, early notification of special performances, and so on. Attached to the free ticket should be a message communicating the advantages of becoming a subscriber and an invitation to a reception with the performers and staff members where these patrons will be encouraged to subscribe. Even if most frequent ticket buyers decide not to subscribe, they will probably purchase more single tickets than they would have otherwise.[16]

Single-Ticket Purchase

Once an arts organization has exhausted its possibilities for attracting committed patrons, there are invariably seats left to be sold for each performance. In fact, although subscription revenues still significantly exceed single sales, arts organizations have been growing more reliant on single-ticket buyers. In 1995, subscription revenues at sixty-six theaters grew 0.8 percent from the previous year; in the same period of time single-ticket revenues surged 14.4 percent.[17] During the eight years from 1986 to 1994, attendance as a percentage of capacity at the Chicago Symphony Orchestra ranged from an impressive 94 to 100 percent. However, during the same period, the proportion of house capacity filled by single-ticket purchases has risen from 6.5 to 14 percent.

Some people *like* being single-ticket buyers, and organizations that have always focused their efforts on subscribers are beginning to respond to this fact. Some theaters have begun to structure their season schedules around the shift toward single-ticket sales by scheduling additional nonsubscription weeks of plays they predict will have box office appeal—musicals, shows cast with prominent actors—to maximize potential single-ticket sales. However, organizations must be careful when allotting time extensions because it is dangerous to rely on predictions of single-ticket sales.

In addition to general publicity, some organizations target specific audience segments for individual productions. To build a black audience for *Boesman and Lena*, the Manhattan Theater Club invited black opinion leaders from churches, schools, and cultural institutions, and asked for help in getting the word out to their constituents. On one Labor Day weekend, the company rented a seaplane to fly a banner over

Fire Island and the Hamptons to publicize *Lips Together, Teeth Apart,* a play set at a beach house on eastern Long Island. This gimmick gave the show prominence, it helped sell tickets, and it reached people who never ordinarily come to the theater. One theater offers complimentary tickets to hairdressers, a nearly cost-free way to reach an excellent source for word-of-mouth recommendations. By carefully targeting audiences for each production, the organization will guarantee that marketing expenditures for single-ticket sales produce good returns.

Attracting single-ticket buyers is also the first step in involving the gradual subscriber. Once people have attended a performance, they can be contacted by mail or phone to become members or flex-plan buyers. They may be lured by the promise of productions similar in nature to those they attended in the past, famous forthcoming guest artists, or the for-subscriber-only benefits. Infrequent attenders, if not responsive to such letters and calls, should not be forgotten. Maybe the problem is not with the offer, but is a matter of personal constraints such as time commitments or life cycle stages that may change in a season or two. Most important, the organization must learn to listen to these uncommitted patrons to discover if there are ways to meet their needs and increase their involvement. The organization must broaden its definition of what a committed patron or subscriber or frequent ticket buyer is, to include the patrons' own definitions of these concepts.

Group Sales

Group sales provide arts organizations with the opportunity to target specific audience segments in significant numbers for individual productions or for subscriptions. Groups may attend for social, fund-raising, or educational purposes; many organizations, corporations, and schools center activities around a performing arts event. Many people who are unaccustomed to attending the performing arts find the experience comfortable and enjoyable when they are among friends. For that reason, group sales offers are a wonderful way of attracting people who ordinarily would not attend on their own. For example, for *The Baltimore Waltz* and *The Destiny of Me,* both of which have gay themes, The Circle Repertory Company promoted group sales to the Gay Men's Health Crisis, the Lambda Legal Defense and Education Fund, and other organizations. The company has found that the effort helps boost sales in general, not just for gay-themed plays.[18]

The commercial sector, including corporations, retail, manufacturing, and service enterprises, provides many opportunities for developing group sales. Companies can use season or series tickets in a variety of ways: for executives and their spouses as gifts or for entertaining clients, as prizes to members of the sales force for outstanding achievement, as annual gifts to certain important customers or clients. A subscription series will be gratefully remembered each time the recipient attends a performance throughout the season. As an alternative to gifts, a company may want to purchase a block of subscriptions or individual tickets and resell them to employees at a lower price, absorbing a portion of the cost. Businesses may also be encouraged to purchase subscriptions as "scholarships" for needy students or disadvantaged persons in the community.

Sometimes companies are not approached about purchase of block tickets for fear that marketing efforts might interfere with fund-raising efforts. However, tickets offer opportunities and benefits that contributions do not, and ticket purchase often comes from a different budget than contribution money so that one has little or no effect on the other. Actually, a business supporting an arts organization with contributions usually likes to "show off" its support by buying blocks of tickets for special events and by giving away gift subscriptions. For businesses that are not contributors, involving them through ticket sales is a logical way to bring them into the organization and build future commitment.

Another viable opportunity for arts organizations to gain groups of subscribers is to encourage other nonprofit organizations to sell subscriptions on commission. Very often, an organization will take over an entire theater or purchase a large block of tickets for a single performance, purchasing the tickets at the group discount and reselling them at a premium as a fund-raiser. This practice has limited benefit to the arts organization, because it is a one-time event. Instead (or additionally), organizations as diverse as community, social, religious, health-related or sports clubs, school groups, junior leagues, and so on, can be encouraged to sell subscriptions to the arts organization to earn a percentage of the return. Since this will create a new ongoing base of support for the arts organization, the cost of the commission is a negligible factor. Consider how the Indianapolis Symphony Orchestra carried out such a process.

SELLING SUBSCRIPTIONS ON COMMISSION	The Indianapolis Symphony Orchestra (ISO) invited a large number of nonprofit organizations to take part in the symphony's season-ticket campaign. The groups that participated were paid a 15 percent commission on each new subscription they sold. Clubs were provided with copies of a sales brochure that could be enclosed with a cover letter in a mailing to their membership and/or distributed at club events. Orders were returned to a representative of the club, who recorded them before forwarding them to a representative of the ISO's club benefit committee, who also made a record of them before turning them over to the symphony box office for processing. Commission checks were issued at the close of the subscription campaign in October.[19]

Arts organizations pursuing this approach have gained thousands of new subscribers, and, in the process, have added thousands of dollars to the coffers of the participating nonprofit organizations.

GROUP SALES PERSONNEL

A group sales campaign may be conducted from within the organization by box office personnel or by someone hired specifically for this purpose; or it may be conducted by a professional group sales specialist contracted by the organization. A large organization usually conducts group sales from within the organization, assigning a staff person to the project. But when the Oregon Symphony turned over this function to the four ticket agents in its box office, group sales increased the first season from $15,000 to $45,000. Due to their inherent complexities, group sales had been frowned upon by the box office when they were sold by someone else. Now, each of the four ticket agents receives a 2 percent commission on every group sale; the agent who actually fulfills the order receives an additional 2 percent. The ticket manager distributes the group sales leads to the agents, and they call the leads when they're not busy with their other box office duties. Because they know the inventory so well, the agents can develop strategies to sell seats that they believe might go unsold otherwise. The extra income this provides the box office staff is a strong motivation for them to pursue these opportunities.[20]

A smaller organization may find that full-time staff is overextended and that there are disadvantages in hiring someone part time, especially since that person will not be readily available to respond to inquiries. In such a case, the organization may prefer to contract out this function to a professional group sales specialist. One theater conducted a cost-benefit analysis of the two options, which is presented below.

COST-BENEFIT ANALYSIS: TWO APPROACHES TO GROUP SALES

A theater presents four plays per year averaging six-week runs each, six performances per week. The house has 250 seats, so there are 9,000 available seats per production. The theater has approximately 4,000 subscribers and would like to develop a group sales plan to increase its audience base.

OPTION I: CONTRACTING WITH A PROFESSIONAL GROUP SALES ORGANIZATION

(Based on a nine-week contract, beginning six weeks before the opening of Play 1 and running through the third week of the show.)

Fixed expenses:

Materials: Bulk mailing, typesetting, printing, phone, fax, postage.	$1,000
Personnel: $100 per week fee.	$900

Variable expenses: 10% commission.

Number of tickets sold	400	600	800	1,000
Gross	$6,000*	$9,000	$12,000	$15,000
Commissions	600	900	1,200	1,500
Fees	900	900	900	900
Net revenue	4,500	7,200	9,900	12,600
Personnel cost	1,500	1,800	2,100	2,400
Per ticket cost	3.75	3.00	2.63	2.40
Per ticket percentage	25%	20%	18%	16%

*These estimates are based on $15 ticket price and ignore materials costs.

Benefits:

- Resource of 6,000 names for mailing list.
- Trained personnel for telemarketing, mailings, accounting.
- Contracts available for several-week periods. Not necessary to maintain all year round.
- Valuable procedural information and resources the theater can use at a later date if management decides to revert to in-house group sales.
- Reduces management supervisory time by taking off premises.
- Renegotiable per show or per year.

Costs:

- $1,900 fixed cost per production plus variable expenses.
- Loss of revenue to theater for large sales and internally generated resources.

OPTION II: AN IN-HOUSE GROUP SALES PROGRAM

Hire group sales person for 18 hours per week maximum (to maintain part-time status and to avoid benefit package requirement).

Fixed expenses:

- Materials (assume similar to Option I even though mailing list is shorter): $1,000.
- Personnel: $1,300 for 9 weeks ($8 per hour 18 hours per week). $7,488 annually based on 52 weeks.

Variable expenses:

Sales commission to be negotiated to act as incentive.

Benefits:

• Cost-effective when large number of sales are generated (must sell 3,000 tickets to break even, given Option I personnel costs).

Costs:

• Fixed, long-term personnel costs.

• Difficult to hire someone on seasonal basis.

• Mailing list of 1,000 (Option I has 6,000 names).

• List development required to develop resources (labor and time intensive).

• Training required for promotional skills, letter writing, tele-marketing, contracts, and accounting procedures.

• Ongoing management supervision required.

• Reduced availability for response to inquiries and required substitution by regular office staff.

RESULTS:

As a result of this analysis, the theater contracted with a professional group sales provider for two plays (two nine-week periods). The manager decided to monitor the program on a regular basis in order to evaluate its effectiveness and to keep complete records that could be used if the organization converts to an in-house system in the future.

Some organizations employ a third option—using volunteers to manage group sales. In certain unique cases this option can function well, especially in very small organizations that are largely run by volunteers and that offer few performances annually. But as a matter of policy, this option is not recommended. The same costs apply to volunteers as to part-time employees, but to a greater degree. It is harder to commit volunteers to regular time schedules, to the long-term involvement that would lead to relationship-building benefits, to job training, and to management supervision. Many organizations that have used volunteers for group sales have found that in the long run, when nonmonetary costs are taken into consideration, it is less expensive to hire a professional.

GROUP SALES PROCEDURES

Whether group sales are conducted in-house or by an outside professional, certain procedures should be followed. One theater developed the following list of responsibilities and procedures for its group sales personnel.

GROUP SALES PERSONNEL: RESPONSIBILITIES AND PROCEDURES

DEVELOPING SALES

- Develop an extensive list of potential target groups and generate a computerized mailing list.
- Customize plans for target groups (seniors, corporations, students, etc.).
- Write and send promotional material targeted to various interest groups.
- Follow up mailings with phone inquiries.

MANAGING SALES

- Mail contracts, confirmations, and payment requests. Include information regarding benefits and requirements.
- Arrange transportation if needed.
- Coordinate with restaurants, hotels, caterers to meet special group needs.
- Check deadlines for payment and follow-up.
- Keep accurate, complete, timely accounting records.
- Communicate with box office manager regarding all sales.
- Provide group information and requested program stuffers to house manager.
- Report regularly to managing director.
- Keep complete card file or computer record of all inquiries and sales by

  Name of organization and size of group

  Contact person

  Performance data (date, program, time of day)

  Special concerns or needs

  Time of year group makes programming decisions
- Send follow-up letter after performance thanking group, asking for satisfaction/complaint report, promoting other productions.

BACKGROUND INFORMATION

Group sales personnel should have the following organizational information available for writing copy and for responding to inquiries:

- Logistical information:

  Prices, space capacity, date availability

  Return/exchange policy

  Forms of payment accepted

  Foul-weather cancellation policy

  No-show policy

  Rules and regulations of theater (minimum age, late seating policy, food restrictions, cameras, etc.)

- Promotional Information:

  History and mission of theater

  Description of facility with seating chart

  Benefits of group patronage

  Statements from satisfied group patrons

  Information from past productions, reviews, awards, photos

  Order form

Gift Certificates

Offering gift certificates is an effective way to encourage current patrons to bring their family, friends, employees, business associates, and visitors into the organization. Loyal attenders may see the gift as a strong incentive for their friends to try out the organization. Also, such gifts capitalize on the recent trend of giving *experiences* rather than tangible items to celebrate occasions.

THE OFFER

Certificates can be offered for single tickets, for subscriptions, or for flex plans. They should be offered year round but promoted intensely during the holiday season. A gift certificate plan usually includes a discount offer to the purchaser for multiple orders. Rather than offering a 20 percent discount, offering five certificates for the price of four will bring more people into the hall more often. Certificates can be sent to the recipient, identifying the donor, or to the donor directly. A sample gift certificate letter to subscribers follows.

GIFT CERTIFICATE PROGRAM SAMPLE SUBSCRIBER LETTER OR NEWSLETTER ARTICLE

GIVE THE GIFT OF MUSIC, THE EXCITEMENT OF A LIVE PERFORMANCE!!

Dear Subscriber or Patron:

As a frequent patron of the arts, you do not need to be convinced of the joys of attending our concert performances. Now we are offering you the opportunity to share that exciting and entertaining experience with others: friends, family, students, teachers, employees, business associates, visitors. With the gift of a concert series, occasions can be celebrated and remembered all year long: holidays, anniversaries, birthdays, graduations, and thank yous.

Our program is *totally* flexible to meet your needs. You may purchase a gift certificate for an individual concert or for an entire season subscription. A certificate may be used for *any* performance, according to availability. A subscription may be used by one person for four concerts, by four persons for one concert, or any other combination that suits your needs. Of course, we encourage our patrons to experience the full range of our musical offerings.

Discounts are also available to our gift certificate patrons. Purchase four certificates at one time for either individual tickets or subscriptions and you will receive one complimentary certificate of equivalent value. All certificates are good throughout this season.

We will be happy to send certificates directly to you or to your recipients. Just fill in the requested information, enclose a check or credit card information, and you will have given a gift that will be enjoyed, appreciated, and long remembered.

Sincerely yours,

(Signed by board president or managing director)

PROMOTING THE OFFER

Since current attenders are the most likely to respond to a gift certificate campaign, the offer should be made available to subscribers through regular and special mailings and at all performances. Consider the following promotional opportunities.

- Include promotional material and an order form in a packet with season tickets to subscribers.

- Place a sign at the ticket desk or box office with order forms nearby.

- Promote gift certificates on the outside of the ticket envelope used for single-ticket sales.

- Before performances and during intermissions, have volunteers available to sell certificates at a visible central location in the lobby.

- Include gift certificate information in the printed program or as an insert.

- Publicize certificates through record stores, local restaurants, music schools, and other appropriate local resources.

- In addition to subscribers and single-ticket buyers, offer certificates to corporate sponsors and to organizations participating in group sales.

An arts organization's current patrons—whether long-term subscribers or first-time attenders—are its marketer's greatest asset. Patrons' preferences, needs, and concerns should be carefully monitored so that their needs are met and their satisfaction and commitment levels grow. Current patrons are also an important resource for locating and attracting new attenders. Each organization should study its patrons' demographics, lifestyles, and interest groups and design offerings that will attract additional members of key audience segments.

[1] Danny Newman, *Subscribe Now!* (New York: Theatre Communications Group, 1983).

[2] Danny Newman, *Subscribe Now!* 17.

[3] Bradley Morison and Julie Gordon Dalgleish, *Waiting in the Wings* (New York: ACA Books, 1987), 138.

[4] Donald Michaelis, *Association of College, University and Community Arts Administrators Bulletin,* 1976.

[5] Adrian B. Ryans and Charles B. Weinberg, "Consumer Dynamics in Nonprofit Organizations," *Journal of Consumer Research* 5, Sept. 1978.

[6] Travis Hurst, Sara Malm, Tim Strevell, and Jennifer Wolfman, "Chicago Symphony Orchestra," group research project, J. L. Kellogg Graduate School of Management, March 1994.

[7] Morison and Dalgleish, *Waiting in the Wings.*

[8] Thanks to Cheryl Havlin, marketing director of the Saint Louis Symphony, for providing much of the information in this section.

[9] John Zorn, "Audio Tapes Increase Sales," *Arts Reach,* Aug./Sept. 1994, 4–5.

[10] John Zorn, "Sneak Preview Performance Boosts Subscription Renewals," *Arts Reach,* Aug./Sept. 1994, 3–4.

[11] Newman, *Subscribe Now!* 100.

[12] Sid Smith, *Chicago Tribune,* July 19, 1992, Sec. 5, p. 3.

[13] Steven Samuels and Alisha Tonsic, "Theatre Facts 1995," *American Theatre,* April 1996.

[14] Adam Glaser, "How the University Musical Society Engineered a 70% Subscriber Increase in One Year," *Arts Reach,* Feb./March 1996, 5–7.

[15] Glenn Collins, "New York's Nonprofit Theaters Turn to Gimmicks to Lure Subscribers," *New York Times*, Dec. 22, 1992.

[16] John Zorn, "Come Fly with Us: Upgrade Single Ticket Buyers to Subscribers," *Arts Reach*, Premiere Issue 1992, 10–12.

[17] Samuels and Tonsic, "Theatre Facts 1995."

[18] Collins, "New York's Nonprofit Theaters Turn to Gimmicks."

[19] Newman, *Subscribe Now!* 221.

[20] John Zorn, "Group Sales Become Box Office Function," *Arts Reach*, Aug./Sept. 1994, 4.

▲●▲

DELIVERING
THE MESSAGE

FORMULATING THE COMMUNICATION STRATEGY

MARKETING IS A PHILOSOPHY, A PROCESS, AND A SET OF STRATEGIES AND TACTICS for influencing behavior—either changing behavior (for example, encouraging attendance at performances of modern music) or preventing it from changing (for example, encouraging patrons to renew their subscriptions). Everything about an arts organization—its programs, packages, employees, facilities, and actions—communicates something. Thus, the whole marketing mix must be orchestrated for maximum marketing impact.

In the preceding chapters, we considered the offer, price, and place components of the marketing mix and saw how these components influence behaviors directly by providing incentives for action or reducing disincentives. But in the vast majority of arts marketing strategies, influencing behavior is largely a matter of *communication*. In this chapter we will discuss the main tools of the communications mix, what factors underlie effective communications, how communication channels should be selected, how the promotion budget should be established, and how the promotion plan's results can be measured. This chapter will serve as an introduction to the rest of Part IV, in which we will examine specific communications tools as they apply to performing arts organizations.

Communication is a matter of *informing, persuading,* and *educating* target audiences about the alternatives for action, the positive consequences of choosing a particular course of action, and the motivations for acting (and often *continuing* to act) in a particular way.[1]

INFORMING

In order to make a decision on whether to attend, a patron needs basic information on the event itself (what will be performed, who will be performing) as well as the date, location, time, cost of tickets, and how tickets may be purchased. Informing is probably most efficiently achieved through advertising media such as newspapers, radio, and direct mail. Information is a necessary ingredient of most communication efforts but can stand alone only for the enthusiasts—the patrons with such a strong interest in a particular art form that they will actually seek out information on future performances without the benefit of extensive promotion. Members of this segment are likely to belong to support groups, subscribe to the season or series, and/or participate themselves in the activity on a nonprofessional basis.

PERSUADING

There are legendary accounts that when Vladimir Horowitz performed recitals in Moscow, one bulletin posted outside the box office was all that was needed to sell out the event in a single day. In most cases, however, prospective patrons need additional incentives to encourage them to attend. All sales promotion techniques, public relations, personal selling, and any advertising that goes beyond basic information is intended to persuade. Persuasion is central to marketing communication.

EDUCATING

For most people an appreciation of the performing arts is learned or acquired over time. This means that the expansion of the audience for the arts requires the development of a level of understanding, appreciation, and enjoyment sufficient to arouse the desire to attend arts events. Nonattenders who are immune to persuasive efforts must first be educated to appreciate the offering. But education is a difficult task. A great deal of information has to be conveyed, it requires a great deal of time and effort, and it often requires changing people's attitudes and beliefs. This is why arts organizations have traditionally focused their efforts on informing and persuading current cultural patrons rather than on the much more daunting task of educating nonattenders.

Each organization must examine its communication style, needs, and opportunities and develop a communication program that is influential and cost-effective.

THE COMMUNICATIONS MIX

The marketing communications mix, also called the promotion mix, consists of four major tools: advertising, personal selling, sales promotion, and publicity. Each tool has its own unique characteristics and costs.

Advertising

Advertising is any paid form of nonpersonal presentation and promotion of ideas, goods, or services by an identified sponsor. Because advertising has so many forms and uses, it is difficult to make generalizations about its distinctive qualities as a component of the promotional mix. However, the following characteristics can be noted:

- *Public presentation:* Advertising is a highly public mode of communication. Its public nature confers a kind of legitimacy on the product and also suggests a standardized offering. Because many people receive the same message, buyers know that their motives for purchasing the offering will be publicly understood.

- *Pervasiveness:* Advertising is a pervasive medium that permits the seller to repeat a message many times. It also allows the buyer to receive and compare the messages of various competitors. Large-scale advertising by a seller says something positive about the seller's size, popularity, and success.

- *Amplified expressiveness:* Advertising provides opportunities for dramatizing the organization and its offerings through the artful use of print, sound, image, and color. Sometimes, however, the tool's very success at expressiveness may dilute or distract from the intent of the message.

- *Impersonality:* The audience does not feel obligated to pay attention or respond to advertising. Unlike personal selling, advertising is able to carry on only a monologue, not a dialogue, with the audience.[2]

Advertising can be used both to build up a long-term image for an organization and to trigger quick sales. It is an efficient way to reach numerous geographically dispersed buyers at a low cost per exposure. Advertising can have an effect on sales simply through its presence. Consumers might believe that a heavily advertised organization or production must be good; otherwise, why would advertisers spend so much money touting the offering? On the other hand, heavy and repeated advertising of a particular performer or performance may be interpreted by some to suggest a desperate need for audience building in the absence of a natural following.

Advertising ranges broadly in cost from relatively inexpensive local newspaper ads to very expensive television commercials.

Personal Selling

Personal selling refers to all attempts by the organization at using personal influence to affect target audience behavior. Personal selling is the most effective tool at the earlier stages of the consumer decision process, particularly in building up preference and conviction, although it is also highly effective at influencing action. Personal selling also has three distinctive qualities not available through advertising.

- *Personal interaction:* Personal selling involves a living, immediate, and interactive relationship between two or more persons. Each party is able to observe the others' needs and characteristics at close hand and make immediate adjustments.

- *Cultivation:* Personal selling permits cultivation of relationships, ranging from matter-of-fact selling relationships to deep personal friendships. In most cases, the sales representative artfully woos the target audience. While tactfully applying pressure to induce an action, he or she normally keeps the customer's long-run interests at heart.

- *Response:* Personal selling makes the target audience member feel under some obligation to respond, even if the response is only a polite "thank you."

These distinctive qualities come at a significant cost, as personal selling can be the organization's most expensive customer contact tool. Salespeople such as telemarketers must be well trained and highly motivated in order to function effectively for the organization and volunteers acting as advocates for the organization must be nurtured and cultivated over a long period of time. Yet, when personal selling efforts are well planned and well targeted, their costs are minimal compared to their benefits. See Chapter 10 for examples of effective personal sales plans.

Sales Promotion

Sales promotion consists of short-term incentives such as coupons and premiums to encourage purchase or sale of a product or service. Although there are a wide variety of sales promotion techniques, they have three distinctive characteristics in common:

- *Communication:* Sales promotions gain attention and usually provide information that may lead the consumer to the product.

- *Incentive:* They incorporate some concession, inducement, or contribution that gives value to the consumer.

- *Invitation:* They include a distinct invitation to engage in the transaction *now.*

Organizations use sales promotion tools to create a stronger and quicker response. They can be used to dramatize product offers and to boost sagging sales. However, their effects are usually short run; they are generally not effective in building long-term preference.

Public Relations

Public relations consists of a variety of programs designed to improve, maintain, or protect the image of an organization or its offerings. The appeal of public relations is based on its distinctive qualities:

- *High credibility:* News stories and features seem more authentic and credible to readers than do advertisements. Public relations can reach many prospects who might avoid salespeople and advertisements. The message gets to the buyers as news rather than as sales-directed communication.

- *Dramatic appeal:* Public relations, like advertising, has the potential for dramatizing and building the image of an organization or offering.

- *Low cost:* The costs for public relations efforts undertaken by an organization with an in-house communications manager are relatively low. Costs include the manager's salary for time and effort spent nurturing relationships with media personnel and keeping them informed and the expense of producing press materials. Additional expenses are incurred if the organization contracts out the public relations function, either on an ongoing basis or for special events.

Since an organization's image and the image of its offerings are especially important in the entertainment world, a well-thought-out public relations program coordinated with the other promotion mix elements can be extremely effective.

Numerous specific tools, such as those listed in Exhibit 12-1, fall within these communications categories. Decisions on which of these vehicles to use, when to use them, and how, must follow from a clear understanding of the communications process.

Exhibit 12-1	SOME COMMON COMMUNICATION/PROMOTION TOOLS			
	Advertising	**Sales Promotion**	**Public Relations**	**Personal Selling**
	Print & broadcast ads	Contests, games, sweepstakes, lotteries	Press kits	Sales presentations
	Packaging		Speeches	Telemarketing
	Mailings	Premiums and gifts	Seminars	Incentive programs
	Catalogs		Annual reports	Special sales events
	Newsletters	Sampling	Sponsorships	
	Brochures and booklets	Exhibits	Publications	
		Demonstrations	Community relations	
	Posters and leaflets	Coupons	Lobbying	
	Directories	Rebates	Media relations	
	Reprints of ads	Installment payment		
	Billboards			
	Display signs	Entertaining		
	Point of purchase displays	Exchange privileges		
	Audiovisual materials	Tie-ins		
	Symbols and logos			

UNDERSTANDING THE COMMUNICATION PROCESS

The communication process consists of five components. According to Lasswell, a communication model answers (1) who (2) says what (3) in what channel (4) to whom (5) with what effect.[3] The major parties in a communication are the sender (the source) and the receiver (the audience or destination). The sender transmits a message (a set of symbols) through a chosen media (the communication channel through which the message moves from sender to receiver). The message is encoded by the sender, who puts the thought into symbolic form; and is then decoded by the receiver, who assigns meaning to the symbols transmitted. The receiver then has a response, or set of reactions to the message. *Feedback* is the part of the receiver's response that is communicated back to the sender. *Noise* is the term for unplanned static or distortion that occurs during the communication process.

Fundamentals of Communication

Management strategist Peter Drucker describes four fundamentals of communication. First, communication is perception. This means that it is the *recipient* who is central to communication. The speaker or transmitter can only make it possible for a recipient or "percipient" to perceive. Perception is based not on logic but on experience; one can perceive only what one is capable of perceiving. Therefore, in order to make communication possible, one must first know the recipient's language or terms.

The situation is further complicated by the problem of selective attention—the recipient will not notice all of the stimuli. People are bombarded by numerous commercial messages from a wide variety of media. The American Association of Advertising Agencies reports that there are 1,600 commercial messages a day directed at the average individual, that 80 are consciously noticed by the individual, and that 12 provoke some reaction. Apparently we have become skilled in screening out the 1,588 unwanted messages a day and at selecting the desired or unavoidable 12. The mass media, driven by advertising, have the sole purpose of breaking through our defenses against their onslaught.[4]

Second, communication is expectation. We perceive, as a rule, what we expect to perceive. The unexpected is either ignored altogether or it is distorted—misunderstood, mis-seen or misheard as the expected. This is the process of selective distortion; people twist a message to hear what they want to hear. Receivers have set attitudes and beliefs, which lead to expectations about what they will hear or see. As a result, receivers often add things to the message that are not there and do not notice things that are there.

Third, communication makes demands. It appeals to the recipient to become somebody, do something, believe something. If communication fits in with the aspirations, values, and purposes of the recipient, it is powerful. If it goes against his or her aspirations, values, or motivations, it is likely not to be received at all, or, at best, to be resisted. Therefore, there is no communication unless the message can tap into the recipient's own values, at least to some degree.

Fourth, communication and information are different and largely opposite, yet interdependent. Whereas communication is perception, information is data. Information is impersonal, rather than interpersonal. The more it can be freed of the human component—of emotions, values, expectations, and perceptions—the more valid, reliable, and informative it becomes. Yet, information's effectiveness depends on the prior establishment of communication. So the most perfect communications may be purely "shared experiences" without any information whatever. Perception, then, has primacy over information. True communication exists when the recipient perceives what the transmitter intends.[5]

Consider how the Columbus (Georgia) Symphony Orchestra utilized these principles in developing an advertising campaign.

COLUMBUS SYMPHONY CREATES A NEW IMAGE

Michael Burks, executive director of the Columbus (Georgia) Symphony Orchestra (CSO) understands that in his community, it is not the classical music or the price of a ticket that is keeping people away from the concert hall, but their lack of familiarity with the experience itself. So Burks created the following ad to be aired on local TV stations during the week before a concert:

The camera scans the audience and focuses on an African-American couple in their late 30s or early 40s. She is in a sequined dress; he is wearing a tux. Both are fidgeting uncomfortably while looking at other audience members. His eyes focus on a college-aged couple dressed casually. The audience can hear the tuxedoed man think: "I know I could have dressed more casually. I sure am uncomfortable." Meanwhile, the younger man's eyes are also darting uncomfortably around the hall, and we can hear him think: "I know I should have worn a jacket and tie."

The announcer then says: "You don't have to feel uncomfortable to enjoy a concert."

This ad functions on two levels. First, it dispels the symphony's highbrow, stuffy image to those unfamiliar with the experience by showing that one doesn't have to dress up or feel the need to "fit in." It's not what you wear; it's *being there* that counts. Second, by incorporating wit and humor, it shows that the symphony experience is not dull and boring.

After the ad was aired, ticket sales jumped by almost 40 percent for that weekend's concert. And several long-time attenders were heard to say how nice it was to see so many young people there.

This example underscores the key factors in effective communication. Senders must know what audiences they want to reach and what approaches and media will reach them best. Their first goal is to gain the attention of the recipient; the next is to modify the recipient's beliefs and attitudes. The sender's goal is to persuade. The more the sender's field of experience overlaps with that of the receiver, the more effective the message is likely to be.[6] Much of what is called persuasion is self-persuasion by the recipient.[7]

Factors in Effective Communication

Fiske and Hartley have outlined some factors that moderate the effect of a communication:

1. The greater the monopoly of the communication source over the recipient, the greater the change or effect in favor of the source over the recipient.

2. Communication effects are greatest where the message is in line with the existing opinions, beliefs, and dispositions of the receiver.

3. Communication can produce the most effective shifts with regard to unfamiliar, lightly felt, peripheral issues that do not lie at the center of the recipient's value system.

4. Communication is more likely to be effective when the source is believed to have expertise, high status, objectivity, or likability, but particularly when the source has power and can be identified with.

5. The social context, group, or reference group will mediate the communication and influence whether or not it is accepted.[8]

STEPS IN DEVELOPING EFFECTIVE COMMUNICATIONS

There are several major steps involved in developing a total communication and promotion program. The marketing communicator must (1) identify the target audience, (2) determine the communication objectives, (3) design the message, (4) select the communication channels, (5) allocate the total promotion budget, (6) decide on the promotion mix, (7) measure the promotion's results, and (8) manage and coordinate the total marketing communication process.

Identifying the Target Audience

A marketing communicator must start with a clear target audience in mind. For example, the audience could be potential buyers, current users, deciders, or influencers. It could be made up of individuals, families, or lifestyle groups. The organization's communications responsibilities also include gaining the support and goodwill of groups such as the press, government agencies, foundations, and the corporate community. The target audience will critically influence the communicator's decisions about what to say, how, when, where, and to whom. The better the marketer understands the target audience and that audience's image, attitude, and beliefs about the organization, the more effective the communications will be.

Determining Communication Objectives

The more carefully the specific objective of a communication is defined, the more effective the communication is likely to be. Possible objectives include making target consumers aware of a product or service, educating consumers about the offer or changes in the offer, or changing beliefs about the negative and positive consequences of taking a particular action. The organization may also want to build consumer preference for their offerings over other options, develop conviction that buying a ticket or a subscription is the right thing to do, prevent discontinuation of behaviors, combat injurious rumors, and enlist the support of funding agencies, governmental agencies, or collaborators such as record stores, restaurants, or other arts organizations.

The ultimate objective, of course, is purchase and satisfaction. But purchase behavior is the end result of a long process of consumer decision making. The marketing communicator needs to know how to move the target audience to higher states of readiness to buy. We can distinguish six buyer-readiness states.

AWARENESS

If most of the target audience is unaware of the organization or its offerings, as in the case of a dance company touring in a new city, the communicator's first task is to build awareness—perhaps just name recognition. This can be accomplished with simple messages repeating the name, but it generally takes considerable time.

KNOWLEDGE

The target audience might be aware of the organization but not know much about it. The dance company may want its younger target audience to know that it presents modern, upbeat, energetic programming, some of which is performed to rock music.

LIKING

Assume the dance company is returning to a city for the second time. If target audience members know the organization and its offerings, how do they feel about it? What is the nature of the word of mouth that was spread by audience members after the first visit? If positive feelings prevail, they can be used to advantage by the communicator. If unfavorable feelings prevail, the communicator should find out why and address the concerns. If the unfavorable view is based on real problems, the dance company will have to fix its problems and then communicate its renewed quality. It is crucial that the message communicated establish realistic expectations. If quality is oversold, the resulting disappointment will be damaging to the organization.

PREFERENCE

The target audience might like the organization and its programs but not prefer it to other available options. In this case, the communicator must try to build consumer preference. Arts organizations combating the growing preference of many people to stay home and watch videos must find ways to stimulate the preference for a live performance.

CONVICTION

Perhaps the target audience knows that this is a terrific dance company and prefers it to other dance companies, but is not sure it wants to attend a dance performance. The communicator's job is to build conviction that attending a dance performance is the (fun, exciting, best) thing to do. The organization might invite community leaders to attend a rehearsal or special event, or might offer additional benefits. An orchestra trying to attract subscribers may invite people to a free concert that overviews the forthcoming season.

PURCHASE

Finally, some members of the target audience might have conviction but not quite get around to making the purchase. They may wait for more information or plan to act later. The communicator must lead these consumers to take the final step. The touring dance company can try to develop a sense of urgency: "Don't miss this opportunity! Only in town for three performances!" Or they may offer tickets at a special low price for a limited time only.

Communication objectives depend heavily on how many people already know about an offering and may have already tried it. If 90 percent of the target market already knows the organization, it would not make sense to devote resources to building awareness in the remaining 10 percent. If there are many knowers who have not tried the offering, reaching more knowers who are nontriers would be a worthwhile objective. This can best be accomplished through sales promotions (discount coupons, sneak previews, and so on). The organization may wish to build retrial and preference among previous triers. An advertising campaign directed to those who have rejected the organization ("Classical music is not for me") may be wasted because the rejecters are not likely to pay attention to the advertising and probably will not come back. Advertising directed to the indifferents ("I didn't like that play but I do enjoy going to live theater") will probably be effective in attracting some proportion of this group to a performance, especially if the advertising makes a strong point to this audience. A personal approach is likely to be more effective in bringing back former triers and lapsed subscribers.

Determining the buyer-readiness states of the target consumers is critical in developing a communication program that will be cost-effective while inducing the desired response.[9]

*Designing
the Message*

After defining the desired audience response, the communicator moves to developing an effective message. Ideally, the message should gain *attention*, hold *interest*, arouse *desire*, and elicit *action* (this is known as the AIDA model). In practice, few messages take the consumer all the way from awareness through purchase, but the AIDA framework suggests the desirable qualities. Formulating the message will require solving four problems: what to say (message content), how to say it logically (message structure), how to say it symbolically (message format), and who should say it (message source).

FORMULATING THE APPEAL

The communicator has to develop an appeal, theme, idea, or *unique selling proposition* (USP). This amounts to formulating some kind of benefit, motivation, identification, or reason why the audience should consider or purchase the offering. The USP is what distinguishes an offer or organization from others. Consider the following appeals:

- "Celebrate the majesty of music."
- "Transcend the ordinary."
- "Every time you take your seat you will be moved to an experience beyond words."

Each of these appeals is so general that it could apply to a multitude of organizations and experiences other than the one for which the ad was produced. Now consider the uniqueness of the following appeals:

- "Climbers dream of Mount Everest; Divers dream of the Great Coral Reef; Music Lovers dream of Carnegie Hall."
- "Who in the world has won 51 Grammys?" (The Chicago Symphony Orchestra).
- The Court Theatre is the place for "Classics that bristle with a new energy."

Each of these appeals identifies a characteristic unique to the organization, communicating a message of an experience that cannot be found elsewhere.

The more direct competition an organization has, the more it is necessary to develop a USP specific to the organization itself. When a symphony orchestra is the only serious music venue in town, a byline such as "Celebrate the majesty of music" may be appropriate, if not compelling. However, messages such as "Transcend the ordinary" and "Every time you take your seat you will be moved to an experience beyond words" could apply as well to a rock concert or a sporting event.

At times, an association with other exciting and entertaining events can be an effective communication device. For example, the Chicago Symphony Orchestra's appeal is that it has won the most Grammys. But consider how the Saint Louis Symphony Orchestra (SLSO) has taken this idea one step further to appeal to a specific target audience. The SLSO may not have won the most Grammys, but it advertises "More Grammys than U2, Pearl Jam, and Janet Jackson combined." For its young target audience, this is an attention-grabbing message and to elicit a response, further copy states that students save 50% on season tickets.

TYPES OF APPEALS

Three different types of appeals can be distinguished. *Rational appeals* engage the audience's self-interest. They show that the offering will produce the claimed benefits, and are exemplified by messages that demonstrate an offering's quality or value. For example, the White Oak Dance Project advertises that "What makes White Oak Dance Project remarkable isn't just Baryshnikov's dancing, but the extraordinary talent of the rest of the ensemble." In the early 1990s, the Steppenwolf Theatre made a strong rational appeal by calling itself "The nation's most important, most consistently successful resident professional theatre company."

Emotional appeals attempt to stir up some emotions—positive or negative—that will motivate purchase. The Milwaukee Chamber Theatre's season brochure asks: "Wanna Play? . . . So do we . . . In the Broadway Theatre Center." The New York Philharmonic uses a lighthearted, humorous approach when it states: "Speeding Tickets . . . Don't get caught without seats for the New York Philharmonic's fall season."

Sexual appeals are being used by some symphony orchestras to "seduce" new and younger patrons into their halls. A brochure for the 1992–93 season of the Pittsburgh Symphony is illustrated with soft-focus photographs of two lovers nuzzling. The text tells a story: "Thursday. Their hearts beat in concert. / Friday. They heard violins. / Saturday. A chord was struck. / Sunday. Each movement drew them closer." The text for the Friday series, headlined "Heartstring," reads: "The feverish drawing of a bow. The pluck of a taut string. One vibrato note hanging tremulously like a breath between lovers." Among the works being marketed with this overheated prose are Brahms' Symphony no. 1 and Shostakovich's Symphony no. 15, which are not noted for their erotic content. Not surprisingly, this brochure offended some of the older subscribers. The following year, the new marketing director, who was hired away from the Pittsburgh Penguins hockey team, adopted instead a strategy drawn from the sports world.

An emotion that has kept many people from attending the performing arts is a sense of inadequacy. This derives largely from the elitism that has been rampant in the fine arts world, keeping the less sophisticated from feeling they are able to "appreciate" certain art forms. Some arts organizations, in trying to attract new patrons, are dealing with this feeling directly. For example, a quote on the back cover of Chicago's Shakespeare Repertory brochure states in part: "(Artistic Director) Barbara Gaines does for Shakespeare what Julia Child does for French cuisine: She demystifies it, popularizes it and turns it into great entertainment . . ."

Whatever the theme, focusing on an emotional appeal remains central. Says Kevin Copps, general manager of Elektra International Classics, "It's a very basic marketing concept. You have a product. It doesn't matter whether it's a deodorant, a breakfast cereal or a (classical) CD. The question is, how do you get the consumer emotionally attached to your product?"[10]

Moral appeals are directed to the audience's sense of what is right and proper. They are often used to exhort people to support social causes. In the arts, moral appeals are most commonly used to encourage school boards to support more educational arts programs and legislators to provide more financial support for arts organizations as well as for arts education. Moral appeals are probably the least effective for audience development purposes, because a "good for you" approach is far less compelling than a dynamic emotional appeal. It is certainly easier to appeal to what people *want* to do than to what they *ought* to do.

STRENGTH OF APPEAL

Some advertisers believe that messages are maximally persuasive when they are moderately discrepant with what the audience believes. Messages that only state what the audience believes attract less attention and at best only reinforce audience beliefs. And if the messages are too discrepant with the audience's beliefs, they will be counterargued in the audience's mind and be disbelieved. The challenge is to design a message that avoids the two extremes.

The marketer should select the best message from a set of alternatives developed. It has been suggested that contending messages be rated on three scales: *desirability, exclusiveness,* and *believability.*[11] The message must first say something desirable or interesting about the product or behavior. This is not enough, however, because many competitors may be making the same claim. Therefore the message must also say something exclusive or distinctive that does not apply to every alternative. Finally, the message must be believable or provable. The desirable feature or features will vary by event and by market segment. By asking consumers to rate different messages on desirability, exclusiveness, and believability, marketers can evaluate them for their communication potency.

BREADTH OF APPEAL

Some messages, such as the Pittsburgh Symphony's seductive season brochure, draw conclusions about the product's benefits or advantages to the consumer. However, drawing too explicit a conclusion can limit a product's acceptance. If the issue is simple and/or the audience intelligent, they might be annoyed at the attempt to explain the obvious. Or, if the issue is highly personal, the audience might resent the communicator's attempt to draw a conclusion. If the Pittsburgh Symphony had continued using its "romance" brochure, it might have driven away patrons and potential attenders who found its message irrelevant or offensive. Conclusion drawing seems best suited for specialized programs where a single or clear target market is intended, such as children's programs or a singles subscription series.

Recent research indicates that stimulus ambiguity can lead to broader market acceptance. The best ads ask questions and allow readers and viewers to come to their own conclusions.[12] Ambiguous use of the word *passion* may, for example, describe the content of the work being performed, such as romantic opera; characterize the patrons' anticipated feelings about the work performed; or relate to something more personal. In other words, when a message is ambiguous, it can mean whatever the recipient wants it to mean. Coca-Cola advertisers knew this when they developed the message "Coke—it's the real thing."

Message Structure: One and Two-Sided Arguments

A message's effectiveness depends on its structure as well as its content. The choice between one- and two-sided arguments raises the question of whether the communicator should only praise the product or also mention some of its shortcomings. One would think that one-sided presentations would be the most effective. Yet, it has been found that

- One-sided messages work best with audiences that are initially predisposed to the communicator's position, and two-sided arguments work best with audiences who are opposed.

- Two-sided messages tend to be more effective with better-educated audiences.

- Two-sided messages tend to be more effective with audiences that are likely to be exposed to counterpropaganda.[13]

Order of presentation raises the question of whether a communicator should present the strongest arguments first or last. In the case of a one-sided message, presenting the strongest argument first has the advantage of establishing attention and interest. This is important in newspapers and other media where the audience does not attend to the whole message. In a medium with a more captive audience, such as an announcement by the house manager before a performance, a climactic presentation might be more effective. In the case of a two-sided message, the issue is whether to present the positive argument first, relying on the primacy effect, or last, hoping to benefit from the recency effect. If the audience is initially opposed, the communicator might start with the other side's argument. This approach will disarm the audience and also has the advantage of concluding with the strongest argument. In high-involvement situations, such as purchasing a season subscription or attending the opera for the first time, the target audience will engage in extensive internal cognitive activity, including consideration of costs and alternatives, and an external search that will make available to them the "other side" of the argument. The marketer should seize the initiative and deal with the other side of the issue rather than leave it to the individual or to competitors. By dealing with the counterarguments in advance, the marketer can "inoculate" the target audience against counterinfluences. If this strategy is to be effective, the marketer must understand what the target audience perceives to be the key costs of the behavior.

The Chicago Shakespeare Repertory put this principle to use for its 1994–95 brochure. Recognizing people's reluctance to attend Shakespearean productions, the company's brochure cover shows a photograph of an actor dressed as Shakespeare, wearing a signboard that says: "Shakespeare is for repressed, uptight, highbrow, pompous bookworms." Inside the cover is a back view with the signboard reading: "YOU'D BE SURPRISED. Shakespeare Repertory turns stereotypes upside down and Shakespeare right side up!"

Two-sided arguments may also recognize other alternatives available to the target audience. For example, the marketer may want to confront the fact that going to the theater or symphony means not going to a movie or nightclub or just staying home to watch TV. Blockbuster Video has made the performing arts communicator's job more difficult with a message that asks people why they should hassle with going out to the theater when they can watch a great movie in the comfort of their own home.

Format Elements

Format elements can also make a difference in a message's impact. Advertisers use such attention-getting devices as novelty, contrast, arresting pictures, and movement. Humor is often an effective attention-getter for any type of message and even rewards the listener for paying attention. It also distracts people from counterarguing. When humor is used, it should be directly related to the message and neither the speaker nor the message's recipient should be the brunt of the joke. Special care must be taken when using humor in advertising: multiple exposures are usually necessary for an ad to be effective, and humor tends to wear out quickly.

An economical way to convey a message is to take advantage of common visual or verbal associations. For example, someone sipping wine is assumed to be of a higher social class than someone holding a beer mug. Someone wearing glasses is supposed to be smarter than someone without them. Colors have symbolism; in the United States, white is pure, gold is rich, blue is soothing, deep pastels are "modern," and so on.[14] Presenters must pay attention to their facial expressions, gestures, dress, posture, and hairstyle. Symbols can help or hurt communicators. The problem, of course, is to choose the right symbols and to be assured that your audience sees them as they are intended. The marketer may wish to conduct focus groups to secure feedback on how the message is actually perceived.

Message Source

Messages delivered by attractive sources receive more attention and are more reliably recalled. In the arts, a well-known and well-liked figure can help bridge the gap to accessibility. Transference is likely to occur so that positive feelings for the ad and spokesperson become positive feelings for the product. In its first year of operation, the Los Angeles Music Center Opera displayed photographs of Dudley Moore, a popular movie star who was starring in one of its productions, dressed in a modern suit rather than in traditional opera costume. This strategy makes opera attendance more compatible with Los Angeles's contemporary lifestyles and its identification with the movie industry.

Messages delivered by highly credible sources are the most persuasive. The three factors most often identified with source credibility are expertise, trustworthiness, and likability. [15] *Expertise* is the specialized knowledge the communicator appears to possess that backs the claim. *Trustworthiness* is related to how objective and honest the source is perceived to be. Friends are trusted more than strangers or salespeople. The spokesperson does not need to possess special knowledge, but should be trusted to report accurately. *Likability* describes the source's attractiveness to the audience. Such qualities as candor, humor, and naturalness make a source more likable. The most highly credible source would be a person who scored high on all three dimensions as Leonard Bernstein did during his leadership of the New York Philharmonic Orchestra.

Choosing the ideal spokesperson is not easy. The effectiveness of a famous spokesperson is limited by his or her popularity, which is likely to wax and wane. If the spokesperson is associated with a scandal, the organization's image is put at risk. One possible alternative is to hedge one's bets by using multiple spokespeople. Also, people like things to fit; they are uncomfortable with cognitive dissonance. If people like a particular spokesperson but dislike the particular offering, they will seek to reduce the discrepancy in their feelings toward the message and the source. They may tend to favor the spokesperson a little less or the offering a little more. The principle of congruity says that communicators can use their positive image to reduce some negative feelings toward an offering but in the process might lose some esteem with the audience.

COMMUNICATION CHANNELS

Messages are transmitted to the target consumer through some medium. The medium may be nonpersonal, like an organization's brochures or newspaper ads, or personal, like the organization's own spokespersons or a patron's family or friends.

A further distinction can be drawn between advocate, social, and expert channels of communication. *Advocate channels* consist of an organization's efforts to influence members of the target market through both impersonal (i.e., direct marketing) and personal (i.e., telemarketing) media. *Social channels* by definition are personal, consisting of friends, family members, business associates, and other people who influence target buyers. *Expert channels* may be independent experts such as music, dance, and theater critics; advocates, such as a conductor acting as spokesperson for the orchestra's upcoming special event; or social, such as a patron's musician friend who is touting a young pianist.

Personal Communication Channels

Personal communication channels involve two or more people communicating directly with each other, either face to face, person to audience, over the telephone, or through the mail. Organizations use personal communication channels because they are effective in individualizing the presentation and feedback. The most persuasive form of personal communication for attracting attendance at performing arts events is word of mouth, conducted most often through social channels. Audience surveys repeatedly find that word of mouth is the most frequently used information source.

There are hundreds of occasions when people will ask others—friends, acquaintances, professionals—for a recommendation. This is especially the case when selecting performing arts events to attend. First, people expect a less biased opinion from personal acquaintances than from advocate sources. Second, personal sources are more likely to have tastes, education, social status, beliefs, and arts exposure similar to those of the opinion seeker than say, impersonal experts such as newspaper critics. Third, personal influence tends to carry great weight; for many people, arts attendance is a social activity with significant status implications.

People whose opinions are frequently sought for recommendations are called *opinion leaders.* Opinion leaders are people who are widely respected within defined social groups. They have a large relevant social network and are highly interconnected in their communities. They are likely to hold office in community groups and often have legitimate power by virtue of their social standing. Effective opinion leaders tend to be slightly higher in educational attainment and/or social status than those they influence, but not so high as to be in a different social class. Opinion leaders are consulted because of their perceived expertise and because they are considered more credible than impersonal or advocacy channels. They have prescreened, evaluated, and synthesized product information. Since they are often among the first to buy new products or attend new productions, they absorb much of the risk.[16]

Arts organizations try to stimulate word-of-mouth exposure through reaching opinion leaders. Thus, the Saint Louis Symphony offers free tickets and membership in the Green Room to African-American ministers whose churches participate in the symphony's community partnership program. Corporate executives may be given special perks if they purchase blocks of seats or stimulate sales among their associates and employees. An arts organization can work through influential community members such as radio announcers, class presidents, and presidents of membership organizations. Patrons can be offered free guest passes with each subscription and can be encouraged to give gift certificates for performances to friends, associates, and employees. Support-group members may be urged to send out brochures to people on their Christmas card lists or to hold subscription sales parties in their homes. A representative from the arts organization can speak at these parties, and peer pressure can be discreetly exerted.

Nonpersonal Communication Channels

Nonpersonal communication channels carry messages without personal contact or interaction. They include media, atmospheres, and events. *Media* consist of print media (newspapers, magazines, direct mail), broadcast media (radio, television), electronic media (audiotape, videotape, videodisc, e-mail, the Internet), and display media (billboards, signs, posters). Most nonpersonal messages come through paid media. After word of mouth, newspapers are the most common source of information about performing arts events.

Atmospheres are "packaged environments" that create or reinforce the buyer's leanings toward product purchase and satisfaction with the experience. Opera houses are often designed to create an atmosphere of elegance and classicism. Experimental plays are often produced in "raw" settings, not just for their low cost but also because they provide atmospheric versatility, spontaneity, and nonelitist comfort.

Public-relations departments arrange *events* such as news conferences, grand openings, and other celebrations to achieve specific communication effects with a target audience. One opera company gained high conversation value when it performed the Triumphal March from *Aida* during halftime at the local university's football game. Similarly, star performers generate conversation when they do well-publicized record or book signings. Channels used to accomplish these objectives will be examined in depth in the following three chapters.

ESTABLISHING THE TOTAL PROMOTION BUDGET

One of the most difficult marketing decisions facing arts organizations is how much to spend on promotion. Danny Newman has shown that for many performing arts organizations, funds are best and most efficiently expended in the preseason subscription campaign, and aimed at gaining and retaining committed subscribers for an entire season.[17] But some organizations, such as summer festivals and presenters with a broad range of offerings, are not well suited to season subscriptions. Arts managers must also take into account the dollar value of seats unsold to subscribers. In order to stimulate sales, a production's available seats must be heavily promoted even before the curtain rises for the first time, before critical reviews are in, and before positive word of mouth can take effect. And since each seat is perishable and becomes unsalable each time the curtain rises, promotional activities must continue right up to the time of each performance. This means that promotional resources must be allocated over the entire period of time during which people make their decisions to attend—from early subscribers to last-minute single-ticket buyers.

Theoretically, promotional budget setting calls for expenditures to the point where incremental revenues from the sale of one more ticket equal promotional costs. In other words, promotional efforts should be made until their expenses exceed the revenue they generate. Unfortunately, this level of expenditure is impossible to calculate in practice. There is usually little information that would allow direct comparison of the drawing power of diverse factors such as the quality of the production, the price of the tickets, and the amount of advertising. However, the principle of incremental revenues should be kept in mind as the promotion budget is developed.

Several factors affect how promotion budgets are determined. One is the organization's stage in its life cycle and its reputation in the community. In the introduction stage, an organization will want to do as much advertising and sales promotion as possible to build awareness and induce trial. A well-established organization with a strong audience base may be able to tone down some of these efforts and focus on past season subscribers, who may be most efficiently reached through direct mail.

Another factor to be considered in budget setting is the event (or series) itself. Some art forms and some specific events have greater drawing power than others, due to a well-known performer, a "war-horse" production, a great review, or some other factor. It is up to the communications manager to determine the most effective level of promotional spending for each event. A highly popular program may require relatively little spending to attract a large audience, while no amount of promotional activity will attract an audience to an undesirable program. Therefore, the promotion budget should be varied from event to event, according to an estimated response to different levels of promotion. Of course, a certain amount of flexibility should be built into the budget planning so that if a production gets rave reviews and/or an unexpected groundswell of word-of-mouth support, the organization can take full advantage and adjust its advertising accordingly.

Arts organizations have several opportunities to help reduce their promotion budgets. First, low-cost or free opportunities for advertising are available to some organizations. Some media will provide a certain amount of free advertising as part of their public service efforts. In some cities, the local trade organization or arts council makes bulk media buys at discount and then provides the space or time to arts organizations at an attractive rate. Community newsletters and state publications are available to some arts organizations. Local businesses often collaborate with arts organizations and exchange free publicity.

Four common methods are used by organizations to set their promotion budget.

THE AFFORDABLE METHOD

Many organizations set the promotion budget at what they think they can afford. However, making the decision according to currently available funding completely ignores the role of promotion as an investment and the immediate impact of promotion on sales volume. It also leads to an uncertain annual promotion budget, which makes long-range market planning difficult.

THE PERCENTAGE-OF-SALES METHOD

Many organizations set their promotion expenditures at a specified percentage of sales (either current or anticipated). In this way, promotion expenditures vary with what the company can "afford." This satisfies the financial managers, who feel that expenses should bear a close relation to the movement of ticket sales, and encourages management to think in terms of the relationship between promotion cost, selling price, and surplus per unit. Despite these advantages, the percentage-of-sales method has little to justify it. It uses circular reasoning in viewing past or predicted *sales* rather than market *opportunities* as the basis for promotion budgeting. It discourages experimenting with countercyclical promotion or aggressive spending. The promotion budget's dependence on year-to-year sales fluctuations interferes with long-range planning and may cause an organization to spend a lower amount than usual at just the time when it may be in the organization's best interest to stimulate support with additional promotional activity.

THE COMPETITIVE-PARITY METHOD

Some organizations set their promotion budget to achieve *share-of-voice* parity with their competitors. This thinking is illustrated by an arts manager who was overheard to say, "If I could afford weekly half-page ads like some of the wealthier theaters in this town, I would have no problem filling my hall." If, indeed, the half-page ads would stimulate enough sales to fill the hall on a regular basis, this manager could not afford *not* to place the ads. She assumes that what the bigger theaters are doing represents the collective wisdom of the industry. But there are no grounds for believing that what the competition spends on promotion and how it chooses to spend its allocation is right for a particular organization. Organizations' reputations, resources, opportunities, and objectives differ so much that others' promotion budgets are hardly a guide.

THE OBJECTIVE-AND-TASK METHOD

The objective-and-task method calls upon marketers to develop their promotion budgets by defining their specific objectives, determining the tasks that must be performed to achieve those objectives, and estimating the costs of performing those tasks. The sum of these costs is the proposed promotion budget. This method has the advantage of requiring management to spell out its assumptions about the relationship between dollars spent, exposure levels, trial rates, and regular attendance.

A major question is how much weight promotion should receive in the total marketing mix (as opposed to more services, improvements in the hall, market research, and so on). The answer depends on where the organization and its offerings are in their life cycles, how unique and differentiated the offerings are, whether there is a strong subscriber base or the performances need to be regularly and individually "sold," and other considerations.

After implementing the promotional plan, the communicator must measure its impact on the target audience. After running a special radio ad or newspaper promotion, the box office personnel may ask all callers where they heard about the production. In audience surveys, patrons may be asked about which periodicals they read, which radio stations they listen to, and where they are most likely to get their information about the performances they attend. More specifically, focus groups might be formed to ask patrons whether they recognize or recall a certain message, how many times they saw or heard it, what points they recall, how they felt about the message, and their previous and current attitudes toward the organization and its offerings.

MANAGING AND COORDINATING THE COMMUNICATION PROCESS

The wide range of communication tools and messages makes it imperative that they be coordinated. Otherwise, the message might be ill timed, lack consistency, or not be cost-effective. For example, direct-mail and telemarketing campaigns for subscription renewals should be carefully timed so that together they reap the greatest possible response in the most cost-effective manner. The style of newsletters should imitate the organization's image as put forth in brochures and advertisements, and the newsletter's content should enhance other new subscriber and subscriber retention efforts.

Arts organizations should strive to achieve *integrated marketing communications.* This calls for appointing a marketing communications director who has overall responsibility for the organization's persuasive communications efforts; working out a philosophy of the role of different promotional tools and the extent to which they are to be used; keeping track of all promotional expenditures by product or service, promotional tool, stage of product life cycle (for example, first, second, and third year of a new flex plan), and observed effect, as a basis for improving further use of these tools; and coordinating the promotional activities and their timing.

Integration of marketing communications will produce more consistency in the organization's meaning to its audiences and other publics. It firmly imposes the responsibility to portray a unified image throughout each of the organization's many activities. And it leads to a total marketing communication strategy aimed at showing how the organization and its offerings can meet the customers' needs and desires.

---

1 Roger A. Strang and Jonathan Gutman, "Promotion Policy Making in the Arts: A Conceptual Framework," in *Marketing the Arts,* ed. Michael P. Mokwa, William M. Dawson, and E. Arthur Prieve (New York: Praeger, 1980), 225–238.

2 Sidney J. Levy, *Promotional Behavior* (Glenview, Ill.: Scott, Foresman, 1971), chap. 4.

3 Harold D. Lasswell, *Power and Personality* (New York: Norton, 1948), 37–51.

4 Ben H. Bagdikian, "How Much More Communication Can We Stand?" in *Ethics, Morality, and the Media,* ed. Lee Thayer (New York: Hastings House, 1980), 175–180.

5 Peter F. Drucker, *Management: Tasks, Responsibilities, Practices,* chap. 38, "Managerial Communications" (New York: Harper & Row, 1974), 481–493.

6 Wilbur Schramm, "How Communication Works," in *The Process and Effects of Mass Communication,* ed. Wilbur Schramm and Donald F. Roberts (Urbana: University of Illinois Press, 1971), 4.

7 Brian Sternthal and C. Samuel Craig, *Consumer Behavior: An Information Processing Perspective* (Englewood Cliffs, N J: Prentice-Hall, 1982), 86–116.

8 John Fiske and John Hartley, *Reading Television* (London: Methuen, 1980), 79.

9 Otto Ottensen, "The Response Function," in *Current Theories in Scandinavian Mass Communications Research,* ed. Mie Berg (Grenaa, Denmark: G.M.T., 1977).

10 Jamie James, "Sex and the 'Singles' Symphony," *New York Times,* May 2, 1993, sec. H, pp. 1, 27.

11 Dik Warren Twedt, "How to Plan New Products, Improve Old Ones, and Create Better Advertising," *Journal of Marketing,* Jan. 1969, 53–57.

12 James F. Engel, Roger D. Blackwell, and Paul W. Minard, *Consumer Behavior,* 5th ed. (Hinsdale, Ill.: Dryden Press, 1986), 477.

13 C. I. Hovland, A. A. Lumsdaine, and F. D. Sheffield, *Experiments on Mass Communication,* vol. 3 (Princeton, N.J.: Princeton University Press, 1948), chap. 8.

14 Edward T. Hall, *The Silent Language* (Garden City, N.Y.: Doubleday, 1973).

15 Herbert C. Kelman and Carl I. Hovland, "Reinstatement of the Communication in Delayed Measurement of Opinion Change," *Journal of Abnormal and Social Psychology* 48 (1953), 327–335.

16 Michael Solomon, *Consumer Behavior,* 3d ed. (Englewood Cliffs, N. J.: Prentice-Hall, 1995), 359.

17 Danny Newman, *Subscribe Now!* (New York: Theatre Communications Group, 1983), 101.

▲●▲

CHAPTER 13

If you think advertising doesn't pay—we understand there are twenty-five mountains in Colorado higher than Pike's Peak. Can you name one?

The American Salesman

I know that half of my advertising is wasted but I don't know which half.

JOHN WANAMAKER

DEVELOPING EFFECTIVE ADVERTISING AND SALES PROMOTION

PERFORMING ARTS ORGANIZATIONS DIFFER FROM MOST ORGANIZATIONS IN THAT they constantly produce new products—stage new productions, present different performers, and so forth. Therefore, they must constantly work to create awareness, build interest, and stimulate sales among their target audiences. They do this by using such communication tools as advertising, sales promotion, direct mail, tele-marketing, and public relations. In this chapter we examine how performing arts organizations can use advertising and sales promotion, respectively, to promote their offerings. In the next two chapters we examine the use of direct-marketing tools and public relations for building audiences.

ADVERTISING

Advertising has many purposes: long-term buildup of the organization's image (institutional advertising); long-term buildup of an ongoing offering such as main-stage productions, second-stage productions, or subscription offers (product advertising); dissemination of information about a particular production, event, or service (classified advertising); or announcement of a special price offer (promotional advertising).

Advertising is defined as any paid form of nonpersonal presentation and promotion of ideas, goods, and services by an identified sponsor. Paid advertising permits total control over encoded message content and over the nature of the medium, plus substantial control of the scheduling of the message. On the other hand, paid advertising permits no control over message decoding by the audience and results in little or delayed feedback on the received message. In most organizations, advertising is handled by someone in the marketing department who works with an advertising agency. This person proposes the budget, approves advertising agency ads and campaigns, and handles direct-mail advertising, displays, and other forms of advertising. The advertising agency's task is to create advertising campaigns and to select and purchase media.

Developing an effective advertising program involves the following steps: (1) setting the advertising objectives; (2) deciding on the advertising budget; (3) designing the message; (4) deciding on the media; (5) deciding on media timing; and (6) evaluating advertising effectiveness.

Setting the Advertising Objectives

The first step in developing an advertising program is to set the advertising objectives. These objectives must flow from prior decisions about the target market, market positioning, and the marketing mix. The positioning and marketing-mix strategies define the job that advertising must do. A complete statement of objectives includes four components:

- *Target:* Who is to be reached (usually expressed as a demographic or psychographic profile)?
- *Position:* What are the offering's merits and what differentiates it from competitive offerings?
- *Response desired:* What audience response is being sought (e.g., awareness, interest, purchase, etc.)?
- *Time horizon:* Within what period should the objectives be achieved?

Consider how the San Francisco Ballet defined the objectives for its *Nutcracker* advertising campaign.

THE SAN FRANCISCO BALLET: ADVERTISING *THE* NUTCRACKER

In 1993, the San Francisco Ballet (SFB) faced a $3.3 million deficit. Since *Nutcracker* ticket sales accounted for 50 percent of the SFB's annual revenue, efforts were under way to exceed previous ticket sales and revenue. The SFB contracted with the advertising firm of Hal Riney and Partners to develop a creative advertising campaign for *The Nutcracker* that would help to create strong awareness of the SFB's sixtieth anniversary and the hundredth anniversary of *The Nutcracker* and build attendance for the 45 percent of seats that are not sold to subscribers.[1]

The specific advertising objectives were as follows:

Target:	Middle-to-upper-income women 25–54 years old with families, with a secondary target audience of adults 18–49 years old.
Position:	In conjunction with the spirit of the Christmas holiday season, capture the fun and the traditional aspects of *The Nutcracker*.
Response desired:	To meet or exceed sales goals of filling 96,000 seats for 33 performances (2,909 per performance). To create broader awareness of the SFB's *Nutcracker* production.
Time horizon:	Generate continuous awareness of the San Francisco Ballet's *Nutcracker* performances beginning the week of Thanksgiving and continuing through the final week of performances.

Many specific communication and sales objectives can be assigned to advertising. These objectives can be classified as to whether their aim is to inform, persuade, or remind.

Informative advertising aims to create audience awareness and knowledge of the organization's programs. Informational objectives include telling the market about a new season or production; suggesting new occasions for attendance; informing the market about a price change; explaining how an offering works, such as a flex plan or coupon offer; describing available services such as parking, an on-site restaurant, or educational programming; broadly disseminating rave reviews; correcting false impressions; reducing consumers' fears; or building an organization's image.

Persuasive advertising aims to create audience preference and stimulate purchase of the organization's offerings. Persuasive objectives include changing target audiences' perceptions of the organization's offerings; persuading customers to purchase *now,* an objective that permeates every season brochure ("Subscribe Now!"); and attracting donations.

Reminder advertising aims to keep consumers thinking about the organization and its offerings. Thus, even a sold-out production is advertised to highlight the organization's success. Similarly, *reinforcement advertising* seeks to assure current patrons that they have made the right choice. In a newsletter or special mailing to patrons or even in a newspaper ad, the organization may reprint good reviews, high attendance records, and so on. This advertising serves to build goodwill that will carry over to future seasons.

Deciding on the Advertising Budget

The proper way to set the advertising budget is to use the objective-and-task approach described in Chapter 12. If the objective is to fill the hall for a highly popular entertainer, one large ad in the Sunday paper may be adequate. If the objective is to build the organization's prestige through association with a popular entertainer, a more intense campaign is in order. If the objective is to fill the hall for a relatively unknown performer and a less popular program, the cost may be prohibitively high and the organization should reevaluate its objective.

Because of the difficulty of measuring the actual effects of advertising, organizations are never sure they are spending the right amount. If the organization is spending too little, the effect is insignificant, and therefore the organization is actually spending too much. But if the organization is spending too much on advertising, then some of the money could be put to better use. In practice, advertising budgets are allocated to market segments according to their respective sales levels or sales potential. It is common to spend twice as much advertising money in segment B as in segment A if segment B has twice the level of some indicator of sales or sales potential. In principle, the budget should be allocated to different segments according to their expected marginal response to advertising. A budget is well allocated when it is not possible to shift dollars from one segment to another and increase total sales.

Organizations must carefully allocate their advertising expenditures to different market segments, geographical areas, and time periods. For example, should a theater place a full-page ad in newspaper sections going to two target neighborhoods or a half-page ad in four target neighborhoods' papers? Should a major advertising campaign be launched before the show opens or delayed in the hope of capitalizing on good reviews?

How much should the organization allocate to attracting current patrons versus new patrons? Arts marketers find it easier to stimulate more frequent attendance among current attenders than to attract new audience members. However, as the mean age of audience members increases, arts marketers need to attract new and younger patrons. This means committing some budget to an objective that is likely to garner a smaller short-term response.

SAN FRANCISCO BALLET: *THE NUTCRACKER* **ADVERTISING BUDGET**	The total budget for advertising *The Nutcracker* was estimated to be $235,900. This included $46,300 for production costs, $76,400 for fees, and $113,200 for media costs. Media spending was allocated in line with historical ticket purchase patterns, with slightly higher levels in San Francisco and lesser in the East Bay, Peninsula, and Marin. However, the East Bay was targeted as an opportunity area.

Should advertising expenditures be increased to match increased spending by competitors? Competitors attempt to outshout each other in the hope of attracting audiences. However, competitive spending assumes that competitors know the appropriate amount to spend. Furthermore, most nonprofit arts organizations cannot compete financially with their larger direct competitors, much less with the for-profit entertainment industry that commands an overwhelming voice in the media.

There are collaborative opportunities for reducing advertising costs. If a theater were to place a single half-page ad in the Friday Arts section of the *Chicago Tribune* by directly contracting with the newspaper, the cost would be $5,915. However, under the banner of the League of Chicago Theaters, which guarantees the newspaper a certain number of ads per month, member organizations can purchase the same ad for only $855![2] In cities and towns where no such trade organizations exist, various arts organizations ought to band together to increase their media clout.

The objective-and-task method requires determining the media tasks that will accomplish the objective. Arts marketers should employ research to assess the potential or actual effectiveness of their advertising expenditures. Consider the following evaluation that one theater made of its radio advertising.

THE SUNSHINE BOYS **IN A SLUMP**	A Chicago-area theater that appeals primarily to an older, Jewish audience produced Neil Simon's *The Sunshine Boys* as its "safe, sure" draw for the season's last play. But the production was failing to draw nonsubscribers. So, in addition to newspaper ads, management bought radio advertising to be read several times during a one-week period by a popular talk show host. To evaluate the radio ad's effectiveness, each person who phoned the box office during the two weeks following the ad's first airing was asked where he or she had heard about the show. Of the 225 respondents, 64 percent said they had heard about it by word of mouth from friends and family, 34 percent from newspaper ads, and only 2 percent from the radio ad. The minimal patronage gained by the ad failed to cover its cost, and the ad was dropped.

Based on further audience and box office surveys, the marketing director made the following recommendations: (1) Advertisements should be concentrated just before a play opens and shortly after the opening. This timing takes advantage of promoting good reviews and creates the best opportunity for word of mouth to spread, which is the organization's strongest promotional resource. (2) "Extra" advertisements should not be added during the run of a poorly received play because their cost outweighs the benefit.

Designing the Message

All effective ads contain certain essentials. Bob Schulberg suggests beginning with Winston Churchill's five rules for successful speechwriting: (1) Begin strongly; (2) have one theme; (3) use simple language; (4) leave a picture in the listener's mind; (5) end dramatically.[3] Creativity is especially important. An ad needs an effective attention-getting device; it also should have built-in associations with factors or qualities familiar to the target audience so that the message will be more easily processed.

EXECUTION STYLES

Any message can be presented in different execution styles, for example:

- *Slice of life:* Shows people experiencing the offering. A summer festival may show a family picnicking on the lawn as the concert is about to begin.

- *Lifestyle:* Emphasizes how the offering fits in with a lifestyle. An ad for a singles subscription series may show young adults standing in small groups and sipping wine during a pre- or postperformance reception.

- *Fantasy:* Creates a fantasy around an offering or the occasion of its use. The Dallas Opera's season brochure was headlined: "Passion in the evening; no regrets in the morning."

- *Mood or image:* Ties the offering to an evocative mood or image, such as beauty, love, serenity, or excitement. No claim is made about the offering except through suggestion. "When my parents take me to the ballet, it makes me feel loved," says one child at the Atlanta Ballet.

- *Evidence of expertise:* Shows the expertise of the organization or its performers, directors, or composers in creating the offering or in mounting productions. It also presents critical or survey evidence that the organization, a particular production, or a performer is highly rated or preferred over other offerings of its kind. The Chicago Symphony Orchestra announces that it has won fifty-one Grammy Awards; theaters advertise their awards and nominations and regularly excerpt phrases from critical reviews that help promote their plays; "Sold Out" banners are placed over performance announcements, testifying to their popularity. (So many people can't be wrong!)

- *Testimonials:* Feature a highly credible, likable, or expert source touting the offering. It may be a celebrity, such as Michael Jordan endorsing Chicago's Lyric Opera ("I'm Bullish on the Lyric"), or an ordinary person praising the offering (an avid runner and Braves fan marvels at the Atlanta Ballet dancers' athleticism).

DESIGNING A PRINT AD

A number of researchers into print advertisements report that the *picture, headline,* and *copy* are important in that order. The picture must be strong enough to draw attention to the ad. The headline must be effective in propelling the person to read the copy. The copy itself must be well composed. Even then, a really outstanding ad will be noted by less than 50 percent of the exposed audience; about 30 percent of the exposed audience might recall the headline's main point; about 25 percent might remember the advertiser's name; and fewer than 10 percent will have read most of the body copy. Ordinary ads do not achieve even these results.

Format elements such as ad size, color, and illustration will make a difference in an ad's impact. A minor rearrangement of mechanical elements within the ad can improve its attention-getting power. Larger-size ads gain more attention, though not necessarily in proportion to their higher cost. Color illustrations are more effective than black-and-white, although some graphic designers have found that two-color ads can be just as effective as four-color and far less costly.

Creative people must find an appropriate style, tone, wording, and format for executing the message. All of these elements must deliver a coherent image and message. Since few people read body copy, the picture and headline must summarize the selling proposition.

To promote its production of Puccini's *Tosca,* the English National Opera wanted its ad to present a "tidal wave of emotion." The ad grabbed the reader's attention as follows:

ADVERTISING

TOSCA

The English National Opera's ad for *Tosca* began with a headline stating:

This is one opera where we suggest you take a box.

Under the headline was a large photograph of a box of tissues. The copy stated: "Since its first performance, audience after audience has sobbed its eyes out. Puccini's *Tosca* conveys the absolute essence of life and loss with manipulative ease. Melodramatic, thrilling, and above all passionate, it's a candidate for the most complete opera ever written. You've almost certainly heard the music. Now we'd like you to take your seats at English National Opera. . . .It's an evening to draw blood from a stone and tears from a desert."[4]

Sometimes an ad can be most effective when it is suggestive. Rather than stating specific benefits or attributes, a suggestive ad allows the consumers to imagine the benefits or attributes meaningful to them. For example, in its direct mailings to subscribers, Concertante di Chicago quoted an excerpt from a review by music critic John von Rhein saying: "For classical programming that is both coherent and enjoyable, nobody does it better than Concertante di Chicago." But, how many people would be motivated to attend a concert by "coherent" and "enjoyable" programming? So for future mailings, the excerpt was reduced to: "Nobody does it better than Concertante di Chicago." Now, "it" can be whatever the consumers want or imagine it to be.

Consider the direct-mail brochure created for the San Francisco Ballet's *Nutcracker* production.

<table>
<tr><td>

THE SAN
FRANCISCO
BALLET:
DIRECT-MAIL
BROCHURE

</td><td>

The direct-mail brochure for the San Francisco Ballet's *Nutcracker* was a cleverly conceived two-fold piece. On the cover it said:

"A Dream, the Way It Was Meant to Be Danced."

After the first fold was opened, the copy changed to:

"A Dance, the Way It Was Meant to Be Dreamed."

</td></tr>
</table>

DESIGNING RADIO ADS

Well-written radio ads can lead listeners to imagine themselves at an event, enjoying its ambience. Advertisers should take advantage of radio's unique ability to let patrons hear a sampling of the performance. Patrons may even hear a familiar piece of music that prompts them to attend a live performance in a way a print ad could not have done.[5]

Although subtle suggestion may be a virtue in print advertising, Schulberg recommends a more direct approach in radio advertising. "The entire thrust of the announcement must be geared to developing response. If the objective of a commercial is to draw requests for a brochure, the commercial should talk about the brochure. If the commercial is selling a subscription, this should be clear throughout the entire 60 seconds." Schulberg says that a radio ad should be created as if you were addressing one person. He suggests that a radio ad should be designed with the following tips in mind:

- Mention your organization's name several times.

- Include a deadline by which time the listener must respond ("Only two days left to purchase the few remaining tickets to the biggest event of the season!").

- The most important part of a radio ad is the ending. Everything should build up to it.

- Repeat the phone number three times. End the ad with the third repetition, since the last sounds of an ad will linger in the listener's mind for a few seconds.

Deciding on the Media

Because message design makes some assumptions about which media will be used, presumably some thought will already have been given to the media that most effectively reaches the target audience. Media selection involves three steps: choosing the media categories, choosing specific media vehicles, and media scheduling.

CHOOSING MEDIA CATEGORIES

The first step calls for allocating the advertising budget to the major media categories. In order of their advertising volume, they are newspapers, television, direct mail, radio, magazines, and outdoor media such as billboards and posters. Marketers choose among these major media categories by considering the following variables:

- *Target audience media habits:* Many concertgoers listen to classical music and public radio stations; teenagers listen more to rock stations and television.

- *Product or service:* Media categories have different potentials for demonstration, visualization, explanation, and enhancing believability. A color ad in a magazine may be the most effective medium to show off a newly renovated auditorium, whereas a short television ad may be the most effective way to promote interest in a Broadway musical.

- *Message:* A message announcing tomorrow's concert requires ads in newspapers or on radio. A message containing a great deal of information about the next season's program might require direct mailings or special newspaper inserts.

- *Cost:* Television is very expensive; newspaper advertising is relatively inexpensive. What is most important, of course, is which medium will yield the highest returns per dollar spent.

SOMARC (Social Marketing for Change) has summarized the advantages and disadvantages of the major media (see Exhibit 13-1).

Media categories must also be examined for their capacity to deliver reach, frequency, and impact. *Reach* is the number of different persons or households exposed to a particular media schedule at least once during a specified time period. *Frequency* is the number of times within the specified time period that an average person or household is exposed to the message. *Impact* is the qualitative value of an exposure through a given medium (a theater's ad in the *New Yorker* would have a greater impact than one in *Good Housekeeping*).

Media selection is the problem of finding the most cost-effective media to deliver the desired number of exposures to the target audience. The media planner must consider a number of trade-offs. With a given budget, what is the most cost-effective combination of reach, frequency, and impact? Reach is more important when introducing

Exhibit 13-1

STRENGTHS AND WEAKNESSES OF ALTERNATIVE MEDIA

Strengths	Weaknesses
Television	
• High impact	• High production costs
• Audience selectivity	• Uneven delivery by market
• Schedule when needed	• Up-front commitments required
• Fast awareness	
• Sponsorship availability	
• Merchandising possible	
Radio	
• Low cost per contact	• Nonintrusive medium
• Audience selectivity	• Audience per spot small
• Schedule when needed	• No visual impact
• Length can vary	• High total cost for good reach
• Personalities available	• Cluttered
• Tailor weight to market	
Magazines	
• Audience selectivity	• Long lead time needed
• Editorial association	• Readership accumulates slowly
• Long life	• Uneven delivery by market
• Large audience per insert	• Cost premiums for regional or demographic editions
• Excellent color	
• Minimal waste	
• Merchandising possible	
Newspapers	
• Large audience	• Difficult to target narrowly
• Immediate reach	• Highest waste
• Short lead time	• High cost for multiple use
• Market flexibility	• Minimum positioning control
• Good upscale coverage	• Cluttered
Posters, billboards	
• High reach	• No depth of message
• High frequency of exposure	• High cost for broad use
• Minimal waste	• Best positions already taken
• Can localize	• No audience selectivity
• Immediate registration	• Poor coverage in some areas
• Flexible scheduling	• Minimum one-month purchase

Source: *Practical Guide: A Program Manager's Guide to Media Planning,* produced by the SOMARC Project, The Futures Group International, 1995, under contract to USAID CCP-3051-C-00-2016-00. Reprinted with permission.

new productions or services or going after an undefined target market. Maximizing reach has the best results when the purchase is planned, when there is high interest and loyalty on the part of the patrons, when the organization is mature and clearly superior, when the ad is simple, and when there are few competitors and therefore an uncluttered marketplace. One can extend reach by going on several radio stations at the same time (called *roadblocking*) or by advertising at several different times of day to reach the widest variety of listeners.

Frequency is more important where there are strong competitors, a complex story to tell, high consumer resistance, or a frequent purchase cycle. High frequency pays off for unplanned purchases, when there is low interest and loyalty, or when the product and/or the campaign is new. Advertising repetition deals with the problem of forgetting by putting the message back into memory. Many advertisers believe that a target audience needs a large number of exposures for the advertising to work. Too few repetitions can be a waste, since they will hardly be noticed. Krugman favors three exposures to an advertisement:

> The first exposure is by definition unique. As with the initial exposure to anything, a "What is it?" type of cognitive response dominates the reaction. The second exposure to a stimulus . . . produces several effects. One may be the cognitive reaction that characterized the first exposure, if the audience missed much of the message the first time around. . . . More often, an evaluative "What of it?" response replaces the "What is it?" response. . . . The third exposure constitutes a reminder, if a decision to buy based on the evaluations has not been acted on. The third exposure is also the beginning of disengagement and withdrawal of attention.[6]

Here Krugman means three *advertising exposures*—i.e., the person actually sees the ad three times. This should not be confused with *vehicle exposures,* namely, the number of times the person has been exposed to the vehicle carrying the ad. If only half the readers look at the ads, or if readers look at the ads only every other issue, then the advertising exposure is only half of the vehicle exposures. A media strategist would have to buy more vehicle exposures than three in order to achieve Krugman's three "hits."[7]

Assume a Chicago theater places ads in three local newspapers. The *Chicago Tribune* has circulation of 710,000; the *Chicago Sun Times* has circulation of 625,000; and the *Chicago Reader* has circulation of 137,000. Reach and average frequency can be calculated as follows: Assume that there is overlap (called duplication) of readership between the *Tribune* and the *Reader* of 80,000; between the *Sun Times* and the *Reader* of 40,000; and virtually no overlap between the *Tribune* and the *Sun Times*. By subtracting the duplication (120,000) from the gross audience of 1,472,000 (710,000 + 625,000 + 137,000) one derives the reach of 1,352,000 people or households. Average frequency can now be computed. Assume the ad is placed for three consecutive weeks. The gross audience equals the reach multiplied by the average frequency (1,472,000 × 3 weeks = 4,416,000), so the average frequency is about 3.27 (4,416,000 ÷

1,352,000). Thus, our three-vehicle schedule provides 4,416,000 exposures, reaches 1,352,000 different people or households, and reaches each household or person an average of 3.27 times.

To determine the impact value of each vehicle, the theater conducts an audience survey. It discovers that more patrons read the *Tribune* than the *Sun Times* and that frequent arts attenders are more likely to seek out the *Reader*—a free weekly distributed in bulk to various locations. Therefore, the *Tribune* and the *Reader* have a higher impact value (higher advertising exposure per vehicle exposure) than the *Sun Times* for this theater. Radio is considered to be the prime media for a strategy that emphasizes frequency. Most people listen to only one or two stations, so they are likely to hear repetitions. Also, radio is intrusive at the time of consumption, making the exposure value high.

Advertisers have long debated the trade-off in budgeting for reach versus frequency. Until recent years, it was common to favor a reach approach. Budgets were adequate to ensure reasonable frequency and still achieve high levels of reach. But as media costs have escalated dramatically in the past several years, advertisers have begun to reduce reach in order to insure adequate frequency levels. In the performing arts, multimedia advertising is usually more effective than single-media advertising. Radio advertising can be used just before and after brochures are mailed to call attention to them to build subscriptions or memberships. A radio ad can direct a listener to see a print ad for details or for a coupon. Reference to a print ad is especially useful when the radio spot is short or when there is more information than can be retained during one or two hearings.

SAN FRANCISCO BALLET: *THE NUTCRACKER* BROADCAST AND OUTDOOR MEDIA STRATEGY		
	Spot TV:	Spot TV will be utilized for its mass reach capability and visual appeal to create awareness of *The Nutcracker* performances.
	Spot Radio:	Spot radio will provide frequency and ticket purchase information concerning dates, prices, and performance times to drive sales. Sixty-second units allow for a detailed message to communicate the broad appeal of the ballet. Spot radio offers the flexibility to change tags, announce promotions, or provide a call to action (purchase).
	Outdoor:	Outdoor stationary billboards, a two-sided mobile billboard to be driven through the downtown San Francisco shopping district, and bus shelter billboards will be used for added awareness with a visual image. The mobile billboard will also broadcast the *Nutcracker* theme and cut through ordinary traffic noise.

SELECTING SPECIFIC MEDIA VEHICLES

The next step is to choose the specific media vehicles within each media category that will produce the desired response in the most cost-effective way. The wide array of radio stations, TV channels, daily and weekly newspapers, other publications, and Internet advertising spell a condition of extreme media fragmentation, which may allow advertisers to reach special-interest groups more effectively but which raises the cost of reaching general audiences. To help make choices among the available media, the media planner relies on services that provide estimates of audience size, composition, and media cost. Audience size can be measured in several ways:

- *Circulation:* The number of physical vehicle units through which advertising is distributed.

- *Audience:* The number of people who are exposed to the vehicle. (If the vehicle has pass-on readership, then the audience is larger than the circulation.)

- *Effective audience:* The number of people with the target's characteristics who are exposed to the vehicle.

- *Effective ad-exposed audience:* The number of people with the target's characteristics who actually saw the ad.

Media planners normally calculate the *cost per thousand* people reached by a particular vehicle. Assume a theater company decides to use local newspaper advertising. A half-page ad in the *Chicago Tribune* costs $5,915; a half-page ad in the *Chicago Reader* costs $1,120. With a reach of 710,000, the cost per thousand for the *Tribune* is $8.33; with a reach of 137,000, the cost per thousand for the *Reader* is $8.18. So the *Reader* ad is nearly equal in cost, in terms of the potential audience it reaches.

Several adjustments have to be applied. First, the advertiser should consider *audience quality;* for a *Nutcracker* advertisement, a magazine read by 100,000 mothers with children aged 5–12 would have a higher exposure value than a magazine read by 500,000 elderly men or college students. Second, the exposure value should be adjusted for *audience-attention probability.* For example, readers of cooking, gardening, and fashion publications pay more attention to advertisements than do readers of news magazines. Third, the exposure value should be adjusted for the *editorial quality* (prestige and believability) that one publication might have over another. Fourth, the exposure value should be adjusted to account for the magazine's ad placement policies and extra services (such as special editions and lead time requirements).

Creativity is clearly needed in choosing media. In the absence of hard data, one must make subjective judgments about a vehicle's effectiveness. It is useful to construct a scenario of how consumers go about choosing cultural events to attend and then to speculate about when and how advertising messages should appear.

Deciding on the Timing of Media Exposure

In timing the use of media, the advertiser faces a macroscheduling problem and a microscheduling problem. The macro problem is that of *cyclical* or *seasonal* timing. Audience size and interest vary at different times of the year. Most marketers do not advertise when there is little interest, but spend the bulk of their advertising budgets just as natural interest in the offering begins to increase and when it peaks. At times when there is much habitual purchasing, such as for subscription renewals, lead time for advertising should be greater and advertising expenditures should be steadier, peaking before the sales peak. The timing of advertising for individual ticket sales is more complex. Interest must be stimulated as far as possible in advance of the opening to fill seats before word of mouth and (hopefully) good reviews have a chance to help the advertising effort. Advance advertising is especially important when there is a low subscriber base and when there will be few performances of each production, such as with orchestral concerts. Then advertising must help build demand through the production run and for less popular performance days and times.

The microscheduling problem calls for allocating expenditures within a short period to obtain the maximum impact. For example, how should advertising be spaced during a one-week period? Consider three possible patterns. The first is called *burst advertising* and consists of concentrating all the exposures in a very short period of time, say all in one day. Presumably, this will attract maximum attention and interest; and, if recall is good, the effect will last for a while. Choosing the day of the week depends on the performance day(s) the advertiser is trying to promote and on knowing when the target audience makes its purchase decisions. Are people more likely to decide on Monday or on Friday what they will do on Saturday night?

The second pattern is *continuous advertising,* in which the exposures appear evenly throughout the period. Continuity may provide the highest level of exposures and reminder value, but also carries the greatest costs. The third pattern is *intermittent advertising,* in which intermittent small bursts of advertising appear with no advertising in between *(flighting)* or continuous advertising at low weight levels is reinforced periodically by waves of heavier activity *(pulsing).* These intermittent strategies draw upon the reminder value strength of continuous advertising but at lower cost, and many advertisers feel they provide a stronger signal than a continuous approach.

THE SAN FRANCISCO BALLET: *THE NUTCRACKER* MEDIA TIMING: SPOT RADIO

- Spot radio will air continuously from the week of Thanksgiving through opening week. Additional spot radio will air during the first half of the final week to push ticket sales to performances not sold out.

- Flighting: Point levels will be increased during key periods such as the week of Thanksgiving and opening week.

- Spots will air continuously from 6:00 A.M. to midnight, with heavier weight levels when listenership is greater, such as morning and evening drive time.

- Selective programming on jazz, light/soft rock, and news stations, along with traffic updates, will reach commuters when alternative media consumption is low.

- Spots will air on approximately 6–7 stations, 20–25 times per week. Average frequency will be 8.7 vehicle exposures.

Advertising on the Internet

In the short span of its existence, the World Wide Web has become a major marketing tool and its use is expected to grow astronomically over the next several years. A Web site provides myriad benefits for performing arts organizations and their publics. "Its efficiencies are stunning," says Robert Bourne, president of Pegasus Internet, Inc., which provides Internet services to, among others, the New York Philharmonic, the San Francisco Symphony, the Ravinia Festival, the Brooklyn Academy of Music, the Metropolitan Opera, and the European Mozart Foundation.[8] Bourne notes that maintaining and updating a Web site for one year costs only about $5,000 to $6,000—less than the cost of a one-page print ad in the *New York Times.* For that modest price, the organization can provide in-depth text, photos, sound, and interactive capabilities. Furthermore, a Web site provides worldwide reach and perpetual frequency, which virtually no organization can afford through any other medium. Each site can be readily analyzed for the number of "hits" it has received; on which pages; for how long; and whether the users have dialed in from commercial, educational, or international lines. In addition, zip codes of the dial-up number can be retrieved. One major orchestra has been receiving about 100,000 hits a month with visitors from fifty countries. An arts organization's Web site also provides attractive sponsorship opportunities, although they are difficult to value because they have no precedent and site traffic cannot be evaluated for specific demographic information that would indicate whether the sponsor's target market is being reached.

The San Francisco Symphony has one of the most complete Web sites available at the time of this writing. Visit the site at http://www.sfsymphony.org or surf the following description of the site.

THE SAN FRANCISCO SYMPHONY'S WEB SITE

At the San Francisco Symphony's Web site, a visitor can explore a wide variety of information. There is an overview of the symphony, including a photograph of orchestra members at the Golden Gate Bridge, the mission statement, historical information, milestones, and messages from the Maestro and the symphony president. Upcoming concert and event highlights are followed by concert listings for the entire season and concert hall information, including directions to the hall and seating charts with views of the stage from various seating areas; listings of nearby restaurants and lodging; and on-line links to hotels, restaurants, and other attractions. Ticket information features a special discount ticket offer for Web visitors and an order form that can be phoned, e-mailed, or faxed to the box office. (Credit card information is obtained through a secure process.) There are biographies of Michael Tilson Thomas and past conductors, and descriptions of orchestra members, the youth orchestra, and the chorus. Visitors can even listen to excerpts from San Francisco Symphony recordings and browse through a list of nationally syndicated San Francisco Symphony radio broadcasts. The latest in San Francisco Symphony news and press releases are available at the click of a mouse. Also available is information on the symphony's educational programs, sponsorship and volunteering opportunities, memberships, and administrative personnel. Through links to other Web sites related to classical music, browsers can access indexes, other symphony orchestra sites, and beginners' guides to music, composers, and recordings. Finally, contact information allows the visitor to send e-mail directly to the music director, the ticket services director, the marketing director, the public relations director, the director of information services, the director of education, or the development director. The visitor can also arrange to be added to the symphony's mailing list.

What more is yet to come? Robert Bourne says that the technology exists now for an arts organization's on-line schedule to be made interactive, so that the concert schedule can be dragged into the visitor's personal organizer software. And before long, symphonies and opera companies (maybe even theaters and dance companies) will be offering audio (and video) excerpts from upcoming programs. The possibilities are endless.

Evaluating Advertising Effectiveness

The final step in the effective use of advertising is evaluation. The most important components are copy testing, media testing, and expenditure-level testing. Copy testing can be done both before an ad is put into actual media and after it has been printed or broadcast.

COPY PRETESTING

The purpose of ad pretesting is to make improvements in the advertising copy to the fullest extent possible prior to its release. The copy should be evaluated to see how well it meets the following criteria:

- *Attention:* How well does the ad catch the reader's attention?
- *Comprehension strength:* How understandable are the words and sentences to the target audience?
- *Follow-through strength:* How well does the ad lead the reader/listener to read/listen further?
- *Cognitive strength:* How clear is the central message or benefit?
- *Affective strength:* How effective is the particular appeal?
- *Behavioral strength*: How well does the ad suggest follow-through action?

An effective ad must score high on all these properties if it is ultimately to stimulate buying action. Too often, ads are evaluated only for their attention-getting or comprehension-creating abilities.

To gather information about the strength of an ad, marketers may show or mail a set of alternative ads to a panel of target consumers or advertising experts and ask them, "Which of these ads do you think would influence you most to buy the offering?" Or a more elaborate form consisting of rating scales may be used, asking respondents to evaluate the ads' attention strength, comprehensibility, cognitive strength, read-through strength, affective strength, and behavioral strength, assigning a number of points (up to a maximum) in each case. Alternatively, since advertisements are often viewed in a group setting, pretests with focus groups can often shed light on how a message is perceived as well as how it might be passed along. The focus-group technique also has the advantages that its synergism can generate more reactions than a one-on-one session, it is more efficient because it gathers data from six to twelve people at once, and it can yield data relatively quickly.

Pretesting, however, requires subjective judgments and is less reliable than the harder evidence of an ad's actual impact on target consumers. Pretesting is more helpful for screening out poor ads than for identifying great ads.

AD POSTTESTING

The purpose of ad posttesting is to assess whether the desired impact is being achieved. One is tempted to use sales as the measure of success. But sales are influenced by many factors besides advertising, such as the nature of the offering itself, price, availability, and the competitive climate. The fewer or more controllable these other factors are, the easier it is to measure the effect of advertising on sales.

Ads may be posttested for their copy, media, and expenditure levels. To test copy and media, marketers may ask consumers of the media vehicle to recall advertisers and products contained in the issue or broadcast (ad recall) or to point out what they remember having seen or read before (ad recognition). But these methods test only the *cognitive* outcomes of advertising. To posttest the effectiveness of alternative messages or media in influencing *behavior,* the advertiser may use techniques such as these:

- Place mail-back coupons in the advertisement. Each coupon should carry a code or post office box address that varies by message and medium.

- Ask target audience members to mention or bring in an advertisement in order to receive special treatment (such as a price discount or free parking).

- Ask individuals to call for further information (on which occasion they can be asked where they saw the ad, what they remember, and so on).

- Stagger the placement of ads so that this week's attendance or sales can be attributed to ad A while next week's can be attributed to ad B. This is also an effective method for assessing alternative expenditure levels.

To further test expenditure levels, staggering may be done by geographic area, so that the organization spends more in some neighborhoods and less in others. These tactics are called *high-spending tests* and *low-spending tests.* If the high-spending tests produce substantial sales increases, it appears that the organization has been underspending. If they fail to produce more sales and if low-spending tests do not lead to sales decreases, then the organization has been overspending. These tests, of course, must be accompanied by good experimental controls and must last sufficiently long to capture lagged effects of changes in expenditure levels.

Marketers can learn a great deal about the effectiveness of alternative message and media strategies by designing experiments coupled with careful posttest measures and by accumulating their insights over time.

SALES PROMOTION

Sales promotion comprises a wide variety of tactical promotional tools, mostly short-term, designed to stimulate earlier or stronger target market response. Overall, sales promotion tools make three contributions:

1. *Communication:* They gain attention and usually provide information that will, it is hoped, lead to trying the product.

2. *Incentive:* They incorporate some concession, inducement, or contribution that is designed to represent value to the receiver.

3. *Invitation:* They include a distinct invitation to engage in the transaction now.

Two tickets for the price of one attracts new triers and increases the repurchase rates of occasional users. Special gifts with a new subscription, discounted dinner-theater packages at nearby restaurants, and subscriber parties reward loyal customers.

The *incentive* is the core benefit of the sales promotion. An incentive can be defined as something of financial or symbolic value added to an offer to encourage some overt behavioral response. The marketing challenge is to design an incentive that attracts the target audience *and* serves the organization's long-run interests.

Consider the sales promotion efforts of the Los Angeles Philharmonic carried out through their annual radiothon.

SALES PROMOTION AT THE LOS ANGELES PHILHARMONIC

In 1993, the Los Angeles Philharmonic raised $170,000 in donations and new subscriptions through its "radiothon." To stimulate the new subscriptions, generous premiums, such as compact discs and dinners at local restaurants, were offered. (The premiums were donated, but production costs and newspaper advertising associated with the radiothon cost the organization $100,000.)

Many of those who responded to the subscription offer were first time concertgoers, attracted not by the musical offerings but by the premiums. As a result, 70 percent of these new subscribers were lost after the first year, a much higher drop-off rate than is usually experienced by the organization. Said marketing director Stephen Belth in response, "The more gimmicks it takes to bring them in, the harder it is to hold on to them."[9]

Planning Sales Promotions

To avoid such pitfalls, the marketer must analyze several factors. The first step is to specify the *objective(s)* for which the incentive is undertaken. If the organization has excess capacity and wants to sell tickets for upcoming performances, it may announce half-price tickets or two tickets for the price of one for this week only. If the goal is to stimulate interest over the run of a production, marketers might stuff programs with discount coupons for patrons to share with their friends. If the objective is to promote trial among never-attenders, an orchestra may offer a free concert in the park, a special concert that samples the upcoming season, or a "singles" reception with performers after the program. If the objective is to encourage patrons to resubscribe early, additional discounts or other special perks may be offered until a specified date.

The next step is to specify the *recipient* of the incentive. For example, when stimulating group sales, should the incentive be offered to each group member, to the membership group itself, or to the sales agents?

The marketer must also determine the *form* of the incentive—whether it will consist of free or discounted tickets, special events, or gifts. The more closely the incentive is tied to the organization's desired outcomes, the more effective it will be in the long run. Therefore, offering one free ticket with every five ticket stubs saved is likely to stimulate more frequent attendance than the offer of a mug or a T-shirt.

The marketer must also determine the *amount* and *duration* of the incentive offer. Too small an incentive is ineffective and an overly large one is wasteful. The amount may be graduated to vary with the consumer's economic circumstances or interest in the offer. In such cases, the market must be carefully segmented so that the offers can be controlled and so that other segments are not offended by them. Special discounts to teens and seniors for certain performances are commonly accepted practices of this kind. The organization may want to limit the time span and availability of the incentive offer. If half-price tickets are always available the day of the performance and the public knows that the house rarely sells out, the organization will have difficulty ever selling tickets at full price. If 50 percent discounts are offered to new subscribers, the marketer must determine whether this offer will have to be repeated in subsequent years in order to keep those subscribers. In general, the marketer must carefully analyze whether the short-term value of the offer is worthwhile to the organization in the long run.

Major Promotion Tools

Consumer promotion tools regularly used by the business sector are highly useful in the nonprofit arts sector as well. This section describes some of the major consumer promotion tools.

SAMPLES (FREE TRIALS)

Offering a free sample is usually the most effective way to introduce a new product or to introduce new people to the offering. For arts organizations, a sample is usually inexpensive to provide, since filling an empty seat carries little or no cost. A theater may enclose two free guest tickets with each subscription so that patrons will encourage their friends to attend. An orchestra may sponsor a free concert in a targeted neighborhood.

COUPONS

Coupons are certificates entitling the bearer to a stated saving on the purchase of a specific offering. Coupons can be mailed separately, enclosed with tickets, inserted in magazine and newspaper ads, or combined with offers from other organizations. Coupon books may be purchased in advance, entitling the bearer to stated discounts under certain conditions. The Ravinia Festival sells coupon books in advance of and two weeks into the season at a 20 percent discount. The coupons can be redeemed for tickets throughout the summer season. The Los Angeles Philharmonic sells "Philharmoney" coupons for $20 each that are redeemable for the best seats available at the time of purchase. Experts believe that coupons should provide at least a 15 to 20 percent saving to be effective.

PRICE PACKS

Price packs are offers to consumers of savings off the regular price of an offering. They can take the form of reduced-price packs, such as single tickets sold at a reduced price (such as two for the price of one) or a subscription with five plays for the price of four, or banded packs, in which two related products are banded together (such as a theater performance along with a meal at a nearby restaurant). Price packs are even more effective than coupons at stimulating short-term sales.

HALF-PRICE SALE AT PENN STATE	At the start of each school year in September, the Center for Performing Arts at Penn State has a one-day-only half-price ticket sale. Not all events are available for half price; just the events that need a little extra promotion. The event is made fun and festive for the fifty to one hundred students who wait in line at any given time throughout the day. An annual theme is conceived highlighting one of the events on the season. When the musical *Buddy* was presented, the staff dressed up in fifties garb, a fifties vintage car was parked in front of the theater, and Bazooka Joe bubble gum was given away. The next year, the musical *Oklahoma* was promoted with a horse-drawn surrey. The sale is a success each year, establishing a sense of excitement and encouraging students to buy early and frequently.[10]

PREMIUMS

Premiums, or gifts, are merchandise offered at a relatively low cost, or free, as an incentive to purchase a particular product. Free premiums may be offered, for example, as gifts with a subscription or contribution or as a special perk at a performance. Consumers are also offered for sale all kinds of premiums bearing the organization's name: T-shirts, mugs, tote bags, and so on.

PREMIUMS FOR FUN AND AWARENESS BUILDING	The Performing Arts Center at Penn State developed a marketing campaign to attract younger audiences for its classical music series. The campaign image featured a graphic of a Beethoven-like bust wearing sunglasses, and prominently featured the tag line "COOL CLASSICS in the hot summer." Sunglasses marked with the series name and logo were given away to students who purchased concert tickets. Students wore the sunglasses, talked about the series, and stimulated further sales.[11]

TIE-IN PROMOTIONS

Tie-in promotions are collaborative offerings between two or more organizations or between arts organizations and the business or public sector. Economic impact studies have shown that for every dollar spent on a performing arts ticket, another $10 to

$12 is spent on related businesses such as restaurants, parking facilities, and even the dry cleaners.[12] So it is only natural that such businesses would collaborate with arts organizations patronized by their current and potential customers. The San Jose "Arts Card," described in Chapter 7, jointly benefits a number of organizations and businesses as well as the consumers they serve.

PATRONAGE AWARDS

Patronage awards are values given in proportion to one's patronage of the organization. Consider the frequent ticket buyer program described in Chapter 11, which provides free tickets after a minimum number of tickets have been purchased (similar to the airlines' frequent flyer plans). Some orchestras and opera companies have exclusive "green rooms" where contributors at certain levels may dine before a performance or have drinks during intermission. Other patronage awards may be the opportunity to have dinner with the artists after a performance or eligibility for the best seats in the house.

Benefits of Sales Promotion

Sales promotion provides important benefits to organizations and their consumers. Promotions enable organizations to fill empty seats and adjust to short-term fluctuations in supply and demand. They induce consumers to try new offerings, and they promote greater consumer awareness of products and prices. They permit organizations to adapt programs to specific consumer segments. They build partnerships among arts organizations and local businesses. Sales promotions also enhance the patrons' experiences. Consumers enjoy the satisfaction of being smart shoppers when they take advantage of price specials. Successful promotions create a sense of excitement about an event, a season, or an organization—and an eagerness to return.

---

[1] The information on the San Francisco Ballet's Media Plan for its 1993 *Nutcracker* production is courtesy of Hal Riney & Partners Advertising, San Francisco, California.

[2] Advertising costs quoted in this chapter are as of 1994.

[3] Laura R. Zarco, "Radio: The Cinderella Medium," *Arts Reach*, Feb./Mar. 1993, 10–12.

[4] Maddy Morton, "Aida Comes Alive," *International Arts Manager,* Nov. 1994, 26.

[5] Bob Schulberg, *Radio Advertising: The Authoritative Handbook* (Lincolnwood, Ill.: NTC Business Books, 1989).

[6] Herbert E. Krugman, "What Makes Advertising Effective?" *Harvard Business Review,* Mar./Apr. 1975, 98.

[7] See Peggy J. Kreshel, Kent M. Lancaster, and Margaret A. Toomey, "Advertising Media Planning: How Leading Advertising Agencies Estimate Effective Reach and Frequency" (Urbana: University of Illinois Department of Advertising, paper no. 20, Jan. 1985). Also see Jack Z. Sissors and Lincoln Bumba, *Advertising Media Planning,* 3rd ed. (Lincolnwood, Ill.: NTC Business Books, 1989), chap. 9.

[8] Robert Bourne, personal communication, April 1996.

[9] Stephen Belth, personal communication.

[10] Rick Feingold, "Promotions That Sizzle," *Arts Reach,* Feb./Mar. 1994, 18–19.

[11] Ibid., 19.

[12] Reported by Schuyler G. Chapin, Commissioner of Cultural Affairs, New York City at a meeting of the Arts and Business Council of Chicago, Sept. 13, 1994.

EMPLOYING DIRECT MARKETING AND DATABASE MARKETING

CLASSICAL ADVERTISING, IN SPITE OF ITS REACH, IS LIMITED IN ITS ABILITY TO serve the strategic communications goals of the marketer. Mass media can easily miss significant segments of the target market. Since ad messages must be broad-based in order to appeal to diverse patrons, it cannot establish one-to-one relationships with specific groups or individuals. In fact, some marketers claim that as a result of changing households, complex products, new ways to shop and pay, intense competition, and declining advertising effectiveness, mass marketing is obsolete.

Direct marketing provides an answer to many of these problems. Direct marketing, usually accomplished through direct mail and telemarketing, is the best way to nurture contacts, obtain sales, and procure information about patrons. Selling via personal communication has been used successfully throughout the ages; with modern telecommunication tools, personalized computer-generated letters, and the many applications of a customer database, the scope of direct marketing techniques is nearly limitless.

This chapter discusses the advantages of direct marketing; how arts organizations can effectively make use of direct marketing—including mail, telemarketing, and integrated direct marketing; and how they can develop and maintain productive customer databases and marketing contact lists.

ADVANTAGES AND TOOLS OF DIRECT MARKETING

Performing arts organizations are major users of direct marketing. The reasons are clear when one views the several advantages of direct marketing:

- *Selectivity:* Direct marketing allows greater prospect selectivity. A direct marketer can send one letter to first-time subscribers, another to long-term subscribers, and still another to onetime single-ticket buyers. The marketer can buy a mailing list containing the names of almost any group: people who rent the classics at their local video store, millionaires, people who work downtown and live in the suburbs, people who are empty-nesters, and so on.

- *Personalization:* Direct marketing provides the opportunity to personalize and customize the message to different persons and groups. *Romeo and Juliet* can be described to Shakespeare lovers as one of the Bard's greatest plays; to musical theater–goers as the "original" *West Side Story;* and to high school students as a story of doomed teenage lovers.

- *Relationship building:* Direct marketing can be used to build a stronger relationship with each customer. A theater can encourage a onetime theatergoer to try a three-play package; and a two- or three-time theatergoer to subscribe to five plays for the price of four. The theater can contact lapsed subscribers to discover how better to meet their needs. By appealing to customers' individual needs and preferences, marketers can increase consumers' interest, frequency of attendance, and loyalty.

- *Timing:* Direct marketing can be timed more precisely than advertising to reach prospects at the right moment. For example, a theater can offer long-standing subscribers a new second-stage series before the season begins. However, the marketer may wish to wait until after the first play of the season to promote a second series to new subscribers.

- *Attention:* Direct marketing material receives a higher percentage of readership than advertisements because it reaches better prospects. In addition, consumers are more likely to pay attention to messages that are specifically directed at them. This targeted approach reduces the waste inherent in any mass media advertising campaign, often resulting in lower marketing costs.

- *Research:* Direct marketing permits testing alternative media and messages (headline, salutations, benefits, prices) in the search for the most effective approach. And the direct marketer knows whether the campaign has been profitable because the response can be measured.

The most common direct-marketing tools are direct mail and telemarketing. Direct mail has the advantage of being virtually limitless in scope and relatively inexpensive per piece: an organization can increase its mailing from 10,000 to 100,000 pieces for little more effort, and if the list is well selected, the payback will more than cover the additional cost. Telemarketing is more expensive but has the advantage of being more personal and more interactive, helping the organization to build relationships with its customers. Integrated direct marketing incorporates the strengths of direct mail and telemarketing in one campaign. Database marketing enables an organization to achieve much more target market precision than mass marketing, segment marketing, or niche marketing. The organization can send fine-tuned marketing offers and communications to small groups or individuals and nurture a closer relationship.

MANAGING DIRECT MAIL

Direct mail is used in audience building to sell an offering, usually a subscription or membership; to collect or qualify leads for further follow-up, such as with response cards; to communicate some interesting news, such as a special performance, an award, or a rave review; or to reward loyal customers with a gift, such as two free tickets to a dress rehearsal. Direct mail is commonly and effectively used for fundraising purposes as well, as will be discussed in Chapter 18.

Well-conceived, well-executed, and well-targeted direct mail is the primary tool for customer retention and renewal. Susan Mathieson, marketing and communications director of Chicago's successful Lyric Opera, believes that direct mail is and always will be the workhorse of subscription campaigns. In a survey of five hundred performing arts presenters, direct mail was found to surpass all other marketing methods in effectiveness, followed by paid advertising, unpaid promotions, telemarketing, posters and handbills, and direct sales.[1] Direct mail is a necessary component of a telemarketing campaign and is important to use in conjunction with mass media approaches to promotion. Arts marketers are effectively focusing more and more of their efforts on segmenting available mailing lists, developing new resources for lists, and creating appropriate mailings for their target segments.

Consider how immediate and effective a response the English National Opera achieved through direct mail.

DIRECT MAIL SCORES AT THE ENGLISH NATIONAL OPERA

In a period of just a few months, Maddy Morton, the new marketing director at the English National Opera (ENO) helped stimulate a 30 percent increase in ticket sales for the 1994 season after instituting a box office monitoring system. Everyone who called to book a ticket was asked where they heard about the performance—mail, poster, press, or broadcast. The effectiveness of each medium was then plotted.[2]

The monitoring showed that direct mail to ENO's 70,000-name list was by far the most effective marketing tool. Morton then engaged an independent consultant to identify an additional 25,000 names consistent with the current audience profile. These people were mailed the repertory brochure, increasing the percentage of the marketing budget allocated for direct mail from less than 20 percent to almost 30 percent.

Posters, which were accounting for about 27 percent of the £850,000 annual marketing budget, were generating only 3 percent of sales. However, Morton decided not to drastically cut the poster budget because the posters "perform a branding function which is not quantifiable, but without which we risk damaging the effectiveness of our more tactical activities."

Target Customers

Direct marketers need to determine the characteristics that distinguish customers and prospects who will be most able, willing, and ready to buy. Bob Stone recommends applying the R-F-M formula (recency, frequency, monetary amount) for rating and selecting customers from a list.[3] The best customer targets are those who bought most recently, who buy frequently, and who spend the most. Points are established for varying R-F-M levels, and each customer is scored; the higher the score, the more attractive the customer. Names may be selected from among the organization's own lists, from lists exchanged with other arts organizations, or from lists purchased from mailing list brokers. Direct marketers typically buy a subsample of names from a potential list and do a test mailing to see if the response rate is high enough. Direct mail allows for easy testing and measuring of results. The Lyric Opera of Chicago found, to its surprise, that it gained a better response from new members of the Art Institute than from longtime Art Institute contributors who were not regular museum visitors.

To target new prospects, the direct marketer can use various segmentation criteria. Good prospects can be identified on the basis of such demographic variables as age, gender, income, education, and where they live and work. Geodemographic list building allows the marketer to target neighborhoods of culture enthusiasts. Segments based on consumer lifestyles, such as the culturally and socially active, are being used creatively and effectively by many organizations to identify potential customers for whom the organization's offerings should be appealing.

Once the target market is defined, the direct marketer's task is to obtain names of good prospects. Whether the target market consists of previous attenders who are part of the organization's own house list or prospects to be sought from outside lists, direct marketers need good list management and acquisition skills. Some strategies and tools for developing comprehensive and up-to-date lists are presented at the end of this chapter.

Components of Direct Mail

Direct-mail researchers have carefully studied how to effectively use the following key components of a direct-mail program: envelope and contents, cover letter (headline, salutation, body copy, postscript), brochure (offer, body copy, front cover, back cover, order form), response card, and special mailings.

THE ENVELOPE AND CONTENTS

The first challenge of the direct-mail marketer is to interest the recipient in reading the mail piece. The most common consumer response to a direct-mail piece is to throw it away. The typical recipient spends about twenty seconds deciding whether to give the mailing serious attention. The marketer must stimulate enough interest on the envelope's exterior that people will be motivated to open it. The envelope should contain a clear, compelling, short message. The marketer may put the headline or main selling proposition right on the envelope, and/or arouse reader curiosity with teaser copy.

Consider the following examples used by various performing arts organizations:

- "Urgent! Dated renewal information enclosed."
- "Create your own series and save up to 20%."
- "Subscribers get up to two plays free!"
- "Subscribe now. Celebrate all year."
- "Wanna Play?"
- "Exercise your imagination."

At the Lyric Opera, the past-the-deadline renewal letter is enclosed along with a copy of the season brochure in an 8½-by-11-inch envelope that says in bold red lettering: "30,217 Lyric subscribers have already enrolled for the fabulous 94/95 season . . . and you can still get in if you subscribe *NOW! (details inside)*." Under this copy is a sketch of a man running while holding on tightly to his seat (emblazoned with the Lyric logo) while a crowd of people are chasing after him (presumably after the seat).

On average, recipients take about eight seconds to scan and open the envelope. For the next four seconds, enclosures are unfolded and the reader builds up judgments about the contents even before a single word has been read. The final eight seconds consist of the first run-through: reading the pictures and headlines, finding short answers to the reader's unspoken but already present questions, such as "What are the advantages? Does this offer apply to me? Is it better than other similar offers? What will it cost me?"[4] The marketer should be sure to use pictures, headlines, captions, and other methods to express the offer's advantages as strongly and succinctly as possible.

If the package has "survived" the first twenty seconds, the recipient is likely to undergo a more comprehensive process: reading blocks of text and gaining more in-depth information. This is when the body copy of the letter or the brochure's descriptions are put to test. After reading the copy in some detail, the reader will do one of three things: throw it away, place an order, or file the mail piece away to be reconsidered at a later date. Putting something to the side is better than throwing it away, but what is out of sight is also out of mind. Responses are usually brought about only by a new external stimulus. This is why Danny Newman advises mailing brochures to the same household several times in one season.

THE LETTER

The direct-mail piece is the modern-day equivalent of the personal sales call. The letter represents the "contact stage." Because of this, direct-mail campaigns, even with elaborate brochures, almost always bring in a higher number of responses when they contain a separate letter. The Lyric Opera of Chicago sends not only a brochure but also a carefully crafted letter and a return envelope. Through these letters, marketing director Susan Mathieson has *doubled* the response from such key groups as lapsed subscribers, single-ticket buyers, donors who do not attend, and people who call asking for information.

Bob Stone offers a seven-step formula for writing a successful letter:[5]

1. Promise a benefit in the headline or in the first paragraph. Most people won't read an unsolicited letter unless they see a clear benefit.

2. Enlarge on the most important benefit. If the lead is relevant, you can build interest without reader diversion.

3. Give details about basic product features. If you expect readers to take action, they must know what they are getting.

4. Support your statements with proof. You can dispel the normal reader's skepticism if you can support your claims with demonstrable facts.

5. Tell readers why they should act. By introducing a sense of urgency, you can put the readers in a receptive frame of mind before you get to the closing.

6. Rephrase prominent benefits in your closing. By summing up the main benefits, you reinforce preferences built previously.

7. End with a call for action. Use a strong, urgent closing. This is your moment of truth.

The headline   Some letters carry headlines, which act as good attention-getters when they are succinct, catchy, and to the point. A tactic resembling a headline is the so-called Johnson box. It consists of a sentence or two above the salutation that summarizes the proposition's main points. The headline makes sure that the offer's highlights and benefits are not buried in copy.[6]

The salutation   One of the first things the reader sees is the salutation. The Lyric Opera varies the salutation in its letter to each target group. One letter is addressed to "Friends of Lyric" and says: "I know that you have purchased Lyric Opera tickets in the past, and now I would like you to seriously consider becoming a full-fledged member of the Lyric family by joining us as a season subscriber." Another letter is addressed to "Former Subscriber" and says in part: "I know that you have been a Lyric subscriber in the past, and there has never been a better opportunity for you to 'return to the family.'"

The body copy   On reading a letter, the reader immediately has many questions, which build up into a silent dialogue: "What will I get out of this for myself?" "How will it help me to find out about or experience something new?" "Is this right for me?" "Will I find it comfortable and enjoyable?" "Will it provide me with a personal advantage?" The marketer should always give an answer that either spells out the advantages or arouses curiosity. The organization's claim to offer something the customer wants will make sense only if the advantages of the offer are immediately apparent to the reader.

Next, people have questions—which vary from segment to segment—about the product itself: productions, performers, pricing, packages, locations, and amenities. The offerings should be clearly described, especially in the case of organizations that have a multitude of offerings.

It is important for the marketer to balance information about personal benefits and about product features in the letter. The more readers know about the offering, the less the personal benefits should be emphasized. When a product's features are obvious (an evening with Luciano Pavarotti, a production of an award-winning play), the consumer can usually infer the benefits. The letter should be long enough to do the selling job but not so long as to erode reader interest. It should have a personal tone, creating a bond of familiarity between sender and receiver.

The letter's opening paragraph gets the most reading. It should introduce the main theme and create a desire to continue to read. The letter may open with a benefit promise or an interesting statement. The Lyric Opera says: "Twenty-five thousand people have already subscribed. You, too, can be a part of our enthusiastic subscriber family if you respond today!" The letter's body copy can then enlarge upon the subject, present data to support the selling proposition, and urge the reader to take immediate action. At the end of each letter, clear and compelling instructions should be given: "See for yourself by filling in the reply card and returning it to us today." "Pick up the phone and call our subscriber hotline at . . ." The recipient's job should be made as simple as possible. The forms should require little effort. Postage-paid reply envelopes should be provided whenever possible.

The postscript   Research into how people handle a direct-mail package indicates that readers start at the top of the letter to look at the salutation. They then turn to the end of the letter to see who is writing them. At this point, most eyes are drawn to the postscript because of its proximity to the signature—and more than 90 percent read the postscript before moving back to the top. With this in mind, some direct-mail professionals actually compose the P.S. first and then move on to write the letter's "lead."

The most effective way to write the P.S. is to state simply and precisely the offer's overall marketing concept and theme. The focus should be on the reader's perspective—the major benefit opportunities, what the reader stands to gain by responding to the offer. The P.S. should stand out from the body of the letter, perhaps handwritten by the signatory in a contrasting ink color. The tone should be warm, friendly, and energetic, and all this should be written in a few lines with short words and sentences so that it can be read quickly and easily. At the Lyric Opera, the first subscriber renewal letter has the following postscript: "Remember, if you submit your renewal by February 28 and pay in full by check, you're automatically entered in our American Airlines draw to Rio de Janeiro or Costa Rica!" In the reminder letter sent out on or about the April 1 deadline, the postscript says: "Please remember, we can only hold your seats until May 1. After this date, we must turn them over to a new subscriber!"

THE BROCHURE

The season brochure is the most basic and effective direct-mail piece for performing arts organizations. It is also the most complex. It serves to stimulate interest and excitement about the organization; to highlight special events of the upcoming season; to list and describe all the productions; to offer all possible subscription packages, subscriber benefits, options for seating locations and dates; to delineate the organization's policies regarding such issues as deadlines and ticket exchanges; to provide an easy-to-follow order form; and, in some cases, to educate the reader about specific productions and about the experience itself. All this must be accomplished in a clear, concise, and interesting manner.

The Saint Paul Chamber Orchestra has created a brochure that resembles a direct-mail instrument used commonly by retailers—the catalog. It is entitled "Feast Your Ears," and its cover offers such "gourmet" items as Vivaldi *The Four Seasons* jam, Mozart *Eine Kleine Nachtmusik* wine, Bach *Overture* cheese, and Pachebel *Canon and Gigue* coffee. Inside, the brochure continues the gourmet theme and catalog format to offer its subscriber benefits, star attractions, performance halls, and each of its subscription series.

The offer　The purpose of a brochure is to sell subscriptions. Danny Newman considers it a "cardinal sin" to offer both subscriptions and single tickets simultaneously. If offered the opportunity to order single tickets as well as subscriptions, recipients may pick the one or two most attractive events, and subscription sales may suffer. Single tickets should be made available after full-season subscriptions and shorter series have been promoted for a sufficient period. If single tickets are mentioned at all in the brochure, it should only be to say that they will be offered after subscribers have had their pick, that seat locations may be less desirable, that single tickets to popular events may not be available at all, and that single-ticket prices are higher because of subscriber discounts. The decision whether or not to offer shorter series along with full-season subscriptions depends on the organization and the nature of its offerings. A performing arts center that presents dozens of different performances each season is likely to sell the most series subscriptions by offering a wide range of package sizes and genre types in its season brochure. On the other hand, a theater that produces five plays each season may be best off waiting to offer three-play packages until the end of the full-subscription campaign. This does not mean that past holders of miniseries and flex plans should be ignored until all subscription orders are in. Rather, they should be contacted early on and encouraged to upgrade to a larger package offering, with the understanding that their plan will again be available once all subscriber orders are filled.

The brochure, which is generally mailed in the early spring, offers a series that does not begin for at least six months and may end more than a year later. It also asks people to make a significant financial outlay, especially in the case of a symphony or opera series. Therefore, an arts organization may stimulate additional subscription sales by providing the option of making a partial payment of one-third or one-half down, with the balance payable when the season begins. The brochure should point out ticket exchange privileges, special discounts, guaranteed seats, and other benefits designed especially for subscribers.

Body copy   The brochure's success is largely dependent on outstanding copy and graphics. When one musical organization faced a decline in new subscriptions, Danny Newman found that the problem lay in the brochure recipients' inability to figure out how to order any of the series being offered. (This problem did not affect subscription renewals because past subscribers had only to check on the form "Please renew my subscription".) After a new brochure was created that outlined series information in a simple-to-follow manner, new subscription sales rose dramatically.

One year, the New York Philharmonic added 10,500 new subscribers, a 500 percent gain over the previous year, due to three factors: greatly increased brochure distribution, a less institutional and more sales-directed tone, and extra clarity in displaying the eleven different subscription series of varying sizes. There were two series of thirteen concerts each on alternate Thursday evenings. They were not listed together just to save space. Rather, each package received a clearly separate display, enabling the prospective subscriber to easily discern the pieces performed and the performance dates of each series.[7]

In describing the plays, operas, ballets and symphonies, the brochure must be colorful and expressive. A potential subscriber must be convinced that a "musty" classic is really full of contemporary meaning and will provide a great evening of superior entertainment. Often, the literal telling of the play's story or a dance's history defeats the marketer's purpose. Rather, the brochure should present vigorous images and impressions of the work's spirit and mood.

Compare the following two descriptions of Shakespeare's *Tempest:*

1. Many critics consider this last work of Shakespeare an allegorical autobiography —a probing of human nature in loveliest poetry.

2. Here's one of the Bard's most scintillating works of genius, offering in quicksilver profusion a procession of frolicking goddesses, clowns, faeries, sprites and spirits, weaving mythically and magically through the tangled, tropical jungle of our subconscious in this pre-Freudian splurge of richly poetic fantasy—all enthralled by the limitless wonders of sorcery—in short, "such stuff as dreams are made of."

The first, more spare description may be informative, but the second is far more likely to instill excitement and sell subscriptions.[8]

The organization should employ similar techniques in featuring (1) its guest artists: their prestige should be used to the fullest degree possible to sell subscriptions and to elevate the organization's own image; (2) its fine-quality resident company (each musician in our orchestra is a star!) and (3) special features about the organization itself: what makes it unique, special, compelling, and what is worth celebrating (a 25th anniversary, a newly refurbished hall, a scarcity of tickets because of the organization's recent great successes).

The front cover   Dramatic photographs, catchy headlines, and/or rave reviews are often used on the front cover to attract interest and to focus on what makes the organization and its upcoming season both distinctive and special. On the cover of its 1994–95 season brochure, the Lyric Opera of Chicago features a dramatic four-color photo from a scene of *Aida,* announces its "Gala Fortieth-Anniversary Season," and quotes Rodney Milnes of London's *Courvoisier's Book of the Best,* saying: "Widely regarded as the best opera company in America."

The back cover   The brochure's back cover is another "front," depending on which way it is taken out of the mailbox. It provides the marketer with a major opportunity to effectively showcase important information. The Lyric Opera features another dramatic photo, lists upcoming season stars, highlights subscriber discounts, and announces "An incredible 102% of seats sold for each of the past six seasons! Only subscribers are guaranteed seats!" The back cover can also provide more detailed information. On its 1994–95 season brochure, the Chicago Symphony Orchestra says: "We take care of You!" and describes thirteen subscriber benefits.

The Saint Paul Chamber Orchestra uses its back cover to humorously and sensitively dispel some common myths about classical music concerts. The back cover of the 1990–91 season brochure included the following:

**SOME
COMMON
MYTHS ABOUT
CLASSICAL
MUSIC
CONCERTS**

- **They're boring.** How can you call passion, romance, and adventure boring?

- **I'll look like I don't belong.** The only way you'll look out of place at the SPCO is to wear a Viking helmet. And nothing else.

- **I won't see anyone there I know.** That's what you think! You could see your boss, your favorite local celebrity, even your high school sweetheart at the SPCO.

- **I'll need a degree in music to appreciate it.** Do you have to be a gourmet chef to enjoy a fine meal?

- **I won't know when to clap.** When in doubt, clap! Thirty-four musicians are playing their hearts out for you. Your applause means everything.

- **It's a pain in the neck to buy tickets.** Buying SPCO tickets could hardly be easier. Just get out your credit card and reach for the phone.

- **SPCO concerts are always sold out.** We are not always sold out. But with nearly 14,000 subscribers, the best seats *do* go fast. Join us now!

- **It's too expensive.** You can subscribe for *as little as $6 a concert.* With prices like that, we guarantee we won't pinch your pocketbook.

- **I'll look strange going alone.** It's that Viking helmet! At any given concert there'll be 100 people going on their own. Or even more. (The "Fanfare" previews are a good place to get acquainted.)

**Now that we've exploded these common myths,
pick up the phone today and
call our subscriber hotline: 291-1144.**

The order form   The brochure must include an order form. The most logical position for the form is inside the brochure. It should not be placed on the back cover—the recipient should not be confronted with ordering information before reading about the repertoire, the artists, and the arguments for subscribing. Abbreviations should be used with great care, because the potential subscriber may not be familiar with box office terminology. The type should be plain and large enough to be read clearly. The form's contents should conform carefully to the ordering information and descriptions of offerings listed in the brochure's main body. The form should not be cluttered or used as a questionnaire to obtain information not pertinent to the order itself. The arts organization's telephone number should be boldly printed on the order form. Remember that the phone works both ways; patrons should be encouraged to call to place their order or to have their questions answered.

The response rate   What response rate should be expected for a brochure mailing? It is difficult to answer the question in general because there are so many variables. Does the organization have a loyal, long-standing subscriber base? Does it have a good reputation or is it little known? Can the brochure capitalize on the excitement of a new building, a Tony Award–winning play, a renowned star? Is the repertoire appealing to a broad cross section of the targeted audience? How attractive is the offer in terms of discounts and other benefits? How selective is the mailing list?

From the most selective lists, the new subscriber response may be as high as 2 to 3 percent. When marketers lower their requirements for list quality in order to increase their reach, the response rate is much lower. Marketers at Chicago's Lyric Opera are even pleased with a 0.3 percent subscription response from lists purchased from a wide variety of commercial sources. (It is important to note that these figures represent the number of subscriptions purchased, not the number of envelopes returned: each envelope is likely to contain two subscription orders.)

With a 2 percent response rate, a marketer might conclude that 98 percent of the campaign effort was wasted. However, that is not necessarily the case. The brochure presumably has some effect on awareness and intention to buy at a later date. It may enhance the organization's image and arouse interest in its offerings. It may educate and inform the recipients and prepare them for later purchase. The recipients may become more sensitive and alert to the organization's mass media advertising, to reviews and public relations efforts, to word-of-mouth recommendations, to telemarketing that is strategically timed to follow up direct-mail efforts, and to future direct-mail efforts.

The costs   The costs of a quality brochure mailing can be controlled. An arts organization does not need to print a fancy four-color brochure in order to get results. A well-conceived, two-color brochure that says the right things and has broad distribution may be equally effective in gaining subscribers. Because printing costs can vary widely, multiple printing sources should be checked. In some instances, a private or corporate donor will underwrite the brochure. If that is the case, care must be taken that the arts organization will receive the same attention as paying customers and that delivery will occur according to the arts organization's schedule.

Once a brochure is designed and printed, the costs for producing extra copies drop dramatically. One way an organization can decide when to stop producing and mailing brochures, including second, third, and even further copies to certain target segments, is to determine when the various mailing lists begin to bring in a negligible response. At this point, the organization may consider using a response card as a less expensive and possibly more effective direct-mail tool.

THE RESPONSE CARD

Mailing a colorful, full-season brochure filled with details may not be the most cost-effective way to attract new subscribers. If people have not attended in the past or know little about the organization, information about all of its programs, benefits, prices, and packages is likely to overwhelm the reader. Full-season brochures mailed to "cold" leads have a notoriously low response rate. A response card is an effective way to reach potential subscribers at a lower cost. The card also provides an opportunity for the reader to *request* more information. Once someone has responded to this offer, he or she has taken a step, however small, toward commitment. The Detroit Symphony Orchestra mailed 100,000 brochures to its best new prospects and 300,000 response cards to the rest. Four to 5 percent of response card recipients requested further information, and of that group, 30 to 40 percent become subscribers!

The response card should spark the reader's interest. The card can range from a flashy, four-color, three-fold piece to a one-color postcard. The card presents information about highlights only—some celebrities who will be appearing, a special event, or a unique benefit. The headline might read: "Fill It Out . . . Send It In . . . Hear the Music!" Instructions may say: "Return This Card for Your Free Brochure to Our Exciting 1997–98 Season." Offering a free brochure is likely to attract the most qualified prospects. Experimenting with other incentives such as a pair of ticket vouchers, a discount coupon, or even an entry into a drawing could improve the results.

The easier the card is to fill out, the higher the response will be. However, the respondent should be asked to fill in his or her name, address, and daytime and evening phone numbers rather than using a "peel-off" label, so that the organization can capture the phone numbers. The organization's phone and fax numbers should be in bold print. The return section should be perforated so that the respondent does not have to search for scissors. The card should have prepaid postage.[9]

The best approach is to send a response card to the organization's "colder" leads —the bottom half to two-thirds of the out-of-house list. This includes other arts groups' single-ticket-buyer lists because those customers are not likely to subscribe right away but can be cultivated over time. If possible, test mailings should be sent more than once to the same list in the same season. The low cost of response cards allows the organization to increase frequency of their use. If someone has been on the in-house list for three years and shown no activity, a response card should be sent to find out if they would like to remain on the list. Response cards can also be inserted into the local daily and weekly newspapers, arts and business journals, and the public broadcasting station's newsletter. This approach is less targeted than a mailing, but its much lower cost may justify its use.

SPECIAL ANNOUNCEMENTS

Arts organizations also send out mailings announcing special events or offers of special interest to target groups, such as annual *Nutcracker* or *Christmas Carol* productions, which are generally not included as part of a regular subscription series. Organizations may offer loyal subscribers the opportunity to purchase early tickets or extra tickets for highly demanded performances. ("The Cleveland Symphony Orchestra invites you—a contemporary music lover—to four extraordinary programs of new music conducted by Pierre Boulez!") Once the season has begun, organizations may design special three-concert packages, coupon packages, and other appropriate offers for targeted mailings.

At the Lyric Opera, subscribers to certain shortened series received a letter that said in part:

> Dear Friends,
> . . . if ever there was a director with the Midas touch, it is certainly Harold Prince! . . . Needless to say, I am thrilled to have him directing our *Candide*. . . . I know that you do not have a subscription series that includes *Candide,* and I encourage you to attend! . . . Most of the *Candide* performances are completely sold out, but happily there are still good seats left on Tuesday, December 20, which is why I am writing to you today. . . .

Special mailings can be sent virtually all season long to current subscribers, to special-package buyers, to single-ticket buyers, and to prospective patrons. Unless the organization has filled virtually all its capacity with subscribers, the direct marketer's job is just beginning when the subscription campaign ends.

MANAGING TELEMARKETING

A survey of twenty-nine major U.S. orchestras found that an average of 30 percent of total subscription income comes from telemarketing.[10] According to Patti Gessner, marketing director of the San Francisco Symphony, 80 percent of new subscriptions result from telemarketing efforts, as compared with 20 percent just a few seasons ago. A major factor increasing the importance of telemarketing is that subscriptions, which averaged ten to twelve concerts five years ago, now average six or seven concerts per season. This means that more subscribers are needed to fill the same number of seats. So marketers are reaching out to more people unfamiliar with the composers and the repertoire. Whereas a direct-mail piece can do little more than list programming information (the San Francisco Symphony's brochure offers twenty-three different subscription packages), telemarketers can talk to prospective patrons, distinguish between offerings, and help them make an appropriate selection. Also, telemarketers can solicit current subscribers to share their concerns and ask questions, and thereby increase their likelihood of renewing.

The amount of emphasis to place on telemarketing depends on several factors. How routinized is the renewal process among current subscribers? How strong is the current subscriber base? Does the organization offer small packages, say of three or four concerts, that can be further customized? Were current subscribers brought in originally by telemarketing? Given the higher contact cost for telemarketing, privacy issues, and the multitude of organizations using telemarketing, precise list selection and targeting is critical.

Telemarketing's success at selling subscriptions is based upon the simple fact that it eases the decision making and purchase process. Telemarketers lead a prospect through the process of selecting packages, number of performances, night of the week, seating selection, and price. The caller also describes the product in a concise and attractive manner, highlighting particular performances or explaining unknown works. Probably the most effective inducement is to offer the patron an exact seat location. This adds urgency to the sale, since the preferred seat might not be available tomorrow.[11]

After the Detroit Symphony Orchestra's (DSO) sorely run-down hall was restored and a new music director was engaged, marketing director Tom Gulick focused on rebuilding the orhcestra's severely eroded audience base. Telemarketing was a key component of his new subscriber and renewal campaigns, and by December 1, 1994, eighteen thousand hours had been logged by telemarketers for that season's campaign. Telemarketing was not used to "cold call" names purchased from external nonarts lists. But it proved effective with past purchasers of a DSO concert ticket and those who attend other performing arts. It also was effective in increasing the renewal rate among first-year subscribers, an important task for the DSO since typically only 40 percent of first year subscribers renew. Gulick has found that the people who responded to telemarketing for their first subscriptions are likely to be more responsive to a personal phone call than a direct-mail piece at renewal time.

The Caller

Effective telemarketing depends on choosing the right telemarketers, training them well, and providing them with incentives. Stephen Dunn, whose firm supervises telemarketing at many arts organizations, rarely, if ever, hires individuals who are trained in selling stocks, aluminum siding, and the like over the phone. Rather, his firm advertises in the local paper for articulate, motivated people who have a knowledge of the particular field and an interest in the organization. Applicants hired include high school students, actors, musicians, professionals between jobs, and retired people. They are screened twice: once over the phone to determine if they have pleasant voices and sound enthusiastic; then in more depth in person. One symphony marketing director said she got her first job as a telephone operator because she could pronounce the Russian composers' names!

Training the callers is an important and ongoing part of a successful telemarketing campaign. At the San Francisco Symphony, telemarketers are provided with background information on the composers and the performers, and audiotapes of certain pieces being performed. Telemarketers are instructed to listen to the people they call—to pick up key words of interest or concern, and to detect their preferences. They are then able to respond with such comments as:

- "This composition may be contemporary, but it is lyrical and easy, enjoyable listening."
- "If you enjoyed that dance company last year, I am sure you will be intrigued and highly entertained by . . ."
- "You probably have not heard of this conductor, but he is well respected in Europe and is dynamic to watch."

Providing incentives to the callers is also critical. Telemarketing is hard and often stressful work, creating frequent caller turnover. It is not unusual for a telemarketer in an eighteen- to twenty-week campaign to quit work after only six to ten weeks. Therefore, whatever incentives can keep callers sharp and motivated are worthwhile. For example, the telemarketing supervisor can build up enthusiasm by offering prizes to top performers or to the first one who gets an order.

Medium- to larger-size organizations often employ professional firms to handle the day-to-day management of the telemarketing campaign—hiring, training, and monitoring callers. But most of the smaller organizations conduct their own campaigns in-house. One advantage these smaller organizations have is that with a smaller patron base, where the task is less daunting, key members of the organization can be called upon to assist in telemarketing efforts.

Imagine how pleased a first-year subscriber would be to receive a call from one of the orchestra's musicians or a repertory company's actor. The performer could introduce him- or herself, say they hope the patron is enjoying the season, offer an interesting anecdote about a performance, offer to answer questions, and encourage the patron to resubscribe. Similarly, members of the board can be called upon to make key phone calls, such as to long-standing patrons who have allowed their subscriptions to lapse. The personal contact and interest exhibited by these respected parties is sure to generate a more positive response than would an anonymous caller.

Performers are not always willing to take on this added responsibility, but many find it rewarding to help the organization build customer satisfaction and loyalty in this unique way and to have personal contact with some of their patrons. It has the added benefit that feedback from the patrons helps the callers to understand their issues and concerns, such as programming or performer preferences, that management deals with on a day-to-day basis.

The Call

The opening lines of the telephone call are critical; they should be brief and lead with a good question that catches the listener's interest. The telemarketer needs to know how to end the conversation if the prospect seems to be a poor one. The call should be made at the right time, which is usually late morning and afternoon for reaching businesspeople, and the evening hours of 7:00 to 9:00 for reaching households. Patrons can be called at dinnertime, but the question, "Is this a good time to talk?" can mitigate the awkward timing of the call. Most importantly, a customer service approach should be maintained. Whatever the response of the person called, the contact should always be courteous and informative. Responsible organizations should go to the trouble to delete from their telemarketing lists those patrons who ask not to be contacted by phone.

Joseph White, president of a telephone fund-raising firm, believes that considering "no" as a final answer from a call recipient can be a major mistake. For three nonprofit organizations, White sent follow-up letters within three weeks after the phone call to current and lapsed members who had refused to pledge support. The letters generated a 9.9 percent, a 4.9 percent, and an 8.6 percent response. The telephone contact, although not successful at the time, generated a delayed reaction. Although these efforts were mainly geared toward gaining contributions, the same principle can work for subscription campaigns as well.

A letter should be mailed very soon after the contact is made by telephone. It should thank the prospect for accepting the phone call and should reinforce the offer's highlights and major benefits. Also, if the person was obviously angry at being called, the letter should include an apology—followed, of course, by an invitation to subscribe. The package should include a detached reply device and a preaddressed, postage-paid business reply envelope.[12]

Telemarketing and the Law

The Federal Trade Commission is now considering regulation of various aspects of telemarketing, namely, restricting hours of calling, requiring disclosure scripts where the caller must say by whom he or she is employed, banning the use of automatic dialers (which use computer messages and random dialing), and creating a national "do not call" list that would have to be merged/purged against all telemarketing lists. Not-for-profit organizations will be exempt from these regulations for the near future, but after a few years, this exemption will probably disappear. However, any organization will always retain the right to contact its "members" (those who have expressed interest in its product or service) in any manner it wishes, including by telephone. So, no matter what restrictions come from the FTC, an arts organization will retain the right to call its in-house file, assuming people have provided their phone numbers. Therefore, arts organizations should plan for this eventuality by developing a prospect campaign as a key element of the direct-marketing strategy.[13]

The Incoming Phone Call

The telephone works both ways. In fact, after mailed subscription renewals, the next-highest number of tickets are sold via calls that come *into* the organization. Organizations are therefore looking into how they can provide more and better information and service to their calling customers and stimulate interest in additional offerings.

THE BOX OFFICE

Typically, when a patron phones the box office of a nonprofit performing arts organization to purchase tickets, the ticket order is handled in an efficient manner, period. But the incoming call also provides an opportunity to promote preconcert lectures, box meals during the intermission of a long production, dinner reservations at a nearby restaurant at a special rate, or recordings of the music being performed that can be mailed out with the tickets. A well-trained box office attendant can also use this opportunity to recommend other productions. For example: "If you like contemporary music, you shouldn't miss Pierre Boulez conducting his own compositions." Finally, rather than concluding the conversation by reminding the caller that tickets are nonrefundable, box office personnel can end on a positive note, saying they hope the caller enjoys the concert and comes back again soon.

TELEPHONE PREVIEW SERVICES

Through survey questionnaires and focus groups, several symphony managers have found that patrons, whether longtime loyal audience members or occasional concertgoers, often want more information about the programs than is available in brochures and advertising. Knowing that one of the biggest barriers for newcomers was the feeling that they had to be expert in classical music, Lincoln Center Productions developed a new way for people to learn about the concerts and become familiar with some of the music. People can phone the "Classical Connection"—a well-publicized phone number—and enter the four-digit date of the concert that interests them. They then hear a brief spoken introduction from WQXR personality Gregg Whiteside, followed by an excerpt from the music to be played at that performance. Then, customers can transfer to the telephone charge service to buy tickets or receive information.

To make the Classical Connection program operational, the marketing director enlisted two partners. The *Village Voice,* the leading alternative newspaper in New York, which had already set up similar services for nightclubs and restaurants, established the back-office mechanics of the service. WQXR-FM, the only all-classical music station in New York, provided the recordings for the one-minute spots. Additionally, both partners were willing to publicize the service in their respective media in exchange for visibility at Lincoln Center and in selected marketing materials. In the first ten days of operation alone, more than a thousand calls were made to the line and more than twenty-five hundred minutes of previews were heard. And, significantly, more than 15 percent of the callers asked to be transferred to the box office.

The Plymouth Music Series of Minnesota, which commissions many new pieces and often performs seldom-heard works, introduced "Dial-A-Preview," a three-minute audio program about each of its six concerts, with music samples and discussions by the artistic director, Philippe Brunelle. The *Plymouth Star-Tribune* provides six phone extensions, each of which plays three-minute tapes of one of the concerts. The caller, unfortunately, cannot connect with the box office because most calls are placed when the box office is closed. Yet, before the final concert of the 1993–94 season, more than a thousand people dialed the preview and the Plymouth Music Series sold standing room for the first time in its history.[14]

An important additional benefit of phone preview services is the ability to evaluate the marketing campaign. Based on the number and timing of the incoming calls and demographic information from people who follow up and purchase tickets, marketers can analyze list and media selection, the timing of mailings and ads, and the relative interest in each concert. Of course, other factors such as media interviews with guest artists affect the number of calls received. But over several years, the data will help the organization fine-tune its marketing strategies.

INTEGRATED DIRECT MARKETING

Too often, direct marketers rely on a single advertising vehicle and a "one-shot" effort to reach and sell a prospect. An example of a single-vehicle, single-stage campaign would be sending a onetime mailing offering a subscription series. A single-vehicle, multiple-stage campaign would involve sending successive mailings to a prospect to trigger purchase. Some arts organizations send their season brochure several times to one household to get reluctant subscribers to renew and potential subscribers to commit. At the Los Angeles Philharmonic, 76 percent of subscribers respond to the first mailing, 3–4 percent to the next mailing, and 1–2 percent to later mailings. Each of these later mailings is considered effective enough to justify its cost. But direct marketers at the Los Angeles Philharmonic increase their effectiveness by utilizing a multiple-vehicle, multiple-stage campaign, a technique called *integrated direct marketing*. Consider the following integrated direct marketing sequence:

Paid ad with response mechanism → Direct mail → Telemarketing → Ongoing Communication

The paid ad creates product awareness and stimulates inquiries. The organization then sends direct mail to those who inquire. Within forty-eight to seventy-two hours following mail receipt, the organization phones, offering to give further information and seeking an order. Even if the prospect is not ready to buy, there is ongoing communication. This use of *response compression*, whereby multiple media are deployed within a tightly defined time frame, increases message awareness and impact. Multiple media are used because different people respond to different media.

When the Detroit Symphony Orchestra receives response cards requesting further information, the season brochure is sent out immediately, accompanied by a personal letter from the marketing director. Within two to three weeks, telemarketers follow up the mailing with a personal call. To keep this schedule running smoothly, response cards are sent out in "wave" mailings, so that the telemarketing staff does not get backlogged.

An Integrated Renewal Campaign

For its subscription renewal campaign, the DSO integrates various direct-marketing techniques as follows:

1. In January, the marketing director sends subscribers a personal letter thanking them for subscribing and offering them vouchers for two free guest tickets to a concert in the spring. (The vouchers must be redeemed by mail or in person, so that the box office can capture the names and addresses of the ticket holders.)

2. On March 1, the first renewal mailing goes out in the form of a full-season brochure, accompanied by an invoice, a special offer (in 1994, special purchase of the orchestra's 75th-anniversary book), and a deadline for response on April 15.

3. On April 1, past subscribers who have not responded receive another invoice accompanied by a short letter from the marketing director with the theme, "We haven't heard from you."

4. As the deadline approaches, telemarketing begins. The first names to be turned over to telemarketers are those who are least likely to renew: first-year subscribers with short series. Long-term subscribers are saved for last, after being sent at least one more reminder letter. The reason: most often these loyal patrons haven't gotten around to sending in their form and do not need the added "push" of a more costly personal phone call.

5. Further mail pieces are sent out in waves, so they can be followed up on a timely basis with phone calls.

An Integrated Full-Season Campaign

In the two-year period from 1991 to 1993, the subscriber base of San Francisco's American Conservatory Theater (ACT) fell by nearly 20 percent, from 16,564 to 13,376. Several factors contributed to this erosion: the long-term closure of the Company's Geary Theater after the 1989 earthquake; several seasons of performing in venues inconsistent with ACT's image; a change in artistic leadership; increasing competition from the Bay Area arts community; and a continued economic recession throughout California.

For the 1994–95 season, marketing director Robert Sweibel decided to capitalize on the following factors to rebuild his subscriber base: the appealing selection of plays, including the Pulitzer and Tony award–winning *Angels in America;* the long-awaited reconstruction of the Geary Theater; new subscriber benefits; and a well-conceived direct-marketing campaign. The campaign is described in the following example.

ACT ATTRACTS MORE THAN 7,500 NEW SUBSCRIBERS FOR 1994–95 SEASON[15]

THE GOAL

ACT set a goal of 14,374 subscribers for the 1994–95 season. Since the subscriber base from the previous season was 13,376 and the renewal rate was projected at 71 percent, this meant that ACT had to attract nearly 5,000 new subscribers.

THE RENEWAL CAMPAIGN

The renewal campaign featured the following new benefits:

- Performance rescheduling (ticket exchange) by telephone—ACT became the only major performing arts organization in San Francisco to offer this service by phone.

- Discounts to subscribers for purchase of extra tickets.

- Discount program with area merchants increased from two merchants to twelve.

- A formalized partial payment plan.

- A half-price student subscription.

- Guaranteed low-cost nearby parking.

The campaign, conducted from March through June, consisted of two renewal notices, the first with an "earlybird" drawing opportunity to win a free subscription, followed by a telemarketing effort. Ultimately, 9,587, or 71.7 percent of subscribers, renewed.

LAPSED SUBSCRIBERS AND MULTIPLE SINGLE-TICKET BUYERS

In April, ACT identified the 6,912 best prospects for new subscriptions (lapsed subscribers and repeat single-ticket buyers) from its database. Each prospect was sent a fully personalized letter package inviting them to subscribe. A special added benefit was included: a dated drawing opportunity to win a weekend getaway at an upscale San Francisco hotel.

The letters were mailed first class, 1,000 per week, so that within a week of each drop, prospects could be contacted by the telemarketing staff. By mid-June, the direct-mail package had attracted 536 new subscribers—a 7.8 percent response rate. The immediate telemarketing follow-up generated another 648 new subscribers.

INFREQUENT ATTENDERS ON THE IN-HOUSE LIST

In June, ACT sent a season invitation, an inexpensive self-mailer with a built-in, postage-paid reply envelope, to 43,243 house-holds on its database. Over an eight-week period, the piece attracted 870 new subscribers for a response rate of 2 percent. Telemarketing to a statistically valid sampling of the database generated several hundred more subscriptions.

NEW LEADS

To attract new leads, ACT designed a large, sixteen-page, four-color brochure with a postage-paid reply envelope stitched into the center. The cover photo featured *Angels in America.* Copy was heavy, but easy to scan. An introduction emphasized the theater's recent critical and popular successes, its imminent return to the Geary Theater, and the forthcoming season. Play descriptions followed, one per page. The back of the booklet was devoted to complete details of ACT's subscriber benefits and ser-vices, a large order form with easy-to-follow, numbered instruc-tions, and other necessary copy. There was no "fine print." Phone and fax orders were encouraged in bold type.

To meet their goal, ACT marketers determined that they needed to greatly increase the number of brochures mailed to new leads, which historically had garnered a 0.5 percent response rate. Acquired lists—mostly from trades with other arts organizations—were increased from five to eighteen, and many smaller arts organizations were included for the first time. The lists were merged and purged, and, in early August, with the sea-son to begin at the end of September, the brochure was mailed to 220,000 households. After Labor Day, the "multiples"—the 40,000 households whose names appeared on more than one list—were mailed a second copy of the same brochure.

The fall brochure attracted 4,205 new subscribers for a response rate of 1.6 percent. Of those, 53.5 percent joined for the full season, comparing favorably with the previous season's 47.2 percent. The urgency created by the timing of the brochure —much later in the preseason than usual—was considered cen-tral to the campaign's success.

THE RESULTS

As of October 23, ACT had enrolled 16,805 subscribers—117 percent of its original goal and the highest subscriber rate since the mid-1980s.

DEVELOPING A MARKETING DATABASE SYSTEM

A customer database is an information-intensive, long-term marketing tool.[16] Many marketers confuse a customer mailing list with a customer database. A customer mailing list is simply a set of names, addresses, and telephone numbers. A customer database contains much more, including customer lifestyle, demographic, and financial information; purchase transaction records; and promotions and media response characteristics. Modern database marketing uses the database as a cornerstone of current and long-range marketing efforts. Each database should be designed around the organization's marketing requirements.

Ways to Use a Database

When a marketing communications program is database-driven, it is customer-driven; it allows the marketer to target the correct offer to the correct consumer. Jackson and Wang have identified the following ways to use a database as the central tool of marketing communications.[17]

IDENTIFY THE BEST CUSTOMERS

A database allows the marketer to look at customer data using recency, frequency, and monetary analysis. How recently has the customer bought a ticket (or subscription)? How frequently does the customer purchase tickets (or subscriptions)? How much money has the customer spent per purchase and over time? This data allows the marketer to direct communications to the right customers.

DEVELOP NEW CUSTOMERS

By tracking information about current customers on the database, the marketer can develop a customer profile. The profile can then be used to identify other people whose characteristics closely match those of current customers.

ENHANCE AVAILABLE INFORMATION

Database enhancement consists of the overlay of information added to customer and prospect records. Customer data can be enhanced with demographic information compiled by such companies as Donnelley Marketing, Metromail, and R. L. Polk, and with psychographic information such as that provided for the PRIZM clusters described in Chapter 4. For example, assume a symphony is offering a rush hour concert and wants to send a mailing to its target audience. By enhancing its currently available customer information (name, address) with U.S. Census Bureau data, it can identify the people who travel thirty minutes or more to work. Other data sources can be used to add information on occupations, ages of family members, and so on. The marketer may even want to research the brand names of cars owned or athletic shoes worn by rush hour concert attenders to help attract corporate sponsors.

DELIVER A MESSAGE CONSISTENT WITH PRODUCT USAGE

The database allows the marketer to target communications based on usage patterns. New and infrequent patrons can be stimulated to more frequent attendance by the use of price promotions. Moderate-usage customers may be encouraged to feel a part of the organization. Communications to frequent attenders may be designed around their long-term loyalty.

DEVELOP COMPLEMENTARY-SELL OPPORTUNITIES

By analyzing past purchase behavior, the organization may discover, for example, that people who like jazz are the most likely to attend world/ethnic concerts or performances of music by young composers. The organization may use this information to develop new series for specific target markets or to advertise specific performances to the best prospects. After the English National Opera installed a computerized box office system in 1993, its marketers identified all the people who came to see *La Boheme* and mailed them brochures for *Tosca*. The strategy generated £10 in direct sales for each £1 spent on the mailing.[18]

CONDUCT ONGOING RESEARCH

Mass marketers usually know very little about their customers. However, a well-run database program allows the marketer to easily and regularly access in-depth information about individual customers, their buying patterns, and their responses to various marketing efforts. This, in turn, allows the marketer to make better informed marketing decisions.

INTEGRATE FUNCTIONS

Too often, the marketing department's and the development department's databases are incompatible. When information cannot be linked, opportunities are lost. For example, when two fifth-row center seats have just become available for a sold-out performance, the box office personnel should know, just by keying in the next caller's phone number, whether that person is an infrequent attender or a long-term subscriber and major contributor who deserves special treatment.

Database Systems for Performing Arts Organizations

Specially designed database systems are expensive. According to Andy Brolin, director of marketing for Prologue Systems (a major provider of arts marketing and fund-raising database systems), the start-up costs for licensing the software and purchasing and installing hardware for a typical eight-user-station system is approximately $75,000. However, before managers of lower-budget organizations despair over such numbers, they should consider the following factors.

RECOUP COSTS

An in-house ticketing database allows the organization to retain the per order service charges that now provide a hefty profit for Ticketmaster and similar ticketing bureaus. Even a reduced service charge can help the organization recoup much of its initial investment.

NEW REVENUE

A database can be such an effective tool for increasing attendance by current patrons and for building new audiences that the increased revenue can pay for the system many times over.

COLLABORATIVE OPPORTUNITIES

The most expensive portions of the database system are the software licensing costs and the server, which centrally stores the information. According to Brolin, if ten small arts organizations were to share these costs and have one or two workstations each, the cost to each would approximate $20,000. The server could be placed in a mutually agreed upon location, and each organization would have its own access codes. Access codes can be designed to restrict access to data within organizations as well as across them. For example, the development director may want box office personnel to know if a subscriber is a major contributor, but may not want the box office to know how much money that subscriber donates. Organizations may be reluctant to share their customers' attendance and contribution history with other organizations, but may be willing to share such information as a subscriber's address change or physical access requirement.

Collaboration also increases research opportunities. A trade organization, foundation, arts alliance, or arts and business council could access information from all the collaborating organizations to study consumer ticket purchase trends. This information would provide a broader perspective on the artsgoing public and their attendance behavior than the information available to any one organization in the consortium.

CORPORATE PARTNERSHIPS

An arts organization may find a corporate partner willing to subsidize some or all of the costs of database marketing, as in the case of the collaboration between the Detroit Symphony Orchestra and the EDS Corporation described in Chapter 7.

ADAPTING EXISTING SOFTWARE

Many arts organizations that cannot afford a specially designed system have ready access to standard database software such as Lotus, Excel, or Quattro Pro. Technical assistance will be necessary to encode levels of information and access, and data integration will be much more difficult to achieve, but even a relatively simple system is far better than no system at all.

*Developing
Contact Lists*

In order to promote its offers to appropriate current and potential attenders, the organization should maintain a full range of lists and update them on a regular basis. The main lists are house lists, external lists, and specially created lists.

HOUSE LISTS

House lists are generated from the organization's current patrons. They should be broken down as follows.

1. *Single-ticket buyers:* Single-ticket buyers who purchase by phone or mail should automatically have their names, addresses, and phone numbers recorded in the organization's database, along with information about each performance attended. Box office personnel are sometimes reluctant to request this information from single-ticket buyers who come to the box office in person. But not one ticket buyer's name should be lost needlessly. The best prospects for future sales are those who have attended a recent performance and those who attend most frequently. The organization can encourage these prospects to purchase more single tickets in their interest areas or to purchase miniseries or flex plans.

2. *First-year subscribers:* Since first-year subscribers are far more likely to lapse than longer-term subscribers, they should be given special attention throughout the year.

3. *Two-plus year subscribers:* These subscribers, although the easiest patrons for the organization to maintain, should not be taken for granted and should receive special "subscriber family" benefits as their subscription time lengthens. These subscribers are also the most likely source for contributions and volunteering.

4. *Lapsed subscribers:* Lapsed subscribers should be tracked as to the season they dropped out, how long they subscribed, which types of plans they held, and whether they contributed to the organization. This information will help the organization develop appropriate efforts to recapture their interest.

5. *Group sales buyers:* Detailed records should be kept on the preferences and needs of these groups.

6. *Special plan buyers:* People who hold coupons, memberships, flex plans, miniseries and other offerings should be contacted for renewals and encouraged to participate in higher commitment offerings.

EXTERNAL LISTS

Arts organizations can obtain additional lists from a variety of sources.

Exchange lists   Arts organizations are increasingly reaping the benefits of exchanging lists with one another, realizing that the most satisfied arts patrons are those who frequent the performances of multiple organizations. When selecting other organizations to contact for list sharing, the marketer should match up as many

characteristics as possible: the dollar value of the performances, the types of performances offered, the zip codes of frequent attenders, and so on.

Rental lists   Organizations can rent lists from commercial sources. For example,
a symphony can rent a list from Blockbuster Video of people who rented the movie
Amadeus or who are interested in romantic movies. Readers of art, literary, gourmet
cooking, and gardening magazines may be likely prospects because of the aesthetic
crossover. However, these lists must be tested because some magazine readers are
homebodies and do not attend live performances. Lists can also be rented from mail-
order houses. Young, upscale, active people purchase from Lands' End and similar
catalogs. For an aesthetically inclined, art-loving market, the Museum Store of the
Metropolitan Museum has a prime list. The mail-order business has become so extensive that the possibilities are endless.

CREATING LISTS

Arts organizations can create new lists by generating leads in various ways. Such lists
have a great advantage over external lists because they consist of people who have
expressed some level of interest in an organization's offerings.

1. *Coupon ads:* Ads with coupons may offer a purchase discount, a season brochure,
   or some other item. Those who respond can be added to the organization's
   database. The cost of the offered item is a small price to pay for an interested
   name.
2. *Broadcasts:* Radio broadcasts may make similar offers and provide a phone number for people to call for information.
3. *Lead cards:* Lead cards (or name cards) can be used in a variety of ways. They can
   be left at the box office, placed in programs, or distributed at corporate sponsors'
   offices, area restaurants, local libraries, and so on. They can be placed on tables
   located in the lobby with a sign reading, "Please leave your name and address so
   we can notify you of our future performances."[19]

SELECTIVITY OF MAILING LISTS

Whether conducting a major new-subscriber campaign or attempting to attract
lapsed subscribers, the organization should prioritize its lists according to the likely
response rate. The organization should not necessarily eliminate the lists with the
lowest response rates. According to Stephen Belth, marketing director of the Chicago
Symphony and formerly of the Los Angeles Philharmonic, a 0.5 percent response rate
is considered good for direct mail; a 1 percent response rate is profitable in the first
year. For telemarketing, which is more costly to implement, a 3 percent to 4 percent
response rate is profitable. Remember that the profitability of a one-year subscribership is only a small fraction of the lifetime value of each subscriber who stays with
the organization. Even if it costs, say, $50 or more to attract a $60 subscription, the

annual renewals, contributions, and potential for bringing new people into the organization can far outweigh the cost.

As organizations collect lists from multiple sources, the lists should be checked for duplications. The more duplication there is between the lists, the more likely it is that those people will be good prospects. It is advisable to test a suspect list before doing a full-fledged mailing or phone campaign. It is not unusual for 25 percent of addresses to change each year, so if a list has not been updated annually and if the names have not been merged and purged, its worth will be greatly reduced.

RENTING OUT YOUR MAILING LISTS

Many arts organizations, including Lincoln Center, Carnegie Hall, and the Los Angeles Music Center, rent their lists, generating from 25 to 50 cents per name every year.[20] That means a 50,000-name mailing list will gross between $12,000 and $25,000 per year. Yet, most arts organizations do not take advantage of this significant revenue-generating opportunity.

A common misconception is that an arts organization may offend its board members or upper-level donors by renting their names to businesses. In fact, these patrons tend to be on countless other mailing lists—their names are probably being rented several times a day, with a credit card company, magazine, or retail store generating the revenue from the list rental. Out of respect for the patrons' privacy, the organization can include a statement in its brochure or newsletter saying: "We sometimes release our mailing list to other organizations who are offering products or services which we believe are of interest to our patrons. If you do not wish your name to be released for any reason, simply write us a note and let us know."

Generally, an organization contracts with a professional list manager to implement a selective list rental program. List managers advertise the list along with information regarding price, geographic counts, and mail date availability. Billing, collections, and sales reporting are also the list manager's responsibility. The arts organization—the list's owner—retains total control over the list. The owner must provide written consent each time the list is released. To monitor the appropriate use of lists, the list manager and the owning arts organization can "decoy" the list. Whenever the list is rented, it should include fake names. If the renter was supposed to use the list only once, then only one letter should arrive at a fake name address.

The better the condition of the organization's list, the more money it will generate for the organization. Good condition means that the list is cleaned regularly of undeliverable names and is frequently updated with new buyers. If the list is productive for other mailers, they will rent it again and again. If the list is poorly maintained, its effectiveness for outside use and for the organization's own mailing purposes will be significantly limited.

Two factors are essential to make database marketing work. First, the marketer must get top management to approve the investment and ongoing cost and get organizational acceptance and support for a new way of doing marketing. Second, after a database system has been set up, the organization must continuously upgrade its data and its database management system in response to the dynamic nature of the market environment.

[1] "Profile of Member Organizations," Association of Performing Arts Presenters, 1991–92 membership survey conducted by AMS Planning and Research, Washington, D.C., 45.

[2] Maddy Morton, "Aida Comes Alive," *International Arts Manager,* Nov. 1994.

[3] Bob Stone, *Successful Direct Marketing Methods* (Lincolnwood, Ill.: NTC Business Books, 1979), 323–325.

[4] Siegfried Vögele, "Handbook of Direct Mail" (London: Prentice Hall International Ltd., 1992), 86–88.

[5] Bob Stone, *Successful Direct Marketing Methods,* 4th ed. (Lincolnwood, Ill.: NTC Business Books, 1988), 344.

[6] Herbert Hatzenstein and William S. Sachs, *Direct Marketing* (New York: Macmillan, 1992), 245.

[7] Danny Newman, *Subscribe Now!* (New York: Theatre Communications Group, 1983), 120–165. Much of the information in this section of the brochure was taken from this source. Please see Newman's book for a more thorough discussion of the topic.

[8] Newman, *Subscribe Now!* 135–136.

[9] Charlie Wade, "Prospect Cards Boost Bottom Line," *Arts Reach,* Dec. 1992, 8–10.

[10] "Telemarketing Practices of Major Orchestras," compiled by the Atlanta Symphony Orchestra, *Arts Reach,* Aug./Sept. 1993.

[11] Stephen Dunn, "Telemarketing Power," *Arts Reach,* Premiere Issue, 1992, 16–18.

[12] Joe White, "When 'No' Doesn't Mean 'No' in Telephone Fundraising," *Arts Reach,* Apr./May 1994, 10.

[13] Dunn, "Telemarketing Power," 16.

[14] "David Rivel and Lisa Wallace, "Telephone Preview Services Break New Ground," *Arts Reach,* Oct./Nov. 1994, 5–6, 19.

[15] Robert Sweibel, "A.C.T. Attracts over 7,500 New Subscribers for 1994–95 Season," *Arts Reach,* Oct./Nov. 1994, 17–19.

[16] Rob Jackson and Paul Wang, *Strategic Database Marketing* (Lincolnwood, Ill.: NTC Business Books, 1994).

[17] Ibid., chap. 4.

[18] Morton, "Aida Comes Alive."

[19] Thanks to Stephen Belth, marketing director, Chicago Symphony Orchestra, for providing much of the information used in this section.

[20] Jeremy Barbera and Bob Budlow, "Why Rent Your Mailing List?" *Arts Reach,* Dec. 1992, 6–7.

C H A P T E R   1 5

*Good public
relations is about
identifying the real
message.*

MARGARET LARSON

IMPROVING IMAGE AND VISIBILITY THROUGH PUBLIC RELATIONS

PUBLIC RELATIONS, LIKE MARKETING, IS A RELATIVELY NEW ORGANIZATIONAL function, although its roots go back to the times when the arrival of kings was heralded in advance by their messengers. Formalization of public relations functions began in the late nineteenth century when businesses established lobbying (equivalent to advocacy in the arts world) and press agentry functions to influence legislators and journalists to support positions favorable to their interests.

Later, companies began to recognize the positive value of planned publicity in creating customer interest in the company and its products. Publicity entailed finding or creating events, preparing company- or product-slanted news stories, and trying to interest the press in using them. Recognizing that special skills are needed to develop publicity, companies began to add publicists to their ranks. Somewhat later, the emerging sciences of public opinion measurement and mass communication theory permitted more sophistication in the conduct of public relations. Public relations practitioners began to recognize the value of conducting research into public opinion prior to developing and launching public relations campaigns.

Eventually, public relations departments were created to integrate the work of the various subspecialists—researchers, publicists, lobbyists—and to coordinate efforts among the organizations' publics. But it was not until the 1980s that the public relations function achieved an explosive growth, fueled by the simultaneous recognition of its intrinsic value by corporations and the development by marketing public relations professionals of programs that precisely support marketing strategies. This realization, in effect, stimulated the merger of PR into marketing and put an end to a long-standing love-hate relationship between the two functions.

MARKETING PUBLIC RELATIONS

In a recent survey of five hundred arts presenters, unpaid promotions were ranked as the third most effective marketing tool, closely following first- and second-ranked direct mail and paid advertising.[1] As advertising costs continue to rise and the advertising audience reached continues to decline; as increasing advertising clutter reduces the impact of each ad; and as marketers continue to place more emphasis on *marketing* PR techniques, it is anticipated that before long, PR will exceed advertising in effectiveness.

Historically, public relations has been treated as a *reactive* function. Public relations personnel get out press releases as needed, fight "brush fires" as they emerge, and cope with individual and group complaints. This reactive stance has many negative consequences. The environment, rather than the organization, sets the public relations agenda; the organization's image is defined by its response to special situations rather than by the creation of a set of carefully designed messages over a long period of time; and the organization's responses to crises are not guided by a long-term strategy.

An *active*, market-oriented public relations stance avoids these problems and assures that the organization has control over how others see it. Tom Harris defines marketing PR as follows: "Marketing public relations is the process of planning, executing and evaluating programs that encourage purchase and consumer satisfaction through credible communication of information and impressions that identify organizations and their products with the needs, wants, concerns, and interests of their publics."[2]

Whereas the main function of marketing is to influence *behavior*, the task of public relations is to form, maintain, or change public *attitudes* toward the organization or its products. According to the International Public Relations Association, "Public relations is a management function of a continuing and planned character, through which . . . institutions seek to win and retain the understanding, sympathy and support of those with whom they are or may be concerned."

Benefits of Marketing Public Relations

Public relations can make a memorable impact on public awareness. PR can place stories in the media to bring attention to a product, service, person, organization, event, or idea. Publicity has several qualities that make it an important part of the marketing function. First, it may have higher credibility than advertising because it appears as normal news and not as sponsored information. Some experts say that consumers are five times more likely to be influenced by editorial copy than by advertising. PR tends to catch people off guard who might otherwise avoid sponsored messages. PR also serves to extend the reach of advertising, to break through commercial clutter, to complement advertising by reinforcing messages and legitimizing claims, and to tell the product story in greater depth. It is effective in arousing attention, as it comes in the guise of a noteworthy and often dramatized event.

PR requires a fraction of the cost of advertising. The organization does not pay for the space or time obtained in the media. It pays for a staff to develop and circulate the stories and manage certain events. If the organization develops an interesting story, it could be picked up by all the news media and be worth the equivalent of a great deal of money in advertising. PR is also less expensive than direct mail. The smaller the organization's promotion budget, the stronger the case for using PR to gain share of mind.

In the performing arts, PR can help to prepare the artsgoer for what is on stage. Says publicist Donald Michaelis, "You must not fail the artistic director, the performing artists or the institution by inadequately preparing the audience. You are interpreting the product. A critical part of the process is accessing a play to the attenders. We don't tell people how to react or what to think. Instead, we try to give a road map to help the attender."[3] Articles in newspapers and periodicals are an important resource for helping to achieve this goal.

PR can also play an important role in attracting the nonattender. Says Michaelis, "Nonattenders were not asking for a change in the kind of plays that were being produced. Instead they were asking for help in getting to them. . . . We assumed that the public understood our language. . . . The notions of masterpieces, classics, seasons, good audiences, and so on, do not necessarily mean the same thing to outsiders. There is a different frame of reference for those on the outside, and an anxiety about entering what appears to be a closed group."

It is up to the PR director to work with the media to create approaches to the productions that use language that will be familiar, comfortable, and appealing to the reader or listener. Before formulating a communication, a public relations person must ask such questions as: Who is the audience (both media and public)? What do we know about them? How sophisticated and intelligent are they? What are their attitudes? beliefs? preferences? habits? How persuadable are they? What are their expectations?[4]

The Tasks of Marketing PR

Public relations serves many different functions, some of them overlapping. Generally, PR is the systematic promotion of organizational goals, products, images, and ideologies. Public relations activities fall into three distinct categories: image PR, routine PR, and crisis PR.

IMAGE PR

Image PR tries to shape the total impression someone has of an organization. For example, image PR may attempt to:

- *Revitalize, relaunch, and reposition the organization and its products:* Public relations for the Joffrey Ballet Company's production of *Billboards,* danced to music by rock star Prince, helped to attract new and younger audiences to its performances and to stimulate demand for other dance productions as well.

- *Build consumer confidence and trust:* Rave reviews at home and on tour; stories about awards and sold-out performances, and about a company's directors, productions, and/or performers being in demand elsewhere may help to position the organization as a leader and expert.

ROUTINE PR

Routine or ad hoc PR comprises most of the efforts by the public relations manager to promote individual productions, performers, and special events. Routine PR attempts to achieve a specific goal beneficial to the organization by actively and sometimes aggressively influencing certain target publics. Some of its goals are:

- *To introduce new products:* Advance media articles about upcoming performances are critical for building interest and excitement and for selling tickets before a show opens, reviews are printed, and word of mouth has a chance to spread.

- *To communicate new benefits:* A symphony that had trouble selling tickets for its Valentine's Day performance positioned its concert as the perfect prelude to love. It also offered a red rose to every woman who attended. In one day, the symphony sold two hundred additional tickets, all to young couples.

- *To involve people with products:* An orchestra may provide news accounts of the renovation of its hall; human interest stories about performers, playwrights, composers; and so on, to make people seem more a part of the action on stage.

- *To cultivate new markets; to reach preexisting target markets:* For example, a theater may choose to promote its lead actress in her nearby home neighborhood newspaper.

- *To tailor marketing programs to local audiences:* When the National Dance Theatre Company of Jamaica performed at the Brooklyn Performing Arts Center, the PR director worked closely with people in the Jamaican community. The Jamaican consulate mailed announcements in envelopes with its own return address and appeared on local radio stations to talk up the performances. Caribbean restaurants promoted the performances and offered to sell tickets, as did the Caribbean Chamber of Commerce.

CRISIS PR

Crisis PR attempts to protect the organization and its management, artistic personnel, and board members from problems that shake the very foundations of its survival. Crisis PR helps the organization to prepare to deal strategically with serious problems as they arise and to deal with the media and the organization's other stakeholders during and following a crisis situation.

IMAGE

According to public relations strategist William Rudman, "Image leads to our survival and growth, or to our failure. The way our institutions are perceived has much to do with how many tickets we sell, and to whom, and how many contributions we receive, and from whom."[5]

Much of the time, an organization's image problems are self-inflicted. Say arts marketers Brad Morison and Kay Fliehr, "What muddies the water is that many organizations have not clearly defined what they want to be, nor do they come to understand who they really are. It is inevitable that the public's image will be confused, and steps taken to improve it will be difficult."[6] In such cases, the board, artists, and staff must reach a consensus on the organization's mission and turn that mission into long- and short-term plans for meeting specific goals. Once an organization is clear as to what it is about, it is up to the public relations manager to communicate that image.

Historian Daniel Boorstin describes an image as

> a visible public 'personality' as distinguished from an inward private 'character.'. . . The overshadowing image, we readily admit, covers up whatever may really be there. By our very use of the term we imply that something can be done to it: the image can always be more or less successfully synthesized, doctored, repaired, refurbished, and improved, quite apart from (though not entirely independent of) the spontaneous original of which the image is a public portrait.[7]

In this sense, reality is "constructed." In creating an image, public relations managers and journalists work with facts to develop stories, perspectives, or opinions; always looking for a fresh and exciting angle; often preferring human interest stories over "substance." The image's "truth" comes from its congruence with the ideas, perceptual processes, beliefs, and self-interests of the audience.[8]

Naive managers and marketers often assume that good ideas, good productions, good composers (or playwrights or choreographers), and good performers have a persuasive power all their own ("See how many Grammys we have won!"). They believe that if presented effectively, this "truth" will be recognized and accepted and the source of what is "good" (the arts organization) will be rewarded. A more realistic view is that images gain power from their appropriateness to the audience to which they are presented.[9]

Characteristics of an Image

Boorstin describes six characteristics of an image: it is synthetic, believable, passive, vivid, simplified, and ambiguous.

AN IMAGE IS SYNTHETIC

It is planned, created especially to serve a purpose—to make a certain kind of impression. This characteristic is exemplified by the trademark or brand name: "The Met" (The Metropolitan Opera) or A.R.T. (American Repertory Theatre). A trademark is a legally protected set of letters, a picture, or a design, identifying a particular product. Unlike other standards, trademarks can be owned. One task of PR is to disseminate, reinforce, and exploit them.

AN IMAGE IS BELIEVABLE

It serves no purpose if people do not believe in the image that the organization is trying to convey. One of the best paths to believability is understatement. One prudent public relations director takes advantage of the increasing use of superlatives to make his own hyperbole seem a conservative truth: "Ask someone who has heard her perform," or "This orchestra is not very good . . . simply the best there is."[10]

AN IMAGE IS PASSIVE

Because the image is already supposed to be congruent with reality, the producer of the image (namely, the organization) is expected to *fit* the image—rather than strive toward it. The consumer of the image (a potential customer, for example) is also supposed somehow to fit into it. Once an image is there, it becomes a more important reality than the organization itself. In the beginning the image is a likeness of the organization; finally the organization becomes a likeness of the image, and its conduct seems mere evidence.

When the Standard Oil Company of New Jersey sponsored the New York television program *Play of the Week*, it was building its image as a public-serving corporation. The production of plays had nothing to do with the production of oil. But the average consumer has only the vaguest notion of the actual activities of this vast, complex corporation, so its public image substitutes for more circumstantial notions of what it does.

Sometimes image building is concentrated in a key individual rather than in the organization itself. This is especially true in the case of a strong, charismatic leader like Robert Brustein, the highly respected artistic director of the American Repertory Theatre.

AN IMAGE IS VIVID, CONCRETE, AND SIMPLIFIED

The image should be simple and graspable. One or a few of the products, the persons, or the organization's qualities must be selected for vivid portrayal. The most effective image is simple and distinctive enough to be remembered.

AN IMAGE IS AMBIGUOUS

In order to suit unpredictable future purposes and unpredictable changes in taste, an image should, according to Boorstin, "float somewhere between expectation and reality, between the imagination and the senses." It must be a receptacle for the wishes of different people. The fuzzier the image, the more people can clarify it by making it what they want it to be. Whether it is fact or fantasy, the purpose of the image is to overshadow reality. These characteristics apply whether the organization is describing one of its productions, a performer, or itself. Consider the examples in the following sections.

A Production's Image

The following is a blurb by publicist Susan Bloch for a production of *Playboy of the Western World.*[11]

> A moonstruck dreamer starving for his place in the sun finds it, by chance, in a town hungry for heroes at any cost. Synge's folk tale for all time slyly captures the fire and joy of the Irish mystique as it compassionately satirizes the contradictions of a world gone topsy-turvy. Primitive, lyrical, romantic, and cynical, this masterful play of great wisdom and gorgeous language will be staged by John Hirsute.

Examples of Boorstin's image characteristics abound in this description:

- Believable: *Slyly, compassionately, masterful.*
- Passive: *. . . finds it, by chance . . .*
- Vivid and concrete: *moonstruck dreamer, fire and joy, primitive, lyrical, romantic, cynical.*
- Simplified: *masterful play of great wisdom and gorgeous language.*
- Ambiguous: *Irish mystique, contradictions, topsy-turvy.*

A Person's Image

The young Russian pianist Evgeny Kissin was named 1995 Instrumentalist of the Year by *Musical America*. Aspects of Kissin's image were clearly presented in a feature article in *Musical America*'s annual directory. Some excerpts follow:

- *Vivid, concrete:* "In highly Romantic repertoire he demonstrates an instinctual flair and natural gracefulness—in addition to jaw-dropping technical control."
- *Simplified:* Describing the "young prodigy," music critic Harold Schonberg said, "Suddenly I was in the presence of greatness. . . . The boy had everything."

- *Believable:* "The effect on audiences is heightened by the shy, even awkward stage presence he projects. At 23, his movements to and fro the piano—a bit mechanical but clearly earnest—convey a youthful vulnerability that is instantly endearing. He is equally shy and equally endearing in person."

- *Ambiguous:* "What does the future look like from here? All expectations on his behalf are of a deepening musicality and an even greater range of repertoire. . . . I am curious," said the interviewer, "to hear how you will put your personal stamp on Viennese classics." Responded Kissin with a chuckle, "I am curious too!"[12]

Upon reading this article, one wonders if interviewer Stuart Isacoff, himself a pianist and composer, is a public relations specialist or just innately understands "such stuff as dreams [or images] are made on."

An Organization's Image

When positioning an organization and creating its image, the marketer should take into account the needs of prospective customers—show the consumer "what's in it for him." Image marketers must keep in mind that their goal is to remain honest while being creative and convincing, never deceptive. This is important not only for the obvious ethical reasons, but also for the sake of customer satisfaction. If the organization does not deliver what the image promises, the customer will be far less satisfied than if expectations had never been set so high. See Chapter 5 for a discussion of ways to analyze, measure, and strategize an organization's image.

PUBLICITY

The publicist must learn to think strategically. Specific communications objectives should be set for specific audiences for each season, production, or event. A clear, continuing program of releases and stories should be developed for each planning period. Not all stories that are interesting to the publicist or to the organization's administrators should be brought out if they do not help promote the organization's long-term interests. Timing of publicity efforts is crucial. More important than getting into the paper on a daily or weekly basis is to time "publicity breaks" that bounce off the other marketing components: the brochure, the radio spot, telemarketing, special events, and so on, to create synergy among all the aspects of the campaign.

A public relations manager cannot underestimate the amount of time and planning that is required for successful publicity efforts. A well-conducted publicity campaign does not begin a week or two before the show opens; it is an ongoing effort, characterized by constant nurturing and planning for the future.

Working with the Media

Getting news items into the local press or on television or radio is itself a marketing task. As such, the publicist must start with the immediate audience—the media—and must understand what reporters are looking for in a news story. The media rely on public relations personnel to provide them with material. People used to believe that there were only so many "events" in the world. Says historian Daniel Boorstin, "There was a time when the reader of an unexciting newspaper would remark, 'How dull is the world today!' Nowadays the reader says, 'What a dull newspaper!' "[13] The enterprising reporter is expected to *find* a story. The public relations director can assist the reporter in this task by setting up interviews, by unfolding the human interest stories behind commonplace events, and by discovering the "news behind the news." The better the PR director is able to meet the reporters' needs, the more likely the media will help meet the organization's PR goals.

A good publicist must be in regular contact with the key columnists, critics, editors, and producers in the community to build relationships and keep them informed about the organization's activities and motivations. Long-term cultivation of relations with media gatekeepers helps get news items reported and assures full and accurate coverage. Favorable attitudes on the part of these gatekeepers can be particularly valuable when a crisis arises or a "scandal" is uncovered. Among the prime characteristics journalists will seek for any story are: the interest of the subject to their audience; the possibility for dramatization through pictures or live interviews; the clarity and exhaustiveness of any press release, including supporting materials, statistics, etc.; limited need for further "digging"; and the possibility for exclusive coverage—either for the entire story or for a specific angle.

Following are some tips for working with the media:[14]

- The key to an effective publicity campaign is advance planning. Space and time restrictions necessarily limit the amount of material that can be used by the media. The PR manager should prioritize the events and issues that best serve the organization's goals, and devote efforts to gaining media coverage accordingly.

- Know the media—read, watch, listen—and become familiar with each media organization's style, orientation, strengths, and limitations. Know which regular columns and broadcast programs are appropriate for the events and will give information about the organization. Know what kind of audience each media person addresses. Don't call everyone with each new idea; the story you pitch must be compatible with the type of program or publication you solicit, or else rejection is inevitable.

- Be selective. Overkill can cause the media to give you less coverage in the future. Not all events call for a full-scale publicity campaign, and if you overemphasize a minor story, you may have trouble getting coverage for a genuinely newsworthy program. Mike Martin, the news director for KRBE-FM in Houston, Texas puts it this way: "Remember, if you flood me with stuff that is not important, you're diluting my interest. Then I'll take anything you send me as probably not important. If you hit me with only important stuff, stuff I need, stuff I can use, that's important to the community, I'm going to pay more attention when I see your logo on the envelope."[15] "On the other hand," says *Charlotte Observer* critic Tony Brown, "some journalists appreciate being kept up on a week-to-week basis. You never know when there is a slow week coming up and journalists might need a nugget of information to flesh out a column. Journalism is a capricious business."

- Know each medium's own deadlines and preferred formats for submitting information for calendar listings and articles. Establish your own deadlines to take advantage of theirs. Keep all media information up to date, such as whether one outlet will give your organization public service announcements if you are buying space or time from a competing media organization.

- However tempting it may be to fax your publicity material to the press, many journalists do not like to receive uninvited faxes. They have a limited number of receiving machines, and a glut of unwanted releases can tie up their machines and keep them from getting important news. When you are *invited* to fax material to journalists, take advantage of the opportunity to help them meet their own deadlines.

- When phoning a journalist to make an initial contact or to follow up on a mailed release, find out first if the journalist is on deadline or is free to talk, and then be brief and to the point. Figure out what to say in ninety seconds that will spark their interest, possibly adding a new "twist" to a follow-up call. Media people get hundreds of calls a day; even if you have spoken with a journalist several hours before, remind him or her of who you are and the reason for the call.

- When you make an exploratory call to a journalist, try to have three or four different story ideas so you have a better chance of providing something of interest. Journalists know the interests of their publics and may have personal preferences that affect their responsiveness to various ideas.

- Once you have been turned down, even for an important story, do not argue with the journalist, as doing so will only alienate him or her. But, if you are able to discover a whole new angle to the story, test it out on some colleagues to make sure it is really different and meets the organization's needs—then call the journalist again and make your pitch.

- Journalists are not responsible for selling tickets. Don't ask them to help you promote a show that is not selling well.

- Never tell a media person what she or he should write about. As you get to know the personalities of the various media people you deal with, develop an idea of what kinds of stories they like to cover. Send a written suggestion pointing out interesting aspects of a production, event, or human interest story.

- Point out opportunities for the journalist to contribute his or her own "spin" to the story.

- Consider the fact that some journalists like to dig further to cover a story well; others do not. Journalists should be presented with not only the facts of the story but a range of peripheral material that may fulfill their specific needs and interests. This material could include photos or photo opportunities, profiles of key figures in the story, lists of reference material, or floppy disks with new release materials in each journalist's own word processing language.

- Don't criticize the critic or review the reviewer. The critic or reviewer has the task of evaluating your product on behalf of the public, not on behalf of the organization. The power inherent in the critic's position is one of the realities of the business. Yet, many critics and reviewers have extraordinary understanding of and sensitivity toward the pressures and issues affecting performing arts organizations. They are generally receptive to receiving information and being kept up to date on the organization, its programs, and its performers. If you disagree with a reviewer, talk with him or her directly on a calm, professional basis. The dispute should not be taken to the editor, publisher, or station manager—this will make an enemy, rather than an ally, of the reviewer.

- Have one, and only one, person from your organization as your media contact, so that the media is not deluged with different requests, releases, and even arrangements for buying space or time from the same organization. Such confusion reflects badly on the organization. However, make key people in the organization, such as the executive director, available to the journalist when requested.

- The organization's tax returns and other information in the public domain should be readily available to journalists upon request.

- Let the reporter know that a certain artist is available for an interview. The PR person may brief the artist in advance, but should not sit in on interviews, because journalists do not like to be monitored. Avoid rewarding or punishing a journalist with access to a star. Says critic Tony Brown, "Punishment by withholding information is a dangerous game."

- Invite media people to rehearsals or send them a script.

- Schedule events to take advantage of slow news days such as holidays.

- Opening night invitations should go out to the media three to four weeks in advance. Include date, time, address, and an RSVP request with the name of the person to whom they should reply. Keep a running list of the respondents to guarantee that seats will be available for them when they arrive. Different newspapers have different policies regarding purchase of tickets for their critics, although arts organizations generally offer them tickets free of charge.

- Send a yearly press kit and/or letter to reporters and editors listing your name, address, and daytime and evening phone numbers. Include a short description of the organization, its offerings, and its upcoming annual program. Press kits can be contained in simple two-pocket folders available at office supply stores. Label the kits with the company's logo, and, when promoting new productions, also put the show's title on the cover. Include the following staple items: (1) press release on the production; (2) photos of the artists or production; (3) copy of *Stagebill* or show program with biographies of performers, author, director and designers; (4) press releases on additional programs such as a children's production, acting school, lecture series, outreach program, etc., being offered by the organization currently or in the near future.

Shrinking Media Coverage for the Arts

Although the public relations function has grown in importance and impact in recent years, the media resources available to arts publicists have dramatically shrunk. "Publicity today is a heartbreaking profession," says *New York* magazine critic Peter G. Davis.[16] One veteran publicist maintains that the newspaper business's editorial stance is killing the performing arts business. From 1991 to 1993, the classical performance and recordings space in the Arts and Leisure section of the Sunday *New York Times* was cut in half. As newspapers struggle to retain readership, the percentage of coverage is veering sharply to the more popular arts—especially pop music and film. Says *New York Times* editor James Oestrich, "I really feel sorry for these [PR] people. . . . I am their job, to a large extent. There are just not that many publications around, and I can't be all things to all people. I feel every day of my life in this job that I am letting down publicists, artists, writers—I'm letting down everybody, because I don't have the space to do more." Publicist Alix Williamson graphically describes the frustrations of her job:

> I get an idea. Then I write a letter about that to a given editor. I don't get an answer, so I start to call him. I call him not once but twelve or fourteen times. He never returns the call. Finally one day I'm lucky and get him on the phone, and he asks what I'm calling about. I tell him, "It's about the letter I wrote to you on such-and-such a day." "Well, what was it about?" he asks, and I repeat the gist of it. "Well," he says, "that sounds like a good idea—would you mind writing me another letter about it?" So I write another letter, and I go through another sixteen calls until I get him on the telephone.
>
> Now this whole business is absurd. It is a waste of my time, it is a waste of his time, and it doesn't get anybody anywhere. If people were at least courteous and just said, "I got your letter—we can't use your idea," that would be the end of it, and I wouldn't bother them again and [would] save a lot of time and money.

New York Times critic Allan Kozinn counters this publicist's complaint by saying, "You feel guilty not calling them back, but there are more publicists today than ever, and some days there will be fifteen or twenty messages on my machine. If I were to call them back, I wouldn't get any work done. We don't have secretaries, we have a smaller staff than we used to, but the work hasn't diminished." To further save time, canny critics and editors press down on the envelope of a press release to see its headline, and toss it if it's of no interest. Others automatically throw away any envelopes addressed mechanically. So the more sophisticated PR people individually type envelopes to the most important members of the press. One savvy press agent sends postcards.

Many in the press complain of publicists who haven't done their homework. Says Edgar Vincent, "Any publicist ought to know the character of the publication he's dealing with. If a publicist pitches the same pitch on one particular artist to *Opera News* as he would to the *New York Times* or the *Daily News* or *Vanity Fair,* he ought to be kicked out of the business. You do different ones for different publications, because the philosophy of the editorial staff is different, and their perception of their readership is different. You have to know with whom you are dealing, for God's sake."

Alternative PR Strategies

Creative public relations managers have found some new solutions to shrinking arts coverage, such as placing features in alternative newspaper sections, creating collaborative features, and capitalizing on holidays to promote the organization and its productions. In addition to gaining visibility for specific arts events, such coverage has served other important goals: reaching new audiences and giving underwriting efforts, educational programs, and even capital campaigns an unexpected boost. Also, these alternative strategies have often led to larger feature stories than would otherwise have appeared and have created new relationships with different editors and writers.[17]

ALTERNATIVE SECTIONS

One San Francisco public relations firm has achieved coverage for musicals, comedies, and dramas in the sports, business, food, home, and news sections of local newspapers. The food section is an ideal place to reach the all-important female reader—whom surveys repeatedly identify as the prime decision maker for theater attendance. In one case, a "cooking lesson" was held for actors at a major restaurant chain, where the actors learned traditional Tuscan culinary tricks for an on-stage kitchen scene. The restaurant—a sponsor of the production—got valuable food-section exposure, and the play was touted to a perfect potential audience.

The corporate takeover drama *Other People's Money* played to Wall Street audiences in New York but failed to draw financial types in San Francisco until an interview with the star actor (whose personal corporate background coincidentally paralleled the play's story line) was published in the business section.

COLLABORATIVE FEATURES

One of the publicist's problems comes from "returning to the well" too often for coverage of repeated events such as *Nutcracker* or *Christmas Carol* productions or annual festivals. Collaborative features offer an alternative by giving a new twist to an old story. One successful approach was to promote together all the Shakespeare festivals offered in San Francisco's Bay Area. Each year, the publicist returned to regional and in-flight magazines with glowing reports on this burgeoning center for outdoor Shakespeare.

In another instance, features on "Alternative Holiday Shows" were pitched to rescue small productions in danger of getting lost among the *Nutcrackers* and *Christmas Carols*. The freshness and ingenuity of this approach led the *Noh Christmas Carol*, a vivid depiction of the Dickens classic performed in traditional Japanese Kabuki Noh style, to be featured in all the local dailies and on the cover of the major Sunday entertainment section.

To make a collective feature like this work, the publicist must come to the media with the bulk of the research completed, including dates, times, and box office information for the group of attractions. The feature's benefits are shared by all the events mentioned, and the approach creates an opportunity for coverage that would not have existed otherwise.

HOLIDAYS

The media are always seeking new angles for covering oft-repeated and predictable events. Every arts publicist should see this as a bonus opportunity to gain additional coverage while helping out the local journalist. For example, one Valentine's Day, a theater provided a feature on "marriages made backstage." On Mother's Day, one theater offered a free ticket to any mother accompanied by her offspring, utilizing both the holiday and price promotion strategies to gain publicity.

Arts publicists may find that in creatively seeking new outlets for publicity, they are actively building new audiences and giving current audiences a different and fresh perspective on the organization and its offerings.

OTHER MEDIA

There are many opportunities besides the standard media for communicating with the public about the organization and its offerings. Consider asking for mention in souvenir programs for sporting events and other cultural events. Seek placement on bus shelters, bus benches, taxi panels, marquees at schools, banks, and other public and private buildings, community bulletin boards, grocery bags, and so on. Send news releases to church and synagogue bulletins, chamber of commerce publications, and service club newsletters.

Companies and individuals that contribute to the arts organization can be instrumental in promoting the organization through their business's internal documents, or even on headers of their fax memos. Leaflets can be inserted in billing envelopes by major employers. Leaflets can also be placed on college campuses and at shopping centers, doctors' offices, building lobbies, health clubs, libraries, and grocery checkout stands. Many arts organizations are more than willing to display brochures from other arts organizations in their own lobbies.

Promotional Tools

Public relations managers have several tools at their disposal to utilize in their image-building and visibility-increasing efforts. The primary tools are the event, the press release, public service announcements, interviews, photographs, and speeches.

EVENTS

Events are important tools for public relations managers. Public relations managers help reporters identify natural events and stories that occur in the life of an organization. PR managers also make news happen, in effect, by creating events. Consider the event created for the Cleveland Ballet.

FIREWORKS FOR *THE NUTCRACKER*

To breathe some new life into an old warhorse, *The Nutcracker*, the Cleveland Ballet added a New Year's Eve party to its December 31 production one year. Ticket prices included entertainment by a rock group, a Dixieland band, and a swing band; refreshments featured champagne, liquor, and hot hors d'oeuvres; and New Year's Eve paraphernalia including noisemakers and hats were distributed.

To publicize the party, the promotion department kept the Nutcracker, the Mouse King and Maria constantly on the road with personal appearances in malls and businesses. The May Company, a major downtown department store, turned its whole store into a Nutcracker Suite, using costumes and sets made especially by the Cleveland Ballet for promotional purposes.

The pièce de résistance of the publicity effort was having a wooden, life-size replica of the Nutcracker climb to the top of an office building near the theater, followed by fireworks at the stroke of midnight.

Although it rained that night, many people came out for the event, including three commercial broadcast stations. People called all the following week to buy tickets for the remaining *Nutcracker* performances.[18]

Several advantages can be gained by creating events. An event can be created to obtain news coverage, such as when a music director participates in the formal groundbreaking for a new performance hall. Its timing can be arranged for the convenience of the reporting media. The success of such an event is measured by how widely it is reported. An event can be created to celebrate the organization's history or triumphs, or to dramatize a particular program or personality. A theater's gala thirtieth-anniversary party broadcasts that it has a long and successful history; an arts organization may sponsor a book or record signing by a featured playwright or singer. Events can bring people together on sociable occasions and bond people to the organization. They can also stimulate word of mouth about the organization and its offerings.

Events make images—however planned or contrived—more vivid, more attractive, more impressive, and more persuasive than reality itself. When used effectively and sparingly, events can go a long way to help imprint the organization's personality on the target public's mind.

A celebrity constitutes an event. Operatic arias do not attract crowds; Placido Domingo and Luciano Pavarotti do. People do not flock to hear the Tchaikovsky Violin Concerto; they flock to hear Itzhak Perlman, Isaac Stern, or child prodigy Sarah Chang. This helps to explain why many highly talented artists have not been able to establish careers: they have not been able to establish an image and big name. Star appearances are events because they spawn other events. When a star dines at a local restaurant or signs copies of a recent book or compact disc, it becomes an event for the media, which, in describing it, mention and thereby promote the upcoming performance, elevating the organization's visibility and prestige.

Creative PR directors can use events to help talented, lesser-known performers develop their own "dramatic reality." Large organizations have the PR personnel and financial resources in place to support the artists they believe in, and this should be a part of their mission. They need not rely only on well-known performers to attract audiences. There are multitudes of highly talented artists in their midst, anxious for opportunities to perform for relatively low fees. Also, by removing the personality from center stage, managers can focus their efforts on building new interest in the artistic experience itself, which can carry over from composer to composer and from playwright to playwright, rather than only from star performer to star performer.

THE PRESS RELEASE

The press release is the basic tool for communicating with the media. The press release has a style and form all its own; it should never resemble an ad or a feature story. A press release's job is not to sell or entertain, but to inform; it should be concise, to the point, and free of background "filler." In writing a press release, the PR manager should avoid hyperbole, but should take advantage of favorable reviews or notices from leading critics. An endorsement from a reputable third party always lends credibility to the publicist's claims.

Each press release is competing for attention with dozens of others each day. Unless the message is immediately discernible, the release will be passed over in favor of one more readily understood. A cluttered, poorly organized release also looks unprofessional and reflects badly on the organization. A press release should contain the following elements:

- *Name of organization:* Whenever possible, send press releases on letterhead; otherwise, type the name of the organization in the upper left-hand corner of the page.

- *Contact name and phone number:* Underneath the organization's name, type your own name or the name of someone who will be available to answer follow-up calls. If you list another person, be sure that she or he has read the release before it goes out. Type your phone number clearly underneath the contact name; do not expect the recipient to search the letterhead for the number.

- *Date:* Type the date on which the release is sent out in the upper right-hand corner.

- *Exclusivity notice:* Situations that call for exclusivity are rare. If you do have a story that lends itself to an exclusive cover pitch, send the prospective journalist a standard press release, then contact him or her in person or over the phone to offer exclusive information. An alternative is to type EXCLUSIVE TO: (in all caps and underlined) followed by the name of the person and the name of the media organization immediately below the contact name on the unique press release. Never mark anything "exclusive" if you intend to send the same information—even in an altered form—to anyone else. If you do, you will damage your own credibility and that of your organization.

- *Release date:* If you want publication of the release to coincide with a specific event, or if there is a tie-in with a particular date, this should be noted. Either "FOR RELEASE ON OR AFTER (date)" or FOR IMMEDIATE RELEASE should be typed in. If the release is about a special announcement—say, the naming of a new artistic director—do not provide the journalist with any information that you would not want publicized in advance. The journalists' job is to report anything newsworthy as soon as they hear it, and of course their preference is to be the first to do so.

- *Headline:* The headline should include as much vital information as possible (without assuming paragraph proportions) and should clearly indicate the tenor of the story to follow. It should be written in the present tense, even if the report is of a past or future event, and should use the active rather than the passive voice. For example: APPLE TREE THEATRE OPENS FIFTH-ANNIVERSARY SEASON WITH MIDWEST PREMIERE OF "ANNA KARENINA" or APPLE TREE THEATRE ANNOUNCES EXTENSION OF RECORD-BREAKING SPRING SHOW, "KEELEY AND DU." In general, copy that is clever and/or funny should be avoided. It doesn't look professional and often confuses and annoys the reader. However, at times, this technique can be used effectively. The Manhattan Punch Line, a New York theater that was devoted to comedy (it no longer exists), sent out "un-press releases," listing stars, then saying: "Only kidding folks—we don't know who will be there." Some media people picked up on these releases and actually printed the "information," stimulating interest in the organization.

- *Body copy:* In fashioning the press release, follow the journalist's rule of thumb, the inverted pyramid. Include all the critical information (the who, what, when, where, and why) in the lead or opening paragraph, then move through the rest in descending levels of importance, concluding with the least essential points in the shortest paragraphs at the end. This structure is helpful to copy editors, who, when pressed for space, can simply cut copy from the bottom, assured that the crucial information will remain intact. Always double-space type and leave wide margins. Don't use the back side of the paper. Be sure to cover the following points: name and address of organization; name of production; opening and closing dates (include a brief description of show; author, director, actors, where applicable (always double-check the spelling of every name in the release); performance days and times; ticket prices and special rates, where applicable; and box office hours, address, phone number. This would be the proper order for a standard release announcing the opening of a new show. If the purpose of the release is to announce a change of cast or performance dates or the introduction of a senior citizen discount package, the order would be adjusted to feature the most important information. If you use more than one sheet of paper, type -MORE- on the bottom of the page, number the pages, and at the conclusion, type a series of symbols such as # # # . This is the journalistic fashion for signifying "the end."

To get feedback on press releases (and public service announcements), include a business reply or stamped postcard with the material. To make the process even easier for the journalist, run off a duplicate set of mailing labels and place one on each of the cards, so the media contact doesn't even have to fill in his or her name and address. Ask them to check boxes to let you know the following: (1) if and when they used the piece, (2) whether they want more like it, and (3) if they want you to call them to supply further information. Be sure to leave a space for comments. The answers can help you evaluate your publicity material.[19] To get feedback from those journalists who do not take the time to fill out the cards, ask them a few questions on the phone or at your next performance.

PUBLIC SERVICE ANNOUNCEMENTS

Although air time on radio and TV is expensive to purchase, the broadcast media are usually quite willing—even eager—to give air time for public service announcements (PSAs). There was a time when radio and TV stations were required by the Federal Communications Commission to give air time to nonprofits. Although this is no longer the case, the media like to be seen as good community citizens, and also to fill otherwise empty air time with interesting material.

On-air time is highly coveted, and the number of organizations competing for it is tremendous. It is crucial that PSA material be prepared properly in order to be considered for use. Many local and national advertising agencies and production houses are willing to donate their services to developing PSAs. Whether PSAs are prepared in-house or by an outside agency, the following tips should be kept in mind:

- PSAs of differing lengths should be offered. The more variations you submit, the better your chances for getting on the air. Indicate the reading time at the top of the page: ten seconds (25 words), twenty seconds (50 words), thirty seconds (75 words). Never send anything without reading it out loud and timing it several times first. Names that may be difficult to pronounce should be spelled out phonetically.

- Check deadlines. Most stations require a long lead time for PSAs, often as much as six weeks prior to the event.

- Check with the public affairs director of each station as to their PSA policies. Some stations air PSAs randomly throughout the day; others have community calendars or bulletin boards where they air many such announcements collectively. Cable stations in particular use this latter format, and many have specific forms that must be filled out and submitted if your PSA is to be considered for inclusion.

- It is against the law to mention raffles, door prizes, and lotteries.

Radio station owners may find that providing public service announcements or low-cost advertising to performing arts organizations can help them to meet their own goals. In one case, a radio station carried out a spot-announcement effort for a theater over a period of several months. The effort not only helped to boost sub-scribership, but also resulted in a significant increase in single-ticket sales, which had been extremely poor. The station owner was then able to make the argument to potential commercial sponsors, "If I could sell subscriptions to this theater, which has always had difficulty marketing its product, can you imagine what I could do for your product?"

As an incentive, a performing arts organization may offer to trade so many sub-scription tickets for so many announcements. The station may then use the tickets as prizes in contests or as gifts to advertisers. A performing arts group with a previous record of considerable unsold seating capacity is in a good position to enter into special deals of this type. In addition to filling otherwise empty seats, it is an opportunity for the organization to attract new audiences.[20]

Major symphony orchestras raise huge sums of money annually through symphony "radiothons," during which an FM classical music radio station gives over an entire weekend to the symphony for the playing of live music by orchestra members and other performers in the community, the playing of recordings on request (with contributions accompanying each request), feature interviews with music "personalities," and offers of special perks for subscribing and for various levels of donations. Such radiothons are highly effective in building visibility for the orchestra and its spokespeople, earning donations, and attracting new subscribers.

INTERVIEWS

An often effective vehicle for publicity is the media interview. It was recently reported that there are 4,250 local news and talk shows on 988 television stations in the United States. On these shows, 10,200 guests appear annually.[21] The public access channels on TV are particularly eager to find and use such guests. Sometimes the guests are celebrities or newsworthy individuals; often the guests are simply experts on some subject, or people with a simple story to tell. Arts organizations can provide to the media a number of subjects and guests over a year's time to satisfy their voracious appetite for program material. Visiting artists at theaters and musical performances are always in demand. Anything offbeat generally has a much better chance of gaining time or space to tell the organization's story than a subject that has already been worn out in the media. To successfully pitch a story to a talk show producer or guest coordinator:

- Keep pitch letters to one page.
- Use background information and statistics to show how and why your suggestion is important to the audience. Provide brochures and related news clippings that help sell the idea as timely and provocative.
- Suggest a few thought-provoking questions to be asked during the interview.
- Follow up your letter with a phone call to the producer or coordinator, and be prepared to sell your idea.
- Send stations a list of possible discussion topics and experts to deal with each one.

Once your interview has been approved for airing:

- Bring along visual aids or props to help enliven a television segment.
- Make sure your guest or representative has seen or heard the show prior to the day of his or her appearance.
- Routinely remind the talk show contact that you exist and that your people are available.

PHOTOGRAPHS

Photos are more than just visual supplements to features and reviews; often they tell a complete story themselves with only the aid of a caption. When pitching a story to the press, the publicist should be sure to alert the photo desk to any photographic opportunities that may exist. In some cases, coverage results exclusively from the interest of the photo editor.

The publicist should try to come up with a visual angle for every event or program connected with the organization. Whether the media sends a photographer or not, the organization can have its own photographer on hand to record such events as an opening-night party, a rehearsal with a visiting celebrity, a special announcement by the artistic director or president of the board, or an enthusiastic standing-room-only audience. The organization should keep an archive of such materials for future promotions. It is important to have a photographer familiar with the organization who can be counted on to have the photo shoots run smoothly while the publicist is busy with other matters.

SPEECHES

Public relations managers can generate many firsthand contacts by providing the organization's volunteers, board members, staff, or artists as public speakers. A large organization may have its own speakers' bureau and provide its services on an ongoing basis throughout the community. To develop speaking engagements:

- Identify the potential audiences in your area such as service clubs, cultural associations, social clubs, churches, business associations, schools, or libraries. Chambers of commerce may have listings of such organizations in your area.

- Develop a list of speakers in your organization and possible topics on which they can speak. For example, many opera companies have specially trained volunteers who lecture on each upcoming production in various communities. Similarly, orchestral musicians, theater directors, choreographers, actors, dancers, and others may provide ongoing programs to educate people about their offerings.

- Send a notice of the speakers' bureau to program coordinators for your potential audiences. Use your speakers' bureau mailing list for publicizing your programs and fund-raisers, and for other direct-mail purposes.

- Develop a comprehensive checklist or worksheet for each speaking assignment, covering the date, exact location, specific start time, whether to expect questions and answers, audience size, program length, and the name and phone number of the contact person.

- Capture the names and addresses of people who attend the speaking engagements for the organization's mailing list.

The Public Relations Manager

Many arts organizations handle all of their public relations in-house; others choose to hire an outside professional PR agency. One of the biggest mistakes an organization can make is to underestimate the amount of time and planning that goes into successful public relations. Therefore, an organization that chooses for economic reasons to do publicity in-house, using already overextended personnel, may work against its own best interests. Either adequate time must be allotted for an in-house person to handle a myriad of details on a timely basis, or a professional PR person or agency should be hired. In any case, the ultimate responsibility for the planning and direction of all publicity efforts belongs in-house.

When hiring an outside publicist, the organization should look for someone with a proven track record with the performing arts—someone who clearly understands the special needs and opportunities of this field. In order to avoid any gaps or overlaps in service, a written agreement should spell out all responsibilities and fees. One member of the in-house staff should be designated to act as the PR liaison to avoid the confusion that inevitably results when more people are directly involved. Management should meet with the publicist on a regular basis; every other week is usually adequate. Management can assemble a calendar indicating deadlines for press releases, photographs, PSAs, opening-night invitations, and so on, and help the publicist to develop story ideas and identify new audiences that may be targeted for specific productions or other offerings. While current productions are being publicized, planning of PR strategies for upcoming productions (and seasons) should be under way.[22]

There are several precautions every publicist should take to ascertain that the information he or she disseminates is correct and to protect against future questions about the publicity material. First, the publicist should get information for press releases, PSAs, and other publicity materials in writing and follow up all conversations, both within the organization and with media contacts, by writing confirming memos. These are valuable ways to avoid misunderstandings. Second, if other people in the organization have to approve the publicity material, the publicist should ask them to initial it. When the organization quotes someone in a news release, the person should be sent a copy ahead of time, along with a note asking them to initial the release and send it back. Third, the publicist must keep copies of everything written, including memos and interview notes, particularly if others are quoted.[23]

CRISIS MANAGEMENT

Crises are an integral part of organizational life. No organization, regardless of its size or the nature of its operations, is immune to crises. As stated by one observer, "If you are not now in a crisis, you are instead in a pre-crisis situation and should make immediate preparations for the crisis that looms on the horizon."[24] A crisis not only disturbs the smooth operation of the organization but at times may even threaten its survival. Crises can be caused by a range of internal and external factors including mismanagement; inappropriate policies, strategies, and practices; scarcity of financial resources; swift economic, legal, or political changes; credit squeezes; significant changes in the nature of market competition; sharp drops in attendance and in sales levels; labor strikes; and loss of credibility with consumers. Because crises tend to be highly publicized, sharply affecting the organization's public image, crisis management has grown as a specialty area within the public relations function.[25]

Characteristics of a Crisis

Not all stressful situations are crises. An organization may be burdened with pressures that are relatively routine and should not be confused with a crisis. How does a crisis differ from a noncrisis situation? First, a crisis creates a new situation that cannot be handled effectively by old rules and that usually requires drastic measures to correct. It may call for the replacement of top management, drastic budget cuts, major programming changes, or other major steps. For example, the revived Honolulu Symphony is dramatically different than when it closed its doors in 1993. The 1995–96 season budget is $2 million—one-third of the $6 million spent during the 1992–93 season. Services for the orchestra members have been sharply reduced from their previous forty-two week seasons to eighteen weeks for the 1996–97 season. But the Honolulu Symphony Society has retired a large portion of the orchestra's debt; an endowment of $5.6 million has been raised; goodwill, financial support, and concert attendance are growing in the community; and the interim executive director is "cautiously optimistic" about the orchestra's new beginning.[26]

Second, the urgency of a fast response is characteristic of most crisis situations. A crisis situation presents a dilemma: the response has to be sound, effective and well thought out, but it must also be fast and forceful. Crises are often predictable. In the majority of cases, there are direct and indirect warnings and signs that either go undetected, are dealt with inadequately, or are ignored altogether. Typically, crises brew for some time before they surface and eventually explode. If a crisis occurs that was fully or partially predictable, the management team and its decision-making process must have failed to detect and/or prevent the crisis.

It is crucial to correctly diagnose and understand the cause of a crisis. Many organizational and environmental problems that are not financial in nature tend to surface as financial crises. Under most circumstances a financial squeeze is a consequence rather than the cause of a crisis.

THE VANCOUVER SYMPHONY ORCHESTRA: ANATOMY OF A CRISIS

In the recession era of the early 1980s, the Vancouver Symphony Orchestra (VSO) suffered reductions in corporate and individual contributions, and government funding failed to increase. To make matters worse, the VSO began to witness a substantial fall-off in subscriptions and lost its contract for supplemental work with the Vancouver Opera Association. This loss of earned and contributed income came at a time of heightened financial need, because the orchestra had recently negotiated a greatly expanded forty-week contract with its musicians.

In January of 1988, facing an accumulated debt of $1.7 million on a budget of about $7 million and unable to meet staff and musicians' payrolls, the VSO suspended its operations. The Symphony filed for a holding proposal under the Canadian Bankruptcy Act, and the board of directors submitted their resignations. While subscription revenues from an ongoing campaign could have been diverted to cover wages payable, the VSO would have managed only to dig a deeper hole for itself. The decision to suspend operations helped the board avoid accusations of negligence for soliciting subscription funds without reasonable likelihood of honoring its obligations.[27]

Although crises can be life-threatening to organizations and/or their management, some organizations come out of a crisis stronger and healthier. Successful crisis management can sensitize managers and board members to the strengths and weaknesses of the existing system, highlight the need for better controls, and boost the morale of managers, who gain a sense of accomplishment by coping with the crisis.[28]

THE VANCOUVER SYMPHONY ORCHESTRA: FACING THE MUSIC

Over the next six months, the VSO's fortunes turned. The mayor's office established a twelve-member Symphony Recovery Task Force in early March 1988, which was charged with assessing the VSO's viability and developing a strategy for its reemergence. The task force was made up of community business leaders and political figures and was assisted by an advisory panel of arts administrators and music professionals. The group's recommendations, including broad restructuring of the staff and board, formed the basis for the new symphony. Encouraged by the promise of extensive organizational change, and faced with little likelihood of receiving more than $300,000 from an asset liquidation, the VSO's creditors, including more than six thousand 1987–88 season subscribers, recommended forgiving the accumulated debt. As loan guarantor, the provincial government was obligated to pay off the bank debt while the federal Department of Communications provided the VSO with more than $500,000 in seed money to begin again.

Managing a Crisis

Effective crisis management is a difficult, urgent, involved, complex, and time-consuming task. It demands objectivity, flexibility, creativity, persistence, commitment, courage, teamwork, and willingness to change and adopt unconventional and unpopular options. It calls for tough and drastic decisions and important sacrifices.[29]

When considering matters that affect the general public or the community, such as closing down a symphony or theater and leaving subscribers stranded with unusable tickets, managers are ethically obligated to disseminate complete and accurate information as quickly as possible. With a crisis of an internal nature, such as the downsizing of the organization causing some employees to be fired, professionals may target messages to employees through face-to-face meetings or personal letters. When issues affect both internal and external publics, employees may feel torn between loyalty to an employer and concern for personal well-being or job security. Managers must use a combination of internal and external media to address all who are involved.[30]

THE VANCOUVER SYMPHONY ORCHESTRA: ORCHESTRATING CHANGE

In the wake of suspension, the VSO confronted the challenge of placating a number of disgruntled parties. Subscribers and donors felt cheated out of two-thirds of a season, musicians faced unemployment without sufficient warning or preparation, the provincial government had lost patience with the orchestra's reliance upon bailouts, and the Canada Council continued to voice concern over the lack of a coherent plan for corrective action. In order to successfully work through the crisis, the symphony had to curry favor with each of these groups.

The first step the new VSO undertook was to redefine its mission statement, develop a statement of artistic direction, and outline guiding principles as part of a five-year business plan. Next, a search committee was formed to find an appropriate successor to music director Rudolph Barshai, whose controversial tenure at the VSO added fuel to the building crisis.

A new contract with the musicians' union was negotiated before operations resumed. The contract was a flexible, five-year agreement, but some senior managers feared that its terms were excessively generous to the musicians in light of the VSO's ongoing financial difficulties. Fortunately, only four musicians left the VSO during the suspension period.

Dealing with the Press

First and foremost, an organization should cultivate positive relationships with the media and other important publics on an ongoing basis. When a crisis occurs, these relationships may result in fairer (or more favorable) reporting of crisis events and in more objective interpretations of the organization's decisions and actions in a crisis situation.[31] The crisis manager should try to understand the press and its needs; remember that it is the journalist who controls what will be printed or broadcast about the crisis. Dean Rotbart, a former *Wall Street Journal* reporter, suggests that reporters can be bought, but that *information,* not money, is the medium of exchange. Think before you talk—but do talk if you possibly can. Saying little is better than saying nothing, and explaining why you can't talk is better than stonewalling.[32]

Planned communication with the press that is honest, open, cooperative, and responsive to the reporters' deadlines is the key to bringing some degree of control back to the organization and to helping the organization through its difficulties rather than further complicating them.

THE VANCOUVER SYMPHONY ORCHESTRA: THE DISSONANCE REVERBERATES

The many ongoing personnel and financial issues at the VSO in the mid-1980s had prompted its board of directors to adopt a clandestine attitude. Despite such precautions as "confidential" letters, board events were regularly leaked to the press by dissident members.

Similarly, when contract negotiations failed at the beginning of the 1985–86 season, management proceeded with a lockout. The lockout lasted only nine days, but by then a contentious atmosphere had been well established. A musicians' representative read the following statement to the press: "The musicians feel that the crisis everyone is facing is not only financial but also a crisis of confidence in management, a crisis of hope for the future, and a potential artistic crisis. . . . If any of these crises continue, the VSO will either die a sudden death through bankruptcy or a slow death through attrition. Inevitably, the musicians will go elsewhere to secure a better future." As a result of this negative publicity, contributions and subscription renewals dropped precipitously, adding to the VSO's problems.

The following list is a guideline for dealing with the press in times of crisis.

FIFTEEN WAYS TO DEAL WITH THE PRESS

1. *Make the chief executive responsible for press relations.* That means he or she must often speak for the organization, routinely and in times of crisis, and delegate enough authority to make the PR spokesperson a credible source.

2. *Face the facts.* If you err, admit it candidly. Avoid hedging or excuses. Apologize, promise not to do it again, and explain how you're going to make things right.

3. *Consider the public interest in every operating decision.* Your reputation depends far more on what you do than on what you say. Act accordingly. The senior PR expert should have a seat at the table when decisions are made.

4. *Be a source before you are a subject.* The time to make friends with reporters is long before trouble hits. Get to know the people who cover your organization, educate them, help them with their stories, and give them reason to respect you. Determine which journalists deserve your respect and trust.

5. *If you want your views represented, you have to talk.* Reporters are paid to get stories, whether you help or not. When you clam up, they must depend on other sources.

6. *Provide journalists with names of follow-up sources—both inside and outside the organization.* Providing names of independent outside sources may cause short-run problems for the organization, but (a) the journalist in all likelihood will find sources anyway (often more hostile ones), (b) providing outside sources will increase the credibility of the present message, and (c) most important, the PR specialist will more likely be seen (except by the most cynical journalists) as someone who is basically concerned about meeting the *journalist's* needs, not just about selling a story. The customer-oriented news source is someone who tries to help.

7. *Respond fast.* You can't influence a story once its deadline has passed. Nor will you appear credible if you seem to be stalling. In a crisis, figure that you have a day to get your story out.

8. *Cage your lawyers.* They will always tell you to keep your mouth shut. But in many crisis situations your potential legal liability may be trivial compared with the risk of alienating your patrons, donors, and other publics.

9. *Tell the truth—or nothing.* Nobody likes a liar.

10. *Don't expect to bat a thousand.* PR is a game of averages, so be content if you win most of the time. Even the most flattering story will likely include a zinger or two, and even the best organizations get creamed now and then.

11. *Don't take it personally.* The reporter is neither your enemy nor your friend: He or she is an intermediary between you and the people you need to reach. And forget about your ego —nobody cares about it but you.

12. *Control what you can.* Release the bad news yourself, before some reporter digs it up. Use your selective availability to reporters as a tool. Set ground rules every time you talk. If the public isn't buying your message, change it. Dealing with the press is dealing with perceptions.

13. *Know who you're dealing with.* The press is not monolithic. Do your homework on journalists before you talk to them, reviewing their past work and talking to other managers they have covered.

14. *Avoid television unless you feel free to speak candidly.* Even then, learn to present your views in the ten-second sound bites that are the building blocks of TV stories. Use simple declarative sentences and ignore subtleties. Whenever possible, favor live TV shows over those that can edit your remarks.

15. *Be human.* Reporters—and the public—usually will be more sympathetic to a person than to an organization. Your mistakes will as likely be forgiven as criticized. Remember that people love to root for underdogs.

Source: Adapted from Stratford A. Sherman, "Smart Ways to Handle the Press," *Fortune*, June 19, 1989, 72. © 1989 Time Inc. All rights reserved.

Planning for a Crisis

Not every crisis can be anticipated. But an organization prepared to deal with crises is in a better position to deal with emergencies and handle media inquiries when they do occur. It is up to public relations professionals to put in place a systematic, practiced approach long before a crisis hits. Anthony Katz recommends the following ten steps to complete crisis planning.

TEN STEPS TO COMPLETE CRISIS PLANNING

1. *Gain the support of top management.* The public relations professional's first and perhaps most important role is to convince top management of the need for detailed preparation, even when business is thriving and a crisis seems unimaginable. Without this top-level commitment, it is difficult to prepare fully.

2. *Enlist the employees.* An internal organizational policy is mandatory for crisis planning, including what employees should do if disaster strikes. Employees should be instructed where to direct media calls and what to say—or what not to say—if they find a reporter on the line.

3. *Perform risk assessment audits.* Thorough preparation must include identification of the most likely vulnerabilities. Talk to people within and outside the organization to determine potential trouble spots. Questions to ask include: What are the greatest risks to the organization? What specifically might happen? What groups will be affected? How severe is the impact likely to be?

4. *Conduct issues management programs.* Situations such as a musicians' strike, an outraged community reaction to an avant-garde play, or the retirement or firing of a well-liked conductor can adversely affect an organization's image, ticket sales, fund-raising capacity, and reputation. Therefore, crisis planning must include an issues management program to anticipate, identify, and address how to deal with problems before they become emergencies.

5. *Develop a communications plan.* Detailed communication blueprints, developed before a crisis strikes, are central to the ability to respond quickly to a crisis. This is especially critical, because all lasting perceptions of an organization in crisis are established in the first few days. The keys to crisis communication are speed, accuracy, thoroughness, consistency, and credibility. Review the plan periodically and revise it when necessary. The plan should include

   Identification of potential steering-group members to take charge during a crisis.

Streamlined internal communications, such as a task force whose leaders are empowered to speak with authority.

One spokesperson to present a unified message.

Communication strategies with relevant external audiences such as the media, governmental agencies, funding agencies, volunteers, audiences, and other stakeholders.

Carefully sequenced communications to each of these external audiences.

Updated media and other stakeholder lists.

6. *Ready your public opinion research.* The organization's messages and actions in a crisis must fully account for the attitudes and opinions of its key audiences. Therefore a mechanism must be put into place as part of crisis planning to sample quickly the opinions of these publics.

7. *Conduct mock crisis drills.* Crises will be less paralyzing if key employees and board members know what to do. Therefore, simulated crises should be conducted in formal, day- or half-day-long sessions with various members of the organization, including top management, top artistic personnel, board members, and supervisory-level employees. Practice company actions and responses to various scenarios utilizing role-playing that represents sensitive community groups.

8. *Train for media appearances.* The media has a huge influence on the public's perceptions of an organization during a crisis. The organization's spokesperson can be trained for media interviews based on the critical areas uncovered during risk and issue audits. The spokesperson should become familiar with the types of questions that can be expected from different audiences under various scenarios, and practice communicating the messages the organization wants to get across under those circumstances.

9. *Plan for direct communications.* Direct communication with target audiences may be essential for the organization to get its messages across without the filters of the media and with the certainty of reaching those audiences. These communications may include the organization's comments on such sensitive issues as why the crisis happened and what the organization is doing about it. The more detailed these messages can be, and the better they address both the needs and

the sensitivities of the targeted publics, the more effective they will be. Provisions should be made for such direct communications via mail, advertising, newsletters, or a combination of media. The plan should identify suppliers such as printers that have fast turnaround times, and should include steps for obtaining mailing lists and internal approval for copy, among other things.

10. *Consider postcrisis communication.* Crises pass, but their effects often linger. Crisis preparation, therefore, should include steps for identifying those audiences that will require follow-up communication as events wind down, and for ensuring that such communication is actually carried out. For example, plans should be developed for addressing disgruntled donors, newly lapsed subscribers, and employees and performers whose morale is low.

Source: Adapted from Anthony R. Katz, "Checklist: 10 Steps to Complete Crisis Planning," *Public Relations Journal,* Nov. 1987, 46–47. Reprinted with permission.

An added benefit of crisis planning is that through the process, the organization is likely to become more sensitive to issues stewing under the surface, and thus to identify and focus on its problems and perhaps avert escalation to crisis proportions.

Public relations is a critical part of an organization's communication mix, and its effectiveness depends upon close cooperation between the public relations manager and the organization's other key managers. Public relations is the organization's primary tool for shaping public opinion and often can play a dramatic role in stimulating audience response.

[1] "Profile of Member Organizations," Association of Performing Arts Presenters membership survey conducted by AMS Planning and Research (Washington, D.C., 1991–92), 45.

[2] Tom Harris, *The Marketer's Guide to Public Relations* (New York: Wiley, 1991), 12.

[3] Donald Michaelis, *Divergent Views on Promoting the Performing Arts* (New York: ACUCAA, 1976).

[4] For more information on communication strategies, see Charles Conrad, *Strategic Organizational Communication* (New York: Holt, Reinhart & Winston, 1985).

[5] William Rudman, "Essentials of Effective Public Relations," in *Market the Arts!* ed. Joseph Melillo (New York: FEDAPT, 1983), 163.

[6] Brad Morison and Kay Fliehr, *In Search of an Audience* (New York: Pitman, 1968).

[7] Daniel Boorstin, *The Image* (New York: Vintage Books, 1992), 187.

8 Robert Jackall, "The Magic Lantern," in *Moral Mazes: The World of Corporate Managers* (New York: Oxford University Press, 1988), 172–173.

9 Charles Conrad, "Analyzing Organizational Situations: Introduction," in *Strategic Organizational Communication* (New York: Holt, Reinhart & Winston, 1985), 202.

10 Examples adapted from Boorstin, *The Image.*

11 Rudman, "Essentials of Effective Public Relations," 165.

12 Stuart Isacoff, "Evgeny Kissin," *Musical America Directory* (New York: K-III Directory Corp., 1995).

13 Boorstin, *The Image,* 7.

14 Adapted from E. G. Schreiber, "Promoting the Performing Arts," and "Rhoda Weiss's Public Relations Tips for Nonprofit Organizations," in *Media Resource Guide,* 5th ed. (Los Angeles: Foundation for American Communication, 1987), 39–41; and Dianne Bissell, *Marketing Promotions Guide* (Chicago: League of Chicago Theatres, 1985), 51–55.

15 David R. Yale, *The Publicity Handbook* (Lincolnwood, Ill.: NTC Business Books, 1991), 5.

16 Sedgwick Clar, "The Publicist's Complaint," *Opera News,* Sept. 1993, 20–27.

17 Carla Befera, "Alternative Public Relations Strategies Help Combat Shrinking Arts Coverage," *Arts Reach,* June/July 1994, 20–22.

18 Nancy Depke, "Marketing Ballet When New in the Neighborhood," *Dance/USA,* Mar. 1985, 6, 15.

19 Yale, *The Publicity Handbook,* 39.

20 Danny Newman, *Subscribe Now!* (New York: Theatre Communications Group, 1983), 201–203.

21 Timothy Manners, "TV Talk Show Tour Extends Marketing Reach," *Marketing News,* Aug. 16, 1985, 1.

22 Bissell, *Marketing Promotions Guide,* 51–52.

23 Yale, *The Publicity Handbook,* 31.

24 Steven Fink, "Coping with Crises," *Nation's Business,* Aug. 1984, 52R.

25 Claudia Reinhardt, "Workshop: How to Handle a Crisis," *Public Relations Journal,* Nov. 1987, 43–44.

26 "Honolulu Symphony Reactivated," *Symphony,* May–June 1996, 14–15.

27 Andrew F. Cypiot, under the direction of Robert Augsburger, "Vancouver Symphony Orchestra," A and B, case studies, Stanford Graduate School of Business, 1991.

28 Hooshang Kuklan, "Managing Crises: Challenges and Complexities," *SAM Advanced Management Journal,* Autumn 1986, 39–44.

29 Ibid.

30 Reinhardt, "Workshop: How to Handle a Crisis," 43–44.

31 James A. Benson, "Crisis Revisited: An Analysis of Strategies Used by Tylenol in the Second Tampering Episode," *Central States Speech Journal* 39, no. 1 (Spring 1988), 50.

32 Stratford A. Sherman, "Smart Ways to Handle the Press," *Fortune,* June 19, 1989, 69–72.

▲●▲

PART V

MANAGING THE ORGANIZATION

CHAPTER 16

▲●▲

There is nothing more difficult to take in hand, more perilous to conduct, or more uncertain of success than to take a lead in the introduction of a new order of things, because the

innovation has for enemies all those who have done well under the old conditions and lukewarm defenders in those who may do well under new.
MACHIAVELLI,
The Prince

There is a dynamic tension between stability and change that is managed with a strong bias toward change. Order without rigidity is the goal.
J. E. McCANN[1]

DESIGNING AND MANAGING A MARKET-EFFECTIVE ORGANIZATION AND ITS VOLUNTEER PROGRAMS

IN ORDER FOR EFFECTIVE MARKETING TO TAKE PLACE, AN ORGANIZATION MUST BE rationally structured and competently managed. Responsibilities and relationships must be clearly understood and regularly evaluated by the key players. The key managers, board members, and artistic personnel must have the proper philosophy toward strategic planning and the proper skills for implementing plans. It is also necessary that the organization manage a volunteer program to amplify its limited resources.

MANAGEMENT STRUCTURES OF ARTS ORGANIZATIONS

An arts organization's management structure depends on several factors: its age, size, growth rate, specific industry (i.e. opera, theater, etc.), and how these factors interact with each other. Performing arts organizations vary from small dance companies and theaters operated and managed by the artists themselves, their board of directors, and one or two part-time employees, to large symphonies and opera companies with a full complement of professional staff members, similar to a business corporation. Some small organizations remain small—a chamber music group that offers four to six performances a year may never have the need or the budget for a full-time professional staff. Other organizations, like an opera company or a presenter who offers a large quantity and/or wide variety of performances all year long, will need to start out with a complete and experienced staff of management professionals.

Organizational Charts

In a small organization with two or three employees, an organizational chart may not be necessary. But an organization with five or more employees should develop a chart to establish lines of authority and reporting as well as chains of accountability. In a large organization, an organizational chart is especially important. Because direct supervision of every employee is not possible, the chief executive must delegate some authority and accountability. Figure 16-1 shows the organizational chart of the Orchestral Association in Chicago as it existed through 1994. This chart clearly demonstrates to whom the board of directors and the executive director have delegated responsibility and to whom each person must report.

Upon the retirement in 1994 of Joyce Idema, director of marketing and public relations, executive director Henry Fogel revised the organization's structure. He changed the position title of director of marketing and public relations to the more inclusive vice president for communications. He decided to have Stephen Belth, this new vice president for communications, report to Michael Gehret, the newly named vice president for development and marketing, rather than directly to him. According to Mr. Fogel, these two top-level, externally oriented functions are equal in importance and responsibility, but he felt that the new reporting structure would stimulate better and more consistent communication between these two strongly interrelated functions. Figure 16-2 shows the new organizational chart adopted in 1995.

Job Descriptions

In every organization, it is essential that job descriptions be written for all staff members. A job description should provide a full understanding of the roles, responsibilities, and objectives of a position, delineating its authority, accountability, and relationships with other positions. Some managers argue against job descriptions. Job descriptions take a long time to write and require extensive discussions with staff. Furthermore, each time there is a shifting of responsibilities, the descriptions have to be rewritten. But job descriptions are useful in several important ways.[2] The very process of writing job descriptions may reveal that the job responsibilities envisioned for a single person are unrealistic. Once all the tasks are written down, it becomes easier to juggle responsibilities and work loads. Job descriptions promote effective operations by highlighting gaps and minimizing duplication of effort. They define the relationships between individuals and within and among departments,

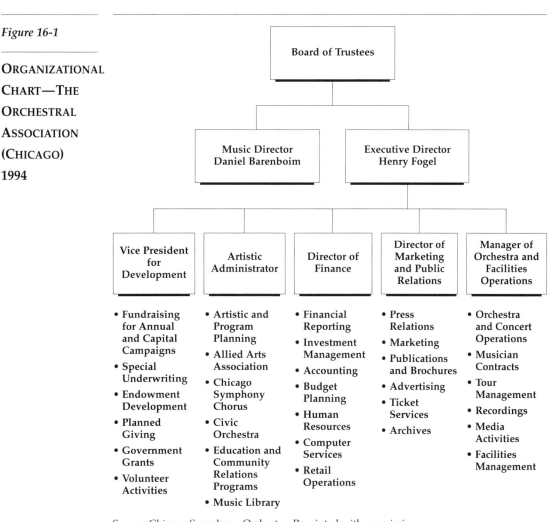

Source: Chicago Symphony Orchestra. Reprinted with permission.

and they provide a basis for formally measuring performance and for maintaining an equitable compensation program.

Job descriptions protect the organization's employees by providing a clear understanding of what is expected of them. Employees are evaluated based on an assessment of the tasks listed in the job description, and cannot be dismissed for not performing a task not listed. Commonly, an employee can expect to be consulted before any changes are made in the job description, especially if the change involves additional responsibilities. Job descriptions also protect the organization, outlining in writing expectations that, if not lived up to, constitute indisputable grounds for dismissal. A job description also helps the supervisor to be objective and to evaluate

Figure 16-2

THE
ORCHESTRAL
ASSOCIATION —
REVISED
1995

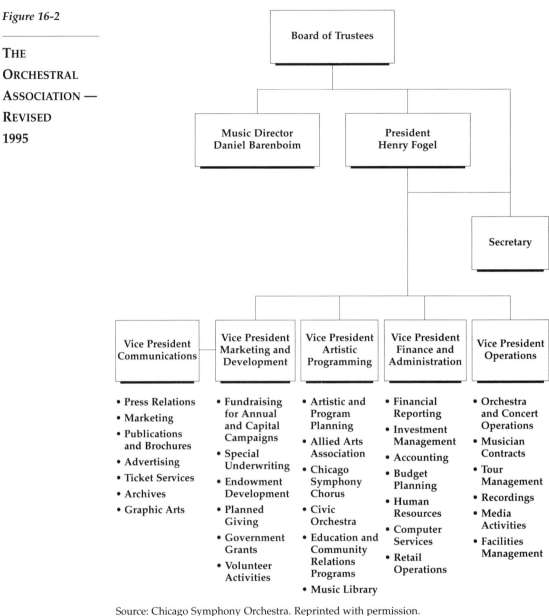

Source: Chicago Symphony Orchestra. Reprinted with permission.

employees based on their performance rather than on more subjective feelings about the person. To make sure that all job descriptions are up to date, the executive director and departmental directors may plan to review them annually and recommend changes to the board of directors that require board approval.

Marketing's Relations with Other Departments

In principle, the various functional managers, board directors, and artistic directors should interact harmoniously to pursue the organization's overall objectives. In practice, interdepartmental relations are often characterized by deep rivalries and distrust. Some interdepartmental conflict stems from differences of opinion as to what is in the organization's best interests and from unfortunate departmental stereotypes and prejudices.

The marketing department is often the subject of such prejudices. Marketers are often accused by artistic directors of a willingness to compromise the art in order to attract a broader audience. Audience surveys are viewed skeptically as the marketer's attempt to "prove" that the audience would like more comedies and fewer classics, or more classical music and less contemporary music. Marketers, however, are generally trying to use the results of their surveys to create higher satisfaction and greater accessibility for their customers through features such as preconcert lectures, flex plans, rush hour concerts, and better targeted positioning strategies—fully respecting the organization's artistic integrity.

Board members and financial managers who pride themselves on being able to evaluate the cost-benefit implications of various business actions are often frustrated by marketing expenditures. Marketing managers ask for substantial budgets for advertising, direct-mail campaigns, sales promotions, and telemarketers without being able to predict with certainty how many sales will be produced by these expenditures. Marketers often see financial people as overly conservative and risk averse, causing many opportunities to be lost, both for the short term and for long-term market development. Financial people see all marketing expenditures as expenses rather than investments. They would be wise to adapt their financial tools and theories to support strategic marketing.

Board members often place a strong emphasis on fund-raising at the expense of marketing efforts. This is especially true in smaller organizations with little professional staff. Board members ask their friends and business associates for donations on an ad hoc basis, recruiting contributions at cocktail parties and on the golf course. Marketing requires strategic planning and a myriad of details to be taken care of on a consistent basis in order for a campaign to be implemented. Marketing requires an initial financial investment; fund-raising does not.

Development directors may also work at cross-purposes with marketing departments. The Vancouver Symphony Orchestra's (VSO) Friends Campaign, which targeted smaller individual donations, actually eroded the VSO's subscription base by "grabbing" the best benefits and leaving none for the subscribers. With the arrival of a new marketing director, the Friends Campaign became the responsibility of the marketing department. Once both campaigns were being coordinated by one person, benefits were strategically apportioned and the timing of the Friends campaign was changed so that the campaigns would be complementary.[3]

Many managers, artistic directors, and board members are product-centered in their thinking. They say, "We have such a terrific product. We have received such consistently great reviews. We have done so much promotion. Why can't we draw larger audiences?" At some point, many of these organizations take steps to become market-driven. Yet often they don't succeed. Why? In many organizations, the executive directors, artistic directors, and key board members do not really understand marketing.

In order to successfully develop a marketing culture, an organization must take several steps. Smaller organizations are not likely to have the resources to carry out all these steps, but in any organization, a marketing culture and mind-set is possible.

Top management must want better marketing and understand it. The chief executive officer's leadership and commitment are critical. The CEO must convince the organization's top managers and board members that better marketing is needed. The CEO must personally exemplify strong commitment to customers and reward those in the organization who do likewise.

Appoint a marketing task force. The CEO should appoint a high-level marketing task force to develop programs for bringing modern marketing practices into the organization. The task force should include the CEO, the finance director, the development director, the chairperson of the board, an executive board member to act as marketing liaison, and a representative of the artistic personnel. They should set objectives, anticipate problems, and develop an overall strategy. The committee should meet on a regular basis to measure progress, to take new initiatives, and to be sure that marketing, artistic, and financial goals are coordinated.

Get outside help and guidance. The organization would benefit from outside consulting assistance in building a marketing culture and in developing strategies. Consulting firms and individual arts consultants have considerable experience in helping organizations improve their marketing orientation and plans. Sometimes larger consulting firms will do work for arts organizations on a pro bono basis.

Change the reward structures in the organization. The organization will have to change department reward structures if it expects departmental behavior to change. As long as the finance department focuses on short-term revenue surplus, finance personnel will oppose major marketing investments designed to build more satisfied and loyal customers.

Hire and retain strong marketing talent. The organization should consider hiring well-trained marketing talent from the outside. And, when budget constraints require downsizing, the organization should not consider its marketing director expendable. Rather, in difficult times, marketing may be the organization's second most important managerial function, after the CEO. Because people are reluctant to contribute to an organization at risk, increasing earned revenue may be the key to the organization's survival. And, if the general manager has to do support-level activities, little time or energy will be left for building or rebuilding. Boards often feel that volunteers can do the marketing work. But what corporate executive would permit a volunteer who is not professionally trained to perform managerial tasks?

Install a modern marketing-planning system. In order to integrate marketing thinking into the minds of the organization's key managers and board members, a modern market-oriented planning system should be installed. Then appropriate marketing strategies and sales forecasts can be developed. Some arts professionals refuse to cooperate with marketing managers, and, on some occasions, they actively seek to frustrate such efforts. According to Robert Kelly, "They are an 'enemy within,' not because they consciously wish to place their arts organizations in jeopardy but because their blind resistance to marketing may, in the end, have that consequence. To survive the crisis in the arts, sophisticated management and marketing will be required."[4] To avoid the commoditization of culture, arts professionals must become more, rather than less, heavily involved in the marketing decision-making process when it affects the areas for which they have responsibility. This is the only way to make certain that artistic standards are not compromised when marketing decisions are taken. Avoidance will lead to ineffectual marketing rather than to an absence of marketing altogether.

Over time, it is hoped that arts administrators will come to appreciate what marketing can and cannot do. Given that the arts audience is limited while leisure offerings continue to expand, even the most sophisticated marketing cannot be expected to fill the hall for every performance or solve an organization's financial problems. But, by taking marketing seriously, integrating marketing with the organization's other functions, and installing better marketing procedures, the organization can be far more successful in achieving its audience-building and financial goals.

Organiza-
tional Size
and Its
Implications

All organizations, whether commercial or nonprofit, share certain marketing problems and can learn from one another. For example, performing arts organizations, airlines, and restaurants all feature a perishable product that cannot be stored, emphasize an experience over tangible factors, and need to smooth demand levels to fit available capacity at any given time. At the same time, arts organizations face issues far different from commercial organizations. For example, while a restaurant may customize its preparations to accommodate the tastes and preferences of its patrons, a nonprofit performing arts organization will generally present its "menu" according to the vision of its artistic leader.

Even among arts organizations, the issues differ widely. In addition to the factors that distinguish each organization from even its most direct competitor, an organization's size has many implications for how it functions. Here we will contrast the characteristics of small, medium, and large organizations.[5]

SMALL ORGANIZATIONS
Smaller organizations are often organized around (and founded by) a guiding artistic figure who sets the organization's policy and style. This often results in a more passive board of trustees, as in the situation at the Eugene O'Neill Theater Center,

described later in this chapter. Most larger organizations have a strong artistic leader to set their style and a strong executive director who works with the board of directors to set policy.

Small organizations are usually newer and less well established. Because not much capital is needed to start a small theater or dance group, they tend to crop up on a regular basis, especially in major cities. A number of volunteers (often the performers themselves) can get together, rent a space, and put on a performance, all at little cost. The paid staff often consists of one or a few part-time and underpaid employees. As a result, the group's fixed costs are low, but its financial position is somewhat shaky.

Many smaller organizations are "creator organizations," existing for the purpose of creating or performing new works.[6] They are committed to the artistic product and to its producers (the acting ensemble, the musicians), more than to the audience. By contrast, larger arts organizations are more concerned with performances that will help them build larger audiences.

Small organizations promote ticket sales largely through word of mouth. Often they distribute free tickets to target audiences to generate awareness and interest. Small organizations tend to have a narrow product focus and thereby appeal to a relatively narrow audience segment. Knowing the target audience makes it easier for small organizations to use targeted publications, radio stations, and mailing lists. But this focus is likely to prevent their building a larger audience.

Smaller organizations focus more on critics and other influential, artistic people. A rave review does not guarantee a large audience, but makes it easier to obtain funding from local foundations and arts councils. On the other hand, several bad reviews can destroy a small organization. Occasional negative reviews of a large organization, especially one with a strong subscriber base, tend to hurt much less.

It is difficult for a small, founder-led, volunteer-run organization to maintain that status for very long. After a while, the founder wants the security of a reasonable salary. The active volunteers want paid staff to take over many of their day-to-day activities. Generous board members may want to see if the organization can "sink or swim" on its own. One small theater had a supporting contributor who, when drastically cutting his annual donation, said that the theater was like one of his children. He had been happy to support it through its infancy and childhood, but now he wanted it to become more self-supporting.

Small organizations that become artistically successful receive pressure from both the artists and the funders to expand. But expansion involves risks, not the least of which is the loss of artistic creativity. Artistic expression begins to take a backseat to presenting productions that will pay for larger rents and salaries.

MIDSIZED ORGANIZATIONS
Orchestra consultant Thomas Wolf believes that large orchestras have inherent strength and small orchestras have inherent flexibility, enabling them to survive

current reductions in funding and audience size. However, observes Wolf, many midsized orchestras have big ambitions but few resources. Consider the factors that led to the 1992 closure of the Sacramento Symphony.

THE
SACRAMENTO
SYMPHONY:
THE DEMISE
OF A MIDSIZED
ORCHESTRA*

By the end of 1992, a downward spiral characterized by increasing deficits and growing acrimony between musicians and management led the Sacramento Symphony to file for bankruptcy. Bad memories of previous bailouts caused the city and county governments to refuse to be financial saviors once again. A generous line of credit, extended in 1990 along with a subsidy, had not been repaid. Besides, the city and county were too financially strapped themselves in 1992 to consider offering more aid.

As the capital of California, Sacramento is a government town. It is not a corporate town or a town of inherited private wealth. It has no tradition of private philanthropy in the arts. So no effort was made to launch a major fund-raising campaign to save the orchestra.

Many people foresaw the Sacramento Symphony's demise. The orchestra had modeled itself on major orchestras in large urban centers. It had lengthened its season and extended and expanded employment for its musicians. It had based its audience size estimates on the area's population, but learned too late that simply counting noses is not very reliable.

*See Chapter 19 for a discussion of the rebirth of the Sacramento Symphony

Sacramento was among the fifty to sixty U.S. orchestras that are most vulnerable —those with budgets between $2 million and $8.5 million. Between 1966 and 1991, these midsized orchestras more than doubled their number of annual concerts. The driving force was not ticket demand, but the increased number of guaranteed services to musicians, which created a need for marketing departments to continuously comb the landscape for ticket buyers.

Most larger orchestras, with budgets ranging up to $40 million, are located in major cities that have a large capital base and a huge philanthropic capacity. These cities are capable of supporting even those celebrated performing arts organizations with large operating losses. They often have long-standing traditions of concert attendance, and benefit from civic pride that makes the loss of an orchestra unthinkable. Many of the largest orchestras are internationally recognized institutions whose survival is considered essential to the vitality of the art form. The Sacramento Symphony was none of these things.

On the other hand, the Sacramento Symphony bore little resemblance to the smallest symphony orchestras, those with budgets under $2 million and with the built-in flexibility to adapt in times of financial stress. Most small orchestras operate on a per service arrangement with their musicians. Instead of establishing an employment contract that assures a minimum number of paid appearances over a fixed number of weeks, they hire musicians on an as-needed basis. They do not commit themselves to burdensome work agreements, and they enjoy remarkable flexibility with respect to fixed costs.

LARGE ORGANIZATIONS

The management structure of large arts organizations is much more institutionalized, and they are much less personally run than smaller organizations. This does not mean that managers of larger organizations are less personally involved in their organizations. It does mean that a change in a director or board chairman is likely to have less effect on the organization's long-term direction or fund-raising ability than a comparable change in the smaller organization. Larger organizations are in a better position to make long-term commitments and plans and to engage in capital and endowment campaigns. Larger organizations are not necessarily in a stronger financial situation than smaller ones. However, they are more assured of continuity of funding from a wide range of sources and are less at risk than smaller organizations when one grant or gift decreases or is withdrawn.

Bigger organizations enjoy a larger subscribing audience and are more likely to attract casual attenders and tourists. Their offerings are scheduled more often, which allows for flexibility in attendance and ticket exchange options. Larger organizations typically feature a broad product line and thereby appeal to a larger public than small organizations. For example, the Boston Symphony Orchestra (BSO) operates its usual subscription series during the winter, a Pops season in the spring, the Tanglewood summer music festival with outdoor concerts, and an advanced music school. The BSO also makes recordings and performs on tour, and its first-chair players combine to form the Boston Symphony Chamber Players. Each of these activities has a different marketing focus and target audience.

There is a strong tendency toward unionization in the larger arts organizations. They are also likely to own and maintain their facilities and to have large professional staffs. These factors contribute to a high ratio of fixed-to-variable costs, putting great pressure on marketers and fund-raisers to generate consistent if not growing revenue streams.

MANAGING GROWTH AND CHANGE

Often an arts organization finds that it must change in order to capitalize on its successes. It cannot afford to remain frozen in its present structure and procedures. At such a point, management and board members must ask such critical questions as: Where has our organization been? Where is it now? And what do the answers to those questions mean for where we are going?

Phases of Growth

A performing arts organization grows through several distinct phases, marked by changing roles and responsibilities of the board of directors and the staff.[7] During each phase, there is evolutionary growth without major changes in organizational practices. This is followed by a transitional phase marked by substantial turmoil in organizational life. Traditional management and board practices that were appropriate for a smaller size, earlier time, or crisis-free situation, are brought under scrutiny by frustrated top managers and disillusioned board members.

Consider the following evaluation that was made of board and staff problems at the Eugene O'Neill Theater Center in Waterford, Connecticut.

THE FOUNDER'S PREROGATIVE, THE FOUNDER'S DILEMMA

The Eugene O'Neill Theater Center in Waterford, Connecticut, was founded in the 1960s by George White, who has served throughout its history as its executive director. White has been a strong leader—managerially, artistically, as the primary fundraiser for the organization, and as its major financial backer. Mr. White's willingness to lend the center approximately $145,000 and to personally guarantee its bank debt has not only kept the center open, but has sustained its artistic focus, as opposed to a focus on generating revenues. Artistically, the O'Neill continues to make significant contributions to the theater world, both domestically and internationally. Despite economic hardship, the creative spirit and vision that drove the O'Neill when it was first started are alive and well after thirty years.

However, most of this spirit is limited to the artistic programs. The center's financial situation is chaotic due to overall cutbacks in arts funding, to cost overruns on a building project, to slow collection and/or writing off of pledges, and to the fact that the O'Neill is reliant on the pledges of six individuals to pay off its existing debt. Daily crises have doused much of the excitement of working at the O'Neill, sapping the energy of staff and board members. To reenergize both parties, the arrival of a new managing director and development director has been trumpeted. While these people may have brought hope with their arrivals, instituting cutbacks for cost containment purposes, upgrading computers, and instigating new programs, the underlying systems and structures at the center have not changed. The resulting frustration has caused frequent staff turnover in recent years.

The board of trustees, however, has done little to respond. Undoubtedly, its members have heard about the "fire drills" of day-to-day operations, and they recognize some of the inefficiencies, but the board has failed to become sufficiently involved to diagnose the core problems and implement positive change. The behavior of individual board members and board functioning as a whole remains consistent with that of years past.

For many years, the equation of George White's name with the O'Neill Theater Center was the founder's prerogative. He was totally involved in proposing artistic and construction projects, raising money, selecting benefits, chairing the board, and managing the staff. In the center's current financial situation, such strong identification has become the founder's dilemma. The board members must devote themselves to separating the O'Neill, the organization, from George White, its founder and life-support system. The O'Neill must be able to stand alone, supported by its board and its manager, not its founder. Such a transition will not only relieve Mr. White's burden; it is also crucial for establishing the processes necessary for the center to operate in today's nonprofit theater environment.[8]

PHASE I: GROWTH THROUGH CREATIVITY—CRISIS OF LEADERSHIP

In Phase I, the founder and the board *are* the organization. Board members type letters and press releases, write checks, and raise money. The attorneys on the board write the articles of incorporation and bylaws; the accountants do the books. In Phase I, active, involved, hard-working board members may be the nonprofit's most valuable commodity.

The new organization typically has minimal staff who work long hours for low pay. Yet their relationships are collegial, and they experience a high degree of professional and emotional reward from being a part of a worthwhile organization and making a difference. The staff and board often operate "family style," each serving as a cheering squad for the other.[9]

In the birth stage of an organization, the founders' emphasis is on creating, producing, and presenting their product. But as the organization grows, the founders find themselves burdened with unwanted management responsibilities. The increasing number of employees cannot be managed exclusively through informal communication; new accounting procedures are needed for financial control; additional funds must be secured through more extensive fund-raising efforts; more complex and long-term marketing strategies must be developed and implemented. Some organizations fail at this stage. A charismatic leader or major funder may depart without providing for succession; the organization may fail to search for or find another person who can lead the organization into the next stage.

PHASE II: GROWTH THROUGH DIRECTION—CRISIS OF AUTONOMY

Phase II begins when a fledgling, grassroots organization undertakes to become more businesslike in its operations. The operations are complex enough to require professional management, so the organization hires a chief executive officer and other staff members. Job descriptions and policy manuals are written, accounting systems are developed, budgeting becomes a key issue, and work standards are adopted. Communication becomes much more formal as a hierarchy of positions is built. Many performing arts organizations are in Phase II. They have built professional staffs and have formalized their policies, plans, and accounting systems. They have managed to attract grants from several funding sources including foundations, state and local art agencies, and corporations, in addition to individuals.[10]

During this phase the board focuses on developing new personnel policies, setting up audit review committees, and paying general attention to the organization's growth. A much clearer differentiation evolves between the board and the administration. This may cause serious difficulties if boards intrude into administrative areas or vice versa. Toward the end of Phase II, board members may feel that they are merely rubber-stamping the decisions of administrators, and may miss the emotional satisfaction they previously experienced when they were more involved in the organization's operations. Long-term employees who experienced the freedom and job satisfaction of Phase I may be uncomfortable with the organization's increasingly businesslike nature. Their professional skills may no longer be adequate. Staff discomfort may be exacerbated by an executive who overcontrols and overdetermines the organization's direction and services.

PHASE III: GROWTH THROUGH DELEGATION—CRISIS OF CONTROL

Phase III evolves from the successful decentralization of the organization. The organization typically has reached a size where there are several managers or project supervisors for day-to-day operations, budget planning for programs, and functional responsibilities such as marketing, fund-raising, and educational activities. There is a need to empower the employees—in effect, to recapture some of the energy of Phase I by heightening motivation at lower levels. During this phase, the board usually decentralizes and diversifies as well. Separate committees may be established for various fund-raising functions, such as special events, individual giving, corporate giving, and so on. A well-connected, wealthy board member may be the most important addition to a board at this phase.

The crisis of Phase III occurs when the management and/or the board begins to develop a sense that it is losing control. As a result of increased autonomy, communication with the top has become less frequent and is often accomplished by memos, brief visits, and formal staff meetings. Autonomous programs and advisory boards have become so self-directed that they are not complementing one another in furthering the mission of the organization. For example, it is common at this stage for marketing and fund-raising personnel to work at cross-purposes because they do not coordinate the timing of their campaigns or their respective appeals.

This is a difficult time for board members. Committee chairpersons argue with one another and with the president of the board. Often, Phase III conflicts center on the fact that funding may have to be curtailed for a project for which a particular board committee has developed a deep sense of ownership, such as a new theater space. Sometimes, subcommittees become invested in projects to the extent that they overreach their responsibilities, intruding into areas of administrative prerogative.

The Phase III revolution is under way when top management seeks to regain control over the total organization. Some executive directors attempt to restore centralized management, but the effort usually fails because of the vast scope of operations. The organizations that move ahead usually adopt a specific strategy. The Dance Theater of Harlem achieved success at this phase by being open about its financial problems. After it decided to lay off most of its staff, the remaining staff and board members developed a detailed financial report for the theater's major donors that outlined the causes of the crisis, the amount of money needed, and how the money would be used. The board president and the staff focused on trying to involve the board members more and to make better use of the technical assistance that they could provide. The goal was to keep board members interested without allowing them to become too involved in running the organization.

PHASE IV: GROWTH THROUGH COORDINATION—CRISIS OF RED TAPE

Phase IV is a time of coordination. During this phase, the evolutionary period is characterized by the use of formal systems for achieving greater coordination and by top executives taking responsibility for the initiation and administration of these new systems. Often, functions such as data processing are centralized, and marketing and fund-raising are better coordinated. Accounting and budgeting become more sophisticated with more emphasis on the bottom line, on program-based budgeting, and on frequent and thorough financial evaluations.

For the board, there is a greater degree of integration and communication. For example, one orchestra board created positions for three vice presidents, each of whom is responsible for several related board committees. This structure encourages more frequent communication with an executive level officer and better integration between related committees. Board orientations are also much more structured. Often, there are planning retreats for board members that focus on the total mission of the organization.

The Phase IV crisis occurs as procedures become too weighty and the extensive red tape creates dissatisfaction among the staff and board. Distance develops as top management loses touch with the day-to-day efforts of employees. Procedures take precedence over problem solving, innovation has declined, and the organization has become too complex to be managed through formal procedural systems. Board members are likely to feel disconnected from the organization's artistic services and they may feel they are overinvolved in business operations, which often are the sole subject matter at board meetings.

PHASE V: COLLABORATION

The final phase emphasizes strong interpersonal collaboration in an attempt to overcome the red-tape crisis. Its evolution builds upon a more flexible and behavioral approach to management. There is a strong focus on quick problem solving through team action. Teams are combined across functions for task-group activity, key managers hold frequent and spontaneous conferences, and real-time information systems are integrated into daily decision making. Experiments and new practices are encouraged throughout the organization.

In this phase, several staff members openly interact with the board, and relationships between board and top staff members are flexible and comfortable. Responsibility is differentiated as the board focuses on organizational policy and the staff generally works on administration, management, and program implementation.

Managing Change

A large majority of arts organizations operate in the first, second, and third phases of organizational development. Most arts organizations remain relatively small throughout their lifetimes, and their growth is generally slow and is limited in scope.

The critical tasks for the management and the board are to be aware of these stages, to recognize when time for change has come, and to welcome the tense periods of transition that provide the pressure, ideas, and heightened sensitivity to the need for new practices. Management must be willing to dismantle current structures before the transitional stage becomes too turbulent.

These same principles apply to downsizing, or "negative growth." Often, during a financial crisis, a manager will downsize by firing several employees without changing other aspects of its operations or programming. This will serve only to create a deeper crisis as the remaining staff and the disillusioned board members are expected to carry on "as usual" but with a heavier load of responsibility in an ever-worsening environment. Managers must understand the need for a more thorough analysis of how management, the board, and artistic personnel can best achieve the organization's mission within the limits of its human and financial resources.

Most important, rather than trying to hold on to what has worked in the past, managers and board members need to understand that change is inherent in organizational life. This is no simple task, because the passage of time contributes to the institutionalization of managerial and board-member attitudes, making behavior difficult to change. But by understanding an organization's historical developments, its current status, and their own changing roles, the organization's leaders can better prepare solutions and coping strategies for its next stage of development.

ACQUIRING AND MANAGING VOLUNTEER SUPPORT

A major problem facing nonprofit managers is that they lack adequate time, personnel, skills, and financial resources to carry out their mission. To be successful, they have to augment these resources by securing the voluntary assistance of others. Volunteers can help in a myriad of ways: contributing their professional skills to managerial tasks, fund-raising, providing assistance in the office, planning special events, ushering, and so on. Volunteers can also help arts organizations build audiences through their connections in the community. For example, in 1988, the Volunteer Council of the New York Philharmonic initiated the Symphony Club to draw previously uninvolved young professionals to symphony concerts. Council volunteers put together a list of three thousand names of people they knew in the 25- to 40-year-old category, and hand-addressed and stamped a mailing offering them a special club subscription. The volunteers included handwritten notes or business cards along with the invitations. Within weeks of the mailing, and well before the deadline, the goal of two hundred subscribers, at $75 apiece, had been reached.[11]

For the most part, securing volunteer assistance is a marketing task. Those who could assist must be brought to the point where they agree to exchange their time and services for certain benefits. While the elevated status of an arts organization offers a positive platform for seeking help, the organization must also offer other benefits. This is due in part to the fact that all nonprofits have real competition. Marketing professionals, lawyers, or accountants who may be enlisted to serve on the board of an arts organization offer time to other organizations as well as participate in many other activities during their discretionary time. To get their help, the nonprofit marketer must offer benefits that exceed the costs that volunteers expect to bear.

Recruiting Volunteers

Recruiting of volunteers should proceed in the same strategic way as any other marketing task. The organization should understand its own mission and its strengths and weaknesses. It should then research its environment: social trends, its competitors, and its target customers. Then, in light of this input, it must choose target segments and develop an attractive volunteer program.

The most important step is understanding the target volunteer market. This means understanding who the volunteers are, why they volunteer, and how to "speak" to them. For example, New York City's Second Stage has used a brochure that imitates a personals ad to attract "adventuresome New Yorkers looking for an intimate relationship." In the brochure, the theater claimed to offer "great looks and terrific quality."[12] The organization must focus on satisfying prospective volunteers' needs, not just the organization's needs. Said one sensitive trustee: "Volunteerism is a quid pro quo business. The organization gets something, but we don't get it for nothing—we have to give something back. A volunteer wants meaningful responsibility and wants to be taken seriously. The minute we take a volunteer for granted, we are in trouble."[13]

Thomas Wolf provided the following list of reasons why people volunteer:[14]

- *Sense of self-satisfaction:* Many people like to use their free time in ways that bring them personal satisfaction and allow them to develop a positive self-image. Some volunteer because they want to feel needed, others like to keep busy in a way that is useful, and still others want to earn the respect of their peers and friends while doing something useful for the community.

- *Altruism:* Many people from all economic strata believe that helping others is a necessary part of a complete and good life. For some individuals who have little cash to spare, volunteering provides the only way to express such altruism. Others may combine volunteering with the giving of cash.

- *Companionship/meeting people:* Another important reason why individuals volunteer is to meet and mix with other people. Volunteering can be a viable way for people who have lost a spouse, young professionals, and people who have just moved into a new community to widen their circle of acquaintances and develop personal bonds or a more active social life.

- *Learning about a field:* Some individuals who have an interest in a particular field see volunteering as an excellent way to learn more about it, particularly if training and learning opportunities are built into an organization's volunteer program.

- *Creating/maintaining an organization:* Some volunteers are entrepreneurs who devote their energies to creating nonprofit organizations and helping them grow and thrive. Pride in their organization's success and continued expansion is often a prime motivating factor in their volunteer activities.

- *Developing professional contacts:* Some people use volunteer jobs as a way to make contacts that may lead them to clients or other kinds of business or professional associations or opportunities.

- *Getting ahead in the corporation:* Many profit-sector corporations view employee volunteer service as an important way for the company to make a contribution to the community. Young executives and other company representatives are encouraged to volunteer; those wanting to move up the corporate ladder know that a volunteer position can be a real asset on a résumé. A study conducted by the Points of Light Foundation found that 92 percent of the nation's largest companies engage in efforts to encourage their employees to volunteer, such as awards or commendations to employees for volunteer service and "lending" employees to help a nonprofit with a specific project.[15]

- *Getting training/experience:* For some people, a volunteer position is a route to finding a paying job. Young people, people who have been out of the labor force for some time, or people wishing to change professions will sometimes use volunteer opportunities as a way to further these personal goals. They may learn a task, gain a marketable skill, or secure a recommendation for future employment.

- *Providing entry to a particular organization:* Volunteering may be the necessary first step on a ladder for people interested in a paying job or a seat on the board.

- *Social status:* There is much prestige associated with certain organizations, and their volunteers represent an elite group within the community. Associating with these volunteers can mark a person as being part of a desirable social group.

- *Pride:* Pride in an organization's artistic achievements and an identification with excellence can be strong motivators. People like to volunteer for organizations that they consider it a privilege to be involved with.

Motivation and willingness to volunteer are not enough; something must bring about actual involvement. In a study undertaken by Gallup, volunteers reported learning of their present activity through the following means:[16]

Asked by someone	40.4%
Participated in the organization	39.3%
Family or friend benefited	27.6%
Sought on their own	19.2%
Saw an advertisement	5.3%

Many potential volunteers simply have not been asked. An organization can increase volunteer participation by carefully targeting the people it wishes to reach and approaching them through appropriate contacts and media. The organization should emphasize the benefits that would motivate each target group to respond to an opportunity to volunteer.[17] For example, an organization may contact retirees and senior citizens through senior citizen centers, retirement counselors, personnel offices, churches, and synagogues. The media likeliest to reach this group are neighborhood and daily newspapers, direct mail, flyers, posters, and speakers' bureaus. Volunteer recruiters may emphasize that life experience is needed, assignments are appropriate and interesting, interactions with other people are involved, and recognition is provided for the important work they do. To attract college students, organizations may contact student leadership, campus organizations, and faculty. Appropriate media for reaching them include school newspapers, posters, flyers, electronic mail, and events such as mixers. College students are likely to be motivated to volunteer by being given benefits as course credit or field experience, career exploration, involvement in community issues, and short-term projects.[18]

Smaller organizations may find that by collaborating and offering a broader range of benefits, they can increase their volunteer base and volunteer satisfaction. Starting with one hundred members in 1980, the Saints: Volunteers for the Performing Arts now have a membership of more than a thousand and have increased the number of activities they offer. The Saints provide volunteer support for small nonprofit Chicago theaters. The Saints serve as ushers, provide meals to actors between shows, help with bulk mailings, distribute flyers, help run food concessions, and provide a helping hand wherever it may be needed. They also combine their financial resources and make group donations to selected theaters.

The volunteers also benefit. They receive a newsletter at least ten times a year listing many volunteer opportunities; they can attend several meetings per year featuring speakers on the performing arts, as well as three parties per year. Volunteers have preferential ushering sign-up for at least fourteen theaters, exclusive ushering at Orchestra Hall, exclusive "greeting" at the Auditorium Theatre, weekend field trips to see theater in other cities, opportunities to socialize with people interested in the performing arts, and a feeling of "belonging" to the performing arts community.

Staff–Volunteer Conflicts

The use of volunteers is not an unmixed blessing for a nonprofit organization. Tensions can arise between volunteers and full-time staff. Many volunteers have the attitude that because they are donating their services to the organization (1) they don't really work for the organization and so shouldn't be *told* what to do—rather, they should be *asked* if they would be willing to do something; (2) they should have a great deal to say about the content and timetable for their assignments; and (3) they deserve continuous appreciation for their generosity and commitment. Further, some individuals volunteer not because they really want to help, but because they have been coerced into volunteering by an employer or peers or because they wish to add an item to their résumé. One manager of a large volunteer force has developed what he calls his "rule of thirds." One-third of his volunteer force works avidly with very little direction and encouragement. One-third will work only with considerable motivation and are only effective with careful supervision. And one-third will not work at all under any circumstances and are best ignored (unless they are causing morale problems among those who do work).

Problems arise when members of the professional full-time staff look upon the volunteers as second-class workers. Professionals have offered such opinions as

- Volunteers are dilettantes. They may perform lethargically or impulsively but do not have to live with the consequences of their behavior.

- Volunteers who come from occupations in which they boss others will not easily take direction. At the same time, those volunteers who are accustomed to being directed in their work lives look to their volunteer jobs as a chance for independence and control.

- Volunteers who come from the leisure classes often consider themselves to be better than the professional staff and are less willing to perform menial tasks like stuffing programs with flyers or counting receipts.

Volunteers may require more supervision and attention than the staff thinks should be needed. One symphony director describes the case of the volunteer who, in October, insisted on getting immediate information from the staff for the May fund-raiser she was organizing. The requested information took time to prepare, and the staff was overloaded with upcoming projects. The director understood that the volunteer took her job very seriously and wished to be valued for her efforts. The director also knew that the staff had several other high-priority tasks to accomplish. The director had to evaluate the relative importance of keeping the volunteer happy versus meeting the staff's needs.

Professionalizing the Volunteer Function

The solution that experienced volunteer managers recommend is simply to treat volunteers as much as possible as professional, full-time workers indistinguishable from paid staff. Among other things, this means using the following standards and managerial practices.

Orientation. A general orientation should include a packet of information about what the organization does and how it is run, including an organizational chart and bylaws, background reading material, a tour of the facility where the volunteer will work, a tour of the office, a meeting with staff, and a group meeting so volunteers can get acquainted with one another.

Appropriate training and supervision. Training varies with the job's complexity and the volunteer's experience, but should always begin with a discussion of the written job description, in order to answer the following questions: What is the job? What is its purpose and how does it contribute to the organization? What are the steps necessary for completion? With whom does the volunteer have to work and to whom is the volunteer accountable? How much time is involved (hours, days, months), and when is the job to be completed?

Performance goals and benchmarks. The organization should set specific performance goals and benchmarks for the volunteers. Volunteers should be clearly informed of these goals and of their responsibility in helping to achieve them.

Evaluation and control. The most difficult task in managing volunteers is informing them that if they do not perform satisfactorily in their job, they will be released or assigned elsewhere. Such a situation must be handled delicately. Management must explain the nature of the problem and may give the volunteer another chance, reassign the volunteer to a more appropriate position, or simply tell the volunteer that his or her services are no longer needed.

Both volunteers and professional staff respond favorably to the professional style of volunteer management. Most volunteers like to be taken seriously and challenged. They appreciate the opportunity to be well trained and well supervised. Full-time paid staff appreciate management's firmness and the fact that they, too, can treat the volunteers seriously. Performance standards for both groups improve enormously and the nonprofit's effectiveness, efficiency, and morale rise noticeably. In fact, the organization's volunteer positions become all the more coveted.

The New York Philharmonic dramatically reorganized its volunteer program, resulting in a larger number of volunteers and greatly increased efficiency. By accommodating the schedules of working people, by providing work schedules and job descriptions and mapping out responsibilities, the orchestra managed to attract young professionals and other volunteers of good quality and ability. Today more than 40 percent of the Philharmonic's volunteers are working professionals. These volunteers value their time and expect the organization to know what it wants from them.

Peter Drucker argues that "the steady transformation of the volunteer from well-meaning amateur to trained, professional unpaid staff member is the most significant development in the nonprofit sector."[19] Drucker says that to attract the knowledge-able worker who will be the backbone of the volunteer movement in the future, nonprofits must treat volunteers as professionals, give them chances to put their competence and knowledge to work, provide them opportunities for advancement up the volunteer career ladder, and provide meaningful recognition of their achievements. Drucker says that volunteers must get far greater satisfaction from their accomplishments and make a greater contribution precisely because they do not get a paycheck. He concludes:

> We hear a great deal about the decay and dissolution of family and community and about the loss of values. And, of course, there is reason for concern. But the nonprofits are generating a powerful countercurrent. They are forging new bonds of community, a new commitment to active citizenship, to social responsibility, to values. And surely what the nonprofit contributes to the volunteer is as important as what the volunteer contributes to the nonprofit. Indeed, it may be fully as important as the service . . . that the nonprofit provides in the community.

Retaining Volunteers

An arts organization must pay particular attention to the problem of retaining present volunteers. One approach is to survey "dropouts" to ascertain why they left. Another is to conduct periodic assessments of present volunteers' satisfactions and dissatisfactions. False expectations are a common source of dissatisfaction. This is sometimes attributable to the recruit's own unrealistic fantasies about what it will be like to be part of the opera company's lecture corps, or organize a fund-raising event, or to give one day a week in the symphony store. But just as often the culprit is the nonprofit organization, which paints an excessively optimistic picture in order to successfully recruit volunteers.

In order to retain volunteers, arts organizations should (1) foster a sense of personal accomplishment by making sure that each volunteer is matched to appropriate tasks, and (2) show volunteers on a regular basis that their work is appreciated. Awards luncheons, special receptions with performers, mentions in the organization's annual report and press releases, and framed certificates of merit are ways the organization can indicate its appreciation.

To make the most of their scant resources, nonprofit arts organizations must attract and retain committed volunteers who are willing to work for no pay at all. Whatever their motivations for volunteering, volunteers are most likely to make the required extra effort when they feel their work is valued and contributes to the overall goals of the organization.[20] William Shakespeare anticipated volunteerism when he said "He is well paid that is well satisfied."

1. McCann, J. E., "Design Principles for an Innovating Company," *Academy of Management Executives* 5, no. 2, 88.

2. Thomas Wolf, *Managing a Nonprofit Organization* (A Fireside Book, Simon & Schuster, 1990), 89; and Frederick J. Turk & Robert P. Gallo, *Financial Management Strategies for Arts Organizations* (New York: American Council for the Arts, 1984), 65.

3. Andrew F. Cypiot, under the direction of Robert Augsburger, "Vancouver Symphony Orchestra," B, case study, Stanford Graduate School of Business, 1991.

4. Robert F. Kelly, "The 'Enemy' Within . . . Marketing in the Arts," *Proceedings*, First International Conference on Arts Management, Montreal, Aug. 1991.

5. Phillip Hyde and Christopher Lovelock, "Organizational Size and its Implications for Marketing Strategy in the Arts," in *Marketing the Arts*, ed. Michael P. Mokwa, William M. Dawson, and E. Arthur Prieve (New York: Praeger, 1980), 75–92.

6. Paul Hirsch, "Production and Distribution Roles among Cultural Organizations: On the Division of Labor across Intellectual Disciplines," *Social Research*, Summer 1978, 315–331.

7. Larry E. Greiner, "Evolution and Revolution as Organizations Grow," *Harvard Business Review*, July–Aug. 1972, 37–46; and Michael R. Ostrowski, "Nonprofit Boards of Directors," in *The Nonprofit Organization—Essential Readings*, ed. David L. Giles, J. Steven Ott, and Jay M. Shafriz (Belmont, Calif: Brooks/Cole Publishing, 1990).

8. Caleb E. White, "The Eugene O'Neill Theater Center: From Founder's Delight to Founder's Dilemma," report for the J. L. Kellogg Graduate School of Management, May 1994.

9. Anne Lowrey Bailey, "Crises Test Trustees," *Chronicle of Philanthropy*, Jan. 29, 1991, 1, 30–33.

10. Paul J. DiMaggio, "The Impact of Public Funding on Organizations in the Arts," Yale Program on Non-Profit Organizations Working Paper 31, Yale University, 1981.

11. Alvin H. Reiss, *Arts Management: A Guide to Finding Funds and Willing Audiences* (Rockville, Md.: Fund-Raising Institute, 1992), 14–15.

12. Ibid., 13–14.

13. Wolf, *Managing a Nonprofit Organization*, 71.

14. Ibid., 70–71.

15. Jennifer Moore, "92% of Big Companies Encourage Volunteer Efforts, Survey Finds," *Chronicle of Philanthropy*, June 30, 1992.

16. *Giving and Volunteering in the United States* (Washington, D.C.: The Independent Sector, 1988).

17. Nancy Macduff, *Volunteer Recruiting & Retention, A Marketing Approach*, 2nd ed. (Walla Walla, Wash., MBA Publishing, 1993), 101.

18. Carol Matusoff Consultants, *Principles of Orchestra Management* (Washington, D.C.: American Symphony Orchestra League, 1989).

19. Peter F. Drucker, "What Business Can Learn from Nonprofits," *Harvard Business Review*, July–Aug. 1989, 91.

20. Wolf, *Managing a Nonprofit Organization*, 78–80.

▲●▲

CHAPTER 17

Managing in accordance with a strategic plan is a learned art. The longer you use the tool, the better you are able to manage with it.

R. HENRY MIGLIONE

Good thoughts are no better than good dreams, unless they be executed!

RALPH WALDO EMERSON

MARKETING PLANS, BUDGETS, IMPLEMENTATION, AND CONTROL

IN CHAPTER 3, WE DISCUSSED THE FIRST STEPS OF THE STRATEGIC MARKET planning process, namely analyzing and determining the mission, objectives, and goals to which any strategy must contribute; and tools for assessing the organization's strengths and weaknesses to respond to current and future opportunities and threats presented by the external environment. By identifying the organization's strengths and weaknesses, managers can determine what the organization does well so that it can do more of the same, and what it does poorly, so that it can improve. An environmental analysis helps managers understand the organization's milieu, over which it has little or no control but to which it must adapt. By reaching a consensus on the organization's purpose and its core competencies; by identifying its customers and what they value; and by characterizing the economic, competitive, political, and cultural climate; the organization can determine long-range goals, program priorities, and financial requirements.

After conducting a strategic analysis, an organization must undertake three major steps to complete the strategic market planning process: market planning, implementation, and control. The purpose of this chapter is to address those steps.

MARKET PLANNING

Market planning is the process of determining specific objectives and goals for the relevant planning period, formulating the marketing strategy to achieve the goals, and establishing detailed programs, tactics, and budgets. Consider the situation facing the Steppenwolf Theatre in the 1994–95 season. An analysis of the organization's strengths, weaknesses, opportunities, and threats allowed the board, artistic director, and senior staff to develop goals and strategies.

THE STEPPENWOLF THEATRE FACES CHANGE	Chicago's highly regarded Steppenwolf Theatre rode a wave of success for many years, amassing awards for its productions and playing to nearly sold out houses. By the 1989–90 season, with its 298-seat house 92 percent subscribed, Steppenwolf was building a new 510-seat theater. Much excitement surrounded the opening of the new space, and by the first full season in the new hall (1991–92), the number of subscribers soared from 13,121 to 18,175.

After two seasons, the tide began to turn. For the the 1994–95 season, renewal rates had dropped to a low of 55 percent, from an average over recent years of 80 percent. New subscriptions were also down, and Steppenwolf had only 13,929 subscribers. Single-ticket purchases during that season were also weaker than they had been since the earliest years.

Three main problems contributed to this situation. First, many of the patrons new to Steppenwolf as they launched their new space were "soft" subscribers. Their interest was based on the excitement over Steppenwolf's new building and the glamour of its Tony award for the production of *The Grapes of Wrath* that the ensemble took to Broadway. Once the excitement wore off, so did much of their interest in the theater. Second, since gaining Hollywood and Broadway fame, many of the founding ensemble members had not been around to help keep the theater on track artistically. During the seasons from 1992 through 1994, the quality and style of many of the productions disappointed both the critics and audience members. Customer complaints were not heeded, much less acknowledged, and even many long-standing loyal patrons dropped their subscriptions. The bad reviews and word of mouth also severely affected single-ticket sales. For the first time in Steppenwolf history, one play was closed a week before its subscription run was complete in order to cut financial losses. Third, the theater industry as a whole was facing an erosion in audience size, to which no theater was totally immune. Steppenwolf not only needed to maintain its audience base, but needed a continuation of its previous growth rate in order to fill the seats in the new hall.

It was clear that Steppenwolf needed to rebuild. During the 1994–95 season, the board and senior staff analyzed what had made the theater great, where they had gone wrong, and what they could do to turn their situation around. They decided to focus on two primary areas: artistic development and changing people's attitudes and perceptions about the theater. Steppenwolf's bold, raw, and powerful image as a high-quality, on-the-edge theater company would be the basis for its new success.

Determining Specific Goals and Strategies

Once the organization has disseminated its overall vision and goals throughout the organization, then management's challenge is to determine specific goals and strategies for the relevant planning period. Goals indicate where an organization wants to go; strategy answers how to get there. Each strategy must be refined into specific programs.

STEPPENWOLF: STRATEGIES FOR CHANGE

Several strategies were selected for artistic development. An artistic advisory board of three founding ensemble members was formed to coordinate play selection with the artistic director. Funds were earmarked to hire a dramaturge to assist in play development. The company would start planning new seasons farther in advance so there would be more room for critical selection. Play readings would be held for emerging playwrights and directors, and subscribers would be invited to view some of these works in progress. Subscribers would also be invited at no charge to attend a lecture series about each of the season's plays. The smaller Studio Theatre would be used to help nurture fine, young, local theater companies and provide them with a high-quality venue and marketing support. In return, by "curating" which shows and companies would be presented, Steppenwolf could select from a wide range of adventurous programming with a minimum of financial risk, since all the upfront work of play selection, casting, and producing would be taken on by the other companies.

To build Steppenwolf's new image, marketing director Tim Evans planned several changes. New, bold graphics for the logo and the subscription brochure design would be developed. Exciting photographs from past productions would be hung in the lobby, and other cosmetic changes would be made to make the theater more inviting. Major efforts were being undertaken to improve customer service, and customer service consultants from the retail and hotel industries were engaged to work with personnel at all levels of the organization.

In determining specific strategies, it is important that the organization correctly identify the issues that affect each target market. For example, arts managers may attribute declining audience size to the impact of television and videos on the younger generations, to the lack of arts education in the schools, to shortened attention spans, or to changing lifestyle demands. Symphony managers who conclude the problem is shortened attention spans may try to attract younger audiences with shorter and livelier works on the programs. Those who think the commute to the suburbs is the problem may offer rush hour concerts to attract people before they go home for the evening. Those who think declining interest in classical music is the problem may conclude they are fighting a losing battle and continue doing what they have always done so as not to sell out. Thus, the causes the managers think explain the organization's situation will influence the choice of marketing strategy.

Decision Making

Good choices are dependent on the quality of the decision-making process. There is general agreement that better decisions are based on in-depth information. Yet many managers "grab at the first available straw, only to discover that it's a short one." Alvin Reiss describes this problem as a reliance on the "instant solution."[1] Consider the following examples:

- An organization copies another art group's promotional idea without researching its effectiveness and without adapting the idea to its own specific situation.
- When faced with a new and desirable community involvement program, a manager may recite the all too familiar "no money" response, rather than seek ways to implement the program using community-based collaborations.
- A marketing director judges a new ad campaign by her "gut" reaction.
- A marketing director requests a budget based on last year's budget, rather than on this year's opportunities.

Decision makers often select a solution that is acceptable or reasonable, though not necessarily the best choice.[2] Due to the complexity of most situations, time constraints, and the multiple decisions that managers must make, most decision makers utilize simplifying strategies.[3] This is appropriate for many decisions; however, important decisions should be made more carefully. The following model outlines the steps in rational decision making.[4]

1. *Define the problem.* It takes good judgment to accurately define the problem. Too often the problem is defined in terms of symptoms rather than underlying causes. It has been observed that "a problem well defined is half-answered."

2. *Identify the criteria.* Managers must identify the appropriate criteria for judging alternative courses of action. For example, in advertising a new production, managers must evaluate the alternative media (radio, newspapers, direct mail, the Internet) not only in terms of their cost but also in terms of their reach and frequency effectiveness.

3. *Weigh the criteria.* Importance weights must be attached to the respective criteria. For example, how much weight should be given to audience satisfaction versus performers' satisfaction versus financial results?

4 *Generate alternatives.* The next step is to generate alternative solutions. Here some creative brainstorming may greatly enlarge the number of realized alternatives.

5. *Make a choice.* Select the alternative that best meets the defined criteria.

The rational model of decision making requires significant levels of information gathering and analysis. What happens when fast decisions must be made? One solution is to skimp on information gathering and analysis. Managers could look at the limited information available to them, consider only one or two alternatives, and decide. The decision will be made quickly but with less confidence.

Another approach is to limit conflict that might otherwise drag out decision making. Minimizing conflict seems likely to accelerate choice. But repressing conflict may result in a lack of support for the decisions that are taken. Furthermore, research indicates that moderate conflict may yield more innovative and more appropriate solutions. A third approach is for a manager to act autocratically. However, this tends to isolate leaders and to result in a lack of support for the choices made.

Kathleen Eisenhardt has analyzed how managers actually do make fast, yet high-quality, strategic decisions.[5] She contends that fast decision makers use simple, powerful tactics to make effective and efficient choices. First, some fast decision makers use as much or more information than their slower counterparts. They gain this information in several ways. They rely on regular—daily or weekly—performance reports, such as ticket sales information. They may require frequent staff meetings—two or three per week. Such frequent communication helps managers stay aware of what is happening daily and enables them to spot problems and opportunities and acquire a deep, intuitive grasp of the business, which, in turn, helps them react quickly and accurately to changing events.

Fast decision makers search for and debate multiple alternatives. Some decision makers will introduce alternatives that they do not support, for the purpose of encouraging debate. This process has several benefits, in that it allows for quick comparative analysis, builds confidence that all reasonable alternatives have been considered, and allows for a fallback position if the primary choice doesn't work out.

Another factor in efficient decision making is seeking advice from a colleague or consultants with broad experience in and knowledge of the field. Seeking advice from members of the executive board fosters a climate of trust and demonstrates discretion. It can boost a decision maker's confidence in making difficult choices and avoid delaying the decision making.

When facing conflict, fast decision makers employ a method of conflict resolution called *consensus with qualification* to resolve deadlocks among individuals. In this two-step process, managers talk over an issue and attempt to gain consensus. If consensus occurs, the choice is made. If not, the manager with the most power in the situation makes the choice, guided by input from the rest of the group. As long as the others believe that the person making the final decision has the appropriate power, they will be satisfied to have had a voice in the process, even if their opinion did not prevail. This conflict resolution method balances the managers' desires to be heard with the need to make a choice.

The Marketing Plan

Once strategies are formulated, the next task is to plan marketing programs. This process consists of basic decisions on marketing expenditures, marketing mix, and marketing allocation. It requires effectively combining the organization's resources to produce annual plans and budgets that work toward achieving the organization's overall goals. For the marketing manager, it also requires deep understanding of how best to meet the target market's needs and preferences.

A structured marketing plan serves several important purposes. First, when a plan is written down, inconsistencies, unknowns, gaps, and implausibilities can be readily identified and dealt with. Second, it provides an anchor—stability in the midst of change. It is a basis on which to measure progress and to incorporate change as the market and the organization's own goals change. Third, it helps focus management on the organization's annual goals, changing market conditions, and key marketing issues. A common complaint among marketing professionals is that their focus on day-to-day affairs causes them to lose sight of the big picture. Fourth, it leads to an implementation timetable that ascertains that tasks and goals are completed by certain times.[6]

FORMULATING MARKETING PLANS

Marketing plans may take on different formats depending on the managers' needs, but each plan should focus on identifying key issues, mobilizing resources, and measuring results. The marketing plan will approach each aspect of the marketing mix in a way that will position the offering effectively for the target market. To create a plan, the manager will (1) identify potential alternatives for achieving the organization's goals, (2) determine the financial implications of these alternatives, (3) decide which alternatives to pursue, and (4) decide on the marketing mix (the four Ps: product, price, promotion, and place) and marketing expenditures for each objective and/or program.

Marketing plans will have several sections, the most common of which are executive summary; current marketing situation; opportunity and issue analysis; objectives; marketing strategy; action programs; projected budgets, including statements of revenues and expenditures; and controls.

Executive summary. The planning document should open with a short summary of the main goals and recommendations to be found in the body of the plan. This permits upper management and board members to grasp quickly the major thrust of the plan. A table of contents should follow the executive summary.

Current marketing situation. This section of the plan presents relevant background data on the market, products, competition, distribution, and macroenvironmental factors. Data are presented on the size and growth (or decline) of the total market and on market segments over the past several years. Data are also presented on customer needs, perceptions, and buying-behavior trends. Each product is described in terms of sales, prices, and distribution. When appropriate, major competitors are identified and described in terms of their size, goals, product quality, marketing strategies, and other characteristics that are helpful for understanding their intentions and behavior. Locations where performances are presented and where tickets are sold are described and evaluated. Broad trends affecting each product and key target market are identified.

Opportunity and issue analysis. On the basis of the data describing the current marketing situation, the marketing manager identifies the major opportunities/threats, strengths/weaknesses, and issues the organization faces for each of its offerings during the time frame of the plan.

Objectives. At this point, management knows the opportunities and issues and is faced with making basic decisions about the plan's objectives. Two types of objectives should be set: marketing (such as reattracting lapsed subscribers or upgrading the organization's image) and financial (such as revenue maximization or full cost recovery). (See Chapter 3.)

Marketing strategy. The manager now outlines the broad marketing strategy or "game plan." The basic strategy can be presented in paragraph form or list form, covering the major marketing tools. Following is a hypothetical strategy statement based on the Steppenwolf Theatre's marketing objectives.

STRATEGY STATEMENT

Target market:	Long-term subscribers whose subscriptions have lapsed in the past two years.
Positioning:	A bold and powerful theater company, one of the country's best and most reliable.
Product:	On-the-edge programming selected by a committee of Steppenwolf's renowned founding members, those who made the theater great.
Price:	Competitive, no increases, discounts for early subscriptions.
Distribution:	Cosmetic changes in the lobby to make it more inviting and comfortable.

Sales force:	Increase telemarketing efforts by 20 percent for personal contact with lapsed subscribers.
Service:	Quick and courteous. Create a response mechanism for all customer complaints.
Promotion:	Create a new direct-mail campaign with a personalized letter for each target market. Increase advertising and direct-mail budget by 20 percent.
Marketing research:	Allot expenditures to increase knowledge of customers' attitudes and behavior and to monitor changes in their attitudes and perceptions of Steppenwolf's image and product offerings.

In developing the strategy, the manager needs to discuss the plans with others whose cooperation and support are necessary for implementation. The financial officer can indicate whether enough funds will be available; the executive director must be willing to dedicate the necessary resources and to support the concept of the program.

Action programs. The strategy statement represents the broad marketing thrusts that the manager will use to achieve specific objectives. Each element of the marketing strategy must now be elaborated to answer: *What* will be done? *When* will it be done? *Who* will do it? *How much* will it cost? *What kind* of benefit and *how much* benefit will it generate for the organization?

Budgets. A budget is an organization's plan of action expressed in monetary terms. Budgeting is a complex process that will be discussed in depth later in this chapter.

Controls. The last section of the plan outlines the controls that will be applied to monitor the plan. Typically the goals and budgets are spelled out for each month or quarter so that results can be reviewed each period and progress can be tracked. Some control sections include contingency plans. A contingency plan outlines the steps that management would implement in response to specific adverse developments that may occur, such as offering reduced-price promotions or other key benefits. The purpose of contingency planning is to encourage managers to give prior thought to some difficulties that might lie ahead.

A MARKETING PLAN IN ACTION

The Chicago Baroque Ensemble is a small organization, run by its board of directors without a paid professional staff. The board president contacted the J. L. Kellogg Graduate School of Management at Northwestern University to gain assistance from arts management students in developing a marketing plan. Three students interviewed board members to learn about the organization. They then created, administered, and analyzed audience surveys, segmented the audience base, and made recommendations for targeting and positioning the offerings to these segments. Finally, they provided the organization with the following elements of a marketing plan: a situational analysis, an audience analysis, and recommendations for marketing mix and positioning opportunities. Their plan, presented here, includes a follow-up response from the organization two months later.

A MARKETING PLAN: THE CHICAGO BAROQUE ENSEMBLE	**THE SITUATION** The Chicago Baroque Ensemble (CBE) was founded in 1992 after the demise of City Musick and Basically Bach, two local Baroque groups that folded in the early 1990s. CBE hopes to succeed where the other two groups failed by pursuing a strategy of quality and fidelity to the Baroque style while maintaining a fiscally conservative style of management.

The organization's informally stated mission is to "give high-quality performances of Baroque music."

The ensemble, which consists of five members (violin, cello, string bass, harpsichord, and transverse flute), has enjoyed excellent critical reviews in its short history. It presents three performances per year each at the Union League Club in downtown Chicago (during the Monday evening rush hour) and at the Mary and Leigh Block Gallery at Northwestern University in suburban Evanston (on Sunday afternoons), as well as live radio broadcasts and special events.

The CBE has received a highly positive audience response to its rush hour concerts at the Union League Club, but still has considerable excess seating capacity there. The ensemble plays to standing-room audiences at the Block Gallery. Largely because of capacity constraints at the Block Gallery, CBE is considering moving to a bigger North Shore location. Subscriptions for either series of concerts offer a 20 to 50 percent discount, and increased savings are available for students, seniors, and Block Gallery/Union League Club members.

The marketing objective is to identify strategies for increasing audience size and for increasing revenue.

AUDIENCE ANALYSIS

There are many similarities in audience responses to the attributes of CBE performances at the two performance locations. A vast majority of respondents at both concert venues feel that the performance location and time is convenient, and more than

90 percent find the performances to be of high quality. More than two-thirds expressed agreement or strong agreement that they enjoyed the reception before or after the concert.

Yet the audiences for the two venues are markedly different. In general, Block Gallery attendees are older and somewhat less affluent, but attend the arts much more frequently. Union League concertgoers are more event-oriented, and many are motivated by avoiding the evening rush, finding something chic to do for the early evening, or being seen at a socially prestigious location.

Another major difference between the two groups is ticket purchase behavior. More than 70 percent of Block Gallery attendees purchase tickets two weeks or more in advance, compared to less than one-quarter of Union League concertgoers. Subscription rates at the Block Gallery and the Union League Club are 50 percent and 26 percent of capacity, respectively.

Attendees at the Union League Club find the intimate parlor setting to be charming and comfortable. However, the modern art that is frequently exhibited at the Block Gallery is seen as incongruous with and distracting from the CBE's musical offerings. Additionally, the seating at the Block Gallery is perceived as uncomfortable. Convenience of parking is far more important to Block Gallery attendees than to Union League attendees. Many people walk from work or take public transportation to the Union League Club. Those who drive do not expect parking to be readily available at this congested downtown location.

AUDIENCE SEGMENTATION

Three audience segments were identified at each venue:

Union League Segments

- *Prime Earners* (56 percent). Aged mid-forties to late fifties, 75 percent have annual income over $100,000. Not ardent supporters of the arts, they primarily attend for social and networking reasons. Most make spontaneous single-ticket purchases. Most hear about the concert by word of mouth and 50 percent are invited to attend by a friend.

- *Traffic Avoiders* (21 percent). This segment's primary motivation is to find something to do while the evening rush winds down; they rate the time of the concert as one of the most important factors in attending. They report virtually no other arts attendance, but have a high rate of subscription to the CBE (60 percent). Most of this segment heard of CBE through written formats, divided evenly between newspaper listings and direct mail. Traffic Avoiders span the age spectrum, with a higher concentration at the upper end of the range.

- *Working Trendies* (25 percent). Like the Traffic Avoiders, this segment does not frequent arts events, but they are younger —in their thirties to mid-forties—and their purchase behavior is more spontaneous; 70 percent purchased their ticket at the event. They are fairly wealthy for their age group (more than half have an income between $50,000 and $100,000).

Block Gallery Segments

- *Solid Supporters* (67 percent). This segment is in the same demographic group as the Prime Earners, but their motivation for attendance is different. Thirty-eight percent of this group are frequent arts attenders and 35 percent named their interest in Baroque music as their primary reason for attending. Fifty-eight percent of Solid Supporters are subscribers. They heard about CBE through a friend (36 percent), through direct mail (29 percent), and through the newspaper (22 percent).

- *Young Traditionalists* (21 percent). This segment is in the same age bracket as Working Trendies, but is more interested in artistic activities. Fifty-nine percent attend the arts with high or medium frequency, and like the Solid Supporters, 60 percent are subscribers to CBE. The majority of this segment report musical content as the primary reason for attending. They have a wide range of incomes, with approximately one-third reporting in each of three categories: over $100,000; between $50,000 and 100,000; and under $25,000.

- *Comfortable Retirees* (11 percent). This is the smallest segment, and is made up of people over age 65. This group is financially comfortable but is less affluent than the others. Rather than being arts supporters, most are looking for something to do for an afternoon. Like the other Block Gallery segments, they have a high subscription rate (56 percent). None of the Comfortable Retirees heard about the concert from a friend. Rather, 45 percent learned about it through the newspaper and 33 percent through direct mail.

RECOMMENDATIONS

Mission: The CBE should develop a formal mission statement that better defines the organization's purpose and benefits.

This will assist them in maintaining an overall consistency in light of varied audience needs and motivations.

Venue: It is recommended that the CBE locate a larger and more appropriate North Shore setting to replace the Block Gallery. Audience size cannot be developed until capacity is increased. The new venue should reflect the intimate, traditional parlor setting of the Union League Club. It is important that the new location be as convenient as the Block Gallery and provide adequate parking.

Pricing: The CBE should consider raising its ticket prices. Current pricing is predominately viewed as inexpensive (17 percent) or fair (75 percent), which indicates that customers would be willing to accept an increase. Furthermore, a higher ticket price is consistent with a high-quality image. Higher ticket prices would help to offset some of the promotional costs and subscriber discounts.

Targeting Recommendations: Specific audience segments should be individually targeted to help the CBE most effectively use its limited resources to reach potential customers. Promotional materials, such as separate brochures and special mailings targeted to each segment, can highlight aspects of the product attractive to each group. In order to implement such a targeting strategy, the CBE must organize its mailing list by segment and be able to identify subscribers and single-ticket buyers.

Union League Club

- *Prime Earners.* Considering that 50 percent of the Prime Earners heard about the concert through word of mouth, incentives should be provided for current attenders to attract others. Each subscriber should be provided with a complimentary guest ticket. Gift certificates to individual performances and gift subscriptions should also be offered to this segment to tap into their network of friends and business associates. CBE should contact downtown businesses to solicit corporate sponsorship. CBE would offer each company a block of reserved seats at each performance, a networking opportunity before or after the concert, and its name printed in the program. In return, the company would encourage its employees to attend the events and offer the concerts as opportunities for entertaining clients or job candidates.

- *Traffic Avoiders.* Because this group has a high subscription rate (60 percent), CBE should focus on maintaining their loyalty. As with the Prime Earners, by providing these subscribers with complimentary tickets for friends, CBE is likely to build a larger subscriber base. To attract other Traffic Avoiders, CBE should contact local downtown businesses for permission to post concert information on company bulletin boards. The posters should emphasize the proximity and time convenience of this "on the way home" event.

- *Working Trendies.* This segment's at-the-event ticket purchasing behavior indicates the importance of spontaneity and convenience to this group. It is important to keep them aware of upcoming concerts close to the time of each event. In order to build commitment, a flex plan (use one ticket for three performances or three tickets for one performance, etc.) may be attractive.

Block Gallery

- *Solid Supporters.* In addition to regular subscriber benefits, CBE should offer these long-term subscribers something special to make them feel a part of the organization. For example, CBE could host an invitational event at which patrons meet the musicians and participate in an educational opportunity, such as learning the differences between period and modern instruments. If relationships are well cultivated, this segment can become a good source of contributions to CBE.

- *Young Traditionalists.* This segment is a good target for enlarging the subscriber base because the Young Traditionalists have a developing interest in the arts. The CBE should encourage this group's involvement in the organization and help them learn about Baroque music. Short preconcert lectures and receptions would be attractive to these patrons and would help develop their commitment. The CBE can keep in touch with this group primarily through direct mail but may add some personal contact as they become long-term subscribers. This segment has the potential to become contributors and board members in the longer term.

- *Comfortable Retirees.* This segment consists primarily of subscribers. However, since their overall interest in the arts is low, the CBE's emphasis should be on maintaining relationships to keep resubscription rates high. Early-bird discounts for subscribers may be effective with this segment, since many are on a fixed income.

FOLLOW-UP

Shortly after this marketing plan was presented to the CBE, a new mission statement was developed and a different North Shore venue was located.

> **Mission:** "To bring into a person's life a sense of dignity and civilization."

In redefining CBE's mission, executive director Jerry Fuller explains that the CBE concert experience extends far beyond the period music that is performed. The music, the ambience of the setting, and even the nature of the promotional materials all contribute to a respite from our busy, harried lives. In this chaotic world where bad news prevails upon our consciousness, the CBE experience is soulful, spiritual, dignified, and civilizing. In keeping with this mission, the CBE makes no pleas for financial support while instruments are in the room. The company's logo is elegant and understated, and no mugs or T-shirts are sold. Says Fuller, "Such things are fine for the ballpark, and the ballpark certainly has its place. But we're not a ballpark."

The Michigan Shores Club was reserved for the CBE's upcoming North Shore concerts to replace the nearby Block Gallery. The Michigan Shores Club has an intimate, traditional parlor with 30 percent more seating capacity. It features valet parking and an adjacent parking lot.

Source: Adapted from a marketing plan prepared by Kurt Naas, Nicole Neuefeind, and Marie Scanlan at the J. L. Kellogg Graduate School of Management, March 1995. We wish to thank Jerry Fuller and the Chicago Baroque Ensemble for sharing their experiences and information.

Budgeting

A budget has three basic functions. First, a budget records in monetary terms the organization's realistic objectives for the coming year or years. Second, it serves as a tool to monitor the organization's financial activities throughout the year, providing a benchmark for managers and the board as to whether financial goals are being met. Third, it helps the organization predict the effects of marketing strategies and tactics with more confidence over a period of years.

The budgeting process is integral to the program planning process as the organization's resources are allocated and programs are dropped or added, weakened or strengthened. The budget operates on two levels. On the policy level, a budget defines in detail how the organization's financial resources will be used to accomplish the strategic plan. Budget formulation is also influenced by questions of efficiency: How much will the program cost? How much money must be raised? How much can be earned? What will be the schedule of disbursements and income over the life of the program?[7]

COMMON BUDGETING PROBLEMS

Budgeting in arts organizations can be characterized as a balancing act of meeting the organization's objectives to the fullest possible extent within the limits of its financial capacity. But while attempting to maximize the use of their limited resources, managers commonly make certain mistakes in carrying out the budgeting process.

Excessive emphasis on new programs   A common budgeting problem in arts organizations involves attitudes toward existing versus new programs. Existing programs are assumed to be a fundamental part of the organization's operations and therefore are accepted virtually unexamined. In contrast, proposed new programs, often modest in comparison to existing programs, are subject to close scrutiny and negotiated endlessly by staff and the board. New programs are trying to find budgetary room within the confines of the organization's total resources, which most likely are already stretched to capacity. With all attention directed to proposed new programs, the unbalanced emphasis serves to institutionalize existing programs.

For example, a consulting group (pro bono) advised board members of a young theater to begin a direct-mail campaign offering a subscription or membership plan to all past attenders. (The theater had no management staff other than a part-time administrative assistant.) The initial campaign effort was estimated to cost $5,000–7,000 and was expected to nearly break even in the first year. However, many members of the board said that the organization could not afford to undertake this effort. Virtually all of the organization's $48,000 marketing budget is spent on print advertising. Although the effectiveness of this advertising expenditure is uncertain and remains unresearched, board members were reluctant to commit even 10 to 15 percent of their advertising funds to a project that was expected to have significant long-range benefits and whose results would be readily measurable. To assure that knowledgeable, up-to-date decisions are made regarding resource allocation, both existing and new program activities should be thoroughly assessed in the budgeting process.

Incremental/decremental budgeting policy   Normally the budgeting process begins with an estimate of revenues. For example, an organization's financial officer estimates that because of decreased grant support and because the current year's ticket sales did not meet projections, the total funds available next year will be 10 percent below the current level. As a result, all attention is focused on how to cut 10 percent from expenses. A common response is that the 10 percent reduction (or

10 percent increase in good times!) should be shared equally by all budgetary units in the organization. This approach to budgeting is flawed because it assumes that all items in the budget should have equal priority. Here the focus is on the decrement or the increment rather than on the needs and importance of each budgeted function. Equal cuts are likely to foster overall mediocrity.

Late preparation   Budgets are often prepared at about the time the new fiscal year begins, long after key decisions, such as committing to next season's shows or hiring new staff, are made. To use the budget merely to record actions already taken is to obtain only a portion of the benefits that can be derived from the budgeting process. Budgets should be prepared and approved by the board as early as new programming decisions are being made.

Lack of participation   Frequently, budgets are prepared by one member of the professional staff, usually the business officer or the director. Limited discussion occurs regarding programmatic needs and changing priorities and, as a result, decisions are made without full information.

   All key staff and board members should participate in the budgeting process to assure that the budget accurately reflects the organization's short-term goals and plans. Full participation also encourages commitment to accomplishing those plans.

Failure to take key variables into account   When preparing budgets, arts organizations often fail to plan for the impact of variables both within and outside of its control. For example, a symphony may hire a relatively unknown soloist to save money. However, the budgeters must consider that fewer tickets are likely to be sold than if a famous performer were hired, so anticipated revenue from the event should be revised downward. Also, environmental factors such as a rainy season for an outdoor summer festival or the NBA playoffs taking place at the same time as a jazz festival are contingencies that should be allowed for in the budget.

Lack of consistency and direction   For some arts organizations, budgetary practices and procedures are not clearly defined. Budget forms and instructions should be standardized and understood by all who have responsibility for budget items. Once budgets are submitted, they should be reviewed by the director, the business manager, and appropriate board members. Meetings should be held between the budget reviewers and submitters to discuss and explain any necessary adjustments. Sometimes program managers set revenue budgets lower than expected to avoid the appearance of failure. They may also set expense budgets high to attract more resources. It is up to the director and board executives to create an environment in which all program managers will be motivated to project budgets as accurately as possible.

Lack of periodic review   In some arts organizations, the budget is "put to rest" once it is completed and approved by the board. However, the budget should be used regularly as a tool to review how well the organization is doing according to its budgeted plan. By comparing actual expenses and revenues on a monthly or quarterly basis with those projected in the budget, the organization can determine possible trouble areas before they get out of hand.

View of budget as inflexible   Budgets should not be considered as carved in stone or unchangeable once written. Rather, they are flexible and need to be adjusted in consideration of changing circumstances. Although the plan itself must be taken seriously—or else it is of no value—change must be a built-in factor. For example, a theater's marketing manager plans an advertising budget for the entire season, attributing certain costs to each of its productions according to anticipated demand. Assume that one play becomes an unexpected hit and its run is extended three extra weeks. The marketing manager increases the advertising budget for that show to get the word out about its great success and its extended run. The costs for this advertising can be allocated to the additional revenues it will help generate.

TYPES OF BUDGETS

An organization may use one or more types of budgets, the most common among them the traditional line-item budget, the program budget, and a PPBES (planning, programming, budgeting, and evaluation system).

The traditional (line-item) budget   The line-item budget lists all expenses by their object or source, such as salaries, benefits, travel, supplies, phone, rent, postage, printing, and so on. Revenues are treated in a similar manner and are listed in such categories as ticket sales, concessions, contributions, and grants. This type of budget is flawed in that it does not indicate how expenses and revenues are allocated across the organization's various functions.

The program budget   A program or project budget distributes revenue and expenses across the organization's functional areas and programs, such as regular season, touring, special events, education, and fund-raising. Such a budget gives managers much more information than the line-item budget. For example, it may show that touring is operating at a deficit while special events are operating at a surplus. Or it may show that fund-raising expenses are too high for the amount of revenue they generate. This can lead to a reprioritization of various activities and programs and an analysis of how to increase the cost-effectiveness of various projects.

For the program budget, a portion of staff salaries, office rent, utilities, and so on, may be allocated to various regular season productions, educational activities, tours, and other projects. For example, staff members estimate the percentage of time spent on each activity to allocate salary costs and the percentage of space taken up by each activity to allocate rent. Care must be taken not to overdo the monitoring of each phone call and postage stamp, which causes frustration and wastes time. Monitoring may be useful for short periods of time to get a rough approximation of what percentage should be applied to each program. The expenses that cannot be reasonably applied to specific programs should be placed in a general "administration" category. The program budget can be extremely helpful with fund-raising, because donors prefer supporting specific programs to providing general operating support. With a program budget, general operating expenses can be attributed directly to specific funded programs.

Combining line-item and program budgets   Table 17-1 shows how a line-item budget and a program budget may be combined, displaying the distribution of costs among various items for each program. For example, a line-item budget will show how much the organization spends each year on printing and mailing; a program budget will show how much is spent each year for the season's opening event; and the combined budget will show how much is spent for printing and mailing for the opening. This enables management to understand and evaluate each program's costs in detail.

PPBES   The planning, programming, budgeting, and evaluation system (PPBES) is an adaptation of the program budget, allowing it to be planned and evaluated in relation to multiple objectives. Often, expense budgets are provided for programs that generate no direct revenue. For example, a symphony may introduce a new concert series designed to attract younger audiences, to develop broader interest

Table 17-1

EXAMPLE OF A PROGRAM BUDGET AND LINE-ITEM BUDGET COMBINED

	Salaries/ Benefits	Rent/ Utilities	Supplies/ Materials	Travel	Printing/ Postage	Total
Subscription Series						
Workshops						
Showcase						
Touring						
Fund-Raising						
Total						

among current patrons in new music, and to provide educational opportunities to enhance the patrons' experiences. The criteria for the program's success may be the amount of audience crossover from more traditional programs and/or the number of patrons new to the symphony, not necessarily the amount of revenue earned. A PPBES system allows managers to evaluate programs on the basis of such varied objectives.

THE BUDGET AS A CONTROL TOOL

In order for a budget to be a useful control mechanism, it must be broken down into periodic increments corresponding to the financial statements. Comparisons should be made throughout the year between the budget and the financial statements. Most organizations do not have resources to fall back on when it is determined that budgeted revenues have not been met or that expenses have been excessive. So the board and staff must be prepared to take action when the financial statements indicate a significant deviation from the budget. If the board and staff fail to take aggressive, corrective action, the board is shirking its responsibility and the budget has become a meaningless formality.

BUDGETING PRINCIPLES

Several principles serve to guide managers in formulating budgets.

Balanced budget   An organization needs at least a balanced budget in order to remain solvent. A balanced budget means that the total budgeted revenue equals the amount budgeted for expenses. Managers may knowingly choose to operate certain programs at a financial loss. But when they do so, they must plan for other programs to compensate for expected shortfalls so that the overall budget is in balance.

Budgeting a deficit   Some nonprofit organizations incorporate a deficit—where total expenses exceed total revenues—into the budget. In such cases, funds for operations are provided by some form of indebtedness in the form of loans, unpaid bills, using advance ticket sales receipts, or "borrowing" from restricted funds. These are all obligations that the organization will eventually have to meet if it is to avoid bankruptcy. Since the budget reflects the organization's goals, operating under a deficit means that the goals are not being fully realized.

Some nonprofit organizations create a deficit as a strategy for raising funds. They intentionally overspend and create a crisis situation that will attract the needed financial support. Although this strategy may have been effective in the past, in the current era of accountability, good planning and fiscal prudence are highly valued, and even long-standing, loyal donors are no longer sympathetic to this approach.

Contingency/reserve fund   A contingency/reserve fund should be included in the budgeted expenses. It has been recommended that between 5 and 10 percent of the organization's budget should be set aside for this account. The size of the contingency fund varies according to the following factors:

- The size of the budget (larger organizations can allocate a smaller percentage).

- The predictability of levels and sources of income (the less predictable the income, the larger the contingency/reserve fund should be).

- The stability of the organization (the more unstable, the greater the contingency fund).

- The extent to which expenditures are fixed in advance (the more flexibility, the less the contingency fund).

- The experience of the current management (the less the experience, the greater the contingency fund).

This fund can be used in two ways. First, it can be used as a backup for unexpected circumstances such as a huge snowstorm the night of a major event, resulting in single-ticket sales far below projected levels; unforeseen legal expenses; or cash flow problems that occur when the organization must pay bills before it has the income to do so. Second, at the end of the fiscal year, any money remaining in the fund becomes a reserve to be invested for future growth and to help carry the organization through tough times.

Determining costs   There are two common methods for determining program and activity costs. The first approach, called *incremental budgeting,* is used for activities the organization has carried out in the past. It relies heavily on previous years' actual expenses and income. The manager investigates changes in the line item costs of each program, such as printing and paper costs, postage, advertising fees, and so on. If administrative costs are built in to program budgets, salary and rent increases should be included. A percentage should be added for other inflationary costs. Similarly, costs may be reduced incrementally. For example, an organization may choose to switch from a four-color brochure to a two-color brochure to save money.

The second approach, called *zero-based budgeting,* requires that each line item of the budget be calculated from scratch. This is not only necessary for new projects, but is also useful for reevaluating ongoing expenses. With a zero-based budget, staff members start with a budget of zero and must justify each amount they request.

The most effective method to determine costs is a combination of these two approaches. Previous expenses are extremely useful in planning the upcoming budget. Yet each budget item should be carefully examined to see if it can be reduced or if anticipated benefits can be achieved more efficiently some other way. Budgeters find it is most realistic to estimate costs on the high side. It is also important to account for the fact that new programs and activities will add to administrative costs such as staff, space, and office equipment.[8]

Budgeters must also take into account both their fixed and variable expenses. Since variable costs are more adaptable than fixed costs, managers often balance their budgets by varying their costs per production, service, or program. However, arts managers must not fail to recognize the interdependence between the income and expense sides of the variable budget. Suppose the first crack at the budget of a large orchestra shows a deficit and a decision is made to cut $100,000 from the guest artist expense. However, no reduction is made in projected ticket sales income. When the original budget was planned, the ticket sales were predicated on a specific roster of artists. Replacing Andre Watts with John Doe will certainly result in lower ticket income. But that part of the budget wasn't revised. At year's end, everyone seems shocked that ticket sales didn't meet projections. The most accurate and revealing method of budgeting variable costs is to compare them to projected income on a precise event-by-event basis.[9]

IMPLEMENTATION

A brilliant strategic marketing plan counts for little if it is not implemented properly. While strategy addresses the *what* and *why* of marketing activities, implementation addresses the *who, where, when,* and *how.* We define marketing implementation as the process that turns marketing plans into action assignments and ensures that such assignments are executed in a manner that accomplishes the plan's stated objectives.

A set of skills must be practiced throughout the organization's functions, programs, and policies to achieve effective implementation. Managers must have *diagnostic skills* to help determine whether a strategy is implementable. *Allocation skills* are used in budgeting resources (time, money, and personnel) to various functions and programs according to standards of efficiency and effectiveness. *Monitoring skills* are used in managing a system of controls to evaluate the results of marketing actions. This topic will be covered later in this chapter. *Organizing skills* are used in developing an effective working organization. Understanding the informal as well as formal organization is important to carrying out effective implementation (see Chapter 16). *Interacting skills* refer to the ability of managers to get things done by influencing others. Interacting skills include applying effective behavior patterns during the implementation process, and effective use of the organization's power structure and of its leadership.

Diagnostic Skills

Many "best-laid plans" fail to see the light of day. Plans to innovate may fizzle out when management or board members are reluctant to commit funds to recommended projects. Plans to improve quality may get no farther than some airy rhetoric. Without successful implementation, a strategy represents merely lost time and frustration to those who develop and support it. Thus, a strategy is not truly well conceived if it is not *implementable.* The factors that allow for successful implementation must be considered during the formulation process itself. A strategist must be able to look ahead and ask, "Is this strategy workable? Can I make it happen?" If an assessment leads to the answer "no" or "only at an unacceptable risk," then the formulation process must continue.

To make this analysis, a strategist should take several factors into consideration. In assessment of the strategy itself, a strategist should consider

- *Complexity:* How many factors must be managed to enact the strategy?
- *Divisibility:* Can the strategy be divided into subcomponents?
- *Reversibility:* Can the plug be pulled on the strategy if it doesn't work?
- *Consistency:* How internally consistent is the strategy? Does it relate closely to strategies the organization has undertaken in the past? Does its success depend on resources currently available in the organization? Diversity is harder to manage.
- *Stakeholder agreement:* How will it look at the board of directors meeting? To the artists? To the public? To the donors?

In determining whether a strategy is implementable, the strategist must also consider the complexity, uncertainty, instability, and hostility of the environment. Internal organizational factors to be taken into account include leadership continuity, quality of decision making, quality of management information systems, and the nature of the organization's reward systems.

Behavior Patterns for Effective Implementation

A plan is a commitment to action—a commitment by people with their own ideas, attitudes, preferences, concerns, and needs. Steps must be taken to lend a sense of realism, motivation, and confidence that the new direction can be achieved. People must see the strategy's relevance, feel they are capable of implementing it, understand the required behaviors, know whether they have achieved the objective, and be rewarded for doing so. Hambrick and Cannella have identified several patterns of behavior that promote effective strategy implementation:[10]

- *Obtain broad-based inputs and participation at the formulation stage.* Widespread participation helps to secure intellectual and social commitment to the new course of action, as well as to highlight the major issues expected to arise during implementation.
- *Carefully assess the obstacles to implementation.* There are both internal and external obstacles to consider. The success of a strategy depends on the material and human resources within the organization. The organization may have the wrong configurations of systems and procedures, or inadequate human resources or financial backing. Equally important, there may be political resistance from those who stand to lose something of value if the new strategy is implemented; ideological resistance from those who believe the new strategy is ill fated or violates

deeply held values; or blind resistance from those who are intolerant or afraid of change. Management must also consider the possibility of external resistance from contributors, government agencies, audience segments, competitors, suppliers, or other parties. Opposition from any of these groups may limit or undermine the expected benefits of the strategy.

- *Make early moves across the full array of implementation levers.* These include resource commitments, policies and programs, structure, people, and rewards.

- *Commit adequate resources.* The commitment of resources is crucial to the success of any new strategy, for it signals true commitment to the strategy. Many strategies fail because resources are not decisively allocated to support them.

- *Design policies and programs.* The strategy must be translated into concrete action plans and assignments within the organization's various departments. Within the marketing department, the strategy should be converted into discrete plans and policies in the areas of product development, pricing, promotion, distribution, and service.

- *Put appropriate structures in place.* The new strategy will often entail developing new groups and relationships. New information systems may also be required to improve decision making and maximize the likelihood of successful implementation.

- *Provide for rewards.* The impact of incentives and rewards must be factored in. Rewards can be formal, such as incentive schemes, promotions, or commissions; or informal, such as private or public pats on the back, a sense of pride, and enthusiasm. People often work in nonprofit organizations for the intangible rewards they receive; if these are missing, motivation may be lacking.

- *Recruit the best people.* Some plans require special skills for their implementation. Additions to the team, training and development programs, personal coaching and counseling, and replacement of individuals are among the options available. Additionally, all persons involved in implementing the strategy must have the personal characteristics of ability to deal with messy problems, willingness to work hard, creativity, flexibility, and tolerance for ambiguity.

- *Sell, sell, sell the strategy to everyone who matters—upward, downward, and outward.* Managers, staff, and board executives must be sold on the merits and viability of a strategy. External stakeholders such as customers, the media, and regulatory agencies must also be sold on supporting the plan. These external parties are no different from insiders in their potential for skepticism and anxiety about the new strategy. If these parties are kept well informed, unfavorable reaction can be greatly reduced or eliminated.

- *Fine tune, adjust, and respond as events and trends arise.* Be prepared to adjust the strategy for changes in the environment or in the behavior of affected individuals or groups. Because all contingencies and eventualities cannot be envisioned at the outset, a strategy should come with broad guidance systems but should allow for spontaneity and responsiveness as well.

Power Relationships

Power, an influential factor in all organizations, can be defined as the ability to get another individual, group, or entire organization to do something that might not be done otherwise.[11] Power is often associated with negative concepts, such as strong-arm tactics or political clout, but it has a much broader meaning. Power is the result of possessing and controlling resources valued by another party. A has power over B to the extent that A controls a resource valued by B. Conversely, interdependence exists when each controls a resource that is valued by the other.

TYPES OF POWER

Power is not determined entirely by one's formal position in the organization's hierarchy. Informal, relational power also exists. Several types of resource-based power can be distinguished.

Reward power   Reward power is based on one's ability to provide valued resources in the form of rewards or recognition in exchange for a desired action. In an arts organization, these rewards may take the form of major contributions by donors or granting agencies to support an attractive project, or rave reviews from critics.

Coercive power   Coercive power is based on the threat to punish if a party does not take a desired action. It is illustrated by a musicians' union threatening to strike or a major donor threatening to withdraw financial support if the organization does or doesn't do something. Coercive power should be viewed as a "last resort"; its exercise generally produces poorer results in the long run than does reliance on other types of power.[12]

Expert power   Expert power is held by those who possess valued information, knowledge, or ability. In the arts world, experts may include critics, consultants, and other specialists who usually operate outside the organizational system. They may be resented by arts managers who regard *themselves* as the experts.

Legitimate power   Legitimate power is held by those who are empowered by the organizational or social system. They govern at the consent of the governed. Such a person is seen as having the right to make decisions. An artistic director, for example, usually has the power to reject productions that are recommended by the board of directors. The executive director has the power to hire and fire employees. And the board has the power to hire and fire both the executive director and the artistic director.

Referent power   Referent power is held by persons and organizations who are highly respected or admired. Referent power has many implications for arts organizations. Prestige is a core qualification for the president and other executives of the board. There is often an "honorary" chairperson as well, someone who lends his or her name to the organization's letterhead but is otherwise basically uninvolved. This person is often the mayor or the CEO of a large corporation. Prestigious arts organizations can attract prestigious board members; and prestigious board members in turn add prestige to the organization. Referent power is normally a highly effective tool for garnering support, involvement, and even loyalty. Sometimes a performing arts organization will feature a famous performer to elevate its visibility and its credibility. The excitement usually dies down, however, after the star leaves town, and may do little to build long-term interest in the organization unless other stars are brought in on a regular basis.

LEVELS OF POWER

The amount of power found in a person or situation depends on several factors. *Centrality* is the degree of access a person has to important individuals and relevant information. *Criticality* is the degree to which a person would be difficult to replace. *Visibility* refers to the degree to which the person has wide recognition in the minds of relevant publics. Finally, *flexibility* is the degree of discretion a person exercises over the use of a resource. Effective leadership requires an understanding of each of these sources of power and the levels at which they are operating in a given situation.

Leadership

A leader of an organization has two primary tasks: *external leadership* is the translation of external needs into an internal vision, and *internal leadership* is the translation of vision to employee action. The leader must be able to motivate followers and show them a path to their goals. Being a leader requires an understanding of the motives of the followers.

Leadership is not just a responsibility of top managers. Every employee must be empowered, and feel empowered, to think and behave as a leader within his or her domain. In order to *be* empowered, an employee must have a full understanding of the organization's mission, goals, and constraints. In order to *feel* empowered, an employee must be given the freedom to do a certain amount of independent decision making and must be given slack for a certain amount of error. A capable organization reflects leadership qualities in all departments and at all levels. The leadership capability of the organization then becomes the integration and sum of the abilities of all its individual leaders.

An important characteristic of good leadership is the capacity for change. Managers must show a capacity to learn from past experiences, the ability for self-assessment, and the ability to experience continuous learning. By being self-critical, managers can learn from both their successes and their failures. Managers must learn about themselves, and not just about the issues at hand. Strong leaders supply a vision, change or reinforce the organization's culture, have the courage to devote resources to new projects and services, and have the courage to abandon losing ones. A good leader knows that the best idea is meaningless unless it can be translated into action.

CONTROL

Performance is the ultimate test of any organization. Says Peter Drucker, "The discipline of thinking through what results will be demanded . . . will protect the organization from squandering its resources."[13] This last step of the strategic market planning process, that of reviewing and adjusting the strategy and tactics and measuring performance, should actually be taken into consideration throughout the process. As we embark on various strategies, our information is necessarily somewhat limited. As experience and further knowledge are gained, strategies and tactics should be reevaluated in light of new information. Frequent evaluations can serve to either validate a current approach, stimulate the modification of approach or of the goals themselves, or even to encourage the abandonment of a strategy altogether.

An organization should establish three levels of performance control: short-range or periodic, to assess progress and the effectiveness of operational marketing plans on a daily, weekly, monthly, or quarterly basis; midrange, usually annual; and long-range or strategic control, usually every three to five years. Many of the control processes and tools used for annual plan control are also used for shorter-term control. The marketing audit is the primary tool in the strategic control process.

Periodic and Annual Control

The short- and midrange control process is driven by an approach called *management by objectives.* Four steps are involved. First, management sets monthly or quarterly goals. Second, management monitors the organization's performance in the marketplace. Third, management determines the causes of serious performance deviations. Fourth, management takes corrective action to close the gaps between its goals and performance. This could require changing the action programs or the goals, or even dropping the program.

Sometimes a strategy should be abandoned altogether. Too often, management keeps investing additional resources, both human and financial, in order to salvage an ineffective project, thereby draining resources from more productive efforts. It is far better to accept a loss early than to continue on an unproductive course of action. The time and expenses already invested are "sunk costs," that is, they are historical, *not* recoverable, and should not be considered when evaluating the best course of action. According to Max Bazerman:

Our reference point for action should be our current state, and we should consider all alternative courses of action by evaluating only the *future* costs and benefits associated with each alternative. The tendency to escalate commitment suggests that managers need to take an "experimenting" approach to management. That is, as a manager, you should make a decision and implement it, but be open to dropping your commitment and shifting to another course of action if the first plan does not work out. This means constantly reassessing the rationality of future commitments and learning to identify failures early.[14]

Management starts the control process by developing aggregate goals for the planning period, such as increasing the number of subscribers. It is then up to the marketing manager to determine the meaningful criteria and the prerequisites for success. For example, the subscription department may have specific goals for increasing renewals, attracting new patrons with flex plans, and converting single-ticket buyers to subscribers. During the relevant period, managers receive reports that allow them to determine whether their goals are being reached, and if not, to take the necessary corrective actions. Various control tools are available for managers to use in this process. Three common quantitative control tools are sales and revenue analysis, expense analysis, and ratio analysis. Two useful qualitative measures are customer satisfaction tracking and a marketing effectiveness/efficiency review.

SALES AND REVENUE ANALYSIS

Sales and revenue analysis is the effort to measure and evaluate the actual sales and revenue being achieved in relation to the goals set by season, specific performance, audience type, and so on. For example, the manager may wish to track whether early subscription renewals are meeting current goals and how they compare to the previous season. If early renewal goals are not being met, the marketing manager may choose to increase direct-mail and/or telemarketing efforts to this group. Analysis by audience type may mean that if too few students attend the university's concert series or if certain areas of the city are underrepresented at the summer music festival, the reasons should be sought out. Management should avoid jumping to conclusions without some research. Too few students attending the concert series could be due to any number of causes: high ticket prices, inadequate advertising and publicity, low interest in the season's performers, competing social events on the same evenings, and so on. The appropriate corrective actions would differ for each cause.

EXPENSE ANALYSIS

The budget can help to determine whether the organization is setting reasonable expense targets and to track actual spending and receipts against planned targets. Variances between actual and budgeted performance serve as a signal to management and the board that attention is required, whether the variance is positive or negative. Positive variance (where actual spending is lower than planned amounts) may either be the result of laggard performance in program implementation or may indicate cost savings in relation to anticipated expenditures. A negative variance may indicate either cost overruns or lower-than-expected revenues. Either of these conditions, if not dealt with in a timely manner, can create serious financial problems for the organization.

At the Steppenwolf Theatre, subscription drive expenses are broken down by various categories. In the 1994–95 season, 13,929 subscribers were recruited at a total cost of $248,681 or $17.85 per subscriber. The breakdown was as follows:

Category	Cost	Number of Subscribers	Cost Per Subscriber
Early renewal	$10,952	3,400	$3.22
Official renewal	$10,593	4,200	$2.52
Telemarketing	$61,391	3,157	$19.45
New subscriptions	$54,771	1,483	$36.93
Flex plans	$7,000	606	$11.55

New subscribers are important to Steppenwolf, even though they are the most costly subscribers to recruit. The organization increased its new-subscriber budget for the 1995–96 season to $85,050 for a goal of 1,800 subscribers. In other words, it planned to spend $30,000 more to capture an additional 317 subscribers, at a cost of nearly $100 per additional new subscriber. As interim results of the subscription campaign were tracked, revisions to the budget were made. By the end of July 1995, the campaign had recruited 2,100 new subscribers, exceeding the goal by 300 subscribers. This reduced the cost per new subscriber considerably, to $49.

RATIO ANALYSIS

Analysis of ratios concerning various functions and programs can be used to compare progress by production, by season, or on a year-to-year basis and determine their relative effectiveness and efficiency. An organization may analyze whether, for example, total ticket sales revenue for the year increased or decreased as a percentage of total combined earned revenue and contributed support. This is known as the ratio of *net total revenue to total revenue and support.*

The key ratio to watch is *marketing expense to sales.* For example, a marketing manager may track ratios of telemarketing to sales, advertising to sales, marketing research to sales, and promotions to sales. The marketing manager will be interested in the expense-to-revenue ratios of various marketing programs. At the Steppenwolf Theatre, in the 1994–95 season, the subscription campaign yielded revenues of $1,423,730 for a cost of $248,680, that is, an expense-to-revenue ratio of 17 percent. For the following season, projections were for revenues of $1,621,200 and expenses of

$295,000, an expense-to-revenue ratio of 18 percent. (Printing and postage costs had increased considerably, accounting for the 1 percent increase in costs.) By the end of July 1995, expenses remained as budgeted, but revenues of $1,810,000 exceeded expectations, which brought the expense-to-revenue ratio down to 16 percent.

An arts organization may also wish to compare the expenses and revenues associated with various programs to the organization's total expenses and revenues. This helps determine whether the programs are receiving a growing or dwindling share of the budget. The numerator is the category of expense, such as outreach programs, a ballet school, special events, or operating expenses. The denominator is the organization's total expense budget. The marketing manager should analyze such expenses as print advertising, promotions, direct mail, telemarketing, and so on, as a portion of each program budget or of the entire marketing budget.

CUSTOMER SATISFACTION TRACKING

The preceding control measures are largely financial and quantitative in character. They are important but not sufficient. Also needed are qualitative measures that monitor changing levels of customer preference and satisfaction so that management can take action before such changes affect sales. The main customer satisfaction tracking systems are the following:

- *Complaint and suggestion systems:* Market-oriented organizations record, analyze, and respond to *all* written and oral complaints that come from customers. The complaints are tabulated, and management attempts to correct whatever is causing the most frequent types of complaints. If the complaints are program-related, this information is shared with the artistic decision makers. Market-oriented organizations try to maximize the opportunities for consumers to complain so that management can get a more complete picture of customer reactions to the products and services. Systems should be developed so that those who have regular contact with customers, such as box office personnel and telemarketers, thoroughly record all complaints and suggestions.

- *Customer panels:* Some organizations run panels of customers who have agreed to communicate their attitudes periodically through phone calls or mail questionnaires. These panels are more representative of the range of customer attitudes than the input to customer complaint and suggestion systems.

- *Customer surveys:* As a part of audience surveys, some organizations periodically include questions that ask respondents to evaluate the friendliness of the staff, the quality of the service, and so on. This system allows management to identify weaknesses in the organization's customer service.

MARKETING EFFICIENCY AND EFFECTIVENESS REVIEW

The final step in the annual control process is to evaluate how effectively and efficiently the organization's activities have accomplished its goals and how they might be better conducted in the future. Marketing effectiveness is not necessarily revealed by current sales and revenue performance. Good results could be attributable to being in the right place at the right time rather than to effective marketing management. Marketing improvements might boost results from good to excellent. Conversely, a marketing department might have poor results in spite of excellent marketing planning. Replacing the present marketing managers might only make things worse.

Peter Drucker recommends that, to evaluate the *effectiveness* of each major program or activity, the managers ask:

- If we weren't already doing this—if we were not already committed to this—would we start doing it now?
- Are we working in the right areas? Do we need to change our focus?
- What have we learned and what do we recommend?
- What, if anything, should we do differently?[15]

To evaluate the *efficiency* of specific projects, managers should raise such questions as:

- Are higher revenue projections achievable?
- What additional sources of revenue are possible—raising fees, devoting extra efforts to existing activities, initiating new programs, providing new services?
- Can expenditures be reduced by cutting certain costs?
- Can alternative approaches be used to improve efficiency and thereby lower costs without affecting quality?

In evaluating one program activity against another, the board and staff should be careful about using the criterion of cost-effectiveness. This criterion is useful for analyzing such factors as direct mail versus print advertising, for example. But from a larger perspective, the organization's mission may dictate that managers should carry on activities and programs that are *not* cost-effective, such as educational programs or performances of new music in a half-empty hall. The primary criterion should be a program's relationship to the mission of the organization, its purposes, and its goals.[16]

Strategic Control: The Marketing Audit

From time to time, organizations should undertake critical review of their overall marketing effectiveness. Marketing is an area where rapid obsolescence of objectives, policies, strategies, and programs is a constant possibility. Each organization should periodically reassess its overall approach to the marketplace. An important tool for this process is the marketing audit. The marketing audit assists managers in assessing the organization's current internal state and its environmental conditions. An internal analysis leads to an understanding of the past use of resources—programs, staff, volunteers, facilities, and finances—and helps identify opportunities for strengthening performance.

This audit is not at all like an accounting audit, which looks for errors, deceptions, or other evidence of mismanagement. Instead, the marketing audit is a forward-looking document that indicates to management what can and should be the focus of strategic efforts in the coming months and years. It is a down-to-earth set of guidelines to point the organization in directions consistent with the best marketing wisdom and experience. A *marketing audit* is defined as a comprehensive, systematic, independent, and periodic examination of an organization's marketing environment, objectives, strategies, and activities with a view to determining problem areas and opportunities and recommending a plan of action to improve the organization's strategic marketing performance.

The marketing audit is *comprehensive:* it covers all the marketing issues facing an organization, not just the one or two obvious trouble spots, such as pricing or public relations. The value of a truly comprehensive audit becomes apparent when unanticipated strengths or weaknesses are identified, often to the surprise of management.

The marketing audit is *systematic:* it involves an orderly sequence of diagnostic steps covering the organization's marketing environment, internal marketing system, and specific marketing activities. The audit is structured to start with the broadest issues with the most general impact on the organization, and proceeds to cover functional details. Most important, this diagnosis is followed by a corrective action plan involving both short-run and long-run proposals to improve the organization's overall marketing effectiveness.

The marketing audit should be *independent:* it is normally conducted by an outside consultant or by an inside party who has sufficient experience, credibility, and independence to attain top management's confidence and the needed objectivity. Performing arts organizations, however, tend to have little or no budget for outside consultants and tend to have small management staffs who work closely together, leaving little room for locating an "independent insider." In such a situation, separate audits can be undertaken by well-informed members of the management and the board of directors. Their combined information can be analyzed and discussed in a committee of the whole, with a primary goal of maintaining honesty and objectivity.

The marketing audit should be carried out *periodically,* rather than only when there is a crisis. This allows the organization to be proactive and continually create benefits, as well as to react effectively to current and pressing problems. Ironically, some organizations are thrown into a crisis partly because they have failed to review their marketing operation during good times.

A marketing audit may be requested by a funding agency or a governing body, but most often the request is generated by the management of the organization itself. Because the audit, like a photograph, represents the organization at a particular point in time, various aspects of the audit should be continued on an ongoing basis, and other aspects should be repeated as situations change or new information becomes available.

COMPONENTS OF THE MARKETING AUDIT

The marketing audit examines six major components of the organization's marketing situation, as described below. The major auditing questions for each component follow.

- *The marketing environment audit* analyzes major macroenvironmental forces and trends in the key components of the organization's task environment: its users, funders, competitors, and other constituencies.

- *The marketing strategy audit* reviews the organization's marketing objectives and marketing strategy to appraise how well they are adapted to the current and forecasted marketing environment.

- *The marketing organization audit* evaluates the capability of the marketing organization for implementing the necessary strategy for the forecasted environment.

- *The marketing systems audit* assesses the quality of the organization's systems for analysis, planning, and control.

- *The marketing productivity audit* examines the profitability of different marketing entities and the cost effectiveness of different marketing expenditures.

- *Marketing function audits* make in-depth evaluations of major marketing-mix components, namely products, price, distribution, advertising, sales promotion, and public relations.

A MARKETING AUDIT

PART I. MARKETING ENVIRONMENT AUDIT

Macroenvironment:

A. Demographic

1. What major demographic developments and trends pose opportunities or threats for this organization?

2. What actions, if any, has the organization taken in response to those developments?

B. Economic

1. What major developments and trends in income, prices, savings, and interest rates are affecting the organization?

2. What major changes are taking place in the sources and amounts of contributed income (from individuals, corporations, private and public foundations, and government agencies)?

3. What actions has the organization taken in response to those developments and trends?

C. Political

1. What recent legislation has affected this organization?

2. What federal, state, and local agencies should be monitored for future actions relating to the organization?

3. What actions has the organization taken in response to these developments?

D. Cultural

1. What changes are occurring in consumer lifestyles, values, and educational opportunities that might affect this organization?

2. What actions has the organization taken in response to these developments?

Task Environment

A. Users, Funders, and other Constituencies

1. What is happening to overall market size, growth, and geographical distribution? Has the audience base (and the subscriber base, if appropriate) been growing, shrinking, or staying the same over the past several years?

2. How do the audience size and the subscriber base (as a percentage of available seats) compare to the local and national averages for similar organizations?

3. What are the major market segments? What are their expected rates of growth? Which are high-opportunity and low-opportunity segments?

4. How much of the consumer volume is repeat versus new business? What percentage of consumers can be classified as light users? Heavy users?

5. How do current customers and prospects rate the organization and its competitors, particularly with respect to reputation, product quality, service, price, and personnel?

6. How do different classes of customers make their buying decisions? How do users find out about and decide to try the organization's offerings?

7. What are the evolving needs that customers seek to satisfy in this market? Can you prioritize these needs in terms of customer preferences?

8. What actions have been taken by the organization to meet these needs? What benefits does the organization offer to each segment? To private and public benefactors? To volunteers?

9. What publics (financial supporters, media, government agencies, citizen groups, ethnic groups, suppliers, personnel internal to the organization) represent particular opportunities or problems for the organization?

10. What steps has the organization taken to prepare to fully benefit from public opportunities and to deal with potential crises?

B. Competitors

1. Who are the organization's direct competitors (namely, other performing arts groups that have a similar product, audience base, location, time frame for presentations, and price structure)?

2. What are the objectives and strategy of each major competitor? What are their strengths and weaknesses?

3. What are the sizes and trends in market shares?

4. Who are the indirect competitors to the organization (other types of performing arts, other forms of entertainment, other leisure-time pursuits)?

5. What trends can be foreseen in future competition and substitutes for the organization's product?

PART II. MARKETING OBJECTIVES AND STRATEGY AUDIT

A. Organizational Objectives

1. Is the mission of the organization clearly stated in market-oriented terms? Is the mission feasible in terms of the organization's opportunities and resources? How well is the mission understood by the organization? Are there any plans for major changes in the organization in the next five years?

2. What are the organization's major strengths and weaknesses?

3. Are the marketing objectives appropriate, given the organization's competitive position, resources, and opportunities? Do they lead logically to clearly stated marketing objectives?

B. Marketing Strategy

1. What is the core marketing strategy for achieving the objectives? Is it a sound strategy?

2. Has the organization established both short-term (one season) and long-term (five years) goals?

3. Are enough resources (or too many resources) budgeted to accomplish the marketing objectives?

4. Are the marketing resources allocated optimally to prime market segments, territories, and products of the organization?

5. Are the marketing resources allocated optimally to the major elements of the marketing mix, offering sufficient quality, service, sales force, advertising, promotion, publicity, and distribution? Does the organization carry out periodic reviews of the efficacy of its operations and evaluations of its resource allocation decisions? How, and with what results?

PART III. MARKETING ORGANIZATION AUDIT

A. Formal Structure

1. Is there a high-level marketing officer with adequate authority and responsibility over those organizational activities that affect the customer's satisfaction?

2. Are the marketing responsibilities optimally structured along functional and end-user lines? Is the system designed for better service to customers or for internal convenience?

B. Functional Efficiency

1. Are there good communication and working relations between the marketing department and other key functional areas?

2. Are there any personnel in marketing who need more training, motivation, supervision, or evaluation? How much and what kind of outside input and training in marketing does the staff get?

3. Are there any problems between marketing and other operational areas, such as financial management, that need attention?

PART IV. MARKETING SYSTEMS AUDIT

A. Marketing Information System

1. Is the marketing intelligence system producing accurate, sufficient, and timely information about developments in the marketplace?

2. Is marketing research being adequately used by managers? What information does the organization have about its markets and other publics?

3. Do managers understand the types and capabilities of various market research techniques? Do they have the skills to develop and analyze them in-house? If not, are they aware of the resources available for contracting out this function?

B. Marketing Planning System

1. Is the marketing planning system well conceived and effective?

2. Is sales forecasting and market potential measurement soundly carried out? Are quotas set on a rational basis?

C. Marketing Control System

1. Are the control procedures (monthly, quarterly, seasonal, etc.) adequate to ensure that the annual plan objectives are being achieved?

2. Is provision made to analyze periodically the profitability of different products, markets, and territories (for touring companies or those who perform in more than one location)?

3. Is provision made to periodically examine and validate various marketing costs?

4. What quality control procedures does the organization have?

PART V. MARKETING PRODUCTIVITY AUDIT

A. Profitability Analysis

1. How profitable are the organization's different offerings (subscriptions, single ticket sales, presented versus non-presented events, tangible products such as T-shirts, books, CDs, other souvenirs, royalties, joint venture profits, food service, etc.)?

2. What is the profitability of various customer markets and territories?

B. Cost-Effectiveness Analysis

   1. Do any marketing activities seem to have excessive costs? Has a cost-benefit analysis been made for each type of marketing expenditure? Are the expenditures tracked regularly? Could cost-reducing steps be taken? Can certain money be better spent in other areas?

   2. What are the organization's sources of contributed income? How have the percentages of support from the various sources changed over recent years? How much time and effort does the marketing function expend for each of these sources? Are these expenses justified in terms of the return?

PART VI. MARKETING FUNCTION AUDIT

A. Product

   When answering the following questions, consider such product features as subscriber discounts, ticket exchange privileges, parking, facility features such as acoustics and leg room, additional benefits such as restaurant discounts, and tangible products. Also, consider the core offerings in terms of the product mix for each performance, for each series, and for the entire season.

   1. What are the product-line objectives? Are these objectives sound? Is the current product line meeting those objectives?

   2. Are there particular products or services that should be phased out?

   3. Are there new products or services that are worth adding?

   4. Could any products benefit from quality, feature, or style improvement?

B. Price

   1. What are the pricing objectives, policies, strategies, and procedures? To what extent are prices set on sound cost, demand, and competitive criteria? What are the procedures for establishing and reviewing pricing policy?

   2. Is pricing demand-oriented? Are there variations by market segments, time of use, number of performances attended?

3. What discounts to the basic fee structure are offered and with what rationale? What discounts are offered by competitors?

4. Do the customers see the organization's prices as being in line or out of line with the perceived value of its offer?

5. What short-term promotional pricing policies are used and with what effect?

C. Distribution

1. Is the performance space in the best location(s) considering the current and potential audience? Are current venues adequate and the most appropriate for the type of product the organization offers and suitable to its audience?

2. How can the current performing space be improved to create ambience and comforts for the audience? What steps have been taken in this regard?

3. What feedback has been garnered from customers, either solicited or unsolicited, regarding inadequacies and possible improvements? List objectives in this area according to whether they are short term or long term, and according to costs versus expected benefits.

4. Should the company expand the number of locations in which it performs? What touring options, either local, national, or international, are available to be developed by the company?

5. How does the organization rank its various geographic service areas in terms of priority of demand and best return on resources?

6. Are services related to information, reservations, and payment decentralized and convenient to target audiences?

7. What other resources are available to the organization for developing earned income through distribution (selling rights to original productions or choreography, coproducing with other companies, distribution of educational programming materials, etc.)?

D. Advertising, Sales Promotion, and Public Relations

1. What are the organization's advertising objectives? Are they sound? realistic?

2. Is the right amount being spent on advertising? How is the budget determined? Is cost-effectiveness tracked on a regular basis?

3. Are the ad themes and copy effective? What do customers and the public think about the advertising? Does it generate interest? purchase?

4. Are the advertising media well chosen? Are results of advertising monitored and reviewed on a regular basis?

5. Does the organization have a paid or volunteer advertising agency? What functions does the ad agency perform for the organization?

6. Is sales promotion used effectively? Are a variety of promotional tactics being used (direct mail, telemarketing, cooperative efforts, etc.)? Is promotion designed for and directed to different markets?

7. Is there a well-conceived public relations program? Are PR opportunities regularly and frequently taken into consideration?

8. What system is used to handle consumer inquiries resulting from advertising and promotion? What follow-up is done? Does the organization engage in internal marketing to keep the staff and volunteers up to date on all events, plans, and possible public concerns?

9. What is done about negative feedback from consumers about the organization's staff or services? How are complaints handled? What kind of follow-up is done?

10. Does the organization have crisis management systems and trained personnel in place?

MARKETING AUDIT PROCEDURE

The marketing audit procedure involves several steps: (1) gathering background information, (2) gathering data, (3) analysis, and (4) writing and presenting a formal report.

Backgrounding and initial management contact   The auditor should begin by holding discussions with key management personnel and, if appropriate, others who have requested the audit to ascertain the nature of the information they are seeking and their expectations as to what should be included in the final report. The auditor should enlist full management support for obtaining all pertinent data and for making use of their valuable time. A checklist of the basic information to be requested should be prepared in advance. Any previous studies of the organization that are available, including past marketing audits, should be reviewed.

The auditor should plan a site visit (or several visits) for firsthand observation and arrange interviews with staff and knowledgeable insiders. The auditor may find it useful to observe staff meetings and meetings of the board of directors in order to observe the organization's culture and the manner in which issues are handled. Executive board members can provide a perspective from a point of view other than that of management, and, because their concerns are central to the organization, this avenue should not be left unexplored. Administrative assistants, box office personnel, and so on, may be the best resources for day-to-day details of the operations.

During this initial stage and as further interviews are held, it is important for the auditor to learn from key management personnel and executive board members what their vision is for the organization. Their responses may clarify whether there is agreement or dissension as to the mission and core activities of the organization, and whether it may become the auditor's responsibility to encourage consensus building on the organization's most basic values and issues. Certain key people may have their own agendas, which would not otherwise be made known and which could undermine the achievement of the organization's mission.

MYOPIC VISION?

Two key board members, who are among a suburban theater's largest contributors, are eager for the theater to move to the heart of the nearby city's theater district, a congested, yuppie area about twenty miles away. Managers and other board members believe such a move would be incongruent with the theater's core strength—its loyal audience base—and would most likely undermine the theater's survival, not to mention its success. The auditor administered a patron survey, which verified that the theater draws 75 percent of its audience from the local community —mostly older patrons for whom a convenient and accessible location are important. She presented to these two board members this irrefutable evidence that their "vision" would be counterproductive for the organization.

The auditor may find it enlightening to attend performances, both in the evening and for a matinee, to get a feel for the audience and how they are handled by box office personnel, ushers, and concessionaires; and to view the general comfort level, accessibility, and traffic flow within and without the facility. It would also be useful to observe box office procedures for a period of time to analyze how calls, computers, and paperwork are managed and to interview box office personnel to determine what issues are pertinent to them and to gain their insights.

If a friendly, open, and nonthreatening relationship can be developed between the auditor and members of the organization, information can be gleaned about the culture, the effectiveness of the personnel, and the nature of various interpersonal relationships and their effects on the organization.

Data gathering   Data gathering assists management in objective and effective decision making by removing the guesswork and dispelling preconceived notions. An auditor may gather primary data by interviewing key staff and observing press briefings, box office transactions, and announcements before performances. He or she may also review advertisements, direct-mail pieces, and benefits offered by the organization and its competitors. The auditor may choose to conduct an audience survey to gauge audience reaction to specific aspects of the organization's offerings. Focus groups are also an effective source of primary data, and an auditor may choose to interview groups of current or potential members.

The auditor may also review secondary data: the organization's financial data, box office tallies, fund-raising results, subscription drive results, personnel reports, and other internal documents. Externally available secondary data may range from items specific to the organization such as awards and reviews, to more general information from such sources as demographic studies, census reports, arts industry studies, and trend analyses.

The availability of valid and useful data is often a major weakness in many organizations. If this weakness becomes obvious as a result of the first audit, a primary goal of the organization should be to put simple information-gathering systems in place immediately. A specific audit form should be used to record the data from these investigations. This standardized document will facilitate comparisons from audit to audit and across units within a single audit. The examinations should be based on up-to-date inputs and information, and, whenever possible, should include a review of data going back several years to help detect trends in attendance, pricing, revenues, contributions, and other more subjective areas such as critical reviews and competitive comparisons.

Analysis   Once interviews and observations have been completed, the data can be analyzed and recommendations can be formulated and reviewed with key personnel. (See Chapter 3 for several approaches to the strategic analysis process.) If managers are opposed to or highly reticent about following the auditor's suggestions, they can work with the auditor to find a viable alternative. If managers are merely surprised, the analysis period will give them time to get used to the ideas and begin to develop support among other members of the organization.

Final report and presentation   The final report should contain several distinct elements. An executive summary should, in one to two pages, present the audit's major findings and recommendations. A more detailed presentation of the findings should follow, backed up by both primary and secondary data obtained and analyzed throughout the process. These findings can be presented according to the categories of the audit form, and recommendations may follow each section. An appendix at the end of the document may contain exhibits, reports, questionnaires, tables, or sample materials to back up the audit report itself. The auditor has the primary responsibility to make sure that the final report is clearly and thoroughly understood. This means that the report itself should be stated in direct, simple, yet compelling language.

Since various recommendations may be applicable across the functions of the organization (such as marketing, accounting, box office, stage management, and development), a separate and comprehensive recommendations section should follow the systematic findings. In this section, each recommendation should include the functional areas it affects and the personnel required, budgetary estimations, and a time frame for starting and completion. Additionally, the recommendations should be presented briefly in the form of a time line for short-range, long-range, and ongoing projects, to help management identify where and when certain resources should be devoted.

The recommendations should be relevant, affordable, and otherwise feasible. This refers not only to the objective realities of the organization, such as budgetary constraints, capabilities of personnel, and potential audience and fund-raising increases, but also to the attitudes of management. If key decision makers are personally averse to even one major recommendation, the entire audit may be rejected as inappropriate. Therefore, the auditor must attempt to be sensitive to both the interests and the flexibility of strategic personnel.

The audit should be discussed in person, on a one-on-one basis or in small groups with top management and other interested parties. A meeting of the board of directors should be called specifically for the purpose of discussing the audit report. Copies of the report should be sent to the members well enough in advance so that they have time to study it and formulate questions. The auditor should be present at the meeting and should be given the opportunity to make an initial presentation of the highlights of the report and to field questions from the membership. Such discussion will ensure that major ambiguities are cleared up, that there is no misunderstanding of the auditor's recommendations, and that organization members understand what is required of them to implement the necessary changes. Finally, face-to-face presentation offers an additional opportunity to secure feedback about the report, which may or may not necessitate revision.

PUTTING THE AUDIT TO WORK

Once the auditor has completed his or her task, the work for management and the board has just begun. All too often, the incentives and excitement created by the audit fade away as members of the organization respond to pressing needs and neglect to take the time to become more proactive in their approach to the management process. A thorough marketing audit is a valuable and powerful tool for use by the organization's decision makers. But there is a danger that the nicely bound "final report" will be seen as a final product, rather than as the first step in a process that requires detailed planning and carefully conceived implementation.

Both the organization itself and the environment with which it interacts are perpetually changing, and it is up to the marketing manager, top management, and the board of directors to be aware of the current pulse and sensitive to opportunities and threats for the future. Therefore, the audit document should be seen as a crucial element of the strategic market planning process. It should be used and reevaluated regularly so that it is as flexible, adaptable, and changeable as the environment in which it exists.

---

[1] Alvin H. Reiss, *Arts Management* (Rockville, Md.: Fund Raising Institute, A Division of Taft Group, 1992) 29.

[2] J. G. March and H. A. Simon, *Organizations* (New York: Wiley, 1958).

[3] A. Tversky, and D. Kahneman, "Availability: A Heuristic for Judging Frequency and Probability," *Cognitive Psychology* 5 (1973), 207–232.

[4] Max H. Bazerman, *Judgment in Managerial Decision Making* (New York: Wiley, 1990).

[5] Kathleen Eisenhardt, "Speed and Strategic Choice: How Managers Accelerate Decision Making," *California Management Review* 32, no. 3 (1990).

[6] David E. Gumpert, *How to Really Create a Successful Marketing Plan,* 2d ed. (Boston: Inc. Publications, 1994), 42–43.

[7] Herrington Bryce, *Financial and Strategic Management for Nonprofit Organizations*, 2d ed. (Englewood Cliffs, N.J.: Prentice Hall, 1992), 453.

[8] Thomas Wolf, *Managing a Nonprofit Organization* (New York: Fireside, Simon & Schuster, 1990), 150–151.

[9] Henry Fogel, "When Bad Things Happen to Good Orchestras," *Symphony Magazine,* Apr./May 1988, 50.

[10] Donald C. Hambrick and Albert A. Cannella, Jr., "Strategy Implementation as Substance and Selling," *The Academy of Management Executive* 3, no. 4 (1989), 278–285.

[11] Louis W. Stern, and Adel I. El-Ansary, *Marketing Channels,* 4th ed. (Englewood Cliffs, N.J.: Prentice Hall, 1992), p 268.

[12] Stern and El-Ansary, *Marketing Channels,* 272–286.

[13] Peter Drucker, *The Five Most Important Questions You Will Ever Ask about Your Nonprofit Arts Organization* (San Francisco: Jossey-Bass, 1993).

[14] Bazerman, *Judgment in Managerial Decision Making,* 72, 83.

[15] Drucker, *The Five Most Important Questions,* 51, 53.

[16] Thomas Wolf, *Managing a Nonprofit Organization*, 155.

P A R T   V I

▲●▲

_____

SECURING
THE FUTURE

▲●▲

CHAPTER 18

Apply to all those whom you know will give something; next to those whom you are uncertain whether they will give anything or not; and show them the list of those who have given; and lastly, do not neglect

those you are sure will give nothing; for in some of them you may be mistaken.
BENJAMIN FRANKLIN

Business investments in the arts are not just a sign of success . . . they are a way to it.
BUSINESS COMMITTEE FOR THE ARTS

ATTRACTING FUNDS AND OTHER RESOURCES

ALTHOUGH FUND-RAISING IS GENERALLY NOT THE RESPONSIBILITY OF THE marketing department, the task of attracting funds is a marketing-like function. An organization must develop a good product (or cause), identify appropriate target markets, and communicate with and exchange benefits with those target markets. Yet not all fund-raisers practice the marketing approach.

Organizations typically pass through three stages of orientation toward fund-raising. First is the *product orientation stage.* Here the prevailing attitude is "We have a good cause; people ought to support us." Money is raised primarily by top board members and the executive director through an "old boy" network. A few loyal donors supply most of the funds. A part-time employee or board members with grant-writing skills appeal to agencies and foundations for support. This model is commonly found in small organizations and those in early stages of development.

The next stage is the *sales orientation stage,* in which the prevailing attitude is "There are a lot of people out there who might give money, and we must go out and find all of them and convince them to give." The organization appoints a development director who hires a staff. This staff raises money from all possible sources, typically using a "hard sell" approach. The fund-raisers have little influence on the organization's policies or personality; their job is to raise money, not to improve the organization. A majority of arts organizations are in this phase.

Finally, organizations enter the *strategic marketing stage.* Here the prevailing attitude is "We must analyze our position in the marketplace, concentrate on those donor sources whose interests are best matched to ours, and design our solicitation programs to supply needed satisfactions to each target donor group." This approach involves carefully segmenting the donor markets, measuring the giving potential of each donor market, assigning responsibility for developing each market, and developing a plan and budget for each market based on its potential. Many larger arts organizations have moved into this stage as their fund-raisers have become aware of the differences between a sales approach and a marketing approach. However, the strategic marketing approach to fund-raising should not be limited to large organizations with sizable staffs. Even small organizations that rely on volunteer fund-raisers should take a customer-centered approach in their fund-raising efforts.

It is clear that an organization has a strategic marketing orientation in its fund-raising when it treats its current and potential donors not as targets but as potential partners. Sophisticated fund-raisers recognize that they need not only individual gifts and grants but also lasting *relationships* with their target markets. The nature and quality of these relationships has become ever more important in recent years as the competition for the donor's head, heart, and hand have grown enormously.

This chapter describes the four major donor markets and how they operate; and discusses how the organization can develop a fund-raising strategy and program and evaluate the effectiveness of its fund-raising activities.

ANALYZING DONOR MARKETS

The four main donor markets are individuals, foundations, corporations, and governments. Smaller arts organizations tend to focus their fund-raising efforts on one source—wealthy individuals. Larger organizations tend to solicit all sources, and in fact, hire separate managers to be responsible for each donor market. Ultimately, they seek to allocate the fund-raising budget in proportion to the giving potential of each donor market.

Individual Givers

Individuals are the major source of all charitable giving, representing nearly 83 percent of giving. In 1992, individuals contributed $8.81 billion for arts, culture, and humanities. During the years 1990–94, while corporate and governmental contributions to theaters decreased, individual giving rose 33 percent. In fact, individual giving to theaters far outpaced the recent annual increases for individual giving to all philanthropic causes.[1] The nonprofit theaters' fund-raising success among individuals can be attributed to the personal relationship that many longtime subscribers and theatergoers develop with the organization, as well as to the dedication existing among the trustees and other volunteers. As a result, theater development departments are concentrating more of their resources on cultivating and soliciting individuals.

WHY PEOPLE GIVE

It is important for organizations to develop a good understanding of why people give. The simple answer "altruism" tends to mask the complex motives that underlie giving behavior. According to fund-raiser Harold Seymour, "What people want most is simply to be sought. Also, every individual needs to feel that he is a worthwhile member of a worthwhile group. Certainly if your appeal misses these two universal aspirations, you'll miss many targets and have a much harder time. Play them well and consistently, and you'll go far."[2]

Fund-raisers have identified a diverse set of reasons why people give:

- *Need for self-esteem:* Some people build their self-esteem and self-image through giving. Giving creates a good feeling, the opposite of which would be shame or guilt.

- *Need for recognition from others:* Some people have a strong need to belong. Giving helps them build their social status or prestige in the eyes of others. They wish to be recognized publicly for their good deeds.

- *Pride of association:* People give out of pride in being associated with a particular organization, its programs, and its personnel. Pride can be nurtured by special communications and ceremonies.

- *Sense of community responsibility and love for the arts:* People may give because they believe strongly in the value of the arts and feel morally responsible to support them. Even people who rarely or never attend the symphony or ballet may believe in the importance of these art forms to the community and may help sustain them.

- *Good business:* Many business owners gain image-building benefits and visibility by supporting worthwhile organizations.

- *People-to-people givers:* Some people give because they are asked by someone they like and respect.

- *Required to give:* Some people are required to give at work; they are pressured by superiors to donate part of their checks to a nonprofit organization.

- *The nuisance giver:* Some people give to get rid of the solicitor. This is an important reason why telemarketing and personal selling is so effective: mail can be ignored; a caller cannot.

- *Family tradition:* Some people give to an organization because their parents always did.

- *Financial planning considerations:* Some people give as a result of financial planning considerations such as tax deductions.

Most people give for more than a single reason; however, belief in an organization's goals and offerings is usually the primary inducement. However, to expect unsolicited contributions for a worthy cause is a great mistake of many organizational leaders. When surveyed as to why they gave to an organization, people most often say it is *because they were asked.* Consider how the San Jose Repertory Theater benefited by simply asking subscribers for donations.

SUGGESTING DONATIONS WITH SUBSCRIPTIONS	The San Jose Repertory Theater has gotten its subscribers into the habit of donating. New subscribers see a suggested donation of $15 on their statements. This amount is low enough to be an impulse buy and is an easy amount to add to a season subscription. As subscribers renew over the years, the suggested donation amount increases to a level determined by the development department, such as from the $15–$35 level to the $35–$50, and then $50–$75. Subscribers let the organization know when their comfort level is reached by simply including the amount they donated the previous year. (Occasionally subscribers cross out the suggested $75 donation and include a check for $500!) Through this practice, the Rep brought in $90,000 in donated income in 1992, up from $40,000 three years before. Where once 30 percent of subscribers would contribute the suggested donation amount, now 65 percent do.[3]

The various motives for giving provide marketing strategy clues for fund-raisers. Donor markets can be segmented by motive, and appropriate messages can be developed. For example, people who like to belong might respond to a message inviting them to "join our family" and to invitations for special events with key artists, board members, and management personnel. People who believe in the value of supporting the arts may respond to an organization that promotes its awards and its extensive educational programming. People who like to be recognized should be offered special name recognition (e.g., a scholarship fund, room naming, etc.) in exchange for a sizable gift. A person who loves the arts but shuns publicity and has no direct heirs is a good prospect for a bequest solicitation.

THE GIFT AS A TRANSACTION

A donation should be viewed as a *transaction,* not as a *transfer.* Some people give and say that they expect nothing back. But actually, most people have expectations. They expect the organization to use the money efficiently and to show gratitude. Even the anonymous giver may privately enjoy the self-esteem that comes from being "big enough" to give money without requiring recognition.

According to a study conducted by Carnegie Mellon University, most donors, no matter what their motivation, want additional considerations:[4]

- Thoughtfulness: don't call during dinner hours.
- Information: let them know the impact of their gifts, how they were used.
- Special appreciation for first-time gifts.
- Acknowledgments: a phone call without a solicitation.
- News about the organization.
- Reminders about pledges: preferably a brief reminder notice.

People are likely to give more when they are clear about the organization's mission. People understand the mission of the Red Cross or the American Cancer Society. But a theater that presents a classic one month, an avant-garde play the next, and follows with a Broadway revival is likely to confuse people as to its mission. Also, patrons may not be aware of the educational outreach efforts and other important products and services that help the organization realize its mission.

Too many organizations ask people to give to them because they are needy—in effect, begging for support. The crisis mentality of years past when people readily and repeatedly wrote checks specifically to help organizations survive (until the next crisis) is much less cogent in an era of accountability. Donors no longer reward good intentions; they reward good results. People expect arts organizations to be fiscally responsible and realistic in their budgeting. They want to support programs of value; not help an organization limp along to survive.

WHO GIVES?

All kinds of people are potential givers. In 1993, 75 percent of Americans reported that they gave money to charities the previous year. Forty-eight percent of that money came from households with incomes under $30,000. Another 14 percent of Americans revealed they would have given money, but nobody asked them! On the average, people give between 1 and 2 percent of their income to charities.[5] People with low incomes actually give a larger proportion of their annual income than wealthy people do.

Fund-raising consultants John Ryan and Thomas Olson suggest that an organization's wealthiest patrons, whom they call the "decision makers," frequently contribute less than they might because their contributions are almost invariably paid from annual income rather than from their assets. To maximize gifts from these individuals, the organization should encourage them to make major gifts to capital and endowment campaigns from their stocks and bonds and other assets. An arts organization's best prospects for annual giving are its "affluent devotees." These people are the vice presidents of major corporations, owners of substantial closely held businesses, and professionals. They have been subscribers and donors to the organization for many years. They usually contribute to a few, select groups, and their interest in a specific arts organization often centers on their love of the art form.[6]

A 1989 study of the Philadelphia cultural community revealed that as people earn enough to begin to support charitable organizations, they start by donating to educational, religious, health, and human service charities, and incorporate cultural support into their giving once they have more disposable income. More than 50 percent of cultural donors reported annual household incomes of $50,000 or more. Only 33 percent of donors to other charities reported equivalent earnings. Cultural donors were found to be much older (more than half in their 50s) than donors to other charitable organizations (23 percent over age 50). Cultural donors are also more likely to be married and less likely to have children at home.[7]

It is the responsibility of fund-raising managers to get to know which groups are most likely to give to their organization. For example, philanthropic giving has traditionally been considered the domain of wealthy white men. Fund-raisers tend to target the "man of the house" when seeking contributions. Yet, recent studies have shown that 55 percent of donors are female.[8] This fact can be attributed to the unparalleled growth in the economic clout of women, both in earnings and financial control. Fifty-seven percent of all women work; the proportion of female executives doubled from 5 percent in 1970 to 11 percent in 1990; and the average pay for female executives and managers rose 18.3 percent over the fifteen-year period that ended in 1993, while pay for their male colleagues rose just 1.7 percent. Furthermore, women continue to make between 70 and 85 percent of the spending decisions in the majority of American households, for everything from durable goods to charitable giving.[9] Since the majority of performing arts attenders are women, they are a viable target for fund-raising efforts.

It is important to decide not only *whom* to target, but *how* to approach them. Fund-raisers need to understand how best to communicate with each of their target groups. There are significant differences in communication styles between men and women. For example, men believe that conversation should have a definite purpose—to solve a problem or fix a situation. For women, conversation is a means to further understanding others and being understood themselves.[10]

TYPES OF INDIVIDUAL DONATIONS

Fund-raisers distinguish between small, intermediate, and major donors. Many fund-raisers prefer to concentrate all or most of their energy on large potential donations, believing that attracting a few large gifts would produce more funds than attracting many small gifts. A common claim among fund-raisers is that 20 percent of the givers generate 80 percent of the gifts. This is applicable both to large organizations that have a core group of major contributors along with a large group of small contributors, and to small organizations that rely heavily on their "inside" supporters.

However, for organizations that rely on a few major donors, the loss of even one of them can be destabilizing. Therefore, many organizations expend an inordinate amount of effort to attract small gifts to offset their dependency on a few large gifts. Clearly, the fund-raising manager must regularly reevaluate the potential return, over both the short and the long term, of various fund-raising strategies.

The characteristics of small and major gifts and the appropriate solicitation process for each are very different. Whereas the small gift solicitation focuses on the *organization's* annual and shorter-term needs, the major gift solicitation process focuses on the *donor's* longer-term needs and agendas. Small gift givers are customers of the organization; major givers are stakeholders in the organization. Small gifts tend to be made regularly—usually annually—and may range from one dollar to a few thousand dollars. Major gifts are often a one-time "stretch" gift and involve a commitment of significant financial resources—usually to a capital campaign or an endowment drive. Small gift prospects are solicited by letter or phone; major gift prospects are solicited in person. Small gifts are usually given in cash from current income; major gifts are often given in appreciated assets from capital. Small gifts are solicited cyclically according to the organization's short-term deadlines; major gifts may take anywhere from several days to several years to solicit, according to the donor's financial circumstances. Small gifts are generally unrestricted and may be used at the organization's discretion; major gifts are almost always restricted, the funds being earmarked for specific projects according to the donor's interests.

Annual campaigns raise funds to support an organization's operating budget and ongoing special projects. It is difficult to sustain donor interest and excitement for annual drives, because donors are asked to make a gift each year for similar reasons. The Lyric Opera of Chicago deals with this problem by having the annual appeal come from a star performer rather than from the general director.

On the other hand, capital campaigns create the most excitement because new, expanded, and renovated facilities are tangible and highly visible. They also provide naming opportunities for donors—from the concert hall itself for the key contribution, to individual seats in the theater. Some organizations even sell feet of cloth for the stage curtain in exchange for a certificate and/or mention in the newsletter.

Organizations have attempted to make their annual fund drives more appealing by combining unrestricted giving with specifically named opportunities. Intermediate and large level annual donors can be invited to support operating budget line items such as computer maintenance, printing expenses, a portion of the office rent and advertising costs, utilities bills, specific salaries, and so on.

SMALL GIFT FUND-RAISING

Small gift fund-raising serves several functions: it provides the organization with income, it increases public awareness of the organization, and it uncovers potential new volunteers and major gift givers. Unlike many upper-level givers, small gift contributors do not receive public recognition, significant appreciation, or leadership posts as rewards for their gifts. They are usually motivated by a belief in the organization, its mission, and its offerings. When they are financially able, many small gift givers move into higher gift ranges.

The more personal the solicitation, the more gift income is received. Types of solicitation ranging from the most personal to the least personal are (1) visits by someone known to the prospect, (2) visits by someone unknown to the prospect, (3) phone solicitations, and (4) direct mail.

It is important that the cost and effort expended by the organization match the expected return. If 80 percent of money raised comes from only 20 percent of the donors, this means that the other 80 percent of donors are providing only 20 percent of the funds. Therefore, small gift fund-raising campaigns are normally conducted by less expensive means such as direct mail and telemarketing.

There are two types of direct-mail campaigns: new prospect campaigns and renewal campaigns. The organization's expenses for new prospect campaigns are rarely recouped by the contributions resulting from the original solicitation. Rather, the campaign repays itself over time through renewals, similar to the value over time of gaining new subscribers. (See the discussion of the lifetime value of subscribers in Chapter 11.) Before undertaking a new prospect mailing, the organization should evaluate whether there are a sufficient number of potential new prospects to warrant the expense of acquiring the mailing lists; designing, printing, and stuffing the direct-mail package; and buying postage.

Direct-mail campaigns should be conducted annually and must be carefully timed so as not to conflict with the annual subscription drive and other organizational activities. Additional solicitations may be made during the year, but they should request support for a special project or need, in contrast to the annual request for general support. (See Chapter 14 for a more complete discussion of direct-mail methods.)

In addition to standard mail and phone campaigns, fund-raisers may undertake special efforts to increase the size and number of individual contributions. For example, patrons and donors can be invited to commemorate birthdays, anniversaries, graduations, and job promotions with a gift to the organization. Commemorative gifts should be acknowledged in newsletters and program guides so that the organization can share in the celebration and thereby build a personal relationship with the donor.

Organizations should periodically revise the minimum contribution levels for eligibility for certain benefits. In July 1994, the Lincoln Center Theater in New York raised the minimum required donation for joining its giving club from $1,250 to $1,500. The increase will bring in at least $125,000 more in operating funds for the theater each year. About five hundred people belong to the club, which offers benefits in exchange for unrestricted gifts. The increase in the required minimum donation caused no drop-off in membership, probably because the members value the benefits so much.

MAJOR GIFT FUND-RAISING

Large gift prospects are the lifeblood of any fund-raising campaign. Fund-raisers must continually identify and cultivate new prospects as the present large gift donors eventually find new interests, relocate, change financial status, or die. Seeking the large gift involves a careful personal selling process, often over long periods of time. Says L. Peter Edles, "Since donating money is not instinctive, giving is something that people learn how to do. Fund-raisers teach people to give by conditioning them to raise their philanthropic sights continually."[11]

People often consider fund-raising as *asking* for money. Actually, asking is only one of several steps in the strategic process of major gift solicitation. One of the solicitation models used by many fund-raisers involves six steps: *discover and qualify, plan, involve, ask, negotiate and close,* and *thank and plan.* Fund-raisers first identify a wealthy individual who could conceivably have a strong interest in the organization. They identify others who might supply information and arrange an introduction. They cultivate the person's interest in the organization without asking for any money and evaluate his or her capability for making a major gift. Eventually, they do ask for money. The "ask" step normally involves dealing with objections. Upon receiving the gift, they express their appreciation and lay the groundwork for future involvement. An analysis of how to accomplish each of the six steps follows.

THE STRATEGIC PROCESS OF MAJOR GIFT SOLICITATION

1. Discover and Qualify. During this first step, the fund-raiser identifies new prospects and gathers and analyzes relevant information about each one. Research should include information about these characteristics of the prospect:

- *Capacity:* What are the prospect's financial resources, income, real estate holdings, etc.? What form of assets might the prospect use to make a gift?

- *Interests:* What have been the prospect's giving patterns in the past, at what types of organizations? Identify the prospect's business, hobbies, clubs, and family relationships.

- *Priorities:* What are the prospect's key needs? deep-down desires? values? lifestyle? Is the prospect putting children through college or supporting elderly parents? What is the person's age and health status?

- *Peer relationships:* These are investigated to determine who should be on the solicitation team: the person(s) to whom the prospect is not likely to say no.

2. Plan. A plan is often the most neglected step in the major gift solicitation process, but it is absolutely necessary. The purpose of the plan is to

- Identify a realistic gift target (Five percent of adjusted net worth is possible, but 1 percent or ten times the prospect's largest annual gift is usually the target. Exceptions to this formula are such factors as a recent inheritance or a situation of high income and low assets).

- Identify which of the prospect's interests match the organization's prioritized goals.

- Determine what this prospect will need to *know, feel,* and *experience* (corresponding to his or her head, heart, and hand) in order to stimulate a major commitment.

- Develop an approach to also involve the spouse if she or he is a potentially significant factor in gift decisions.

- Select the best potential volunteer for the prospect.

3. Involve. This is the stage at which the prospect is cultivated and a bond is created with the organization and its representatives. To complete this step, the fund-raiser must

- Specify the prospect's current attitudes and concerns about the organization.

- Clarify the prospect's needs and interests that can be satisfied by meaningful participation in the organization.

- Estimate how much future involvement and cultivation will be required before the "ask."

- Keep the prospect in a comfort zone throughout this cultivation phase, and maintain a focus on the prospect's own needs.

- Evaluate whether different or additional organizational representatives should be brought into the solicitation process.

4. Ask. Before the formal "ask" takes place, the solicitor should undergo a five-step process to get the appointment:

- Send a letter to set up the phone call. The letter prepares the recipient for the ensuing call, since a surprise call often results in either flight or fight. It also prepares the recipient for the call's agenda. The recipient should at least recognize the name of the letter writer, and the letter should indicate the person's link with the organization.

- Plan the approach for the call. The caller should put herself in the prospect's shoes to identify when (time of day) and where (home or office) the prospect would prefer to be approached. The caller should have her previously sent letter and her calendar in hand.

- Make the phone call to request an appointment. If the prospect is not in, the caller should not leave her phone number and request a return call. The prospect should not be made responsible for making the call to set up an appointment.

- Address immediate objections and issues and agree on a time to meet in person. Concerns should be acknowledged immediately, but the caller should not attempt to solve problems over the phone. Rather, issues of concern can be used as a reason to get together.

- Confirm the date, time, and place of the appointment with a follow-up note.

During the actual solicitation, the prospect is invited to consider an investment in the organization by giving a specific amount of money over a specific period of time for a specific project. People should be told not how much they *should* give, but how much the solicitor *hopes* they will want to give or what others at their level are giving.

The fund-raiser has several options in deciding which type of "ask" best fits the prospect's circumstances. Here are some suggested ways to solicit the gift:

- *The component of a larger plan:* Show the bigger picture and the role that the prospect can play by participating. The prospect might be invited to partner with a group of friends or associates in order to be responsible for a larger portion of the need.

- *The initial commitment:* This is a growth option for a younger or overcommitted donor. It allows the donor to make a smaller contribution now and heighten involvement at a later date.

- *The option list:* The solicitor may present three options, all at the same price level, to test for interest—such as a capital drive, an endowment fund, or a special project.

- *The priority list:* The solicitor may offer several projects, each at a different level of giving, and indicate what can be accomplished at each level.

- *The gift vehicle:* The solicitor may suggest a planned gift or a conditional pledge. A conditional pledge may be appropriate in such a case as when the prospect has indicated he is about to sell a real estate holding or will contribute if his new business goes well.

- *The single item:* The solicitor may suggest a single option at an exact amount. This technique can only be used when the prospect's interests and financial capabilities are well known.

5. Negotiate and close. This step involves leading the prospect to a commitment by removing remaining objections, addressing concerns, making any necessary alterations to the original request, and obtaining professional help, such as legal counsel and investment advice. There are three type of closes the solicitor may use.

- *The sole objection:* When the prospect is holding back because of concerns about a particular matter, the solicitor should make the condition of satisfying the objection a pledge in and of itself.

- *The recommendation close:* When the prospect cannot move beyond indecision, the solicitor may make a specific recommendation such as "I suggest you make a pledge of $5,000 and pay it over five years."

- *The assumptive close:* When time has passed without a response, the solicitor may choose to take the somewhat risky step of assuming a pledge, and ask for feedback from the prospect simply for details of the agreement.

It is important for the solicitor to keep in mind these points:

- Large gifts require several calls. It generally takes anywhere from eighteen to twenty-four months of active cultivation before a relationship with a prospect is mature enough to result in a major gift.

- The most important discussions and deliberations go on when the seller isn't present. Whereas closing "techniques" may increase the chances of making a sale with a low-level donor, with major donors they reduce the chances.[12]

- The absence of a response should not be interpreted as meaning "no." The donor may be saying, "not now." Don't give up on donors; commitment may come at another time.

6. Thank and Plan. During this final phase of the major gift fund-raising process, the solicitor expresses appreciation and recognition for the gift and lays the groundwork for future involvement. To complete this step, the fund-raising manager should

- Specify to the donor what types of personal attention will be shown.

- Identify areas where ties between the organization and the donor should be strengthened.

- Create a plan and assign accountability for the actions identified above to the organization's personnel.

- Examine what further interests and needs of the donor may be served by another gift.

Source: Adapted from *The Skill and Art of Major Gift Fundraising* (Pasadena, Calif.: The Russ Reid Company and Paul V. Edwards, 1990). Reprinted with permission

The value of building relationships with donors and paying them special attention is highlighted by the following example. One nonprofit organization found that mailing birthday cards to people who had given $1,000 or more prompted some of the donors to make an additional gift, with no strings attached. In one case, a donor responded with an additional $1,000; another donor gave $10,000 after receiving a birthday card. The personal attention required to keep track of major donors' birthdays, special anniversaries, the birth of a grandchild, and so on, is minimal, especially compared to the goodwill and the donations that such efforts generate. Since major donors tend to be community and business leaders, the organization's staff members and volunteers should regularly scan the local newspapers for mention of special events that should be acknowledged and/or commemorated.

SPECIAL EVENTS

Special events, usually in the form of benefits or galas, have been a popular fundraising strategy for centuries. Handel's *Messiah* was first performed in 1742 as a benefit for "relief of the prisoners in several gaols, and for the support of Mercer's Hospital in Stephen's Street, and for the Charitable Infirmary on the Inn's Quay."[13] Demand for tickets was so high that sponsors tried to make more space by asking ladies to attend without hoops under their skirts and gentlemen to attend without their swords! The £400 raised from this performance paid for the release of 142 debtors from prison. For these prisoners, the Messiah had truly come!

Selling special event tickets requires only that the fund-raisers sell the event itself —at a premium price—unlike asking for donations to support the mission of the organization. However, special events should be linked to the organization's mission: the opera gala may feature special arias and duets; the theater's dinner benefit may feature vignettes from an upcoming musical or comedy.

Special events are a good way to attract current and potential donors who are motivated by the social and business networking aspects of a contribution. They are also a good way to attract new people to the organization while asking for a relatively small commitment of time and money. Special events are fun to plan and provide a valuable opportunity for the organization's volunteers to work together and build binding relationships. They are also an important opportunity for gaining press coverage, thereby building awareness about the organization.

Although special events have many benefits, their disadvantages must be carefully considered before the organization takes on new events or even repeats long-standing events. Special events can lose money because they are costly to run. They are highly labor-intensive. Although they are often managed by volunteers, they still require staff input, which takes time away from other work. Events can also take fund-raisers' time away from asking for individual gifts, which may be more lucrative. They may distract major donors from considering larger gifts, and may turn off smaller donors for whom the price is too high. Specific thematic events exclude people: dances exclude those who do not like to dance; casino nights exclude those who disapprove of gambling. Says fund-raising expert Joan Flanagan, "The only way to include everyone is simply to ask for money."[14]

PLANNED GIVING

In the past few years, bequests have been growing at the highest rate of all charitable gifts. Experts predict that funding from bequests will triple in the next decade. Surveys show that 89 percent of Americans give to charitable organizations, and they give to between eleven and fourteen charities each year. Americans with a will remember two to five charitable organizations in their will. Usually, the ones not included in the will are left out because nobody asked.

Once an organization has built a broad base of annual donors and major gift givers, it should consider asking for planned gifts. A donor plans now to give money later, most often in the form of a bequest. Planned gifts are usually assigned to the organization's endowment fund, which accrues principal and distributes a portion of its interest—usually about 5 percent—to the organization's annual operating budget. Bequests account for at least five out of six planned gifts. Other opportunities for planned gifts are life insurance, annuities, and trusts, or such complex instruments as pooled income fund agreements, charitable remainder annuity trusts, and revocable charitable trusts, in which donors give cash, securities, or real estate to an organization in return for a tax deduction and income for themselves or another person.

Planned gifts provide advantages to the donors and the organizations. The donors get credit now for a big gift that is not realized until after their death. They may strengthen their financial condition through reduced taxes. And they can be motivated to do something they feel they ought to do. The organization receives the benefits of knowing that large amounts of money will be coming in the future, ensuring financial stability and providing an impetus for long-range planning and more serious financial management.

Managing planned giving requires a working knowledge of current tax laws, insurance options, and investment opportunities. The fund-raising staff may recruit legal, insurance, and investment experts on the board to assist in these matters, or may hire fund-raising counsel with expertise in planning and managing a planned-gifts program. Special software is available to fund-raising managers that is designed to calculate tax deductions and annual payouts of different planned-gift options.

The most likely prospects for planned giving are board members, donors who have given for at least three to five years, and people who have exhibited both an interest in the organization and the ability to make a planned gift. Planned giving experts say that the best prospects for bequests are seventy-three-year-olds. Statistically speaking, they are an average of three to four years from becoming "actuarially mature."[15] Other good prospects are people updating their wills, which usually occurs at the time of certain events such as inheriting money or property, marriage or divorce, or being diagnosed with a life-threatening illness. About half of all Americans (and one-third of all lawyers!) do not have a will, and the fund-raiser can provide potential donors the service of urging them to write a will. Since planned gifts sometimes come from unexpected sources, the organization should include basic information and a phone number to call about the bequest program in each newsletter, annual report, and program. Once a year, a letter that specifically addresses the issue of wills should be sent out to likely respondents.

Fund-raisers must discipline themselves to visit prospects and follow up with them about planned gifts. Because the organization may not see a result for five to twenty or more years, fund-raisers must keep in mind that the key to success is patience and persistence in asking.[16]

Foundations

Foundations are established for the express purpose of giving money to worthwhile causes. They are the second-largest source of giving to the arts, providing funds to cover 8 percent of the expenses of the sixty-eight sample theaters in the 1994 Theatre Communications Group study. Between 1990 and 1994, foundation giving to those theaters increased 84.4 percent, by far the most significant five-year growth of any income source and a much larger increase than in charitable giving overall.[17]

Many foundations are established for a specific purpose and support only programs that meet their strategic grant-making policies. As social conditions change, these foundations adjust the focus of their giving programs. This restrictiveness has intensified in recent years. The percentage of foundation grant dollars awarded for general operating support dropped from 17 percent in 1987 to about 12 percent in 1994.[18] As a result, arts organizations are experiencing more and more difficulty in attracting important general operating support from foundations. In order to attract foundation support, managers frequently *develop* projects that are less than central to the organization's mission. Although these projects tend to be worthwhile, they may cause managers to lose focus of the organization's objectives and goals, stretch their human resources—and managers rarely budget for the additional staff time needed to manage these special projects—and often get the organization no closer to meeting its ongoing budgetary needs.

Foundations fall into four groups:

- *Family foundations* are set up by wealthy individuals to support a limited number of activities of interest to the founders. Decisions tend to be made by family members, their counsel, or both. A variation on this type of foundation is the "hybrid family foundation," in which nonfamily trustees play an integral role in determining grant-making policies.

- *General foundations* are set up to support a wide range of activities and are usually run by a professional staff. General foundations range from extremely large organizations such as the John D. and Catherine T. MacArthur Foundation and the Ford and Rockefeller Foundations, which support a wide range of causes, to more specialized general foundations that give money to a particular cause, such as the Lila Wallace Reader's Digest Fund, which is the largest private donor to the arts, making annual gifts in excess of $30 million.

- *Corporate foundations,* set up by corporations, are allowed to give away up to 5 percent of the corporation's adjusted gross income. The giving policies of a corporate foundation are usually consistent with the corporation's goals and interests.

- *Community foundations* are set up as a vehicle for pooling bequests from many private sources, including individuals, corporations, foundations, and nonprofit organizations. A community foundation is governed by a board of community representatives. Individuals who contribute to the foundation have the option of restricting the types of gifts made from their funds or allowing the foundation's staff and board to make all grant-making decisions.

Foundation grants may be annual or multiyear. Small foundations commonly give annual support, while larger foundations generally prefer to fund special projects over several years. Arts organizations must be aware that a substantial five-year foundation grant is likely not to be renewed as foundations move on to new projects and new areas of interest.

With more than 27,000 foundations in the United States, it is important for the fund-raiser to know how to locate the few that would be the most likely to support a given organization or project. Many foundations publish information on their funding policies, areas of interest, and application requirements. It is important to review these guidelines carefully so that the grant proposal addresses areas of concern to the foundation. The best single resource for researching foundations is known as the Foundation Center, a nonprofit organization with research centers in New York, Washington, and Chicago. In addition, materials describing foundations and how to approach them are available in many libraries around the country and on the Internet. The most important materials are listed here.

- *The Foundation Grants Index,* which lists the grants that have been given in the past year by foundation, subject, state, and other characteristics. The fund-raiser could look up the performing arts in general, or more specifically, dance, music, or theater, and identify the most active foundations in each area of giving.

- *The Foundation Directory,* which lists 6,615 foundations that either have assets of over $1 million or award grants of more than $500,000 annually. The directory describes the general characteristics of each foundation, such as type of foundation, types of grants, annual giving level, officers and directors, location, particular fields of interest, contact person, and so on.

- *The Foundation News,* which is published six times a year by the Council on Foundations and describes new foundations, new funding programs, and changes in existing foundations.

- *Fund Raising Management* and the *Chronicle of Philanthropy,* periodicals that publish articles on fund-raising management and provide information about new grants made.

The key concept in identifying appropriate foundations is that of *matching.* The arts organization should search for foundations matched to its interests and its scale of operation. Too often, a small organization will send a proposal to a major national foundation that prefers giving fewer larger grants than many smaller ones, when it would be better off approaching a regional foundation. But sometimes small organizations help major foundations to meet their giving objectives. Consider the approach of the Ford Foundation, as explained by its president, Franklin Thomas.

THE FORD FOUNDATION NURTURES NEW WORK

The Ford Foundation spends $7 million annually in the United States and overseas for the arts, to "nurture a new generation of exciting art that embraces America as it really is." In all cases, grant recipients must demonstrate high artistic standards.

The grants, a mixture of general and project funding, are intended to support artistic vitality and new work through collaborations between artists in the United States and their counterparts in Africa, Asia, and Latin America; strengthen the financial stability of arts organizations; expand the civic role of the arts and artists; and preserve cultural traditions so they may enrich contemporary artistic activity.

Typical groups receiving funds in recent years are the Alvin Ailey Dance Company, Appalshop, the Brooklyn Academy of Music, the Festival of Indonesia, Jacob's Pillow Dance Festival, Lincoln Center, the National Arts Stabilization Fund, the Nonprofit Facilities Fund, the Satyajit Ray Archives, the Smithsonian Institution, South Africa's Market Theater, and the West Africa Museums Project.[19]

Writing successful grant proposals is a fine art, and many guides are currently available to help the grant seeker. Some state and local arts agencies provide grant-writing workshops for their applicants. Each proposal should contain at least the following elements: (1) a cover letter describing the history of the proposal, and who in the foundation has been contacted previously, if anyone; (2) the proposal, describing the project, its uniqueness, and its importance; (3) the budget for the project; and (4) the personnel working on the project, with their résumés. The proposal itself should be compact, individualized, organized, and readable. In writing the proposal, the organization should be guided by the criteria used by the particular foundation in selecting among the many proposals it receives. By knowing the relative importance of the respective criteria, the proposing organization can do a better job of selecting which features of the proposal to emphasize.

Among the most common guiding criteria used by foundations are:

- Is the organization qualified to implement the project?

- Is it able to use funds effectively and efficiently?

- Is the organization's board of trustees capable of providing leadership?

- How long will the organization require support from the foundation?

- Will the project be self-supporting, or will it develop other means of grant support after a reasonable amount of time?

- Does the project address foundation concerns and help the foundation to meet its own goals?

Contacting foundations on the occasion of a specific proposal is only part of the "relationship marketing" that each organization should carry on with its funders. Once the organization has received a foundation grant, it is important to submit progress reports, updating the foundation on the status of the project and highlighting new developments. Reports should be accompanied by appropriate budgets and selected supplementary materials. Each interim and final report should be as thorough as the original proposal.

Corporations

Corporate giving differs from foundation giving in a number of important ways. First, corporations regard gift giving as a minor activity, in contrast to foundations, for which it is the major activity. Second, foundations are usually more willing than businesses to consider providing seed money for experimental projects. Corporations often avoid supporting controversial or unpopular programs that do not provide them with the desired type of visibility; foundations do not require the extensive public relations benefits from their grants that businesses demand. But like foundations, corporations are increasingly trying to meet their own social agendas through support of the arts; 45 percent of businesses surveyed in 1994 reported that they encourage the arts groups they support to collaborate with other nonprofit groups dealing with education, health and human services, and the environment, compared with 11 percent in 1991.

Corporate contributions to the arts fluctuate according to economic conditions and philanthropic priorities. For example, corporate giving to the arts among businesses with annual revenues of $1 million or more grew to $698 million by 1985, then, following the recession of the late 1980s, dropped to an average of $518 million in the years 1991–93 and in 1994 increased to a high of $875 million. Although business managers expect their contribution levels to continue to rise in the next few years, future funding decisions will be affected by the interest level of senior executives and employees, limited resources, pressure to fund other areas such as health and human services, and concern about a lack of measurable business benefits.[20] Such fluctuations make it difficult for arts organizations to depend on a specific level of support over time.

Yet, with 47 percent of the nation's companies supporting the arts with a median gift of $2,000, it is clear that businesses support the arts for sound business reasons as well as altruistic ones. In a national survey conducted by the Business Committee for the Arts (BCA) in 1994, companies gave the following reasons for supporting the arts: to demonstrate good corporate citizenship (74 percent), to enhance the quality of life in their community (66 percent), to enhance their image and reputation (46 percent), to strengthen employee relations (22 percent), to increase business networking opportunities (21 percent), to increase sales (19 percent), to reach important constituencies (18 percent), to promote products and services (17 percent), to enhance employee creativity (13 percent), and to increase media coverage (9 percent). Businesses also receive a tax savings by contributing to charitable causes—the IRS allows deductions of up to 10 percent of their adjusted net income. However, it appears that this tax advantage is not a major incentive for business contributions.

Arts organizations tend to consider large national and multinational corporations as their best opportunity for contributions, yet the BCA survey results indicate that nearly three-quarters (73 percent) of the total dollars contributed to the arts in 1994 came from smaller companies with $1 million to less than $50 million in revenues. Businesses state a preference for supporting local rather than national or international arts organizations (93 percent), arts organizations with which employees volunteer (60 percent), and arts organizations that offer employee benefits such as lunchtime performances and reduced ticket prices (28 percent).[21] In recent years, the diversity of arts disciplines supported by business has increased. Theater, museums, and symphony orchestras receive the highest levels of business support (about 17 percent of all business philanthropy), while opera, other music, and dance receive the lowest levels (about 5 percent).

TYPES OF CORPORATE SUPPORT

Business support of the arts may take the form of general support, service in-kind support, employee matching gifts, and/or sponsorships. Sponsorships and some examples of noncash support were covered in Chapter 7 because they represent important collaborative opportunities for arts organizations.

General support   Some corporations make grants to arts organizations to help cover their operating expenses. This money is typically paid out of a business's annual contribution budget. It may take three or more years of repeated appeals to a likely prospect before a general support grant is made. Corporate budgets are planned well in advance, and analyses must be made as to the appropriateness of the fit with corporate goals.

In recent years, corporations, like foundations, have become less enthusiastic about paying for overhead expenses such as salaries, administrative expenses, and rent, and have been restricting the use of their gifts. Companies often want to help but do not want to see their money go into a "black hole." Creative fund-raisers are developing innovative ways to make corporate donors more interested in paying for basic operating expenses. One nonprofit organization in Louisville, Kentucky, has arranged with two local businesses to cover its utility costs; one pays the phone bill, the other pays the electric bill. The bills are sent by the organization to the sponsoring companies, which write their checks directly to the utility companies. Business people who want to be sure that their funds cover specific expenses are finding such arrangements highly attractive.

Service in-kind support   By providing noncash contributions in the form of management expertise, technology, volunteers, and products, corporations can increase their giving to the arts even when budgets are tight.[22] Significantly, most companies that donate goods and services are doing so in addition to their grants, not in place of them.

Arts organizations can approach businesses for in-kind support: goods (asking a furniture company for furniture or a computer firm for PCs or software), expertise (asking an advertising agency to provide pro bono work for a special project or an accounting firm to help set up a new organization's books), services (asking a printing company for free printing or printing at cost), and space (asking a company for use of some office space or its auditorium for a program). An arts organization should be able to get some of its office equipment, marketing research, advertising, and so on free or at cost if it can identify the right corporate prospects to approach and demonstrate how the businesses can gain visibility and an enhanced profile by linking up with the arts organization's image, appeal, and customer base.

APPROACHING BUSINESSES FOR FUNDS

According to the BCA, 82 percent of the decisions about philanthropy are made by the chairman, CEO, owner, or a partner of the business. The surest entrée for an arts organization is to contact the chief executive officer through a board member, personal friend, or business colleague. Board members are key intermediaries in approaching top-level executives. The development director should survey each of the organization's board members to determine what business contacts might provide fund-raising opportunities. Whether personal contacts exist or not, the fund-raising manager should research the firm thoroughly and determine how he or she can create and frame proposals that fit the business's own interests. Consider how the Washington Civic Symphony creatively attracted corporate support.

ART IN THE SERVICE OF BUSINESS

In the old days, princes used to pay composers to write music for the kings so that they could earn the right to sit next to the king at the king's reception. Today's new princes are the corporations.

Milton Kotler, president of the board of directors of the Washington Civic Symphony, recognized an opportunity to gain support for his orchestra in the fact that a number of U.S. companies were signing deals with the Chinese government. He phoned the Chinese Ambassador to the United States in Washington and asked for permission to hold a concert in his honor. The ambassador responded enthusiastically and provided the orchestra with the business cards of the people in U.S. companies who had made deals with China. Seven individuals from such corporations as Ford, Westinghouse, and New York Life were invited to attend the concert and sit with the ambassador at a private reception, in exchange for a $5,000 donation. Executives at other companies donated $1,000 each to attend the reception and concert.

Some corporations handle the many requests for support by setting up a foundation so that corporate officers are not personally drawn into decision making about gifts. Others with a well-established philanthropic function have a specific senior staff member such as a vice president for community relations or a marketing director, who is given responsibility for corporate donations. And, as more companies move toward a team approach in their business operations, decisions about philanthropic activities are increasingly being made by employee committees.

Effective corporate fund-raising requires that the arts organization know how to identify good corporate prospects creatively and efficiently. Of the millions of business enterprises that might be approached, relatively few are appropriate to any specific organization. Furthermore, most organizations do not have the resources to cultivate more than a handful of corporate givers.

Arts organizations must also be aware of what factors are important to potential business funders. Business leaders have indicated that arts organizations could work more effectively with them by making more reasonable requests for support, by submitting funding proposals earlier, by providing budgets, and by providing lists of other business supporters. Arts organizations should also make an effort to better understand the company's funding guidelines and its business goals and objectives, and to work with the company to develop programs that meet business needs. Another important factor to keep in mind when seeking and managing corporate contributions is the issue of accountability. The organization should report to its funders its short- and long-range goals, the effectiveness with which those goals are being met, and how future funds will be applied to help meet the goals. Arts organizations should report to their funders what they were able to accomplish as a result of the support. Donors will appreciate the feedback (especially when the organization's financial report is good news), and the more they trust the organization's use of their donations, the more willing they will be to provide funds in the future.[23]

Government Funding

Government support to the arts is available at the federal, state, and local levels and through some community agencies.

FEDERAL FUNDING

At the time of this writing, federal funding is at risk of being eliminated as Congress debates whether or not to continue supporting the National Endowment for the Arts (NEA). Although federal funds for the arts have shrunk significantly in absolute dollars in recent years, the NEA remains symbolically significant far beyond the financial reach of its grants. Each dollar granted by the NEA generates another eleven dollars in matching and challenge grants by other funding sources. An NEA grant is also highly valued as an imprimatur connoting artistic excellence.

A *matching grant* generally means that an organization is required to raise at least 50 percent of the costs of a given project, equaling the amount of the NEA grant. The matching income may come from private sources, revenues from ticket sales or other income-producing activities, and the value of project-related in-kind services. NEA *challenge grants* require a three-to-one match, with the exception of awards for capital projects, which require a four-to-one match. The recipient organization has from one to four years to raise the matching funds, depending on the amount of the grant and the nature of the project. The NEA also stipulates that challenge grant matching funds raised by the organizations must represent new and increased monies.[24] Because of its severe budget cuts, the NEA is discontinuing matching grants after 1996.

The NEA publishes annually its very detailed funding guidelines, which contain information on the application process and deadlines, typical grant sizes, eligibility requirements, and the program areas for which funds are available.

STATE ARTS COUNCILS

Most state arts agencies support individual artists, community arts activities, and arts organizations in their state. They also provide information on arts activities, publish annual lists of art fairs and festivals, and disseminate information relating to various kinds of technical and management assistance available. State funds for the arts have shrunk even more than federal funds in recent years. In the sixty-eight theaters surveyed by the Theatre Communications Group, for the five-year period from 1990–94, state funds were reduced 8.9 percent while federal funds dropped 6 percent (compounded rate adjusted for inflation). In May of 1996, the NEA announced a 40 percent cut in grants to the states, dramatically restricting the already limited support that state arts agencies are able to provide.

COMMUNITY SUPPORT

There are approximately two thousand community agencies in the United States, many of which are private, nonprofit organizations, not branches of city or county governments. Their goals, programs, and organizations reflect their unique communities. Some community agencies make grants to artists and local arts organizations. Others conduct annual united fund drives among local businesses on behalf of the community's arts organizations. Most of these agencies provide a local clearinghouse for cultural information, act as cultural advocates, and offer administrative and technical services to their artists and local arts organizations.

Other Funding Sources

Arts organizations may find that they can attract funding from such sources as social clubs, professional groups, alumni groups, singles groups, and employee groups. Small arts organizations can increase their number of individual donors and unrestricted gifts by linking up with an organization that can provide an endorsement and access to its members. Such a group may be encouraged to "adopt" an arts organization and attend programs and develop fund-raising activities for a year (or more). An association with a performing arts organization provides group members with the entertainment and social aspects of performance attendance and the opportunity to support a worthwhile community organization. Special events can be planned by the arts organization to honor its "adopters," thereby building increased loyalty and encouraging larger donations in the future.

One alumni group interested in learning about classical music, developing opportunities to socialize and network, and practicing philanthropy is forming a unique relationship with the local symphony. The alumni group will attend select performances, before which they will be presented with a lecture series about classical music by knowledgeable staff members. After each performance, a special wine and dessert reception will be held for the alumni and their guests. The symphony will benefit by gaining new audience members, by educating more discerning and loyal audiences for the future, and by developing a new generation of funders.

SETTING GOALS AND STRATEGIES

Good planning is essential for achieving fund-raising goals. Whether an organization is conducting its annual campaign, initiating a capital drive to subsidize a new building, building an endowment, or seeking foundation, government, or corporate support, there are several steps that the organization and its fund-raisers must complete. An effective campaign requires that fund-raising goals be defined, that feasibility studies be undertaken, that financial goals be set, that a strong case and timetable for the campaign be developed, and that the fund-raising team be identified and recruited.

Setting Fund-Raising Goals

A fund-raising campaign is usually designed to meet a specific organizational goal, in addition to its total monetary goal. Mal Warwick has identified five different strategies that an organization may pursue:

- *Efficiency:* An efficiency strategy means that the organization is focused on raising money at the lowest possible cost per dollar raised. This goal may be short-sighted —it can make it impossible for the organization to grow. Growth generally requires a large investment for identifying and nurturing new donors.

- *Stability:* Stability is a major concern for arts organizations in today's environment of funding cutbacks. When the organization's long-term survival is at stake, most of the fund-raising effort and creativity should focus on ways to diversify the base of support and build the most viable opportunities. This process may be expensive, but is well worth it.

- *Visibility:* If the objective is to gain broad-based public support, it can often be best achieved through visibility. The fund-raising program should be designed to help gain public attention and executed in ways consistent with the organization's image. This strategy is likely to be most useful to an arts organization during a large capital campaign when efforts are geared toward building awareness of and interest in a new building project.

- *Involvement:* Donor involvement is a key to building loyalty and support. Fund-raising strategies ought to be reviewed for the contributions they make to involving donors in the organization's affairs.

- *Growth:* Growth may refer to growth of revenues, growth in the number of donors, or both. The fund-raising program will be shaped by the demands and costs of sustaining a high rate of growth.

Most arts organizations pursue two or more of these goals simultaneously. For example, the organization may want to ensure its long-term survival and to raise money at the lowest possible cost per dollar raised. However, the priorities must always be clear, because the methods for achieving each of these goals may be contradictory. The more goals any organization is trying to achieve at any one time, the less effective the campaign will be. In fact, it is impossible for any organization to achieve all five goals simultaneously. [25]

The Feasibility Study

Each organization undertaking a major campaign should conduct a feasibility study. Aside from setting a goal to raise a specified amount, there are many factors that must be taken into account to create and sustain an effective campaign. The feasibility study should attempt to establish the following:

- The total likely response for campaign giving
- How much each donor segment might give
- The identity of major gift prospects
- The identity of leadership candidates
- A timetable and sequence for solicitation
- Elements of the case statement and all support documentation required
- Staffing and budget required
- Public relations support plan
- When and how campaign consultants will be needed

More than one-half of the organizations who conduct first-time feasibility studies led by professional consultants are told to defer their campaigns. These organizations generally wait anywhere from six months to five years, during which time they make fund-raising conditions more conducive to running successful drives. For example, after analyzing the results of fifty interviews with prominent community leaders, a feasibility study for a capital campaign drive for a symphony orchestra concluded that

> Although those interviewed see the Board of Trustees as highly supportive, many people doubt that enough members will make major gifts to a capital campaign. Many . . . are especially concerned that two other major capital projects are now in progress elsewhere in the area. They believe that scheduling a third drive at this time is inappropriate. It is recommended that until the symphony is assured of additional major gift donors, the capital fund drive be delayed. A second feasibility study should be initiated when appropriate.[26]

Setting Financial Goals and Standards

Every organization wants to achieve at least its goal or better. Goal attainment makes the organization appear successful in the community, and it provides an important recognition opportunity for volunteers, which also helps in recruiting new volunteers. Often, the development officer favors an ultraconservative goal so that he or she will look good. The organization's president, however, is tempted to set a high goal to induce the development office to work hard. Yet, both paid staff and volunteers can be motivated or frustrated by high goals.

The crucial factor in *reaching* the goal is the appropriate *setting* of the goal in the first place. For the annual fund, each year's goal should be at least 3 percent larger than the previous year's, just to keep pace with inflation. Most organizations set their overall goal 10 percent higher each year, although with the funding cutbacks of recent years, many organizations are working hard just to maintain previous levels. For the capital campaign or the launch of a new endowment drive, the goal should be set by feasibility, not by financial need. This means that the campaign goal for the renovation of a symphony hall is determined not by what the project *costs,* but by an intensive, up-front, realistic evaluation of how much can be *raised.* So, if the project costs $25 million and the symphony board and management determine that they can raise only $15 million, the orchestra should downsize its plans or divide the project into two phases to be funded and constructed five to ten years apart.

How does an organization determine how much can be raised? One common rule of thumb applied by many experienced fund-raising managers is to use the top gift as a benchmark for the entire campaign, with the top gift representing 10 percent of the total goal. So, once an approximate goal is set, the top gift is recruited. If it comes in significantly higher or lower than anticipated, the goal should be revised.

After the top gift has been made, test solicitations should be conducted for several of the largest gifts in the drive, which set the standard of contributions for the entire campaign. Prospects should be those with the most loyalty and the highest dollar potential. These top solicitations are important for three reasons: (1) Major donors make gifts in direct relation to those of the leadership and their peers. For example, the Greens are asked to give $300,000. When they find out that the Browns, who are wealthier than they, only gave $250,000, the Greens give $200,000. (2) Until people make their own gifts, they are in no position to solicit others—and the top giving prospects are likely to become the major solicitors for the rest of the campaign. (3) Approximately one-third of the goal should be contributed by the top ten donors. Unless this occurs, it is not likely the overall goal will be attained. Until the top several prospects have been effectively solicited, the rest of the campaign should not be initiated.

Standards should be set for each giving group, namely the top ten donors, other major donors, active donors at lower levels, inactive (infrequent or lapsed) donors, and new prospects. The standards set for each group depend on the size and appeal of the organization and the giving potential of each group. For capital campaigns, it has been customary to say that a third of the money comes from the top ten gifts, the next third from the next one hundred gifts, and the last third from everyone else.[27] (More recent experience indicates that a 40–40–20 split among these three groups is closer to reality.)[28] As goals have risen higher and higher, more is expected from fewer people. This "rule of thirds" is illustrated in Table 18-1.

Table 18-1	**THE GIFT RANGE CHART**

Campaign Goal: $9,000,000

Number of Gifts	Dollar Amount	Goal	Comments	
1	$1,000,000			
2	500,000	$3,000,000	Top 8 gifts	(0.5%)
5	200,000			
10	100,000			
20	50,000	$3,000,000	Next 70 gifts	(4.8%)
40	25,000			
60	15,000			
100	10,000			
125	5,000	$3,000,000	All other gifts (1,385)	(94.7%)
250	1,000			
350	500			
500	100			
Total 1,463		$9,000,000	1,463 gifts	(100%)

An organization's donor base is often visualized as a pyramid, with a small number of major donors at the top and a broadening base of small contributions at the bottom. The shape of this pyramid will depend on whether the organization has a broad-based constituency (like a major symphony orchestra) or a narrow constituency (like a young avant-garde theater). Some analysts say that giving behaviors are moving toward more larger gifts and fewer smaller ones. For this pattern, a pagoda is a better representation of giving patterns than the pyramid.

Quotas should not be set until there has been sufficient demonstration of giving patterns to lend the final figures some basis for credibility and ready acceptance. In addition to the giving capacity of the target donor base, the organization must also take into account the factors that go beyond the raising of money itself: constituency relationships, quantity of volunteers and their fund-raising ability, and the organization's reputation and competitive situation.

Each quota should have a "cushion" built in. While some giving will be above expected levels (large campaigns often have at least one big windfall gift), some giving will fall below. Harold Seymour recommends that the separate quotas should add up to as much as 120 percent of the publicly stated goal. This cushion principle should apply as well to the number of prospects required for the needed number of gifts at each level. At the top, for example, there should be four or five prospects for every needed gift. Seymour indicates that for annual campaigns, about half the givers tend to come up with about the same amount they gave the previous year, about 15 percent tend to give less, 25 percent give more, and about 10 percent of the givers are new to the organization or have lapsed and returned.

It must be kept in mind that the overall goal in any annual campaign is not nearly as important as the dozens of goals that get established in terms of unit quotas. It is the successful battles that win the war.

Making the Case

A central part of good planning is making the case for the campaign. Most important, the campaign must be infused with *relevance, importance,* and *urgency.* Maximum attention and response will be achieved if the purpose of the campaign is relevant to a public need and to the personal interests, loyalties, or concerns of its own natural constituency. The campaign should also project a clear image of importance, both in its own field and within its wider sphere of influence. Potential contributors must believe in and have a highly positive response to the organization's mission and goals; they must identify with its reason for being. Importance answers the question, Why us? Clearly communicating relevance and importance makes it possible for the case to do what Seymour says it must in order to be effective—catch the eye, warm the heart, and stir the mind. A case can be both relevant and important and still be ineffective if its urgency is obscured or intermittently conveyed. With all the competition for the donors' dollars, it is important they know why their money is needed *now.*

Each fund-raising campaign needs a case statement. The case statement, which should be included in campaign brochures, grant requests, speeches, and publicity releases, should amplify why the drive is being held, what it intends to accomplish, and who will benefit. The statement should be brief, succinct, and straightforward. The following case statement was written for a theater group that wanted to raise funding for an outreach program.

An Outreach Program: The Case Statement

The history of our repertory company is a story of upholding the traditions of highest quality, professional theater while setting ticket prices the public could afford. Since the next generation of serious theatergoers will come from today's young people, we feel a responsibility to help stimulate both children and young adults to become involved in this art form.

Next season two innovative outreach programs are planned to attract a youthful audience. The first involves a tour of black communities. By using a specially equipped theater bus, members of the company will stage forty performances of black folk stories in parks, streets, and playgrounds in some ten upstate

communities. These stories depict the imaginative folklore of
black people in both Africa and the United States.

Additionally, the full repertory company will present two distinguished contemporary dramas and conduct directing and
design workshops following the performances at ten eastern
seaboard colleges.

To obtain the funds necessary to produce these presentations,
we have begun a major fund-raising drive to gain support from
individuals, foundations, and corporations.

The case statement, although it summarizes the campaign's goals in a compelling way, rarely motivates prospects to make major contributions. Prospects should
also be provided with information that answers all the important questions about
the campaign, reviews the arguments for support, explains the proposed plan for
raising the money, shows how gifts may be made, and indicates who is leading the
campaign.[29]

The Timetable

Every campaign must have a timetable for partial and complete goal realization and
a specific ending date (whether or not the goal has been realized). Campaign managers should remember that whatever there is plenty of time to do will probably
never get done. When the campaign is formally ended, some last gifts are likely to
come in from the holdouts—those who were reluctant to participate but who do not
want to be left out. Also, neither volunteers nor staff can be expected to go on and on
soliciting funds until inertia takes over. One effective way to manage the time factor
in a campaign is to divide it into phases: victory can be declared for phase I, and
phase II can be accomplished at a later date. Time is an important motivator, and the
timetable should be extended only if there is a well-analyzed strategic reason to do
so, meaning a strong potential for future success.

The Fund-Raising Team

Fund-raising is a team activity; both paid professionals and volunteers have important roles to play. There is often concern that if volunteers solicit the bulk of the contributions, the professionals will be unable to justify their positions and salaries.
Some professionals can also be heard to say that "it is easier to do it myself," and do
not take advantage of all that volunteers have to offer.

THE DEVELOPMENT STAFF

The fund-raising manager, often called the development director, has an overall
responsibility for planning and managing all the organization's fund-raising efforts and working closely with the board of directors. Professional fund-raisers plan
goals and strategies, maintain databases, research prospect information, train volunteers, work with volunteers on individual solicitations, seek and manage corporate
sponsorships, write grant proposals, implement follow-up efforts with donors, and

conduct campaign evaluations. Development directors are also responsible for coordinating their efforts with other staff members—for example, setting short-term cash-flow goals with the finance director and coordinating benefits offered, mailings, and telephone campaigns with the marketing director.

Larger organizations have several development staff members, who generally specialize in donation categories such as corporations, major donors, planned giving, or annual direct-mail campaigns. Other staff members manage such functions as public relations, research, and volunteer coordination.

VOLUNTEERS

The most important volunteer fund-raisers in an organization are the members of the board of directors. Fund-raising talent among the board can be developed in two ways: by recruiting talent from the outside and by training leaders from the inside. Joan Flanagan recommends that when building a board, the nominating committee seek to recruit leaders who can give the board a balance of the "Four Ws": *work*—people willing to ask for money, organize events, and do other fund-raising work; *wealth*—people willing and able to give big money; *weight*—people with power in the community whose names can open doors; and *wisdom*—people who are experts in the fund-raising field.[30]

All board members should contribute to the organization. Personal donation levels can be set according to each member's giving ability, but a donation of some amount from each board member is psychologically important to the success of the campaign. Board members should be solicited for their contributions annually by the board chair.

Board members should provide contacts in the business sector and at foundations, and should identify prospects for individual donations. They are also responsible for making appeals for contributions to prospects identified by the development director and to some of their own contacts.

Some organizations create a special honorary board, whose prestigious members simply lend their names to the organization. The name of a celebrity on the organization's letterhead is an endorsement that opens doors for recruiting volunteers and donors.

Some organizations create other volunteer groups with special fund-raising goals. These may be called committees, guilds, auxiliaries, or specially named boards. Some of these groups have their own annual fund-raising goals for the general fund; others raise money for special projects. Performing arts groups that attract audiences from outside their own communities often establish volunteer groups in outlying areas to raise money and to build audiences. For example, the Santa Fe Opera has fund-raising committees in California, Colorado, and New York. The Stratford Festival in Ontario has an active group of Shakespeare fans raising money in Chicago.[31]

Other volunteers are often recruited to assist in making solicitations and for planning special events such as benefits and telethons. Organizations should clearly outline what is expected of the volunteers and prepare them for making effective solicitations. They should understand the motives for giving, should be given profiles of the prospects and methods for approaching them, and should be provided a forum to practice in a role-playing situation. Volunteers should be well informed about the organization, its goals, its programs, and its financial status.

CONSULTANTS

Major organizations usually retain consultants before and during capital and endowment campaigns and to help oversee annual campaigns. Consultants do not replace the organization's own fund-raising staff or volunteer leaders. Their role is[32]

- To implement a feasibility study to see if the organization should be holding a campaign.
- To assess the organization's fund-raising potential.
- To supply a fund-raising plan suitable to the organization, including such factors as goal setting, strategies, approaches, and procedures.
- To give continuing direction, making certain that plans are carried out, deadlines are met, volunteers are knowledgeable, and strategies are revised when necessary.
- To contribute communications skills, such as copywriting, graphic design, and creating audiovisual presentations; and to analyze the efficacy, efficiency, and cost-effectiveness of present communications programs or those proposed by other providers.
- To train volunteers when such expertise is not available within the organization.
- To troubleshoot. Consultants are expert in diagnosing and recommending cures for a troubled campaign.

It is the key leadership and professional fund-raising staff who know the organization's current and potential donors and who best represent the organization in making solicitations.

EVALUATING FUND-RAISING EFFECTIVENESS

Each organization must make a continuous effort to evaluate and improve the effectiveness of its fund-raising strategies, especially in the face of increasingly sophisticated competition and scarce funds. Several factors can be used to evaluate effectiveness.

Percentage of Goal Reached

The first and simplest step is to see how close the organization has come to achieving its goal. This analysis should be done not only for the overall goal, but for the goals set for each donor segment. Many organizations track their results as often as monthly. For annual campaigns, it is useful to compare results to those of previous years in order to track trends, identify opportunities for growth, and identify areas to strengthen.

Number of Donors

Each organization hopes to increase the number of donors each year. The organization must find ways to improve its results with former donors, to identify how best to attract new prospects to make up for those who have lapsed, and to increase the overall number of contributors.

THE RENEWAL RATE

The renewal rate is the single most important indicator of the health of the fund-raising program. It is a measure of donor loyalty, not of gift size. The development office should keep track of the quantity and percentage of renewals among first-year contributors, two- to five-year contributors, and those who have contributed for more than five years. The manager can then track renewal trends and answer such questions as: Is the multiyear renewal rate increasing? Is the first-year rate moving up? Is the donor base aging? What percentage of renewed subscribers are making donations to the organization? Answers to these questions can help target areas of focus for upcoming campaigns.

THE ATTRITION RATE

The converse of the renewal rate is the attrition rate. The development office should track how many past donors are no longer contributing. If this number is growing at a much more rapid pace than new donors can be attracted, the organization's support base is eroding. Even with a strong base of loyal, generous supporters, managers may find that a continuing drop-off in the number of donors can place the organization's survival in danger in a few short years.

As the organization reaches farther from its core of supporters to attract funds, the response rate gets smaller and smaller. Therefore, following up on lapsed donors is a crucial function for the development office. Lapsed donors should be interviewed and asked to identify the importance of such factors as: "No longer enjoy many of the performances," "Do not like the donor benefits I received," "Not treated well by the organization's representatives," "Was not asked," and so on. Each reason suggests a possible plan of action to bring back lapsed donors and to retain those at risk in the future.

Gift Size

The development office should review the size distribution of gifts and target certain classes of gifts that deserve special effort in the coming period. Gift size can be analyzed from several perspectives.

AVERAGE GIFT

A major objective of the fund-raising organization is to increase the size of the average gift in given donor segments. By comparing the average first-year gift with the average multiyear gift, the fund-raising manager can track trends over time. It is important that the average gift size be segmented by gift-size category. Assume an annual fund-raising campaign in which $750,000 was raised from 7,500 donors. Averaging this total implies an average gift of $100. However, the organization may have reached this amount by receiving $1,000 from each of 250 people and $69 from each of 7,250 people. Or it may have received 700 gifts of $1,000 and 6,800 gifts at $7.35. Each of these response rates suggests a different fund-raising strategy for the organization.

UPGRADES AND DOWNGRADES

The fund-raising manager should note individual donor behavior by counting how many donors upgrade or downgrade their contributions each year. These groups should then be segmented by certain common characteristics (age, income, length of donor history, subscriber status, and so on). While seeking to increase its overall gift size each year, the organization should also target its most likely prospects for larger gifts. Identifying the characteristics of those who are likely to upgrade allows the organization to invest in its best opportunities.

GRADUATION RATE

In most fund-raising programs, there is a boundary between what is considered a small contribution and what is considered a major gift. For some organizations, that boundary may be at the $50 level. For others it may be $1,000 or even higher. Wherever the line is drawn, the principle is the same. When a donor "graduates," passing from one territory into another, *something should happen.* That something may be a personal phone call from the president or a member of the board. It may be automatic admission to some honorary status or exclusive benefit. Whatever that something is, it is—and should be—a big deal.

Therefore it is important to determine and monitor the organization's graduation rate. First, a graduation level should be set. The organization should be prepared to stick with that level over a number of years, so that its analysis will be consistent over time. The dollar amount should be set so that it is achieved by no more than 2 percent to 10 percent of the active donors.

Then the development office should count the number of donors who—for the first time—contributed gifts within a recent twelve-month period that were at or above the graduation level. This number should be compared to the number who first gave a gift at or above the same level during the previous twelve-month period to determine whether the graduation rate is going up or down. (The manager may look at a single gift over the twelve-month period, at cumulative gifts, or at both.)

Some organizations find it useful to track the graduation rate on a monthly basis and focus their fund-raising strategies accordingly.[33]

Expense-to-Contribution Ratio

The ultimate financial goal of fund-raising is net revenue, not gross revenue. Many large donors, including corporations, look at this key ratio before they decide whether to support an organization. A low expense ratio can be a potent marketing feature because donors like to support an organization's programs, not the costs of raising money. Also, by comparing costs to revenue for various fund-raising projects and over time, the fund-raising manager can identify the most cost-effective programs.

For example, assume an organization incurred expenses of $104,000 in one year to raise $228,000. In this case, the expense-to-contribution ratio was $104,000/$228,000, or 46 percent. The following year, the organization spent $124,000 and raised $340,000 for an expense-to-contribution level of 36 percent, improving the cost-effectiveness of its campaign by 10 percent. By spending only $20,000 more, it raised an additional $112,000!

Each program—direct mail (acquisition), direct mail (renewals), telethons, benefit events, personal solicitations, and so on—should be evaluated in this manner and tracked over time. (In determining costs, it is important to include a prorated portion of the salaries of all paid personnel involved in the campaign.) This will help managers evaluate the cost-effectiveness of their various efforts, identify opportunities for growth, and identify those projects for which the costs outweigh the benefits received.

Other Measures of Fund-Raising Success

The numbers do not tell everything that the executive director and the board need to know in evaluating fund-raising effectiveness. Mal Warwick suggests that the executive director answer the following important questions to determine how "in touch" the fund-raising department is with the organization's and its donors' needs:

- Are your fund-raising resources commensurate with your organization's goals? Can you honestly say your resources are adequate to match the scale of your goals, so that you're not underfunded?

- Does every member of the board, without exception, contribute money at least once a year? If those committed to the organization do not lead, others cannot be expected to follow.

- Does your funding come from several different sources or channels, with no single source accounting for 60 percent or more? Funders' interests (and financial status) change, donors die, and it is therefore dangerous for an organization to be heavily reliant on one or two funders.

- Are you raising money from reliable, predictable sources to cover your fixed expenses (overhead), and, if necessary, funding optional programs from less predictable sources? Fund-raising methods and appropriations must be geared to meet the organization's continuing needs.

- Do you have enough cash to pay your bills at any given time, plus a reserve fund to allow for contingencies? Funding goals should be set not just to meet the organization's annual budgetary needs, but to meet those needs at various points in time throughout the year.

- Does your organization receive bequests (gifts from the wills or estates of deceased donors)?

- Is one senior-level person clearly designated as responsible for planning and monitoring the fund-raising efforts? Fund-raising doesn't just happen. It is a complex activity, undertaken by both staff and volunteers at various levels of responsibility. The process must be coordinated to increase efficiency and effectiveness and to help avoid turf wars. Most important, relationships with donors require continuity.

- Do thank-you letters to your donors go out within forty-eight hours of the receipt of the gift? Donors notice.

- Do you have the names and phone numbers of your top ten donors at your fingertips?

- Do you know how, where, and by whom your donor giving records are maintained, and what information is on file?

- Are your organization's fund-raising activities scheduled in advance and carried out according to schedule? Fund-raising campaigns must have deadlines and closure in order to keep volunteers, staff, and donors motivated and in order to meet the organization's goals.

Throughout the twentieth century, many generous donors have contributed large sums to guarantee that the arts they love will survive and prosper. As these funds have become more scarce and competition has grown, fund-raisers must regularly evaluate their organizations' best fund-raising opportunities; they must strategically, creatively, and methodically design and implement fund-raising programs; and develop and maintain meaningful relationships with current and potential donors. In this way, arts organizations can best assure that they will meet their contributed income needs.

---

[1] Barbara Janowitz, "Theatre Facts 94," *American Theatre,* Apr. 1995, 10.

[2] Harold J. Seymour, *Designs for Fund-Raising,* 2d ed. (Rockville, Md.: Fund Raising Institute, 1988), 6.

[3] Butch Coyne, "Optimizing Suggested Donations," *Arts Reach,* Oct. 1992, 15.

[4] John Miller, Director of Development, Carnegie Mellon University, Pittsburgh, Pa. (newsletter).

[5] Joan Flanagan, *Successful Fundraising* (Chicago: Contemporary Books, 1993), 17.

[6] John Ryan and Thomas Olson, "The Affluent Devotees," *Arts Reach,* Feb/Mar. 1995, 5.

[7] Philadelphia Arts Market Study commissioned by the Pew Charitable Trust, 1989.

[8] "The Mind of the Donor," Barna Research Group Ltd., Glendale, Calif., 1994, photocopy.

[9] E. Janice Leeming and Cynthia Tripp, *Segmenting the Women's Market: Using Niche Marketing to Understand and Meet the Diverse Needs of Today's Most Dynamic Consumer Market* (Chicago: Probus, 1994).

[10] Judith Tingley, *Genderflex: Men and Women—Speaking Each Other's Language at Work* (New York: Amacom, 1994).

[11] L. Peter Edles, *Fundraising: Hands-On Tactics for Nonprofit Groups* (New York: McGraw-Hill, 1993), 53.

[12] Neil Rackham, *SPIN Selling* (New York: McGraw-Hill, 1994).

[13] Peter Jacobi, *The Messiah Book* (New York: St. Martin's, 1982), 37.

[14] Flanagan, *Successful Fundraising,* 54–61.

[15] Mal Warwick, "How Much Choice Do Donors Want?" *Nonprofit Times,* Mar. 1995.

[16] Flanagan, *Successful Fundraising,* 174–185.

[17] Janowitz, "Theatre Facts 94," 11.

[18] Holly Hall, "The Struggle to Raise Operating Funds," *Chronicle of Philanthropy,* Jan. 26, 1995, 33.

[19] Franklin A. Thomas (President, Ford Foundation), Letter to the Editor, *New York Times,* Dec. 29, 1994.

[20] The BCA Report, "National Survey: Business Support to the Arts" (New York: Business Committee for the Arts, 1994).

[21] The BCA Report, "National Survey: Business Support to the Arts" (New York: Business Committee for the Arts, 1992).

[22] Craig Smith, "The Emerging Paradigm," *Corporate Philanthropy Report,* Sample Issue, Feb. 1995.

[23] Hall, "The Struggle to Raise Operating Funds," 33, 35.

[24] Carolyn L. Stolper and Karen Brooks Hopkins, *Successful Fundraising for Arts and Cultural Organizations* (Phoenix, Ariz.: Oryx Press, 1989), 91.

[25] Mal Warwick, "Which Fundraising Strategy Is Right for You?" Changing America, Berkeley, Calif., 1995 (workshop).

[26] Edles, *Fundraising,* 63.

[27] Seymour, *Designs for Fund-Raising,* 5.

[28] Ibid., annotations to the second edition.

[29] Ibid., 42–43.

[30] Flanagan, *Successful Fundraising,* 36–37.

[31] Ibid., 39.

[32] Edles, *Fundraising,* 29.

[33] Mal Warwick & Associates, "How to Calculate Your Donor Graduation Rate" (Berkeley, Calif., 1995).

▲●▲

CHAPTER 19

Without an
audience, is it art?
JANE ALEXANDER

It takes great
audiences to make
great artists.
WALT WHITMAN

AUDIENCES FOR NOW—AUDIENCES FOR THE FUTURE

Is THERE A GROWING CRISIS IN THE ARTS? THAT QUESTION WAS ASKED AS EARLY AS 1955 at the annual symphony convention in Cincinnati, where orchestra managers expressed concern that the growing popularity of television would severely cut into concert attendance. In fact, the three decades that followed were the largest period of growth in performing arts history. Today, in the face of other new forms of leisure competition such as VCRs and compact disc recordings, changing lifestyles with more demands on people's time, funding cutbacks, and diminishing arts education, many people again believe the arts are facing a growing crisis.

Some performing arts organizations truly are in crisis. Some face the loss of a performance hall or of a major funding source, or life-threatening situations. Midsized orchestras find themselves unable to sustain the rampant growth of the 1980s and are struggling to reengineer their structures and downsize their budgets. But the struggle of one organization or even a group of organizations does not sound a death knell for the industry as a whole, any more than the troubles faced by such companies as IBM and Chrysler in the early 1990s meant that the entire computer and automobile industries were at risk.

History shows that arts organizations have remarkable resilience in the face of adversity. In the 1993–94 season, the Royal Opera House (ROH) in Britain managed to declare a financial surplus and its work gathered critical acclaim. But just a few short years before, the ROH had budgeted for a $1.6 million deficit and its artistic standards had been vigorously criticized.[1] In Chapter 16 we described the 1992 bankruptcy of the Sacramento Symphony. But by 1993, the symphony was reformulated, and, by the end of the 1995–96 season, it had again become a fixture in the community. One might attribute the resilience and longevity of arts organizations to the stabilizing influence of their funding sources. But this would not explain how organizations like the Royal Opera House and the Sacramento Symphony have survived or come back to life despite severe funding cuts. It is their capacity to adapt to changing external and internal environments and to reposition themselves in creative and dramatic ways that has been the key to their success.

THE REBIRTH OF THE SACRAMENTO SYMPHONY

After the Sacramento Symphony filed for bankruptcy in December 1992, the musicians formed their own Philharmonic and presented their own concerts. But, presenting a great performance of a Beethoven symphony, they found, is not adequate for filling the hall. Before long, the musicians acknowledged that they needed professional management. By the summer of 1993, the Sacramento Symphony reorganized with a new board of directors, 10 percent of whom were musicians; a new executive director, who, as general manager of the Buffalo Philharmonic, had played a leading role in that orchestra's revival and reorganization; and a popular new music director. The reorganized Sacramento Symphony became a very different institution from the original. The symphony's commitment to inclusiveness, outreach, and education is a recognition that its success depends on its mission to serve the whole community.

A direct result of the symphony's commitment to community outreach is its World View Music Festival, which salutes the musical traditions of the area's African-American, Asian-American, Latin-American, Jewish, and Greek populations. This series achieved such instant success that by its second season, it moved from the symphony's small hall to its large performing space.

Other innovative programs were designed with an eye on new and culturally diverse markets. The "Jeans and Beer" series, which mixes familiar classics with pop, Broadway tunes, and folk music, is held in an old movie house. Audience, orchestra, and guest artists come attired in blue jeans, ticket prices are kept low, and attenders are welcome to snack during the concert, as they do at the movies. (Eating has not been distracting to other patrons, because everyone tends to be quiet and considerate.) Audience members mingle with players at the free postconcert performance parties and receive a complimentary Samuel Adams Boston Lager courtesy of the Boston Beer Company, one of the series sponsors. Attendance was up 25 percent by the series' second year.

Achieving similar success is the Mocha and Mozart series, which offers classical chamber music and free coffee drinks, sponsored by Java City. Dress is informal, and free postperformance parties with the musicians, informal lectures, and refreshments are provided to ticket holders. In other efforts to reach out to new audiences, tickets are offered for $6 between 6:00 and 6:30 P.M. on the day of the concert, and subscribers to the Sunday afternoon series are welcome to bring a child for free.[2]

The symphony's board and managers also focused efforts on regaining the trust of former subscribers and donors, some of whom had lost up to $1,000 worth of tickets when the symphony closed its doors. Due in part to an aggressive telemarketing campaign, many subscribers were lured back. The symphony also established increased individual and corporate support as a major goal. Particular emphasis was placed on building relationships with individual donors and on further developing the symphony's roster of corporations that sponsor concerts, series, and programs such as the "Heartstrings Program," which makes reduced-price tickets available to corporations for distribution to disadvantaged youth.[3]

When the symphony reorganized, its season was shortened by six weeks and musicians absorbed $500,000 in salary cuts to balance the budget. Even so, an anticipated $400,000 in annual support from the city and county did not come through, and the symphony was battling to reduce its deficit by that amount. At the end of 1994–95, the musicians and staff agreed to further salary cuts. Since musicians are well represented on the board of directors and are fully aware of the symphony's financial issues, and since they did not want to repeat their past crisis, they were willing to make the concessions necessary for the symphony's health.

By the end of the 1995–96 season, the symphony had again

become a fixture in the community, boasting strong advance subscription sales and an increase of 52 percent in ticket revenue in the three years since reorganization. The budget was balanced for the first time in twelve years, and contributions from business leaders totaling nearly $1 million allowed the symphony to retire its accumulated deficit. Said Board President Jack Courson, "We were facing the brightest future ever."

Postscript: In August 1996, negotiations began for the musicians' contract for the next three seasons. Although the musicians were fully aware of the symphony's financial condition, and the board's offer was based on a year-long analysis of proven expense and revenue patterns, the new negotiating team elected by the musicians had a far different attitude from that of their predecessors. Cooperation turned to intransigence as the terms presented by the board to the musicians were flatly rejected by a vote of 64 to 6. The musicians issued three counterproposals, each requesting extraordinary increases, with progressively higher increases in years two and three. No work rule changes or benefit reductions were deemed acceptable.

By September 5, 1996, the board concluded there was no basis for believing than an acceptable agreement could be reached at the bargaining table, and the Sacramento Symphony Association filed court papers requesting Chapter 7 Bankruptcy, in effect dissolving the eighty-four-year-old organization.[4] Said symphony board member Frank Washington, "The economics and politics of a symphony orchestra tend to frustrate the efforts of even the most innovative turnaround artists."[5] "Unfortunately," says Lynn Osmond, the symphony's executive director, the musicians' negotiating team "could no longer buy into our vision of a better future."[6]

Despite the tragic, untimely closure of the Sacramento Symphony, what the arts face today in the midst of spiraling costs, funding cuts, and greater competition for audiences is not a terminal crisis, but what Peter Drucker calls the "challenge of accountability."[7] In the past, arts organizations have successfully looked to others for solutions to their problems. When the arts enjoyed rapidly growing audiences and readily available funding sources, arts managers had the luxury to operate a less than professional managerial environment. But cries for financial help and ineffectively targeted and positioned appeals to prospective audiences are no longer answered as readily. Pointing a finger of blame at the public for a decreasing interest in performing arts offerings and at the funders for changing priorities will not help to solve the problems.

Rather, arts organizations must become more accountable for their actions and inactions. They must be *proactive:* they must plan, listen, continually create and recreate, rather than being *reactive.* Holding on to what has worked in the past and making changes only when a situation has become critical is no longer defensible.

In this chapter we discuss the two major challenges that arts managers face today. First, arts organizations must *reach outward* to become major providers of arts education to youth and adults, with a goal of creating understanding and accessibility and making art an integral part of people's everyday lives. Second, arts organizations must *look inward* to professionalize their management and marketing, to approach their tasks strategically in light of a continually changing environment, and to learn how best to be responsive to the needs and interests of their publics.

EDUCATION IN THE ARTS

This book has focused on marketing the arts—on ways to bring the art to the public and the public to the art and on ways to present culture to a broader, more diversified, and ever-changing marketplace. However vigorous the marketing program, it is the love and appreciation for the art itself and art's sustaining, nurturing, fulfilling, and satisfying qualities that bring people back time after time and make the symphony, the theater, the opera, and dance a necessary part of people's lives. For arts fans—those who understand the nuance of Schubert, enjoy the line of Balanchine, find inspiration in the insights of Samuel Beckett, are moved by the auras of Miles Davis—attending such performances is stimulating, exciting, and irreplaceable. For other patrons, arts attendance may be in response to social pressures, status striving, the excitement of glamorous people, the bargain of a membership, and the promise of a richer life.[8] But in the absence of a real love and appreciation for the arts, continued patronage cannot be guaranteed, for the attenders' needs can be met, and probably better satisfied, elsewhere.

Importance of Arts Education

Central to a love and appreciation of the arts is a deep understanding of the art forms themselves. A 1996 study of the effects of arts education on participation in the arts clearly indicated that the richer one's arts education, the greater one's participation in the arts. Arts education was found to be the strongest predictor of arts creation and consumption, stronger even than socioeconomic status, race/ethnicity, and gender.[9] Education is the key to making art meaningful, important, and necessary. Before the invention of the gramophone record, music lovers contented themselves by playing Beethoven symphonies in four-hand arrangements for piano in their homes. Their numbers may have been far smaller than the orchestra audiences of today, but they were not simply passive listeners and their actual knowledge of the music was greater.

Today, not only are fewer people directly involved in playing music, but arts education programs in the nation's elementary and high schools have been dismantled, and the focus in colleges and universities has shifted away from the liberal arts. In a 1989 National Endowment for the Arts report, 75 percent of Americans said they had never had any art appreciation classes and 43 percent had never had art lessons. If arts education has always been spotty, experts say things are worse now.[10] This is despite the fact that studies have shown that students who had four or more years of art and music education scored 34 points higher on verbal SAT and 18 points higher on Math SAT.[11] And although arts supporters argue that art classes teach the very qualities that educators believe can reinvigorate American schools—analytical thinking, teamwork, motivation and self-discipline—arts education is dismissed as a frill. Not only that: many people are afraid of the arts—we were told as kids that we had two left feet, couldn't carry a tune, colored outside the lines. What was a natural form of self-expression for generations of individuals, and what continues to be so in more "primitive" societies where people feel free to sing, dance, and weave baskets, has become depreciated and repressed in our more "advanced" society.

Ultimately, the best way to educate people about art is to expose them directly and often to artistic experiences. Zelda Fichandler, director of the Arena Stage in Washington, D.C., had this to say about the importance of theater:

> Theater is educational in that it teaches man to recognize, by means of the events acted out before him, his own human condition, to understand that condition and to have compassion for it. Theater is educational in that it causes a change to be brought about within the nature of man, so that he becomes more knowledgeable, more sensitive, more responsive, more enlightened, more aware. . . .
>
> To think isn't enough. You have to think feelingly. To know what those thoughts mean feelingly. You can't change the way people think by talking to them. So you put them through an experience and hope they come out a little different from the way they were before. It's not to make them feel good about themselves, but to make them *ask* about themselves. [The idea is] to create sensitive people capable of transforming their world a little bit by knowing about themselves.

Because the live performance experience is integral to the arts organizations' educational process, it may well be that arts organizations are the best-suited educational institutions for creating an appreciation and love for the arts and for building future audiences.

So arts organizations and the artists themselves must try to fill the gap created by changing priorities in the schools. Says Susan Franano, general manager of the Kansas City Symphony, "Ten years ago I would have said that it was not the responsibility of arts organizations to do education. But the reality is that the educational system is not providing even a rudimentary arts education, and somebody had better pick up the challenge. That includes educating adult audiences through programming, pre-concert lectures, and printed materials."[12] The two challenges are to educate current attenders and to educate the next generation.

Educating Current Attenders

Because repeated arts attendance is the result of satisfying experiences, it is important that current audiences appreciate and understand what they see and hear. Also, since attendance is encouraged by word of mouth, it is important that patrons feel secure about discussing the performances. Says Henry Fogel, president of the Chicago Symphony Orchestra:

> How often have we heard someone say something like this after a classical music concert: "I didn't really like it, but I don't really know that much about it, so I'm not a good person to ask." Or worse: "I'd like to go to the symphony, but I don't know enough about music." . . . We must recognize that certain music is difficult, and make special efforts to help our audiences connect to it, rather than making them feel inferior for not responding to it. . . . We can make it more immediate and meaningful by provoking constant thought and discussion in our program notes, in special articles in our programs and at pre- and postconcert discussions (and isn't "discussions" a better word than "lectures"—isn't anything a better word than "lectures"?). We can also explore these ideas at meetings of our volunteer groups, at annual meetings, at board meetings, even at receptions and in the community. We have constructed the damned pedestal over many years; we have to be aggressive in ripping it down.[13]

Many organizations are effectively tearing down their pedestal of pretension with a major commitment to educating their patrons and increasing accessibility to the art. Some examples follow.

PROGRAMS AND EVENTS

Dance Cleveland offers a variety of educational programs for its subscribers, its members, and even its single-ticket buyers. Members and subscribers receive mailings that provide general information on the company and its choreographic style and point of view. They can borrow from the company's video library, which features tapes of upcoming artists and programs. This prepares them to better enjoy the live performance and helps them decide which programs are most appropriate for their children and guests. Artists' promotional tapes are shown at Dance Cleveland events, at various business sites, and to the trustees. Before each performance and during intermission, a video previewing upcoming dance companies and artists is played for interested patrons.

Before concerts, artists often perform in the community, at schools, in malls, and in office buildings to promote and discuss their work, bringing dance into a setting that is familiar and comfortable to a wide range of people. Some visiting dance companies offer residency activities for area schools, community and senior citizen centers, juvenile detention facilities, and the community at large. A residency may take the form of lecture-demonstrations, master classes, open rehearsals, or other activities preferred by the visiting artists. On the day before an opening, fifty to one hundred selected patrons, subscribers, and single-ticket buyers are invited to meet visiting artists at an informal reception in a private home, where the artists may speak briefly and display their work on video. These gatherings provide an opportunity for guests and artists to become acquainted in a comfortable setting.

For some programs, Dance Cleveland hosts preconcert discussions featuring dance scholars who provide background on the evening's performance. This format was used for the Glasnost Festival Ballet Tour, since the audience was unfamiliar with the company's work and would benefit from preparation about its "spare" style of presentation. Following each show, postperformance discussions are held among the artists and the audience. The discussions help foster a positive rapport between artists and audience members and create an understanding among the audience of what they have seen on stage. During the discussions, audiences are encouraged to develop their opinions and respond emotionally. Artists then help them put their thoughts into context, in words they can grasp, helping to build a bridge between the audience's thoughts and the artists' intent.[14]

PROGRAM NOTES

The San Francisco Symphony has taken up the challenge of focusing people's attention on the musical experience with its specially designed program notes. Most U.S. orchestras have contracts with program producers whereby the orchestra has control over about half of the program for the concert notes and the rest of the program is filled with stories of more general interest designed to sell the advertising. However, the San Francisco Symphony controls its entire program and employs a full-time musicologist and two other full-time writers, who produce ten pages of high-quality copy on special subjects such as the great American symphonies. These programs cost the orchestra about $200,000 a year, but, says executive director Peter Pastreich, "You look out during a performance and one third of the people are sitting reading the program—no matter what you give them. How can you say you don't care what they read? Is it a luxury to put something in front of them that focuses them back on the orchestra, on what they're hearing?"[15]

THE MUSIC DIRECTOR AS EDUCATOR

Leonard Bernstein, as music director of the New York Philharmonic, was the first conductor who dared to speak to the audience from the podium. But his talks were so meaningful to his audiences that Bernstein helped to establish a means of communication that many conductors have since adopted. Kurt Masur, the current conductor of the New York Philharmonic, has been a willing partner in the drive to present the orchestra as friendly, responsive, and accessible. At the Rush Hour and Casual Saturday concerts, Masur has adopted what he calls the "verbal program note approach" to deal with the feelings of intimidation felt by novice concertgoers. Says Masur, "You can talk to the audience so the audience doesn't feel that those people onstage are a little bit far away, doing holy music."[16] Gibes Masur, "New York has the best coughing audience in the world." Masur is convinced that such behavior is symptomatic not of a tickle in the throat but "a lack of attention, of expectation," attitudes that can be nurtured beforehand by communication.[17]

Kirk Muspratt, resident conductor of the Pittsburgh Symphony, believes that reaching out to the community goes far beyond talks from the podium. Muspratt goes out of the hall to address Rotarians, schoolchildren, teachers, and volunteer groups. His aim is not only to educate about music, but also to cultivate the community's trust in the orchestra. Explains Muspratt,

> For me, it's a matter of investing in people. The time has come in Pittsburgh for us to expand what we do to include more of our community. Music is phenomenal, whether Bach or Joplin. Anybody, whether they're 5, 35, or 95, if they have just a few tools and a little exposure, will love it. We don't ever have to apologize for Bach or Bruckner. We just expose the audience to the music, treat people in an intelligent and respectful way, and give them something that will be emotionally uplifting and appealing. The investment means getting people to trust you and your taste and the quality.[18]

USING MULTIMEDIA

Community access cable television and public television and radio can provide forums for composers and orchestras to introduce new repertoire to potential audiences. As interactive video and CD-ROM become more developed, more widespread, and less expensive, orchestras will be able to utilize such technologies to communicate with audiences and to provide opportunities for interactive learning experiences.

Leonard Slatkin, music director of the Saint Louis Symphony Orchestra (SLSO), has videotaped preconcert conversations to educate his audiences about upcoming concerts. Because videotapes are expensive to disseminate and because air time is scarce and costly, the SLSO has developed a creative solution in partnership with a local TV station. The videotapes are aired on TV as public service announcements, free to the orchestra, when a half hour or more of air time is easy to come by—at 4:30 A.M.! Subscribers are informed of the airing well in advance. They can record the program while they are asleep and then view it at their leisure. Not only does this system bring the program to the audience at negligible cost to the SLSO, but no viewers miss the program because of time conflicts. The broadcasting has been enthusiastically received, and it is estimated that thousands of people participate.

*Educating
the Next
Generation*

Performing arts organizations have historically provided special children's concerts, usually for school groups. But educating children has never been a priority in the orchestra world. It has often been left to volunteers rather than professional staff. Performances for children have been minimally funded, underrehearsed, and dismissed as "just kiddie concerts" by musicians and music directors. Says Gary Good, former executive director of the Milwaukee Symphony, "A generation ago, the typical one-shot approach of the children's concert worked well. Now general music has disappeared in the schools. The minimal knowledge that students used to bring to concerts has disappeared. A generation ago, we talked about sonata form at youth concerts. Today, we have to tell them what a violin is." However, even in the early 1970s, studies conducted at Lincoln Center's Elementary and High School Programs showed that exposing children to a few live performances had little impact on cultivating their interest in the art form.[19]

In response, arts organizations have begun to take up the cause of providing meaningful, ongoing arts education opportunities. And they are finding that when arts education works, it does more than cultivate interest in the arts. The study of art can combine critical thinking and creative problem-solving experiences with creative expression. The communication, clarity, and cooperation that come from viewing, making, and enjoying art help prepare children for more productive lives. Arts education helps to make people more creative, improves quality of life, and even helps to keep kids in school. The arts have been credited with reaching students who don't have the desire or motivation to learn. For example, due to the popularity of the Arts Enterprise Zone, the Kennedy Center's local initiative in Washington's Anacostia neighborhood, attendance in regular classes has increased from 60 percent to 90 percent.[20] And when children are taught to become dancers, musicians, and artists, they learn not only the self-discipline needed to succeed in school but also the skills needed to get and keep a job in an increasingly complex world of work. Students learning to dance are learning to work cooperatively, to deal effectively with complex direction, and to develop self-discipline.

PROGRAMS

Many arts organizations have begun to rethink their educational missions and to experiment with new educational strategies. Some have even developed extensive, in-depth programs that are in use in many communities. The John F. Kennedy Center for the Performing Arts in Washington, D.C., has developed a major program called Performing Arts and Schools: Partners in Education, which brings together presenting organizations and school districts in more than thirty states to strengthen the role of arts in education. The program's initial focus is on educating teachers, based on the belief that teacher education is an essential component of any effort designed to increase the artistic literacy of young people. Each participating school district has devised an evolving program that addresses specific needs in its community. The Music Center of Los Angeles County spent three years to develop

Artsource, an educational program designed to place the arts at the heart of an integrated kindergarten-through-eighth-grade curriculum.[21]

ARTSOURCE: THE MUSIC CENTER STUDY GUIDE TO THE PERFORMING ARTS

The fifty-eight units in the Artsource study guide are unified by a focus on five universal themes: "Transformation," referring to a change in the appearance, thinking, or character of a person, animal, idea, situation, place, or object; "Enduring Values," encompassing the standards and principles that are considered important in life, such as love, aesthetics, justice, honor, spirituality, and the search for truth; "Freedom and Oppression," centering on the struggle and balance of power between individuals and between groups of people, including concepts such as war and peace; "Power of Nature," including the entire natural world, its laws and its mysteries, as well as man's relationship to it; and "The Human Family," embracing all that is human, including emotions, dreams, the family structure, relationships, work, games, culture, and history.

Each Artsource program unit focuses on the work of an accomplished artist in dance, theater, or music. Units include written materials about the artist's life—where he or she grew up, what brought him or her to the arts—and about the artist's creative process. Each unit includes information about the cultural context for the body of work and a sample of selected work presented in audio, visual, or textual form. The art is linked to multiple subject areas within the school curriculum with sample discussion questions, a glossary of terms, multidisciplinary activity and study options, and additional references. For example, the glossary for the theater section includes such terms as *commedia dell-arte, non-traditional casting,* and *pantomime.*

Teacher lesson plans are offered on three levels. Level one is for younger grades or for students with little background or experience in the arts. These plans are fundamental but can be developed at the instructor's discretion. Level two requires some specific arts vocabulary, increased skills, and a fundamental knowledge of the elements of the art form being addressed. Students can develop their own aesthetic perceptions and judgments; activities require group cooperation. Level three draws upon the students' analytical abilities and stimulates creativity. The student has more responsibility to comprehend, communicate, apply, analyze, synthesize, critique, and evaluate.

One unit is developed around Chuck Davis, choreographer, ethnologist, and founder of the African American Dance Ensemble. In the Chuck Davis unit, students are taken through a basic history lesson on African culture and geography. They experience storytelling, movement improvisation, sound, and music, and experiment with exercises in building leadership skills through dance. While an accompanying video shows a chorus of dancers moving to the tempo of African drums, individual students are led across the stage, mimicking the frenetic yet perfectly controlled movements of their leader.

The Davis unit, like many of the others, links creative elements to other curriculum areas. In this case, the traditional "Bacteria Chant" uses an African vocal art form to teach the physical properties of one-celled plants.

The market for Artsource is the educators themselves, who are primarily reached through the Music Center's biannual Institute for Educators. The institute is a four-day series of live performances in theater, music, and dance; its educational component includes participation workshops with artists and educators, training in classroom applications, and small group seminars, and uses Artsource units as the primary teaching resource. Described by teachers as "powerful, practical and compelling," the Institute provides them with the basic resources to become more creative educators and to draw out the individual child's voice through new ways of thinking about the world.

With fine, comprehensive programs such as Performing Arts and Schools: Partners in Education and Artsource, much hard work in this area has already been done. Whether organizations adapt preexisting programs to their own needs or develop their own arts education programs, the following aspects of high-quality, effective programming should be kept in mind.

SETTING STANDARDS

Mitchell Korn, a national arts education consultant, has developed a set of ten standards for effective arts education. Korn believes that these standards suggest a method by which arts education programming can best be assembled and implemented in today's schools.

1. Arts programs should be comprehensive and sequential. Contrary to the traditional "exposure" program, in which children experience a single arts presentation in their school auditorium, sequential and comprehensive arts education

provides many connected experiences and lessons that are a regular part of class-room life.

2. Schools should strive to integrate art into the entire curriculum. An integrated arts curriculum means that arts are taught in conjunction with other academic subjects, each giving greater meaning to the other. A school might also want a separate arts curriculum that stands on its own, equal to math or science. Either way, the arts can be taught as an essential part of a child's education.

3. Teachers are incredibly important; they provide continuity and success in a child's arts education. Teachers need incentives to learn the skills they need to teach the arts. In addition, combining arts with other academic subjects can help relieve the time pressure on teachers to cover everything demanded in the curriculum.

4. Arts programs are an important vehicle for understanding and respecting the many cultures that contribute to American life. The arts of Africa, Asia, Latin America, Native America, and Europe help children understand their own roots and respect others.

5. As children make art, they learn to solve problems and to think critically. They develop disciplined work habits as they observe, analyze, make art, and reflect on its meanings. They learn the human values of discipline and hard work, developing habits they can carry well beyond their school days.

6. Partnerships between arts organizations, artists, and schools combine essential resources to set standards and provide resources for good arts programs.

7. Teachers, artists, and arts organizations need time to plan good arts programs. Good programs can take twelve months to plan before beginning.

8. Artists need training to teach children. Their preparation has been in their discipline (music, drama, dance) and has not usually included teaching skills. They need help choosing age-appropriate materials and activities for children.

9. The arts organization should not lower its standards, but instead should make high standards accessible to children.

10. The arts education program must address a need within the school. Arts organizations must listen to schools and build appropriate programs.[22]

Based on these standards, Mitchell Korn has created an arts education program for the Milwaukee Symphony.

ARTS IN COMMUNITY EDUCATION

A comprehensive and revolutionary arts education program initiated and managed by an arts organization is Arts in Community Education (ACE), created by Mitchell Korn for the Milwaukee Symphony. The ACE program is built on outreach, teacher involvement and training, community collaboration, and alternative musical experiences. Its goal is to establish a sequential, continuing arts education program, from the first grade through the twelfth. The curriculum is designed to be integrated into reading, science, and math classes, rather than adding a discipline. A favorite ACE story tells of a first-grader who spotted an ordering principle in a math lesson and exclaimed, "That's ABA form!" (symphonic sonata form).

ACE schools, ranging from inner-city to wealthy suburban schools, were chosen through a competitive application process and pay four to five dollars per student to participate. The program was started in the kindergarten and first grade, and one grade will be added each year. New curriculum materials are sent out several times each year, and teachers meet for mandatory in-service education sessions twice a year.

The curriculum is built around particular pieces of music to be heard again at concerts specially designed for ACE participants. The kindergarten theme is "The Family of Music," covering audience members, musicians, composers, and conductors. In first grade, children study "Musical Tales," and learn about storytelling through music. In the second grade, the theme is "Detectives," and concentrates on problem-solving skills.

To complement the curriculum, ensemble programs are presented in the schools by Milwaukee Symphony musicians, who select repertoire and write interactive programs that follow the curriculum guidelines. Later, when the students come to the concert hall, the musicians stand in the lobby with their instruments, greeting the children and cementing the relationship.

A major challenge of the program has been the training of the ensemble members. Musicians who are not used to talking are forced to think about what they do in an entirely new way. Yet more musicians than ACE needed have volunteered for the program. And talks are underway about putting ACE services into the orchestra's master agreement.

INITIATING AND IMPLEMENTING AN ARTS EDUCATION PROGRAM

Any plan for the development of an arts education program should involve school administrators, parents, and teachers, as well as the arts organizations. Teachers should be involved from the start as partners in the program. They can identify points of connection for arts in the curriculum and plan ways to make those connections work. Program planners should take inventory of what local schools already provide in the way of arts education and of the regular curriculum that arts programming will be designed to complement.

Parent networks should be set up so that the vital family connection can be brought into the project. Parents can get involved in arts projects in several ways: working on in-school projects such as murals; participating in field trips as chaperones and guides, thereby taking leadership in extending the value of those experiences; collecting information to publish an arts calendar. Some schools schedule arts workshops for parents to increase their knowledge and encourage their participation in their children's schoolwork; parents are welcome to join children in any of the school arts activities. At the George Howland Academy for the Arts, an elementary school on Chicago's West Side, principal Anita Broms has created a developmental arts program for teachers, children, and parents. One result of this cooperative program is that the local school council and a group of parents produce an original play and perform it for the students each year.

Arts organizations in the community and artists coming on tour should contact the schools to offer to develop outreach programs. Since the arts can play an important role in teaching and transmitting cultural values and traditions, organizations that focus on specific cultures have much to offer the schools. It is advantageous, when possible, to bring programs into the schools that invite students to participate, not just observe. It benefits the children to be actively involved.

Once a plan has been developed, including project goals, a funding proposal should be written. The proposal should indicate who the arts educators will be, the nature of their activities and programs, and how often they will have contact with the students. A detailed budget should accompany the proposal.

ISSUES IN CREATING A WORKABLE PLAN

The factors that most commonly prevent arts education programs from getting under way are time, space, and money. Planners should look creatively at ways to restructure the use of these resources to make them work for the program. If teaching time is raised as an issue, look resourcefully at how teachers now utilize their time and how that time can be restructured to provide more opportunities to focus on the arts. The more the arts are integrated into the regular curriculum, the less time will be required specifically for the arts program. Space can also be "expanded" creatively. The school playground could become an arts arena in warm weather. The gym is an appropriate arena for dance. And when music and dance are added to physical education, children become more engaged in learning. Some arts programs are held before and after school when more space is available and children from different classrooms can be brought together.[23]

Finally, many fund-raising opportunities are available for arts education projects. Many foundations and corporations are delighted to fund projects that unite the arts, education, and cultural values. With federal and state arts funding decreasing, schools have received state and federal assistance through school improvement funds, gifted and special education grants, bilingual funding, and community and school alliance grants. One school in San Bernardino County was able to access county desegregation and integration funds by establishing an arts magnet program that drew students of all ethnic backgrounds.[24] Sometimes money can even be found within a school's already tight budget. For example, the library may purchase a specialized collection about the music of cultures studied in social studies classes and videos of arts performances. With good planning, creative solutions can be found to make arts programs viable.

THE ARTIST AS EDUCATOR

While facing a continued dwindling of resources for traditional arts education, teachers and administrators are turning to individual artists and presenting organizations to provide the necessary resources and training. In some cases, individual artists have taken the initiative in fulfilling this role. Consider the following examples.

The young violinist Midori donated some of her fees to start a foundation dedicated "to bring classical music and its artists closer to the everyday lives of children." She is working on a curriculum guide for music school graduates who work with children. She has also tried to teach cooperation by having her accompanist play his part on the piano first, then playing hers, and then having the two play together to show how much more interesting it becomes. Says Midori, "To make music real for children, they have to be directly exposed to musicians."[25]

Choreographer Eliot Feld believes that ballet can help inner-city children and that inner-city children can help change the face and image of ballet. Since 1978, Feld has auditioned more than 120,000 third- through fifth-grade students from the New York City public schools and has enrolled 6,000 of them in classes. The New Ballet School's students reflect the racial composition of the city schools, whose students are 80 percent nonwhite. Although most children drop out of the program before reaching the advanced level, a handful have gone on to perform in Mr. Feld's contemporary dance company, and one danced with the entourage of pop idol Madonna. The school not only helps the children develop their artistic skills but also teaches them concentration, self-discipline, and a sense of their own potential for accomplishment. The school's $680,000 budget is supported primarily by grants from foundations, corporations, and government arts funds.[26]

Some symphony orchestras have taken on the responsibility of running music schools for their communities. Says Bruce Coppock, executive director of the Saint Louis Symphony Orchestra, "We don't presume to have the answers for the public schools, but we do know that the preservation of music education is absolutely critical to this industry, and that it's important for broader societal reasons as well." Continues Coppock, "Imagine if you're an eight-year-old kid taking lessons, and you have access to a member of the Saint Louis Symphony. That's a real education."[27] The Saint Louis Symphony rejects the notion that orchestras can enhance their audiences only by adding more pops concerts and repertoire geared solely to nontraditional audiences, contending that the educational mission of the orchestra is far more central to audience development than the playing of pops concerts. True to its mission and its name, the Saint Louis Symphony Community Music School provides private lessons, group classes, and ensemble opportunities for 2,600 students in six locations around the city and its suburbs.

Several orchestras have developed formal relationships with local music academies. In some cases, as in Saint Louis, the orchestra owns and manages the school; in others, the two organizations cooperate on permanent or temporary programs. Faculty members at the schools include orchestra players and other local professional musicians. Typically, tuition covers only one-half to three-fourths of total expenses at these schools. The balance comes from endowments or grants by foundations and businesses, which are delighted to support educational programs run by organizations as prestigious as the symphony orchestra.

THE ARTS ORGANIZATION AS EDUCATOR

The role of the arts organization as the purveyor of music education raises many questions. Can symphony musicians, dancers, singers, and actors be trained in order to participate meaningfully? Can new orchestra members be interviewed for their communications skills as well as auditioned for their musical talent? How many students can realistically be served? How much money can be raised to support the programs and for how long can the funding be sustained?[28] These questions may not be answered for years, but given the current dearth of arts education in the schools, it is incumbent upon arts organizations and the artists themselves to fill the gap.

There has been much public controversy as to whether art itself must change to fill the growing number of empty seats in the concert hall, to attract younger people, and to attract funds from those sources most responsive to the social and political issues of our times. If artists and arts organizations take up with zeal the responsibility for educating young people about art, in the very process of doing so they will develop enthusiastic audiences, attract funds, make people more culturally aware and sensitive, and guarantee that great art will endure for generations to come. And arts educators must keep in mind the words of Igor Stravinsky, who warned that "the trouble with music appreciation in general is that people are taught to have too much respect for music; they should be taught to love it instead."

MARKETING PRINCIPLES AND THE ARTS

Throughout this book we have described strategies and tactics to help arts managers, marketers, and board members become more effective and efficient in proactively managing their organizations and in reaching out to their publics. Many of the ideas represent some of the best practices currently in use. But what works well for one organization may not suit another organization's situation. And because environments change and people's needs, interests, and desires change over time, the best practices of today may be less appropriate tomorrow. Therefore, it is crucial that arts managers and marketers fully understand and internalize the following universal and enduring principles that underlie each and every successful strategy.

Manage for the Mission

Managing for the mission means that an organization takes no decision or action that is not informed and inspired by its mission statement. The mission is the organization's purpose or reason for being. Every mission statement reflects two things: the competencies and attainment levels sought by the organization, and its purposeful commitments to various stakeholders. Each member of the organization must understand, support, and be able to articulate that mission.[29] The organization uses the power of the mission to bring people together and to direct their energies toward a common purpose. If an organization devotes a disproportionate amount of its resources to activities that do not support the mission, then the organization is supporting only the institution itself and not its reason for being.

Focus on Core Competencies

Second only to its mission, an arts organization should focus on its core competencies. It is important to concentrate on only a few things, to do them well, and to communicate effectively what those strengths are. This is the basis for programmatic emphases as well as for the collaborative efforts we discussed in Chapter 7. Consider how the Rochester (Minnesota) Symphony achieved a major goal by combining its strengths with its opportunities.

ACHIEVING GOALS WITH A FOCUS ON CORE COMPETENCIES

The Rochester Symphony wanted to expand the number of concerts it presents. Based on the results of an audience survey and pilot concerts developed to help identify musical voids in the cultural scene, the symphony inaugurated a chamber music series. The chamber series gave Rochester Symphony members a new touring opportunity. Many small towns have neither the finances nor the facilities to host a full symphony orchestra. But they can afford to bring a chamber orchestra into a local church, where much of the chamber orchestra repertoire can enjoy appropriate acoustics and atmosphere.[30] In addition to achieving programmatic innovations, the better players were provided an opportunity to work on a higher musical level, providing satisfaction to the performers and the conductor.

By focusing on quality musical experiences, the Rochester Symphony was able to broaden its audience base, provide additional satisfaction to its musicians, and increase the earned revenue generated for the organization.

*Understand
the Nature of
the Business*

Although arts organizations must focus on their core competencies, too rigid or narrow an interpretation of its role has been the downfall of many a company and many an industry. Says music critic John von Rhein, "Some already consider the symphony a cultural dinosaur—*Orchestrasaurus rex* lumbering to extinction in the waning years of the century."[31]

Out of such concerns, in 1992 the American Symphony Orchestra League created a national task force of more than 150 people who work directly with orchestras (musicians, board members, executive directors, marketing directors, etc.) and people who brought in expertise from outside the orchestra field (music school deans and other educators). For nearly a year, the task force conducted a series of issue forums in which members discussed and debated what directions the nation's orchestras should take "to assist the orchestra field's dynamic progress into the 21st Century."[32] Their report, "Americanizing the American Orchestra," resulted from those forums. In a section entitled "Why talk about change?" the report stated:

> In the face of shifting community needs and cultural agendas, orchestras are finding that their current missions and programs lack meaning for many people. Larger numbers of citizens see the orchestra in their community as a benefit to "other people," not themselves, and the repertoire as representing "other people's music," not music they wish to spend time and money to support. . . . It is vital to begin to see the shaky financial status of many orchestras as merely symptomatic of the orchestra field's need to address its role in American society.
>
> Without significant change, orchestras could easily become both culturally and socially irrelevant, and the orchestra field would have missed an opportunity to evolve into a revitalized musical and cultural force in this country. . . . However, discussions about how to fix things are often mired in inflexible and destructive dichotomies that juxtapose "classical, old, European, high art" music against "popular, new, American, low culture" music; music for adults against music for children and youth; and professional musical activity against musical participation by amateurs. Such limiting constructs may discourage many people from participation in and support of American orchestras. They belie the American spirit of energy, innovation, and inclusion, and can dim an orchestra's vision of what is possible.[33]

The task force challenges orchestras to look beyond old patterns and ways of doing business to discover and develop new relationships, new sounds, new missions, new repertoire, and new presentational opportunities. Some of its recommendations have been highly controversial and have been subject to severe criticism from the press. The *New York Times* music critic Edward Rothstein denounced the report as a "disgrace" and "thoroughly wrongheaded," suggesting that it is nothing but a panicked response by a "cynical managerial class capitulating to the philistines of political correctness."[34] But the report will have been a great success if it ignites a productive discussion among everyone in the orchestra field to refine and redefine the nature of the business of the symphony orchestra.

Commit Resources to the Marketing Function

Marketing success requires a wholehearted commitment of funds, well-trained personnel, and trust in the marketing function itself. An arts organization cannot muster or maintain a strong audience base without full-fledged campaigns that include direct mail, telemarketing, well-designed, high-quality brochures, advertising, and special offers designed to attract and retain patrons. Central to effective marketing is a commitment to marketing research. Market research is an investment the organization must make to develop, execute, and monitor intelligent marketing plans and thereby to sustain and increase its audience.

Typically, an arts organization earns 50 percent of its revenue from ticket sales and gains the other 50 percent from contributions. And because nonprofit arts organizations often reach out to broader and larger audiences as a part of their mission, one would assume that the organizations would dedicate at least as many resources to marketing as to development functions. But marketing budgets tend to be underscaled. This situation exists despite the fact that many organizations find that meeting their funders' needs detracts them from their core purpose and competence. Many funders have their own agendas for the programs they support—such as outreach programs, programs with a multicultural emphasis, or programs that put the funder (usually a corporation) in a good light. Arts organizations also dedicate much time and effort to writing lengthy and complex grant proposals to government agencies, which at the local, state, and federal levels combined only contribute about 3 percent of the operating costs of arts organizations.

By dedicating more human and financial resources to the marketing function, organizations can focus more directly on their core competencies and build their audiences in the process. With strong audience support, granting agencies become less important. With a stronger audience base, arts organizations can focus less on the issues central to their corporate, foundation, and government funders. In other words, they can focus on the purpose of their art: communication with the audience. This will allow for greater long-term organizational stability and will better serve the public as well.

Focus on Quality

The most important factor to the success or failure of an artistic product is its quality. The product that has a quality advantage is destined to capture and rule the minds and hearts of the marketplace. Cutting corners in a way that adversely affects the artistic quality of an organization is the sure road to failure. Quality is far more important than marketing tools such as price and promotion. Marketing strategies may attract customers, but if the experience itself is not satisfying, promotional techniques will not bring them back. And spending advertising and promotion dollars on behalf of an inferior product is futile if not counterproductive.

Know the Customers

An arts organization must know its consumers—its current and potential audience members. A performing arts group must start by listening to the heartbeat of its community: what people like and dislike; what they find attractive, what keeps them away; which segments of the community are most likely to be interested in its core product; which segments can be lured with augmented product features.

Larger arts organizations usually have the resources to employ sophisticated market research techniques to measure and describe their current and potential audiences. But even the smallest organizations with minimal resources can conduct in-house surveys and focus groups, obtain grants for further research, and study published reports on audience characteristics and preferences.

The most successful arts organizations are those whose products and services are directed at separate, distinct, and reachable segments of the population and whose offerings are positioned from the customer's viewpoint, not the organization's.

Create Accessibility

An important message of this book is how to create access for the current or potential customer to the product. Instead of focusing on the product—"We have a great product so you should come" (the elitist, product-centered viewpoint)—the organization should focus instead on the target audience and *their* issues, concerns, needs, and preferences. Instead of saying "This is good for you," we need to translate the way the product is offered to the public so that the message they receive is "This is good." That means understanding the public's comfort levels, what *prevents* them from attending, and ways to ease the access.

Remember that reality is what the consumer *perceives* it to be, that the solution is not in the product or in the marketer's own mind, but inside the prospect's mind. Success may well lie in the details: offering a performance at a convenient time, emphasizing casual garb, or surrounding the performance with familiar faces and comfortable settings. Some organizations create more access simply by selling tickets at grocery stores or through peer groups and employee organizations. In these examples the core offering is not even an issue. Accessibility is improved through augmented product features and through effective positioning.

Understand the Organization's Internal Biases

Artists and arts managers are often guilty of an attitude that prevents arts organizations from effectively reaching out to "less serious" audience segments. A common perspective held by artistic directors and arts managers is that art and entertainment are two different things. They imply that art is serious and entertainment is not. The public then draws the conclusion that art cannot be entertaining! Said Clifford C. Nelson nearly twenty years ago, "Whether one believes in the so-called elitist view of the performing arts (i.e., support for creative excellence and activity), the so-called populist view (participation by more and more people in the arts), or whether one thinks the arts should be "popular without being popularized," the fact remains it is the public that will resolve the future role of the arts in our society."[35]

Leonard Bernstein's *Candide,* which was presented by the Lyric Opera of Chicago during the 1994–95 season, has also been performed on musical theater stages. Critic John von Rhein asks: "Is *Candide* an operetta, a musical comedy, a music theater piece, or what?" Responds Timothy Nolan, who starred in the Lyric Opera production, "Like *Sweeney Todd,* when *Candide* is done in an opera house, it's an opera; when it's done in a music theater venue, it's music theater." Says director Harold Prince: "I don't know why people have to categorize."[36]

Similarly, Henry Fogel, president of the Chicago Symphony Orchestra, has accused the American orchestra business of promoting pretension in a country dedicated to unpretentiousness. "We are so grimly serious. We alienate listeners. No other art form has so intimidated its audience. People are afraid to have opinions. We have to stretch listeners but remember too that merit exists not only in the abstruse. We have to stop demeaning music that appeals to the public and demeaning the public that likes it."[37]

So arts managers and marketers must understand the impact of their own attitudes upon the publics they are trying to reach. They should be sensitive to their own emotions, predispositions, and biases as well as those of their publics when selecting their target markets and positioning their products. The marketer's task is to find ways to connect with the audience so they will be receptive to the offerings and not be put off by interfering attitudes.

View Changing Needs as Opportunities —Not Threats

As customers' needs change, so must every organization's marketing strategy. And marketers must view change as an opportunity, not as a cause for concern. According to Jack McAuliffe, marketing director of the American Symphony Orchestra League, total subscription purchases at U.S. symphonies during the 1994–95 season were roughly equivalent to what they were several years before in the heyday of the full subscription purchase. The difference is that in the past, one person bought tickets to twelve concerts. Now four people buy tickets to three concerts. That means more patrons need to be sought and more work needs to be done by the marketing departments. But it also means more potential contributors and more opportunity for building frequency of attendance. So while full-season subscriptions have been declining in recent years in response to the customers' expressed preference for more spontaneity and lower time commitment levels, farsighted marketers have been offering flex plans and miniplans. These options attract new patrons and help to maintain a level of frequency, commitment, and loyalty among lapsed subscribers without eroding the subscriber base at all.

Those who warn against flex plans, memberships, and other "partial offers" believe that full-season subscribers are necessary to fill the hall for all productions and allow for experimentation. But these critics are looking only at the organization's side of the equation. *Arts organizations must be responsible to the needs of their audiences.* Each and every current and potential arts patron—including single-ticket buyers— should be respected, listened to, appreciated, and then, when possible, nurtured into higher levels of commitment. If arts organizations do not respect and meet the public's changing needs with respect to how the product is offered, there will be an ever-diminishing audience to share in the artistic experiment. So in the long run, such change can only serve to strengthen the organization, not to weaken it.

Take the
Long-Term
View

Successful marketing requires a long-term view. Arts organizations commonly recognize the need to attract young audiences. But educating children is costly, and targeting younger audiences is likely to imply smaller packages, lower ticket prices, and lower donation levels—in the short run. However, in the process of absorbing these costs, the organization is building a strong and broad foundation for its future and for a time when these younger people will have more leisure time and more discretionary income to pay higher ticket prices and make substantial contributions.

In New York City, high school students can buy tickets to performing arts events through Ticketmaster outlets for just $5 each, or two tickets for $5 Mondays through Thursdays. The program is sponsored by High 5 Tickets to the Arts, a nonprofit organization working with major support from Ticketmaster, the Citicorp Foundation, the New York Times, Time Warner, Sony Music Entertainment, and the Coca-Cola Company. The program features a wide range of cultural events including theater, dance, classical music, modern music, and even the circus. Among the dozens of performing arts organizations participating in the program are the New York Philharmonic, the New York City Ballet, the Brooklyn Academy of Music, Alvin Ailey Dance Theater, Circle Repertory Company, Jazz at Lincoln Center, the 92nd Street Y, Carnegie Hall, the Big Apple Circus, and the Broadway musical *How to Succeed in Business without Really Trying.* The arts organizations receive no payment for the tickets they allot for this program; they receive exposure and the opportunity to help build interest, enjoyment, and the proclivity for arts attendance among the next generation of arts ticket purchasers. Corporate sponsors demonstrate how much they value the program by the extent of their in-kind support: Ticketmaster contributes its services and the New York Times provides about half a million dollars worth of advertising annually. By December 1995, the third month of the program, High 5 had sold one thousand tickets, had collected a mailing list of five thousand people who called a toll-free number to ask for information, and had received many calls from cultural organizations around the country interested in emulating the program.

In Cincinnati, a program entitled Enjoy the Arts/START is also designed to stimulate attendance among the young. For a low membership fee in Enjoy the Arts, high school students are entitled to discounted tickets for many cultural events, some free tickets, workshops, and meet-the-artist receptions. On-site performances and staff presentations are also offered at more than eighty area schools annually. Once the students graduate, they are eligible to join START (Sample the Arts), a membership organization for adults age thirty or younger and geared primarily for young professionals. Members may purchase two tickets for the price of one for the entire year to the Cincinnati Ballet, Cincinnati Chamber Orchestra, May Festival, Opera, Playhouse in the Park, and Symphony starting seven days before the performance of their choice. Members also receive over $400 worth of free ticket vouchers good for themselves and a guest to specific events at some of the participating organizations and a 10 percent discount on tickets for selected Broadway shows. A bimonthly calendar of performances, events, and exhibitions is mailed to members; information is also made available through a twenty-four-hour hotline. More than a thousand twenty-somethings, who report that they joined START to save money and to become more active in the arts community, are currently members.

Integrate the Arts into Everyday Lives

An anthropologist has found a remote African tribe that has zero literacy in the community at age twelve and 100 percent literacy at age fourteen. All courting in this society is done in written form, so once the children reach puberty, they all quickly learn to read and write.[38] We can learn an important lesson from this tribe for finding ways to make art central to people's lives. The more we can integrate access to the arts with our everyday lives, the more people we can bring in.

For example, after the bombing of the Murrah Federal Building in Oklahoma City in the spring of 1995, the Oklahoma City Philharmonic performed music of Beethoven, Rachmaninoff, Ravel, and Bach in the official ceremonies broadcast internationally, and many of the musicians, as soloists and in ensembles, performed for many of the private memorial services held for individual members of their community who had perished.[39] Their musical contributions helped to comfort the mourners.

Many arts organizations have found effective ways to integrate their offerings into the lives of their publics, albeit in somewhat less compelling ways. The New York Philharmonic invites families to integrate music into their weekend outings with its casual, inexpensive, one-hour Saturday afternoon concerts. The American Symphony Orchestra ties in its musical themes with literature, politics, history, and other interests common to its audience members. The "home base" for Dancing in the Streets is wherever a target audience can be found.

In addition to reaching out to individual audience segments, arts organizations must become active, involved members of their communities. They should have representatives on the local chamber of commerce participate in the Fourth of July parade and perform for patients in local hospitals. When a community event is being staged, such as the grand opening of a new store, or when a young public official is speaking before a crowd, performing artists and presenters can lend their expertise by helping to stage events and by coaching public speaking. In return, they will benefit from awareness, familiarity, and gratitude, which will translate into new audiences, new funders, and new sources of gifts-in-kind. Such efforts will weave the arts into the very fabric of the community. Each of these activities will create new opportunities for exposing people to art and showing them how art is integral to our everyday lives, our experiences, and our feelings, which in turn will make the artistic experience compelling to a broader number of people.

*Focus on
the Art*

The focus of this book has been on the arts organization, for the organization brings the art to the public and the public to the art. However, it must be remembered that it is the art itself that has the power—the power to move the soul, lift the spirit, expand the mind. Art is an open system; it constantly creates, cajoles, undermines, confronts, challenges. And great art endures, transcending time and space. The power of *Hamlet* has only intensified in the four hundred years of societal growth and change since its creation.

Yet the organization is a closed system. It is controlled, systematized, resistant to change. That resistance must be broken down. Arts organizations must continually change to retain their effectiveness. They must change their internal structures, their ways of doing business, sometimes even their missions. Above all, they must *listen* to their constituents.

Pierre Boulez says that "it is a sign of weakness in a civilization that it cannot destroy things." Similarly, Daniel Barenboim claims that "this mania for keeping everything shows a lack of courage, courage which is needed in order to use the experiences of the past as stepping stones to the vision of the future."[40]

If the essence of art is the relationship between the artist and the audience, the arts organization must be vigilant in pursuing both the artists' and the audiences' best interests. Our programs should be developed not with the purpose of keeping the institution *alive,* but of making it *viable.* In the end, our accountability is to the artists and their publics—not to the organization. By attempting to alter public perceptions of our institutions, we only scratch the surface of the challenges we face and, at best, create short-term solutions. By educating our publics about the art we treasure and by being sensitive to the continually changing needs of various audience segments, we can build enthusiastic and loyal audiences for the future. And by doing that, we can guarantee that art will thrive and prosper.

The challenge: bring order to the whole through design . . . composition . . . tension . . . balance . . . light . . . and harmony. . . .

So many possibilities.

STEPHEN SONDHEIM
Sunday in the Park with George

1 Richard Pulford, "Losing the War of Words," *International Arts Manager,* June 1994, 37.

2 Judy Gruber, "New Lease on Life," *Symphony,* Mar./Apr. 1995, 59–60.

3 Lynn Osmond, executive director, Sacramento Symphony, personal discussion, June 1995.

4 Sacramento Symphony, "Sacramento Symphony Association Files Bankruptcy Papers," Sept. 5, 1996, press release.

5 Frank Washington, "Maybe the Symphony Went Beyond Sacramento's Means," *Sacramento Bee,* Sept. 12, 1996.

6 In discussion with Lynn Osmond, executive director, Sacramento Symphony, Sept. 1996.

7 Peter Drucker, as quoted by Frances Hesselbein on Mar. 18, 1995, at a meeting of the National Society of Fund Raising Executives, Chicago.

8 Sidney J. Levy, "Arts Consumers and Aesthetic Attributes," *Marketing the Arts,* ed. by Michael P. Mokwa, William M. Lawson, and E. Arthur Prieve (New York: Praeger, 1980), 44.

9 Louis Bergonzi and Julia Smith, "Effects of Arts Education on Participation in the Arts," Research Division Report #36, National Endowment for the Arts, Seven Locks Press, Santa Ana, California, 1996, pp. 32–47.

10 Susan Chira, "As Schools Trim Budgets, the Arts Lose Their Place," *New York Times,* Feb. 3, 1993.

11 Luis R. Cancel, "Radicals Have America's Arts and Culture in Their Sights," *Update: American Council for the Arts,* Jan. 1995.

12 Susan Franano, "Up to Date in Kansas City," *Symphony,* Mar./Apr. 1993, 48.

13 Henry Fogel, "How Can We Assure the Future of Classical Music in America?" *Inside Arts,* Nov. 1993, 36.

14 Stephanie Brown, "Building an Audience for Dance," *Dance/USA Journal,* Summer 1991, 24.

15 James Odling-Smee, "Listen to the Music," *International Arts Manager,* Aug., 1993, 25.

16 Heidi Waleson, "Facing the Future," *Symphony,* Mar./Apr. 1993, 40.

17 Kurt Masur, "The Beauty of Life," *International Arts Manager,* May 1994, 23.

18 Sandra Hyslop, "On the Road to Conversion," *Symphony,* Jan./Feb. 1995, 46.

19 Heidi Waleson, "Orchestras Go to School," *Symphony,* Sept./Oct. 1992, 23.

20 James D. Wolfensohn, "Visions," *Inside Arts* 5, no. 1 (Spring 1993), 36–37.

21 Kendis Marcotte, "Making the Grade," *Inside Arts,* Nov. 1993, 29–32.

22 Barbara Radner and Philip Prale, "Arts and Learning: The Vital Connection," *Chicago Tribune,* Education Services Supplement, Mar. 24, 1993.

23 Ibid.

24 Marcotte, "Making the Grade," 32.

25 Nadine Brozan, "Violinist Wants to Zing Strings of Children," *New York Times,* Jan 23, 1993.

26 "Finding Ballet Dancers in the Inner City," *Chronicle of Philanthropy,* July 28, 1992, 4.

27 John Felton, "Mandate for Education," *Symphony,* Mar./Apr. 1995, 37–40, 50–51.

28 Heidi Waleson, "Orchestras and Education," *International Arts Manager,* Mar. 1993, 20.

29 Peter F. Drucker, *The Five Most Important Questions You Will Ever Ask about Your Nonprofit Organization* (San Francisco: Jossey-Bass, 1993), 12.

30 Jere Lantz, "Appropriate Programming: The Music Director's High-Wire Act," *Symphony Magazine,* Apr./May 1983, 84–88.

31 John von Rhein, "Musical Dinosaurs?" *Chicago Tribune,* July 18, 1993.

32 "Americanizing the American Orchestra," report of the National Task Force for the American Orchestra: An Initiative for Change (Washington, D.C.: American Symphony Orchestra League, 1993), 4.

33 Ibid., 4–5.

34 Ibid.

35 Clifford C. Nelson, quoted in the preface to W. McNeil Lowry, *The Performing Arts and American Society* (Englewood Cliffs, N.J.: Prentice Hall, 1978).

36 John von Rhein, "Voltaire Unstuffed," *Chicago Tribune,* Nov. 20, 1994.

37 Bernard Holland, "For Symphonies' Survival, Major Changes Urged," *New York Times,* June 19, 1993, Arts, p. 13.

38 Reported by Nick Rabkin, program director for arts and culture, John D. and Catherine T. MacArthur Foundation, during a speech in Chicago, Nov. 1994.

39 Catherine French, "A Gift of Music: Orchestras in the Community," *Symphony,* July/Aug. 1995, 124.

40 Daniel Barenboim, *A Life in Music* (New York: Scribner's, 1991), 171.

▲●▲

NAME
INDEX

▲●▲

ORGANIZATION
INDEX

▲●▲

───────────────

SUBJECT INDEX

▲●▲

ABOUT THE
AUTHORS

PHILIP KOTLER IS THE S. C. JOHNSON & SON DISTINGUISHED PROFESSOR OF International Marketing at the J. L. Kellogg Graduate School of Management, Northwestern University

Dr. Kotler is currently a member of the Board of Governors of the School of the Art Institute of Chicago; a member of the Getty Trust's Advisory Committee for the Getty Leadership Institute for Museum Management; a member of the Advisory Board of The Peter F. Drucker Foundation for Nonprofit Management; and a member of the Advisory Board of Copernicus, a leading marketing research firm. He has been chairman of the College of Marketing of the Institute of Management Sciences, a director of the American Marketing Association, and a trustee of the Marketing Science Institute.

Dr. Kotler is the recipient of many awards and honors, including Marketing Educator of the Year (from Sales and Marketing Executives International), Leader in Marketing Thought (from the academic members of the American Marketing Association), and the Viktor Mataja Medal of the Austrian Advertising Research Association. Dr. Kotler has received honorary degrees from The Athens University of Economics and Business, the University of Zurich, and DePaul University. Each year, the Academy of Health Service Marketing awards the Philip Kotler Award for Excellence in Health Care Marketing to a leading practitioner. Also each year, Istituto Europeo per il Marketing awards the Philip Kotler Award to the company in Italy that exhibits outstanding marketing performance.

Dr. Kotler is the author of fifteen books, which have been translated into more than twenty languages, and more than one hundred articles, several of which have received best-article awards, in leading journals such as the *Harvard Business Review, California Management Review, Business Horizons,* and the *Journal of Marketing.* Among his best-known books are *Marketing Management, Principles of Marketing,* and *Strategic Marketing for Nonprofit Organizations.*

Professor Kotler has consulted for such companies as IBM, Apple, General Electric, Ford, AT&T, Motorola, Honeywell, Bank of America, Merck, Ciba-Geigy, J. P. Morgan, DuPont, Westinghouse, and Merrill Lynch in the areas of marketing strategy and planning, marketing organization, and international marketing.

JOANNE SCHEFF IS AN ADJUNCT ASSOCIATE PROFESSOR OF ARTS MANAGEMENT at the J. L. Kellogg Graduate School of Management, Northwestern University, where she is also the faculty administrator for executive education programs for arts managers.

Ms. Scheff is a marketing and management consultant for arts organizations and for foundations and corporations that work with the arts. Her consulting has included a study of marketing strategies for the San Francisco Symphony, the San Francisco Ballet, the San Francisco Opera, and the American Conservatory Theatre as well as projects in marketing analysis, planning, and strategy for several theaters and chamber music groups. Scheff has been a guest speaker and workshop leader on topics in arts marketing and strategic collaborations at conferences and schools in the United States for such groups as the National Coalition of United Arts Funds, the Arts Services Office of the Cincinnati Institute of Fine Arts, Arts Midwest, the Michigan Orchestra Association, the Arts and Humanities Special Interest Group of the National Society of Fundraising Executives, the organization of arts marketing directors of the Boston area, the Nonprofit Division of the American Marketing Association, and the Masters in Arts Administration program of the Art Institute of Chicago as well as for arts management conferences in Toronto, London, Paris, and Santiago. She is a member of the scientific committee of the International Association for the Management of Arts and Culture (AIMAC).

She has had extensive experience as a member of the board of directors, executive financial officer, executive vice president, endowment drive chairperson, endowment fund trustee, and fund-raising chairperson at several cultural organizations. With Philip Kotler, she is the co-author of the *Harvard Business Review* article "How the Arts Can Prosper through Strategic Collaborations" and the *California Management Review* article "Crisis in the Arts: The Marketing Response."